A
HISTORY
OF THE
FAMILY

A
HISTORY
OF THE
FAMILY

VOLUME TWO
THE IMPACT OF MODERNITY

Edited by
André Burguière, Christiane Klapisch-Zuber,
Martine Segalen, Françoise Zonabend

Introduced by Jack Goody

Translated by Sarah Hanbury Tenison

Polity Press

English translation © Polity Press 1996
First published in France as *Histoire de la famille*
© Armand Colin Éditeur, Paris, 1986

This translation first published in 1996 by Polity Press in association with
Blackwell Publishers

Published with the assistance of the French Ministry of Culture

Editorial office:
Polity Press
65 Bridge Street
Cambridge CB2 1UR, UK

Marketing and production:
Blackwell Publishers
108 Cowley Road
Oxford OX4 1JF, UK

ISBN 0 7456 06342 (vol. I)
ISBN 0 7456 06350 (vol. II)
ISBN 0 7456 15430 (2-vol. set)

A CIP catalogue record for this book is available from the British Library.

Typeset in 10 on 12pt Sabon
by Wearset, Boldon, Tyne and Wear
Printed in Great Britain by Hartnolls Ltd., Bodmin, Cornwall

This book is printed on acid-free paper.

Contents

Acknowledgements

The authors, translators and publishers wish to thank the following who have kindly given permission for the use of copyright material.

Institut National d'Études Démographiques for data from *Population et sociétés*, June 1982 and January 1983.

Institut National de la Statistique et des Études Économiques for the table, 'Groupes domestiques en France' from M. Villac, 'Les structures familiales se transforment profondément', *Économie et Statistique*, February 1983, p. 40.

UNESCO for abstracts from items 1.3 and 3.2 of the *UNESCO Statistical Yearbook 1994*. Copyright © 1994 UNESCO.

Every effort has been made to trace all the copyright holders but if any have been inadvertently overlooked the publishers will be pleased to make the necessary arrangement at the first opportunity.

Introduction

Jack Goody

A part from the division between what Claude Lévi-Strauss calls the 'horizontal' and the 'vertical', there is another division that inhibits the study of the changing systems of the modern world: the division between kinship and family. In books covering the whole field, kinship is usually assigned to anthropologists and family to sociologists, with their contributions touching at only a few points.

This situation results from the general trend of many nineteenth-century studies which assumed that there was no 'family' in early societies. Though these assumptions have now been discarded, they continue to influence the topics studied by different sets of specialists. Anthropologists pay great attention to marriage preferences and but little to age at marriage. Demographers look closely at age at marriage but tend to treat preferences, if they discuss them at all, as statistical rather than normative.

A rapprochement between these attitudes, and an effort to extend the scope of the earlier restricted paradigms, are being forced upon the separate specializations by two main considerations. First, the development of historical demography has meant that historians, demographers and sociologists need to understand something of pre-industrial patterns even if only to establish a baseline for the study of Western societies. How can we talk about the disappearance of the 'extended family' without understanding the nature of wider kinship ties in pre-industrial societies? How can we understand the demographic transition without a thorough examination of the pre-transition structure?

Secondly, anthropologists have had to come to terms with a range of observational data which made clear the universal significance of the domestic domain and the fact that it was never simply a microcosm of wider social groupings. While moving from the general levels of analysis of earlier times, they have had to take account of the radical changes taking place in societies throughout the world, and to plot the course in particular localities of what William Goode has called 'the world revolution in family patterns'.

The results of this merging of interests between sociologists and anthropologists, demographers and historians, are brought out in the present volume and I shall try to draw together several themes from the work discussed in the individual chapters.

What happened in Europe and the other countries of the world when they encountered the onslaughts of modernity? The development of writing, the rise of the state and the expansion of industrial capitalism, colonization and urbanization are some of the onslaughts discussed in the following chapters.

Some of these factors may not have had a direct effect on family relations, but they nevertheless acquired great indirect importance. Thus writing, when controlled by the clergy, enabled the Church to impose a collection of rules on European as well as on colonized societies, in Meso-America for instance. In this way a certain homogeneity developed between cultures, while the gulf widened, depending on the particular social groups and classes, between norm and practice, and between varying degrees of acceptance of the norm.

By insisting on the universal nature of these family and matrimonial norms, the Church had a profound influence on the process of conversion; in so doing, it accumulated, during the early modern period at least, property which had been alienated from newly converted individuals and families. Some features, which are often considered characteristic of the western European family (and by some historians as only characteristic of the English family), were developed either as a condition or a consequence of this process. I refer here to 'individualism', 'free choice of spouse' (meaning *consensus, affectio*, love itself), liberation from parental constraint and the 'privatization of marriage'. These features are particularly clear in Shakespeare's *Romeo and Juliet*. In fact, the monk who performs the marriage and intrigues to prevent the other alliance arranged by Juliet's parents from taking place, is fulfilling the wishes of two individuals who are marrying for love rather than for honour's sake. The source of the Romeo and Juliet theme can be traced back to Boccaccio, and is both Elizabethan and medieval; it is not only Anglo-Italian but European, and draws its inspiration from the Church's intervention in the affairs of private individuals at the expense of kinship networks.

This privatization of marriage is associated with the ease and frequency with which it is dissolved. When the choice of spouse is left to the partners themselves, society is pressurized into allowing them to change their minds. The growing frequency of divorce at the present time must be viewed in relation to the longer life-span of couples, and, until recently, to the tendency to marry younger and to engage in precocious sexual relations. Couples are married for far longer periods than formerly, but, where marriages were previously dissolved by death, nowadays divorce performs this task. The consequences are the same: in Sweden, the incidence of step-families following divorce and remarriage is nowadays as great as it was in the old agrarian societies, following widowhood. Divorce, however, does not prevent the partners (husbands at least, since wives suffer some loss of freedom by getting custody of the children) from rapidly contracting new unions. They thus perpetuate the very widespread model of widowers soon remarrying and widows hardly at all, or only once their children have grown up (as in Upper Provence in the eighteenth century), or never at all (as in India).

To understand our world, we cannot neglect either the past or other cultures. Whatever changes take place in Europe or Africa, India or Japan today, are doing so from different points of departure, against the background of different experiences. In western Europe, where age at marriage had been characteristically late for both males and females, the figure has been dropping until recently. In Asia, where age at marriage was early for both sexes, it has risen. In Europe where divorce was at one time virtually impossible, the rates have risen dramatically; in Japan the opposite has happened.

It is also a mistake to reject the study of otherness. Only by looking at other kinds of family, for example, the polygynous family of Africa, or even at non-marriage in other cultures, can we really understand some basic features of our own. We are not the first to have high rates of divorce and a plethora of lone-parent families.

A central theme raised by many contemporary observers is whether we are witnessing the total disappearance of family, marriage and kinship. The attempt to write off kinship, which for present purposes I under-stand as extra-household relations, is long-standing. We have certainly seen, over the long term, and in several parts of the world, the disappearance of larger, organized groups of kin such as clans and lineages. The efforts of the descendants of Scottish émigrés, of the Protestant bourgeoisie expelled from France and of black Americans to seek out their genealogical roots, and sometimes to introduce collective gatherings of distant 'relatives' are no functional substitute. However, continuing ties between a wider range of kin are often of much greater importance in other parts of the world, even under contemporary transformations of the political, productive and ideological systems, where they may be of major significance in influencing paths of migration from country to town or from one country to another.

In Europe such ties are often of greater importance in the countryside than in the town (that is, where the countryside is not merely a dormitory extension of the town). But even for those living in the metropolis, a limited range of kin outside the household remains a dominant part of an individual's network of relationships, often becoming more prominent for the very reason that households themselves are smaller and their members linked in a more fragile manner.

One recurrent theme of writers on the emergence of the modern family is the reduction in the size of the household (or consumption group) and family (or number of children). The number of children is closely linked to the decline of infant mortality and to changing patterns of women's labour, to new techniques of contraception, to attitudinal changes and to new modes of support, especially in old age. These factors are also related to the size of the household, and influence decisions on what individuals live together. But even though households have become smaller, in every 'advanced' society we find some larger units of communal living. In earlier times these were often single-sex institutions such as monasteries, colleges or military units. The popularity of 'communes' of a cross-sexual kind, based upon the co-operation of couples and their children, has in recent years often been connected with a socialist ideology. Hence their attractiveness for Russia in the 1920s, earlier for Polish Jewish socialists (leading to the founding of the Israeli *kibbutz*), then for the promoters of the people's communes in China between 1958 and 1961, and in an attenuated form for the young Swedish (and Danish) middle class. Most of the last-mentioned group were established in opposition to the family, although they have been less successful in this respect than in modifying the boundaries of the household. Such forms of communal living also have an obvious appeal to religious groups, as well as to lone-parent families, battered wives and other vulnerable parts of the population, partly for mutual support, partly for external protection.

In earlier times, the larger units found in rural areas were often the result of the co-residence of two or three generations in the same house (as in eighteenth-century Provence) or in adjacent dwellings (as in twentieth-century Sweden). This often happened where each generation earned its living by taking over the farm or workshop from the parents. Obviously proximity and dependence could give rise to conflict and co-operation.

In the contemporary West, relations between adjacent generations of old and young are somewhat easier, since neither is entirely dependent on the other. The old have their own income in the form of state or occupational pension. They can convert their wealth, even the value of their house, into an annuity. They then need no help, and they leave no inheritance. While parents may live apart from their children they tend to live nearby. In Sweden in 1975, 9 per cent of over-seventies lived with their kin, some 6 per cent in institutions, and the great majority (85 per cent) in their own homes. But these were not totally isolated; nearly half of all retired people in Sweden (two-thirds of those with children) have a child living within 15 km; only about 6 per cent live alone and lack frequent kin contacts.

The contributions to the present volume, original in their scope as well as in their treatment, show the situation in Asia to be very different despite the shock of modernity. It is not surprising to find children looking after their parents in China, with 80 per cent of its population in the countryside. But even in highly industrialized Japan, as in Sweden, with nearly 70 per cent in the towns, some 60 per cent of parents were recently living with or near an adult child. The figure is on the decrease, and would drop more rapidly if pensions and homes for the aged were more common.

A further aspect of the relations between generations, largely deriving from medical advance, results from the increasing length of life; children are less likely to be orphaned and more likely to know their grandparents than ever before. Since parents live longer, children are unlikely to inherit until they themselves are approaching retiring age. Conflicts, however, are less important than under domestic modes of production (where the family living is earned at home), since in general the new generation is not dependent upon the senior for the transmission of the means of production. Parents are no longer directly responsible for training children to take over a family enterprise. Through schooling and the diversification of jobs and opportunities, such training is undertaken outside the house. In Europe parents are left with a vague responsibility for moral education, and even that is often thought to be the business of school or church.

Meanwhile adolescence is prolonged and entry into work delayed, not only by temporary troughs in the business cycle and the lack of opportunities resulting from long-term changes in the structure of economic activity but because of the extended period of choice and training. If the support for training (or unemployment) comes from outside the family, children are likely to quit the parental home before establishing a family-type group of their own. They may retain a notional base in that home, especially where they depend upon the family for some additional support, and sometimes because of a shortage of other housing, but this phase is generally brief, though it may be repeated at the break-up of a marriage or cohabitation when there are children. In other words the break up of the domestic group no longer turns on the 'marriage' of children, or even on their starting work. Independence comes earlier, providing a prolonged and autonomous 'adolescence' which merges into cohabitation and possibly a delayed marriage. But the formalization of the union is no longer connected with the transfer of property or responsibility (as in many agricultural communities), or with the movement of a spouse into the parental home, or even with the establishment of an independent residence. Not much hangs on marriage, unless it is the recognition of a union for bureaucratic purposes or the formal legitimation of children. Even that has become of little significance. In Sweden approximately half the children are born out of wedlock. There are some tax advantages in being a lone parent.

One reason why marriage has become of less significance has to do with property considerations. In general, even those that have property, which for the middle class consists mainly of the house in which they live (in England and Sweden the working class are more likely to rent, as most did in formerly socialist countries), keep it for their old age in order to ensure that they do not have to be looked after by their children. Property is retained till death rather than distributed *inter vivos*, in order to cope with a long post-retirement period.

It has always been the case that 'marriage' has meant different things to different people. In simple societies, the change of status is often enacted in a public ceremony, but in more complex societies, the state may require certain formalities, the Church others, while the community itself may recognize unions established in less formal ways. The policies of the state have been strongly influenced by ideological factors. In some parts of the world, the reform of family and marriage has been seen as an essential part of the process of modernization, whether promoted by socialists, religious bodies, colonial administrators or general reformers. Partly this has been seen as a question of modernizing morality, of doing away with abhorrent customs like the binding of feet in China and Indian widows throwing themselves on their husband's funeral pyre. On the other hand, some practices, such as parental choice, have been set aside in favour of freedom in the choice of partner, because they have been considered to run counter to the natural rights of any individual. All in all, there has been a substantial degree of consensus across a wide range – autonomous conjugal families, agreement of bride and groom, monogamy in marriage: easy divorce, equality of the sexes and of siblings. Some of these changes have had the force of law behind them, others the support of a reforming segment of opinion. But they have not gone unopposed, most openly in India, and some earlier relaxations in China have been modified, partly for reasons of policy, partly in reaction to more general sentiment; secular rituals have grown up around the act of marriage: abortion and divorce have become more difficult.

While some of these changes have been the result of ideological pressures, the revolt of the young and the decline of parental control must also be seen as linked to general social changes – in the economy towards wage employment, in residence towards the town, in education towards schools and in the political system towards public control. One aspect of particular importance is the increased entry of women into the labour market.

In rural and pre-industrial economies, women have always 'worked', not only at what we call 'domestic work' but also by joining in a family enterprise in craft production, home manufacture or outwork, in which the children also took part. Even in pre-industrial societies some women worked outside the house, in manufacture and domestic service, as entertainers (dancing, sex, etc.). But this was a minority, often of low status, or during a particular phase in their lives. Early industrialization brought women into the 'labour market' in greater numbers, working outside the house especially in textile manufacture, where physical strength was not essential. Despite the domestic role assigned to women in middle-class ideology, participation in the labour force has spread rapidly from the working classes. In Sweden today there are almost as many women (83 per cent) between twenty-five and fifty-four working as there are men (95 per cent). Women are more often in part-time and lower-paid jobs, but the effects on family life (though they may be concomitants rather than consequences) are radical.

The number of births per woman has gone down drastically since the early twentieth century. The drop in infant mortality meant that fewer births were necessary to achieve the 'ideal' family size, but the effective family size also decreased, leading to smaller sibling groups. This decrease was made easier by the development of contraceptive techniques and the widespread practice of abortion in some western societies.

The 'ideal' may be a function of either family or state policy. In Europe families nowadays consist of a smaller number of children, irrespective of religious and political differences. In some countries the state is more immediately involved, either by family planning propaganda or by more direct means, such as the much resented sterilization campaign in India in the 1970s and the more recent, and more closely supervised, attempt of the Chinese government to implement a one-child family (at least in urban areas, and at least for one generation). The latter policy is dictated by the socio-economic problems that arise as a result of raising the standard of living when the population is increasing rapidly. In addition, there is sometimes more general concern about the relationship between people and resources. The long-term effect upon surviving children (predominantly male) of having no siblings, no uncles and no aunts (at least in the narrow sense) can only be guessed at.

Other governments in the West have taken a different line in view of the relative stability of their populations, and have even offered special payments to large families; while this is explicitly a welfare measure, it is also pro-natal. In Africa, neither governments nor families have paid much attention to the numbers of children born, misled perhaps by the standard calculation of population density, for in terms of technology and resources that density is high and increasing more rapidly than in any other part of the world. The results are only too obvious; most of Africa depends on imported food, much of it with the aid of more developed nations. Without this aid its people face shortages and starvation.

The family has undergone major demographic, legal and interpersonal changes in the twentieth century. These changes have to be seen both against the past and in a world context. Domestic groups may no longer be at the centre of the production process in many parts of the world, but, as the following chapters show, they have by no means disappeared as the basic units of consumption, of living together and of reproduction. They are the most universal and the most intimate source both of tension and support.

PART I

Europe and the First Modernity

ONE

The One Hundred and One Families of Europe

André Burguière and François Lebrun

The history of the family in the countries of Europe between the sixteenth and nineteenth centuries developed within a demographic context which has become well known through the systematic use of the few viable censuses and cadasters, and above all of the baptismal, marriage and burial registers kept in many dioceses in several European countries since the end of the fifteenth century. Registers were not, however, brought into general use until the second half of the sixteenth century when the decrees of the Council of Trent were applied, thus duplicating in some areas previous instructions from the civil authorities. In any case, the situation could vary widely from one country to the next. In Italy, censuses, cadasters (the Florentine *catasto* for instance) and viable parish records have often existed since the fourteenth century; in Poland, by contrast, baptismal and marriage registers began to be kept only at the end of the sixteenth century, and have been preserved only in exceptional cases. The exploitation of these different sources over recent decades has allowed historians gradually to prise out the demographic structures of the past and to conclude that there was such a thing as a demographic system on a European scale in the past. This system may be understood at best from the beginning of the sixteenth century (the sources before then are inadequate): during the nineteenth century it gradually gave way to the new structures which characterize the European populations of today. This 'European demographic system', the term coined by the English historian Michael Flinn (1981), has a number of distinctive features.

The first section of this chapter (to p. 19) is by François Lebrun. The remainder is by André Burguière.

Death Carries off a Child. Until the late eighteenth century, the high rate of infant and juvenile mortality (a quarter of all children died before their first birthday, and another quarter before the age of twenty) was a terrible and inexorable reality common to all social levels. Sixteenth-century wood engraving. Bibliothèque des Arts Décoratifs, Paris. Photo: J. L. Charmet.

The demographic framework

Demographic structures

Nuptiality conditioned the birth rate to a far greater degree than it does nowadays. Extramarital births were few in number, generally less than 2 per cent of all births in rural parishes, and about 5 per cent in the towns, albeit with marked variations according to country and region and a fairly general increase, especially in the towns, from the 1760s onwards. The first marriage, which more often than not joined two young people from the same or neighbouring parishes, was celebrated much later on in life than was previously thought on the basis of certain royal or aristocratic marriages. In all the countries of Europe in the eighteenth century, the average age for men at their first marriage was around twenty-nine or thirty; for girls it was twenty-five or twenty-six. Recent research has shown that the age for both sexes was decidedly lower in the sixteenth century, and that there was a gradual rise in age between the end of the sixteenth and the end of the eighteenth century, with certain exceptions such as England, where the average age at first marriage fell from 1740 onwards, leading to an accelerated growth in population. In the same way, in most countries of Europe, it was a temporary lowering of the age at marriage that enabled the breaches made by death to be filled in the aftermath of the great demographic crises. Nuptiality thus emerged as the great self-regulating mechanism of past populations, just as the later age of girls at their first marriage is one of the key elements of the European demographic system. Indeed, by cutting at least ten years off a woman's reproductive period, compared with marriage at puberty, this later age constituted, in Pierre Chaunu's famous words, 'the great contraceptive weapon of classical Europe'.

Furthermore, given that breast-feeding was the rule in the countryside, where more than 80 per cent of the population of Europe lived, it too contributed to limiting fertility, since a breast-freeding woman is more often than not temporarily infertile. Finally, the average age of mothers at the birth of their last child was everywhere around forty, sometimes even slightly less. This explains why, in the best cases (when the family had not been broken up by the death of a parent before the mother had reached her fortieth year) the average number of children in this type of family, known as 'complete', was about seven, which corresponded to one birth every two years, and not one every year, as used to be thought in accordance with the misleading concept of natural fertility. This average number is reduced to four or five if one takes all families into account, not just those called 'complete', but also those broken up prematurely by the death of one or other spouse.

This average number of four or five children was, however, only just sufficient to ensure generation renewal, given the high level of mortality in the first years of life. During the seventeenth and eighteenth centuries, in France and in most European countries, one child in four died before it reached its first birthday. England was lucky in this respect, since the rate there was one in five. This terrible loss was especially prevalent at birth and the following days. Neonatal mortality, defined as the rate of mortality during the first month, was 150–80 per 1,000, or one child in every five or six. In almost every instance, it was a case of endogenous mortality, when the infant is the victim of inherited defects or, more often, of accidents occurring in the course of birth. Birth took place under conditions which exposed mother and child to great hazards as soon as there were complications. Generally speaking, midwives were unqualified, and baffled by even slightly difficult cases. In any event, no one seems to have been aware of the dangers to which both mother and child were exposed through ignorance of the rules of hygiene. The situation was the same in every class of society, so that infant mortality was as high among the rich as in the working classes. We have evidence of this in the high proportion of cot deaths among the royal and princely families of Europe, with all the consequent problems of succession.

After the first month, infant mortality was basically exogenous, the result of illness or accidents after birth and unrelated to the birth process. Even after the first birthday, an age used by demographers to calculate infant mortality but not in itself significant, the death rate remained very high throughout childhood, especially at weaning, so that of 1,000 children born alive, little more than 500 would survive to their fifteenth year. In England, however, the situation was decidedly better than on the continent. Table 1 has been compiled using averages calculated from a variety of studies and shows the number of survivors at different ages for every 1,000 live births before 1750 in England and in France (Flinn, 1981).

These figures mean that in France, no less than in most countries of continental Europe, of the four or five children born on average to a

Table 1 Number of survivors at different ages per thousand births before 1750 in England and France

Survivors	at 1 year	at 5 years	at 10 years	at 15 years
England	799	668	624	—
France	729	569	516	502

family, two or three at most would be available to replace their parents.

After adolescence, death was less frequent. Even so, the death rate remained high, and the causes were many for all adult men and women. In the working classes, the basic diet of bread or broth, which was barely enough to sustain life, meant that people were vulnerable to every sort of infection. Among the more fortunate, it was often an excessively rich and unbalanced diet which led to illness. With everyone, peasant or prince, disease was the great bringer of death. Chest infections, gastro-intestinal disorders (notably the dreaded dysentery), tuberculosis, cancer and venereal diseases, not to mention plague epidemics, ravaged the population, all the more so as the art of healing was still in its infancy and medicine often totally ineffectual.

One of the consequences of this high death rate for adults of all ages was that marriages were frequently curtailed. Widowhood and remarriage, the lot very often of the survivor, were common experiences: in the seventeenth and eighteenth centuries at least one marriage in four was a remarriage. In the absence of divorce, which did not exist either in Catholic countries or *de facto* even in Protestant ones, most marriages were terminated by death, which turned the family into a far less stable and protected unit than one might imagine. Quite the contrary. The chief feature of the traditional European family was its instability, the successive blows dealt it by death: the loss of infants whom their brothers and sisters could scarcely have had time to know, and the frequent ending of marriages by a husband's or wife's death. While it has been claimed that the family unit was very often reconstituted, and very quickly too, the problems posed by remarriage for both the bereaved partner and for the children remained. Here indeed are the 'splintered families' which come to light when one reconstructs the families living within the confines of one parish: over a period of ten or twenty years couples could form, break up and re-form, with the children of two or even three different unions being brought up together (Baulant, 1972).

Nevertheless, during normal periods, the number of deaths was slightly less than the number of births, which would have permitted some population growth. Unfortunately, brutal demographic crises recurred at fairly regular intervals to disrupt these tentative trends towards expansion. Differing but often connected reasons such as shortage, famine or the violence of war could cause the normal number of deaths to double, triple or quadruple for the space of a few months, while the number of marriages and conceptions would dwindle sometimes to nil. Once the crisis was over, its effects would gradually be effaced as a result of marriages and births multiplying. Overall, the 'ordinary' death rate and the crisis death rate combined in the long term to condemn the population to stagnation, subject to significant short-term variations.

The evolution of the European population

The evolution of the European population in the course of the three centuries examined here may be explained within the framework of these structures. The first fact to note is the general increase in population from the mid-fifteenth century to the last decades of the sixteenth. In most cases, however, this rise should not be mistaken for more than a simple recovery after the 100 years of misery which most European countries endured after the Black Death in 1348 and, in France and its neighbours, the long-drawn-out conflict with England rightly known as the Hundred Years War. Within almost unaltered demographic and socio-economic structures, this recovery was made possible by a more favourable economic situation. Although war, famine and plague had not disappeared, the crises which they provoked were less frequent and less serious until around 1560–80.

At about that point or a little later, the general population rise in Europe was interrupted. New outbreaks of plague were largely responsible. Epidemics occurred all over Europe in 1564, 1580, 1586, 1599 and 1604, i.e. five great epidemics in forty years, compared with only one on this scale during the previous hundred. The most serious outbreak was the one which ravaged Atlantic Europe from southern Spain to northern Germany between 1596 and 1604. After a fairly general quiet period between 1605 and 1625, exceptionally long-drawn-out and deadly epidemics broke out between 1625 and 1637 and between 1647 and 1652. By extrapolating from the figures compiled during the Provence epidemic in 1720, Biraben (1976) tried to evaluate the number of deaths attributable to plague in France between 1600 and 1670: he calculated that the number was between 2,300,000 and 3,300,000, and that around 1,000,000 occurred in the years 1628–32 alone. In northern Italy, especially in Milan, tens of thousands of victims fell to the 1630–1 epidemic. In Spain, the 1647–52 outbreak, which struck the whole kingdom apart from Catalonia, killed more than a million, or one fifth of the whole population. Towns were especially vulnerable: in London, in 1665, 70,000 to 100,000 inhabitants died, out of a total of 400,000. In the countryside, although the effects are more difficult to quantify, they seem to have been more selective, one parish being decimated while a neighbour escaped entirely, probably by rigorously shunning all contact with the outside world.

Around 1580 the 'little ice age' began, so named by Le Roy Ladurie

(1967) because a slight cooling of the climate in Europe gave rise to many more harsh winters and poor summers than before. This deterioration in climatic conditions was felt especially sharply between 1580 and 1600, when it gave rise to a series of subsistence crises which degenerated into famines throughout western and central Europe. To compound the disaster, war brought desolation and death to every place where soldiers and armed bands marched and fought. This was the case in France with the Wars of Religion between 1560 and 1598, and in the Low Countries where the War of Independence was fought against Spain by the northern provinces between 1566 and 1609. The effect was especially strong in most of Germany, rent by the Thirty Years War between 1618 and 1648. The demographic effects of those decades were dramatic: German towns lost on average almost a third of their population, and the countryside about 40 per cent. Although the war in Germany ended in 1648, it continued between France and Spain until 1659, which meant that the devastation continued until that date in Alsace, Franche-Comté and Lorraine, which lost half their population between 1635 and 1660. Poland was the victim of a series of invasions by its neighbours between 1648 and 1662, and in western Europe, England, France and Spain were rent by the civil wars of the 1640s and 1650s, with all the violence inflicted by undisciplined armies.

The disappearance of plague from western Europe from 1670 onwards (apart from the epidemic which ravaged Marseille and part of Provence in 1720), constituted a major event in the history of the European population. In the same way, the consequences of war for civilian populations tended to lessen with the strengthening of discipline in the armies. These two positive factors did not, however, protect western Europe from demographic crises sparked off by epidemics of dysentery, typhoid, measles or typhus, or by subsistence crises degenerating into famine, and often, by a combination of both factors.

Under these conditions, it may well be assumed that the sum total for a long seventeenth century running from 1580 to 1720 was negative in many countries, notably in the German states, which were bled white by the Thirty Years War, in Italy, which suffered terribly from plague, and in Spain, which was permanently weakened by the expulsion of the Moors, by emigration to the New World and by plague epidemics. During this period, France went through a switchback evolution, between a base population of 16–18 million inhabitants to a ceiling of 20 or 22 million, a level which, although never exceeded, was often reached only as the result of recovery after a crisis. As for England, where the standard of living was markedly higher than in the rest of Europe, the crises were less frequent and less deadly. This accounts for the demo-

Table 2 The population of some countries in western Europe from the sixteenth to the nineteenth century (in millions)

	1550	1680	1820
England	3	4.9	11.5
France	17	21.9	30.5
Low Countries	1.2	1.9	2
Spain	9	8.5	14
Italy	11	12	18.5
Germany	12	12	18.1
Western Europe*	61.1	71.9	116.5

* British Isles, France, Low Countries, Belgium, Germany, Austria, Switzerland, Italy, Spain and Portugal.
Source: E. A. Wrigley, 'The Growth of Population in Eighteenth-Century England: a Conundrum Resolved', *Past and Present*, 98 (1983), pp. 121–50.

graphic growth during the sixteenth century, which continued during the first half of the seventeenth century and increased the population from 3 million in 1551 to over 5 million in 1656. The second half of the seventeenth century, however, was marked by stagnation and even a slight fall due, among other causes, to the effects of the 1658 and 1665 plagues and the demographic crisis of 1679–81.

From around 1720 the population of Europe began to grow again nearly everywhere. The difference between this and previous rises was that this time, it was not a recovery but a real take-off, the start of a population boom which has not ceased since. This was especially the case in France, where, in spite of stagnation and local setbacks (notably in the west), the 'four-century-old platform of 20–2 million inhabitants' was definitively crossed with 24.5 million in 1740, 28 million in 1790 and more than 29 million in 1800. This was also the case in England, where the growth rate, which was slow until 1740, speeded up spectacularly, bringing the population up from 5.5 million in 1741 to more than 8.5 million in 1800. Not only did the English population grow much faster than the French, but the growth came from a different cause: a very marked increase in the birth rate, itself due to the lower average age at first marriage and to the reduced incidence of lifelong celibacy. This expansion of the English population, a 'silent incitement to growth', should be related to the Industrial Revolution which began at the same time. In France, the population growth can be explained not by a rising birth rate (which, on the contrary, started to fall in the 1760s with people setting voluntary limits to their families, and was much more moderate than in England), but by a lower death rate, which fell slightly between 1740 and 1770 and much more rapidly after 1790.

To sum up: in the European demographic system the family, which more often than not was founded late and was soon broken off by death, appears as the great demographic regulator, while heavy infant mortality constituted a pitiless corrective to a high level of fertility. It was only in the second half of the eighteenth century that these structures started very slowly to disintegrate, in different ways in different countries, thus allowing the general rise of the European population to begin.

Mapping the family in its various forms

In the 1960s, any historian dealing with the family since the sixteenth century would have spoken of the gradual rise of the modern nuclear family in Europe under the influence of the economic transformations and the 'modernizing' effect of the state. Common to most sociological theories was a belief in the passage of the traditional family, featuring large and complex domestic groups, into the present-day restricted family, with the residential group limited to the conjugal unit, which provides for both biological production and social reproduction. Some of the older theorists saw this passage as a sign of decadence (e.g. Le Play, 1875), others as the more or less beneficial march of progress (Tönnies, 1887; Durkheim, 1950; Parsons, 1937).

This evolutionary vision appeared to be proved by the newly acquired history of mentalities and population history. Philippe Ariès, one of the first to stress the diversity of family traditions in France in a study published in 1948, saw that a new concept of childhood was confirmed during the eighteenth century in the educational and affective behaviour of the elite classes (see, 'L'Enfant et la vie familiale' in Ariès, 1960). According to him, this altered sensibility corresponded to the affirmation of bourgeois values, which distinguished more clearly between age groups and social classes, and isolated the conjugal unit from the old solidarities of kinship and neighbourhood. This new mentality postulated a rejection of the cosy muddle of communal life in older forms of society and a new concentration on the conjugal group.

Nuclear families were precisely what demographic historians found when they applied the 'Louis Henry' method of 'reconstituting families' from a documentary base, the parish records, which provide serial data from the mid-seventeenth century onwards. Reconstituted families, reduced to their biological histories, supplied the demographer with a handy observation point for the study *in vitro* of the rhythms and mechanisms of reproduction among earlier populations. But, by a natural tendency to reify the instrument constructed by themselves, demographic historians ended by acting as if their reconstituted families were real families, and thinking that all families in the modern age were nuclear in structure.

English historians were protected from this illusion by the inadequate nature of their demographic source material. Less well equipped than their French colleagues for studying the family as a cell for biological reproduction, because of the gaps in their parish registers, they preferred to exploit their censuses, which are older and more numerous than those compiled by the French monarchy, in order to analyse the family as a domestic group.

Laslett (1972) undertook a great comparative study which undermined the old evolutionist cliché that the modern nuclear cell is derived from an extended and complex family. If one looks just at the size of households, it may be said (as demonstrated in the relevant chapters in volume I) that the restricted family was dominant in much of Europe from the Middle Ages. If one takes a look at the structure of households, meaning the greater or lesser complexity of forms of co-residence (involving several core units, close and more distant relatives, etc.), it is clear that several family models presenting different forms of organization and allocation of authority coexisted in Europe from the Middle Ages. The nuclear model dominated very largely in north-western Europe. It was much less common in central and southern Europe, and in eastern Europe it was sometimes even in a minority. There is evidence that France enjoyed a more marked cultural heterogeneity than other European nations, and encompassed both forms of family tradition: the north of the country belonged to nuclear territory, whereas southern France showed a clear preference for complex forms (stem-families, *frérèches*, etc.).

It would be paradoxical to reduce the history of the forms of family organization during the three centuries in which Europe experienced its first flowering of modernity, to structural, if not fixed traits. Our vision of how things were depends on the state of research, and on the researchers' state of mind. The many papers and debates elicited by the Cambridge Group and its research (see the opening chapter by Françoise Zonabend in volume I), which react against the old evolutionist stereotype, tend to concentrate on the study of structures, family models and their internal coherence. The synchronic nature of the sources that can be used to describe domestic groups tends to reinforce the anti-evolutionism of the analyses; they are censuses, fiscal rolls and listings of inhabitants, all of which multiplied in Europe from the sixteenth century onwards. These sources, however, rarely come in series. Although they present us with a multitude of instantaneous records of the composition of households in the different parts of Europe, the juxtaposition of all these 'snapshots' reveals geographical contrasts more easily than evolutionary clues.

May it not be claimed that geographical contrasts themselves bear the marks of some sort of evolution? The new family model was not created, as was long thought, by the main components of the 'first modernity'. These included: the stabilization of the demographic system through better regulation (especially the implementation of delayed marriage) and the acquisition of a growth profile in the course of the eighteenth century; the development of towns; the rise of mercantile capitalism and its growing influence over the forms of production, and the strengthening of the state apparatus. All of these, however, put the existing family models to the test. In some places they were able to call on their capacity to adapt, in others on their ability to resist.

The Stepmother. The cruel stepmother whose misdeeds convulse the family group in this picture by Greuze also appears in eighteenth-century popular tales, novels and bourgeois drama, nourished by imaginations haunted by the memory of childhood experience. In a society in which almost a quarter of all marriages were remarriages, one child in every two ran the risk at some stage of incurring the dubious guardianship of a stepfather or stepmother at some stage. Engraving by Le Vasseur after J.-B. Greuze. Bibliothèque Nationale, Paris

By emphasizing the developmental gaps, and even the dependent relations, between west and east, the more intensive modernization of north-western Europe brought a whole new light to bear on the cultural bedrock underlying these differences, and the contrast between several dominant family models in particular.

Delayed marriage, for instance, a key element in the arsenal of regulations which allowed Europe to stabilize its fluctuating population, was established in western Europe by the sixteenth century. In southern Europe this happened later and more slowly, and was limited to reducing the wide age gap between spouses. In eastern Europe, on the other hand, it was so little in evidence that Hajnal (1965) was able to use it as the keystone of the matrimonial model proper to western Europe established by him, and as the secret mainspring of its modernity.

While it cannot be claimed that delayed marriages and their corollary, a smaller age gap between spouses, acted in favour of the nuclear family all over western Europe, they did at the very least strengthen the autonomy of the couple, setting it at the centre of the family network. In eastern Europe, on the other hand, the custom of early marriage and the persistence of a difference of age between spouses, which was maintained by frequent remarriage, prolonged the dependence of young couples on their parents and on formulae for co-residing with them.

The socio-economic transformations of the period call for comments of a similar nature. The spectacular maritime expansion of the western sea-front in the sixteenth century, which was stimulated by the discovery of America and expansion overseas, set the whole of Europe in motion. It unlocked the provinces, intensified the commercial irrigation of the continent and favoured the simultaneous circulation of goods, men and ideas. It caused a decisive shift of Europe's economic centre of gravity to the north-west. This involved a promotion of the mercantile bourgeoisie which set up a new form of domination of the countryside by the towns, and to the dissemination of the Reformation which put value on individual responsibility and the spirit of enterprise. It is no coincidence that these features, which traced the modernity of the north-western perimeter of Europe, coexisted with family structures in which the nuclear model often predominated.

There was some congruity between the arrangement of the nuclear family and the new demands made by society. Without going as far as Macfarlane (1970) in claiming that the Promethean individualism which gave rise to the Industrial Revolution had long been germinating within the English nuclear family, it nevertheless may be supposed that the family model which had been rooted in that part of Europe since the Middle Ages, and the pre-capitalist dynamism which can be observed there from the sixteenth century onwards, did indeed have a mutually stimulating effect.

During the whole of this period, however, Europe retained its essentially agricultural base. The growth of the state, as of the towns, was nourished above all by what could be levied from the countryside: wealth in the form of taxes and rents, and people as well. In France, as in most European countries, the towns kept a much higher mortality rate than the country, which meant that they could not ensure a positive rate of replacement. Even so, whether active or not, whether favoured by the economic situation or not, they all saw their populations grow during the course of the century. This growth was possible only thanks to the flow of rural immigrants throwing themselves into the 'urban mortuaries' (Chaunu).

This was but one feature among others of the countryside's increased dependence. From the end of the sixteenth century, the history of the

Concord. A very idealized (because allegorical) representation of a family meal in a prosperous household of the bourgeoisie or lesser nobility. The round table symbolizes the perfect unity among the members of the family group. Note that even in this prosperous milieu (witness the richness of the furniture) the same room serves as both dining room and bedroom. Engraving by Boissart. Bibliothèque Nationale, Paris.

European peasantry was marked by economic contraction and social regression, expressed in rhythms and formulae which varied according to region. In England, which offers the most classic instance of the penetration of the countryside by capitalist structures (according to Karl Marx's famous description), property rents replaced manorial dues: the lord turned into a gentleman farmer. He took in and enclosed his demesne, put his lands to grass in order to engage in speculative farming and, with the connivance of the property-owning peasantry, the free-holders who had resisted eviction, brought about the enforced enclosure of the common lands.

In France, too, the peasants had been subjected to the onslaught of revived seigneurial and bourgeois claims and the rise of ground rents. They were, however, better able to protect their commons from being swallowed up by greedy landowners, except in some regions such as the Gatine (in Poitou) or Sologne, where a movement analogous to the English enclosures developed in the seventeenth century. At all events, in both England and France – for it was in the great cereal-growing plains of

Payment of Dues. A seigneurial office cluttered with files containing every detail of debts, dues and other obligations owed by the lord's dependants. Note the watchful serenity of the lord as he reads his accounts, whilst his clerk, at his side, looks down on the peasant throng; the peasants, fearful and deferential, bring their dues in kind or in coin. This is a complete tableau of seigneurial domination, which was enjoying a strong revival when Pieter Bruegel II painted this picture. Giraudon.

northern France that the ground rents were most extortionate – the great majority of the peasants who had to face this offensive by the aristocracy and the bourgeoisie lived in nuclear families.

In the English case, the nuclear family acted as a real school of individualism and encouraged the children to leave home as soon as possible, thus loosening the grip of kinship and neighbourhood solidarities, the web woven around village society. The nuclear family hastened the dissolution of this society into capitalist structures. In France, however, the nuclear family remained solidly enclosed in the peasant community and formed part of it. The differences between the social customs of the nuclear family in England and France may be illustrated, if not explained, by the differing evolution of inheritance practices observed in the countryside. In England, the habit of transmitting the farm to a single child, which started in the fourteenth and fifteenth centuries when the population was small, land plentiful and wages high, was maintained after the population had recovered. Since farms had grown in size, it was now possible to accumulate enough movable wealth to give money to those children who were prepared to move elsewhere, and thus to preserve the unity of the inherited land (Howell, 1976). This practice made the whole idea of leaving the land bearable, and that of co-residence unacceptable. It maintained a flow of emigration which was merely hastened by the enclosures.

In France, on the contrary, the pressure of population imposed formulae for subdividing inheritance. This can be observed from the way customs evolved, at the beginning of the sixteenth century in particular, and from the disappearance of the principle, in Orléans–Parisian law, of excluding dowered individuals; and especially from the success in the countryside of innovations of urban origin. The only way of preventing farms from being reduced by subdivision to sizes below the minimum necessary for survival was reliance on the use of common land and on endogamous marriages. Both factors helped consolidate the nuclear family and the village community.

When looked at within the whole dispossession movement which affected the peasant world from the end of the sixteenth century onwards, the nuclear family appears as a supple structure. Depending on the way in which it was articulated in the local society, it could easily adapt to the new conditions of lordship, or as the link in a network of resistance and protection. This observation may also be applied to southern and eastern Europe, where the degradation of the peasant condition was more spectacular, and to other forms of social organization: the extension of *métayage* (*mezzadria* in Italy), and the formation of huge *latifundia* in Castile, Andalusia and in southern Italy at the expense of the peasants who alienated their property or their privileges as tenants in return for better debt repayment terms or for the protection of a powerful man. This constituted a process which has been called, in their case, 'refeudalization'.

The most clearly feudal system was the one established in eastern Europe from the Elbe to the Urals, and from the Baltic to the Danube, in regions settled more recently, and by populations of mixed origins. There, war and political insecurity enabled the aristocracy of *boyars* or magnates to appropriate land and men, or to have them assigned to them by the rulers. Forced labour dues enabled landlords to extract considerable surpluses from their immense demesnes by direct exploitation. These surpluses were basically cereals destined for the international market.

Where the landlord's grip was tightest, a high percentage of complex households may be found. As with the nuclear model in north-western

Saying Grace, engraving from the second half of the seventeenth century, by C. Duflos after a painting by Charles le Brun. This is a pious engraving evoking the rechristianization of society through the family, as advocated by Catholic reformers. This (somewhat idealized) peasant interior gives a fairly accurate picture of contemporary table manners. The father, mother and three children (only the eldest is seated) all eat out of the same dish, using wooden spoons. J. L. Charmet.

Europe, we are dealing with an ancient structure which had existed before the socio-economic transformations of the early modern period. In Tuscany at the beginning of the fifteenth century, the Florentine *catasto* of 1427 reveals that 44 per cent of *mezzadri* households were of the extended or multiple type; this tendency was not specific to the *mezzadria*, and similar rates may be found among small property-owners and *affittuari* (Klapisch-Zuber, 1972). On average, however, *mezzadri* households had more children than the others.

The ancient households of Russian serfs, which combined vertical and horizontal complexity, are revealed to us by the registers of the Michino demesne compiled at the beginning of the nineteenth century (Czap, 1983). They cannot be attributed to the sole effect of serfdom, since this family model was equally successful in regions, such as the edges of the Urals, where the peasantry had avoided serfdom.

The extended or complex family appears to be particularly well adapted to an economy of great estates, in which levying dues (in whatever form, whether as part of the produce, as in *métayage*, or as labour dues, as in Polish or Russian estates), relied on the contribution of an unpaid workforce. The more numerous the family, the greater the available workforce. Great landowners thus favoured the widest forms of co-residence among their peasants, encouraging early marriage and preventing young people from leaving.

Since the peasants themselves thought that the only way of raising their income was by increasing the family workforce, they too moved in this direction. In terms of economic rationality, however, their calculation only served to strengthen the system of exploitation bearing down on them. It is, however, rare for family strategies to follow a purely economic rationale. In the case of peasants who were established in a domanial economy, the individual's sense of security and immersion in the group, which he could derive from belonging to a great house, cannot be ignored. These families had turned themselves into bastions in periods of uncertainty when protection by the state or by a lord was not available. Furthermore, the inertia mechanism inherent in every institution had ensured that this feeling survived even when the reality had changed, and generated a system of values in which the family was invested with all the tasks and all the rights pertaining to the social environment.

The developmental gap between the north-western perimeter and the rest of Europe, which was established during the period under consideration, consolidated the contrast between a largely predominant nuclear model in the north-west and a greater frequency of extended or complex family forms elsewhere. It did not, however, create that contrast. It is the nature of the statistical sources available for studying family structures with their many lacunae, as well as the desire to break with the received notion of a linear and uniform trajectory from the extended family to the nuclear family, which has inspired most recent research. This means that it is at the moment difficult to discern precisely what did change in the forms of family organization in Europe during the modern period.

An evolution at different speeds

Is it really necessary to shelve all ideas about the evolution of family structures when tackling the history of a period so fertile in major mutations affecting the social and mental structures of Europe? Some historians of the family are not resigned to this, proposing instead a comprehensive scheme of evolution. We shall mention only two attempts, by Edward Shorter and Lawrence Stone. The concept of modernization, which Shorter (1977) applies to the family sphere in order to qualify the transformations accompanying the passage to industrial society from the mid-eighteenth century onwards, alongside judicious hypotheses about the pioneering role of the proletariat in the invention of a new affective model (romantic love), is based simply on reviving Tönnies's old evolutionist thesis ('from community to society').

The interpretation proposed by Lawrence Stone (1977) is more circumscribed in space and more firmly centred on our period, as it reconstitutes the history of the English family from the beginning of the sixteenth century to the end of the eighteenth. At first sight it appears to adopt the same procedure as Shorter: Stone outlines a three-tiered diagram (open lineage family; restricted patriarchal family; closed nuclear family) which integrates all the signs of change into a compre-hensive evolution and postulates the family's progressive passage from an extended to a restricted structure. It is a surprising postulate when one recalls the insistence with which Peter Laslett and the Cambridge Group established the antiquity of the nuclear model as the dominant type of household in English society.

Stone, however, does not envisage this evolution as a linear and ineluctable advance towards a greater respect for individual autonomy and more harmonious relations between individuals. The passage to the patriarchal family, for instance, which in his view owed much to the new religious climate, reinforced the subordination of wife and children to the head of the family and the hierarchical nature of their relationships. One sign among others of this hardening was the introduction of corporal punishment into educational practice, even in the universities.

Furthermore, contrary to Shorter and his fluid concept of 'modernization', according to which all levels of reality change at the same time, Stone attempts to determine and to document in the case of every mutation the instance which constituted the principal site and motor of the change. In this context, he presents his concept of the 'restricted patriarchal family' as the joint product of a transformation of political and religious attitudes. The reinforcement of monarchical power, the diffusion of humanist ideas about the legal state and sovereignty, transferred to the person of the king or the nation a great part of the ties of affection and loyalty which bound the individual to his kindred and the protection of his lord.

Parallel to this, the Anglican doctrine of holy matrimony, which broke with the ancient Pauline depreciation of the state of marriage, exalted the value of the conjugal tie. Just as it turned the sovereign into the religious head of the kingdom, it turned the husband into the religious head of his family. Arguments against each of Stone's hypotheses may be found: he can be criticized for attributing to the elite classes an exclusive ability to invent new ways of feeling and thinking, and for envisaging the diffusion of cultural models simply as a 'percolation' from the upper classes down to working people. To him, however, we owe the attempt to reconstitute the evolution of family life with all its distinctive features by stipulating for each period the level at which, and the process by which the change was made.

The most ambiguous aspect of his approach is that it is applied essentially to analysing family attitudes, but employs terms to describe them which apply to organizational structures and forms. According to Stone, it is the psychological architecture of family reality which constitutes an object of historical research: what, in other words, exposes it directly to the evolution of the political organization of a society, to its intellectual or religious climate. This evolution is one which follows several rhythms simultaneously. It undergoes the relatively brief fluctuations of intellectual and sentimental fashion, and of the generation effect. It is at this level that the most visible changes are attested, and sometimes demonstrated by the actors themselves in their correspondence, diaries and writings – in short, in the documents to which Stone pays the most attention. His history of the English family is a pertinent reconstitution, such as Philippe Ariès had undertaken for the French family, of an intellectual and sentimental journey.

Family reality can, however, also be grasped in a long-term history, one involving unconscious testimony and principles of organization. Not only do these family structures alter more slowly, but their purpose is to resist change and to ensure their transmission and reproduction. Since they are taken for granted as part of the fabric of everyday life, they are not mentioned in the documentation of the period, and the historian often has to make do with hypotheses.

Households: size and social power

What was new about this period was that it produced the first stirrings of a preoccupation with statistics: it has left us with vast numbers of documents (tax records, lists of inhabitants, manorial and domanial registers), on the basis of which the study of family structures is possible. The statistical source material is very unevenly distributed, being, for instance, more plentiful in England than in France, but it can be found (and this makes it even more precious) in those parts of Europe like the Scandinavian and Baltic countries, or the Austrian possessions, where qualitative sources, such as Stone was able to make extensive use of in the case of England, are particularly rare.

When these sources are capable of being arranged in series and of providing contrasts, they generally reveal the least recorded if not the least conscious family practices. Their special advantage is that they are not restricted to the upper levels of society, which formed part of the literate world and had both the leisure and the habit of self-expression, but that they are able to 'photograph' all the domestic groups within a parish or a region at a given moment.

It would be naive to think that, by passing from personal testimony to serial sources, the historian is able to leave all ideological muddle behind him in favour of the certainties of objective reality. Censuses tend to treat family categories with Procrustean ruthlessness, and translating a whole gamut of indigenous concepts about the domestic group and kinship relations into the census-taker's categories (intended for tax collection, Church administration, etc.) multiplies the risks of error and mis-understanding. As with any other document, they need to be read with vigilance and critical acumen.

Let us take the case of Paewelia Michkli Michel, a dependent farmer on the Lihula estate at Karusa, a parish in northern Estonia. In the 1782 census, he appears as head of the household with his wife and three daughters, his father and his sister. 'Reconstituting' his family, however, reveals that two of his three daughters were really his step-children (his wife's children by a previous marriage), and that the person who claimed to be his father was actually the father of his wife's first husband. This 'revision of souls' thus makes no distinction between children born of several marriages. In some parishes, the children or kin of the head of the family living at home are referred to simply as menservants or maids (Palli, 1983).

In these instances, the census-taker was concerned to discover the size of the workforce each hearth was able to provide for forced labour dues. For him, then, it was more important to distinguish between the active and the inactive members of the household than to record their precise relationship to the head of the family. Whether identifying a group of producers, taxpayers or church-goers, the census will always present an incomplete picture: a function, in algebraic language, of the domestic group.

But did not the domestic group itself, conceived as a residential unit, correspond to at least a partial definition of what made up a family? In the Hungarian census of 1804, for instance, the family unit was not defined by co-residence but by commensality. It was frequently the case among the peasantry that a married son working alongside his father would continue to take his place with his family at his parents' table, but would live separately in a house built on the same parcel of land as his parents'. The Hungarian countryside presented a huge range of family combinations, in which co-possession, co-farming and co-residence did not necessarily coincide.

This extreme example illustrates the extent to which the notional family, by virtue of its functions and extensions, extended beyond the residential unit. What we call 'family' covered a reality which could move rapidly over several forms of solidarity. One family would unite all those linked by blood or a common ancestor, another those living under one roof and sharing the same interests as producers or consumers. Ambiguity is built into the language. In the sixteenth century the word 'family' was still close to its Latin meaning of *domestic* group, not a group of relations. Although the term went on gradually to absorb some of the solidarity of blood relationship, this was because the world of citizens progressively replaced that of 'cousins', as Stone wrote. The kinship tie, which henceforth had to compete with other solidarities like attachment to ruler, nation or social class, had atrophied and in part fossilized. Its most visible, everyday and well-worn form tends to be confused with domestic solidarity.

For a long time it was believed that the families of pre-industrial Europe were much larger than our own, and that this was due to their great fertility. Frédéric Le Play, who provided the myth of the extended family with a theoretical basis, claimed that the average mother gave birth to between fifteen and twenty children in the course of her married life. This hypothesis has been discredited by demographic historians since the publication of Pierre Goubert's works. Delayed marriage, prolonged lactation and a high mortality rate which broke up many marriages and removed half of all young people under twenty years of age, all made it extremely difficult merely to replace the old generation.

Families which handed their children over to wet-nurses, meaning the upper classes in particular, but in the eighteenth century also the urban middle classes who ran shops and workshops, tended to be more prolific. In Lyons, the baby-a-year which has been dismissed rather too quickly as a myth by demographic historians, reappeared in the eighteenth century among butchers' families: twelve, sixteen, twenty births per family were frequent. Without achieving quite such heights, the silk workers in the parish of Saint-Georges also seem to have been very prolific, with an average of 8.5 births for every complete family (Garden, 1970).

Mortality was higher in the towns, and death was quick to wrest these surplus births from urban families, hitting the poor harder than the rich. Curiously enough, though, apart from Tuscany in the fifteenth century, this social indexation of mortality, though frequently observed by demographic historians, is almost never confirmed by the number of children per household. In the hundred English parishes observed between 1574 and 1821, gentlemen, at the top of the social scale, had more children than paupers or workmen, but fewer than clergymen and farmers (Laslett, 1972). The same has been observed in France, in the provostship of Valenciennes under Louis XIV. The number of children did not vary according to the head of the family's social status (Dupâquier, 1979b).

At the end of the seventeenth century, Vauban in France and Gregory King in England were nevertheless convinced that the size of households was related to their social rank. King postulated an average of forty persons in the households of lords, sixteen for baronets and eight to mere gentlemen. His estimates were exaggerated, but the principle was sound: the average size of the English household between 1576 and 1821 was 4.7 persons; it rose to 6.6 for gentlemen, and fell to 3.9 for paupers. The correlation may in fact be verified almost anywhere: in fifteenth-century Tuscany, where the size of households increased according to their wealth (Klapisch-Zuber and Herlihy, 1978); in sixteenth-century Hungary, where the township of Szigetvar provides a striking instance in the 1551 census (Andorka and Farago, 1983); in France under Louis XIV, where the largest households in the provostship of Valenciennes belonged to husbandmen, being swollen by their many resident servants (on large farms, three-quarters of all menservants and half of all maidservants lived in). Artisan and worker households were of about average size; the smallest were those of the poor and of widows (Dupâquier, 1979b).

Thus it was not the fertility of a married couple which determined the size of a household, but their ability to gather more people than just their own progeny under one roof. The size of households was an indicator not of demographic vitality but rather of social influence. It was their wealth which allowed the upper classes to keep a large number of servants and to take in unmarried relatives. This superiority may be observed numerically in agglomerations where a degree of social segregation prevailed. In Györ, in eighteenth-century Hungary, households were definitely larger in the town centres where the well-to-do middle classes lived, and in Vienna this was also the case in the aristocratic Herrengassen quarter.

On the other hand, when a noble or bourgeois house distinguished itself from the mass and asserted its pre-eminence, it disappears from statistical averages. This was the case in England, where the gentry, unlike most other European nobilities, preferred life in the country. Averages obtained from the 'hundred English villages' give an impression of great uniformity, of a population made up of restricted families. The peasants, however, had quite the opposite impression of the imperious presence of the lord's castle in every English village, or in every four out of five villages, according to Laslett.

At Goodnestone-next-Wingham, in Kent, the vicar compiled a census of one of the three gentleman households in 1676. This was Squire Hale's, and included twenty-three persons, fifteen of whom were servants. Since these servants were on the whole very young and were almost all from the parish, it may be said that one in every five households at Goodnestone was under some obligation to Squire Hales (Laslett, 1969). This modest gentleman, who was not even the landowner, is illustrative at his level of the ostentatious dimension of the aristocratic household. Plenty of servants, as well as the fact that he kept some of his relations under his roof, did not reflect any economic purpose, but rather a social obligation. Using manpower to excess was evidence of one's power, and of generosity to families with children to place.

The size of households other than those belonging to the elite classes was linked to their wealth, but was measured by their productive capacity, not their spending power. In western Europe, the large peasant households belonging to yeomen in England, or to *laboureurs* in France, contributed to their wealth and social dominance. In central and eastern Europe, however, household sizes no longer necessarily coincided with social rank. At Villgraten, a township in the Austrian Alps devoted solely to stockraising, and therefore needing plenty of labour, the size of households in 1781 varied in exact proportion to the size of herds (Schmidtbauer, 1983). At Nagykovacsi, a Hungarian village near Buda, in 1769 serf households were the largest, with an average of 7.5 persons, and the free population had the smallest households, with 5.5 persons for peasant property-owners and 4.2 for labourers. In this region, those peasants who had been reduced to serfdom were often the wealthiest (Andorka and Farago, 1983).

However, it was not wealth in itself which induced a family to grow larger; it was the nature of the relationships binding it to its estate. In Poland, the Baltic countries and the Austrian Empire, large household establishments and small conjugal families could both be found on the large estates. Following a trickle-down method of land exploitation, large households delegated their forced labour dues to the smaller ones, enabling them to use their own workforce on their own tenures.

In modern Europe, the size of the domestic group increased dramatically, not as a result of serfdom, but of all those systems of land exploitation in which the size of the workforce determined both the tenant's income and the landowner's dues. This was the case, for instance, with the *mezzadria*. In fifteenth-century Tuscany, *mezzadri* households were markedly fuller than those of other peasants. In the eighteenth century, in the Abruzzi (at Morro d'Oro), they were almost twice as large, with eight persons per household as against 4.9 for the population as a whole.

The nuclear family never crossed the Oder

The Austrian Alps, central Hungary and the Abruzzi are all remarkable for their high levels of large-size domestic groups. Although these regions belonged to three different agrarian systems, they all shared the same need for an extensive workforce. Most of the households in these three regions were poly-nuclear. At Villgaten in Austria, only 2 per cent of farms with few animals consisted of multiple households, whereas in those owning more than fifteen animals, the proportion was 47.5 per cent. At Morro d'Oro in the Abruzzi, the proportion of multiple households in the population as a whole was 25 per cent; among the *mezzadri* it was 66 per cent. Conversely, it was not the small size of the households which determined the anthropological unit of English society, since half of the English population in the sixteenth and seventeenth centuries lived in families of six or more members; it was the small number of complex households, which never rose above 20 per cent and was generally less than 10 per cent.

This homogeneity was not present in France. In the 1732 *gabelle* (salt-tax) registration in the Paris Basin, the average number of 3.5 *gabelle*-payers per hearth (since children below the age of eight were exempt) was exceeded in Perche, in the Bray country and in Berry. According to

Dupâquier (1979a), this points to a higher percentage of complex households. The contrast is heightened when one compares northern with southern France. Seven urban and rural parishes in the north, Normandy and the Paris region, which were counted in the seventeenth and eighteenth centuries, were divided into 77 per cent nuclear households and 8 per cent complex households. Six southern parishes in Périgord, Rouergue, Provence and the Pyrenees in the same period consisted of 51 per cent one-family households and 41 per cent complex households.

The propensity to live in complex family groups extended much further south than France. In Italy in the eighteenth century, these represented one fifth of all households in the Bologna region and more than half in some parts of Tuscany. The propensity increased the further one moves towards eastern Europe. In Germany and Austria, although the nuclear model was statistically in the majority, the proportion of groupings comprising three generations, a couple or a widow and married children, was never negligible. This tendency was linked to a custom frequent among peasants of handing over their farm to one of their children on reaching an age when they wished to retire, but continuing to live under the same roof.

In Austria in the late eighteenth century, 12 per cent of hearths included at least one retired parent. The proportion was smaller in the north-east, where the custom of inheritance by the last-born child predominated (20.4 per cent of the extended households in the Metnitz region in 1757), and was especially high in the Alpine zone: at Zell am Ziller in Tyrol in 1759, almost half of all households were of the extended type. The success of this formula can be explained both by the strong need for a family or servant workforce in a pastoral economy dedicated almost exclusively to stockraising, and by lax seigneurial control. In the subalpine region, where a domanial economy prevailed, the lord encouraged widowed peasants to remarry in order to maintain his capital in manpower. In Tyrol, on the contrary, the farmer had more freedom of choice and often preferred to remain on his own in charge of his farm, apart from taking on a servant to perform those tasks which had fallen to his wife. Such pressure as he was subjected to came not from his lord but from his children, the eldest especially, who opposed any idea of their father remarrying.

Hungary was more complex. Here, ethnic and religious diversity and the rich variety of forms of family co-operation meant that the physiognomy of the domestic groups differed from one village to another. On the great plain, the high number of complex households seems to have been dictated by the economic conditions of a sparsely populated region.

Farms tended on the whole to be large and, in order to achieve a degree of division of labour and to engage in stockraising, they needed to be able to rely on a large family workforce.

Can one really talk about a model of family organization specific to eastern Europe? It is possible to find a few features common to the area between southern Serbia and northern Estonia, passing through Poland and Russia: features such as the average size (eight to nine persons) of the household, which was much higher than in western Europe, and a strong propensity towards multiple households, both being extreme forms of tendencies in evidence in central Europe. On the other hand, the situation varied so much between regions and periods that it is difficult to think in terms of a homogeneous model.

Two parishes in Estonia, Karuse (3,000 inhabitants in 1686) in the north and Vändra (976 inhabitants in 1683) in the south, give us a measure of the contrasts which may be observed within the same region. At Vändra in the late seventeenth century, the average number of persons per household was reckoned at 7.4, but at 11 on farms since, apart from the twenty-seven labourer families who lived separately but were included within their employers' households, a certain number of farms were held by co-farmers (*Hälftner*) who were not necessarily related or co-resident. In this province, 65 per cent of households were nuclear, 23.5 per cent were multiple, and 6.5 per cent extended. At Karuse by the end of the seventeenth century households were clearly smaller (six persons on average). Northern Estonia had abandoned co-farming. In 1710–11, Karuse was ravaged by the plague, as was a large part of the region, and lost two-thirds of its population. After this sharp fall, the size of households climbed back to an average of 6.9 persons in 1739, and reached eight in 1795.

In this period, the parish, which included four estates, consisted of 48 per cent nuclear, 39 per cent multiple and 13 per cent households of the extended type. A century earlier, the proportion of nuclear households must have exceeded 50 per cent, but would still have been smaller than at Vändra. Which of these two examples came closer to the regional norm? We do not possess comparative data for Estonia, but we do have a 1797 'revision' for the neighbouring province of Courland two years after its annexation by Russia, which included forty-one estates and 2,824 farms. Half of the hearths were nuclear (50.4 per cent), one third were multiple (31.8 per cent) and one sixth were extended in type. Of the two parishes, therefore, it was Karuse with its more numerous complex households, which came closest to the Baltic standard (Palli, 1983).

It is useful to be able to distinguish, when the documentation allows it, between farms in which several conjugal groups co-operated without fully co-residing, and farms in which everyone lived under one roof in a complex household. As far as the family was concerned, however, did this involve two completely different structures? If one considers co-residence to be the major criterion for determining the family sphere within which relationships of authority were organized and reproduced, and feelings of solidarity and intimacy were nurtured, should one not also allow a degree of shared experience among the members of a household establishment who rubbed shoulders daily but lived separately? Like the members of a complex household living under one roof, they too were placed under a single authority and shared the same interests.

The family model of the Baltic estate is distinguished most clearly from that of the Russian serf by the use of servant labour, as illustrated by research into Michino, an estate of four villages in the Ryazan region early in the nineteenth century (Czap, 1983). The *dvor* was both a farm and a household, being a unit of production adjusted to the size of a family. It was in the interest of the head of the family to gather as many people as possible under one roof, because serf tenures, being constantly redistributed, were calibrated according to the size of the family. This was also in the lord's interest, because the productivity of a household (meaning the size of the workforce available for forced labour dues) increased with its size.

Furthermore, the estate existed within a closed circuit: 90 per cent of girls who got married were born on the estate, and masculine emigration was almost nil. The population was grouped into large household establishments, beyond which there was nothing. The few nuclear families which did exist were either accidental or temporary situations. In 1814, the average household contained nine persons, a size which remained stable until half-way through the century, apart from a slight drop in 1843 due to the combined effects of cholera and poor harvests. However, 70 per cent of the population lived in households larger than the average size, and 18 per cent in households of more than fifteen persons.

Of all families, 7.6 per cent were of the nuclear type. Contrary to what happened in western Europe, these families did not consist of young couples with small children, but corresponded to the debris of complex families which had split up as a result of disagreement. Of these, 10.8 per cent were of the extended type: some did show a stem-family profile (for instance, a widowed father living with one of his married sons). Such families were, however, rare, because the principle of the stem family, which consisted of choosing a single heir to avoid splitting up the farm, was completely counterproductive in a system under which the land allotted was constantly adjusted to the size of the family.

The overwhelming majority of households (74 per cent) were of the complex type, a good half of them constituting patrilineages through the association of parents with several married sons. While one estate cannot represent the whole of Russia, we have enough indicators from other places to show that this was not a regional or local anomaly. The propensity to live in multiple families had been stimulated, as we saw, by the domanial economy and the system of serfdom. It certainly increased in the course of the eighteenth century. In the Vologda province in 1678, 58.5 per cent of all households were single families. By 1717, the proportion was only 39.2 per cent. This family model was, however, not integral to serfdom. In western Siberia, where serfdom had been avoided, the proportion reached 76 per cent of households in the Surgut district by the mid-eighteenth century, and 85 per cent in the Beriozovo district. Nor was it linked to socio-economic conditions. In the Ryazan province, the households of state serfs, whose economic system was very different from that of other serfs, were noticeably the same size as households in Michino.

The entity which we have, perhaps wrongly, treated as a model, corresponds in reality to the statistically superior or important frequency of one type of household. What threshold may, however, be applied when it comes to deciding what type of household represents the dominant or preferred model? Some researchers were encouraged by the earliest works testifying to the ancient roots of the nuclear model to state that, in every society at least half of all households were of the nuclear type – for reasons which are related more to demographic mechanisms than to cultural choice. In the light of recent research into the Baltic lands, Russia and Hungary, we now know that this law did not apply to eastern Europe and is disputed with regard to central Europe.

Nevertheless, it is obvious that if the nuclear model is taken as dominant in every area where it accounted for more than half the households, we can no longer take account of the important cultural contrasts between western and central Europe or, for instance, between northern and southern France. Sociology has taught us to distinguish between the norm and the average, the most frequent practice and the preferential practice. In the French Pyrenees during the nineteenth century, the stem family, considered the ideal family model, was realized in less than 20 per cent of domestic groups. On the basis of a study conducted on a village near Lavedan, where Le Play (1875) thought he had discovered the archetypal stem family, it has been demonstrated that most of the 'houses' adopted successively, during the course of their domestic cycle, the forms of a stem family, a conjugal family, and finally a multiple family. As soon as the economic situation allowed, however, they would rearrange themselves into their preferred organizational form, that of the stem family. The preferred model was not necessarily the most prevalent. How, then, is preference to be defined if statistical distribution does not constitute an adequate indicator? The classification of households proposed by Laslett, which has turned out to be an extremely useful tool for conducting comparative studies into the ordering of domestic groups, has here reached the limit of its usefulness. It allows one to describe the composition of each household type, but not to grasp its internal coherence, the degree of its openness to the outside world and its ability to perpetuate itself, what, to use Le Play's own words, constituted its 'stability' or 'instability'.

Young people in service: the secret agents of the Western household

These features can often be spotted in serial sources. For instance, Hajnal (1983) retained three in his model of the Western family, which develops the model of the Western marriage elaborated by him twenty years earlier. He made the West move far towards the East, because he observed that, in the pre-industrial period, his model gave way to an Eastern model on the further side of a line drawn from St Petersburg to Trieste. According to him, this model was not defined by the form assumed by the domestic group, but by the conditions under which it shaped and reproduced itself. These were, firstly, delayed marriage; secondly, neolocal residence; and thirdly, placing young people in service with other families until they married. During the last few years, much emphasis has been laid on the role of delayed marriage, in early modern western Europe, in increasing the couple's autonomy and promoting their conjugal relationship. On the other hand, few specialists had perceived the significance of circulating children in service before Laslett invented the expression 'life-cycle servant' to describe the phenomenon. Many family books or autobiographical accounts in France, England and Germany refer to this practice in the seventeenth and eighteenth centuries. Restif de la Bretonne tells us about his father's move to Paris when an adolescent. As the eldest son of a well-off Burgundian peasant, he was placed in service with his cousin, who was an usher in the capital.

Ralph Josselin was the vicar of a rural parish in Essex who kept a diary. It provides us with invaluable evidence about the private life and state of mind of what could be termed the English middle class in the seventeenth century. In it he tells us how he bound the elder of his two sons as an apprentice at the age of fifteen and placed two of his four daughters in service at fourteen and thirteen (Macfarlane, 1970).

On the other hand, there is little reference to the widespread nature of this practice before the end of the eighteenth century: in the mountain villages near Zurich, the custom of placing children aged six and over with weavers to earn their living (*Rast geben*) was linked to the demand for labour during the proto-industrial period, and was thus fairly recent. Elsewhere, however, the practice formed part of a very old tradition. This was the case among the small peasants of the Vorarlberg region, who took their young children aged between eight and sixteen to the Ravensburg market in spring to auction them off as servants to the big farmers, and came to fetch them back at the end of autumn (Shorter, 1977).

In England, a census conducted in 1381 in Rutland refers to the presence of servants in 20 per cent of hearths, a similar proportion to that found between the sixteenth and nineteenth centuries. The practice was more widespread in deprived regions and levels of society. It allowed poor households to rid themselves of part of the burden on their family while providing a relatively cheap labour supply for other families in need of manpower, for instance, while their own children were still small. However, the main result of this practice – and, for some, the chief purpose – was educational. In the countryside, it was as successful with the rich as the poor; good Flemish farmers living at the end of the *ancien régime* would place their sons with husbandmen in Artois for one or two years to learn something of French language and manners. At all levels of society, families exchanged their children to teach them *savoir faire* and give them some experience of life: '*coqs de village*', artisans, shopkeepers and lawyers all did it, and so did the gentry.

Why did parents feel this need to give others the task of educating and socializing their adolescent children? First of all, it was clearly the idea that technical and social apprenticeship required a prolonged initiation of the child in the outside world. Taking adolescents out of the family circle was intended to make them adaptable; and it was thought that the loss of the family's emotional support would equip them for the rigours of life.

To this was added the conviction that when the years of cosseting were over, during which the young child was left to the mother's attentive and permissive care, his education turned into a training process – a matter for men which required authority, even brutality. While the father could provide all this, there was a risk that the affection he felt for his own children would impede his obligation to be severe. This was why he preferred to hand the rod over to someone who was not hampered by the emotional bonds of fatherhood – to a stranger if need be. An Italian traveller in England in 1500, on discovering this custom that was so alien to his own culture, wrote, 'I think that they do this because they value their own comfort and are better served by strangers than they would be by their own children' (quoted by Stone, 1977).

Many authors have stressed the violence to which children were subjected by their parents, masters and employers in the past. Recently a historian has been influenced by the psychoanalytic approach to go so far as to state that the condition of a child until the dawn of the twentieth century was one long martyrdom (de Mause, 1974). It is hard to say whether the modern period saw a rise in violence towards children, or whether they had always been subjected to large doses of brutality. On the other hand, from the sixteenth century onwards, it is possible to distinguish a rise in reasoned or pedagogical violence. Stone has described this process in England very well, with the introduction of corporal punishment in public schools and colleges. Education by blows was justified in theory by a pessimistic vision of human nature, inspired by the Christian doctrine of original sin. In its Protestant variant, especially that of English puritanism, the doctrine encouraged even greater rigour.

This 'educational' violence could be found on the farm and in the workshop under a more uncouth and disorganized form: abusive sanctions, wounds and broken arms which sometimes left a child maimed for life. Memoirs written by former apprentices are numerous, for instance, in eighteenth-century Germany, where the hatter Anton Reiser, the jeweller Kloden and others all insisted on the brutality of their masters. 'Apprentices, especially in small workshops', Kloden exclaimed when recalling his youth at the end of the eighteenth century, 'I knew only too well that they were the slaves of Europe' (quoted by Müller, 1969).

States and municipalities started to legislate against this sort of abuse. A Prussian law decreed that the master must not go beyond 'what the father of a family would permit himself'. In reality, though, the educational model which inspired this violence originated in the family; schooling and the placing of young people in service constituted two aspects, in part competing and in part combined, of the same tendency of families to transfer to others the task of completing their children's education. England and the Scandinavian countries were the most literate regions of Europe at the end of the eighteenth century, as well as those in which the phenomenon of the life-cycle servant was most widespread.

Perhaps this avoidance behaviour, which consisted of transferring to others the violent tasks deemed inseparable from education, should be examined more closely. Can it be explained by a desire to remove the

crises of adolescence from face-to-face family dealings (especially relations between father and son)? Was it that these crises, which are feared
and ritualized by every society, were here resolved by transplanting
them? At a deeper, possibly unconscious level, it may have been a dread
of incest that drove parents to remove their children at the approach of
puberty in order to protect their family from the risks of dangerously
powerful sexual impulses.

For the child, the earlier his experience of servant status, the more
important the part it played in forming his personality and view of the
world. In the Bedfordshire village of Cardington in the late eighteenth
century, a quarter of all boys were placed in service between the ages of
ten and fourteen. In the Salzburg region during the same period, they
started at the age of nine (boys earlier than girls), and most children left
their families from the age of twelve.

The experience was both damaging and educational: it injured the
special bonds which tied a child to his or her family, even when the new
family recreated a loving climate and a similar style of authority (the
master assumed some of the father's powers and duties). The exclusive
and bonding childhood sense of belonging to the circle of close relations
gave way to an acute awareness of autonomy – and soon to an assertion
of it. Placing adolescents in service schooled them in individualism.

It was also an educational experience, because it taught the young to
separate work relations from parental relations. Put in a situation where
these no longer coincided, they discovered sooner the contractual nature
of their obligations to the master, clothed though they were in a moral
and affective garb. It is difficult to say whether this practice created a
psychological terrain favourable to a market economy and to capitalist
work practices where it was current. However, it can be said that the
surviving aspects of a family concept of economic relations, which recur
in paternalistic doctrines and experiences during the industrial period,
had a looser hold in regions where the practice of the life-cycle servant
had been diffused.

Where the placing of young people had spread widely and been
assimilated to an apprenticeship system, every social level was affected.
In the Danish island of Moen in 1645, 19 per cent of farmers' children
and 36 per cent of labourers' children aged between ten and fourteen
were placed in service. Between the ages of twenty and twenty-nine, 46
per cent of farmers and 80 per cent of labourers' children were servants
(Hajnal, 1983).

For those who came from prosperous backgrounds, servant status
represented a temporary drop in social status. This demotion had an
initiatory value. Boys were employed to perform subordinate tasks (but

Illustration for Restif de la Bretonne's *La Paysanne pervertie* (1784). The home of a prosperous peasant, as described by Restif on the basis of his own upbringing. The seating plan for this large family bespeaks an etiquette no less rigorous or subtle than that found at court. Bibliothèque Nationale, Paris.

never household duties), as shepherds for instance, and they would take on the inferior status that went with them. In the young Restif's family the domestic hierarchy imposed an etiquette 'as well regulated as the setting of the duchesses' stools at the court of Louis XIV' (Le Roy Ladurie, 1975). It determined the table settings at supper, for instance, with the cowman and the shepherd coming at the end of the list, after the carters and the vineyard workers, and just above the two serving-girls.

Although his drop in status was only temporary, because the farmer's son recovered his social status on marriage and became equal if not superior to his former employer, at the same time it was marked enough to teach him the value, the relativity and the flexibility of all social hierarchy.

Children were sometimes placed with distant relatives, but more often with neighbours or local friends. This circulation gave rise to other exchange circuits, reciprocal gifts, even producing spouses (it was not impossible for the young man to end by marrying into the family where he had been placed as a servant), or it flowed into existing circuits. In every case, it forced the domestic group to open up widely to the society around it, to become outward-looking instead of turning in on its kinship network. It favoured ties of a social and diffuse nature, which have to be constantly renewed and extended at the expense of blood ties, which are made once and for all.

In regions where such placing was common, most servants were young and single. Five per cent of English children between the ages of ten and fourteen (in the seventeenth and eighteenth centuries), 10 per cent of Norwegians (1801), 20 per cent of Icelanders (1729) and more than 30 per cent of Danes (1787–1801) were in service. The proportion for those aged between twenty and twenty-four varied from 33 per cent for Norwegians to 54 per cent for Danes. In total, it can be estimated that one adult in two, in this part of Europe, had experienced servant status at some time during youth, and that the permanent proportion of these life-cycle servants was greater than 10 per cent of the population: servants represented somewhat less than 10 per cent of the population in Norway in 1801, 17 per cent in Iceland in 1729 and 18 per cent in Denmark at the end of the eighteenth century. They represented 14 per cent in England during our period (1754–1821) and about the same proportion in the Low Countries. In France, they seem to have been more numerous in the north, where the nuclear household predominated, than in the south: at Montplaisant in Périgord in 1644, where less than half of all households were nuclear, the proportion of servants was only 5.8 per cent. They amounted to 12.6 per cent in Longuenesse in the Calais region in 1778, where more than three-quarters of all households were nuclear. In

Provence during the same period (1770) they numbered only 5.7 per cent.

In Germany, Austria and even further east, in the Baltic lands, servants also exceeded 10 per cent of the population in some places.

These figures are of uncertain value, being sometimes too high (as when ages were not mentioned and life-cycle servants were confused with professional servants), and sometimes inadequate, as in the case of young people placed with a relation, who were generally designated by their kinship tie and not their servant status. This is why the Europe of servants, which according to Hajnal extended very far eastwards to a line running from St Petersburg to Trieste, ends by putting very different family cultures together.

Were there two, four or three models?

Laslett has tried to reconstitute a European geography of the best-articulated family forms. In order to elaborate his models, he combined four basic criteria (age at marriage, the age difference between spouses, the birth rate and the remarriage rate) with a certain number of secondary criteria such as the way domestic groups were formed, their family structure and their socio-economic profile (1983a).

This allowed him to distinguish four types (more in the nature of tendencies than models) which shared the European area during our period. They were:

A western type based on delayed and neolocal marriage, the nuclear household and the circulation of children in service. It corresponds to the north-western perimeter where the model defined by Hajnal is established with all its western attributes.

A 'mid-western' type which dominated in central Europe, both Germanic and Baltic, and differed from the previous one by its favourable attitude to the stem family.

A 'Mediterranean' type, characterized by the early age of girls at marriage, a wide age gap between spouses and a certain resistance to remarriage, and by more numerous complex families.

Finally, an eastern type, similar to the one which Hajnal places on the further side of the St Petersburg–Trieste line.

The point about this typology is that it acknowledges the intermediate formulae encountered across Europe, which do not really fit into either of the two models defined by Hajnal. But what it gains in descriptive coherence, it loses in localization. For instance, if one tried to define the characteristic particular to southern France in relation to northern France, which had adopted the 'western' nuclear model, one would have to connect it to the 'mid-western' type which favoured the stem family, not the 'Mediterranean' type. This 'mid-western' type, on the other hand, did not cover all Germany (since the north was predominantly nuclear) nor all Austria, even less all Hungary. As for the 'Mediterranean' type, it is more suited to the south of the Italian peninsula than to the regions north of the Apennines, and is ill-adapted to the Iberian peninsula. It suits Catalonia much less than Andalusia, not to mention Portugal, where the labourers on the great estates of Alentejo practised early and neolocal marriage and lived in nuclear households, whereas among the small property-owners of the north the stem-family system and delayed marriage were current.

As with all social indicators, the geographic distribution of family structures is revealed by the effects of dominance, of contrasts, whose impact and irregularity vary according to whether they are observed at the level of a continent or of national entities, a region or a micro-region. In Lower Saxony, for instance, two practically neighbouring micro-regions presented radically opposite structures at the end of the seventeenth century. In the Calenberg region, where a single child generally inherited the property, the stem family was the preferred formula, realized in 28 per cent of households in 1689. In the countryside around Göttingen, on the other hand, the farms were generally smaller and were divided between all the children; households were 90 per cent nuclear (Berkner, 1976).

On a European scale, it would seem more useful to distinguish between forms of family organization according to their cultural peculiarities rather than their geographical location. Instead of retaining Hajnal's two models and Laslett's four, it seems more profitable to return to the three basic models defined by Le Play: the nuclear model based on delayed neolocal marriage and centred on the conjugal group; the 'stem-family' model linked to the permanence of a 'house' or property transmitted to a sole heir; and the 'communitarian' model (which Le Play calls patriarchal) characterized by complex households of various forms and great size (lineage groups in which the parents co-reside with several married sons and *frérèches* containing several married sons and daughters and their families).

The nuclear family's vocation was to open up to the surrounding society, thanks to the practice of placing its children and of circulating servants. It was also the most flexible structure (Le Play would have called it unstable) and the one most redolent of the spirit of enterprise, since each new couple had to establish a home of their own. This model dominated the whole of north-western Europe during the modern age.

Stem families sometimes placed their children in service with other families too, but this did not involve real reciprocity. In their case, placement was prompted less by concern to complete their children's apprenticeship than by the need to remove them from the succession. Only the heir was called on to co-reside with his parents after his marriage, while waiting for them to die or to retire. This procedure was called *Leibzucht* in certain regions of Germany, and *Ausnahm* in Austria, and was especially common in the whole German-speaking area. The stem family was, however, the preferred form of family organization for large stretches of the mountainous or pastoral parts of Europe, places where the habitat was more often than not dispersed. It may be encountered between northern Portugal and the Baltic, passing via southern France and the Alpine zone.

Where the Baltic lands are concerned, the situation is debatable. The frequently considerable size of households, their complex and poly-nuclear structure, and the demesne system they fitted into, with forced labour dues, all constituted features related to the communitarian model. However, in certain regions such as Latvia, the farm would be trans-mitted to a sole heir (*Wirth*), with the other children moving away to work as farmhands (*Knechte*), thus giving the family group a stem-family profile.

In principle, the 'communitarian' family excluded recourse to servants, because its very reason for existing corresponded to the necessity of accumulating a large number of unpaid workers – consequently family members – in order to exploit serf tenure (in Russia or Poland), a system of *métairie* (in Poitou, Limousin, Auvergne and central Italy), or an undivided demesne (such as the tacit communities in Bourbonnais, Franche-Comté and Valois, or the Serbian *zadruga*), whose income depended on the level of labour invested. This model was not necessarily linked to dependent status, since it can be found just as frequently among peasants reduced to serfdom or precarious tenures as among farmers or landowners who had chosen non-division; and in Russia this type of family was just as prevalent in regions which had escaped serfdom.

The economic logic underlying this model dictated that children could not leave home. Legrand d'Aussy wrote about a tacit community in the Thiers region, called Guittard-Pinon, which he visited in 1788:

> Another fundamental law is the one concerning property. Never, under any circumstances, will it be shared . . . should a Guittard girl leave Pinon to marry, she will be given 6,000 livres in money; but she relinquishes her claim to everything . . . The same applies to the boys if one of them

establishes himself elsewhere. This has happened . . . but very seldom. All the members of the family stay put. Since they need many hands to farm their property and do not by any means have enough . . . they do not allow emigration.

This logic encouraged people to marry their children off very early and then to keep them beneath the family roof as long as possible.

When the family did not enforce this of its own accord, the lord or employer took care to do so to protect his own interests. At Michino, a Russian village belonging to Prince Gagarin, the peasants were informed in December 1817 of their lord's command that all unmarried and widowed daughters over fifteen years of age were required to work in the fuller's mill that the prince had just opened on another estate. Nearly all the parents undertook in writing to marry their daughters before Easter so as to avoid losing them. The forms of coercion were different under the *mezzadria* system, but the principle was the same: every reduction in the family's productive capacity was treated as a breach of contract. In 1752, the monks of San Gregorio in Bologna, who owned the land of Sant'Almasio, ended the tenancy of the Rinaldi family on account of the family head's death and the 'departure of a son from the paternal hearth'.

The same landlords had also granted the farm of San Donnino to N. Macchi in 1726–34. They subsequently installed him on a larger farm called Bassa di Camaldo. Two years later, however, Macchi asked to return to San Donnino 'because he has not got a large enough family to farm Bassa di Camaldo, nor the means to pay a servant' (Poni, 1983).

In spite of this chronic instability, the 'communal' model did encourage an autarkic withdrawal into a family universe geared to mobilizing the individual and taking charge of him from the cradle to the grave. Over and above their economic finality, groupings of this type were inspired by a defensive attitude to the social sphere, identifying their obligations of solidarity with their blood ties, and attempting to gather the greater part of their kinship network under one roof.

Family cycles and family tensions

One of the criticisms most often made of the study of family groups as conceived by Laslett is that it relies on a fixed representation of family structures: censuses provide to some extent 'snapshots' of a living and thus constantly changing reality. This method would consequently tend to remove from family groups their evolutionary dimension and the cyclical character of this evolution, which modifies their size and their function at the whim of demographic changes, marriages, births and deaths.

If this criticism involves questioning the extent to which the statistical data underlying our analysis are representative, it does not seem important. Since all the members of the same community were never born or married at the same moment, the chance arrangement of demographic events provides in every instance a sufficiently representative spectrum of the family cycle's different evolutionary stages.

However, the criticism is justified if it aims at making us more attentive to the dynamic dimension of the family group, and more aware of its individual duration. Keeping to the three models identified above, an account of their development cycles makes possible a better understanding of the characteristics peculiar to each, and reveals features which a synchronic approach would never suggest. The shortest and least enduring of the three, but also the most regular, is the cycle of the nuclear family, since every marriage established a new family group. The family grew larger according to the rhythm of its births, but never changed its structure; the tensions and authority clashes which could arise when the children reached puberty were avoided by placing them outside the family.

In France, where this practice seems to have been less common, the children often waited for their father to die before marrying and settling down. This waiting time was made endurable only by the conjunction of the delayed marriage norm and a high death rate; it also allowed the transmission of property and authority and the formation of new households to coincide. In England, however, where the life-cycle servant was a general phenomenon, the marriage calendar and the calendar for forming households were regulated by the labour market. When real wages increased, the rate of saving by young servants speeded up, allowing them to marry sooner. The increased marriage rate then gave rise in the next generation to an increased labour supply, which caused wages to fall. The trends in marriage rates and wages interacted over intervals of thirty years; the marriage rate fell at the end of the seventeenth century; it then rose again and stabilized between 1771 and 1776, then fell again at the beginning of the nineteenth century (Schofield and Wrigley, 1981).

The stem family, on the other hand, which at first sight seemed to provide every guarantee of stability because it was based on the principle of continuity, turned out to be particularly unstable in its mode of development. The most distinctive feature of the model was the co-residence of a young couple with the parents of husband or wife, but this feature occurred only during a part of the cycle at a moment which varied according to demographic and legal conditions. It came later if the rule was ultimogeniture, and earlier if it involved a female heir (girls married on average two or three years earlier than boys) and thus a son-in-law marriage. For demographic reasons, this was the case in 20 per cent of households with only daughters, and for legal reasons in some regions where the right of primogeniture was totally dominant (in the Pyrenees especially) or where the parent had total freedom of choice; in the Gevaudan region, for instance, parents, even if they had sons, could make their daughter their heir in order to realize a favourable option on the marriage market.

Being a truly variable construct, the stem family passed, depending on the head of the family's age, from a complex structure to an extended and then to a nuclear structure. Esparros in the Baronnies is not far from the village of Lavedan where Le Play thought he had rediscovered the miraculously preserved stem family, the prototype, according to him, of the family organization of France under the *ancien régime*. The existence here of the Guilhamets as one family and one house had been attested since the seventeenth century; during the course of the nineteenth century they had passed through all the five types delineated by Laslett: a couple with children (3b); a married son co-residing with his parents (5b); an extended family with one collateral (4c); 5b again; a couple with a grandparent (4d) and finally a widow with children (3d).

Any family group with the ambition to become a stem family had not only to undergo different metamorphoses in order to achieve the ideal form of co-residence with three generations, and to maintain it for a few years, but each transformation also constituted a source of tension and uncertainty about the fate of the household. Tension between the children, between parents and children while the heir had not yet been chosen, if the custom allowed choice, followed by tension between the head of the family and the heir, impatient to take control of his inheritance. At Saint-André-des-Alpes, a market town in Upper Provence, 45 per cent of all marriage contracts entered into in the eighteenth century mentioned the obligation to co-reside with parents, and almost all of them included an *insupport* clause to cover disagreement between parents and the heir (Collomp, 1977).

Research into crime in the jurisdiction of the Toulouse *Parlement* in the eighteenth century (Y. Castan, 1974; N. Castan, 1971), in Gévaudan (Claverie and Lamaison, 1982) and in Upper Provence (Collomp, 1983) has shown the extent to which the system of a sole heir, instead of creating harmony and stability in the family as Le Play thought, engendered a climate of disagreement; jealousy between rival brothers and resentment on the part of younger brothers who had been sacrificed by an unfair father often led to violence. Most crime, however, had its origin in disagreements about co-residence between the parents and the inheriting couple.

Unlike the stem family, the communal family did not insist on stability at all costs. In the case of the *mezzadria* system, for instance, the *mezzadri*'s concern to maintain a constant relationship between the size of the family and of their farm meant that they were constantly moving around, attracted by a larger farm or cutting back to a smaller one after a loss in productive capacity. On the large Russian estates, families did not move, but the size of their tenures was constantly readjusted according to each household's working capability.

Of these three models, the communal family was nevertheless the most stable, or rather the least responsive to the progress of the family cycle. It was not demographic events (marriage of the sons, death of head of household, etc.) which tore the household apart and gave rise to new family groups, but psychological tensions. At Michino, a Russian serf village, all new households were formed in the same way: when an existing family group split up as a result of conflict, generally following the marriage of a second son and the difficulties faced by the new couple in co-residing with the rest of the family.

Breaking away from the communal family was both a permanent threat and the only way of founding a new household. The threat was not restricted to Russia and the demesne system. It was conjured up in France in the eighteenth century by the peasants belonging to the *métayage* communities of Limagne and the tacit communities of Bourbonnais, in order to secure a marriage dispensation from Clermont officialdom: take for instance the widow of a *métayer* (share-cropper), who wished to remarry a cousin, and declared that the community to which she belonged 'has existed for sixty years, its members are incapable of rendering accounts', and that the only way in which she could safeguard her interests was by marrying within her kin (Poitrineau, 1980). Concerning the tacit communities, a vicar wrote that 'harmony between members is their guarantee of survival' in support of a request for a dispensation. These large household establishments were not, any more than the stem families, havens of peace and human warmth. The mantle of patriarchal power, which was not generally passed on until the death of the patriarch, concealed the frustration and renunciation of adults obliged to remain under the family roof, people whose marriages more often than not were made to confirm the stability of the group rather than to meet their personal inclinations.

The seeds of conflict were here as many as in stem families. If their crises resulted less often in crime, it was because the logic of communal family groups and the behavioural model which it elicited, tended to ignore the family cycle, or to render it ineffectual. In the case of the stem family, which was simultaneously inegalitarian and selective, crises gave rise to personal strategies making for competition and confrontation.

The test of economic transformations

According to Chayanov (1966), the peasant family was structured by a constant effort to adapt its production to its cyclical evolution, but the logic of our communal model serves to contradict this well-known theory about peasant economy. Kula (1972) said the following about the great Polish estates of the eighteenth century: 'They give the impression that the composition and structure of the family adapt to the invariable

The Son Punished (1777–8) by Greuze. The eldest son is driven from the family home by his ageing father, while his mother and the other children try to intercede in this dramatic confrontation between father and son. A classic instance of the conflict of authority which occurred in the middle-class families whose lives and sentiments Greuze illustrated, in relation generally to the choice of a trade or a spouse. In the peasant world such conflicts arose more often when a married heir lived with his parents. Musée du Louvre, Paris.

resources of the family's productive forces.' As in Russian estates, it was often the lord who imposed on peasant families measures designed to maintain their productive capacity.

The lord forbade girls to make exogamous marriages, which would take them from the estate: the 1733 regulation for the villages of Zegree and Rataje, belonging to the city of Poznan, stipulated that peasants were not to marry their daughters into other jurisdictions, but only into estates belonging to the city. The lord rehoused orphan children on his own authority, and he forced widows to remarry, as in the Ros regulation of 1804: 'Guardians are enjoined to marry off the widow within the year, and she must be warned that if she is not married with the space of a year . . . all her property will be put up for auction.'

Similar constraints were applied to the 'communal' households of western Europe. In the mid-eighteenth century, for instance, a *coparsonnière* widow in a Limagne *métairie* could declare to a Clermont official that she 'has to provide hands in order to compete with her brothers in farming their estate' and that she will be ousted if her marriage does not take place. The same situation applied to the *mezzadri* families (as we saw in the case of the lands belonging to the monks of San Gregorio in Bologna) who risked eviction or transfer to smaller farms if the head of the family died or an adult son left home.

The communal family demonstrated the same ability to withstand economic fluctuations by closing its gaps and compensating for a fall in its income by increasing its investment of labour to counteract the disruptive effect of the domestic cycle. Economic tensions strengthened the communal structures' tendency to immobility, which in its turn engendered economic immobility. When demographic growth caused wages to fall and levies to rise, the loss in peasant revenue, which in this case was masked by a larger investment in manpower, was revealed only by an increase in the size of households. This may be observed in the eighteenth century of the *métayage* area in central France, in that of the Italian *mezzadria*, in the great Baltic estates and, a little later, in Russia.

In spite of the nuclear family's greater flexibility (or because of it) the social edifice which it supported was affected to a far greater extent by the economic changes of the eighteenth century. This is demonstrated by a micro-regional study of three villages in south-western Norway, in which nearly all the families were nuclear at the start of the eighteenth century, and exchanged their children by placing them in service (Dyrvik, 1983); Etne, a parish of big farmers who combined stockraising with crop-growing; Sauda, consisting of smaller peasants engaged in stockraising and forestry; and Torvastad, a village of peasant-fishermen on the coast. The demographic surge which accelerated during the second half of the eighteenth century gave rise in all three villages to an increase in the number of labourer households without land. One might have expected it also to produce an increase in the adolescent population in service. The opposite happened in Etne and Sauda. In these two purely agricultural parishes, the inflation in the number of available wage workers caused wages to fall and competed with the system for placing adolescents in service. Even when young servants' wages were low, it became more profitable for a farmer to employ agricultural workers on a seasonal basis when work was plentiful, than to feed a servant all year round. At Torvastad, on the other hand, where the farms were on average smaller, the servant situation remained stable, and labourers found employment as sailor-fishermen. As for those peasants who engaged in fishing, they continued to need a servant to accompany them out to sea during the slack farming season, or to stand in for them on dry land.

No complex household could be found among the property-owning peasants of Sauda in 1758; in 1801, 38 per cent displayed a stem-family profile. In the event of the land being sold, Norwegian law gave the eldest child the privilege of buying it back at a low price after an interval of twenty years. Population growth transformed this possibility into a rule and immobilized the property market. The institution called *kar*, by which the parents could spend their retirement *in situ* by ceding their farm to their heir in return for a substantial life income, became general. Co-residing with their parents and taking on the high cost of supporting them was the price young people paid to get land which had otherwise become unobtainable. Faced with the crisis, the stem family was the least unattractive solution for the eldest children of the propertied class. For the others, it meant migration.

The practice of resorting to life-cycle servants was in retreat in the eighteenth century over the whole of north-western Europe, in places where it had ensured the stability of the nuclear structure. In England, where widowed parents, grandparents or collaterals were appearing in ever greater numbers in households in place of servants, the reduction was less marked in stockraising regions, which mobilized a very large permanent workforce. The pressure of population was, however, turning farmers away from stock towards cereals. Since the mid-eighteenth century in England, however, and in the first half of the nineteenth century in most of western Europe, the Industrial Revolution was attracting surplus peasants, who had been deprived of their land or their employment, to the manufacturing centres, where they went to swell the growing armies of the urban proletariat.

Prior to, or alongside this process, the industrialization of the countryside which accompanied and stimulated the population growth of the eighteenth century had specific effects on family structures. This was perhaps more clearly the case for the stem-family system than for the nuclear family.

Whether dealing with Switzerland, southern Germany, Austria or Languedoc, the threat posed to the stem family by proto-industrialization related much more to the internal organization of the domestic group than to its ability to redistribute its workforce. First to be challenged were patriarchal power and the pre-eminence of the heir; enhanced employment prospects and non-agricultural incomes robbed land, the heir's privilege, of its attraction, and consequently diminished the power of the patriarch who controlled access to it. Earlier marriage was encouraged. The subordination of wives to husbands was challenged by their common position as wage-earners. In its initial phase, proto-industrialization enrolled men and women, but established a sexual division of tasks: in the textile industry, for instance, the women spun and the men wove. During the ensuing period, however, when the advent of spinning factories forced the increasingly abundant rural workforce to fall back on weaving, it was the women who, by accepting lower wages, squeezed the men out of what had hitherto been their task, and condemned them to fall back on agricultural work. Travellers of the time have reported that in some regions this gave rise to a real inversion of roles, with the men performing domestic duties while their women were busily pursuing the profession of weaving (chapter 9 below).

In such regions, the industrialization of the countryside was soon interrupted by the rise of urban manufacturing centres, leaving only a strong emigratory drive. For the stem family, this represented only a return to normality. Founded on the concern to preserve the continuity and if possible the unity of a property, the stem family condemned most of the children of each generation to find a home by marrying into a neighbouring house or by migration. This was not too harsh in periods of demographic stagnation or depression (in the fifteenth century for much of Europe, in the second half of the seventeenth century in central Europe), but it became impossible in periods of demographic growth. Children excluded from the inheritance were then tempted to secure a right to share, or simply to remain beneath the family roof.

Tension of this type, which reveals a latent crisis in the stem family, can be observed at the beginning and end of our period: in the sixteenth century, on the eve of the Peasant Wars, in Upper Swabia the custom of transmitting land to the child who had remained with his parents to the last (the principle of ultimogeniture) was challenged by excluded children, who could no longer find land elsewhere. To avoid the proletarianization to which they were condemned on leaving home, they demanded the right to stay (Sabean, 1972).

Almost everywhere, and especially in southern France, in the eighteenth century, the stem family was navigating between two evils; dismemberment of the inheritance or landed tenure, and asphyxiation of the family group encumbered with unmarried brothers who stayed on in the heir's service. Waning patriarchs were got rid of; grudges were settled by poison in the soup; grandmothers who did not earn their keep and were too slow to die were helped on their way into the next world by being squeezed between wall and door (a custom called *serrade* in Gevaudan); sisters who had remained unmarried in order to stay under the paternal roof gave birth to illegitimate children, who in their turn were consigned to the hardest menial tasks and were the objects of sexual aggression by neighbours. Much family crime, as studied by Nicole and Yves Castan in the returns of the Toulouse *Parlement*, and by Elizabeth Claverie (in Claverie and Lamaison, 1982), for the Gévaudan district, can be attributed to the gradual suffocation of a family system which could no longer off-load its unwanted members and was submerged along with them.

The demographic flood did not destroy the stem family but took it to its logical conclusion, as happened in Ireland, where it has given rise to an abundant ethnological literature. Ethnologists interested in the Irish stem family often forget that, unlike the Occitan *oustal* or the *volles Haus* of Alpine Europe, it involved a recent mutation which became general in the second half of the nineteenth century: it was the response of a society traumatized by the Great Famine. In the eighteenth century, peasants had followed the English model and divided their inheritance between their children, according to their degree of wealth and to market fluctuations: the land went to a single child and money to the others.

Demographic growth transformed this system of transmission into a practice which was suicidal for a peasant society, and soon rendered it impracticable. If they chose partition, the small peasants ended by splitting up their farms so drastically that their heirs were condemned to poverty. If they preferred to restrict the land to one child and to endow the others, they were forced into debt and alienation of part of their patrimony.

Family logic

The Great Famine provided the terrible sanction for deregulating a system of reproduction which had proved incapable of checking the infernal cycle of demographic overload and pauperization. The stem family in its most rigorous and inegalitarian form came to dominate as a survival procedure: access to land and to marriage 'to the land' was henceforth the privilege of one child only, with the rest forced without compensation into celibacy or emigration. The considerable flow of money sent back to their families by young Irish immigrants to the United States in the 1880s demonstrates that their exclusion was accepted by all, including themselves.

Apart from the stem family, which fed on crisis situations perhaps because in itself it already constituted a crisis structure, the other family forms of Europe appeared extremely vulnerable when faced with the effects of demographic and economic fluctuations. Were one to ask what hidden resource enabled them to reproduce themselves and even to stabilize during the three centuries of our period, one would be tempted to answer: inheritance customs. This idea is popular nowadays, ever since the study of legal traditions has been seized by historians from the grasp of specialists in law. The inheritance customs which regulated the transmission of goods by succession (in wills) or by anticipation (in marriage contracts) ensured the reproduction of family structures under two aspects: under their material aspect by reorganizing the way the heritable property, around which the family groups could reconstitute themselves, was shared out; under their constituent aspect, by classifying individuals (eldest sons in relation to younger sons, boys in relation to girls, the wife in relation to the husband) according to a hierarchical system which proclaimed a particular ideology of the family sphere, and consequently of the social order. Certain customs put a concern for equity between children first (meaning strict equality in the inheritance system), others favoured the continuity of the lineage by circulating property along the lines of filiation, like sap through the branches of a tree (this was the principle of *paterna paternis, materna maternis*). Others, finally, gave priority to continuity and the unity of a house or a farm, and favoured a single heir.

The principles of social reproduction

Historians influenced by structural anthropology who want to reveal the mechanisms of social reproduction, and to rediscover in repetitive and obligatory practices the manner in which a family's social world fits in with its thought-world, could not have asked for more: inheritance customs provide a relatively rigid framework within which individual strategies can be inscribed. At the same time, they circulate material or symbolic goods and systems of representation. They combine obligatory, considered and chance forms. They can be both manipulated and pondered.

From the beginning of the sixteenth to the end of the eighteenth century, customary arrangements enjoyed a sort of golden age. They stabilized and were often set down in writing. Where France was concerned, the distinction which is habitually drawn between the customary law of northern France and the written law of the south, as the heir to Roman law, no longer had any meaning in the sixteenth century, once customs had started to be systematically compiled in the Great Royal Custumal (*Grand Coutumier royal*).

Most states respected diversity of customs and only legislated in exceptional cases, principally in the direction of the landed aristocracy, to limit the concentration of patrimonies or to preserve it. We are thus in the presence of a body of rules whose social efficacy was intact and which presents itself, in its regional diversity, as a fund of pluri-secular concepts.

Le Roy Ladurie (1972), following in the footsteps of the legal historian Yver (1966) and his 'geography of customs', has ventured among the extraordinarily confused inheritance customs of France under the *ancien régime*. The old contrast between the customary law of the north and the Roman law of the south which characterized the legal traditions in their origins had been replaced by a structural division which characterized them according to their underlying ideology: according to the conception of family architecture as an egalitarian and lineage-based pole, as represented by the customs of the west, which never merged the contributions of husband and wife, and circulated property along the lines of filiation; as a preciputary pole localized mainly in southern France, which gave parents, according to traditional Roman law, the power to favour an heir; and as a centrist pole – from all points of view because, starting from the customs of Orléanais and the Île-de-France, it radiated over the Paris Basin – which allowed a choice between dowry and *rappel exprès*, the right to claim a share at the moment of succession, conditional on returning the dowry (Le Roy Ladurie, 1972).

This classification outlines the main sections within the French legal space (in a schematic manner of course, since the picture is complicated by a number of enclaves in the north and east) and reveals clearly its cultural heterogeneity.

It also has the advantage of revealing the family ideology which made sense of these legal solutions: in the egalitarian west, it was attachment to the lineage which prevailed, with every individual deriving his right to part of the inheritance from his membership of a network of blood relatives joined by a common ancestor. Being an 'anti-father' law, it repudiated any testamentary dispositions made by the parents and gave short shrift to the conjugal group whose ties – between spouses as much as between parents and children – it considered as temporary and incapable of being prolonged. This anti-conjugal concept of the family affronts our present-day sensibilities on account of its rigidity, but it acquires a special profundity and a sort of legitimacy of precaution within the demographic context of France under the *ancien régime*. We know, for instance, that a quarter of marriages at the end of the seventeenth century were remarriages, and that half of all children were raised at one time or another by step-parents.

The precipuary law of southern France, on the contrary, exalted the power of the father, even when this was arbitrary. What he intended to preserve by choosing a privileged heir was not the continuity of a lineage but the permanence of a 'house', meaning both land, an inhabited dwelling and patriarchal authority. Alongside the paternal *auctoritas* of Roman law, the spirit of the house (the *oustal* in the south-west) was here affirmed, inspiring in all a sense of being rooted, and in younger sons a sense of sacrifice.

In the Pyrenees during the eighteenth century everyone inherited not only a patronym but also a house name, which was often recognized by the authorities as being equal in status, and which was recorded in parish registers. This name could pass from one patrilineage to another if a 'son-in-law' marriage had taken place, that is to say if a daughter had been made heir (generally for lack of a son) and had married a man who agreed to move into her parents' house. In such cases, the children would inherit their father's patronym and their mother's house name. It could even pass from one family network to another, but it never left the house which, in this cultural area, stood more strongly than blood for the continuity of a line.

The 'centrist' customs of the Paris Basin, finally, rested on an ideology which was both egalitarian and conjugal, because they allowed for choice between taking a dowry or a share of the inheritance. At the time of marriage, the spouses' contributions merged to become common property: at the point of succession, shares were allotted primarily according to 'beds' when the heirs were the issue of several marriages. In both cases, the custom confirmed the primacy of the couple.

Customs were periodically readjusted following pressure from the demographic and social environment. However, the spirit inspiring them and determining the three basic orientations which make up the geography of French customs, was tied to ancient and stable ideological traditions which offered family practices a sort of permanent syntax and conceptual framework.

Inheritance rules were not the only normative discourse within which these ideological structures appeared. They are clearly present in the three concepts of kinship which Champeaux (1933) identified in the formulations of canon and customary law: fraternal kinship or blood kinship, which binds brothers, sisters and first cousins; matrimonial kinship, which proceeds from *copula carnalis* and corresponds to its oldest definition in canon law; finally, individual kinship, which places each individual within a line of descent and counts the degrees of kinship between two persons by connecting them hierarchically through their common ancestor, as in Roman law.

Old Norman law established parental kinship (kin who came into the inheritance) without taking account of the line of equality. Thus the notion of individual kinship and the lineage principle underlying western French customs shared the same ideology. Similar connections can be established between fraternal kinship and the precipuary system which favoured the eldest child, between matrimonial kinship and the optional customs of the Paris Basin.

Non pater et mater sunt truncus, sed frater et soror: this formula taken from a barbarian law code defines fraternal kinship perfectly. It inspired customs like those of Burgundy, which declared that 'kinship does not pass upwards' and insisted that inheritance was to be allotted 'within the same degree'. As a horizontal and, so to speak, synchronic representation of kinship it set up a bond of solidarity between blood relations of the same generation, which in popular usage generally stopped at the third degree according to canon law. Beyond this began the larger circle of kin or *amis charnels*.

This representation is also found behind the right of primogeniture in the idea of a family of brothers ruled by the eldest. Matrimonial kinship based on the marriage bond continued to be hinged on the fraternal concept as though it proceeded from it. In order to become valid in practice, that is to say, to allow the spouses to establish their property and their children to succeed their parents instead of their uncles, it had to settle with the fraternal concept. Peter Damian defined conjugal love as *germanus amor*. As for popular concepts which dictated customs, they often failed to recognize *unitas carnis* (husband and wife as 'one flesh') until the birth of the first child: children and their parents were bound in a fraternal kinship, because they were of the same blood and it was through their own children that the parents themselves entered into the community of blood relatives.

The fact that these two concepts were largely interconnected possibly explains why a number of customs, especially in northern France, were able to evolve early in the sixteenth century, under the pressure of a shrinking property market, from a system of primogeniture with exclusion of dowered children into an optional system which was more conjugal and more egalitarian.

Is it possible to go even further and establish a link in every region between the prevailing inheritance customs and the dominant family model? Where France is concerned, it seems plausible to relate the nuclear structure to the egalitarian customs of the west and the optional customs of the Paris Basin which encouraged everyone to share. It is also clear that the preciputary system which dominated in southern France was related to the stem family.

It is all the more tempting to make the connection in that it appears to rest on a relatively clear and coherent causal relationship. If the inheritance customs had applied only to dividing a property between those entitled to it when the person holding the patrimony died, as is the case nowadays, it is hard to see how they could have shaped the household and ensured its reproduction.

In reality, in most families, from the landed aristocracy to very small tenants with only a patch of land, a hovel or just their knowledge to transmit, these customs made themselves felt from the cradle to the grave. Transmitted through educational practices, they inspired godparent or marriage alliances, the management and division of property and the strategies for its transmission. To ensure one's children's future or that of close relatives, to reward or punish them, to exorcize the precariousness of life by means of far-seeing choices, constituted the purpose of a social gamble in which the desire to maximize one's own prospects and the hope of preserving those of one's closest relatives, the group to which one belonged, were intimately connected.

Let us not forget that the practice of dowering or compensating those excluded at marriage involved the close association of alliance strategies and strategies for the transfer of property. This gave inheritance practices a recurrent influence over all the decisions which punctuated the family life cycle. In the regions of preciputary law, for instance, where testatory power was greatest, the marriage contract often included an anticipatory clause stipulating which of the the future children would inherit, and what portion of the property contributed by the couple would come to him.

From rule to practice: how families interact

Certain historians have grown accustomed to associating the sharing of inheritance with a nuclear structure, and the choice of a single heir with complex structures, for instance by contrasting egalitarian northern

France with the inegalitarian south. Unfortunately, there is a considerable distance between rule and practice: of seven notarial acts involving marriage contracts and wills drawn up at Bordeaux in 1647, each one selected different types of disposition, and together they provide a sort of panorama of all the legal solutions described by Yver for the whole of France.

A master baker gave the usufruct of his property to his wife and provided for an equal division between his three children. A merchant and burgher of Bordeaux gave a third of his property in *préciput* to his eldest son, and provided for an equal division of the remainder between him and his three sisters. A master mason without issue left everything to his wife. A magistrate gave 6,000 livres in dowry to his daughter to marry her to the son of a notary, who himself received from his parents a gift of 3,000 livres and agreed to live with them for six years. A servant girl brought to her marriage savings of 100 livres, which she had amassed herself, and a gift of 20 livres from her employer. A knight, the baron de Landiras and a judge of the *Parlement*, who was marrying the daughter of a Bordeaux *parlementaire*, stipulated in the contract that their first son, if they had one, would receive half of his father's property and 35,000 livres from his mother. In the event of only a daughter, she too would get half the property and would be able to transfer the title to it to her husband. The widow of a barrel-maker who was marrying a peasant from Entre-Deux-Mers brought him 15 livres as her dowry to live 'by the same pot and by the same fire' in a household of nine persons, including her two children from a previous marriage, her new husband's father and one of his brothers, with his wife and children (Wheaton, 1979).

The same gap between custom and practice can be observed in England. Of fifty wills drawn up between 1543 and 1630 in the parish of Orwell in Cambridgeshire, where primogeniture was still the rule, twenty-two involved testators with only one son to provide for: ten transmitted their land to a single person and twelve divided it (Stufford, 1976). At the end of the eighteenth century, when the law had been standardized following pressure from the state, more egalitarian principles were imposed on a large part of Europe and conflicted with custom, which remained attached to the choice of a single heir. There are, however, many indications that peasants keen to avoid excessive division of their lands clung to rules involving exclusion. This was the case in Austria after the great reforms of Joseph II: at Andrichsfurst, a lowland village made up of fairly prosperous arable farms, where primogeniture was the rule, only 34 per cent of the farmers at the beginning of the nineteenth century transmitted their property to the eldest son. At Rappoltenkirchen, a village in Lower Austria inhabited by small wine-growers, the tiny farms encouraged the retention of the practice of transmitting the property to the youngest child. As it was, less than 10 per cent of youngest children (including families with only one son) can be found among those who took on the farms (Mitterauer and Sieder, 1983).

In certain cases, finally, the logic of a particular inheritance system led to such a degradation of the economic and social equilibrium that it ended by imposing in practice safety procedures which were completely at odds with its original principles. This may be observed, for instance, at the end of the seventeenth century and even more clearly in the eighteenth century in the *bailliage* of Pont-à-Mousson in Lorraine, which was ruled by the custom of Saint-Mihiel.

The geography of customs in Lorraine (a transit zone which has been crossed during the course of its history by all the great migrations and by all the armies of Europe) appears as a mosaic of traditions, arranged in an incredibly complex pattern, in which may be found all the principal tendencies enumerated by Yver for France. Like the customs in the west, the custom of Saint-Mihiel prescribed equal distribution of property *de ligne*, but also community of acquests for spouses, as in the Paris custom. In the seventeenth century, the practice was to leave the patrimony undivided for two generations in order not to expropriate the surviving ancestor.

Faced with the risks of family conflict and especially land subdivision, which population growth rendered still more acute, the practice of non-division was extended over three generations; beyond that it was relayed by means of matrimonial strategies designed to reunite or reconstitute a viable farm or subdivided lineage property (Joignon 1984). These strategies could include marriage linkages, meaning marriages between blood relations in the third or fourth degree. One case of a sharing custom which ended up as a non-division practice can be found in the eighteenth century over a great part of the Paris Basin, especially in the wine-growing parishes of the Île-de-France which were ruled by the custom of Paris.

When houses or parcels of land could no longer be subdivided materially, they continued to be divided formally without shifting the occupants. A son who inherited a third of a house, a quarter of a parcel of land, could only hope to acquire a home of his own by marrying a girl from his village who had inherited fragments of the same kind of immovable property, which could be exchanged for other parcels of land in order to reconstitute a house or a smallholding. Hence the frequent occurrence of double marriages (when two siblings or first cousins from the same family married two siblings or first cousins from another), of marriage linkages and more generally, of endogamous marriages which were sometimes drawn up within the prohibited degrees of kinship.

The need for equity

There were numerous reasons why the rule was not observed in practice. There were subjective reasons derived from the moral and affective constraints which influenced parents' decisions. There were also objective factors derived from the demographic and economic situation in which these decisions were made. The opposite tendencies of the egalitarian and inegalitarian inheritance rules have been attributed to a doctrinal and moral basis which they did not necessarily possess. Customs said to be inegalitarian corresponded not to a desire but to a need for inequality. They aimed at preserving the unity of a farm or the power of a house, and they attempted to compensate in one way or another for the injustice shown to those excluded (by means of a dowry or a money portion, by some expenditure on education or training in a profession, etc.).

The injustice implicit in the unequal devolution of immovable patrimonial property was not automatically derived from legal requirements. This can only be appreciated in the light of the economic and demographic conditions of the time, and, more particularly in the case of peasants, of the state of the property market. The customs of primogeniture and of excluding dowered individuals developed in England and France during the fifteenth century, when land was plentiful and workers few. Compensating a younger son with money made it easy for him to set himself up elsewhere by marriage or by putting up money, or to use his *peculium* to launch himself into commerce or a trade. Given the situation at home, with a well-entrenched heir and authoritarian parents, the status of younger son conferred on him a degree of autonomy and mobility which were not necessarily perceived as the lesser part.

In the much more difficult economic situation at the beginning of the seventeenth century and in the eighteenth century, when population growth had made land rents rise and wages fall, the privilege of inheriting was not always an enviable one either. The right to stay with the father, which was a guarantee of security when land was hard to get, could just as often mean the right to work for him for nothing, and to suffer his abusive authority until his death. In Upper Provence in the eighteenth century, Pierre de Chaslan, lord of Moriez, decided at the age of ninety-three to emancipate his second son, who had remained with him and was sixty years old, because he had, as the patriarch acknowledged, attained the age of competence (Collomp, 1983).

In regions where parents were accustomed to transmit the farm to their son fairly early on, as established by various procedures such as *kar* in Norway, *Ausnahm* in Austria or *Vymenek* in Bohemia, which allowed them to take their retirement on the spot, the heir had to pay them heavy life annuities in return for his long-awaited accession to power.

Along with the farm, the heir sometimes also inherited the debts which his father had accumulated, or he would contract debts of his own in order to dower or compensate his siblings. The stem-family system with a single heir, which was adopted by Irish peasants after the Great Famine, represents the most finished form of privilege inversion. The excluded members, whose only inheritance was the right to emigrate, and who passed briefly through England before setting out for America, considered themselves so little disadvantaged by fate that they then felt obliged to help the stem family which had driven them out by sending money home.

When parents were unable to compensate their excluded children with capital or money, they generally invested in some sort of education. Such an investment was modest in the case of Irish children, but elsewhere it could extend to the acquisition of a diploma or mastership. When Pierre Coulet, known as Luque, a small farmer in Hyères in Upper Provence, drew up his will in 1661, he divided his property between his six children and stated with regard to a son who had been placed as an apprentice, that 'he should be content, without being able to demand anything else from his inheritance, since, unlike the other children, he had him taught writing and reading, and given him the profession of hatter, which has cost him much money' (Collomp, 1977).

This concern for equity towards children was expressed, even in exclusion strategies, in forms of compensation or simply by admitting remorse and the desire to justify oneself. It may also be observed among the ruling classes where inequality was much harsher and constituted both a principle of survival and of distinction. In the reform of the nobility of 1668, the procedure in Brittany required as proof of nobility that three regular successions on the noble side be established. In Brittany and in much of France under the *ancien régime*, 'feudal' custom attributed two-thirds of the inheritance to the eldest son, and the remaining third to the other children. In his *Mémoires d'outre-tombe*, Chateaubriand wrote that 'Younger sons divide between all of them one third only of the paternal inheritance . . . and since the same distribution of two-thirds to one third also existed for their children, these younger sons of younger sons soon ended up with a share of a pigeon, a rabbit . . .'

Often the very people who exercised the right of primogeniture in order to maintain the prestige of their lineage would also attempt in their wills to justify their choice to those children whose interests they had been obliged to injure. For instance, the marquis d'Yerre, a noble of Savoy, wrote in 1721: 'I pray each of my children nevertheless to believe that I love them all very tenderly and as much as their elder, although I have not made them joint heirs with him, but I believed that I had to have a single heir to maintain [the property]' (Nicolas, 1978). This evidence of a father's remorse at his duty of violating his affection for his children also shows the emergence of a 'new mentality' which was increasingly attached to an individual concept of justice. This is witnessed also by the rise, in an enlightened Europe, of a current of opinion hostile to the substitution formulae (*fideicommissum, majorat*, etc.) used by the aristocracy in order to protect their patrimonies.

In reality, transmission strategies had to come to terms with a latent need for equality which formed part of the spirit of Christianity and, perhaps more distantly, the fundamentally bilinear ethos of European kinship. Goody (1983) has shown that what was original about European transmission systems, in relation for instance to African systems, was their tendency to circulate property as much through women as through men. Each inheritance custom embodied in its own way a compromise solution between a desire for equity and a concern to ensure the continuity of the patrimony. To make a radical and structural contrast between the inegalitarian character of some customs (those allowing for the right of primogeniture or the choice of a principal heir) and the egalitarian ideal of others (which imposed division between all entitled persons) would be to disregard their common ambivalence, which inevitably surfaced in practice. It would also disregard their instability and inability to adapt to demographic and social fluctuations.

In his essay on the 'geography of customs' (1966), Yver himself indicated that there are limits to a structural approach, taking the case of the 'exclusion of dowered persons'. This practice developed in the fifteenth century in England, northern France and Germany. It constituted a wise precautionary measure on the part of a peasant tied to his patch of ground or to his farm, who ensured its survival by reserving it for the child who agreed to stay with him. In a favourable economic climate, when land was plentiful and wages high, there was nothing unjust about compensating the others with money when they married and left, and thus secured the means for their early independence.

At the beginning of the sixteenth century, the pressure of population made leaving a more risky affair for dowered children, and the dowry itself less profitable. In northern France the custom evolved into an optional system which allowed dowered children to return their dowry in order to secure their share if they felt hard done by at the time of succession. In England, the custom did not undergo the same egalitarian trend and, for younger sons, primogeniture became an exclusion procedure which condemned them to join the proletariat either on the spot or in town. In Germany, younger sons threatened with loss of social status preferred to exercise their right to remain beneath the paternal roof on condition they did not marry.

In England, as in the Paris Basin, the evolution of customs did not challenge the nuclear model. However, the divergent evolution of the law shows the extent to which apparently similar family structures could conceal very different conceptions of the family. In France, the nuclear household was tightly linked to the village community and constituted a stable unit, whereas in England it stimulated individualism, the desire for autonomy and mobility, voluntary or enforced. In Germany, finally, the revolt by younger sons, which played an important role in the Peasant War of 1525, did not deflect the law, but it transformed family structures by asserting their right to remain on the paternal farm; those sons who had formerly been excluded caused household groups to evolve towards a stem family or, in extreme cases, a *frérèche* formula.

Faced with the same demographic situation and endowed with similar traditional customs, England, France and Germany chose three different routes. Explaining this sudden divergence would require a precise evaluation of the power relationships in the three countries between mutually antagonistic social groups, of the particular action of the state apparatus, and the influence of ideological currents which mobilized public opinion, especially in literate and legal milieux.

By the end of the Middle Ages, when economic and demographic expansion made it possible to avoid subdividing farms without excessively injuring the interests of the excluded persons, 'inegalitarian' dispositions such as birthright, exclusion of dowered children and others, which were common in northern Europe (where customs were not much influenced by the principles of Roman law) resisted the economic upturn fairly well, depending on the country and especially on the social strata involved.

They survived best among the nobility because, in their case, preserving the unity of the patrimony constituted a power, or simply a survival objective in periods of crisis; also because the spirit of lineage and the right of primogeniture itself had long been deeply rooted in them. Since the eleventh century, Georges Duby tells us, the Mâconnais nobility had practised a fairly strict form of birthright, by limiting access to marriage and to the landed property to one child only. In certain regions such as

Normandy or Brittany, which derived their inheritance practices from an egalitarian custom, the right of primogeniture was firmly maintained as an aristocratic counterpoint to common practice.

The rise of exclusion practices: an aristocratic phenomenon?

Alongside these legal idiosyncrasies, the aristocracy frequently resorted from the sixteenth century onwards to practices which interpreted or even distorted the prevailing law in order to protect the greater part, or even the whole, of the landed inheritance from being divided between heirs. *Mayorazgos* in Spain, *fideicommissa* in Italy, strict settlement or entails in England and *substitutions* or *fidéicommis* in France were all practices aimed at protecting the inheritance against subdivision or enforced alienation on account of debt.

Substitutions were most fully developed along the most radical lines in Spain, first of all in Castile, where they had already appeared by the fourteenth century with the *majorat*. Although it has been frequently maintained, it is not certain that the Italian *fideicommissa* were introduced by Spaniards, but it is true that they appeared in the sixteenth century at a time when the Spanish hegemony was being established, principally in those regions where its influence was felt (the kingdom of Naples, the papal states and Tuscany).

In France, certain noble houses in the south-west regions, like the Albrets at Lévis-Mirepoix, had resorted to systematic substitution practices since the fourteenth century; others were encouraged to do so when royal apanages were established. In the sixteenth century, the practice of *fidéicommis* was current in southern France, where it was regulated by Roman law, to protect the landed patrimony, in the absence of dispositions similar to the northern ones of birthright and *retrait lignager*, which could be used against younger children demanding their legitimate portion.

According to J. P. Cooper, the author of a magisterial study of the concentration strategies employed by the European aristocracy (1976), substitutions were much less extensive in England because the monarchy, which was already highly centralized by the thirteenth century and even more so by the sixteenth, was able to limit the ambitions of the landed aristocracy. Since 1539, in fact, the Statute of Uses had forbidden nobles who had fallen into debt to exclude their landed property from being mortgaged, and so deprive their younger sons and daughters of any share in the inheritance. In Spain, on the contrary, the law of Toro (1505), which extended the *majorat* practice to non-nobles, formed the starting point for a long period of lax control and favours on the part of the monarchy to the great. Royal power had sacrificed to the aristocracy the interests of the productive social groups (to which the great landowners owed money) as the price of their loyalty and of a few extraordinary contributions (the *donativos*) to the royal treasury. The French monarchy pursued a middle way between the English practice of containment and Spanish favouritism. The *ordonnances* of Orléans (1561) and Moulins (1566) attempted to make substitutions gradual, and to have them declared in order to protect creditors from unpleasant surprises. The *Code Michau* (1629) was intended to prohibit 'rustics', meaning non-nobles, from employing the *fideicommissum*. However, the *Parlement* of Dijon was the only one which agreed to accept it. Simultaneously, attempts to buy the submission of the great were made by applying a policy of granting their children royal pensions and dowries; this system had already been generous under Henri IV, and it was systematically exercised from Louis XIV onwards. These favours, which so effectively disarmed the barons' revolt and enclosed them in a court existence, served to console them for the refusal to allow them to distribute their inheritance.

In the eighteenth century, a general offensive on the part of the new elites, led by the spirit of the Enlightenment against practices that infringed the rights of the individual, came to the forefront everywhere. It varied in effectiveness, depending on the reception accorded to these currents of opinion and on the norms restricting or prohibiting substitutions. In England, each case had to be submitted to Parliament for approval from 1706 onwards. In France, an *ordonnance* by d'Aguesseau in 1747 restricted substitutions to within two degrees and submitted them to tighter control by the *Parlements*. In Piedmont, reforms which had been undertaken earlier on were to end by abolishing the practice of *fideicommissum*. The action taken by states towards these exceptional inheritance practices was dictated by the way in which they conceived the role of the aristocracy and the power they meant to leave it. One may, however, ask whether their policy was not restricted to following and, when needed, to slowing down an evolution which largely evaded their control. The real motors of this evolution were economic. They were firstly the fluctuations in landed income which allowed the heads of aristocratic houses to compensate their daughters and younger sons (with land or money) in growth periods, and drove them to withhold their demesne lands from the share-out in periods of stagnation.

The agricultural recession provoked a general rise in substitution practices. In Spain, the practice of *majorat*, which continued to grow from the beginning of the sixteenth century thanks to the exceptionally favourable attitude demonstrated by public opinion and by royalty, reached a high point after 1640, when economic depression set in. In Italy, the expansion of the practice of *fideicommissum*, which made itself felt in Rome and in the south from the mid-sixteenth century onwards, became general by the beginning of the seventeenth century. In England, in a much more hostile legal context, the aristocracy multiplied its entails during the depression of the second half of the seventeenth century. The advance of substitutions was slower in France, where it coincided with the agricultural crisis in the last quarter of the seventeenth century. It had certainly reached its peak by 1712, when the government introduced obligatory registration of all patrimonies which had been subjected to substitution in order to restrict abuses and to inform possible creditors.

The system was in fact nourished by its own contradictions. It is difficult to see how a refusal to share out an inheritance because it formed the material basis for the power of a lineage, which encouraged the practice of raising the minimum (and if possible only on movable property) needed to pay dowries and portions, could be compatible with the need to increase the prestige of a 'house'. This objective would sometimes involve transferring property to junior branches to enable them to found families, as was the case with the duc de La Rochefou-cauld, who passed the duchy of La Roche-Guyon to his younger son in 1715; this was a comparatively unusual instance of land sharing, which only a few very great houses had the means to adopt. The most common practice, which was applied systematically in Italy for instance, was to endow younger sons with their mother's property.

Cadet branches could in their turn be resorted to, through the mediation of intermarriage, for perpetuating the name and power of a house when the senior branch was left without a male heir. This strategy occurred frequently in Spain where daughters had access to the practice of *majorat*. In 1581 the fifth duke of Infantado, having lost all his sons as children, married his eldest daughter to one of his brothers (the young girl's uncle).

Girls, however, generally presented the main obstacle to concentrating landed patrimonies. They constituted essential trump cards for great families seeking to extend their influence by means of illustrious alli-ances, and they demanded comfortable dowries in order to play this role. Thus they were generally better provided for than younger sons; this was the result of strategic much more than affective choice. Stone has observed that dowries took off among the English high nobility at the end of the sixteenth century. This rise, which accelerated at the time when monetary inflation slowed down, could be felt all over western Europe. In the eighteenth century, this climate of competitive bidding and tension in the marriage market overwhelmed the high aristocracy. In Toulouse, a girl of the middle-ranking nobility could receive the equivalent of three to four years of her family's total income as her dowry. The system could thus be sustained only by strictly limiting marriages. In England, where the aristocracy did not possess ecclesiastical outlets, girls were harder hit by this restriction; between the end of the sixteenth century and the mid-seventeenth, the rate of permanent celibacy among aristocratic women had quadrupled. By the beginning of the eighteenth century it had reached 25 per cent. It was already almost as high among Venetian patrician families at the beginning of the seventeenth century.

In Catholic countries, where the aristocracy could put its daughters in a convent and colonize ecclesiastical profits, the restriction was no less rigorous, but was perhaps more equitably distributed between girls and boys. In Florence, during the sixteenth century, the custom grew up among the great families of only marrying one son, and of dowering one daughter, if possible. In Venice, the percentage of sons sworn to celibacy grew from 18 per cent in the sixteenth century to 64 per cent in the eighteenth. In France, at the beginning of the eighteenth century, 42 per cent of sisters of dukes and peers did not marry (almost as many as among the middle-ranking nobility of Toulouse). These Malthusian efforts were, however, clearly not sufficient to solve the inheritance problems of the top nobility. In France, dukes and peers added birth restriction to marriage restriction. On average 6.1 children were born to each couple during the second half of the seventeenth century; by the first half of the eighteenth, this had fallen to 2.7 children.

The price paid for distinction

One may ask whether these exclusion strategies were effective in the long term. In Poland as in England, the petty nobility which at the start of the seventeenth century was still attached to the practice of equal shares was condemning itself to decline or revolt: we are aware of the role played by the poverty-striken petty nobility in the English Revolution. The case of the ancient Danish nobility, which was also attached to the practice of strict sharing, is particularly revealing. In 1660, it held 97 per cent of all manors. Forty years on, it owned only 44 per cent. Deprived of their property, the men embraced military careers, and often celibacy as well. In 1720 these families owned only half as much property as in 1660, whereas the Danish population had increased by 70 per cent over the same period (Cooper, 1976).

The practice of sharing did not necessarily condemn the nobility to decline. In Hesse-Kassel, the nobility, which respected equal sharing, was able to maintain its rank and its landed seats until the mid-nineteenth century, without limiting marriages (although men married late) or births, and without the practice of *fideicommissum*, by the simple play of population mechanics. Girls were excluded from fiefs but received compensation in money. The strict sharing prescribed for the men did not in reality affect more than a minority of families, since only 40 per cent of nobles during the first half of the eighteenth century, and 45 per cent in the second half, managed to prolong their lineage. Property with no heir reverted to the closest male blood relatives, and gave rise to frequent regroupings. The three estates of Buttlar-Ziegenberg were shared between three brothers in 1690, only to revert to a single brother twenty years later. When Hartmann von Eschwege died in 1770, his six sons became co-proprietors of the estates of Reichensachsen and Jestadt. When the last of the six heirs died, they left only two grandsons; each branch got one estate. In the following generation, however, the practice of non-division was revived (Pedlow, 1982). Sharing or non-division, splitting up followed by reunion, all enabled aristocratic landed patrimonies to be unmade and remade. The same happened in certain peasant societies whose customs stipulated sharing, as with the Lorraine peasants who were ruled by the custom of Saint-Mihiel, thanks to a self-regulatory ability to adjust practice to population mechanics.

We have plenty of examples demonstrating that substitutions were the best means of forging the power and landed wealth of a 'house'. A family from the south of France called Albret, which had fallen into semi-obscurity by distributing so much of its inheritance, developed into the richest and most powerful house in the south-east within twelve generations from the beginning of the fourteenth century. In this case, an adroit policy of acquiring fiefs and property through marriage, which were then integrated in the patrimony and transmitted as a whole to the eldest sons, and in the absence of male heirs to daughters, had brought it by the end of the fifteenth century to the throne of Navarre, and then, a century later, to the French throne. Bernard-Hezi II, the most inventive exponent of this family policy during the fifteenth century, had taken advantage of the *coutume* of Casteljalous, where he established his 'principal domicile', to give five of his twelve children to the Church and to make the other younger sons renounce all claims to his lands (Poumarède, 1972).

One family of the lowest-ranking *noblesse d'épée*, called Gérard de Béarn, whose main property was found in Angoumois and Périgord, had enlarged its landed inheritance between the beginning of the seventeenth century and the end of the eighteenth century by restricting marriage for its younger sons (only six out of twenty-one married), arranging unpretentious alliances for its daughters, and transmitting the estate in accordance with the principles of primogeniture. Their estate was worth 200,000 livres in 1600, and 800,000 in 1788 (Labatut, 1973). However, this strategy was often not enough to save a lineage from decline. The Rigaud de Vandreuils, a family which held twenty lordships in Lauragais in the mid-fifteenth century and had never deviated from the practice of transmitting their landed property in its entirety via the male line according to the rules of primogeniture, had only three lordships left on the eve of the French Revolution.

Among the high nobility, for whom maintaining rank demanded great expenditure on their lifestyle and ruinous dowries, the practice of excluding lands from division and transmitting them to the eldest son was impossible without incurring considerable debt, although this was partly relieved by the generosity of the king. In 1788 the Saulx-Tavane family, in spite of excluding from the *fideicommissum* the lands in Normandy which the first duke's wife had brought, using them instead to pay their debts, received from the king the equivalent of half the revenues from their estates in the form of various pensions (Forster, 1971).

One might indeed ask whether the king of France was not, by these acts of generosity, encouraging the propensity of the court nobility, and most especially of the princes of the blood, to fall into debt in order not to dismember their landed patrimony. In any case, the high nobility's investment, from the mid-seventeenth century onwards, in their partisans' business dealings and in other sectors of financial capitalism, and its role during the eighteenth century in the first enterprises of industrial capitalism (such as the mines), show that the system did not run entirely counter to France's economic dynamism.

In Spain and in central and southern Italy, on the other hand, from the mid-seventeenth century onwards, the practice of *majorat* and *fideicommissum* froze the economy within a *latifundium* agricultural system dominated by an increasingly indebted aristocracy, and drove southern Europe along the road of underdevelopment. As for the Venetian patrician class, since the eighteenth century it had condemned itself by its extreme Malthusian approach: the fact that in every family only the heir could marry resulted in lineages disappearing as fast as among the Danish nobility, with its habit of sharing.

The counterproductive and even suicidal character of exclusion strategies is apparent to us from our retrospective view of the destiny of great families. It is however possible that the actors themselves were more or less aware of it. In the seventeenth century, an English reformer called Benjamin Worsley contrasted in his book *The Advocate* the practice of the Dutch bourgeoisie, who shared their inheritance between all the children without diminishing their prosperity and the continuity of their commercial enterprises, with the English aristocracy and their disastrous practices.

In the eighteenth century, in France as much as in Italy and Spain, more and more voices were raised even among the nobility to denounce a system so manifestly unjust, which condemned the caste whose survival it was meant to ensure, to decline. Was it truly a question of caste prejudice, as its enlightened opponents thought, of a form of behaviour peculiar to the nobility in its desire to establish its difference by means of an inegalitarian ideology and rules of succession, even at the risk of suffering their destructive effects?

One might indeed believe this to be the case, considering the fascination which these practices exercised over the commercial upper middle classes as soon as they aspired to become integrated into the landed aristocracy. The great merchants of London, who traditionally followed London custom which prescribed division of the inheritance into thirds (one third for the widow, one to be divided equally between the children, and one to be left according to the testator's will), were by the end of the seventeenth century frequently adopting restrictive rules in the manner of the landed nobility (Cooper 1976).

This form of mimicry can be found in France during the same period, as for instance in the case of bourgeois dynasties in the Beauvais region such as the Motte and the Danse, who were studied by Goubert (1959). Lucien Motte the elder, a wealthy cloth merchant who showed a forceful spirit of enterprise, died in 1650. His three sons all married merchants' daughters and divided their father's property and business between themselves; of his two daughters, who had been respectably dowered, only one managed to raise herself somewhat above this circle by marrying an officer who had purchased an ennobling office. With the next generation, the rules of the game had changed: of Lucien, the eldest son's six boys, three entered religious orders (two canons and one prior).

The same pattern occurred in the Danse family, whose wealth had its roots in the cloth-bleaching trade. Nicolas Danse's children shared the *bueries* among themselves, or married into the trade, except for the eldest girl, who took the veil in a fashionable convent. This early use of the Church as an outlet may possibly be explained by the considerable role played by land in Nicolas Danse's investments – which had not been the case with Lucien Motte the elder. In the next generation, four of the eldest son Claude's seven boys chose the Church and three commerce. As for his daughters, those three who did not choose 'the perfect state' married members of the new nobility.

In fact, we have any number of examples which prove that the aristocratic custom of transmitting the patrimony to one child only, if possible through the male line, and of not permitting property brought in by marriage to leave the lineage, was equally prevalent among the common people, especially the peasantry. Pedro Manrique de Lara, count of Paredes, made his will in 1539 in which he entrusted to his son Antonio the task of dedicating the property which his wife would bring him to dower his sisters 'as is usual among good *cavalleros, mayorazgos*'. Three centuries later, in 1812, a doctor from Sault in Upper Provence taught his son the same strategy: 'It is necessary that she whom your family and you will chose to be your wife shall possess a fortune which will more or less replace your sisters' dowries.'

In this instance, Antoine de Courtois was giving axiomatic expression to a practice common in the most deprived countrysides of southern France. At Ribennes, a parish in Gévaudan, it determined the majority of marriages in the eighteenth century, and sometimes even the choice of heir. In this land of impoverished and proud *oustals*, where sheepfarming was combined with weaving woollen cloth, marriages provided each house with the opportunity to gamble with their rank within the local hierarchy. Two possibilities were open to them: to raise themselves by securing a particularly desirable spouse and dowry for the heir, and lowering other houses by establishing their children in them with minimal dowries. Where possible, both methods were practised at once.

This is why they waited so long to designate the heir, reserving the possibility of choosing a boy or a girl at the last moment according to the marriage market, in order to attract a dowry. The principle was not to allow either landed property or money to leave the *oustal*, and to repay no more than had been received. The exchange could even succeed in avoiding all transfer of property, as when two families managed to conclude double marriages; for instance, when the heir in one family and his dowered sister were married to the heir and daughter of another, or when, in the case of widowers remarrying, the man gave his daughter to the son of the woman he was marrying.

The circulation of dowries was, however, generally effected over two generations or more: a tailor in Ribennes called Thomas Léger got married twice; his first wife, who gave him six children, had brought him a dowry of 400 livres. His second wife, who had two children, brought him 260 livres. Three of the children married. The dowry which Anne Tranchesec returned to the *oustal* by marrying Thomas, the eldest son and heir, was used to dower his sister and half-sister: Antoinette married the brother of his father's second wife, and Elisabeth married his first wife's brother. The two dowries acquired by Thomas Léger the elder were thus returned to the Jouve and Forestier families.

A much longer cycle is instanced by a dowry paid by the Tichit family in 1680, which returned to it in 1823 after changing hands seven times and passing through six *oustals* (Lamaison, 1979). It may be asked whether returning the dowry after 140 years to the first *oustal* which had put it into circulation was the effect of a coherent – albeit long-drawn-out – sequence of strategic choices or quite simply of chance. Predictive calculations were inculcated into family strategies, as for instance, when noblemen assigned to children intended for the Church property which was then supposed to revert to the lineage, and could easily apply to two or three generations. However, was this still true for longer periods?

One might equally ask what was left of this dowry, which was in any case a modest one, after the monetary mutations of the revolutionary period. The two questions are really a single one. Like the baton passed from hand to hand in a relay race, the dowry was not the real issue but the outward sign of the exchange; its value was above all symbolic. As a simple marker of the matrimonial alliances which structured this society, the dowry, which belonged to nobody because it was constantly having to be put back into circulation, allowed spouses to be exchanged without touching transmissible property.

In societies which were opposed to the subdivision of inheritance, the practice of setting aside the heritable property was often accompanied by a strict sexual division. Among the aristocracy, this comprised the property brought in by wives, including landed property, which was used to dower their daughters. This usage, which has been observed in the case of a ducal family in Burgundy called Saulx-Tavanes in the eighteenth century, had existed among a large proportion of the nobility and the Italian patrician class since the seventeenth century.

It may also be found among peasants; for instance, in the seventeenth century in San Cipriano, a large market town in the Salerno region consisting above all of small landowners, daughters were given money dowries and the land was circulated among the men. In the exceptional event of a property being sold, for instance to provide a girl with a dowry, it would always be to a blood relation through the male line, '*linea et domo mea*'. Consequently very few rents from land are to be found, but many transfers of land occur in wills, marriage contracts and transfers 'between relatives and friends'. Each owner's lands ended by adjoining those belonging to a distant blood relative (Delille, 1983).

Figures of alliance

Sexual discrimination could also apply to customs of subdivision. In Apulia, whose inheritance practices have been compared by Delille

The Marriage Contract. This is the first engraving in the famous series *Marriage à la Mode* by Hogarth, *c.*1745. The Earl of Squanderfield is marrying his son to the daughter of a wealthy City alderman; the earl wants to pay off a mortgage and finance the sumptuous dwelling which can be glimpsed through the window; the tradesman wants his descendants to accede to the nobility. The earl is unrolling his family tree (which goes back to William the Conqueror) before the tradesman's awestruck gaze, while his creditor is returning his mortgage bond. Behind them, the young couple turn their backs on each other in boredom. It is a poor outlook for the atmosphere in their future home. All the furnishings in the room (especially the paintings, which are pastiches of famous works) serve to illustrate the absurdity of the nobleman's pride and to predict the couple's future disunion. Hogarth's satirical verve is here employed to denounce arranged marriages between a newly enriched bourgeoisie and the spendthrift aristocracy, when the only motive is social pretension. Bibliothèque Nationale, Paris.

(1983) with those in Campania, dowry goods, such as furniture or buildings, which circulated among the women, were distinct from other property which was transmitted to sons. The ideal pattern behind this would involve the transmission of patrimonial property from father to son, and of the mother's dowry to her daughter. However, population mechanics made numerous transfers obligatory. When necessary, they preferred to sell the dowry, although this might mean making part of the patrimony into dowry property.

The obligation in some families without male issue of transmitting the patrimony to the daughters encouraged the younger sons of other families to seek out heiresses, thus introducing into the system a tendency to social mobility. Boys tended to marry upwards and girls downwards. However, the social play and the margin of manipulation allowed to families by this sexual division of inheritances was based on the way in which the capital was distributed between dowry and patrimonial property.

Among the richest people, bourgeois or nobles, landed property featured only slightly in dowries (at most one quarter in Paolo del Colle, a village near Bari in 1633) and was represented above all by arable land. Poor folk, especially the *foritani* (labourers), tended on the contrary to dower their daughters exclusively in houses and lands: they gave them their most 'fixing' lands, the vineyards and olive groves, and to the boys they gave cereal-growing land and almond orchards, which were more subject to market fluctuations. Within this circle, where male labour and strength constituted the most precious contribution to the resources of a household, the essential task of matrimonial alliances was to attract this male labour force by transmitting via daughters the most deeply rooted property, which was most capable of fixing them to the spot.

This type of sharing may also be found in the eighteenth century in Piedmont, where women brought in meadows and cattle whereas men inherited cultivated fields. It may be encountered too after the end of the seventeenth century in certain parts of Lorraine, such as the region of Saint-Mihiel, where houses were transmitted preferably to daughters and marriages were, for the most part, uxorilocal. Here, the usage seems to be directly linked to the demographic situation: Lorraine had been ravaged by the Thirty Years War and was a ruined and deserted countryside – many of the houses mentioned in the records were in a state of ruin or poor repair. In order to retain or attract male labour, so indispensable for returning land to cultivation, the most efficient and least expensive means was to offer the men well-portioned wives.

It was not by chance that the three regions referred to above, Apulia, Piedmont and Lorraine, possessed inheritance customs which favoured formulae for sharing: although the shares were not equal, they split up the farms and maintained a constant movement of alienation and acquisition. Inversely to what was happening among the small landowners of Campania, a significant flow of transfers may be observed in Apulia; in Polignano, a village of slightly under 5,000 inhabitants at the start of the eighteenth century, thirty-five to forty sales of land or houses could be counted each year.

These transactions were only seldom undertaken between male blood relatives of the same lineage, as was the case in the Salerno region. In Manduria, a village near Tarento, where Delille (1983) was able to compare the notarial records with the family genealogies between 1570 and 1600, only four sales of this type occur among 500 notarial acts. One, for instance, was drawn up for a churchman, Don Sergio Pasaniso, who ceded an estate to his nephew Gasparo Pasaniso with a clause *de retrovendendo* allowing him to recover his property in the event of the nephew dying without issue. Three-quarters of all sales, however, were conducted between relatives and much more distant connections. The most frequently occurring case involved selling or buying a property from a brother-in-law (the wife's brother or the sister's husband). Such transfers, which preceded or followed a marriage, served to constitute a dowry or to compensate for whatever had provided it. However, the exchange circuits and kinship relations criss-crossed so much that one may ask whether marriages were determined by economic strategy or whether the transactions were shaped by alliance strategies.

This question, which Delille has asked in relation to Apulia, could be put in more or less the same terms about other regions in western Europe where customs prescribing a variously egalitarian division of patrimonies prevailed, and where a significant proportion of the property circulated via the women. These were generally regions of mixed farming (combining stockraising with crop-growing) or of specialized farming, which depended on heavy investment in labour. This was the case, for instance, for the village of vineyard workers in the Paris region, where the subdivision of parcels of vineyards or houses gave rise to an intense dismembering and regrouping activity by means of transfers, sales and compensations closely linked to alliance strategies of a largely endogamous nature, which were constantly tightening and complicating the social network.

In the relatively stable societies of modern Europe, the logic of economic reproduction and the logic of kinship were so evidently and generally interpenetrated that one might ask whether this had not rendered them indistinguishable. Certain features recur in such different regional or social contexts that it is tempting to consider them as invariables, common to all forms of social organization.

This was the case for particular figures of alliance, such as 'remarkable marriages' (simultaneous marriages between two siblings or two first cousins with similarly related partners) or renewed marriage alliances which united (often outside, but sometimes within the proscribed degrees of kinship) spouses belonging to two family lines which were already allied and were keen to renew the tie.

Most of the time these figures corresponded to property arrangements. 'Remarkable' marriages enabled families to avoid, through their reciprocal nature, transferring a dowry and a legitimate portion. Renewed marriage alliances sometimes served, as was the case with the Lorraine peasants in the Saint-Mihiel region, to reunite indivisible property shares in a house or an estate which had been retained over several generations, at a time when the non-division agreement expired. However, the fact that such figures may be found in economic and legal contexts as different as those of Normandy, Burgundy, Brittany, the Paris region, Lorraine, Gevaudan, Upper Provence and Apulia, seems to indicate that homogeneous and, so to speak, elementary kinship rules directed alliance strategies independently of inheritance practices or methods of compensation.

Consanguinity and endogamy

It would be tempting to claim as much for marriages between blood relatives. From the point of view of the Church censor, marrying a blood relative could not be a properly considered action, since it contravened the law of the Church. For the Catholic Church in particular, which retained the most wide-ranging system of proscribed degrees of kinship, consanguinity was defined above all negatively because it covered blood relatives prohibited from marrying. The Roman curia dealt with serious cases and with requests from members of the upper classes, and local tribunals handled requests from ordinary people bearing on more distant kinship; dispensations granted by these courts required a reason justifying the marriage in spite of the impediment to it.

One gathers from reading the Church documents that marriages of this type were in response to choices dictated by family strategy or by passion but very explicitly not to considerations of kinship. There is no reason for thinking that the motives alleged by petitioners were not genuine: marriages requiring a dispensation for spiritual relationship, for instance, were nearly always remarriages, and occurred frequently in the towns, in the world of shops and craftsmen. They would involve a widower or a widow wanting to marry a servant or a journeyman who happened to be godparent to one of the children. The alleged motive, that it involved someone well acquainted with the trade and the family and who would be able to run the business and bring up the child, is entirely plausible. The only factor to be neglected is the events leading up or even contributing to the impediment. Choosing a journeyman living under the same roof as oneself to be godfather to one's child involves creating a pseudo-parental relationship in order to integrate an employee within the family group. Indeed, once the outline had been traced, adapting kinship relations to labour relations might end in marriage, should the need arise, as, for instance, when the *patron* died.

Marriages to relatives within the limits of affinity (meaning marriage to a blood relative of a deceased spouse) were also much more numerous in the towns. In eighteenth-century Paris, the commercial and civil service bourgeoisie were especially involved here. Equally reasonable are the moral reasons given (when the petitioners were sufficiently high-ranking not to content themselves with advancing 'family reasons'), such as 'suspicion of familiarity' or 'frequentation' between a widowed petitioner and the sister or cousin of his deceased wife living under the same roof and caring for his children. Nevertheless, such reasons did not exclude other motives, which were more seldom mentioned. These could be commercial associations (between the husband and father-in-law, for instance) or the grant of offices which accompanied bourgeois marriages. In such circles, professional needs and preferences combined, betraying a tendency to favour alliance relationships in the social sphere just as in economic activities.

Kinship affinity was very like spiritual affinity; it was in an explicit manner and within very precise social circles that marriage strategies relied on kinship networks. The same did not apply to consanguinity. Consanguineous marriages within the aristocracy may be set apart. In France, the great number of such marriages among the dispensations promulgated in the Paris diocese reflects the place held by the nobility in the Parisian population and in Versailles. When very close blood relatives in the first and second degrees (marriage between uncle and niece) or in the second degree (first cousins) were involved, the alliance was generally responding to the need to transfer to a cadet branch (when the elder branch had no male heir) a patrimony which was in danger of being lost to the lineage. As for third-degree dispensations, they can be explained above all by the narrowness of the marriage market in a highly hierarchized society which was keen to keep its ranks closed.

Consanguinity occurred just as frequently in peasant marriages; of all the impediments to marriage, this was the one with which people took the most liberties, although it is difficult to establish the reasons why. Almost all studies have been based on petitions for dispensations, and, setting France and Italy aside, those on a European scale are still too few to attempt an overall evaluation of the phenomenon. Was it above all an effect of the narrowness of the *isolats* in which peasants were accustomed to choose their spouses? This is what the ecclesiastical law treatises of the period appeared to acknowledge, in designating the 'smallness of the place' as the most likely reason for requiring a dispensation.

Contrary to what has long been thought, the level of endogamy in the countryside during the modern period was not always linked to the geographical isolation of the inhabitants. Endogamy was certainly strong in islands and mountain villages, where by the eighteenth century it featured in 70–90 per cent of marriages, but it was often just as prevalent in the villages of the Beauvaisis plain, Lorraine and the Paris region. Endogamy is a voluntary mode of behaviour and not one imposed by circumstances. It owes more to norms, the legal rules presiding over the conclusion of alliances, than to the constraints of geography. Some ethnologists have mooted the hypothesis that societies with 'inegalitarian' inheritance customs are less consanguineous than 'egalitarian' societies: the frequent occurrence of marriages between close relatives would in fact give rise to an excessive concentration of patrimonies and would end by making the circulation of dowries impossible. This hypothesis has yet to be checked against the facts.

Where France is concerned, the impression is that endogamy was related positively to the marriageable population in the parish in regions which favoured single heirs, and negatively in regions where partition was practised. In Upper Provence, in the first third of the eighteenth century, of the 102 marriages contracted at Saint-André-des-Alpes, fifty-five were exogamous and four endogamous. In the neighbouring parish of Riez, where only fifty-nine marriages were registered, nine were exogamous and fifty endogamous.

In Champagne, on the other hand, a comparative study of three villages in the Vallage shows that the rate of endogamy in the eighteenth century was all the higher in that the parish was more populous. In Blécourt, with twice the population, 46 per cent of marriages were endogamous, and in Mossey, with 511 inhabitants, it was 68 per cent (Arbellot, 1970). It has been possible to check this phenomenon against the diachrony which prevailed at Romainville, a wine-growing parish in the Paris region, where a certain slowing-down in population growth in the mid-seventeenth century led to a slight downturn in endogamous marriages (Burguière, 1979). Let us attempt to explain these differential variations: in southern France, where people's sense of 'house' determined their alliance strategies, the need to circulate dowries and to protect their patrimonies required partners and exchange circuits which were all the more numerous in that there were more 'houses' involved. In northern France, it was on the contrary imperative to marry as close as possible to one's parish and, ideally, within it, in order to reconstitute within the same area a viable resource base by reuniting two fragments of a shared farm. Here, the practice of endogamy consisted of marrying just outside the prohibited degree of relationship within the parish or the kin, both of which ended by merging. When the number of marriageable persons within a parish was insufficient, the marriage area overlapped into adjoining parishes.

Like endogamy, consanguinity does not appear to have been linked to any particular inheritance model in peasant society. It may be found as much in regions with a strong sense of 'house', where people tried to circulate wives without transferring property, as in regions where sharing prevailed, where setting up the new couples was the dominant concern. Is it possible to distinguish between several practices of consanguinity? In a country of stem families such as Upper Provence, marriages within the third or fourth degrees of consanguinity were frequent occurrences but were not necessarily endogamous. In Saint-André-des-Alpes, they involved 'marriage linkages' with a variety of 'houses' in neighbouring communities such as Moriez, La Mure and Barrême, and even distant ones like Auzet.

'We are all related, but I do not know how', declared a peasant of Saint-André. Peasants were sometimes united under one patronymic which showed that they shared a common ancestry, albeit a distant and imprecise one, and they classified themselves by branches (such as the Lucque or Chapelier branches in the Colet family), aimed at 'reawakening the alliance' periodically at times when their genealogical memory expired (Collomp, 1983).

In the parishes of the Paris region and Beauvaisis, which were endowed with powerful community structures, consanguinity was a direct effect of endogamy. In Romainville, a wine-growing parish near Paris, where one quarter of all marriages celebrated between 1718 and 1787 required and got a dispensation, in only one case were the two spouses not born in the parish: at least 44 per cent of endogamous marriages in this parish were consanguineous in the eyes of the Church, and in reality it must have been 50 per cent, because the growing tolerance of Church officialdom encouraged some parishes after 1760 not to petition for a dispensation for fourth-degree relatives (Burguière, 1979).

Here, these peasant dispensations involved wine-growers almost exclusively; this was a particularly consanguineous group, and in the eighteenth century it alone provided more than 70 per cent of petitions for rural dispensations in the Paris diocese, and 55 per cent of all the

petitions granted by Church officials in Pontoise. Vineyards were especially 'fixing' on account of the high prices they commanded and the
great disparity in their yields and value according to the nature of the
soil, the lie of the land, and so on. 'One cannot take one's vineyard with
one', a petitioner declared to the Church officials in Paris to justify his
right to choose a spouse from within the parish. Other professional
groups, however, such as the fisherfolk on the Île-Saint-Denis, near Paris,
the charcoal-burners of Cotentin and the peasant nail-makers and
weavers in Beauvaisis all evidence an equally strong propensity to
consanguineous marriages.

The need to marry someone who could bring into the household
property capable of being combined with one's own property – for
instance, a parcel of vineyards or a professional qualification – counted
for much in this systematic application of consanguineous marriages. In
the marriage acts in rural parishes, the *vigneronnes* were often the only
women to be designated by their professional status as a sign of how
greatly their knowledge was valued in the marriage market. However,
the economic stake only served to strengthen and justify the tendency, in
the most stable parts of these peasant communities, to make alliance
relationships correspond with neighbourhood relationships.

'We are neighbours and we know all about one another', two
Piedmont peasants declared to the Church official in Como in the
sixteenth century when they were seeking a marriage dispensation for
their children (Mezzario, 1980). Such marriages bear witness to a
privileged form of attachment for networks of sociability and mutual
knowledge which ended by transforming the circle of neighbours into
kin. It was not consanguinity itself that was sought after in this circle of
'vague relations', but renewing an alliance which legitimized the neighbourhood, and it was the mechanism of marriage linkage that multiplied
the bonds of consanguinity between these allies.

A Church official in Beauvais stated in 1731 about two peasants of
Estry who were soliciting a marriage dispensation that 'a relative is
supposed to have declared that the grandparents of the said petitioners
called each other cousins without knowing whether they were first
cousins or not, without knowing the names of their great-grandparents
and that their said grandparents called every other woman their aunt
without knowing either whether she was a real aunt.' The parish priest
too, who had made his own inquiry, noted at the end of the report that
'in the country, people call each other cousin up to the sixth and seventh
generation.' Deprived of a sense of lineage, the peasants of the Paris Basin
had a short genealogical memory (and one which they made little attempt
to extend before the Church tribunal). Beyond the limited circle of close

relatives who represented for them the prohibited degrees of consanguinity, they relied on an essentially horizontal perception of the
kinship which encompassed the wider bourn of their favoured relationships and which merged with the village horizon. It was within this circle
that they intended to choose their spouses.

If consanguineous marriages are to be considered merely as a sub-
category of endogamous marriages, can consanguinity be anything more
than an automatic and involuntary effect of endogamy? This is not
impossible. The very high rate of consanguineous marriages recorded at
Romainville was not exceptional. It is almost as high in the other little
wine-growing parishes of the Paris region such as Montesson and
Frépillon. The rate thus tends to rise when parishes are smaller, contrary
to the rate of endogamous marriages. Probability studies have been
carried out for non-European micro-populations which officially observe
prohibited degrees of kinship fairly similar to those in the Catholic
regions of modern Europe. Calculations have shown that by establishing
their alliances just beyond or just within the limits of kinship, these
populations were far from exhausting the marriage possibilities available
to them within their own *isolat*, taking official prohibitions into
account.

In other words, what was represented as an inevitable choice on
account of 'the smallness of the place where everyone is related'
corresponds to a preference, a sort of tropism which established its
alliances at the immediate edges of the prohibited degrees of kinship, as if
the social link to which marriage conferred an extra legitimacy, did not
have to be invented but only stirred, renewed and drawn upon within a
network of relationships which had been provided once and for all.

Conquering and co-operative strategies

Social homogamy may perhaps have presented merely the other side of
this tendency towards concluding the closest possible alliances within a
limited circle of mutual acquaintance. Like geographical endogamy, it
was characteristic of the most stable societies, being both cause and effect
of their stability. In eighteenth-century Romainville, for instance, the
incidence of social homogamy exceeded 90 per cent among the wine-
growing population; this was the most numerous and most securely
settled professional sector, in spite of the crisis which affected a large part
of the vineyards in the Paris region during the second half of the century
due to the subdivision and increasing indebtedness of the properties.
Marrying among themselves provided wine-growers with one way of
dealing with the crisis. Among the market-gardeners, on the other hand,

the incidence of homogamy was weak; they had been settled more recently but they profited from the proximity of Paris and its growing demand for their fruit and vegetables (Burguière, 1979).

In Vraiville, a parish of the Elbeuf region which had been affected in the second half of the century by the rise of rural industry, the incidence of homogamy reached nearly 70 per cent among labourers, and 90 per cent among husbandmen, whereas weavers married one another very seldom (8 per cent). They got 30 per cent of their wives from the labourers and 23 per cent from the husbandman class. For their part, the labourers chose 11 per cent of their wives among the weavers, but the husbandmen chose none at all. This form of exogamy, which was aggravated by a very unequal exchange of spouses, can be explained by the emerging work sector to which the weavers belonged and which had not yet acquired much professional status and was not well placed on the parish's social chequer-board. Half a century on (between 1823 and 1852), as a wholly established professional group which was already being affected by the crisis in rural industry, the weavers were marrying within their own circle at a rate of 57.5 per cent (Segalen, 1972).

The same phenomenon may be observed at the top of the social scale. Who indeed would be surprised to find that the dukes and peers of France engaged in particularly closed marriage practices? Their social position was directly affected by the nature of their alliances, since the pre-eminent status given to them by the king and marked by the privileges of their rank was basically dedicated to furthering the antiquity, reputation and power of their families. Between 1589 and 1723, half of them had married as their first wives daughters of dukes or peers, 37 per cent had allied themselves with the *noblesse d'épée* and 14 per cent with the *noblesse de robe*. Not one had ventured outside the world of the nobility or had agreed to allow one of his daughters to do so. Daughters of dukes and peers, who did not inherit the title but could transmit it, represented the trump cards in the society game within a circle which considered alliance policies as simply part of politics.

From this point of view, the function of the daughters of dukes and peers was not to acquire power through their marriages but to assert and confirm this power. This was why they married within an even more restricted social sphere. Half of them were given away within the circle of dukes and peers, and the other half to the *noblesse d'épée*. Their fathers, on the other hand, if one compares the first period (1589–1660) with the second (1661–1723), had laid emphasis both on homogamy (41 per cent in the second period as opposed to 26 per cent in the first) and on interbreeding: 27 per cent were allied to the *noblesse de robe*, starting in

Louis XIV's personal reign, as opposed to 8 per cent in the preceding period (Labatut, 1972).

Such mismatches were of a tactical nature, involving the old-established dukes and peers, not the newly created ones. They were the most willing to marry into the *noblesse de robe*, but not any family: they chose the daughters of secretaries of state and other great clerks presiding over the Council, or the daughters of *Parlement* presidents. In this way they laid siege to the principal seats of power. Even in this circle, for whose members a closed society was one of their reasons for existing, homogamy represented a matrimonial ideal which was freely practised even at the cost of growing consanguinuity, just as among the most

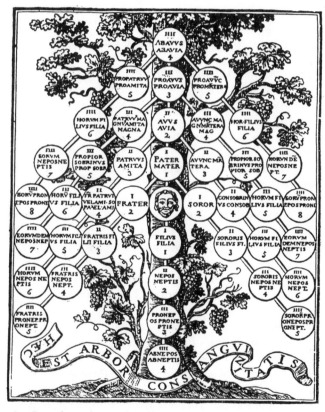

Figure 1   Genealogical tree showing the degrees of consanguinity from *Ego* (represented by a face). Arabic numbers are used for the civil (or Roman) system of computation, which was used to work out inheritance, for instance, and Roman numbers for the Germanic (or ecclesiastical) system, which was used to calculate impediments to marriage.

endogamous peasants; this was not however, a golden rule. According to the depth of their family's roots and their power objectives, dukes and peers did not hesitate to trade power for prestige with a lower-ranking social group.

Depending on whether they were old-established or recent *parvenus*, the upper middle classes also practised strict homogamy or an ambitious matrimonial opportunism. During the eighteenth century, the great Marseille business families, which had been bourgeois so long that they were almost noble, married within their group at a rate of over 70 per cent. On the other hand, the *fermiers généraux* were as keen to ally with merchant families (5 per cent) as with doctors (7 per cent) and general receivers of the finances (5 per cent) as they were with the high nobility (7 per cent). Only 14.5 per cent of them married within their own circle. La Bruyère wrote that 'if the financier's scheme falls through, the courtiers say he is a bourgeois; if he succeeds, they ask him for his daughter.' This quip is confirmed by the figures: 14.8 per cent of the daughters of *fermiers généraux* married within their own circle (i.e. men of the same rank as their own fathers), and more than 28 per cent of them were allied to the high nobility. Durand (1971) wrote that 'Tax farming was not an end in itself for the third estate: it was a social crossroads.' As a mobile and transient group, with no precise career and no hereditary succession (of 156 families counted by Durand, only fifty-five numbered more than one *fermier général*), tax farmers pursued an eclectic and variable matrimonial policy in conformity with their fluid social position.

Some historians such as Roland Mousnier have made social homogamy into a golden rule for Europe under the *ancien régime*, and, thanks to this rule, see marriage as the principal factor in the stability of hierarchical societies. Without wishing to revive the debate about the nature of the classes or orders in the society of the *ancien régime*, a debate which raged among French historians during the 1960s, it is worth observing that homogamy hovered between proximity of rank and proximity of socio-professional status.

Both coexisted easily in an urban environment, where the diversity of work and the specialization of tasks rendered the social hierarchy more visible. In town as in the countryside, they coincided most especially in those groups whose social superiority isolated them from others and who had to get involved in a marriage market which was not limited to the immediate neighbourhood. This was the case for nobles: their alliances were all the less local or regional as their rank was more elevated and they were more present at Court. This was also the case with local notables such as the miller and the *coqs de village*, whose alliance networks extended far beyond the parish horizon.

A family of the merchant middle class in seventeenth-century Holland, portrayed in its familiar everyday surroundings. Rijksmuseum, Amsterdam. By Jan Steen.

In the countryside, where people preferred a spouse from the same area or neighbourhood, some regions favoured social status, others professional status, according to how insistent families were on classing themselves in relation to others in a hierarchical order. Where France was concerned, it does seem that this contrast between homogamy based on rank and homogamy based on social circle reflects the anthropological division between northern and southern France. Can the almost exclusive practice of taking social rank into account when concluding alliances, which one notes in southern France, be explained by the custom of dowering daughters, as Le Roy Ladurie suggests? As he wrote, 'the female dowry is to the male inheritance what interest is to capital' (1982). Thus it would have been necessary, in order to avoid inconvenient and dangerous inequalities, to choose husbands for the daughters from families whose wealth was closely equivalent.

This concern for equivalence was all the more necessary, as Lamaison (1979) has demonstrated, for a peasant community in the Gevaudan, in that the act of paying a dowry obeyed a principle of reciprocity. The *oustal* which received a dowry from another *oustal* took on the obligation of restoring it, either directly by means of another marriage to be concluded later on, with the same house, or by means of a more complex circuit.

However, it may be asked whether the concern to form alliances at an equivalent social level and to put reciprocity into play in the exchange of property and spouses, were features peculiar to the dowry system. The social classification of possible spouses was possibly less systematic in 'egalitarian' France, where, for instance, the status of eldest and younger sons was concerned, but it was marked enough for young people of marriageable age to feel the need to indicate their status by their clothes. From the eighteenth century onwards, peasant formal dress had followed extremely refined demands for ornamentation, including braids, embroideries and facings which were displayed by young people at wedding dances and other ceremonies, and which allowed them to be located with precision in the local hierarchy. As for the principle of reciprocity, it was stated, as we have already seen, by means of practices which can be observed in northern France just as much as in the south. 'Remarkable' marriages, for instance, endowed matrimonial exchanges with an element of symmetry, and marriage linkages served to renew exchanges of spouses between two lines at regular intervals.

The difference was to be found elsewhere, in the idea of relations between family groups which is revealed by their matrimonial strategies. One could draw up a schema contrasting a 'conquering' idea proper to the upper classes, but which could also be found among peasants in southern France, with a 'co-operative' conception proper to northern France.

Those royal or princely marriages which helped to conclude a peace treaty or avoid a conflict represented the extreme form of alliance strategies of the warrior type: like war, they represented no more than the pursuit of diplomacy by other means. However, such a conflict-ridden conception of relations between family groups was not the exclusive privilege of crowned houses. In sixteenth- and seventeenth-century Corsica, the most classic method of ending a vendetta was to draw up a betrothal agreement between the two warring houses. There is no *vera amicitia*, a proverb went, '*senza parentella*', and the *parolanti* (the peace negotiators) were also called *maritanti*. In 1597, for instance, a certain Cilidonia demanded the completion of a marriage which had been contracted in 1583 when she was four years old. Her father Piero had been killed by Cristiano de Brizo, who ambushed him with some of his friends. Peace was subsequently established two years later between some of the victim's relatives and some of the murderer's, who had stayed on the island. Andrea, the murderer's son, was to marry Cilidonia, the victim's daughter, and assign her a marriage portion of 700 livres (Marin-Muracciole, 1964).

Without requiring such a context, permanently tensed between peace and war, to reach a conclusion, marriages among the aristocracy and the upper classes in general, were negotiated in a climate of rivalry and confrontation. The Court at Versailles, as Saint-Simon has described it for us, devoted most of its time and its taste for intrigue to setting up marriage projects. The slightest hint about a possible party for a girl of marriageable age, the slightest rumour about the start of marriage negotiations between two houses set the whole Court in motion, with everyone trying to 'promote their advantage, by means of initiatives for setting him, or improving his position, in the centre of a pressure group or a cabal'. Though these certainly represented the diversions of an idle world, they also constituted power strategies which met the particular conditions of Court society as described by Elias (1974).

In the provincial elite, finalizing a marriage gave rise to a climate of tension and general competition not radically different from that at Court. Nicolas (1978) has been able to reconstitute the diplomatic history of a 'good marriage' which mobilized the whole of high society in Annecy in the mid-eighteenth century, thanks to Canon Favre, the principal architect of the whole affair, who kept a detailed diary of his activities. The two parties involved, Emmanuel Favre and Josette Fernex, were both heirs and had both lost their fathers. The two seasoned marriage-brokers were the heiress's mother, the widow of Antoine Fernex, and Canon Favre, the boy's uncle and a wealthy cleric who had, since his brother's death, become head of the family. Generally speaking, churchmen demonstrated a great sense of family patriotism and they often transferred their unused paternal feelings onto their nephews and nieces. Their excellent knowledge of society and their moral authority made them expert marriage brokers, and just right for this match. It did not matter that anyone of good society in Annecy was capable of providing a fairly exact assessment of the two young people's 'expectations' (each had 70,000 livres in property) or that their marriage had been taken for granted by everyone for ages: the actual finalization of the marriage took many long months.

Among the peasants of southern France, even when minimal dowries and inheritances were involved, the conclusion of an alliance gave rise to similar excitement in the neighbourhood and unleashed a series of equally subtle strategies, manoeuvres and deals, as has been demonstrated for Gevaudan just as much as for Upper Provence.

The general competition which presided over the marriage market was a feature common to these societies, in spite of their being different in other respects. It was due to the fact that they all accepted a strictly hierarchical order, whose criteria for determining rank were imprecise because so numerous. The social gamble was based on this margin of imprecision. No family was absolutely equal to another, though two families could come close in socio-professional status and degree of wealth, but they would diverge again in antiquity and reputation (an especially vulnerable form of capital). In the same way, none of the children they were able to offer on the marriage market would have been the equivalent of another: a younger son was worth less than an elder, a girl less than a boy, a dowered girl less than an heiress, and so on.

Two further features served to complete this hierarchical vision of the social body: a strongly marked sense of 'house' and an agonistic concept of relations between families. The individual was socialized within his family group in an authoritarian and hierarchic framework, which then made it very difficult for him to insert himself into the peer relationships upon which were based neighbourhood solidarities and classifications by age or professional community. The only membership group which he was naturally capable of joining, and the only one capable of transcending his singular social status, was the network of his blood relatives, both departed and living, whose perennial status was symbolized by a house, a farm or a locality which had been occupied by the same lineage for ages.

This exclusive attachment would have been inculcated from his childhood on, and would have inspired in him disregard for himself and devotion to his family of origin, a loyalty which was not without its bitterness and frustrations, but which mobilized a great part of the couple's investment at the expense of other social ties. Not only was the wife never her husband's equal, but their marriage consecrated the passage from one house to another more than it did the birth of a new conjugal unit. The allies could not be added to the blood relatives. They remained separate, partners or rivals if not enemies.

The conclusion of an alliance temporarily ended a situation of confrontation which was perceived by these societies as the traditional and, so to speak, natural form of relationship between family groups. Like the mercantilists who conceived of wealth as a totally inelastic entity and thought that one state could grow rich only at the expense of another, these societies considered that a family could raise itself in prestige, wealth and influence only by bringing other families down. While exchanges in marriage were necessary to calm relations between houses, no marriage constituted the basis of true reciprocity: the house which took a wife would indicate its superiority over the house which gave her. One may also ask whether the codes of honour and revenge which incited families to watch over their daughters' virginity and their wives' virtue, to confound being with semblance, and moral worth with reputation, and which induced the whole of the family group to take responsibility for the past and present actions of one of its members, were not consubstantial with this type of society.

In contrast to this climate of tension and competition were the 'co-operative' strategies of peasant communities, among whom local neighbourhood or age-group solidarities provided an arbitrating and regulatory authority. In such communities, the ritual participation of local people in the conclusion of alliances had remained more vigorous than elsewhere, even when the hostility of the Church authorities had gradually turned it into a quaint survival. 'Barrier' *charivaris* were held to penalize exogamous marriages, and the year's couples were formed by auctions of the marriageable young, a custom condemned by the Synod of Toul in 1665: 'Furthermore they play a game called *Fassnottes* in which they designate at the top of their voices husbands and wives for all the young sons and daughters of the village, such things being neither beneficial nor lawful.' Another practice was reported by Boucquereau, prefect of the Rhine and Moselle region in the Eifel during the Consulate: 'There, on St Matthew's Day, the boys of the commune gather together and auction off each girl, calling them one after the other.'

The object of these rites, which attempted to neutralize the effects of competition, like the family strategies which encouraged prolonged 'frequenting' between engaged couples before their marriage was concluded (in spite of the Church's warnings), was to ensure, by setting up well-matched new households, that the group would reproduce itself and function properly on the basis of reciprocal offerings: exchanges of services, goods and spouses. Such societies deserve to be qualified as 'egalitarian', not so much on account of their inheritance customs, nor for their social structure, which was as complex and hierarchized as elsewhere, but for the ideology which shaped them. People married within their socio-professional circle, but in principle as equals.

The main task of the alliance was to accomplish and strengthen the reciprocal relations upon which the life of the community was founded. Endogamy (reverence for neighbourhood relations) thus prevailed here as the dominant principle. The degree of consanguinity was often close here, even closer than in societies which were dominated by their sense of 'house', but it was not willed nor perceived as such. As Louis Dumont has observed concerning Indian kinship, one could say that marriages with blood relatives were regarded in such societies as marriages with allies. The multiplication of exchanges of spouses among groups of descendants in the same parish or restricted matrimonial sphere, by means of marriage linkages, double marriages, and so on, ended by weaving tighter and tighter ties of consanguinity between the members of these groups. Instead of radically distinguishing between blood relatives and allies in their kinship networks, these communities saw marriage as a means of merging the two groups within a continuum of obligations and sociability which was identified with the social circle.

We have no reason to think that these two types of society, as we see them through the prism of their matrimonial strategies, were established in Europe during our period. They both correspond to ancient social and mental structures. It is, however, probable that some of the major phenomena which gave Europe's first modernity its particular hue, such as the reaction of landowners and the rapid but uneven growth of the state, reinforced the contrasts between these models of social organization.

Like chemical substances, these models were nowhere to be met in the pure state, but they are signs of the dominant tendencies in a family's ideology and practice. The same reservation applies when one seeks to establish a link between behavioural models and models of family organization. There was an obvious affinity between the stem family and strategies for conquest, and between the restricted family and co-operative strategies. In itself, this link is purely tendentious. The pattern of social relations revealed by matrimonial practices should have accustomed us, had this been necessary, to the idea that in trying to describe and classify forms of family organization, we are studying forms of social organization. As in engravings by Escher in which the image at first glance seems to produce its opposite, family forms also enable us to see, starting from their position in the social space, a further form which depicts the very texture of their society.

TWO

Priest, Prince and Family

André Burguière and François Lebrun

As we saw in volume one, the canonical view of marriage was elaborated at the end of the twelfth century. Marriage was a sacrament whose substance was constituted by the mutual consent of both spouses, and its ministers were the spouses themselves. The result was that the parents' consent, even when their children were minors, was not indispensable, any more than the presence of witnesses or the intervention of a priest. When freely exchanged consent was the test, what were known as 'clandestine' marriages became fully valid and the Church, while reproving them, refused to annul them. Furthermore, canon law defined numerous impediments to marriage. Some were totally invalidating disqualifications, notably absence of consent, impotence attested by experts and non-attainment of legal age. Others were prohibitive but could be lifted by papal dispensation; this applied to natural or spiritual kinship within the fourth canonical degree (when there was a common great-great-grandparent), and to affinity or kinship by alliance. Finally, the sacrament of marriage was indissoluble: bodily separation (in Latin *divortium*), which could be pronounced only by a Church tribunal, was not a divorce in the modern meaning of the term and so did not allow the spouses to remarry. Death alone could break the conjugal tie and so permit the survivor to remarry.

The first and third sections of this chapter (pp. 95–113 and 146–58) are by François Lebrun; the remainder is by André Burguière.

The Landlord's Family, engraving by C. Knight, after Stothard, 1792. This picture celebrates conjugal bliss and the simple joys of intimacy, and no longer those of a house's power and a lineage's glory. In Lawrence Stone's view, this new family ideal, founded on conjugal love, first found expression in the English aristocracy. Roger Viollet.

Control of the family by the churches and the state

Matrimonial law: Protestants and Catholics

At the beginning of the sixteenth century, this Christian concept of marriage was fiercely contested by Protestant reformers. For Luther as for Calvin, the Roman Church had created a contradiction by making marriage an indissoluble sacrament, while exalting the ideal of virginity. It was in order to resolve this contradiction that it had gradually forged a complex and restrictive legislation whose justification could not be found in the New Testament and which was contrary, on some points, to Divine Law. These were the reasons behind the reformers' wholesale condemnation of obligatory ecclesiastical celibacy, the validity of clandestine marriages, the multiplicity of impediments, the interdiction on breaking the conjugal tie even in the case of adultery and the Church's affirmation of its exclusive competence in matrimonial matters. For Protestants, marriage was a divine institution, but not a sacrament: it was a state no more or less valuable than celibacy, and a contract based on mutual consent. However, this consent involved too many spiritual and material interests not to be carefully thought over, which implied in the case of minors the consent of their parents, through which the authority of God is expressed. Nevertheless, in such circumstances, the parents were obliged to take care not to put constraints on their children. Protestant moralists, notably Anglicans and Puritans, paid great attention to this point, underlining the grave dangers of forced unions. Around 1560, Joseph Hall, the Anglican Bishop of Norwich, wrote with sadness about the way parents tended to abuse this fearsome authority by forcing their children into loveless marriages in order to promote their worldly interests. He alluded in vivid terms to the likelihood of such young marriage partners having formed prior attachments and thus suffering the pangs of hidden passion: loathing their legitimate spouses, they would be ready to practise any deception that enabled them to commit adultery. As it was, Protestants did in theory allow divorce, but only in cases of acknowledged adultery or of *desertio maliciosa* (prolonged desertion of the conjugal home). In fact, as we shall see, this theoretical possibility was not much used.

These Protestant positions were condemned by the Council of Trent, which reaffirmed in 1547, on the occasion of its seventh session, that 'the sacraments of the Church number seven', amounting to a reminder that marriage was indeed a sacrament. However, it was only in 1563, on the occasion of the twenty-fourth session, that the Council tackled the question of matrimonial law. The members soon agreed to reaffirm the principal points of the Church's classic doctrine. Conversely, the problem of clandestine marriages – ones which had been concluded without the consent of the parents of minors or in the absence of a priest or witnesses – provoked fierce debate and the formulation of several proposals. In fact, although the majority rallied to the view of the French bishops, who demanded that such marriages, notably those of minors without their parents' consent, should be declared invalid, a minority agreed with Jacques Laynez, the Jesuit General, that since free consent by the spouses was the very substance of the sacrament and thus sufficient to validate it, lack of consent by the parents or the absence of a priest could not make it null and void.

Finally, on 11 November 1563, the Council adopted a number of texts which fell, after a brief doctrinal preface, into two distinct parts: twelve short canons and a long disciplinary decree. The canons were drawn up under the formula 'If anyone says that . . . may it be anathema', and condemned all those who denied the following propositions: that marriage was a sacrament (canon 1), both monogamic (2) and indissoluble (5 and 7); that the Church had exclusive competence in matrimonial cases (12), both for pronouncing impediments and granting dispensations (3 and 4), for authorizing in some cases bodily separation (11) and prohibiting the 'solemnity of marriage' at certain times of the year (11). Finally, secular and regular clergy could not contract marriages (9) and the state of virginity was superior to the married state (10).

As for the decretal *De reformatione matrimonii*, it was divided into ten chapters, the first and most important of which is generally designated by its initial word *Tametsi*; it was aimed at clandestine marriages.

> Although it should not be doubted that clandestine marriages, contracted with the parties' free and voluntary consent, are only valid and true marriages so long as the Church has not rendered them null, and that consequently one should condemn, as the Holy Council condemns them, as anathema those who deny that such marriages are real and valid and who maintain falsely that marriages contracted by the heirs of families without their parents' consent are null and that their parents can validate or annul them, the Holy Church has always held them in horror and prohibited them for very just reasons. But the Holy Council, on perceiving that all these prohibitions no longer serve any purpose . . . orders the following: in future, before a marriage is contracted, the vicar proper to the contracting parties shall publicly announce three times in church, during Mass, on three consecutive Sundays, the names of those who are to contract a marriage. After these proclamations have been made, if there is no

legitimate opposition, the marriage will be celebrated in the church . . . As for those who would undertake to contract a marriage other than in the presence of their vicar or of some other priest authorized by the vicar or by the incumbent, and before two or three witnesses, the Holy Council renders them absolutely incapable of contracting anything of the sort and declares that such contracts are null and void, rendering them null and valueless by this present decretal.

In spite of some ambiguity, *Tametsi* managed to distinguish between marriages of minors without their parents' consent and clandestine marriages proper. The Council was content to 'forbid' the former without considering them invalid, but it declared null and void all marriages celebrated without vicar and witnesses. What was more, it imposed prior publication of the three banns and registration of the marriage. It is true, however, that the distinction between marriages of minors and clandestine marriages was above all a formal one, since family heirs who married against their parents' wishes nearly always did so clandestinely.

The nine other chapters of the decretal were concerned with impediments and dispensations (the impediments of spiritual kinship were limited, those of consanguinity and affinity were upheld, but dispensations for them were made easier). They dwelt on the interdiction of marriage 'between a ravisher and the girl he has abducted, so long as she remains in her ravisher's power'; the sufferings of concubines, and the precise definition of the periods when solemn marriage was forbidden (*tempus ferarium*), 'from Advent to the day of Epiphany and from Ash Wednesday to the Octave of Easter inclusively'.

Procreation, the chief purpose of marriage

While the Council judged it neccessary to respond to Protestant attacks with this redefinition and adjustment of canon law in matrimonial matters, it did not feel the need to recall the ends of marriage since these were not challenged by its adversaries. In the Christian view, the family founded on marriage only acquired meaning and legitimacy when children were born. Theologians and catechists of the sixteenth to eighteenth centuries, repeated this constantly. The Agen Catechism (1677) defined marriage in these terms: 'It is a sacrament instituted in order to have children legitimately and to raise them in the fear of God.' The Nantes Catechism (1689) stipulated that 'to make holy use of marriage is but to use it to good ends, which is to say only in the desire to have children who may one day love and adore God.' Procreation is thus truly the first and principal end of marriage, before the happiness of both spouses and their mutual sanctification.

The primacy granted here to procreation is not mentioned explicitly in the New Testament. St Paul does not refer to it when he expands on marriage. Nevertheless, the idea very quickly took root. In the fourth century, according to both St Jerome and St Augustine, a husband sinned if he had intercourse with his wife without the deliberate intention to procreate. There was nevertheless a slight difference between these two Fathers of the Church: St Jerome considered the sin mortal, for St Augustine it was venial. However, this requirement of procreative intent was challenged by later theologians, including St Thomas Aquinas, who recognized the legitimacy of conjugal union with the sole purpose of avoiding incontinence. What was more, towards 1550, the Spanish Dominican Domingo de Soto acknowledged that births could be limited by abstention from all conjugal relations when the spouses were too poor to raise more children than they already had; and the Spanish Jesuit Thomas Sanchez, in his *De sancto matrimonii sacramento* (1602), justified the conjugal act without procreative intent on the part of the spouses so long as they did nothing to avoid conception. He even authorized restrained embraces, meaning 'the huggings, kisses and fondlings customary between spouses to demonstrate and strengthen their mutual love', even if there was a risk of involuntary pollution (but Sanchez's work was placed on the Index as soon as it appeared).

These speculations on the part of theologians were only variations on the central theme, which none of them challenged, namely the condemnation as mortal sin of everything that could divert the conjugal act from its procreative purpose, nobably the practice of *coitus interruptus* or 'sin of Onan'. St Francis of Sales was only expressing general opinion when he wrote in his *Introduction to the Devout Life* (1608): 'The procreation of children is the first and principal end of marriage; one is never at liberty to depart from the order which this requires.' This condemnation of every contraceptive practice allowed room in theory for only one form of voluntary birth control, and only in certain circumstances and under certain conditions: continence within marriage. In fact, however, despite this unequivocal condemnation, there was latitude enough to allow vicars and confessors to apply the principle very cautiously at grass-roots level. Were they supposed to engage in narrow interrogations and possibly dissipate the 'the young spouses' ignorance', as Father Féline prescribed bossily in his *Catechism for Married Persons* (1782), or were they supposed to 'keep silent about these matters unless explicitly asked', as recommended by Alfonso Liguori? Certainly the second way of doing things was most generally employed until the mid-nineteenth century, and could only have helped indirectly to diffuse knowledge of contraception, in France at least. Could a wife whose husband habitually practised *coitus interruptus* accept such conjugal relations without sinning? By replying, even implicitly, in the affirmative, many confessors also opened a breach in the armoury of theoretical condemnation.

In principle, at least, the Protestants' point of view did not differ at all. Calvin took up the theologians' condemnations on his own account and qualified the crime of Onan as 'monstrous'. In *The Whole Duty of Man*, published in 1663, Richard Allestree was echoing St Francis of Sales when he pointed out that, since there are two ends to marriage, the procreation of children and the struggle against fornication, nothing should be allowed to prevent the former. However, in spite of identical condemnations, there were many obvious differences between Protestants and Catholics. Calvin saw the sexual act as a gift of God, which it was meet to 'use joyfully' and which was justified in itself, apart from its final end, which was procreation. The latter involved the full responsibility of the spouses, who should engender only as many children as they could care for and educate. 'The loss of a line or absence of children', Calvin wrote 'would be happier by far than abundance of children, full of tears and groans.' It is obvious, however, that Calvin and the Protestant theologians considered this option of voluntary birth control only in terms of abstention from conjugal relations. Thomas Malthus, himself a cleric, said the same in his *Essay on the Principle of Population* (1803), in which he advocated continence among poor families as one way of reducing the population. This Protestant concept of the couple's complete responsibility in matters of conjugal morality, together with the abolition of confession, resulted in the paradox that although Calvinist, Lutheran and Anglican clergymen married, they could not play the role played in this domain for their penitents, male and female, by celibate Catholic priests.

While respect for nature and the sacred value of life served as foundations for the Church's condemnation of contraception, these great principles served even more to justify condemning abortion and infanticide. Theologians were divided over the point of determining the precise moment of gestation when the foetus aquires a soul. However, this distinction only served to evaluate the nature of the sin – whether or not it was homicide – because in every case it was a mortal sin. This is how Pontas summed it up in his *Summary of the Dictionary of Cases of Conscience* (1764): 'Abortion is the premature delivery of the fruit borne by a woman. He who voluntarily procures an abortion, whether or not the foetus has a soul, sins mortally. He even commits a murder if the foetus has a soul. It is not certain, among doctors or philosophers, about the precise moment when the foetus acquires a soul.' For their part, Protestants saw abortion as a grievous sin which involved 'suspension from the Lord's Supper'. As for infanticide, defined as the killing of a new-born baby by its mother, it was true murder, and all the more grievous in that the child was deprived of baptism in the majority of cases. The exceptional gravity of infanticide – as of abortion of the ensouled foetus – was indeed linked to this deprivation of baptism, involving loss of eternal salvation, which was not the case with the murder of a baptized person.

Baptism

It was the first duty of parents to their children, in the eyes of the Church, to get the new-born baby baptized as soon as possible. Baptism was, in fact, a sacrament which removed original sin, and without which no one could be saved. The ecclesiastical authorities had long accepted that lengthy delays could intervene between the birth and the administration of the sacrament. In the late Middle Ages, they began to worry about the fate of so many children who had thus died unbaptized, at a time when one nursling in four died in its first year, and they made it incumbent on parents to have their children baptized very soon after birth: 'as soon as possible' (*quamprimum*) was what the Council of Trent prescribed in 1547. The practice of keeping baptismal registers in each parish, as early as the fifteenth century in some dioceses, and checking on them during pastoral visitations by the bishop or his representative, made it possible to ensure that this instruction was being followed. By the end of the century, the cause had been won. The child's eternal salvation took precedence over his temporal survival. Since the little ones who died unbaptized were not Christians, this meant not only that their bodies were buried outside the cemetery's consecrated land, but, even more serious still, that their souls were deprived of heaven and condemned to wander eternally in limbo. Baptism had become the indispensable passport to the next world.

If the birth process went wrong and the child was in 'peril of death', the first duty of the midwife, father or whoever was present was to baptize it immediately. Two witnesses were to testify to the vicar that the prescribed forms had indeed been respected. In such cases, the sacrament was reduced to its essentials: the person performing the baptism poured a little holy water, or, if none was available, ordinary water, onto the infant's head or some part of its body if it was still stuck inside its

The Married State, illustration for chapter 11 of the French edition of Erasmus' treatise on oratory. It was one of the many works in which the great Dutch humanist criticized the inadequacies and contradictions of the Church's doctrine on marriage. Ancient Art and Architecture Collection.

mother, and pronounced distinctly the words of the sacrament: 'I baptize you in the name of the Father, the Son and the Holy Spirit.' Although the sacrament was fully valid, such a baptism was called an 'unction' and was considered incomplete. Thus, in the event of the infant surviving, it had to be taken without delay to the church so that the vicar could supplement the ceremony in front of the godparents, who were to give the child their names. What was more, anointing could only be practised when the infant was alive, since the theologians considered it sacrilege to administer a sacrament to something dead. In doubtful cases, however, conditional baptism could be administered with these words: 'If you are alive, I baptize you', etc. This formula must have been much employed, even in the case of still-born babies, for who would risk depriving a soul that was possibly alive of eternal life? The Church also authorized unction, with prior dispensation, when the parents wanted to delay the solemn baptism to enable the mother and distant friends to attend it. Such dispensations were, however, never requested by ordinary people.

These exceptional cases apart, baptism normally had to be administered in the parish church, on the day of birth or the following day, and only very rarely on the day after that. During the ceremony, the baby was given a Christian name by the godfather and godmother. They were in theory called to play an important role in the child's life well beyond the actual day of baptism. In the sixteenth century the baptized child commonly had several godfathers and several godmothers. However, the Council of Trent, in its concern to reinvest godparenthood with all its dignity and value, forbade this multiplication. The Church, in fact, considered the godparents, the possible substitutes for the father and mother, as partially responsible for the spiritual education of the child whom they had brought to the baptismal font. Protestants understood from the doctrine of justification by faith alone that baptism had no claim at all to play the vital role in the economics of salvation which Catholic theologians recognized in it. Neither Luther nor Calvin considered that it could remove original sin or open the gates of heaven. Calvin wrote that it was 'a purely diabolical doctrine because it allows justice without faith'. In any case, baptism was retained as a sacrament by most of the reformers who viewed it as a symbol of the soul's union with God, a sign of the promise of regeneration made to the newly baptized child and a rite of integration into the Church. In this perspective, the baptism of new-born babies could not be justified at all. Nevertheless Luther and Calvin retained it, above all as a rite of presentation to the assembly of the faithful. However, for this no haste was required, since the death of an unbaptized child could not have the same tragic consequences as it did in Catholic eyes. According to Calvin's prescriptions and to the usage of the Genevan Church, all the children born in one week were baptized collectively on the following Sunday, during the sermon. However, this was not a strict rule, and often a much longer period, which could extend to one year, elapsed between birth and baptism. In 1676, at the request of the Church of La Charité, the Synod of Sancerre even deemed it necessary to remind 'all those who have children to baptize, to have them brought to the temple to administer baptism to them on the day of worship closest to their birth, under pain of being grievously censured'. In England, the Anglicans and most Dissenting sects only proceeded to the child's baptism several weeks or even months after its birth, while Baptists administered the sacrament only to persons aged at least fifteen, who professed their faith and repentance for their sins.

The rights and duties of parents towards their children

As well as baptism, parents had a set of rights and duties to their children, which were gradually defined by the Church between the sixteenth and nineteenth centuries. St Paul had already spoken of the reciprocity of duties between parents and children: 'Children, obey your parents in all things: for this is well pleasing unto the Lord. Fathers, provoke not your children to anger, lest they be discouraged' (Col. 3:20–1). For a long time, however, the concept of the authority of the father of the family, as a reflection of the authority of God himself, remained very close to what it had been in ancient Roman law. By recognizing, since the twelfth century, the validity of marriages by minors without their parents' consent, the Church had indeed tended to weaken paternal power, though at the same time reminding children who thus disobeyed that they were sinning grievously. The casuist John Benedicti made it clear in his *Summa of Sins* (1584) that this contradiction was resolved in favour of paternal authority: 'The father can order him, not by threatening to beat or kill him, for his marriage must be free, but the child is bound to obey under pain of mortal sin.'

Nevertheless, from the beginning of the seventeenth century onwards, more and more Catholic reformers were beginning to mention, by way of a footnote to the Fourth Commandment ('Honour thy father and mother') the duties of parents towards their children. In his *Instruction du chrétien* (1640), for instance, Richelieu wrote that 'this command-ment is an obligation not only for children towards their fathers, but, what is more, for fathers and mothers towards their children, in so far as love should be reciprocal.' It is true that some of these duties were already implicit and self-evident, such as material assistance and religious education, but from then on the Church authorities spoke explicitly, and at greater or lesser length, about these parental duties. A good example of this is provided by the bishop of Agen, Claude Jolly's manual, *Les Devoirs du chrétien dréssés en forme de catéchisme*, commonly known as the Agen Catechism (1677). Here is the first part of the seventh instruction:

> *Question.* What are the duties of fathers and mothers towards their children? *Answer.* They owe them four things: food, instruction, correction and a good example. *Q.* What does this food consist of? *A.* To nourish, clothe and raise them according to their condition; to have them taught a trade or a vocation suitable to them. *Q.* What is the instruction which fathers and mothers owe to their children? *A.* They must teach them themselves or through another the principal mysteries of the Faith, the Commandments of God and the Church, the *Pater* and *Ave*, and to flee from sin more than from death. *Q.* What must the father and mother do before engaging their children in a life profession? *A.* They must pray and consult God to know if their children are called to it, and to acquaint them with the obligations of their state. *Q.* In what consists the correction which fathers and mothers owe to their children? *A.* In reproving them and chastising them when they do wrong, with kindness and charity, and not in anger and malice. *Q.* What good examples do fathers and mothers owe to their children? *A.* Abstaining from all evil and doing as much good as they can in their presence.

However, while stressing more than previously the obligations of parents in matters of education (notably that of teaching their children a trade and placing them in a profession suited to their state and vocation), at the same time the Church was tending to encroach on this educational role. This was true in the first place of religious instruction, which was henceforth provided within the framework of parish catechism. While the institution of Sunday catechism under the parish priest's authority only gradually became general in the course of the seventeenth century in France and other Catholic countries, even afterwards the parents, notably the mother, retained in theory an important role, during early childhood at first and subsequently parallel with Church instruction. Nonetheless, as far as the bishops were concerned, the religious instruction of children had to be conducted essentially in terms of the catechism, as the only way of transmitting the truths of the faith uniformly, and of keeping tight control of the process. The multiplication of little schools and the creation of colleges and boarding schools linked to some of them also contributed towards parents' relative dispossession. This was notably so in France: even though school attendance was still weak overall, especially at the elementary level, schooling for children and adolescents seems to have been one of the major facts in the history of education in the three centuries before the Revolution. By then, 'for more and more children, apprenticeship in behaviour and knowledge had been increasingly transferred from the family to the school' (Chartier, Compère and Julia, 1976).

In Protestant countries, the authority of the father of the family was reinforced by the role which he played as the minister of family worship, with Bible readings and communal prayer. An Anglican minister called William Perkins described such families, in which divine services were held, as little churches, as, indeed, a kind of Heaven on earth. Protestants stressed even more clearly than Catholics that parents have not only rights with regard to their progeny, but also duties. They insisted notably on the care with which their children's future was to be prepared. Such a concern was perfectly in line with the rigid warp of Calvinist doctrine, according to which the service of God and the service of men were inseparable, pure contemplation was but a snare of the devil, and the supernatural vocation of each individual involved his vocation to a socially useful trade. In the words of the authors of *A Goudly Forme of Householde Government* (1640), idleness was the mother of all evils and the stepmother of all virtues. They stressed the importance of bringing all children up to be learned, or trained in the sort of work or trade that would one day allow them to earn their livings and better themselves.

However, while enhancing the role of the father of the family, the Protestant Reformation also contributed, before the Catholic Counter-Reformation, to the partial dispossession of the family's educational role. The corollary of the fact that all the faithful had the right and duty to enter into direct contact with the Word of God in the Bible was that they had to know how to read. Reading ability thus became an indispensable priority for Protestants. As early as 1524, Luther launched an appeal to the magistrates in every German town to open and maintain Christian schools. In Luther's view, education in the faith was the duty of parents, and he composed a *Grösser* and *Kleiner Katechismus* in 1529 for their use. For Calvin, on the contrary, school and catechism went together: it was the ministers on whom fell 'the public charge of instructing in church', and first of instructing the children. In order to make their task easier he wrote the *Formulary for Instructing Children in Christianity* in 1541, the first manual drawn up not as a continuous discourse but in question-and-answer form. The weekly catechism by the pastor became an obligatory institution for all children in the reformed churches. Only those who had given proof of their knowledge were admitted to the Lord's Supper.

As far as the parental role was concerned, then, the Catholic and

Protestant Reformations were both working in the same direction, with a few subtle differences. Both worked towards the maintenance and even reinforcement of parental authority, towards an improved definition of parents' duties with regard to their children while respecting children's rights, and towards a relative reduction in their educational responsibilities.

Marriage as a civil contract

In his *Dictionnaire universel* (1690), Furetière defined marriage as 'a civil contract whereby a man is joined to a woman for the procreation of legitimate children: marriage belongs to the law of nations and is practised by all peoples.' Only after this did he add that 'Marriage, among the Roman Catholics, is a sacrament, a sacred and indissoluble tie.' As a civil contract, marriage and all that concerned the family which it founded, was of direct interest to states. In Catholic countries, even before the decisions of the Council of Trent, some of the dispositions of canon law presented problems, especially the exclusive competence of Church tribunals in matrimonial matters, and the validity of clandestine marriages. In France, the *Parlements* did not refrain from intervening in these matters in response to the appeal procedure or in cases of abuse. As for 'son of the family' marriages, i.e. by minors against their parents' wishes, a royal edict of February 1556 declared them 'illicit', which entailed disinheritance. The fact that the French bishops had been unsuccessful in their bid to get the Council of Trent to recognize the invalidity of such unions in 1563 was very much behind the Royal Council's refusal to acknowledge the decisions of the Council of Trent as laws of the kingdom and to submit them to the *Parlements* for registration.

In any case, royal legislation was gradually to adopt on its own account most of the Tridentine prescriptions in matters of conjugal law, although not without giving some of them a tincture of the Gallican theory of marriage. The principal texts were the edict of 1556, the Blois *ordonnance* in May 1579 (articles 40–4), the *ordonnance* called *Code Michau* in January 1629 (articles 39, 40 and 169), the declaration of 26 November 1639 'about marriage formalities' and the edict of March 1697 'regulating the formalities of marriage' (not to mention section 20 of the *ordonnance* of April 1667 and the declaration of 9 April 1736 on the keeping of parish registers). Royal legislation was in agreement with Tridentine decisions about the essential details: the prior publication of three banns, the presence of four witnesses (the Council said two or three), keeping a register 'to provide proof', and the indissoluble nature of the union. It became clear, however, that there were three points of divergence, a fact which was exploited by some *Parlements*. These were the marriage of minors, the role of the parish priest and the competence of the Church. The later laws repeated and strengthened the terms of the 1556 edict, making the age of consent thirty for men and twenty-five for women, and requiring that parental advice must be sought even after these ages had been reached, though it could in the last resort be flouted after 'respectful warnings'. The sanctions against recalcitrant minors were not only civil in nature, notably disinheritance, but also penal, theoretically capital. The presence of the parish priest, as we have seen in the case of the Tridentine decisions, served merely as a witness. This enabled Gilbert Gaumin (1585–1665), a state councillor, to contract his marriage before a notary by compelling his parish priest to witness it. Conversely, the 1639 declaration gave the parish priest an active role and even made him administer the sacrament, since it stipulated that he was charged not only with 'receiving the spouses' consent', but 'conjoining' them. By relying on this text, *Parlements* were to annul marriages '*à la gaulmine*', which were in theory valid in the eyes of the Church. As for exclusive ecclesiastical competence in matrimonial matters, as reaffirmed at Trent, it could not fail to lead to conflict between the two powers. This was why the *Parlements* claimed to be competent to check the validity of certain dispensations granted by the Church in matters of impediment, and to judge annulment proceedings for impotence. However, the civil power's claims were particularly clear where requests for separation were involved. In theory, bodily separation was a matter for the Church, and separation of property for the state. In fact, since most requests for separation involved both bodies and property, royal judges used this as a pretext for claiming competence for themselves. In a more general way, the manner in which relations between monarchy and Church in France evolved from the personal reign of Louis XIV onwards led to some adjustment of the Church position as expressed in the synodal statutes on civil legislation. Thus, by rendering the parish priest's nuptial blessing obligatory, the majority of bishops gave the latter an active role (without, however, making him administer the sacrament). In the same way, they forbade their vicars to celebrate the marriage of minors without having made sure of their fathers' or guardians' consent.

Matrimonial legislation in Protestant countries was that of the Established Church. In England, since the promulgation of the Thirty-Nine Articles in 1563, marriage was no longer a sacrament. It was a simple contract requiring only the consent of both parties, whether or not it was performed in front of a minister of the Anglican Church, a facility which allowed Nonconformist sects to develop. Furthermore, publication of the banns was not indispensable, nor was parents' consent in the case of minors. This lax official stance resulted in multiple abuses and led to the 1753 adoption of Lord Hardwicke's Marriage Act 'for the preventing of clandestine marriages'. From then on, in order to be valid every marriage had to be celebrated before a minister of the Anglican Church, in accordance with the Church's ceremonial, and in the presence of two witnesses; what was more, consent by the parents was made obligatory for minors below the age of twenty-one. Jews and Quakers alone continued to enjoy the privilege of marrying according to their own rites. Other English people – notably minors – who refused to conform to Hardwicke's Act could resort to marrying in Scotland or in Jersey, where it did not apply. This is what the Frenchman François de la Rochefoucauld observed with astonishment when he visited England in 1784:

> Thirty years ago, not only was no priest needed to carry out the marriage ceremony, but even the consent of the parents was not mentioned; the first man to turn up could marry two persons. This is still happening today in Scotland. There the presence of a priest is as useless as is the parents' consent, which causes a great number of young people, whose parents do not want to let them marry according to their inclination, to go every year to Scotland, where all paternal power is without strength and absolutely null.

As for divorce in the full meaning of the term, it was theoretically possible in England, either as a consequence of disqualifications (such as pre-pubertal age, a former marriage, rape, impotence or consanguinity within the third degree), or in the event of adultery by the woman. However, divorce could only be given by an Act of Parliament, which would be forthcoming only if the previous bodily separation had been pronounced by an ecclesiastical court, and if, in cases of adultery, the woman's accomplice had been condemned by a court of law to pay the husband damages and interest. Furthermore, the whole procedure was very expensive. This meant that divorce was available only to members of the very wealthy aristocracy and was very rare, at least until the mid-eighteenth century: seventeen were granted between 1670 and 1749, and 115 between 1750 and 1799. Divorce was considered a threat to the social equilibrium and thus remained more of a theoretical than a real resort. Though they were divided over the notion of indissolubility, Protestant and Catholic states combined to denounce adultery as a violation of the conjugal tie, and more generally all forms of sexual activity outside marriage, which were seen as threats to the structure of the family and consequently to the entire body of civil and religious society.

Civil legislation in favour of the family and child

Apart from matrimonial law proper, states provided very little family legislation. This is why the edict of Henri II of France in February 1556 on termination of pregnancies is particularly important. This aimed at putting an end to the practice of infanticide and ran as follows:

> Having been duly apprised of a great and execrable crime occurring frequently in our kingdom, which is that several women, having conceived children by dishonest or other means and prompted by ill will and bad advice, disguise, conceal and hide their pregnancies, without revealing or declaring anything; and when the time of their parturition and deliverance of their fruit occurs, they give birth secretly, then suffocate, strike or otherwise suppress the child without having imparted the holy sacrament of baptism to it; having done this, they throw it into secret and disgusting places or bury it in profane ground, in these ways depriving it of the customary burial of Christians . . . We have, in order to obviate this, said, commanded and ordered . . . that every woman on finding herself duly accused and convicted of having hidden, covered and concealed both her pregnancy and her childbearing, without having declared one or the other . . . be held and reputed to have murdered her child and, in reparation, be punished by death and the last agony.

In order that 'No one may be able to claim ignorance', provision was made for the edict to be published every three months at all parish masses during the sermon. This was an exceptional procedure and showed the great importance attached to the prevention of infanticide. In England, a law of 1625 adopted wholesale the dispositions of the king of France's edict, but applied it only to illegitimate children.

State action to help abandoned children was rarer still. In France, every foundling was theoretically the responsibility of the Justice in whose fief it had been exposed, and who had either to feed it at his own expense, or to have it brought to the nearest hospital and to pay the cost. However, this responsibility was more often than not evaded. That was why the Moulins *ordonnance* of 1566 prescribed that if the Justice failed to make provision, exposed children should become the charge of the parish where they were 'raised'. Apart from these two laws from the mid-sixteenth century (the 1556 edict and the 1566 *ordonnance*), during the next two centuries legislative measures specifically related to the problems of childhood were rare. By the royal edict of 28 June 1670, the Hôpital de la Couche (maternity hospital), founded in Paris by Vincent de Paul for foundlings, was attached to the general hospital established fifteen years before. In the same way, the few children's hospitals founded at the end of the seventeenth century, often attached to general hospitals, were the result of local initiatives and not of the application of any overall scheme for solving the problem at state level. Conversely, the great movement which induced enlightened opinion in France in the 1760s and 1770s to take an entirely new interest in the problems relating to children, was expressed in a number of legislative measures. This trend in opinion led to a real collective awakening: the killing of children and infants was no longer regarded as impossible to prevent, but as something that could be controlled. The authorities' concern to preserve 'subjects for the king' meant that their first efforts were directed at training midwives. In fact, all those concerned with childhood, with doctors and surgeons in the lead, felt, with justice, that one reason why so many new-born babies died was that the vast majority of midwives lacked any training. In 1762 the Estates of Brittany supported the introduction of an institution for teaching obstetrics to the future midwives of the province. In 1769, Joseph Raulin, the king's doctor, published his *Succinct Instructions concerning Delivery for the Benefit of the Provinces' Midwives*. Between 1767 and 1785 Mme Le Boursier du Coudray, a certified midwifery instructor, was nominated by the king 'to teach the art of delivery over the whole breadth of the kingdom'. She travelled throughout France and stayed two to three months in each major town, where she provided a course of instruction for midwives of the region who wanted to obtain an official certificate. At the same time, she initiated a number of surgeon-demonstrators able to continue the work she had thus begun, by organizing similar courses every year for new students in the area. In Languedoc, where the provincial Estates undertook in 1780 to create free midwifery courses in all the towns in the province, one of the project's supporters expressed himself in these significant terms: 'Since the instruction of midwives has no other object than the public weal it must be supported by the public; thus it is up to you, Messieurs, to provide the necessary funds for their instruction.' The practice of putting babies out to wet-nurses also drew strong criticism, which was accompanied by pleas for maternal breast-feeding. The ill-controlled activities of *recommanderesses* in the large towns, who took charge of recruiting wet-nurses and placing children, were denounced, as were the conditions in the countryside to which the babies were exposed, the absence of supervision and the lack of a professional conscience in so many wet-nurses. Here too, the authorities intervened. The royal declaration of 24 July 1769 'concerning *recommanderesses* and wet-nurses' proved decisive for establishing a general office for *recommanderesses* in Paris, whose directors were charged notably with 'maintaining a continual correspondence between the wet-nurses and the parents, which will enable all of them to concur equally in safeguarding the lives of their children'. People everywhere were concerned to regulate the activities of wet-nurses. The Seneschal's court in Anger, for instance, approved a police order on 22 March 1772 enjoining them to nurse only one baby at a time, and to inform parents of any accidents which might prevent them from continuing to provide milk.

The authorities also made attempts to improve the distressing condition of abandoned children. Since there were too few specialized hospitals in the provinces, the Paris Hôpital took in exposed children from all over the kingdom, who were brought to the capital under even direr conditions than those suffered by children in the care of wet-nurses. This was why two rulings by the Royal Council in 1773 and 1779 prohibited children born and exposed in the provinces from being brought to Paris. Official initiatives for distributing rubella immunizations were conducted within the same context. In 1769, Choiseul instigated a large-scale experiment which was carried out at the military college of La Flèche, with the systematic inoculation of the 400 students there. The experiment was continued every year until the military college was closed down in 1776. These various initiatives, which were connected to the establishment of the Société royale de médecine in 1776–8, is evidence of the new interest taken by the French state in the problems of public health and especially in those of infancy.

To sum up, the sixteenth to eighteenth centuries saw an increasingly tight control over the family by the churches and states throughout Europe. Whereas the Protestant and Catholic Reformations played a major role in the development of an increasingly internalized piety and in the emergence of great inwardness and of 'private life', at the same time they paradoxically granted a growing importance to all forms of collective piety, notably in the family framework. For Lutherans as for Calvinists, the daily prayer and Bible reading enjoined on all the faithful generally assumed the aspect of family worship; the task of presiding over this worship generally fell to the father of the family. Every morning and evening it was he who gathered his wife, children and servants together to read the Bible out loud and intone the Psalms, and his authority extended well beyond this daily role. Catholics, for their part, insisted on the importance of the family, as an institution sanctified by a sacrament, and as the primary and privileged unit of the individual's Christianizing process. The greater power of states in these centuries moved in the same direction. Although most rulers introduced little legislation, they did protect the institution of the family (the impediments to divorce introduced in Protestant countries were significant in this respect) and they used the family as an essential relay in the increasingly necessary task of supervising the individual.

How the couple developed

Hypotheses

Was the couple, like happiness, a new idea in eighteenth-century Europe? Historians have put forward several interpretations of the changes which affected the way the couple developed and of the climate of conjugal life in pre-industrial Europe. Did it involve a rise in individualism, starting in the working classes, among migrants from the country attracted by the emerging industrial centres and liberated from the moral and social constraints of the traditional village society in which they were brought up? Such a concept, as developed by Shorter (1977) in particular, sets this mutation in the eighteenth century, at the start of the Industrial Revolution. It assumes that there was a direct connection between the aspiration to choose one's own spouse and the demands of a capitalist economy, which requires a workforce whose services are freely offered in accordance with market conditions. The model of romantic love which claimed to found marriage on a strictly affective and even passionate base is supposed, in this view, to have been derived from poorer social groups, for whom sentiment replaced considerations of inheritance. It then won over the upper classes by imitation, the effect of fashion or simply the contagion of individualistic values.

Or did it, on the contrary, involve a matrimonial model which took shape among the educated upper classes and trickled down through society to disseminate among working people? By imposing an internalized piety, both the Protestant and Catholic Reformations and humanist opinion trends, it is suggested, converted the elites to individualistic values and laid the basis for a new mode of managing conjugal feelings and relations. Both Protestant and Catholic preachers favoured the promotion of the couple in different ways, the former by denying the superiority of the priestly state over the married state (this was the English Puritans' doctrine of holy matrimony), and the latter by using the archetype of the Holy Family as an instrument for Christianizing private life.

Stone (1977) applied this hypothesis to the British case, which enabled him to credit the English aristocracy with a pioneering role in developing a new conjugal civilization, a role already conceded by some witnesses of the age. The young duc de La Rochefoucauld, for instance, who travelled around England at the end of the *ancien régime*, recorded the custom in English high society of going out to dinner in town or to the theatre in the company of one's wife, as a matter occasioning some surprise to a Frenchman.

Such an interpretation presupposes a slower and older evolution, one which was sensitive to shifts in religious and moral values. Stone tells us that from the end of the sixteenth century, the conjugal unit was promoted by an austere morality which exalted individual asceticism and the head of the family's responsibility and authority. In the eighteenth century, religious values were on the wane, and pleasure and the establishment of earthly happiness were rehabilitated by a hedonistic morality. A more liberal and permissive climate developed which loaded conjugal relations with affectivity and accepted more easily the demands of young people to marry according to the dictates of their hearts.

Was it, on the other hand, a 'process of civilization', to adopt Norbert Elias's (1978) terminology? What is interesting about his much more general scheme of interpretation is that it tries to explain the change in family behaviour, and especially in conjugal life, not simply as the effect of new ideas but as the result of a transformation of state and society. Modern man's 'psychogenesis', which can give an account of how the couple has been re-evaluated, passes via the 'sociogenesis' of the modern state.

Monarchical centralization, which gave the sovereign a triple monopoly in military, fiscal and judicial affairs, brought peace to social life; relations between individuals, which had previously been based on the use of force, were transformed into competitive relationships for procuring favours from the powerful. Open confrontation gave way to guile, thus obliging individuals to acquire greater mastery over their impulses and greater refinement in their thought processes and psychological awareness in order to anticipate and interpret other people's reactions.

According to Elias, seventeenth-century France provided the most finished example of court society; it was the crucible for a new psychological balance in which rational behaviour took precedence over impulsive behaviour. The principles of behaviour and the techniques of self-mastery, which were characteristic of this new balance, were initially the object of treatises on comportment for use by courtiers. This was then transferred, using Erasmus' *De civilitate morum puerilium* as a model, to inspire a new pedagogical approach based on disciplined movement and the acquisition of a sense of modesty (Elias, 1994).

Avoidance of physical contact in social relations, concealment of everything to do with the body's natural functions, modesty and restraint especially in relations with the opposite sex: the new social model, like the moral framework of the religious Reformations and the veil of suspicion which they cast over emotional life and sexuality, had a

The Holy Family, a painting by Andrea del Sarto (1519). This famous work has a theme which was new at the time but was widely promoted by the Church in order to popularize the cult of the Holy Family as a model of family life based on Christian virtues. In the Middle Ages St Joseph was seldom placed to the fore, being an ageing spouse and a father in name only, and popular religiosity sometimes made him into a figure of fun. From now on, however, the important thing about the family was not the quality of the filiation it represented, but of the bonds between the spouses, and between parents and their children. Galleria Nazionale d'Arte Antica, Rome.

repressive influence on the way people handled their impulses. By raising a rampart of dissimulation between personal experience and what was permissible to show in social life, it gave consistency to an intermediate world, a sphere of intimacy over which the couple and conjugal relations secured exclusive rights. Did the economic changes which burst asunder the community constraints of traditional society and liberated the individual, or rather inspired the individual with the need to choose freely, play the motor role here? Or was it the pioneering role of the enlightened elites, who invented a new morality and a new sensibility for the whole of society? Or was it the modernizing role of the state which led the individual to internalize behavioural norms, refine social conduct and discover intimacy?

Perhaps it was all three at once. The last two interpretative models have the advantage over the first that they take account of the whole of our period and envisage a long, non-linear evolution conforming to the shifts which may be perceived in the demographic trend and in the moral and religious climate. After an exuberant start in the sixteenth century, when demographic growth and fluid social relations allowed young people a fairly wide margin of freedom in their sexual life, as in their choice of spouse, came a long authoritarian and ascetic period in the seventeenth century. Convergent efforts by states and churches imposed a general normalization of behavioural forms, using the family as their instrument for moralizing the social body. This moralizing process set value on the married couple and tried to repress all extramarital sexual activity. In the eighteenth century, when religious control was relaxed, a new ideology emerged as the offspring of the Englightenment, which not only favoured the autonomy of the individual and the achievement of earthly happiness based on the cult of sentiment and pleasure, but also brought about the re-emergence of a permissive climate with regard to sexuality and the promotion of the love match as a social ideal. The new rise in premarital conceptions and illegitimate births, which is perceptible from the middle of the century, followed the rhythm of the economic upswing and the process of urbanization.

The idea of a permissive sixteenth century is acceptable, so long as it is made to end about 1560, as is an austere seventeenth century and a liberated eighteenth century, though not till around 1740: this is a very approximate chronology on a European scale of a non-linear evolution made up of constraints and breaks, and not a simple oscillation between repression and relaxation. It was during the long period when an austere conjugal morality and supervision of family life were inculcated, that the frontier between public and private domains became clearer, defining an intimate space within which the couple ceased to be a mere unit of reproduction and became a privileged pole of affection and solidarity. Paradoxically, it was also the religious redefinition of the marriage bond and the Church's efforts at confining sexuality within this conjugal space which created the conditions for the emergence of love matches. When love matches are referred to as the dominant matrimonial model, two distinct aspects are being confused, which ended by merging, but only after following different routes: the first was the notion that young people should be able to determine their marriages themselves; the second, that the bond of love and the marriage bond should be one and the same, and that love is the best if not the sole reason for marriage.

'To keep society one with another'

At the beginning of the sixteenth century, the power of decision in relation to marriage was the object of contradictory pressures reflecting the chaotic vitality of the social fabric. The earlier pattern of negotiating an alliance remained at issue between two family groups, which had to agree among themselves about the transfer of wife and property. The important moment in the marriage came at the *verba de futuro*; this was above all a civil ceremony during which the heads of the family of both future spouses publicly sealed their agreement (the marriage contract or pact) in the presence of a notary or, failing that, of neighbours and close relatives, so as to give the agreement a public character.

Ecclesiastical authority was content to accompany this civil procedure and respect its customary dispositions by blessing the spouses (the *verba de praesenti*) under the church porch or inside the church, thus confirming the agreement which had just been ratified. After all, marriage was the oldest sacrament, as the rituals and theological treatises liked to recall; but it was a sacrament with a weak ecclesiastical content, being administered by the spouses themselves.

As long as the Church, in accordance with Pauline doctrine, had to view marriage as a remedy for concupiscence and an institution willed by God for the reproduction of the species, it tended to relate the sacramental power exercised by the spouses themselves to their carnal union (*copula carnalis*). However, with the advent of Scholastic doctrine, the basis of the marriage bond passed progressively from bodily union to the union of hearts, from copulation to consent by the spouses, and their sacramental power tended to be confused with their voluntary act of agreement.

At the end of the Middle Ages, the theologians put the stress on the consensual character of marriage: this led them to underline the social dimension of the marriage bond at the expense of its biological or prophylactic dimension. This is particularly visible in the debate about the marriage of old persons, in respect of which Parisian theology at the end of the fifteenth century defended a resolutely modern point of view. If procreation was the principal end of marriage, should the Church encourage or even allow marriage between persons no longer capable of procreation? For Martin le Maistre, such marriages were perfectly legitimate because they enabled the spouses to give each other assistance in their old age (Noonan, 1986).

During the same period a similar line of argument led the Church authorities to encourage remarriages and to reaffirm their legitimacy in the face of popular reluctance. This reluctance, which the Roman Church had shared in the past, was expressed by *charivaris*, symbolic retaliation and compensation rites inflicted by the neighbourhood on widowers who remarried. It may be asked whether the large number of condemnations of *charivaris*, found in the synodal statutes of the fifteenth century, indicate an increased popular resistance to remarriages which would then have unleashed a real *charivari* epidemic? It attests at the very least the Church's insistence on favouring this type of marriage, and attempting to get it accepted (Burguière, 1981).

The social conditions of the age – depopulated towns, deserted villages and a climate of general insecurity – which made solitude unthinkable, had largely contributed to this new conviction on the part of clerics that marriage was not the lesser evil or a duty towards the species, but a social necessity, and that its justification could be found within the marriage bond itself in the relationship of mutual assistance and affection which it instituted between two individuals. In the long term, this modification of the ecclesiastical vision prepared the ground for the sanctification of the married state by Protestant doctrine. Lawrence Stone rather over-estimates the contribution and novelty of Protestantism – and most singularly of English Protestantism – when he makes the puritan concept of holy matrimony the essential cause behind the expansion of a conjugal civilization, which occurred earlier in England than in the rest of Europe. Even if the Catholic Church met its Protestant critics by reaffirming at the Council of Trent the most traditional forms of its marriage doctrine, in its pastoral activity it stressed (as one realizes by reading ecclesiastical rituals from the end of the fifteenth century onwards), such reasons for marriage as 'to keep society with one another', which had previously been neglected.

It was difficult for the Church to underline the social value of the marriage bond without stressing the spouses' free consent and reciprocal agreement. This was the reason for the extraordinary burgeoning of the ecclesiastical rite of marriage at the end of the fifteenth century and for the blossoming of numerous regional variants (Molin and Mutembé, 1974). By means of the gestures they performed, the symbolic objects they exchanged and the words of agreement and of reciprocal giving of themselves which they pronounced, the spouses assumed in these rites an increasingly active role at the expense of the priest and relatives, who were now present only to witness and consent. By accepting regional variations and underlining the spouses' role, ecclesiastical ritual was seeking to adapt to the new tendencies of customary law much more than to theological shifts. As it was, the strong move to modernization in the late fifteenth century and the first third of the sixteenth, preceding the systematic compilation of customs and their inscription in the *Grand Coutumier* coincided with a powerful conjugal trend, revealed by the success of the practice of sharing inheritance according to marriage beds in cases of remarriage in Orléans–Paris law, and of the formulae for associations of aquests, for *affrèrement* between spouses. These formulae which may have emerged in the towns as has been demonstrated for the Bordeaux region (Lafon, 1972), but which were given a favourable welcome by prosperous peasants, accompanied the economic and demographic revival: in a society which was socially extremely mobile, they reflected the weight of the 'new men', with no family past or lineage associations; for such men, who were able to choose freely, the conjugal union was precious as an affective refuge and as a unit of production in a boom period when wages were high.

The freedom which prevailed at that time in premarital relations and marriage agreements is fairly well illustrated by *créantailles* (engagements) in Champagne, as described in the cases of clandestine marriages or requests for the performance of engagements which came before officials at Troyes. In 1483 Henriette, widow of Baudonnet Legouge, and Jean Biret had *créanté* (engaged) themselves, employing purely civil but quasi-statutory forms:

> On the eve of the Purification, the accused, while in the home of Henriette's father, said that he would like to take the said Henriette to wife if it pleased her. Henriette replied that she would like to if it pleased her father. Her father said that it pleased him because it pleased his daughter. Then the father told his daughter to sit at table next to Jean Biret then he put some wine in a glass and told Jean Biret to give his daughter a drink 'in the name of marriage' . . . Once this was done, Henriette's uncle said to her, 'Give Jean a drink in the name of marriage as he has given you a drink.' Henriette presented the accused with a drink. He drank from her hand and then told her: 'I want you to receive a kiss from me in the name of marriage', and he kissed her. Then those present said to them, 'You are engaged to one another, I call the wine to mind.'

The father's agreement and his daughter's consent, drinking the wine together and giving a kiss 'in the name of marriage' constituted ritual gestures of agreement whose legal value was entirely familiar to customary law as was the part played by the relatives and friends who attested to the legality of the act and the irreversible character of the agreement ('I call the wine to mind'). Nothing seems to be missing from this 'popular' ceremony – the account of which is so legally perfect that it bears all the marks of a speech in defence – that could prevent it from conforming to the demands of canon law, unless it was the absence of a priest.

This case was a particularly straightforward one because the two partners acknowledged their union. Henriette easily succeeded in having the 'accused' 'adjudicated' to her. However, in many other cases one of the two would deny any agreement and the plaintiff's brief would be much less well substantiated (it was nearly always the woman who considered herself *creantée*). Only rarely was she capable of attesting to the public nature of the agreement, like Marguerite Gueux who claimed in 1495 to have become engaged to Guillaume Foucher at Troyes two years previously during the counterpane-makers' festival: she claimed he had offered her a pear 'in the name of marriage' in the presence of their 'friends'. A witness added that, as soon as she ate the pear, the other women said, 'He's your husband.'

More often than not, the agreement was regularized by the gift of a small object, such as a pewter goblet, a flute, a woollen braid or a branch of sloes; in the absence of anything else, one could give one's body. In 1532, Pierre Pellard, a weaver at Nogent-sur-Seine, and a fairly cheeky, humorous sort of suitor, was said to have declared to Marguerite, the widow of Jacomart, whom he had joined at night in her room, 'I promise you on the faith of my body that I will take you in marriage', and, when she hesitated to give herself to him, it was claimed he added, 'So that you may not fear that I will abuse you, I put my tongue in your mouth in the name of marriage.'

In the ritual gift which sealed the *créantaille*, it was not the object that counted but the giving itself, and more than the giving, the exchange: one witness who referred to a *chanjon* (exchange) which Jeanne Lepage (of Beaufort) demanded of her suitor Jean Ragon in 1529, on the Feast of the Blessed Sacrament, in the 'name of marriage', explained that this was 'a belt which the *créanté* gives to his *créantée*, and reciprocally, and which is called *chanjon* because of this exchange'.

From permissiveness to intimacy

While the accuracy of these depositions may be doubted, the circumstances and reported words and gestures are sufficiently similar from one case to the next for them to be considered as good witnesses to how an agreement to marry was conceived among ordinary people in the sixteenth century. At that time, young people wanting to marry had great freedom of choice; they were not the only ones involved in the decision, but the power to control marriages and to ensure that they were valid was distributed between different authorities which did not share the same system of values or make the same demands. If necessary, candidates for marriage could manoeuvre between the control exercised by the Church, the father or guardian, the kinship network, friends and neighbours, their peer group and professional circle, in order to decide according to the dictates of their heart.

Although these authorities were concurrent they were also tolerant. Young people's access to marriage benefited not only from a state of mind which was favourable to marriage and to the voice of conscience, meaning everything that could encourage individual choice, but from a general climate of sexual permissiveness. Permissiveness with regard to premarital sexual relations is attested to by the great number of clandestine or contested engagements, which were accompanied by 'carnal commerce'. With regard too to extramarital relations, bastardy – although the inadequate serial sources do not allow one to measure its extent – was widespread and fairly well accepted amongst high and low. Prostitution was allowed, and sometimes administered, by the urban authorities as a prosperous and highly acceptable activity. Brothels and stews were denounced by preachers but celebrated by poets, who turned venal lovemaking into a privileged mainstay of masculine sociability.

This climate did not have much to do with what we nowadays call sexual liberation; although it took a benign attitude to male urges, this was at the price of increasing the sexual submission of women, who were exposed to prostitution and rape. Cases of rape, and often of collective rape, came in great numbers before the civil and ecclesiastical courts, because the perpetrators of these misdemeanours were frequently young clerics and their victims 'priests' wives'. These crimes were punished with astonishing leniency with mere fines, usually proportionate to the victim's social status (Rossiaud, 1976).

Prostitution and rape were considered by the authorities as outlets for the sexuality and rebellious mood of the unmarried young which the various institutions for young men (*abbayes de jeunesse* and *reinages*) could not channel. They might at any moment attack women, property or the power of the older men in authority. Population growth, which served to exacerbate the pressure of the rising generations, and the growth of the towns, which attracted an unstable mass of unmarried immigrants, combined to make the young seem threatening.

Thus the authorities' tolerance did not proceed from belief in freedom, but rather from their prudent resignation in the face of a social turbulence they could not control. Added to this was their naturalistic vision of sexuality inherited from medieval Christianity: one cannot fail to be struck by the atmosphere of truculent and good-humoured sexuality which emerges from the literary, pictorial and legal evidence of the time about the love life of great and humble people alike. This atmosphere gradually subsided and faded during the last thirty years of the sixteenth century.

Sexual relations and love life were far from being confused with the world of marriage, either in law, where the old Pauline concept was still vigorous at least as a generally accepted idea, or in fact, for the permissive climate described above allowed the 'carnal act' to wander where it would outside the marriage bed. However, the conjugal tendency promoted by the Church and by some ranks of civil society, and the growing assertion of the tendency to allow young people to marry according to the dictates of their hearts and to respect the couple's autonomy took on a new meaning in this climate of tolerated sexuality and widespread hedonism. More precisely, they prepared the way for an inversion of relations between marriage and sexuality.

Marriage had not yet become the goal of love, as it would when what is called the model of romantic love took shape in the nineteenth century, but it was already no longer considered as a term, as the passage into a legal bond which would extinguish the ardour of desire in the obligations of conjugal duty. Once young people were licensed, by the low level of social retribution and by the ease with which they could meet one another, to follow the promptings of nature and give way to their desires, they were also invited to form their own engagements. The temptation to confuse desire with choice, momentary pleasure with long-term obligation, was strong. In the case of our *créantés* in Champagne, the exchange of a simple object 'in the name of marriage' was enough to turn a feast-day flirtation or a roadside cuddle into an indissoluble union. The ritual giving and receiving of the object symbolizing the engagement here takes on a magic power redolent of alchemy, since it transforms an instant of affective or physical fusion into an eternity of mutual obligations.

The summary ritual of these clandestine or alleged engagements cannot be considered to represent regular practice, since its very inadequacy was the object of litigation. However, the fact that the validity of these pseudo-ceremonies could be discussed shows that we are not far from the normal procedure. There was an obvious disproportion between the insignificance of the ritual and legal formalities of the marriage, and the indissoluble nature of the bond contracted between the spouses. So long as the low level of population and its dynamic rate of growth maintained strong social mobility, the imbalance between the ease with which one could enter into the marriage bond and the irrevocability of the bond thus contracted might seem tolerable; the risk of forming a misalliance was all part of the flexible social interplay which gave the age its tone.

However, as tensions re-emerged and class barriers were raised in an ossifying society, this imbalance seemed increasingly absurd and unbearable. Its absurdity was denounced by humanists as a contradiction which harmed the social order. Their criticism was joined by Protestants when they denied the sacramental dimension of marriage: marriage was a civil institution, and holy not because its sacred content was administered by a priest or by the spouses themselves, but because it was willed by God, as were the other organizational forms of social life. It had to be considered as a civil contract capable of being revoked, binding two individuals and their families.

Thus challenged by the most innovative intellectual currents, the institution of marriage became in the first half of the sixteenth century an inexhaustible subject of discussion in the learned and light-hearted modes alike (witness Panurge's dissertations in *Pantagruel*). An institution such as marriage, as we are nowadays well placed to know, can enter a critical situation in people's minds long before disintegrating in practice.

It is possible, as has often been stated, that Henri II's edict of February 1556 against clandestine marriages and the pressure brought to bear on the Council of Trent by the monarchy, using the French legates as intermediaries, to secure the nullity of all marriages executed without parental consent, was directly caused by matrimonial misadventure at court: Henri II had intended to marry his illegitimate daughter Diane de France, aged seven, to François de Montmorency, when he discovered that the young duke had secretly become engaged to one of the queen's maids of honour. The girl was sent to a convent, and Rome was asked to invalidate the clandestine union, but refused.

The confusion at Court was accompanied by a sense of panic among the upper classes, especially the nobility, at the epidemic of clandestine marriages and the risks of misalliance which it brought. France was not the only state to launch into repression of clandestine marriages. Similar measures were adopted in much of Protestant Europe. In Basle, the

Ehegericht (the tribunal for matrimonial cases which was reformed by Zwingli) adjudicated between 1550 and 1592 in 167 cases of clandestine marriages; in 133 cases it decided on annulment (Safley, 1982). The Council of Trent remained faithful to the doctrine of consent and refused to follow the French legates' proposals, and the conflict between royal legislation and canon law was the main reason behind France's refusal to 'receive' the Council's decisions officially.

However, the importance of this disagreement should not be exaggerated. Though the Church after the Council of Trent refused to annul clandestine marriages, all the measures adopted by it during and after the Council were aimed at strengthening the conditions for validating marriages and at submitting them more closely to the dual control of priest and head of the family. Changes to the rite of the marriage blessing confirmed this trend. At the end of the seventeenth century, Pope Paul V's Roman Rite everywhere replaced local rites which had reflected the diversity of local customs. The actions and formulae of reciprocal self-giving with which the spouses had accepted the autonomy of their mutual vow disappeared and were replaced by the officiating priest's '*ego conjugo vos*'.

The struggle conducted by the bishops in the seventeenth century against rowdy processions, *barrières, charivaris* or 'rough music', 'dishonest songs' and other indecent demonstrations, in short against the popular rites accompanying the religious ceremony, sought to impose an austere and internalized form of devotion. However, it aimed just as much at depriving local solidarities – the village community, the peer group, etc. – of the control they exercised over alliances in competition with that of the Church, the state and, to some extent, their families. The state, being the natural enemy of local powers, could only rejoice at the disappearance of this rival authority and of a diversity which favoured clandestine unions.

The disappearance, or rather the weakening of the control which the neighbourhood exercised over alliances, deprived young people who wanted to marry against their parents' or guardians' will of a possible recourse; paradoxically, however, it strengthened the couple's autonomy. By passing entirely under the authority of the family and of centralized systems, conjugal life turned its back on the neighbourhood and took refuge behind the more clearly defined frontiers of the private sphere. Couples had internalized this transfer of authority by a reflex process of introversion and privatization which rendered them increasingly hostile to intervention by the local community. This may be observed from the growing number of *charivari* cases, from the end of the sixteenth century onwards, which turned nasty and came before the courts. Couples had earlier accepted these light-hearted but cruel disturbances, which often asserted the right to inspect family life by a symbolic action such as knocking down the door or the roof where the newly-weds were staying, because they understood that it was a rite which served to integrate as well as punish them. Now they refused to submit to local law. The idea that neighbours could create an uproar because a widower remarried, or a woman married a younger or poorer man, or chose a stranger to the community for a husband, began to appear to couples as an invasion of their private lives.

Religious regulation and popular traditions

In some respects, the imposition of religious control in Catholic countries was equally aimed at restricting families' power of decision in matrimonial matters, which could appear to run counter to the state's objectives. This is the meaning which must be attached to the gradual disappearance of the engagement ceremony, an old institution which often accompanied the act of signing the marriage contract. Lay people considered the engagement ceremony to represent the sequence which legitimized the union in so far as it sealed the agreement between the families of the betrothed. Whereas the ceremony had become increasingly elaborate from the end of the fifteenth century onwards, given the general desire to adapt the religious rite to civil practice, until it had become almost as important as the nuptial blessing, it was now either reduced to the place allotted it by the Council of Trent or simply suppressed. Families in southern France were less attached to it because they had long become used to making their arrangements to coincide with the nuptial blessing; the bishops there chose to suppress the practice. In northern France, on the other hand, it was upheld and even made obligatory in places where it had not existed, but merely as an occasion for checking the validity of the projected marriage and for moral instruction. Also, to prevent the engaged couple from feeling authorized to live together before their marriage, priests were enjoined to celebrate their engagement very shortly before their marriage (Piveteau, 1957).

Indeed, the main concern of the Church (and of Protestant Churches) was to render sexual activity moral by driving it back within the conjugal sphere and to subject it to repressive rules. This preoccupation was not necessarily shared by families, which were more concerned to control the alliances than to regulate sexual activity. Institutionalizing a degree of permissiveness in the relations between young people was sometimes perceived as the best means of retaining a hold on an age group, which was by nature unstable, and making it co-operate with family strategies.

In some regions such as Corsica, premarital cohabitation was the direct effect of an agreement concluded between families. The engagement contract was often settled well before the betrothed had reached the legal age, in order to seal a peace treaty between two families engaged in a *vendetta*, and it would stipulate that the girl was to be transferred immediately to her future husband's family. This practice was discovered with horror by the priests of the congregation of St Vincent de Paul when they were sent on a mission to the island at the end of the seventeenth century:

> There was still a great abuse among the inhabitants of this island, touching the sacrament of marriage . . . When they were engaged or had only given each other their word, the girl went to dwell in the house of her future husband and persisted in this state of concubinage for two or three months and sometimes two or three years, without going to the trouble of getting married.

The value which the Corsicans set on their daughters' virtue, and the cruelty with which they punished adulterous women, clearly contradicted the impression of licentiousness which they gave the good priests from the mainland when they landed there. Using the girl as security to ensure that the engagement was fulfilled corresponded to an archaic custom, which made the issue most at stake in the alliance that of maintaining the peace which had been concluded.

In other places, young people could meet, and even live together while their families were conducting the negotiations: the agreement was often concluded and the marriage celebrated in church when the girl had become pregnant. The husband and his parents thus entered into the contract in the knowledge that the girl they had chosen could provide them with descendants. In 1567, around the Feast of All Saints, Richard Thomas, a young peasant from Porbury in Somerset, was sowing wheat in the company of Maud Methewaye, one of his father's servants, when he declared to her that he 'wished her belly was as big as that of Joan Asheman [a pregnant girl of the parish]; if she were with child by him, he would marry her' (Houlbrooke, 1984, p. 81). Premarital relations of a probationary nature were frequent in England, as they were in much of northern France and the regions of Aquitaine. Early in the sixteenth century Pierre de Lancre, the famous demonologist of the Bordeaux region, denounced the Basques in the area of Labour for 'the liberty which they take of testing their wives for a few years before marrying them and for taking them on a trial basis'; according to him, this abuse was not unconnected with the witchcraft which plagued the region. His colleague Jean d'Arrerac uncovered this practice in Labour as well as in the 'usages of the land of Sainctonge', and explained it primarily as a customary practice: 'They marry their wives on a trial basis. They do not couch their marriage contracts in writing at all and do not receive any nuptial blessing until after they have lived with them a long time, have probed their habits and have learnt by results about the fertility of their soil' (quoted by Flandrin, 1975).

Those evening gatherings among the peasantry, when boys were allowed to come and murmur sweet nothings to their girls as they sat busily spinning beside their mothers, and the *maraîchinage vendéen* with its code of exaggerated flirtation and caresses exchanged in public, but beneath the shelter of ritual, constituted the vestiges (or rather the

Par vn Sage temperament   DECEMBRE   Et le travail le plus penible

The Evening Gathering, eighteenth-century engraving. The long winter evenings in the country – this engraving illustrates the month of December – were the time for gatherings of neighbours in stables, grottoes or, as here, cellars, where work was combined with entertainment. The young girls were chaperoned by their mothers, who gathered to spin and chat together; they could meet the young men of the village, to dance with them and let them make up to them with impunity. Church authorities had been attacking the immorality of such gatherings since the mid-seventeenth century. Peasant society, on the other hand, saw them as a good way to control relationships between young people and keep a tight hand on matrimonial strategies. Bibliothèque Nationale, Paris.

resurgence) at the end of the *ancien régime* of those premarital liberties, whose extreme form was marriage on a trial basis, which had been permitted and controlled by the neighbourhood. The Church had been trying without success to abolish them for over a century. In 1680 the synodal statutes of the Troyes diocese gave the following ruling on *veilleries* or *escrins*: 'We prohibit men and boys on pain of excommunication . . . to meet with women and girls in the places where they gather at night to spin or work.' Six years later an instruction from the bishop repeated this prohibition by stipulating:

> So that there may be no future ambiguity about what we mean by *veilleries* or *escrins* . . . we mean not only the public places detached from houses and dug into the ground, in which all sorts of persons may enter without distinction, but also the cellars, stables, bedrooms and other domestic places in which the wives and daughters of several families gather at night.

This condemnation was repeated by the bishop of Boulogne in 1744 against 'these nocturnal gatherings which are commonly known as *séries*, where women and girls gather on the pretext of working . . . that men and boys should not be admitted or allowed to turn it into an occasion of dissipation and unregulated behaviour.'

This 'unregulated behaviour' between girls and boys did not necessarily imply that their flirtation went as far as 'carnal commerce'. However, the custom did increase the risk of extramarital conception, and those regions where such permissive premarital sociability was allowed can be spotted by their particularly high rates of illegitimate births and premarital conceptions. This was the case all over Europe in places where girls of marriageable age were allowed to be visited by their suitors at night. The custom was known as *albergement* or *trosse* in Savoy, *Kiltgang* in Switzerland, *Fensternl* in Austria and *Nachtfreien* in Bavaria, and existed in much of the Alpine range and Scandinavia. It is known in particular from descriptions by travellers and ethnographers in the nineteenth century, and confirmed by the very high levels of illegitimacy which can be observed for the same period. The maximum rate was achieved by Carinthia, a real 'European Jamaica' (Mitterauer, 1983), where more than 80 per cent of births recorded in the second half of the nineteenth century were illegitimate.

In some countries at this time, the illegitimacy rate was increased by legislation which made marriage almost impossible for the poor. It could, however, be asked whether, unlike the premarital permissiveness prevailing in England, the Vendée and the Basque country (which was one way of controlling gently and from a distance relations between young people so as to direct them towards the desired alliances), the customs in the Alps and Scandinavian countries were intended to provide young servants with a sexual substitute for married life. It was a fairly restrained substitute, according to a French traveller who observed the custom at the end of the sixteenth century in Germany and reported that couples who thus spend the night together 'sleep chastely'. As in the case of *maraîchinage* in the Vendée, the *Kiltgang* combined intimacy with proximity; banter involving several couples who chaperoned each other, mere light-hearted chatter at the young girl's window, or a more or less chaste night when they would sleep together without removing their clothes. It is unlikely that couples were always content with this anodyne form of eroticism.

In 1603 the bishop of Augsburg denounced 'the abuse on the part of men servants and maids demanding in their contracts the right to visit a person of the opposite sex or at least to converse with them through their window'. What was involved was not tolerance on the part of a lax family authority, but a right claimed by a population of farm hands whose status prevented them from marrying. The custom is not correlated with the religious context; it could be found as much in regions which had remained Catholic as where the Reformation had triumphed. It appears, on the other hand, to have been closely linked to a grazing economy employing a large workforce of farm hands of both sexes working together in the cow byres and on upland pasturages.

This was why religous campaigns to inculcate morality were strongly resisted by local populations, which were all the more attached to their 'vices' as these were part of their social system. Such campaigns gained only temporary and modified successes. In the early nineteenth century, the highest illegitimacy rates were found in Bavaria and Austria, countries where the Counter-Reformation had been particularly intense (Mitterauer, 1983). On the other hand, the Churches' moralizing activity everywhere won them the approval and support of the state.

In France, in February 1556, at the same time as pronouncing clandestine marriages null, Henri II declared war on illegitimate births with his edict 'against women who conceal their pregnancy'. Initiatives on the part of the king and local dignitaries led to the progressive closing of brothels, gaming houses and all public places which could provide cover for extramarital sex. Protestant states did not lag behind in the campaign for morality. In Basle, the marriage tribunal in the second half of the sixteenth century ordered 133 couples to separate on account of 'fornication'. In early seventeenth-century England, the courts instituted proceedings for premarital fornication against couples who declared the birth of a child less than eight months after their marriage.

Was illegitimacy a permanent or re-emergent feature?

The successes of this imposition of religious control were unequal and short-lived, varying with the people involved. The process did, however, profoundly transform mentalities and behaviour. In England a perceptible fall in premarital conceptions may be observed from a sample involving twelve parishes: they represented 25.5 per cent of first births in the second half of the sixteenth century, 22.8 per cent in the first half of the seventeenth century and 16.2 per cent in the second half (Houlbrooke, 1984). It has been possible to measure an even more spectacular fall in illegitimate births in a larger sample of ninety-eight parishes. The illegitimacy rate was 3.2 per cent in 1600–10 and 1.7 per cent in the 1640s at the start of the Civil War. It reached its lowest level of 0.94 per cent during Cromwell's Protectorate, then rose progressively, and in the mid-eighteenth century overtook its level of one and half centuries earlier (Laslett, 1977).

France has no statistical data reaching so far back. Nevertheless, the low level of illegitimate births and premarital conceptions which may be observed in the seventeenth century, and their fairly rapid rise from the mid-eighteenth century onwards, seem to indicate that the Catholic Reformation did manage to discipline behaviour and to impose a model of ascetic behaviour for at least a century, and that the liberation of morals at the end of the *ancien régime* coincided with the relaxation of religious control.

Furthermore, it must be pointed out that the rise of illegitimacy was only really noticeable in large market towns which had been overtaken by rural industry, such as Villedieu-les-Poêles (which had 0.1 per cent illegitimate births in the mid-eighteenth century and 4.1 per cent between 1771 and 1790); in suburbs such as Ingouville (which had a 3.5 per cent illegitimacy rate between 1730 and 1773, and 5.7 per cent at the end of the *ancien régime*); in middle-sized towns like Meulan (0.5 per cent illegitimate births between 1670 and 1759, 2.3 per cent 1760–89) and Saint-Denis (8 per cent on the eve of the Revolution); and in regional centres like Lyon and Grenoble (10 per cent) and Lille (12 per cent) in the same period. In the big towns, the expansion of illegitimate births was a direct effect of urban growth and of the presence of a large immigrant population, which was unstable and poorly integrated. In addition, there was migration on the part of pregnant girls who chose to give birth discreetly in large towns, where, if necessary they could abandon the 'fruit of sin', given the existence of institutions for taking it in. Thus the impact of illegitimacy in the great towns was far greater than the mere number of illegitimate births declared. If abandoned babies are added in, illegitimacy figures of 25 per cent in Toulouse and 30 per cent in Paris on the eve of the Revolution seem probable.

The behavioural changes of the eighteenth century were less perceptible in the countryside. Illegitimacy did sometimes progress to the same rhythm as in the towns. This was the case at Soudeilhes, in Quercy, where 0.9 per cent of births in the seventeenth century were illegitimate. There were 2.1 per cent between 1700 and 1779, and more than 3 per cent by the end of the *ancien régime*. In most regions, however, the rates were static. They remained low in the Paris Basin (around 1 per cent illegitimate births), and were even lower in the west, in Brittany and Anjou. They were higher – and have never ceased to be so – in Normandy: 3 per cent at Troarn from 1658 to 1792; 2.6 per cent at Tamerville 1624–1740; and 2.5 per cent at Port-en-Bessin in the eighteenth century.

Structural disparities appear to set northern France and the more indulgent north-west and south-west against western France and the Mediterranean Midi, which were stricter about illegitimacy. Do these disparities reflect different family attitudes to premarital encounters between young people? At the very least they show up the unequal success of the authorities' efforts to impose rules in the seventeenth century; results were provisional and limited in the countryside and among the upper classes. They achieved more lasting success among the urban middle classes, especially in families connected with the municipal corporations, among whom exhortations to moral order revived their traditions of conformity, and of supervision by the group of its members' private lives.

This strictness was particularly striking in German-speaking countries, where it was primarily aimed against illegitimacy. A tailor of Hildesheim was refused admission to his guild in 1733 because he had been born a bastard and only later been legitimized by his parents' marriage. Ten years later, the corporation of weavers in Lünen forced one of its members, a master weaver, to dismiss an apprentice on account of his illegitimacy. Supervision was no less rigorous in respect of premarital relations. In 1716, a master tailor at Kiel was deprived by the community of his right to practise his trade because his wife had given birth two months after their marriage. In Bremen in 1726, a master cobbler was threatened with the same sanction because his wife was delivered five weeks too early (Möller, 1969).

In central Europe, unlike France and England, this moral pressure was often encouraged by the state and religious authorities, and it persisted into the century of the Enlightenment. Several German states instituted a supervisory system modelled on the *Keuschheitskommission* (chastity commission) set up by Maria Theresa in 1764; this supervision was applied mainly in the towns and eventually infuriated enlightened minds. 'Is it not distressing for a friend of the human species', wrote J. K. Riesbeck in 1784 in his *Letters of a French Traveller in Germany to his Brother in Paris* (a Germanic pastiche of the *Lettres Persanes*), 'to see the policemen on the Prater chasing young couples in the bushes and beneath the trees to prevent any risk of sin?' However, the inquisitorial zeal of the corporations far surpassed anything desired by the public authorities, which can often be observed intervening at the end of the eighteenth century in defence of artisans banned by their corporations, and imposing greater respect for private life.

This movement to impose regulation did not have the same breadth and efficacy or last equally long in different countries and sections of society. For the moment, we shall probably have to abandon any attempt to measure it by precise statistics. However, there is no doubt about the reality of the cultural change which brought emotional life under suspicion for more than a century. It enables us to understand better the explosion of tearful sensibility in the second half of the eighteenth century, which invaded not only painting and literature but also the everyday and unadorned language of letters and songs and the simple words of those who remained outside written culture, as recorded in legal sources. In some countries, especially in central and Mediterranean Europe, Catholic propaganda campaigned to win back souls and tried to enlist the masses by appealing to their emotions; some have seen in this inculcation strategy the mainspring of Baroque aesthetics. The sensibility thus manipulated and canalized, however, was directed strictly at mystical or devotional ends.

What appears dull and commonplace, overemphatic and possibly insincere to us nowadays, seemed at that time, after the long period of repression when emotional life was no longer admitted, to express the desire to trust one's own sensibility and to make personal relations more open.

In order to grasp in depth the importance of this change it is enough to take the marriage cases recorded in a long series such as the Troyes official records, and compare those heard early in the sixteenth century with those of the mid-seventeenth. In the petitions for divorce or fulfilment of engagement promises in the seventeenth century, there was no longer any question of furtive embraces or moments of abandonment, which were noted in the laconic formula, 'promise of marriage followed by copulation'. In 1665, Nicolas Marot no longer wanted to marry Anne Rousselot of Troyes; although 'he holds the respondent to be a good and honourable girl' he 'has no friendship for her'.

That same year Jeanne Pluot of Vauchassis, who had made some promises to Nicolas Lasnier, said she 'never intended to carry them out, since they had been made against her will and out of the respect she bore her father and mother, who had beaten her: she had never loved and still does not love the said Lasnier and would rather choose death than marry him.'

In 1667, Savine Dieu, the daughter of a master trimmer of Troyes, reneged on the marriage promises she had exchanged with Joachim Simon, a master scribe 'which she had only made out of obedience and duty to her father and mother and since . . . the petitioner has not rendered to her the duties which he owed her, this has given rise . . . to her having no inclination or love for the said petitioner'. Such examples could be multiplied; they all adopt the same tone and arguments. The body is absent. On the contrary, 'friendship', 'love' and 'inclination', the sentiment is frequently put forward, but, deprived of its carnal wrapping, it was obliged to furnish proof of its authenticity and licitness. As for objects, which were henceforth deprived of their sacramental power, they were no longer exchanged, but offered, generally to the promised girl. As the gages of their future union or as advances on the dowry, they had to be returned or reimbursed in the event of a broken engagement.

France conforms, Britain rebels

In France the laws regulating marriage established by the monarchy through edicts and ordinances were constantly renewed and made more precise. Their strict application benefited from the vigilant support of the clergy, which applied the reinforced ecclesiastical control of the Council of Trent in all its severity. The institution of marriage functioned well, perhaps too well. Legislation dealing with the 'crime of seduction', for instance, had become so extensive by the beginning of the eighteenth century that it was employed with fearsome efficiency by girls looking for a good match to blackmail the men they wanted to marry.

The royal declaration of November 1730 'concerning the crime of seduction in the province of Brittany and some other provinces of the realm' stigmatized this abuse:

> In Brittany all criminal commerce has been confused with the crime of seduction, and it has given such a great advantage to one sex over the other that the mere complaint by the girl who claims that she has been suborned and the proof of mere frequentation are considered by it as sufficient motive for condemning the accused man to the last agony . . . At the request of the girl who asks to marry the man whom she calls her suborner and at the consent which fear of death always wrests from the condemned

man, a commissioner of the *Parlement* brings him to church with his legs in irons . . .

By the end of the *ancien régime*, mainly in the great urban centres, a growing number of couples were failing to appear before a priest to have their union legalized. 'Concubinage is prohibited by divine and human laws', wrote Sébastien Mercier, 'but good form authorizes it . . . Bishops . . . magistrates, merchants and artisans live in concubinage, and concubines make up a third of the women of the town.' The proportion is very difficult to check. About 1770 a police report in Paris referred to 'a great number of households of poor people who had not been joined by the Church'. The authorities reacted by forcing parishes to provide free marriages for the indigent (Kaplow, 1972). Poverty was undoubtedly the principal reason why couples were driven to do without the legal forms, but it was not the only one. The immigrant's situation, cut off from his original community and deprived of his legal status and any fixed domicile, also prompted him to live outside the law.

According to observers of the condition of the working class, most of them conservatives, who exaggerated the extent of free unions on the part of the proletariat and above all its desire for them, and according to the Society of St Francis Regis, which fought this social evil by dowering poor girls who were trying to return to the strait and narrow path, the popular concubinage which proliferated at the beginning of the nineteenth century was a consequence of the de-Christianizing effect of the Revolution and industrial development. However, the fact that it is familiarly referred to as 'marriage in the Parisian manner' does seem to indicate that the phenomenon was already well established in the capital by the end of the *ancien régime*.

In Great Britain the authorities had never managed to force everyone to celebrate marriage according to the official rules laid down by law. Despite hesitation on the part of Anglican doctrine (about divorce, for instance), and opposition by the Dissenting sects, a stricter form of ecclesiastical control, fairly similar to that stipulated by the Council of Trent, was set up at the end of the seventeenth century. At the same time, the 'lawless churches' which celebrated simulated marriages for Dissenters or simply to make money, were suppressed.

In London, the closure of irregular churches around 1690 ensured that the Fleet parish was flooded with applicants for quick marriages. It has been estimated that 150,000 to 300,000 marriages were celebrated there in the first half of the eighteenth century. While this church was in principle intended for sailors who wanted to get married between two sailings, it provided priest, banqueting room and lodgings at an affordable price for all couples who wanted to marry in secret, either to legitimize a union already established or to avoid the heavy expense of a showy official marriage (Gillis, 1983).

There were other places of the same kind elsewhere in the country, and a parson in Derbyshire about 1750 who would marry people discreetly for a shilling a time. Clandestine marriages, as straightforward substitutes for the private contract which had formerly enabled children to be legitimized, increased markedly at the start of the eighteenth century in those regions where rural industry once again obliged the family group to assume the role of a unit of production. In the iron-working villages of the Midlands and among the weavers of Cumberland and Lancashire, a young person wishing to get married would frequently clash with his parents, who would be reluctant to lose part of their productive capital. The couple sometimes forced their parents' hand by enlisting the community, which for its part wished to prevent the birth of a bastard who would become a charge on the parish.

Hardwicke's Marriage Act of 1753 (see above, p. 110) was designed to put a stop to these abuses and to reinstate patriarchal authority; but it had the opposite effect. By suppressing clandestine marriages, it caused customary forms of marriage, such as 'besom weddings', 'smock marriages' or Welsh *priodas vach* (little weddings), to re-emerge. In the Ceiriog valley in Wales, 60 per cent of births registered between 1768 and 1805 were the issue of this kind of marriage, which had never crossed the threshold of a church.

Contrary to what the Victorian middle classes thought, these marriages were no mere poverty-stricken survivals or mere dressing-up of proletarian cohabitation but a renewal of ancient customs by working people who were either well-qualified artisans or comfortably off, like peasants or traders. For the men, it represented a means of setting themselves up without waiting to succeed their father; for the women, who had been rendered legally incapable outside their husband's authority by Hardwicke's Act, it was often the only way they could hang on to their own property.

It would be a great exaggeration to view the practice of marriage, as most state and religious authorities had regulated it from the seventeenth century onwards, solely in terms of confrontation between parents and children and of repression of adolescent desires. The main preoccupation of parents, as of the public authority, was to preserve, via alliances, the family's social rank and degree of wealth. This was clearly expressed, for instance, by Louis XIII's *ordonnance* of 1629 about abduction which began, 'Wishing to preserve the authority of fathers over their children ... and in future to prevent families of quality being joined with unworthy persons of different customs . . .'

Parental control weighed all the more on children's matrimonial choices in that social status was the issue most at stake. In the countryside this rule was perfectly well known and accepted by everyone; it was recited in proverbs as much as in the chatter of children, as Restif de la Bretonne reports in his monumental autobiography, *Monsieur Nicolas*. As a little boy and dreaming in the 'green paradise of infantile loves', he announced one day to the world that he would later marry Marie Fouard. As she was the daughter of poor peasants, Jacquot, one of his playmates, took it upon himself to drag little Nicolas back to earth and pointed out that his parents would never agree. 'I'm happier being Blaise Guerreau's boy', he added, 'than the son of Monsieur Réti; for I am master of my wishes. You are Monsieur Nicolas, and you'll pay for for that "Monsieur" . . . He who is more suffers more.' Nicolas Restif, as the son of a *coq de village*, would not be able to marry as he wished (Restif de la Bretonne, 1959).

Among the peasantry, love matches were the privilege of the poor. This may frequently be observed in the files of official dispensations from the seventeenth century onwards. Only the poorest or orphans gave the 'friendship' or 'inclination' they felt for each other as the reason for their wish to marry despite impediment. This rule applied equally to the urban environment, where young people of the upper classes were less free in their relationships and the bestowal of their hearts than others.

Sébastien Mercier criticized authors of his day for ignoring this, especially in the case of girls, and for committing a sociological blunder 'by making all the enamoured girls in plays girls of quality', when they were actually depicting 'only the loves of *grisettes*'. In the case of Paris at the end of the *ancien régime*, he stressed the manner in which the status of a marriageable girl altered according to her social background:

> Daughters of the upper bourgeoisie are . . . in convents; those of the second level never leave their mother and have no kind of freedom or familiar communication prior to marriage. Thus it is only the daughters of the petty bourgeois, simple merchants and ordinary people who are totally free to go and come and consequently to make love as it suits them. The others receive their spouses from their parents' hands. The contract is never more than a deal and they are not consulted at all.

His vision is oversimplified. Girls were consulted before being married off in the upper classes as well. In the eighteenth century, concern to take young people's feelings into account in marriage arrangements is perhaps stated more in English high society than in the ruling classes of other countries. This is what Stone thinks, going by the evidence provided by the travellers of the age like the young François de La Rochefoucauld. But were the liberal attitudes of the parents and the serenity which seemed to permeate their relations with their children anything more than the effects of a successful internalization of the social rules of marriage?

In this respect, numerous accounts of exemplary marriages, in which the children's wishes more than met their parents' expectations, can already be found in seventeenth-century France. Thus the maréchal de Noailles reported to his mother in 1687 how easily he had been able to agree with his daughter about choosing a husband: 'After we had suggested all the marriageable young men, and even those we were not aiming at, she told her mother and me that she liked best the comte de Guiche and Monsieur d'Enrichemont, and of these, she preferred the comte de Guiche.'

This was a perfect marriage, or rather, as Mme de Sévigné stressed, not without some irony, in a letter dated 10 March 1687 commenting on the news, a marriage in perfect conformity with the demands of the Catholic Reformation.

> They will be married, there will be no great display of dressing; they will not be put to bed; this task will be left to the governess and tutor. The next day, it will be assumed that everything went well; no one will go and tease them; there will be no witticisms, no nasty jokes . . . She will pay her visits with her mother-in-law; she will not lie on her bed like a village bride, displayed to every tedious visitor.

The birth of the love match?

The story of Saint-Simon's matrimonial gambits is well known, since they are reported by him in his memoirs with an exemplary mixture of zest and candour. The first was a semi-failure: he did not secure, as he wished, the hand of a daughter of the duc de Beauvilliers, but the latter, in his dismay at inflicting a refusal, subsequently 'treated him like a son-in-law'. The second was happier: he secured in marriage the eldest daughter of the maréchal de Lorge, 'supported' (according to the *Mercure galant*) by a dowry of 400,000 livres. In both cases, Saint-Simon had first fallen in love with a family, or more precisely with a head of family, and only then with the girl whom they might want to give him.

In order to ally with the duc de Beauvilliers, he had been ready to marry any one of his daughters, even with a small dowry. Unfortunately, at least according to the would-be father-in-law, the eldest of the girls wanted to take the veil, the second was misshapen and the third too young. As for his marriage with Gabrielle de Lorge, it inspired Saint-

Simon to issue a real declaration of love – for his future father-in-law.

> His extremely distinguished birth, his great alliances . . . an eldest brother
> who is also well considered . . . and, more than all this, the goodness and
> truthfulness of the maréchal de Lorge, so rare to find and so effective in
> him, had made me wish ardently for this marriage . . . to live agreeably in
> the midst of so many illustrious friends and in a pleasant house.

Brought up by an old father and orphaned at an early age, the famous
memoir-writer had every reason for seeking to integrate himself by
marriage into a new family network. However, his old-fashioned education, which is revealed as much by his tastes as in his written style, also
coloured his affective attitudes. His conventional behaviour as a lover is
evidence of a conception of alliance in which the married individuals
served only to mediate the social and affective bond uniting two families.
This view persisted until the eighteenth century among the aristocracy,
where the individual identified with his lineage. It may equally be found
among peasants, as is revealed by this declaration before the Angers
officials in 1757 concerning a marriage under the impediment of 'public
honesty': 'They have declared to us that the families of the young
widower Charles Martin and Jeanne Métivier are closely united and seek
to become more and more attached. Secondly, that the said Martin never
sought to break his first engagement and, since he could not have the
eldest daughter, he wishes for the youngest daughter, out of his attachment to the families.'

Falling in love with a family and falling in love with a person do not
seem to belong to the same affective register. To us, the distance between
the two appears all the greater in that we belong to an age which is
dominated by the myth of love at first sight and by the idea that there is a
cause-and-effect link between love and marriage. Nevertheless, in both
cases, what the individual is expressing, possibly unconsciously, by his
behaviour in love is first and foremost his love for his social destiny.

Was there a difference in the intensity or the nature of this love? The
answer does not lie within the historian's competence. What he observes,
through individual or collective testimonies, is never what individuals
experience deep down in themselves, but only what the behavioural
norms and forms of the age allow them to show. It would be absurd to
claim that no one married for love or that no couple was really in love
before the eighteenth century. Such an affective disposition, however,
constituted neither an ideal nor a necessity. What can be analysed is the
progress by which love, so long considered by religious morality and
popular wisdom as a stranger and even contrary to marriage, set itself up
as the keystone of a new matrimonial model. This evolution did not

proceed from a relaxation of morals or a reaction against the moral austerity promoted by the new forms of devotion, but possibly from the austerity itself, from the internalization of constraints which made the individual more aware of his responsibility and uniqueness. Starting as an anxious awareness imbued with guilt, it was then better assimilated and sought to achieve fulfilment by means of sentimental fusion with another 'self'.

Literature, especially fiction, enables us most easily to grasp how these stereotypes were renewed – perhaps too easily. Although the central narrative theme of the plays and novels of the seventeenth and eighteenth centuries, marriage as such rarely appears to have been studied. The fact that the question of marriage came to the fore as the mainspring of dramatic or romantic intrigue for showing the individual at odds with his destiny or the rules of the social game, in situations of conflict between love and duty, between propriety and authenticity, or between obedience and love, was certainly not unrelated to the evolution of moral values and matrimonial practice.

But to what extent was this the case? To consider the characters of Corneille, Molière or Marivaux as representing the behaviour of their age would to be ignore the function of imagination, which forbids us to view any work as a mere reflection of reality. Fictitious situations do not reflect real situations, but only the significance which their social actors attribute to them. They stage the moral contradictions and psychological conflicts which set individuals at variance, in order to put forward an imaginary solution. As Le Roy Ladurie wrote (1982), literature does not imitate social existence but is normative in relation to it and correlated with it.

Its normative character is particularly vivid in theatrical production, which developed in the seventeenth century in response to a demand for entertainment as well as education. Under the Jesuits' influence, plays became a school activity in colleges, and progressively in most institutions dedicated to educating the elites. Two young persons love one another but their plans for union are countered by authority – their parents or their ruler – who have to decide the issue. In the tragic version (*Le Cid, Horace, Britannicus* or *Bajazet*) the conflict between love and law is unresolved. In the comic version (*L'Avare, Tartuffe, Les Femmes savantes*) the obstacle is overcome by restoring harmony between the love which the young people feel for one another and their parents' decision; the parents are vilified for a while, but are finally made to see reason.

Such is the almost immutable pattern of intrigue which runs through every play in the seventeenth century. It dramatized the two demands of post-Tridentine doctrine in marriage matters: the free consent by the spouses and the authority of their parents. These two principles were confronted – temporarily or insolubly – in the imagination, possibly indicating the necessity for compromise in reality. The most striking aspect of the tragic and comic vision, however, is the indomitable presence of love. Delayed marriage and the Church's efforts to isolate the couple from its circle of relatives worked in favour of greater autonomy of choice and more individual commitment on the part of the spouses.

By the eighteenth century, the contradiction had shifted. It was no longer concerned with relations between parents and children, but with the loving relationship within which the young persons encountered one another to test the authenticity of their feelings. From now on, what ensured a happy ending to the intrigue was the parents' insistence on respecting their children's deepest wishes, if necessary against their own interests, and on promoting their happiness. Even the law no longer had to give way to love, since from now on the only law of marriage was love.

We can see an analogous evolution in the production of novels. The success in England of Richardson's novels in the mid-eighteenth century, especially of *Clarissa Harlowe*, which extolled her refusal of an arranged marriage, was according to Stone a form of plebiscite for the new matrimonial model. Did this plebiscite, however, extend beyond the restricted circle in which literature recruited its authors and their public? 'Peripheral' or 'popular' forms of culture continued to refer to other models. Provençal plays and novels, which enjoyed a sort of Golden Age at the end of the *ancien régime*, employed a dramatic scheme which continued unchanged until the mid-nineteenth century. This was the 'love-square' described by Le Roy Ladurie: a penniless younger son has to procure or invent a fortune by more or less orthodox means in order to marry the girl he loves and who returns his love. He succeeds by eliminating the two obstacles which ritually bar his way: competition from another suitor, who is sometimes an old man and always rich, and the hostility of the loved one's father, who stubbornly refuses to give his daughter to a man of no wealth (Le Roy Ladurie, 1982).

In this scheme, marriage does not present a straightforward opportunity for confronting the rationality of the heart with the irrationality of authority, or children in love with temporarily blinded parents, but love with money. The comic aspect of the story is not provided, as in the classic comedy of the seventeenth century, by the parents' return to reason and so to social harmony, but by a trick or miracle which disrupts the natural order. Love is still incompatible with the social demands of marriage.

Did this scheme of intrigue owe its astonishing longevity to the particular introverted nature of Provençal culture, or, as Le Roy Ladurie thinks, to the particular nature of southern France, arising out of its distance from the central power and its adherence to a particularly rigid model of a *société de rang*? In northern France, as in much of Europe, the imposition of moral and religious control coincided with the consolidation or reconstruction of a hierarchical society, but was perhaps tempered by the more marked intervention, on the ideological level at least, by Church and state, which ensured a certain mediation between individual aspirations and family imperatives.

By extending this hypothesis, one could interpret the triumph of love in the representation of marriage which invaded literature in the eighteenth century as proof that this mediation had succeeded. The social constraints of alliance were henceforth accepted by all and no longer seemed to contradict individual aspirations. Though in reality committed to compromise, love matches recovered their absolute power in the realm of the imaginary. This, however, seems much less the case in popular imagination if one relies on the evidence of pedlar literature. More 'popular' in its public than in its authors, this literature fairly accurately reflects the way mentalities evolved, in so far as the works which it diffused, while often constructed on very old patterns, were constantly reworked to meet publishers' idea of what their readers wanted. The marriage theme holds a major position in them, but is viewed more from a practical than a fanciful point of view. From the *Jardin de l'honnête amour* (The garden of honourable love) to *De l'instruction à l'usage des grandes filles* (Concerning instruction for grown-up girls) (Farge, 1982), this hodge-podge of lessons in deportment and models of declarations of love or proposals of marriage for use by aspirants puts forward in a courtly style which the *précieuses* of the *grand siècle* would not have found amiss, an unconditional apology for family propriety and parental authority.

As for works of entertainment, for instance the street theatre which Jacques-Louis Menetra (1982) enjoyed so much, happily going off to cheer Carlin or Taconnet, they remained faithful to the principles of the *commedia dell'arte*. In them, marriage invariably appears in the guise of the enamoured old man, the deceived husband and the battered wife. The model of the love match does not appear to have had any more influence on the life of the Parisian glazier than it did on his literary tastes. This 'workshop Casanova', who was unable to keep a tally of his female conquests, enamoured widows, forsaken wives, complaisant maids and venal girls, also made a rational marriage: he married a rather elderly provincial bride who brought him 1,000 livres with which to start his own business.

Was he representative? For France we have two clues of a serial nature which tend on the contrary to show that the evolution of mentalities, as illustrated in the literature of the eighteenth century, may also be found in behavioural patterns. These concern illegitimacy and premarital conceptions. The great increase in the number of declared pregnancies – that repressive procedure for unmarried mothers instituted by the monarchy in the sixteenth century – cannot be attributed solely to heavier police supervision. The rise in illegitimate births recorded in parish registers confirms the tendency. Indeed, the circumstances of these unfortunate love affairs, as reported in the declarations, witnessed to a new state of mind. Sometimes it was still a case of affairs with servant girls, seduced by married men or ones whose rank was so far above theirs that marriage was not a possible outcome. However, most often these seduced girls had given themselves to boys of their own age and social circle who had promised to marry them (Depauw, 1972). Illegitimate births had earlier resulted from amorous passions incompatible with married life. Now they were increasingly the product of love affairs which included plans for marriage, that is, of premarital relationships which had turned out badly.

As for premarital conceptions, they were derived more and more frequently from illegitimate relationships which turned out well. Although they were everywhere on the increase from the mid-eighteenth century onwards, it is noticeable that the batch of births very soon after marriage increased at a greater rate than that of births occurring six or seven months afterwards (Flandrin, 1975). In the latter case, the couples involved were about to get married, and had embarked on married life a little before the nuptial blessing. In the case of births soon after marriage, on the other hand, the girls involved may well have been seduced by men who agreed to marry them when they became pregnant.

In both situations, the sexual relationship had preceded the married relationship, which is in principle contrary to ecclesiastical law. It is, however, significant that this illicit behaviour, which was most on the increase and revealed most about the evolution of customs, was the one in which marriage occurred as an almost accidental result of love-making.

It is very difficult to distinguish the transformations affecting pre-marital life at the representational and behavioural level from those which may be observed within married life itself, and from the most important one of all, the appearance of birth control. This had already been reported in the eighteenth century by a few social observers like

Moheau, who deplored the fact that 'these grievous secrets penetrate even into the countryside.' This innovation in the sex lives of couples seems to have been welcomed far earlier in France than in the rest of Europe, and was attributed at first to the relaxation of morals and to de-Christianization. Given that the Church had from the start forbidden infertile sexual relations, and especially the most common contraceptive practice of *coitus interruptus*, some historians advanced the hypothesis that the internalization of this ban made contraceptive methods unthinkable, and likewise the mere idea of resorting to them. These methods had become shameful and clandestine, and continued to be practised only among marginal communities of prostitutes (Ariès, 1960). Other studies soon revealed that birth control was already very widespread by the end of the seventeenth century among the upper classes, not only in France, among dukes and peers and the English high nobility, but also among patricians in Geneva. While this phenomenon may indeed be explained as an aspect of the elites' cultural superiority, it can no longer be put down to to de-Christianization.

A whole series of demographic studies has since enabled historians to date the introduction of birth control among the bulk of the population. It appeared as early as the second half of the seventeenth century, but in a temporary form in Geneva and the English countryside at Colyton, and irreversibly in Rouen by 1700. It is observed from the mid-eighteenth century in several medium-size towns in northern France, such as Meulan or Châtillon-sur-Seine and a little later on in the countryside of the Paris Basin.

In the case of the high nobility, which derived its power from its landed wealth, the need was to prevent the subdivision of patrimonies at a time of crisis when land revenues were falling. For the bulk of the population, birth control was an attempt to react to the stresses of a particularly severe crisis, with price rises and high mortality. This is what Bardet (1983) suggests in the case of Rouen after the 1694 crisis. As for the small French peasant trying to win possession of a tiny plot of land in the unfavourable economic situation of the second half of the eighteenth century, it had to do with his concern to save and preserve his inheritance. There was no shortage of economic motives for family limitation. In Rouen, contraception seems to have begun among new arrivals before reaching the settled inhabitants. It was widespread among notables and shopkeepers from the early eighteenth century, but reached the world of artisans and labourers only half-way through the century. In this matter there was no difference between Catholics and Protestants. Should this change of attitude to life be attributed to the emergence of the spirit of enterprise? Should we stop trying to search religious mentalities for an explanation for the disappearance of what had so long been a religious taboo?

Whether the phenomenon was radically new in the seventeenth century or was merely the reappearance of an old practice, it is unarguable that the time in which the religious Reformations were most active coincided with a long period when the prohibition was respected. However, the influence of the Reformations was uneven and ambiguous. Post-Tridentine Catholicism, influenced chiefly by Jesuit casuists, attempted to explain precisely to the faithful the Church's doctrine in matters of conjugal sexuality and to ensure that the 'sanctity of the marriage bed' was respected by applying inquisitorial confessional methods. Protestant authorities, on the other hand, adopted a stern and distant attitude towards conjugal life. They tried to moralize private life by communicating to the individual an acute sense of sin and a profound awareness of his responsibility, but they refused to see sexual activity as the principal or almost sole occasion of sin. Above all, they meant to allow couples to assume freely the responsibility for their daily lives together. 'You should know', Bridel declared, 'that we Protestant ministers do not allow ourselves to penetrate the secrets of the marriage sanctuary' (quoted in Perrenoud, 1974).

In France, in the second half of the seventeenth century, the Catholic clergy, both rigorist and Jansenist, and deeply hostile to Jesuist casuistry, ended by adopting a similar attitude. Far from feeling indulgent, and filled with holy repugnance to everything to do with sexuality, this hyper-puritan clergy thought that even talking about sex could constitute an invitation to sin. A parish priest called Sauvageon wrote of his parishioners in Sologne that 'it is necessary to question them, but this must be done particularly prudently for fear of perhaps teaching them sins which they have never committed or thought of committing' (quoted in Flandrin, 1975). The best solution was to cover conjugal life with a veil of silence.

This chaste silence during the eighteenth century gradually turned into indifference, or at least a refusal to intervene in the intimate lives of couples, in Jansenist regions where the lower clergy fostered anti-sacramental tendencies among the faithful, in particular refusal of baptism. Though they started from different doctrinal positions, Protestantism and Jansenism both ended up with the same results. By refusing to submit married life to external control, they gave consistency to a sphere of intimacy over which husband and wife secured an exclusive right of co-ownership. Conjugal sexuality was from now on lay territory and morally neutral, since it was removed from all risk of censure; it became the principal issue of this intimacy and the instrument of a more intense and closer affective relationship between husband and wife. There are good reasons for thinking that certain Protestant (in Geneva, for instance) or Jansenist circles were among the first homes for western Europe's great conversion to birth control.

It was not religious attitudes in themselves but their effects on couples' lives and their degree of intimacy which favoured the appearance of contraception. This explanation fits in with the conclusions of several comparative inquiries into the introduction of birth control in different societies in the Third World. In Puerto Rico, in particular, a traditionally Catholic country, contraception spread rapidly; in India, on the other hand, the population is still widely hostile to it, although its religious traditions do not contain any prohibition of the practice. Thus it is not religious tradition but, among other factors, the nature of the couple's relationship and the degree of their intimacy and equality, which may favour the transformation of sexual behaviour or impede it.

In Europe, it can at least be said that the coming of intimacy and 'companionate marriage' and of a new model of a less distant, if not more equal, relationship between spouses, were the indirect results of the new forms of religious behaviour.

Parents and children

Birth and baptism

Before the advances in obstetrics of the nineteenth century, entry into this life remained a formidable trial. The mother had to take precautions during her pregnancy to ensure the health and well-being of the child. Furthermore, certain practices were recommended to ensure successful delivery without excessive pain. Recourse to the saints, most notably the Virgin Mary and St Margaret, was necessary, as was perhaps a pilgrimage to one of their sanctuaries. Many of which preserved a 'holy girdle', that, when worn, ensured an easy delivery. In 1638 the French queen, Anne of Austria, when pregnant with the future Louis XIV, sent twice for the Virgin's holy girdle kept in Puy-Notre-Dame in Anjou. When the actual relic was not available, a belt which had touched it and been blessed could perform the same function.

Childbearing was feared with good reason. While in most cases everything turned out all right, with the 'matron' and neighbours, themselves married and mothers, limiting themselves to reassuring and encouraging the woman in labour and applying recipes to hasten her delivery. Sadly, when nature had not done its task properly, events quickly took a dramatic turn. How could it have been otherwise, given the incompetence of the matrons and, in even the best cases, the relative impotence of the best-qualified surgeons and midwives? The prejudice preventing men, out of decency, from playing any part in childbirth was strong in the sixteenth and seventeenth centuries and only retreated slowly. Nevertheless, during the eighteenth century, the surgeon-obstetrician gradually came to the fore in most European countries. Surgeons even attempted international collaboration and, after 1750, rapidly developed clinical instruction in obstetrics modelled on the great schools of Paris, London, Strasbourg and Göttingen. However, the birth of this 'Europe of obstetricians' should not deceive us: the surgeon's knowledge and capabilities remained rudimentary, and his clients were mostly limited to the upper-class women of urban society, since any intervention by him in the country was prevented by the cost as well as the old prejudices.

Even so, the matron continued to play the main role more or less

Birth as the business of women. This engraving illustrates the treatise by Dr Jean Rueffe *On the Conception and Begetting of Man* (Frankfurt, 1580). It shows the tasks and the persons connected with childbirth. Whether it is the mother or the baby that is being tended, everything is being done by women. Bibliothèque Interuniversitaire de Médecine, Paris.

everywhere. In Catholic countries, she came under the strict control of the parish priest. In fact, he had to rely on her to ensure that the child was baptized properly 'in case of necessity'. This was why no one was allowed to assist women in childbirth unless they had been approved for the purpose by the parish priest. On the other hand, nothing, or almost nothing, was done to ensure that the midwife was technically competent. Outside the large towns, where the surgeons could exercise a modicum of control, the vast majority of midwives operating in the countryside and market towns had undergone no apprenticeship or examination. They acquired all their knowledge at the bedsides of women in labour and by helping older matrons, who passed on their recipes along with their prejudices. This situation was little altered by the spread throughout Europe after 1760 of courses in childbirth for midwives modelled on those by Mme du Coudray, because the midwives thus trained were relatively few and almost all of them, even if they had previously been working in the countryside, set themselves up in towns, where they could find a well-off clientele capable of recognizing and paying for their new qualification. Thus the countryside, where 80–90 per cent of the European population lived, did not benefit.

Furthermore, qualified surgeon-obstetricians and midwives were powerless when confronted with difficult situations. Even more serious was the dilemma which soon emerged in such cases: was the mother's or the baby's life to be saved? Where the Roman Church was concerned, the primary issue was that of ensuring the salvation of the new-born baby by means of baptism. This attitude met with general assent to the extent that a preoccupation, even an obsession, with baptism was solidly anchored in popular consciousness. The frequency of unction in cases of necessity is witness both to this collective awareness and to the great number of difficult deliveries.

The child had scarcely left his mother's body when he was washed all over in front of the fire with a little fresh butter or warm water with some *eau-de-vie* added, while someone else was busy burying the placenta and umbilical cord. After his first washing, the matron might feel inclined to mould the baby's head with her hands to make it rounder and to cut the child's frenum by slipping the nail of her little finger under his tongue. During the following hours, and in the period preceding baptism when the birth could not be considered complete, they made sure that no one cuddled the baby or turned him towards the sun or gave him to his mother to feed; they would simply give him a little honey-water. He had no name, no social existence, being still impure and regarded as incomplete.

It was baptism which really marked his entry into this life; it signified not only his birth into Christian life but also his essential rite of passage through the gift of his first name by his godparents. The child was carried to church, not by his mother who would still be in bed a few hours after giving birth and who, furthermore, would be considered impure until she underwent the ceremony of churching, but by the matron or at least by one of the women who had assisted at the birth. The father, godfather and godmother, possibly the brothers and sisters and a few friends would also be present. Although moving the new-born baby so soon after his birth might, in some cases, constitute a danger to his health, this consideration was of no account. It was better to risk his temporal life than his eternal life, the necessary condition for which was of course baptism.

Before proceeding to the baptism proper, which itself was preceded by a series of exorcisms to drive away the devil and eliminate original sin, the priest would ask the godparents what name they intended to give the child. Choosing the name was very important. It was often the god-father's or godmother's, and more often still the father's or mother's, especially in the case of a first-born child. The stock of first names in actual use was relatively small. In France, about ten masculine first names and as many feminine names met three-quarters of all requirements. Jean and Marie were generally in the lead, followed by Pierre, Jacques and François, and Anne along with the feminine forms of the preceding names for girls. The remainder were less common names, many of them those of local saints whose renown varied in importance. The baptismal name thus held a dual significance, being both magical and religious. It renewed the bond between the living and the dead by ensuring that the same name passed from one generation to the next, and it gave the new Christian a patron saint to protect him and set an example in life. In Protestant countries, where reference to a saint could not carry the same significance, many first names such as Abraham, Samuel, Nathaniel, Sarah, Rebecca and Deborah were taken from the Old Testament. This was the case most notably among French Protestants and the English Puritans.

Early childhood

For the newly baptized child, this was the start of his early childhood until he was weaned. During this essential and difficult period, he was linked to his mother, or a wet-nurse, by a vital bond. It was she, in effect, who wrapped him up, watched over his sleep and his hygiene and, above all, breast-fed him. Until the mid-eighteenth century and even beyond, custom demanded that the baby should be tightly wrapped in swaddling clothes and laid in a narrow cradle to which he was secured. Many are the paintings and engravings, from Denmark to Spain, from England to Italy, testifying to this universal fashion for swaddling clothes, which made the baby look like a mummy. This was done to keep the baby quiet and made it possible to leave him unsupervised, but it was also meant to mould his body. It was feared that without this discipline, he would grow deformed or his little legs would buckle. The little cradle was made of wood, and could be finely worked, depending on the family's social station. It was set on wooden rockers, and was sometimes connected by a rope or a piece of wood to the mother's bed so that she could rock it at night without having to get up. In some regions, the baby was placed in a plain box and suspended from a beam in a vertical rather than a horizontal position. This box, which could be just a sack, could be carried to the fields, where it would then be hung from a tree while the parents worked nearby.

In many poor families, however, cradles, even the most rudimentary,

A Rural Household, seventeenth-century engraving. The way the mother is tipping the baby's body while holding his feet, having come close to the fire to change his nappy and clean him, is one of the most ancient actions of motherhood. Bibliothèque Nationale, Paris.

were an unknown luxury, and the little baby had no other bed than his parents'. Nevertheless, mothers and wet-nurses were at all times strictly prohibited to sleep with their baby in bed, lest he be found suffocated the next morning. The insistence with which the civil and ecclesiastical authorities reiterated this prohibition from the sixteenth to the eighteenth century proves that the habit was very deeply ingrained, in spite of the obvious risks to the baby. In most cases, the practice was undoubtedly followed to enable the child to suck at the breast when he wanted and, above all, to keep him warm and preserve him from the dangers and baleful influences of the night.

Although the bodily care lavished on the nursling was far removed from the rules of modern hygiene, it nevertheless met very precise imperatives, which were to be observed among some working people until the twentieth century. Dirt was generally considered to be beneficial, and babies' heads were seldom washed; the dirt made their hair prettier and protected the fontanelle. The same with lice; they were prevented from proliferating by delousing, but one or two were always left in, because 'lice eat bad blood'. In the same way, children's nails were carefully not cut until they were one or two years old. What was more, since swaddling was a long and difficult operation, the child would only be changed once or twice a day. After all, was not urine, far from being harmful, a remedy employed in traditional remedies? This was why most mothers and wet-nurses dried the wet nappies and used them again without washing out the urine (Loux, 1978).

These customs began to be challenged in France during the 1760s and 1770s, notably with the publication of Jean-Jacques Rousseau's *Émile* and of several dozen works dedicated to the problems of babyhood. Tight swaddling was universally condemned; the adoption of a loose form of swaddling, which was recommended, had the further advantage of allowing the child to be changed more easily and regularly. All the doctors, who were discovering the extreme importance of hygiene for maintaining health, insisted that this was necessary in the case of very young children. Some recommended washing nurslings daily in warm or even cold water. Nevertheless it cannot be said that this campaign had more than very modest results. Except among the well-to-do, the new precepts about loose swaddling and hygiene for babies remained practically a dead letter. The working classes rejected with suspicion these innovations, which qualified doctors, surgeons and midwives were trying to force on them, and they kept to their old practices. The same applied to the business of breast-feeding.

Breast-feeding by the mother was the rule in the countryside, meaning in the great majority of families. Besides, popular wisdom, long before

Rousseau, saw it as the natural extension of pregnancy and the maternal task *par excellence*. It could happen that, in spite of precautions and pilgrimages, the mother's milk dried up for a while, the result for instance of illness. If she could not or would not resort to paying a wet-nurse, she used cows' or more often goats' milk. In any case, after a few weeks of exclusive breast-feeding, the nursling would pass on to mixed feeding. As well as milk, which remained an essential part of his intake, he would begin to be fed various mixtures of gruel, depending on the region.

In town, the practice of paid breast-feeding and of putting the new-born child out to a wet-nurse, which was still restricted to bourgeois families in the sixteenth and seventeenth centuries, spread in the eighteenth to all classes of society. The process may be observed in several European countries, but most markedly in France. In rich or merely well-off families, for whom keeping a wet-nurse at home or paying her wages in the countryside presented no problem, the practice had become so current that to run counter to it would have been to fail to observe the proprieties. Among the working classes it was more often than not a necessary step linked to the mother's work at her husband's side. This was the case, for instance, among the home weavers and in some of the food trades, such as butchers or bakers. Among the Parisians who put their children out to a wet-nurse on the eve of the Revolution, the whole socio-professional range is presented, from nobles and the upper bourgeoisie (relatively few in number since they preferred keeping a wet-nurse at home) to apprentices, passing through merchants, shopkeepers and master craftsmen, the only exception being, significantly, the low-paid. We have already seen how this practice of putting out to a wet-nurse could lead to abuse and negligence, resulting in a notably higher level of infant mortality than among babies who were breast-fed by their own mothers. We have also seen how the authorities tried to remedy the situation. However, the measures they took bore fruit only very slowly and imperfectly, and there were still many justified complaints in the first half of the nineteenth century.

Far sadder still than the fate of children put out to wet-nurses was that of abandoned children. In the sixteenth and seventeenth centuries they came from two sources. They could either be new-born babies abandoned by their unmarried mothers, or legitimate children, often several years old, whom their parents, driven by poverty, could no longer feed. The first page of *Petit Poucet* (Tom Thumb), published by Charles Perrault in 1697, refers to a practice still current at the time: 'There came a very bad year and the famine was so great that poor people determined to rid themselves of their children.' It was normal, under these conditions, to observe a correlation between great subsistence crises, which degenerated into famines, and the maximum number of admissions to the foundling hospitals. From the 1760s onwards, the number of abandoned children increased rapidly. This increase was paralleled by the increase in the numbers of children baptized as illegitimate in urban parishes: in many towns the proportion passed from 2 per cent of all baptisms at the beginning of the eighteenth century to 25 per cent in the decade 1780–9. In Paris, the Hôpital de la Couche (maternity hospital) in 1772 – a record year – noted a figure for admissions of abandoned children equivalent to more than a third of all baptisms registered that year in the capital's parishes. In fact, among those babies abandoned at birth and baptized as illegitimate were many, possibly a third, who were legitimate.

The brutal increase in the number of abandoned children from the 1760s onwards thus corresponded to an evolution in the motives for abandoning them. In the case of illegitimate children, their growing numbers, even when one takes into account the legitimate babies who were baptized as illegitimate, reveal both an increase in extramarital births and a deterioration in the moral situation as applied to the unmarried mother and her bastard, compared with previous centuries. Above all, alongside the real poverty which still lay behind many acts of abandonment (for instance in 1788–9), a new and more complex motivation began to appear. Parents from modest or even well-off backgrounds, members of the middle classes or master craftsmen, would leave their baby at the hospital if they were temporarily short of money and feared that they would not be able to raise this child, the latest-born of several others, as they wished, with the idea of eventually taking him back. Their attitude can be explained by the fact that many parents thought that the residents of children's hospitals were well treated and thus received free the care and education which they themselves would have found it hard to give them. The fact that the reality was quite different and that these unfortunate babies had tragically low chances of survival did nothing to alter matters. It is interesting to note that such an attitude on the part of a number of parents was contemporary with a new interest in children, which has already been mentioned, and was also contemporary with the spread of contraception in France. To the extent that children were now being looked at with new eyes, and that the family was tending to concentrate around them, people wanted to limit their numbers, either through contraception or, in the event of that being refused or failing, by abandoning their unwanted children.

Weaning and the second stage of childhood

For those who managed to avoid the dangers of early infancy, weaning constituted a major stage. It generally occurred around two years of age, often earlier, sometimes later. It corresponded in theory to the growth of the child's first teeth. Except when pregnancy or some other cause intervened, weaning was generally introduced progressively. It came at the end of a more or less lengthy period of mixed feeding when milk was complemented by gruel. Nevertheless, the moment had to come when the child was finally separated from the breast. Several techniques were resorted to in order to make things easier: the mother or wet-nurse would cover her nipples with bitter pastes to disgust the nursling, and at the same time she would try to dry up her milk supply by magical or symbolic means such as applying parsley or wearing a necklace of cork stoppers. Whatever was done, weaning had severe psychological and physical effects. This stage was all the more important if the child had been raised by a wet-nurse in the country and weaning coincided with his return, or rather his admission, to his family, since he would generally have left it a few hours after his birth. Only now would he take the place due to him next to his father and mother, in the midst of his brothers and sisters.

This second stage of childhood, which thus began and lasted until around his seventh year, was that of difficult apprenticeships carried out mainly within the narrow framework of the conjugal family and under the almost exclusive authority of the mother, since the father was not supposed to take care of his younger children. Having been totally weaned from the breast, the child had to get used very quickly to the adult food which was from now on his too. Among ordinary people, this meant dipping his bread into the soup. The child's bread ration would increase as he grew older; by his seventh year he would already be eating his pound a day. Another apprenticeship would be in cleanliness. When the child was weaned, and often before, his nappy was replaced by skirts, for boys as well as girls. These skirts did not normally have any nappies under them. In the countryside, absolutely no rules had been applied in this respect. The child performed his functions wherever he might be, and then gradually learnt to go off somewhere when he felt the urge. His apprenticeship in walking began when he wore his first skirts. Among the well-off, the child would be clad in a padded bonnet to protect him from serious falls; sometimes wooden or wicker frames set on wheels were used for this. In the countryside, no one had worried about this particular apprenticeship, and the baby had been allowed to learn how to walk by himself, on all fours at first, and then up on his legs. People worried only if he was clearly behindhand in this domain, which then justified recourse to the appropriate saint.

The same sort of thing applied to his apprenticeship in language. Precocity in speech and intelligence were generally considered by ordinary people to be worrying signs. However, long delays were also worrying, and magical and religious practices were used to prevent or cure them. Learning how to talk was, in effect, the first and vital stage in the child's socialization. Following the cradle songs which accompanied his sleep during the first months, his first initiation into language consisted of little phrases and nursery rhymes recited by his mother. They were soon followed by songs and stories. The child would feel at ease in this universe where there was no frontier between the imaginary and the real world. Whether sung or told, these recitals were not presented as true, but not as false either. They were filled with more or less accurate allusions to a reassuring environment, but at the same time they introduced an outside world, removed from perceptible reality, and inhabited by imaginary creatures which were sometimes friendly, sometimes terrifying. The mother would consciously use fairy tales as a means of education. Among country people, the main object was getting the child, who naturally moved about as soon as he could walk, to disturb his mother as little as possible in her many tasks. To make him obey and keep quiet, she threatened him not only with the wolf, but also with fantastic beings such as Mélusine and the fairy Carabosse, the ogre and the werewolf. Using fear in this way, accompanied perhaps by physical chastisement, was aimed at inculcating a minimum of discipline in the children, without which communal life within the family would soon become unbearable. Among the aristocracy and the middle classes much more stress was laid on this apprenticeship, which ended by truly conditioning mind and body. The great success of *De civilitate morum puerilium* over the whole of Europe from the start of the sixteenth century is evidence of the importance attached to these new notions of how to behave, as copied from court practice.

Maternal training also included the child's first religious education. In fact, even when Sunday catechism was generally practised under the authority of the pastor or parish priest, it involved only children of seven and over. Before this age, the mother's role was of primary importance. Bossuet addressed parents, and most specially mothers, when he announced the publication in 1687 of his *Catéchisme* for the Meaux diocese: 'Know that you must be the first and the principal catechists for your children', and he laid down their duty in the following terms:

> As soon as they stutter, you must teach them the sign of the cross: it is good too to make them say it in Latin, so that they grow accustomed from the

Chardin was one of the first painters to explore the world of childhood and to express, often in small-format works executed in warm tones, the bonds of affection between mothers and children, thus entering the private world of children. *Grace*, was painted in 1740 and presented to Louis XV. Musée du Louvre, Paris.

cradle to the language of the Church . . . When they start to talk, you must teach them a few questions and answers, one after the other, according to what they can remember, without hurrying or worrying whether they can understand them, because God will give them intelligence in time.

This preliminary religious education within the family was made easier in all Catholic houses, even poor ones, by the presence of a crucifix, which was blessed on Palm Sunday, a few holy pictures of Christ, the Virgin or a saint, and a stoup containing a little holy water. In Protestant households, this role was played by the family Bible, from which the father read out a passage every day, and which was carefully kept in a place of honour.

Apprenticeships

As he grew bigger and acquired greater independence of movement, the child was keener to quit the protection of his mother's skirts. His horizon was expanding beyond that of his family home, and he would start to play with friends of about his own age, his brothers and sisters and neighbours from the village or district. Those games of the second stage in childhood were much more than a mere antidote to boredom; they schooled him for communal life and in comprehending his environment. They were also proof that his family was already no longer playing an exclusive role in the child's education.

This slow and progressive replacing of the family in its educational role was speeded up once the child was seven. At this age, boys gave up their skirts for their first trousers. It was above all the age at which boys and girls were supposed to attain the age of reason or discretion, meaning the ability to tell right from wrong. They were obliged from now on to attend parish catechism classes regularly. It was also the age at which school education began for a minority of children, and their apprenticeship in reading, writing and arithmetic. Finally, for all of them it was the age from which their surrounding village or town quarter was to contribute in an essential way to their socialization. Among working people, in town as well as in the countryside, children now enjoyed an autonomy in relation to their parents, and this increased as they grew older. While they took part, according to their ability, in the family's work, this participation more often than not brought them outside their home, and they were able to carry out their tasks alongside friends of their own age. In the same way, they took part with adults in evening gatherings and festivities. All this constituted an indispensable education conducted outside the narrow circle of the conjugal family in the heart of the village or urban community, and enabled girls and boys gradually to familiarize themselves with the circle in which they were growing up and would probably spend the rest of their lives.

The more formal apprenticeship in a trade could be served entirely within the family, and independently of any teaching institution. This was most often so among peasants, and shopkeepers and in the manual trades. The son of a farmer, a rural weaver or a miller would normally learn the techniques of the trade, which would one day be his, from his father. This education, which began early, was continued until the day the father died, and thus enabled his eldest son to establish himself by taking up the work on the farm, on the market stall or in the workshop. However, there were exceptions. In many regions it was usual for the sons of peasants to be placed at about fourteen as farm hands for a few years with other peasants, friends or often relatives, living in neighbouring parishes. The father would then compensate for his son's departure by hiring a farm hand and would adopt the same educational role towards him as his cousin or neighbour was doing for his own son, who had been sent there. In the eyes of churches and states, the rights and duties of masters and mistresses to their servants were exactly the same as those of fathers and mothers to their children.

For boys who did not want to succeed their father, or who could not do so, their trade apprenticeship had to take place outside the home. In most European countries, apprenticeship was regulated and involved a notarial contract between the boy's parents and his future master. The latter undertook to give his apprentice not only his professional but also his moral and religious training. In fact, placing an apprentice was the equivalent of temporarily transferring paternal authority to his master. From now on the young boy lived with the master and his wife. He ate their bread, slept beneath their roof and owed them the same obedience and respect as his father and mother. Living with the children of the house and perhaps two or three fellow apprentices, was not very different from life at home. Thus the family – whether the natural one or a host family – maintained right to the end the reproductive role assigned to it by society.

PART II

Other Worlds

THREE

Children of the Apocalypse: the Family in Meso-America and the Andes

Carmen Bernand and Serge Gruzinski

The study of the family over more than six centuries of history and in two regions of the American continent which lie far apart may appear a bold enterprise in many respects. Among the numerous questions arising from this choice, two are fundamental and deserve an explanation. Can one compare two societies belonging to distinct cultural zones? Are these societies representative of Latin American populations as a whole?

From an ethnological perspective, the pre-Hispanic societies of the Mexican and Andean plateaux share some general characteristics which differentiate them from the majority of Amerindian populations. The Mexica and the domains under their rule, like the ethnic races contained within the Inca Empire, formed strongly hierarchical state-controlled societies. The Incas' bureaucratic structure, which was intended to strengthen their central control over a vast territory, was certainly not in the same order as the looser administrative network within the Mexica sphere of influence, but, in spite of some differences which cannot be neglected, these two 'empires' were important in a demographic sense. Furthermore, their social stratification and ethnic plurality gave them a degree of institutional and cultural heterogeneity.

To these general structural similarities, belonging to the pre-Hispanic period, can be added the destiny shared by both societies from the sixteenth century onwards as a result of the Spanish Conquista. It was their exceptional human and natural resources which made Mexico, Peru and Bolivia the economic and political basis for the Spanish colonial empire. For the native populations, Spanish domination signified an ideological and political break, and at the same time continuity. The Indian peasants of the colonial period paid tribute to their new masters, and the hierarchical order was maintained in spite of the great social and cultural upheavals. The essential fact, however, was that the particular modalities of religious and cultural integration were most widely accepted by the native Mexican and Andean populations.

It is simply impossible to develop a history of the family from pre-Christian times to the present. This is why we have chosen to present chronologically certain important themes relative to the family, which are both specific to the regions selected and representative of a larger reality, to the extent that they are the result of a unique historical experience of a transformation in mentalities and of indigenous forms of behaviour on a vast scale. We have thus deliberately stressed the imposition of the Christian model from the sixteenth century onwards and the diversity of the reactions and adjustments which it elicited among the indigenous populations.

The family in the prehistoric period

Although there is a great deal of documentation about Meso-America and the Andes, references to the family are few, and hard to interpret. The Spanish chroniclers were mainly churchmen, and they took particular interest in rites and idolatries, at the expense of daily life. Their attention was drawn more to the habits of the ruling elite than to the customs of humble folk, and, in every case, their witness was marked by Christian ideology. In quite a few cases, this bias casts suspicion on their references to life cycles, sexuality and alliances. Thus it is difficult to distinguish between truth and distortion in their descriptions of indigenous families, in which their moralizing intent and every kind of censorship are only too apparent.

A further problem, and not the least, involves the chroniclers' habit of generalizing on the basis of individual instances. How can one pass from an abstract model of the type 'the ancient Mexicans were accustomed to' to a more ethnic type of analysis? We cannot in the present state of our knowledge solve this problem; likewise the historian and the ethnologist who draw their inspiration from these texts can offer only generalizations, while attempting to qualify statements which only seem categorical because the facts are so few.

The family and household group

The Spanish chroniclers of the sixteenth century did not use the word 'family' at all, preferring the terms 'kin' or 'household' (*los de la casa*).

These expressions matched the reported facts more closely. In Mexico, the concept of *nahua* for family implied a production and consumer group possessing a common residence. In this respect, their vocabulary is significant: *cencalli* (whole house), *cencaltin* (people of the same house), *cemithualtin* (people of the same house, of the same courtyard), *cenyeliztli* (people who are together), and *techan tlaca* (household). One should thus refer to family groups rather than to families.

Several family groups occupying different living spaces but bound by the ties of kinship and engaging in co-operative economic and social practices, formed a *cemithualtin*. Their dwellings were grouped around a communal courtyard, and their composition varied perceptibly according to the rules of inheritance, the tributary system, the area of exploitable land and their social status. In Tenochtitlan (Mexico) residential units predominated; they were closed to the outside world and sheltered anything between two and six nuclear families. Each family lived in one or two rooms ranging in size from 10 to 30 square metres. The building would be made of stone and adobe, and sometimes included a first floor. It opened onto the communal courtyard and comprised, apart from the cisterns and attics, a *cihuacalli* (women's house), a collective space which presumably combined kitchen, family altar and reception area. The members of the household would be related and would form a group around a married man. Such households of variable size also included servants and slaves, but the density of the family group was dependent on demographic and economic pressures. Newly married couples resided temporarily with the wife's parents, although this does not seem to have been a general rule of residence over the whole of the Mexican central plateau region.

The chroniclers' texts are terser about the Andean home, and they reflect the Europeans' astonishment at finding disparate forms of housing, which they termed 'disorganized'. In the large towns like Cuzco (Peru), the space was divided into quarters according to a system of partition which obeyed specific symbolic principles. In the villages of the central and southern Andes, different lineages were divided in terms of space according to a ritual dualism. It was a structural complexity which contrasted with the rusticity of their houses, if the Spanish sources are to be believed. The houses were small in size, closed to the outside world and circular, notably in the Collao region.

How was the family group composed? The detailed censuses carried out by the Spaniards during the first years of the Conquista provide precious information on this subject. Thus, in the Huanuco region in Peru, the houses sheltered the conjugal couple, the husband's parents, some grandparents, some widowed or spinster sisters, and a few sick or crippled individuals. The number of children per house was not high: in rare cases when the figure recorded is five, the chronicler adds a personal comment on the numerous progeny. In so far as the censuses date from 1562, it can be asked whether the low incidence of children per couple was not a consequence of the demographic shock following the Conquista.

One real difficulty which one comes across when determining the Andean domestic group is derived from their vertical farming model in the ecological enclaves situated in terraced zones, sometimes a considerable distance apart. In fact, John Murra's work (1978) has made it possible to distinguish a particular form of land appropriation over a discontinuous territory, as a function of autarkic ideals typical of the Andean population. Thus domestic groups would have several residential units situated on the cold lands of the puna (at an altitude of over 4,000 m), in the temperate zones (valleys and slopes at 3,500 m) and the warm zones (about 1,800 m high). However, although we know nowadays that it was current practice in the central and southern Andes for families to be displaced and settled on a seasonal basis, the effect of this mobility on the composition of households is not well known.

Kinship and matrimonial practices

The same applies to the rules governing endogamy and exogamy, which are still poorly understood. It appears, for instance, that in Mexico the lower-class Nahua and Mixtecs married within their community, whereas the nobility was just as likely to marry foreign girls as close relatives, sisters-in-law or cross-cousins. Generally speaking, monogamy in the Andes as in Mexico was the lot of commoners whereas the ruling elites practised plural marriage. Thus it was that, near to Mexico-Tenochtitlan, Nezahualpilli, the ruler of Texcoco, kept 2,000 wives and had 144 children. The Inca, for his part, had a large number of concubines. Without attaining such exceptional proportions, it does seem to have been current practice for two to three wives to co-reside in the houses of men described as 'principal'.

The documentation for Nahua kinship is slender and does not enable us to set up a specific model for this population. The texts collected by Sahagun, the Franciscan chronicler, which also describe the ages of life, must be reassessed critically. In some cases, his Western approach produced flagrant distortions. The fact was that the Indians were accustomed to very diverse matrimonial practices. The Mixtecs, for instance, married their sister-in-law by preference, or even their sister, but these terms could correspond to classificatory sisters. The Tarasc people in Michoacan, unlike other ethnic groups in ancient Mexico such as the Otomi and Mazahua, married among their kin. A young Tarasc girl would be promised from childhood, and, while waiting for her to reach marriageable age, her fiancé would sometimes form a temporary union with her mother. The Nahua disapproved of such customs. On the central plateau, kinship was cognatic and bilateral; the members of a noble house formed one lineage (*tecalli*) and the whole population was integrated into loosely and sometimes contradictorily contoured units, called *calpulli*. Their function was economic, administrative and religious, with a clear exogamic tendency, and they were placed under the aegis of a tutelary deity known as *calpulteotl*. The sources provide a few more meagre clues to the existence of lineages which were fixed to a particular place and possessed sacred objects transmitted from generation to generation.

It is just as difficult to reconstitute Andean kinship. The richest documents on the subject, such as wills, transcripts of trials and genealogies, show how kinship was manipulated in function of the succession law introduced by the Spaniards. For the period before the Conquista, one can glean the odd allusion to noble households and matrimonial practices among the elites, but the bulk of our information about kinship is derived from Quechua and Aymara dictionaries compiled by missionaries. These give us a nomenclature, but there are theoretical problems in passing from a terminology to a general model of alliance. The study of Inca kinship has fed a fertile polemic between two specialists, Lounsbury (1978) and Zuidema (1977). Without entering into the details of the debate, let us take a look at its main theme. The rules of marriage were determined by the *ayllu*, a kinship group comprising all the male and female descendants of a male ancestor down to the fourth generation. Members of the same *ayllu* could not intermarry, an exogamic practice which was respected down to the fourth generation. On the other hand, members of the elite could contract marriages with close relatives, including sisters, as was the case with the Inca. It can thus be stated that parallel descent – masculine filiation for men and feminine for women – played an important role in transmitting certain ritual or landed rights. *Ayllu*, however, were neither lineages nor clans; these kinship bodies organized around a common ancestor were tied to their land of origin, symbolized by the *pacarina* and *huaca*. Furthermore, each group owned luck-bearing objects, *conupa*, which were transmitted from heir to heir, according to inheritance rules about which little is known.

The marriage ceremony was controlled by the state's bureaucratic apparatus, as was characteristic of Inca society. In fact, drawing up a

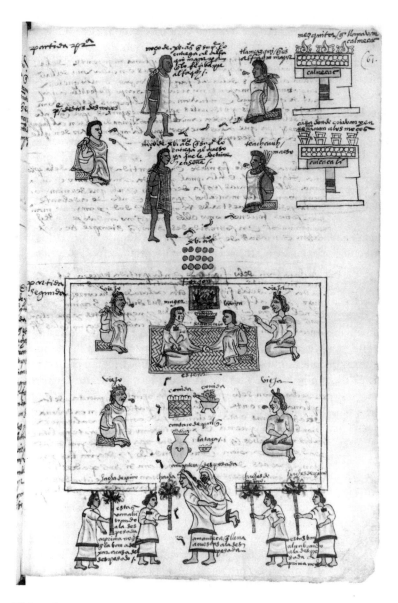

This codex was commissioned by Don Antonio de Mendoza, first viceroy of New Spain (1535–50), and was intended for the Emperor Charles V. Seventy-one pages arranged into three parts, using pictograms and commentaries in Spanish, record the history and customs of the Aztec world. Bodleian Library, Oxford.

census of the ethnic populations of the Tawantinsuyu Empire, which stretched from the south of what is now Colombia to Chile, was a political and economic necessity, because the number of tributaries, chosen among heads of family aged between twenty-five and fifty, was thereby determined. Marriage legitimized a prior union contracted long before, and founded a new family group, meaning a new tributary unit. Individuals were allotted their agricultural tasks before attaining the age of twenty-five or after their fiftieth birthday, but they did not pay tribute directly. They contributed through the specific work performed by them according to age, or by means of services rendered, to the tribute paid by the tributary unit, the household to which they were attached. In the Inca context, where accounting for human and material resources was a matter of state, marriage was made to depend on the will of the ruler or his representatives.

The chroniclers report how in every village, young unmarried persons would be lined up according to sex, and the person representing authority would proceed to distribute the young girls among the lords and principal men, who had several wives already, after which he would allot the remaining women to commoners. The most beautiful girls were destined for the temples of the Sun or the houses of the Inca. This unequal levy of women according to social hierarchy certainly presented problems in terms of demographic imbalance, which must have affected the composition of households. The sources tell us that commoners were left wifeless for a long time 'even after attaining the age for having one', whereas those who married several wives were rightly considered rich. Those with numerous progeny were also considered rich, and, inversely, orphans were called *waccha*, which also meant 'poor'.

Sexuality

Tackling the domain of sexual behaviour is even trickier. However, certain constants emerge. In Mexico, precocious sexual relations were disapproved of, and young nobles were compelled to be chaste, which kept them within the orbit of their paternal homes and of their temple-school, the *calmecac*. To make up for this, married adults enjoyed greater sexual freedom. Female sexuality, on the other hand, was systematically repressed. In ideological terms, the Nahua considered the female sex as the source of harmful energies. The word for woman (*cihua*) contained notions of cowardice, weakness and indecision. Woman was considered insatiable, and hence represented a worrying threat to man, whose vitality was progressively and irremediably sapped by performing the sex act. Ancient Mexican man was distinguished as much by his pronounced taste for human sacrifice as by his unremitting repression with regard to all forms of sexual behaviour external to the couple's reproductive function: abortion, adultery, homosexuality and rape were often punished by death.

Those individuals the group rejected were called *tetzahuitl* (those who provoke seizure and fright); they included homosexuals of both sexes, children born in incestuous unions, adulterers, persons afflicted with sterility, celibates and girls who had lost their virginity before marriage. The child of an adulterous union was supposed to spread unhappiness and fear among his family circle. However, we must draw distinctions here: the most systematic if not the strongest forms of repression were applied to the ruling class, as though moderate sexuality was one of the best ways of preserving the vital energy animating the powerful. In a general way, sexual behaviour, instead of obeying a strict dichotomy of licit and forbidden forms, or of good and evil, was accepted and tolerated or hunted down, depending on the context in which it was manifested. This was why the sacred prostitute was esteemed, unlike women condemned by fate to sell their bodies and other loose women. The myths and great ritual enactments of these peoples were shot through with the same ambivalence, representing as they did behaviour which would have been cruelly punished had it been detected in the context of everyday life. It must not be forgotten that the Spanish chroniclers relied on Indian informers who were Christians and who tended to systematize ancient attitudes, either by idealizing them or by attributing satanic designs to them, muddling such information as we do have about these populations' real practices and value systems.

Inca society seems to have been more tolerant about sexuality. As in Mexico, adultery was severely punished because once a legitimate marriage had been celebrated, the couple had to remain united until the death of one of the spouses. This rigidity is partly explained by political imperatives of state to do with fixing and counting tributary populations. Nevertheless, a woman's virginity was not held in any great esteem, to the extent that a young virgin was to some extent depreciated because no man had desired her. Here too, our judgement must be tempered, because virginity was a necessary condition for young girls dedicated to the worship of the Sun.

Contrary to Mexican customs, in Andean communities unmarried girls took part in collective rites of intoxication accompanied by sexual licence. Furthermore, a number of witnesses mention, without giving precise details, the custom of giving to a young man a woman who would look after him and initiate him into the pleasures of sex. This woman would remain attached to him for the rest of her life and become his 'serving-woman' or concubine. When the families involved were poor, they would entrust a male child to a widow with no descendants of her own, who would take care of his education. These links would be maintained after the young man had married.

References to homosexuality are rare and are in many cases confused with denunciations of sodomy, which appears to have been current among the populations of the Pacific coast. In Quechua, homosexuals were called *ipa*, a term which also meant 'sister of husband' and 'sister of father'.

It is at the moment practically impossible to draw any conclusions from all this. At the most, one could extend and multiply the probes and samples provided above. Our information is full of lacunae, and researchers sometimes produce contradictory interpretations, all of which prevents us from venturing beyond a few constants; even these are close to caricature and reveal the prodigious cultural diversity of the Amerindian world. On the whole, one is constantly confronted by a heterogeneity of situations resulting in a multiplicity of ethnic, social and cultural variables. Polygamy did exist, but it coexisted with monogamy, which was more frequent, just as preferential unions could bring the same individual into alliances which obeyed other factors. Generally speaking, it seems that belonging to a territory prevailed over belonging to a lineage and involved a genealogy of limited depth which would explain, for instance, why alliances were resumed within Inca *ayllu* after the fourth generation.

The Spanish Conquista: demographic catastrophe and colonial exploitation

The most immediate and unquestionably the most spectacular impact of the Conquista took the form of a demographic collapse of staggering dimensions. The experts' estimates vary, but they all agree in stressing the magnitude of the drop in population: according to Borah and Cook (1971–9), the population of Mexico was reduced over little more than a century from 25 million to some 750,000 inhabitants, a reduction of about 97 per cent. Without attempting to assess these figures, we can say that Mexico, the Andes and the rest of Spanish America suffered a demographic cataclysm as the result of repeated assaults, first from the biological impact on people who had no immunity to disease and were regularly decimated by epidemics introduced by Spaniards and black Africans. On top of this came the traumatic shock and state of lawlessness brought about by the disruption of ancient, social, political and (above all) religious structures leading, in the worst cases, to suicide, abortion and infanticide. Let us remember, finally, the heavy toll levied by war, massacre and, most obviously, the daily and brutal effects of the frenzied exploitation unleashed upon this new world.

Without being able to pinpoint it precisely, one may hazard a guess at the impact which this collapse had on demographic structures and on the behaviour of Indian populations. Take the composition of families, for instance: in Mexico, in the Oaxaca region, after the great epidemic of 1576 nearly half of all houses were abandoned and the number of persons per hearth also fell by half. In the Andes, at Huanuco, the average size of nuclear families fell from 6 to 2.5 persons. Again in the Andes, at Chucuito in 1657, young persons of both sexes aged between eleven and sixteen represented only 5.8 per cent of the whole population, when the rate should have been twice this. Early in the seventeenth century, half of all indigenous couples in New Grenada (now Colombia) had no children. In Peru, in some places, two-thirds of the men were missing, while the proportion of widows and unmarried women was excessive. As in Mexico, and even more so in the low-lying warm lands of Spanish America, whole landscapes were emptied of men and women; dwellings and settlements were entirely deserted over long periods. The sixteenth century was thus unarguably a time of demographic upheavals affecting indigenous societies which had been abruptly faced with the destruction, temporary or permanent, of their family groups, with brutal changes to the age of marriage, the wholesale loss of the collective memories which had preserved genealogies and regulated alliances and sometimes even a refusal to live and reproduce.

The ravages inflicted by the death rate were further complicated by the effects of the colonizers' policies. These included enforced deportation of the local workforce to the mines and building sites in the colonial towns, and measures aimed at concentrating the rural populations (referred to as 'reductions' or 'congregations'), which ripped the Indians out of their natural social environment, temporarily or for good. The bonds of life were severed, as with the Peruvian *ayllu*, which based the autonomy of the group on autochthony and recognition of a common ancestor. Once reassembled on new sites chosen by the Spaniards, the Indians were forced, sometimes with great brutality, to discover new ways of organizing their communal space in the chequer-board plan of colonial villages, and sometimes their houses which had separate rooms, doors and windows in the Spanish manner. The new arrangements gave rise to a restructuring in the Western manner of the domestic space and the relationships accommodated within it. However, we should not exaggerate the incidence of these policies ánd the inertia of populations which took every opportunity to return to their former dwellings and escape their conquerors' demands.

The fact remains that the colonial system did not cease to exert its destructive pressures on autochthonous structures: by setting up new forms of urban life, by installing a distinctive labour organization, assimilating from their traditional community more people than one imagines, who were eager to escape the onus of ancestral obligations or, quite simply, fiscal exactions. The colonial towns in which the new rulers were concentrated, the mines and their quick profits, the haciendas which usurped the Indians' lands in the seventeenth and eighteenth centuries and drew whole families within their orbits, the progressive implantation of precapitalist forms of exploitation and the entry into an Atlantic and global economy formed the broad outlines of the colonial framework which is the subject of this chapter. It was a shifting framework, constantly being transformed, which remained under the ascendancy of Indian mortality until life regained the upper hand during the second half of the seventeenth century in Mexico and in the eighteenth in the Andes, and the Church was called to fill a major role in it.

The 'conquest of bodies': the Christian model of marriage and the family

It was in Mexico, which had but recently been conquered, at the end of the 1520s and in the 1530s that the Church first considered diffusing Christian marriage on a large scale as the most effective means of securing the rapid and thorough Christianization of the indigenous populations. It is revealing that the 'conquest of bodies' and establishment of vigilant control over them began very soon to compete with the extirpation of idolatry in the heart of the Mexican Altiplano. As the chronicles and confessional manuals suggest, the inculcation of the Christian marriage ethic and conjugal life became an essential part of missionary strategies, as if the Church had decided that it was easier to mould behaviour than to uproot beliefs.

It is not immaterial that Spanish America, and especially New Spain (Mexico), served as experimental areas for material which had not yet been strictly codified. Reflections by the clergy on the existence and forms of marriage in the pre-Hispanic period; their inquiries into this sphere; their consultations in America and in the mother country; the local councils and papal interventions; their occasionally tentative prescriptions of the applicable rules and a high level of theological writing – all attest to the exceptional importance attached to these questions even before the Council of Trent. Only later on, and on the basis of the

Mexican experience, did Peru have to confront the same problems.

It was thus during the decades following the Conquista and up to the Council of Trent that the Church defined and modulated the system of values, rites and behaviour which was supposed to regulate the Indians' marriages and conjugal lives. A unique and uniform code, valid everywhere, whatever the ethnic people or social status involved, and founded on a written tradition and law, the Christian model could not fail to offend and confound people who had lived in a world of plural practices and diverse rules. It is true that the Christian norms did occasionally present superficial continuities with certain autochthonous practices: the primacy of reproduction was stressed, abortion and homosexuality were condemned without pity, the matrimonial bond was protected and esteemed compared with the opprobrium which was heaped on adulterers.

From another point of view, however, the Church was attacking head-on the prerogatives of ancient ruling groups and communities. It imposed and claimed to control the new rites of passage which punctuated birth, alliance and death. It introduced the strange figure of the priest who became, for the overwhelming majority of the subject populations, the first incarnation of their new social and cultural order. It forbade the Indian elites to practise polygamy and subjected them to the monogamous rule which reduced them to the common level. It interfered in the regulation of kinship systems by setting up a network of prohibitions, modified though they were by Paul III's bull *Altitudo divini concilii* (1537); marriage was prohibited within the second and third degrees of consanguinity and affinity, whereas the Spaniards continued to obey the stricter prescriptions which applied in western Europe. By taking away the right to sanction alliances and depriving traditional authorities of all possibility of intervention, Christian teaching tended to turn marriage into a private matter subject to the free choice of the spouses. As the Franciscan Alonso de Molina stressed, 'marriage must be voluntary and not forced, neither done against the will of those marrying nor under the dictates of fear' (1569, fos. 46v, 47). In this statement can be perceived a conception of the individual and of the couple, a logic of society and salvation, which were as foreign to the Amerindian worlds as they were profoundly subversive. The net result was that preparing for marriage no longer concerned anyone except the couple and the representatives of the Church, thus excluding the local authorities and the family group, even immediate relatives.

Thus it comes as no surprise to see how the missionaries stressed the nuclear family to the detriment of its domestic and social extensions. The gulf between the Christian conjugal core and the Indian household could not have been greater. It is true that the Spanish crown's fiscal preoccupations meant that it was initially interested only in the tributary and residential unit, without worrying about the status of the persons in it. However, from the second half of the sixteenth century, by adding widowers and unmarried men to the list of taxpayers, it modified the internal structure of the family group and promoted its break-up. In the long term, the introduction of private property and the practice of making wills, together with the spread of a salaried class, contributed, among other factors, to the emergence of a Western type of individualism and a privatization of social relations parallel to what the Church was advocating.

To its reductionistic one-dimensionalism, exemplifying every Westernizing process, the Christian model added an even more subtle and totalitarian aim: it connected the regulation of alliances to a strict control over the body by means of circulating the notion of a relationship between self and pleasure which the West calls 'sexuality'. For the clergy and those Indians who were supposed to listen to and understand them, 'the third enemy of the soul is our body . . . the body fashioned from earth and mud [which] does not cease from seeking the thousand disgusting manifestations of the flesh and many other kinds of sin which lead straight to hell' (Anunciación, 1575, p. 216).

The Church was thus claiming strict control over desire and pleasure. It was a matter not only of protecting the stability of alliances which had been concluded under its aegis, but of penetrating within the Indian's inmost self by exploring his erotic dreams, his troubled thoughts and solitary practices, of which he would now have to give an account in the confessional. Thus it was, for instance, that masturbation came at the end of the sixteenth and seventeenth centuries to occupy a growing proportion of the preoccupations of the Indians' confessors in Mexico, whereas in the eighteenth century the same faithful were invited to question themselves on the subject of sadism or desiring their mothers. So, in New Spain in the sixteenth century, and to a lesser degree in Peru, the Church launched its project of submitting entire populations to what we might call in Foucault's terms, 'a mechanism of alliance and sexuality'. Once again, Spanish America seems to have formed an experimental site for the modern age in the West.

Means, obstacles and misunderstandings

The means were not adequate for this project. The Church relied at first on the regular clergy, Franciscans, Dominicans, Augustinians, Jesuits and monks of the Order of Mercy. The mendicant orders left for America armed with privileges granted by the Holy See. They enjoyed practically unlimited competence. They married, ended marriages, dispensed civil and criminal justice; being aware of how difficult their enterprise was, they constantly tried to take the specific features of their territory into account; pragmatic and opposed to rigorism, they perfected a system of dispensations which extended their control over what would otherwise have remained clandestine and thus eluded them. But as an Augustinian asked early in the eighteenth century, 'Were the Indians not people for whom all the rules had to allow exceptions?' (Perez, 1713).

Though their numbers were far from adequate, the regular clergy had found efficient collaborators in the persons of those called *criados* or *ladinos de la iglesia*. Educated by Spanish monks, these natives gravitated to the churches and monasteries and came to constitute a vital link between the Church and the communities. From the 1530s, when marriage was being diffused on a massive scale in New Spain, these persons were instructed to inform the clergy about the kinship relations formed before Christianization; some of them (called licensees) even had specialized knowledge of Christian rites and 'the practice of the tree of consanguinity and affinity'. Other Indians hunted out deviants, pursued concubines, prevented clandestine marriages and investigated impediments of consanguinity which had been concealed by couples wishing to marry. Although the *criados* were only a minority faction within the community, they were accessible to the regular orders and played a key role in the implantation of marriage and the Christian family, and in their modes of adaptation.

For all that, this venture at cultural integration came up against innumerable obstacles. First of all there was the numerical weakness of the Spanish clergy compared with the local populations, even after they had been reduced by epidemics. This led to massive campaigns of baptisms and marriages after only the most superficial indoctrination. The chief means of dissemination at the Church's disposal were based on the word, through catechism, sermons, confession and instruction in schools. It is easy to imagine the linguistic and conceptual obstacles which, often without the monks' knowledge, impaired the transmission of notions as exotic to the Indians as Christian marriage, Western kinship, free will, evil and sin. The numbers of catechisms and confessional manuals printed in indigenous languages multiplied, revealing a considerable effort to adapt to local realities, but they were not enough to bridge the conceptual abyss separating the missionaries' humanist Christianity from Amerindian cultures in their infinite diversity. By deliberately putting the accent on 'metaphysical terrorism', the fear of hell and damnation, in order to ensure observation of the new rules, it was assumed that representations and values had been internalized which were in fact dead letters to many Indians.

In addition to these difficulties there were institutional pitfalls. The regular clergy which had taken charge of evangelizing the Indians was progressively replaced by secular clergy in the course of bitter struggles in which the Indians sometimes took sides. These conflicts went hand in hand with those conducted between the religious orders from the start of the colonial period. Also to be taken into account were the constant tensions between the Church and civil authorities, between the clergy as a whole and the colonists who were more concerned with making a quick fortune than saving souls. The diffusion of Christian marriage cannot be considered apart from the dynamism and contradictions of an emergent colonial society, in which opposite aims merged and clashed. Very soon, then, between discourse and reality, the practice of corruption at the very heart of the Church was to modify considerably the application of Christian norms. By 1537, an ecclesiastical dignitary had cleaned out a Mexican province and was returning to the capital with 'his pockets full of fines from Indian concubines which he intended to appropriate' (Garcia Icazbalceta, 1947, vol. III, p. 200), while the Church's Indians

Baptism of a native by a Franciscan missionary, Codex Azcatitlan (sixteenth century). Bibliothèque Nationale, Paris.

were using and abusing their new authority over the faithful they ruled. The rapacity of these agents of control imposed heavy burdens on populations and their customs during the whole of the colonial period and even into the twentieth century.

From incomprehension to manipulation: how the Indians reacted

Under these conditions it is understandable that the Christian pro- gramme had some trouble actually getting established, and that the Indians were often left perplexed or confused by the demands made on them. The diffusion of the Western notion of impediments of kinship provides the clearest instance of this. In the eighteenth century and in one of the most culturally integrated areas of Spanish America, in the heart of Mexico City, the Indians revealed that they were incapable of understanding and implementing the Christian terminology for kin; 'most of the time they do not know how to explain themselves', the author of the famous *Farol Indiano* confided in 1715. Others con- tinued to ignore that they were not bound by the same prohibitions as the Spaniards.

The confusion could sometimes turn into excess. Towards the end of the colonial period, in the late eighteenth century, the Indians were busily multiplying the occasions for forming sponsor groups, and thus increas- ing the numbers of sponsors, by simultaneously extending the prohibi- tions associated with spiritual relationships far beyond the limits stipulated by the Church. The same thing applied to the inflation of the impediments derived from kinship by alliance, and to the ban (still current in Mexico) on unions between widowers and unmarried women, which had never been proscribed by the Church. It is paradoxical that, whether through ignorance, incomprehension or a desire to submit to the same norms as other groups, the Indians sometimes made the system brought to them by the Church even stricter than it actually was.

Nevertheless it does not appear that the Indians' reactions were limited to expressing their natural incomprehension. Even less did these popula- tions passively accept the model wished on them. From the first years of Christianization, they showed widely varying responses. In Mexico and Peru, some aristocratic groups took refuge in veiled refusals and tacit resistance, continuing to practise polygamy and forming alliances which had now become incestuous. Many felt that the licentious behaviour of the great majority of their conquerors authorized their continuance in their own traditions and privileges. Furthermore their rejection of Christian marriage sometimes formed part of a wholesale strategy to

combat political, religious and cultural integration. The decisive importance of the issues was as obvious to the native nobility as to the Spanish
clergy, despite their conflicting motivations.

Concubinage and forms of slavery were tacitly substituted with
varying degrees of discretion for the traditional polygamy. Although they
married in church, the native lords retained a variable number of women
around them as their concubines, whom they passed off as their slaves. In
Peru, somes nobles dismissed the wife given them by the Church in order
to devote themselves to the women of their choice. This practice was all
the easier in that the plebeian classes were still providing their lords with
Indian women who were employed in their service. In northern Mexico,
an Otomi lord who was baptized in 1527 and married in 1532, was still
keeping four to six consorts in 1538. In 1540, in a part of the country
further from the capital, a Totonac lord shared his life with sixteen or
seventeen concubines, even after his Christian marriage. He kept half of
them under his roof while the rest had a house of their own. What is
more, it would be mistaken to consider concubinage as a practice
peculiar to the ancient nobility. In the same period, and in spite of having
passed through the monks' hands, the notables of Mexico also surrounded themselves with concubines, and the censuses reveal that during
the sixteenth century the Indians' houses in the capital included, as well
as the Christian couple, a slave-girl and her child, when there was every
reason to believe that she was the consort and her child the bastard of the
head of the household.

However deviant the practice of concubinage may appear, by becoming the barely concealed obverse of Christian monogamy, it also opened
the way to the decisive cultural integration of behaviour, as though the
Christian model carried its own 'antidotes' within itself. What is more,
some Indians began very early on to apply one of the major rules
promulgated by the Church to their own advantage: the validity of
marriages which had been legitimately concluded before the Spanish
Conquista. They seized on this pretext in order to temper the theoretical
indissolubility of Christian marriage. After all, what criteria or witnesses
could be applied to identify the first wife, who, according to the Church,
had to remain the recently converted Indian's sole legitimate spouse? The
question was particularly relevant in the case of polygamous Indians, and
the monks proceeded to conduct interrogations which called on the wives
to defend their rights of precedence. It is doubtful whether such
proceedings were effective. According to the Franciscan Bernardino de
Sahagun, 'the [formerly polygamous men] lied about the identity of their
first wife and made up stories in order to marry the one to whom they
were most attached' (1965, p. 581).

Other Indians were more daring in that they extended the Christian rule *ad absurdum*: was it not enough to declare that the union blessed by the Church had not been concluded with one's legitimate wife in order to get it dissolved and to marry the partner of one's choice by passing her off as the first spouse? Yesterday's polygamous men and today's monogamous ones knew how to use the sacrament of confession to formulate their pretended avowals and obtain entire satisfaction by keeping up the pressure.

Another strategy, which was just as effective but came later, consisted of playing off one Christian marriage against another. Indians who had been married in church would announce to the priest that they were already married to different partners. Since their marriage bond no longer existed in the eyes of the Church, they would obtain a dissolution and join the woman they claimed was their real wife. This did not inhibit them sometimes from retracting their statements under the pretext of confusion, or admitting the deception in order to force the priest to return their first spouse, who might in the meantime have concluded another alliance, which gave rise to innumerable imbroglios. This practice had reached such proportions in the bishopric of Michoacan in Mexico that one contemporary admitted his total inability to deal with it in 1561: 'I began by putting it into good order, but I have come across so many cases of this kind that I have finally given up' (Cuevas, 1975, p. 253). While some formerly polygamous men were marvellously capable of exploiting the contents of Paul III's bull on the validity of pre-Hispanic marriages, others were able to benefit from the scruples of the regular clergy who, out of principle and their inability to see clearly, relied on the conscience of the faithful. Clandestine marriage was practised until the Council of Trent, and attracted those Indians who were keen to marry several times and in several places, or to keep up their observance of indigenous rites banished by the Church. The civil and religious authorities felt strongly about this but could not forbid the Indians to follow a custom hitherto tolerated by the Church. Had the Franciscan Motolinia not written at the start of the 1540s: 'That which is celebrated clandestinely is also a marriage' (1971, p. 333)?

Others less brazenly restricted themselves to cheating with some of the rules imposed by the Church. Witnesses could be compliant or manipulated, and an impediment of kinship could be concealed in the interests of a marriage which the Church would normally have forbidden. Some people would conceal the fact that they were already married – and this very early on too. Francisco, an Indian living in the neighbourhood of Mexico City, married in church twice, in 1531 and 1535. After four years of living together, he told his first wife that he had remarried, and advised her to do the same, going so far as to offer her his help. It is clear that his second wedding could not have been celebrated without lies on the part of the new spouses, compliance on the part of the witnesses and silence on the part of the Indian community, and indeed without the absence of the control exercised by the Church during the first years of evangelization. Francisco avoided resorting to the Dominicans who administered his parish in order to celebrate his marriages; he chose a second wife who lived in the capital. In short, he infringed the ecclesiastical prohibition knowingly and astutely, thus reviving and engaging in the practice of bigamy as defined by Christianity. During the first period of colonial society, such remarriages can more often than not be explained by ignorance of the rules. In Peru, where such cases also abounded, some Indians invoked their interpretation of Christian rites to justify remarriage: the absence of *velaciones* (the ceremony of the veil covering the two spouses during the wedding mass) was in their eyes sufficient motive for repudiating their partner.

In the same way, during the sixteenth century some Indians concentrated on deflecting the impediments of kinship, even though the Church had adapted them to the conquered populations. They resorted to lies in order to conceal kinship, or to concubinage to avoid going through the Christian rite. They also knew how (by consummating sexual relations) to force the clergy to apply dispensations and to bless unions considered incestuous by the Church. To that extent it was true that pragmatism and a dislike of rigour sometimes induced priests to connive at some of their flock's ploys.

Though it should not be thought a general rule, the basic fact is that camouflaged polygamy, bigamy and concubinage in the European manner, and the manoeuvres adopted for the annulment of marriages reveal the extent to which some Indians, nobles and plebeians, were able to adapt the strict Christian norm to their personal needs and indigenous traditions, and the ingenuity they showed. From the first decades of colonial rule in the sixteenth century, behaviour of this kind unleashed the silent struggle which, from New Spain to Tucuman in Argentina, was ceaselessly conducted by the Indians against ecclesiastical rule by playing on churchmen's ignorance, and often on the complicity of Spaniards who were prepared to conceal illicit situations so long as they kept a docile workforce. In the first half of the eighteenth century, the Indians of the parish of Santa Maria la Redonda in Mexico City armed themselves with stones, sticks and knives to undermine the indigenous authorities' and parish priest's task of drawing up lists of the faithful. While these lists enabled the treasury to levy tribute, they were also the only means available to the Church of effectively supervising families and individuals. Their continued refusal to submit, interspersed with sporadic outbursts, ensured a relative freedom of movement and behaviour to individuals or whole families who moved around from one Mexican parish to another: 'More than 2,500 Indians go to Communion wholly illegally in other parishes, where they get married, bury their dead and pass themselves off as half-castes, when they are Indians . . . according to the parish registers more than 200 of them have been married for many years but refuse to receive the marriage blessing.' By changing their ethnic identity at will and eluding the vigilance of the parish priests who administered them in theory, these Indians could attach themselves to the parish of their choice if it suited them to mingle with the Spaniards in order not to pay tribute, or they could claim Indian status in order to moderate the parish's rights over them.

Whereas some learnt how to exploit the disorder of a society still under construction, in which institutions tailored for western Europe functioned with difficulty, other Indians finally turned Christian norms into occasionally fearful weapons at the very heart of the new forcible relations which were everywhere emerging.

Here their reaction is surprising by its precocity. Take for instance, the 'Church Indians', those precious collaborators who gravitated around the Spanish clergy and whose mission was to police families. It is known that setting up the institution of Christian marriage, with all the control and repression this involved, guaranteed this substantial sector a position of power which it did not fail to abuse. Others, animated by a variety of motives, were involved in denouncing every kind of contravention to the Church institutions. The Iguala affair, about 200 km into southern Mexico, illustrates fairly well the nature of the conflicts which broke out in many regions of Latin America. Don Juan, the local lord, continued to keep five concubines in 1541, while ill-treating the wife he had taken with the blessing of the Church. Instead of suffering in silence, she received the support of the 'Church Indians' and took the case to the tribunal of the Inquisition. She had understood what action she could expect from the ecclesiastical institutions, and denounced the incestuous ties which Don Juan, as an aggravating circumstance, had formed with an aunt and a sister-in-law. Aware of the rights conferred on her by Christian marriage, the lady claimed from then on that she was exempt from performing her conjugal duties. This sort of reaction suggests that the assimilation of new forms of behaviour and remedies often depended on the practical and immediate effect which the Indians expected to obtain from them.

The accusation of polygamy and incest thus often allowed Christianized notables to put local lords in a bad light. It could be complicated by charges of ill treatment, dissipation and clandestine idolatry. Sometimes the *caciques*' own children betrayed their fathers' concubines and brought about intervention by a Church heavily dependent on its indigenous informers. As such behaviour reveals, the introduction of the Christian institution of marriage and the family into the heart of Indian cultures nourished extraordinarily diverse and contradictory attitudes from the first decades of evangelization. As a result, these simply cannot be reduced to the simple alternatives of acceptance and refusal.

A preliminary reckoning

Any attempt to assess the achievement of the first century of colonial domination would be difficult. This is partly due to our complex reactions as well as to the absence of quantitative data. We know that Christian marriage at the end of the sixteenth century had become a reality in Peru and Mexico. By 1540, the Franciscan Motolinia could claim of the Indians of Mexico that 'almost all of them lived within the law of marriage' (1971, p. 158). Polygamy was being progressively eliminated, often being replaced by concubinage, as we have seen. It is possible that the prohibited degrees of kinship imposed by Christianity restricted certain endogamic tendencies, in particular by proscribing marriage to a sister or sister-in-law. Our lack of information about pre-Hispanic practices and the *de facto* lack of rigour accepted by the Church prevent us from establishing the overall incidence of Christian impediments. Similarly, we know very little about the evolution of filiation. For instance, in the Andean region, the rule of parallel filiation persisted (which requires that women inherit their name and property through the matrilinear line and men through the patrilinear line). By the end of the eighteenth century such customs had largely been eroded by the agnatic system of transmission which contributed to reinforcing patronyms and the father's role. However this view must be qualified in proportion to the abundance of illegitimate unions and to the fact that, in rural regions, loss of virginity was not considered ignominious.

It would anyway be appropriate to inquire into the vicissitudes undergone by the household. Presumably prohibiting polygamy and restricting the range of possible alliances – by eliminating the widows of brothers, nieces and so on – combined to limit the dimensions of the household. Had the Church not forced the wives of polygamous men, their 'incestuous' consorts, to leave their homes with their children? There are some indications that, shortly after the Conquista, many houses in Mexico City contained just one person or only blood relatives, and it is not impossible that the rules of Christian marriage had something to do with this. However, other factors had immense influence on the fate of the household, notably the massacres associated with the Conquista, population displacement and successive epidemics. Nevertheless, by the second half of the sixteenth century, what we see in Mexico City is the return, not the disappearance, of crowded households.

We must be just as careful in our analysis of the evolution of relations and family roles in the indigenous population. It seems obvious that the abolition of plural unions eliminated the status of the co-spouse, who was reduced to the illicit and depreciated rank of the Spanish concubine or *manceba*. The death knell of feminine sociability within the heart of the family space (called *cihuacalli* by the Nahua) had sounded, to be succeeded by the emergence of the Christian wife who, as we have seen, was more exclusive and sometimes determinedly monogamous.

It is also possible that indissoluble monogamy contributed to intensifying the bond between mother and child by conferring on it a unique and exclusive dimension which it may not have possessed before. This would have contained the embryo of a gradual Westernization of the personality, linked to the reinforcement of Oedipal triangulation and the crystallization of affective relations within the heart of the conjugal space which the Church considered so important: father, mother and their children.

Once polygamy had been abolished, the effect could only have been to increase the distance between the mother and the only substitutes for her now considered legitimate, in this case step-mothers, with all the unfavourable connotations the term can involve in the West. One should add that the prohibition of remarriage with a sister-in-law undoubtedly contributed to the affective dislocation caused by a second marriage by preventing the close and familiar figure of an aunt from succeeding a dead mother.

Examining the transformations of the female condition is an equally tentative process. The bishop of Mexico, Juan de Zumarraga, opened schools in 1537 with the purpose of giving young Indian girls a Christian and Western education in order to bring them up to be wives for Indians educated by monks. The experiment failed: the Indians, even the most culturally integrated, refused to unite with these women because, as they claimed, 'they learnt how to do nothing, they took little trouble over their husbands, they did not want to serve them in conformity with their custom which requires that they should support their husbands' (Garcia Icazbalceta, 1947, vol. IV, p. 178). One should not disregard the far greater impact made by those women who lived in concubinage with Spaniards and who abruptly cut the ties uniting them with their community and its rules. This had a direct impact on the process of cultural integration and the creation of the half-caste state, and in the long run it had an impact on the transfer of landed property into the hands of Spaniards and even half-castes. Thus it was that north of the Equator, those Indian women married to Spaniards and half-castes purchased lands from other Indians and transmitted them to their descendants. They played a notable role in that their ethnic origins gave them access to lands reserved for indigenous peoples, which the colonial system of succession allowed them to leave to descendants who were not Indians.

The evolution of the status of wives cannot be dissociated from the growing discrimination between legitimate children and bastards, which was introduced by Christianity. The children of polygamous and 'incestuous' couples who had been removed from their paternal homes by zealous monks were the first of those abandoned creatures who constituted one of the running sores of colonial society and a reservoir of cheap labour for the Spaniards.

On a different level, whereas the ancient practice of polygamy and divorce had authorized transient kinship ties, the Catholic religion codified relations of alliance, and prohibited marriage between relations in the first and second degrees. These prohibitions extended to spiritual parents, notably godparents and parents-in-law. The institution of godparents by the Church was undoubtedly welcomed in Mexico and Peru because of its formal similarities with pre-Hispanic customs. Nevertheless, the spiritual kinship which was implanted in the sixteenth century took the form of a relationship which basically united godparent and godchild, and only later did the significant relationship shift to that between the sponsors who thus constituted the *compadrazgo* (see below). We should be equally cautious about giving undue importance to the diffusion of Christian names through the medium of baptism in the heart of the indigenous populations: in the sixteenth century Indians frequently forgot or failed to use the names given them by the Church and colonial administration.

Indigenous inheritance

The Christian model defined forms of behaviour and laid down prohibitions, duties and roles. However it was impossible for it to control the reality of everyday experience. Furthermore, by turning marriage into the concern of the couple and the Church, so that it was no longer an alliance between groups and families, it turned too much against the family unit, kinship relations and the community, as well as minimizing the constant interaction between all three.

The means available to the Church were too weak to rob the Indian community of the control it exercised over the family group and the conclusion of unions. During the whole of the sixteenth century, the traditional authorities continued to intervene in these domains, and although their involvement was subsequently tempered by the vicissitudes experienced by the Indian ruling groups, their progressive renewal or definitive weakening, it is nevertheless the case that in the eighteenth century the community applied itself to supervising marriages very closely and to transmitting property so as to retain territorial integrity.

In the Andes during the sixteenth century, the *caciques* and notables (*principales*) frequently prevented widows and unmarried women from marrying commoners (*hatunrunas*) in order to keep their domestic and sexual services. The same thing applied in Mexico: the natives were obliged to present victuals and gifts to the notables in their quarter (*barrio*) in order to obtain their permission to marry before they resorted to the good offices of the elders (numbering two or three per *barrio*) who acted as marriage-brokers and collected the commodities intended for the notables. Unfortunately we do not know about the principles governing the local authorities' decisions and directing alliances among the population. Generally speaking, as the Mexican provincial councils of 1555 and 1585 testify, *caciques* and *principales* retained considerable influence in the whole business. We can glean some idea of how widely diffused it was from the confessional manuals which attempted to extirpate these practices. It is known that for a long time indigenous governors did not hesitate to interrupt proceedings in the Catholic ceremony by answering instead of the spouses, a practice which the Church had willy-nilly to tolerate if it was not openly repudiated by the couple.

Around the 1560s, in areas as open to Spanish influence as Mexico City and nearby Texcoco, the marriage-brokers (*tecihuatlanque*) retained a pre-eminent role although we do not know for sure what the links uniting them to the *barrio* authorities were. They were literally 'wife-seekers' who acted as intermediaries between two families by taking on the task of asking in the suitor's name for his intended. It is probable that in places their role considerably exceeded this function and that they acted as interpreters for the community as much as messengers for families. In a wholly different register, that of the repression of deviant behaviour, there were regions where the indigenous authorities were impervious to Christian tolerance and did not abandon the strictness with which they had traditionally pursued concubines and adulterous women. This was the case, among others, in the province of Oaxaca around 1558, where the Indian *alguaciles* and *fiscales* punished transgressors so severely that the Church had to moderate their brutality and report it to the Crown.

During the whole colonial period parents continued to determine the selection of a spouse for their child, and often choose the young couple's dwelling too. They too broke in on the Christian rite when they replied in the place of the engaged couple, as was still current practice in the Mexican countryside in the eighteenth century.

Continuity could be seen just as much in the vital domain of the customs surrounding the conclusion of an alliance and the economics of the gift marking it. Half a century after the Conquista, there could be no question of sealing an alliance without the initial presentation of a gift from the suitor to the parents of his future spouse. The Mexican Council of 1585 was sufficiently exercised by this to issue a stern condemnation of what it considered to be very close to a sort of bride price. The gesture implied a symbol of exchange and consummation which was wholly pre-Hispanic and the clergy was entitled to view it as the manifestation of a 'subtle idolatry' (Duran, 1967, vol. I, p. 78). The practice survived into the eighteenth century in Mexico City in an attenuated form: 'The elders, who are called *huehuechiuque*, meaning factors or marriage-brokers, visit the father of the engaged girl with a dish of cakes, biscuits and wine which is offered to all the relatives of the engaged girl who have been invited' (Perez, 1713, p. 161).

In the same period, practices in the countryside compelled the future son-in-law to do far more: he had to promise to enter the service of his parents-in-law for a predetermined time: 'The husband's contribution was reduced to his strength as a labourer' (ibid., p. 158). During the engaged man's term of service, which the Nahua called *montequitl*, and which contributed a valuable addition to the family unit's workforce, premarital cohabitation was frequent and even obligatory, as it enabled the young man to establish that his fiancée was a virgin, contrary to Christian rules. If this did not happen during the *montequitl*, then the young people would get to know each other during the period of matrimonial stocktaking without the slightest objection on the part of her parents. In this, apart from indifference to the laws of the Church, can be seen a survival of the ancient trial marriages, prior to the Spanish Conquista, which could only result in an alliance in due form.

Certain aspects of the marriage ritual proper also resisted the onslaught of Christian forms by going underground or, more generally, by adapting and accommodating to them. Once again, the Mexican valley towns provide the first instance of this, in that from the second half of the sixteenth century, syncretic practices had been widely diffused in which old and new were juxtaposed. At this date, the conclusion of a

Christian marriage depended, as we have seen, on the outcome of a marriage proposal *al modo antiguo*: after the Church ceremony, an indigenous celebration would take place 'at the home of the men and women elders' who were probably the regular marriage-brokers. Indian customs would be adhered to at this, and the ritual would finish at the young husband's house, to which his bride was brought. From then on, local tradition, in terms of chronological and spatial continuity, was adapted to the Catholic rite. This is how, for instance, the Catholic rite of the veil, *velaciones*, preceded the native gesture which consisted of tying the young man's cape to the girl's *huipil*, or blouse. In its continuing retention of Indian features and the way it was bounded by traditional practices, the sacrament of marriage followed the destiny of the great majority of Amerindian cultures which had, to different extents and various rhythms, been swept up by the flood of cultural integration, syncretism and reinterpretation.

Native blemishes and logic

If it is true that the Spanish Conquista and evangelization brought about the collapse of the authority enjoyed by the native ruling groups within the community, it is less certain that there was any similar impact on a diffuse collection of beliefs which were not encumbered by spectacular and complex rituals or by explicit references to ancient mythologies, but which continued, during the whole colonial period and sometimes beyond, to play a part in the mechanisms regulating sexual and family behaviour.

Whereas the Church submitted the conclusion of alliances to the complex play of canonical impediments, Indian cultures brought their attention to bear on a wholly different domain, one so foreign to Christian categories that the monks either neglected it or failed to recognize its extent. In Mexico, without ignoring the prohibition of incest, though restricting its range, the Indians were concerned about the compatibility or incompatibility of the future spouses' signs. When the two signs coincided, it was thought that they would devour one another, and an alliance would be postponed or cancelled. The people who examined the young couple's signs were experts in ritual calendars, and their intervention played a part in orientating the conclusion of alliances within the community. Similarly, in the Andes soothsayers were consulted before the naming of a child or celebration of a marriage.

Tracing the evolution of defence and control mechanisms linked to the domain of blemishes is a trickier business. However, we can put forward some hypotheses based on the Nahua countryside during the first half of the seventeenth century. The Indians judged adultery as the origin of a 'filthy evil' (*tlazolmiquiliztli*) which contaminated the whole family circle and disorganized the life of the family group and the collective body: the spouse would sicken, struck by the evil *chahuacocoliztli*, domestic animals would perish, the crops would spoil, new-born babies would waste away and food would not cook. Sometimes the mere expression of sexual desire was enough to contaminate the space surrounding the one who had felt it, and all those who crossed it were struck by the evil *netepalhuiliztli*. Thus the signs of death revealed the presence of a deviant to his watchful family circle, although he himself would not necessarily be struck down by bad luck. On the other hand, innocent third parties could pay with their lives for the consequences of transgression, as though it were necessary in this way to unleash or intensify the collective reprobation of those producing the evil forces. The more intangible the deviance, as in the case of sexual desire, the more blind and unpredictable were its repercussions, as if the community had tried to multiply its defences in a situation which could easily elude its control and sanction.

Daily life, too, never ceased to brim over with signs revealing some transgression, which would be hastily interpreted: if mice made a hole in a basket or a calabash, or gnawed its rim, it was a sign of concubinage; if they chewed holes in the man's braids or his cape, in the woman's skirt or blouse, it meant that there was adultery in the home. This was one of many domains which the Church refused to interpret for the Indian populations, who never stopped deciphering their environment in order to avert or to interpret bad luck under all its aspects.

Similarly, the Indians went on resorting to rites capable of wiping out the repercussions of blemishes, such as the purification baths which were administered to the sick. However, we should avoid too static a view of all this. We shall see how insistent most of the evidence is about wiping out the consequences of blemish rather than accusing and punishing the deviant person; they even describe practices which do not fit very well with what we think we know about pre-Hispanic norms: there is, for instance, the Nahua Indian in the seventeenth century who had fallen ill from his wife's sexual excesses and was urged to react to the evil by committing similar acts. It is not impossible that, once deprived of their traditional extensions (corporal punishment and ritual avowals), beliefs associated with blemish were strongly influenced by erotic magic practices. Given that they too had been relegated to the underground, domains which had once run parallel were now intermingled, and the same Indian healers now read the signs, healed or triggered off illnesses, and provoked or contained desires. Thus there would have been a tendency to substitute a concern to remove impurities for the desire to impose social sanctions on the deviant. It may be supposed that the Andes also experienced similar drifts towards erotic magic at the same time as pre-Hispanic institutions and repressions were growing weaker and falling into disuse. Men and women resorted to sorcerers to attract their partners, get rid of rivals, protect themselves with feather amulets called *huacanquis,* induce abortion or render an adversary sterile. The whole of Amerindia suffered a culture shock as a result of the Spanish Conquista, which, while it failed to make a *tabula rasa* of the past, did have sufficient impact on certain indigenous cultures to allow erotic witchcraft to prevail over other forms of social logic.

Complex systems of belief and practice continued to structure the successive stages of reproduction. The Indian midwife acted as the depository of this knowledge and occupied a crucial position which continued to form an important transmitter of indigenous culture. Among the Nahua in Mexico, she imposed sexual abstinence on couples after the third month of pregnancy to prevent sperm from accumulating in the womb and blemishing the baby, causing dangerous complications at birth. The future mother was expressly forbidden to feel excessive agitation and violent emotional reactions; certain bodily practices and foods were banned. On the other hand, she was allowed to satisfy her slightest wishes for fear of subjecting her child to a harmful sense of frustration. Surrounded by the midwife's advice and this network of prohibitions and cautions, the woman was nonetheless responsible for her delivery, which was often dramatic. In the same way, children's growth was the object of a whole web of precautions and rituals which the Church had the utmost trouble in extirpating: for instance, the Cuzco Indians at the end of the sixteenth century, retained the practice of piercing their children's ears when they reached the age of fourteen, and of celebrating their daughters' first menstruation.

In Mexico, as in Peru, the family space managed to a great extent to avoid being penetrated by Christianity. Even though it was very quickly enriched by pious images, which mingled with lineage idols, statuettes and dried plants in the family shrine, the home continued to be a universe of signs waiting to be deciphered, by which one could read the approach of danger or the onset of death from animal noises or incursions. Did not the owl's hooting presage the end of him who heard it, or of his son? Beams splitting and millstones cracking were the harbingers of disaster or death for those living under the same roof. Hearthstones, hearth ashes and warmth were clues suggesting which decisions to take and which forms of behaviour to avoid. Ways of cooking and consuming food took on precise meanings which could implicate the reproduction of the group and its composition, and even its choice of alliances. A *tamal* which stuck would foretell the perils of a birth; a creased *tortilla* presaged the return of a husband; a young girl who ate standing up ran the risk of contracting a distant and unhappy union. Needless to say, these collections of beliefs testified to the extent to which conceptions about the family group, family roles, age groups and sexual distinctions were rooted in the smallest actions of daily life, on which in the final analysis the Church had very little grasp. It is here that one can best measure the gulf separating a Christian model based on free will from the indigenous logic relating individuals to responsibility and misfortune that was based on radically different social organizations and relations to reality.

Half-caste societies: from the unforeseen to improvisation

Founded on the principle of a strict division between the 'republic of the Spaniards' and the 'republic of the Indians', the Spanish crown's cherished project for a colonial society had not envisaged first the appearance and then the proliferation of mixed-blood populations. The overwhelming majority of the first Spanish immigrants was male;

A Hispano-Mexican couple with their mulatto child. Anonymous painting on copper, part of a series on half-caste life, eighteenth century. Museo de America, Madrid.

soldiers, clerics, traders and all types of adventurers. The overwhelming majority of these also brought with them family and sexual practices which were notably distant from the model conceived by the Church – this must not be forgotten – and what the American space provided above all was incomparable freedom of movement and behaviour which they were quick to exploit. Hence those thousands of unions, almost all of them illegitimate, with Indian women, from which were born half-caste children who, if fortune smiled on them, merged into their Spanish or Indian groups, unless they went to make up the first generation of that intermediate unclassifiable sector of half-castes.

The process was complicated by the arrival of tens of thousands of black slaves who mingled with whites, Indians and half-castes in a dynamic process which the colonial state did not manage to halt, or even slow down. The Spanish authorities tried to enclose the mixed population within a system of detailed rules linked to degree of pigmentation, but these proved totally unable to stabilize a fluid reality in perpetual motion. By the seventeenth century this biological and cultural mixing had become one of the major dynamic elements of colonial society over the whole American continent. It cannot be dissociated from the mechanisms of social rise and decline which enabled the half-castes and mulattos to join the Spaniards, or which absorbed the poor whites into these populations. Without denying the strength of racial prejudices which were reinforced in the course of the eighteenth century, it is a fact that individuals found it relatively easy to exchange their racial label for a more esteemed one if fortune smiled on them. It is self-evident that the institution of the family, marriage and particularly the broad gamut of illegitimate relationships occupied a central position in these fundamental complex processes which went to make Latin America.

Promiscuity, concubinage and forms of bigamy

The colonial context, with all its violence, uprooting and constant improvisation, put an indelible mark on whole patterns of behaviour. Whites cut off from Spain and black victims of the slave trade maintained relations in which strength and the imbalance of the sexes – in sixteenth-century Peru the proportion was six or seven Spanish men to one Spanish woman – were far more important than the laws of Christianity. Hence the incommensurable extent of rape, concubinage and prostitution. Indian women who had been picked up in the streets or the countryside and employed as domestics, later followed by black slaves and mulattos, were used by most Spaniards for easy and immediate gratification. This was the general rule in the aftermath of the Conquista, but these practices were maintained, albeit in attenuated form, during the whole colonial period and beyond.

For half-castes, blacks and Spaniards in search of a more stable bond, concubinage was a state equivalent to marriage but less rigid. It involved sharing 'bed and board', to use the phrase of the time. The man benefited from his consort's domestic services and paid the household expenses. Many took to concubinage out of poverty, being unable to meet the demands of the Church before it would celebrate a marriage. Some found it a convenient way of tackling everyday life when they did not own a slave or a servant. Black or half-caste women were sometimes able to use this as a means of linking up with a man of superior birth, sometimes a Spaniard, with whom marriage would have been impossible. Whatever the motives behind it, concubinage and all that it implied in terms of shared experience and pleasure as well as the routines of daily life, constituted a powerful vector for cultural integration.

However, although some cohabitants might have chosen this path in order to avoid concluding an alliance in proper form, others had to put up with it because they were already married. This was not always the case, because bigamy itself offered a means of escape which profoundly marked family and matrimonial behaviour in the Spanish New World. From the first decades of the Conquista, the Indians had discovered in it a means of adapting the strict Christian norm to deep-rooted practices of polygamy and repudiation. Among the Indians bigamy was nonetheless confined to those who had cut themselves off from their original community and disappeared into the anonymity of the towns or mining centres. The supervision exercised by family circle and village limited the emergence of native bigamy. The same did not apply to the half-caste and Spanish world. As solitary immigrants with little wish to encumber themselves with the wives they had left behind in their distant homeland many Spaniards were keen, once they had established themselves in America, to found a legitimate family the better to integrate themselves in colonial society. Bigamy met, as did concubinage, the demands of constant moving, but it also allowed people to use marriage as a means of acceding to a higher and more respected social position.

Among the half-castes and the poorest sections of colonial society, blacks, mulattos and poor whites, bigamy featured constantly in oft-repeated patterns of wrongdoing and destitution. A man's first marriage might have been concluded under social and religious pressure, leading to a stormy conjugal life, unbearable living conditions and the husband's eventual flight. He might be willing to travel great distances in order to lose himself in the crowds of Mexico City, Puebla or Lima, where he might form a liaison with another woman, and then, after months and sometimes years of concubinage, contract a new marriage which would sometimes be disrupted by the reappearance of his abandoned wife or a peremptory summons before the Inquisition. Among half-castes, the sources of bigamy could include their precarious existence, uprooting and mobility, delinquency and flight from justice; there was also the desire to find a young partner and the many strategies for social insertion. Black slaves and mulattos, on the other hand, deserted to escape servitude, reaching urban centres where they could remake their lives by changing identity and wife. Although it destroyed the indissoluble nature of marriage, the practice of bigamy witnessed to the importance attached by colonial society to the marriage sacrament even when it caused the guilty to risk the severity of the Inquisition.

Bigamy was also a specifically 'American' and colonial crime in that it took advantage of the immense space, the thin distribution of the administrative and ecclesiastical presence and the fluidity of major sectors of population which were prompt to move to the new areas of development, the mines, towns and advancing frontiers at the extremities of the empire. One effect of bigamy on families was, in part at least, responsible for the proliferation of fatherless children and families with no head, in which the abandoned mother was forced to live alone and more often than not was driven into concubinage. It reveals, finally, an astonishing faculty for abrupt change and redeployment on a personal level in those people who changed identity, invented families, genealogies and roots for themselves, and concealed their ethnic and social origins the better to elude control by the Church and perhaps to better their condition.

Prostitutes and erotic magic

In a society where concubinage abounded, where bigamy was widespread and where furtive contacts with Indian women, half-castes, African slave-girls and mulattos were commonplace, it is clear that prostitution began as an activity limited to Europeans. Nevertheless it flourished in sixteenth-century Lima and Potosi. By the end of the century, Mexico City numbered no fewer than one prostitute for every ten potential Spanish clients, a remarkable number which can only be explained when one considers that Spanish women, whether orphans, widows or abandoned wives, had no choice of livelihood. The minor professions, retail trade in the markets and domestic service, were naturally reserved for slaves, Indian and half-caste women. Such women, however, would not have found it easy to sell their bodies, even when they were extremely attractive, as was the case with mulatto women, because they were objects of no value. Spanish women, on the other hand, belonged, even if only marginally, to the conquerors' world, and they offered more than their bodies for sale: they offered a way of life, the chance to rediscover in the company of a European woman ways of being and feeling which had once been familiar; the dual pleasure of wiping out for a brief moment all cultural distance and of touching a white woman's more exclusive body.

Clients, prostitutes and procurers belonged within the middle sphere of artisans, lower-ranking officials and small-time traders, all of whom were of European origin in the sixteenth century. This specific aspect of colonial life, which did not exclude the existence of high-class courtesans whose luxurious lifestyles were the talk of the town, seems to have been attenuated in the eighteenth century with the development of urban centres, population growth and the transformations taking place within colonial society, which combined to drive prostitutes onto the streets. There they immediately became a favourite object of repression as the state gradually abandoned its attitude of the previous two centuries. Previously it had taken a semi-tolerant attitude. With a network of brothels under municipal control, it had put greater emphasis on punishing procurers and clients than the women themselves. The end of the Spanish era, however, took prostitution out of its medieval context and away from its European recruits and drove it into 'modernity'.

Concubinage, bigamy and prostitution constituted varying alternatives to Christian monogamy. They cannot be dissociated from a world of parallel practices which claimed to have an effect on sexual desire: this was a world of erotic magical practices which combined recipes from Africa, Europe and America and even the Philippines. At the same time as acting as a corrective to the rigours of religious rule, these practices helped transcend social and ethnic barriers by weaving networks which linked the native supplier to the Spanish consumer, with the mulatto slave acting as intermediary. They softened the effects of sexual and racial inequity by creating a guilty complicity between the Spanish mistress, her black servant and the Indian witch against an errant lover or a jealous husband. In the secret, unforeseen and illicit contacts of erotic magic all sorts of cultural and social dynamics, in which muffled subversion rubbed shoulders with exotic illusion, were started up, without which the evolution of colonial society into a half-caste world cannot be explained.

Black itineraries

The attitudes of black groups to marriage and the Christian family confirmed the crucial importance of the issue in their struggle for survival and emancipation. Taken from their African homes, parted for ever from their families and cultures – and this often before they were even deported to the New World – the blacks had suffered all the agonies of being uprooted. Some managed to reconstitute more or less autonomous societies hidden away in corners of the tropical world where they had escaped from the whites. Most of them, however, remained condemned to promiscuity and the arbitrary will of their masters. Furtive enjoyment, concubinage and sometime bigamy were their lot. However, it would be mistaken to see in all this a mass of people resigned to their fate: from the first decades of colonization some blacks had been aware of the advantages they could draw from the white man's laws and sought to form alliances, both legitimate and illegitimate, with Indian women who, for their part, were free. They knew that Spanish legislation would guarantee the freedom of their progeny. This practice acquired such proportions that the viceroy in Mexico asked the Holy See, in a fruitless bid, to prohibit unions between Indian women and slaves. There could not have been a more flagrant contradiction between the Christian rule and the colonists' interests. Similar behaviour can be discerned among African slave-girls who secured freedom for their children by their Spanish lovers; here too, concubinage and, in exceptional cases, marriage could be used to remove descendants from the world of slavery.

In the sixteenth and seventeenth centuries other blacks used the principle of conjugal cohabitation exalted by Christian marriage to escape excessively demanding owners and inhuman working conditions, and to live with their free wives. Obviously these were mostly from the urban centres who were able to establish contacts outside their owner's house, and used them to penetrate the interplay of colonial institutions and to assimilate Christian values in order to draw the greatest advantage from them. They knew that when its principles were held in ridicule, the Church could be induced to put pressure on their owners and to ensure a minimum autonomy for their slaves. Once again the logic of the institution coincided with the interests of the dominated parties.

Two major tendencies appear to have marked profoundly the behaviour of blacks and mulattos in Mexico and colonial Peru. First, very many of them preferred gaining freedom for themselves or their descendants to maintaining their African identity, which only served to immerse them more deeply in slavery. Concubinage and marriage with half-castes, natives or even poor whites opened a means of quickly entering colonial society and ridding themselves of their African and servile taint. Furthermore the institution of the family advocated by the Church helped them to reconstitute stable family relationships. It is revealing that first- or second-generation negroes spent their lives in servitude without any memory of family; with no brothers or sisters, and most especially no mothers, such people had almost no background at all. Two or three generations on – and this is the case by the beginning of the eighteenth century – their descendants' memory was filled with dozens of names, the names of blood relatives and negro, mulatto, half-caste and sometimes Indian in-laws. This was how they recreated a solid family circle on the basis of the matrimonial and family institutions imposed by the Church. Alongside this process of integration, they were putting down local roots, diversifying their range of activities and implementing discreet 'whitening' strategies designed to allow them, by choosing consorts paler than themselves, to melt into the half-caste world and draw closer to Creole society. All means to this end were valid in the eighteenth century, even falsifying parish records to transform dark-skinned persons of doubtful origin into Spaniards and half-castes. Unlike Brazil, which developed on very distinct ethnic foundations, New Spain and Peru absorbed into their half-caste masses the descendants of slaves who grasped at Christian marriage and its variants as the means of integrating themselves socially and dissipating their specific ethnic origin.

The homosexual fringe

Unlike historians and anthropologists who have reached an unlikely consensus on the subject, we cannot ignore those people whose sexual inclinations led them to live on the margins of normality, whether they were Christian, Spanish or indigenous. As adepts of the 'abominable sin', *pecado nefando*, called sodomites by colonial society and homosexuals in ours, they constituted a minority group from the late sixteenth century, but one coherent enough to allow the authorities to discern in it the spectre of 'conspiracy' and 'epidemic contamination', thereby lumping together Jews, negroes, idolaters and sorcerers. Beneath the phantasms entertained by the Spanish civil and ecclesiastical authorities and the exceptionally laconic references in the sources, a specifically urban form of sociability emerges, one in which neither age nor colour of skin nor social class constituted real barriers. It was a world in which half-castes, mulattos, Indians, Portuguese, Spaniards, students, butchers, tailors, cobblers, hairdressers, servants, slaves, clerics and persons of rank – whose anonymity the sources do their best to preserve – all rubbed shoulders in accordance with their inclinations, forming all sorts of transient relationships. This mingling of bodies provided an unparalleled melting-pot for cultural integration, independently of any institution and away from the collective gaze. It was a world which was constantly being unmade and reformed according to the dictates of occasional chance meetings on the edges of towns, in brothels and the secrecy of the *temascales*, the native steam baths which proliferated in urban agglomerations, or in taverns frequented by transvestites touting for tipsy customers. These shifting and clandestine networks, whose links were woven meeting by meeting, were at the mercy of the slightest denunciation. Repression had already been merciless in some pre-Hispanic cultures, and it came down heavily on deviants caught *in flagrante* or confessing to the act of sodomy. This crime was punished with death until the mid-eighteenth century, being considered by the dominant ideology an attack on nature, society and the king. In 1658, in Mexico City alone, the civil law courts condemned as many as fourteen homosexuals to be burnt to death, and never a year passed without one sodomite being sent to the scaffold.

It is nevertheless a fact that this homosexual society, going by the little we know, evinced in many respects a surprising conformity, as if, despite its clandestine and detested marginal nature, it could not escape the

A Hispano-Mexican family. Anonymous painting on copper, part of a series on half-caste life, eighteenth century. Museo de America, Madrid.

propagation of dominant models and forms of behaviour. The language of love and relations between lovers were copied precisely from heterosexual liaisons; here too, possessiveness, infidelity and jealousy degenerated very commonly into violence. Some might try to reproduce the gestures and gait of Creole or half-caste women. Others might adopt suggestive names like 'chestnut horse' or 'king of France', redolent of machismo; others evoked the memory of loose women as *'la Conchita'* or *'la Zangarriana'*. Homosexual and heterosexual prostitution were closely associated, but without impinging on each other. Finally, religiosity and piety were far from absent from this condemned world. A patron saint's feast day would generally provide an occasion when sodomites would hold secret parties at which they could dance and embrace away from prying eyes.

As well as its conformist tone, this circle, which was deemed totally subversive by the authorities and public opinion, possessed a further feature which has survived to our day: the fragility of a group structured on immediate physical relations, stripped of all social and material foundation and often betrayed by its own members. Since colonial times, these features have put limits on an interclass and interethnic form of sociability artificially sustained by the threat of repression and as easily dissolved by it. This situation comes fairly close to that prevailing in many Latin American countries today despite the tentative introduction of lifestyles imported from New York and California.

We should stress, finally, that the forms and the intensity of the abjection inflicted on this heterogeneous sector cannot be dissociated from the genesis of Latin American *machismo*. Beneath the umbrella of condemnation without appeal by the official discourse which vilified the homosexual act and hunted down sodomists, all sorts of collective attitudes were enlisted and directed even more strongly against effeminate men, *mariquitas* with their tawdry jewellery, turning transvestites into the exuberant archetype, indispensable and ridiculed, of the homosexual. Other forms of homosexuality, however, were less easily spotted and remained largely ignored, for instance those who were forced into marriage and chose to lead double lives at the price of occasional hysterical outbursts which, in the seventeenth century, took the form of blasphemous acts.

The colonial inheritance

Colonial society was a shifting world of disorder and improvisation in which conflicting interests and aims crossed, sometimes cancelling each other out, and divided between *laissez-faire* attitudes, a taste for making quick fortunes and the bitter struggle for individual and collective survival. Its originality lay in the way it juxtaposed the most diverse forms of family life. Some were inspired more or less by the Christian norm, there were the groups of unmarried men newly arrived from Spain, the numerous opulent households of rich Creoles and the varyingly chaotic unions which proliferated in the subcultures of poverty and fringe existence, in a world of vagabondage and street life, of promiscuity in *temascales* and *obrajes* – workshops in which men, women and young children lurked – and of liberties taken in taverns where couples parted and prostitution flourished amid general drunkenness.

During the second half of the eighteenth century, without reaching these extremes of abandonment and cultural dislocation, a family form seems to have taken shape in the better-integrated areas and levels of society. Although it was not yet the dominant form, it seems to us that it should be credited with anticipating future developments. The family unit tended to dwindle to the couple and their children, seeking, with some difficulty, to emancipate themselves from relatives, even at the risk of provoking continuing conflict and material hardship, for instance when a young couple was driven to leave home, and hence to a life on the streets. The woman's position was not an enviable one: abused and deflowered before marriage, as an unmarried deserted mother, a seduced and pregnant widow, a wife raped by her neighbour, the victim of local gossip, or simply deceived by her husband, she could count on no more than the support of her priest and the Church while her community, the civil authorities and often her kin proved indifferent to her fate. Needless to say, the Church thereby became deeply rooted within the female population, while ensuring that it came under its vigilant supervision. It is true that some women did dare to rise against their husbands and take over the management of their family group. These, however, seem to have been in the minority. The exceptional incidence of violence within marriage – meaning battered wives – did not fail to strike all observers and to fill legal archives.

Surprisingly enough, very little about these indigenous and half-caste forms of behaviour could be called exotic. The fact is that, whether directly or indirectly, they revealed the extent to which the Christian conjugal model and the seeds of conflict contained within it had been internalized, while reflecting the progressive erosion of community checks and solidarities as well as of the restraints imposed by the extended family. This was a process which took place principally in the towns and their neighbourhood. On the other hand, conjugal violence in the countryside probably formed the counterpoint to a relatively peaceable sociability at community level, as if the family group, and the couple even more so, functioned as outlets for individual aggression and thus ensured the cohesion of the whole community against aggression from the outside world. The colonial era – whose extraordinary complexity has been greatly simplified here – was in every respect crucial in establishing a unique model and in the multiplicity of the adjustments and interpretations to which it constantly gave rise in the course of three centuries.

The second onslaught of Westernization: secularization

From the second half of the eighteenth century a second wave of cultural integration slowly gathered strength, that of a progressive secularization of power which replaced the evangelizing aims of the Renaissance and Baroque ages with the language of civilization and productivity. This process made its appearance under the enlightened despotism of the Spanish Bourbons, and had won over the towns and elites in the guise of nineteenth-century liberalism before acquiring added impact from industrialization, the exodus from the countryside and the introduction of the consumer society.

The first phase of this secularization process was the dwindling influence of the Church. Under the aegis of the Enlightenment, the Spanish crown had already inaugurated measures limiting the Church's competence by reducing its privileges, ecclesiastical immunity for instance, expelling the Jesuits (1767), extending (this is an important point) the responsibilities of the state in family and matrimonial matters at the expense of ecclesiastical tribunals. The priest's image was diminished by all this, as was the institutional grip which the Church had maintained over families and couples.

Independence, which came a few decades later, disrupted the Church's relations with the new states because, once freed from the *patronato* imposed on it by the Spanish crown since the sixteenth century, it became a power independent of the state, and had either to coexist and come to terms with it or struggle against it. This meant that the Church ceased to identify fully with society, as it had done during the three centuries of colonial rule.

While the Church did not, for all that, cease to represent a major social, cultural and ideological force, it lost much of its economic basis. The introduction of civil weddings with no ecclesiastical sanction and the declared intention of liberals to control education had the effect of stressing an evolution which, with hindsight, appears irreversible, but which should not conceal the authority which Catholicism retained. In

Mexico, the struggles between Church and state reached an exceptional level of violence in the nineteenth century and continued until the 1920s with the *Cristeros'* revolt and the bloody repression inflicted on them. The clergy continued in spite of all this to be supported by large sectors of the population. Furthermore the Church seems to have managed to use the last decades of the nineteenth century to strengthen its roots in the countryside in opposition to a liberalism essentially urban in its ideology and preoccupations. The anticlericalism of the nineteenth century was only put into effect by a minority, albeit the ruling one, and this is still largely the case today. Once again, there is not the space here to give an account of all the different local situations. We shall restrict ourselves to observing the marked weakening of an institution which had lost its uncontested political role but maintained a crucial influence in matters of values and behaviour. The conservative position adopted by the Church on contraception is the most striking instance of this. Nevertheless, the risk is that the new models articulated by the consumer society will erode its predominance much more effectively than all the liberal arguments of the nineteenth century.

The collapse of colonial rule led to many other upheavals. The early decades of the nineteenth century witnessed insurrections which spread out all over the continent. Mexico and especially Peru were bled white by their struggles for independence. Their mining infrastructure was neglected and trade was monopolized by the middle classes. Land remained the only source of available wealth in these countries. Consequently the *libertadores* addressed themselves to this by attacking the colonial legislation which froze the peasant communities' landed property. The legal status of Indian was abolished in 1821, and the indigenous population thereby became citizens of the new states and part of the general legal system. Personal service was abolished, but this important change also involved the suppression of certain privileges, including ownership of land by communities by virtue of ancient legal dispositions. Bolivar declared in 1824 that every Indian now owned his own land, and that the government would proceed to allot individual parcels of land, and would consider all surplus land to be state property. In the event, however, this process of privatization and land distribution developed slowly and won over the Mexican and Andean countrysides in different ways. We should point out here that these measures had as corollaries, on the one hand, the development of large estates or *latifundia*, and on the other, the proletarianization of indigenous peasants who had in many cases been reduced to selling their labour in order to survive. These facts had a special impact on rural families which developed several strategies to adapt to the new conditions.

Another period of strong political evolution was in the first decades of the twentieth century. Growing social oppression in Mexico provoked a revolution which shook the framework of political life and the rural world. South America had to wait until 1952 for the first revolutionary type of agrarian reform to take place in Bolivia.

The era of agrarian reforms was closely connected with another major phenomenon in the history of the family: the population boom and onset of massive and continuous migration from the countryside. Starting in the 1960s, the large urban centres became reservoirs of unskilled labour, because growing urbanization was not accompanied by any form of industrialization capable of absorbing all the migrants. There developed in the urban shanty towns what Oscar Lewis has called a 'culture of poverty' which characterizes sub-proletarian families. Finally, the mechanization of certain rural areas, notably plantations in tropical regions, accentuated the difference between modern agriculturalists on the one hand, and 'backward' indigenous peasants on the other, who are consequently doomed to disappear.

It is within this overall context, which has been surveyed only too superficially here, that we now intend to examine a few themes which do not necessarily exhaust the wealth of the empirical data. They do, however, allow us to discern the tensions and conflicts which overturned and transformed family structures in the course of the last 500 years. We will concentrate successively on the ritual extension of biological ties through the *compadrazgo* system, on modernization and on proletarianization, on the conservatism of family practices and ideology as means of resisting secularization, and finally on the urban migrations and acquisition of new values.

The compadrazgo *system*

The institution of *compadrazgo* is typical of Latin American societies and touches the countryside as much as the towns. Originally the institution was linked to the rituals marking the different stages in a man's life: baptism, confirmation, marriage and burial. On the American continent, baptism and marriage are the essential rites for consolidating godparent relations.

It may seem surprising to be dealing here with a phenomenon whose roots go back to the colonial era, notably to the first decade of the Spanish Conquista. The Franciscans introduced baptism to New Spain and practised collective rites in which an individual's godparents were limited to members of the native elite. The finality of baptism and the godparent relationship which was a direct consequence of it had multiple effects: in principle the new-born child's conversion was enhanced by the influence which the godfather or godmother could exert; by baptism the new-born child was snatched from paganism. Christian godparents seem to have been accepted very quickly by Meso-American and Andean populations, undoubtedly because of superficial similarities between this rite and pre-Hispanic customs linked to the life cycle. The Franciscan Sahagun even used the term baptism to describe the practice of naming the new-born child, which was performed by the midwife who saluted the child's arrival by sprinkling him with purifying water. In the Andes a certain category of relative, including the maternal uncle, played an important role during the haircutting ceremony which conferred status and identity on the child.

It would, however, be mistaken to consider the present-day *compadrazgo* as a remnant of those long-distant practices. In fact, the practice of giving the new-born child godparents underwent a clear evolution during the colonial period without actually acquiring the importance which it assumed in more recent periods, as we have already mentioned. According to Nutini, it was between 1630 and 1810 that the ritual kinship established at baptism between godparents and godchild began to weaken progressively, while the bond between the adults involved in the ceremony grew stronger. These were the godparent and parent couples, referred to in Spanish by the term *compadres*. This term *compadre* even came to extend to the kin of the partners in this relationship. Mutations of this type, which affected the Central American and Andean countries differently, resulted from several variable factors. First, it has been possible to observe, through the history of rural communities, an extension of godparenthood from godchild to other people and possessions, marked by the presence of godparents at the marriage of godchildren, at the blessing of a holy picture or a lorry, or at a ceremony intended to seal a hospitality pact between strangers. In addition, the isolation of rural communities and the closure of opportunities for social mobility drove families to extend their solidarity networks beyond the village sphere and to seek out godparents and *compadres* in different groups more prosperous or powerful than their own. Finally, the growing importance of economic motives proved an incitement to strengthen personal relations carrying obligations and expectations, to the detriment of kinship ties which were no longer able to secure social promotion.

Mintz and Wolff have distinguished in a standard article (1950) between two ideal forms of *compadrazgo*: one between individuals of similar status (horizontal) and one uniting two individuals of different status and rank (vertical). Horizontal *compadrazgo* is dominant in homogeneous societies where social distinctions are not clear-cut. Indeed, examining parish records in certain regions of the Andes not much affected by modernization reveals that baptismal godparents were generally chosen from among kin: brothers and married sisters of one of the two spouses, or grandparents. This is a custom which can also be found in Spain, where godparents have not really evolved as an institution into *compadrazgos*. However, we mut be careful to avoid making too categorical judgements in this matter. In other rural regions, such as those alongside Lake Titicaca, to give just one example, the choice of *compadres* within the kin seems redundant in some ways because it does not create new obligations or new exchanges. We are thus faced with a diversity of practices concerning an essential aspect of the system; the choice (not the imposition) of a new relative with whom the founding couple of a family unit will have privileged relations.

Compadrazgos started to develop in the nineteenth century because kinship ties were no longer as effective for ensuring the group's economic and social survival. In the mid-nineteenth century, in Mexico, Ecuador and Peru, the practice of having the same individual as godparent to several godchildren became widespread. The higher the status enjoyed by an individual (whether administrative or religious, in the system of public appointments, or as landowner, trader or notable), the more important and extensive was the number of *compadrazgo* networks which he would manipulate. A hundred godchildren would not have been an exaggerated number for such a person. It would exemplify the intensity of the mutual help, solidarity and dependence networks linking him to the communities around him. The modern *compadrazgo* is above all asymmetrical. A peasant looks around for a godparent for his new-born child who is capable of meeting the considerable expense of the ceremony; the more elevated he is, the more the godparent's prestige increases, and by extension that of the godchild's family as well. On the other hand, a prestigious individual can avoid such an honour only with difficulty. Not only will he be perceived as miserly, and his prestige will be diminished, but he has in addition a real interest in securing the assistance of his *compadres* through the medium of their spiritual kinship. This is all the truer in Peru, where the agrarian reform of 1872 was undermined in some regions by the existence of *compadrazgo* ties between peasants and landowners. We should end by pointing out that the *compadrazgo* can be compared to a chain whose links are made up of individuals set on different rungs of the social ladder and dispersed over a large geographical area. This was how a trader in Sicuani (Peru) could profit from a preferential price for potatoes supplied by a *compadre*, and could in his turn intercede in the latter's favour by appealing to one of his higher-ranking *compadres*.

In fact, *compadrazgo* is a political institution drawn along lines identical to kinship networks. The mutual help relationship which it favours allows the families involved to leave the social compartment to which they are confined. *Compadrazgo* consolidates the client relationships between *compadres* on the one hand, following the statutory hierarchy, and between godparents and godchildren on the other. These client relationships can serve political interests expressed in a paternalistic language dominated by interpersonal relationships (elections, appointments to municipal posts or the formation of pressure groups) or by traditional celebrations. This is how, in some districts of the Cuzco region in Peru, *compadrazgo* ties are brought up to date on the occasion of carnival festivities. The Thursday, called *compadre* day, followed by 'comrade' day, precedes the mobilization of villages for a battle with stones and whips which has to end in at least one death as a necessary condition for the ritual renewal of the soil. The man with many *compadres* and godchildren is obviously better armed, in every sense of the word, to come unscathed through this confrontation. This example is a good illustration of the link between *compadrazgo* and *machismo*, the glorification of virility which is common to every Latin American country.

Machismo must not be confused with the domination of women by men. *Machismo* embraces a constellation of practices from the submission by women to masculine values, to the consumption of alcohol as proof of virility and sign of resistance, to ostentatious heterosexuality and its corollary, the execration of homosexuality, to masculine friendship and a numerous progeny. *Compadrazgo* favours these last two aspects as much through the solidarity linking the partners involved (men and women) as by the illusion of many descendants which is conferred by the godchildren on their godparents.

During recent decades, the progress of secularization has weakened the sacred aspects of *compadrazgo*. The new generations reject this form of clientship and shy away from the expense of the ceremonies. The respect which exists between godparent and godchild is gradually fading, its only surviving aspect being the economic interest derived by both partners through the provision of mutual assistance. One could also ask – although there are but few studies on the question and they do not allow one to generalize – whether the political function of *compadrazgo* can survive in a rural or suburban context in which union membership is growing stronger by the day.

Modernization and proletarianization

The system of forced labour based on peasant debt did not originate in the nineteenth century, although it was during that period and until about the 1960s in the Andean countryside that this institution developed to touch not only workers bound by contract (*concierto*) but also their family and progeny. *Peonaje* and its Andean variant, *concertaje*, are linked both to the extension of large estates to the detriment of native lands, and to the loss of community resources. The proletarianization of the native is revealed by a change in his relations with wider kinship groups: in so far as liability to repay falls on his restricted family, and especially on his heirs, the consequence of this system is to atomize communities into family groups placed in a dependent situation *vis-à-vis* their employer. In the nineteenth century too, in villages there was a rise in the number of children abandoned at the doors of native or half-caste notables. The records do not tell us about the family conditions which led to such acts, whether they were the work of unmarried mothers or of families with too many children. One can, however, observe in a given population numerous cases of unmarried mothers, as much among indigenous groups as among those qualified as white in the records. In the northern Andes these adopted children take the name of their new parents but are referred to as *huiñachishca*.

The disintegrating effects of *concertaje* on family groups and communities were denounced by liberal politicians from the end of the nineteenth century. Propaganda books were written, inspired by sympathy for the natives, and contributed in the first decades of the twentieth century to rousing a new conscience about the peasantry's poverty in the material as much as the moral sense. In Ecuador, a violent campaign in favour of abolishing *concertaje* drew its arguments from descriptions of peasant families wholly engaged in wage labour (in the *peonaje* system, wages covered only a tiny part of the days worked). Liberals felt that children were the primary victims of such a system, being destined from birth to toil. Indeed, from the age of five, peasant children had to go to the fields to milk cows, as well as taking part in domestic and agricultural work. The liberal challenge was directed just as much against the oppression of women who worked in their employers' fields up to their first birth pangs. This political discourse, which based its arguments on the decline of the family, is of undeniable interest. Their claims, which seem so legitimate to us, were not founded on a faithful representation of the past: both in the colonial period and in pre-Hispanic times pregnant women appear to have worked in the fields up to the last moments before giving birth. As for children, the sources indicate clearly that they took part in agricultural work according to their strength and ability. If we can follow the liberals in distinguishing between wage labour and farmwork within the family unit, the fact remains nevertheless that the essence of the liberal argument consisted of the expression and diffusion of new ideas about the ideal family and the respective roles of women and children. The liberal model of the family was no longer an extended family group but a restricted unit based on the couple and their children, conforming to the laicized picture of the middle-class family. Viewed from this perspective, which aims at involving all the nation's active forces in its economic and social development, the school necessarily plays a primary role. Peasant children have to be released from exploitation on large landed estates and from their families' mental apathy: hence the country school appears as the ideal institution for integrating young people to modern life. From the nineteenth century and the first decades of the twentieth, lay schools were founded in the Andean and Mexican countryside but, contrary to the hopes they had aroused, their impact generally remained weak. There were many reasons for this: the burden of illiteracy, the teachers' inadequate training and the natives' bilingualism, coupled in many cases with ignorance of Spanish, and in many regions, the poverty of families which resented sending their children to school and thus losing a vital source of labour. In fact the peasants have an ambivalent attitude to school; on the one hand, it is linked with the idea of social promotion, and it is thus a matter of prestige for children, notably boys, to be able to read and write correctly. On the other hand, school is viewed as a rival by peasant families attached to their traditional way of life. It is indeed in class that children learn about the norms and values of their national society. 'Bourgeois' or in Mexico 'revolutionary' ideals are represented by the half-caste and urban world, as is everything that can help them forget that they belong to an obsolete, backward and ignorant milieu. Thus school necessarily divides children from their families, which explains the latter's authoritative behaviour aimed at protecting the young by forcing them to perform agricultural and domestic tasks incompatible with continuous education. These are obviously not general tendencies, but then neither is the peasant family homogeneous, and its configuration obeys several parameters: the nature of the landed tenure (landless peasants, small proprietors, middling landowners and rich peasants), the impact of modernization and specific cultural factors. Although all natives are peasants, not all peasants are natives, and peasants try to differentiate themselves from natives with varying degrees of success.

The liberal line of argument about the disintegration of native families made only a very gradual contribution to the transformation of family practices, and even nowadays it would be an exaggeration to talk about turning peasant families into the middle classes in terms similar to those employed to describe the way the lives of French workers have evolved. However, its impact cannot be neglected because, as we have seen with regard to school, liberal discourse has a tendency to devalue the poles of family life, which are treated as archaic and oppressive. This is why the younger generation's ideal is to leave the narrow framework of their community at the price of a subjection which is not always perceived as constraining.

Getting away involves a stage of wage labour. The repercussions of capitalism and its development on traditional rural families have been examined in numerous surveys. Among landless peasants or those with an inadequate landed inheritance, participation by women in waged agricultural work (in sugar cane and cotton plantations in Colombia, Ecuador and Peru) is much more important than in the patriarchal type of family characteristic of the middling landowner or of men who have retained the power of decision, even when their wives contribute to the family's production. This is not surprising: it is the poorest peasants who are forced to leave their village circle to ensure a subsistence for their families through wage labour. When the head of the family leaves for regions of possible employment, his wife becomes the head of the family, manages its meagre plots and ekes out out their income by doing paid work close to home. Women's participation in production through the medium of wages does not necessarily imply an improvement in the female condition, but simply a substantial modification to her status and the role she fulfils. After all, it must not be forgotten that in the great majority of Latin American countries, women are paid lower wages than men, and that the jobs which women get are either less skilled or are held in less esteem. Where the female condition is concerned, it should be observed that wage labour is directly related to the family's poverty, and conversely that better-off peasants who can resort to waged labour exempt women from agricultural work and employ them to cook for all the workers instead.

Let us recall, since we will return to the subject, that the migrations have an effect not only on the role filled by women, but also more generally on the composition of the family group in line with the evolution of traditional divisions of labour. It can happen, for instance, that when all the adults have moved to town the group is reduced only to those grandparents who have been entrusted with the care of the house, the plot of land and the small children.

One particular form of wage labour for women is domestic service, which is related to traditional forms of *concertaje*. This institution is certainly not peculiar to the modern age. For instance, in the rural regions of Peru and Ecuador during the time of colonial rule, Indian women were forced to give personal service in Spanish families for a number of days every year. This form of servitude is in any case not similar to what is referred to nowadays as a type of 'domestic employment'. Apparently the practice of placing peasant girls in service with urban families has undergone a considerable development since the 1950s as a consequence of demographic growth, which has brought increased pressure to bear on the land as well as impoverishing peasant families. Agreements made between families take on a paternalistic, or at any rate a personal, form. For instance, a couple might try to place a young daughter in service with her rich godparents – the vital role of *compadrazgo* is evident here – or with landowners, or they could 'give' the child to notables with a dwelling in the main provincial town or even in the capital. Sometimes the girl might even look forward to this separation with relief. Testimonies gathered from domestic employees in Cuzco in 1980 emphasize the extraordinary violence inherent in family relations in rural areas which we referred to earlier. Girls are frequently beaten by their parents and elder brothers, who also make brutal threats: 'I will tie you to the horse's tail', or 'I hope you die for good' are not exceptional expressions. These relatively recent facts show the extent to which the status of children in in the country differs from that accorded them in middle-class town families. The obligations imposed on children are considerable, and every attempt on their part to escape these family constraints is punished with beatings and abuse, on account of the difficulties and precarious nature of daily existence. In many cases, children regard their step-mother as responsible for their ill-treatment. The high death rate for women in childbirth means that men do indeed remarry and may thus have children from several marriages. The portrait of the jealous and cruel step-mother is thus not simply a theme from folk tales, but illustrates a situation which many children experience with particular anguish.

Violence within the family, applied above all to girls, should not obliterate the opposite attitudes, which can be observed in native homes. Physical contact between parents and children is much more intense in rural families than in urban ones, notably among the better-off. Not only is the child carried by his mother until the age of two, when he is weaned, but parents commonly share their bed with some of their children. Sleeping together to combat the cold and to keep one's courage up is frequently practised by mountain people, who consider solitude to be the worst of the evils which can befall man.

Conservatism as applied to practices

Many peasant communities have gradually abandoned their traditional customs under the impact of modernization and secularization, and have entered willy-nilly a capitalist farming system based on mechanization, technology and wage labour. Conversely other peasant societies have retrenched fiercely within their own values, retaining up to the present practices derived from past ages. These are not so much survivals from pre-Hispanic periods as pale reflections of a colonial world in which the Catholic Church was no longer to play the principal ideological and political role. Two contemporary examples illustrate this situation.

The natives of Q'ero in the Cuzco region of Peru retained their traditional dress until recently. Not having been much influenced by Spanish ways or had much contact with urban civilization, although the men regularly go to town to deal with legal business or commercial transactions, the natives of Q'ero provide an exemplary illustration of the rejection of progress. The way their families are distributed reflects the Andean ideal of economic autarky. Thus a first residential unit formed out of 'principal' houses (*hatun wasi*) is to be found on the cold lands more than 4,000 metres in altitude. *Hatun wasi* consist of three to five dwellings arranged around a communal courtyard and enclosures for animals. The village proper is situated in a lower zone (at approximately 3,300 m); it is a residential centre of about sixty houses arranged according to the typical chequer-board design. Every nuclear family has one house in the village, in which it lives temporarily. Such families also live in the lower warmer zones (between 1,800 m and 2,000 m in altitude), where they farm tropical produce. Their houses are not clustered but dispersed, and their main building materials are timber and reeds.

Among the Q'ero people, cattle play an essential role in structuring family relations. As his children set up their own homes, their father will give them the portion due to them as their inheritance, but will retain the share belonging to the youngest child who is obliged to live with his parents even if he has taken a wife. When his parents die, the youngest son inherits all their furniture to compensate for the assistance he has rendered them.

Since marriage between cousins and even more distant relatives is considered incestuous, the young Q'ero seek their wives from among far-off groups. The young people's choice is consolidated by a traditional ritual: the fiancé's parents visit the girl's family and celebrate with a coca-chewing ceremony, which seals the marriage (*warmichakuy*). Children conceived before the union has been formalized are considered to be of

an unknown father and are referred to by the term *q'aqa*: the new-born
child is laid in cold wrappings and left alone. Any *q'aqa* who survives
such treatment does not live with his parents, because his presence would
bring shame on the family. His paternal grandfather will adopt him in
order to avert conflict, but he is excluded from the share of inheritance
which would have been his had he been legitimate.

Sexual freedom ends with marriage, and a number of beliefs contribute
to reinforce the bonds of fidelity between spouses. Thus the mere
mention of a former lover can stimulate malevolent spirits called *soq'a*
into action, who strike the guilty person with incurable sickness. Fidelity
in marriage, especially on the wife's part, is extolled in many stories, and
every farming calamity is attributed to the wife's dissolute conduct. After
many years of cohabitation, the couple celebrates the Catholic marriage
rite, *casarakuy*, a word made up from a Spanish root and a Quechua
ending. For this occasion, marriage sponsors have to be found, according
to the traditional godparenting system – and to *compadrazgo*. *Casarakuy*
is an indispensible formality for anyone wishing to assume the post of
alcade, one of the highest rungs on the political and administrative ladder
of Q'ero. In former times, religious posts were more prestigious, and the
number of people married in church was greater. Nowadays, with the
decline of Catholicism, the interlude between *warmichakuy* or traditional marriage and *casarakuy* (Catholic marriage) can extend to ten
years. In 1955, of fifty-two couples counted among the Q'ero, only
twenty-eight had been married in church.

The Q'ero case provides a clear illustration of the syncretism of family
practices produced during the colonial period. Whereas their 'vertical'
farming model for different unconnected areas follows the pre-Hispanic
model, the role of cattle, inheritance rules, moral sanctions regarding
bastards and weaving marriage into the system of religious and administrative posts are elements rooted in colonial administration. Contrary
to what the Q'ero people's cultural conservatism would lead one to
believe, the general process of secularization over the whole of Peruvian
society is manifested indirectly in this region by the collapse of the
Church whose ideology gave a meaning to the social relations between
families.

Different conservative findings can be made in the communities of the
northern Andes, notably in the Cuenca and Azogues provinces in
Ecuador. Unlike the Indians of Q'ero and numerous Peruvian communities, the peasants of Ecuador – in the regions mentioned above at least –
have practised endogamic marriage strategies since the end of the
nineteenth century, which is just as contrary to the marriage rules
promulgated by the Church. Although it has always been possible to

arrange a marriage between close cousins, whether cross-cousins or parallel, by purchasing a dispensation, this custom appears to have developed in an astonishing manner in modern times, giving rise to a closed list of alliances. Of course, a closed endogamic system is but one possible strategy, though undoubtedly the most frequent one from the statistical point of view. Some children in the same family will seek to form other unions from motives of status, wealth or simply personal attachment.

From the point of view of kinship, we are in the presence here of a system of alliances of the complex type which is superimposed on a more coercive system based on the need to form preferential unions of the 'elementary' type. All the same, it may be asked whether the numerous instances of marriages with the daughter of a maternal uncle represent the remnants of a pre-Hispanic model or the results of the strong pressure exerted by landed property, whose logical corollary would be to retain the patrimony within the same family group. Marriages with close relatives would thus constitute an effective strategy for fighting against the partition of land, the other strategy being the acquisition of a patrimony outside the community or of a status represented by a foreign spouse's name. On the whole, these peasants play two cards simultaneously: that of closing in and reconstituting their landed tenure, and that of opening up by integrating, through marriage, with better-off or prestigious families.

Suspicion of every technological and cultural innovation constitutes a reaction against the dangers presented to the native community by the dispersal of their young people and their integration into a world of work. This attitude is expressed in terms of envy, a feeling which the peasants fear above all others because it is the motive for acts of witchcraft. The proliferation of spells dates from modern times, if the testimony of the persons involved is to be believed, and the danger affects every family. It is enough to unleash envy when a person distinguishes himself – an aspiration encouraged by the modern ideal of citizen – whether by his work, manner or satisfactory state of health. Anyone who stands out from the crowd is called ambitious, which can only bring him bad luck. In this context, witchcraft is never attributed to the malice of a specialist who could concoct magic potions to destroy these marginal beings, but to the skill of one of the victim's relatives by alliance. Thus witches are always mothers-in-law, sisters-in-law and daughters-in-law, and they are all the more fearsome in that it is impossible to avoid them. The magical substance is added to food, an essential object of exchange between families according to the rules of reciprocity. Witchcraft thus appears in the present age as the negative expression of family solidarity when shattered by modern values and the lure of a social mobility which can only be achieved outside the village circle.

Urban migrations

The migration of rural populations to urban centres goes back at least as far as the colonial period, but since 1940 this phenomenon has acquired unprecedented magnitude over the whole of Latin America. Its causes cannot be examined here; enough to say that transformations in the capitalist economy, speeded-up demographic growth, the dwindling area of cultivable land and the depreciated image of the countryside, with its corollary in the urban mirage, have contributed to drive increasingly large numbers to the towns.

The effects of these migratory movements on the composition and evolution of family groups of rural origin are many, but we will restrict ourselves to tracing their main outlines. Once the family is installed in town, in the best cases the husband has sufficient resources, his wife stays at home and his children will regularly attend the local school. If the husband's income is irregular or not adequate, extended family groups can be seen to form, often gathering several couples under one roof. Such units are large enough to ensure the survival of the different families involved, because they make sharing household tasks easier and allow wives and daughters to find jobs in small local businesses.

Inserting these migrants into the economy has a considerable impact on family structures, modifying traditional sexual roles. In some circumstances, ideological models derived from the middle classes have influenced husbands and induced them to share in household tasks, while their wives have acquired greater autonomy within the family, especially if they work in a factory. Conjugal relations are evolving towards setting up fairer complementary roles between spouses. Living at a distance from the husband's mother, who rules her daughter-in-law in rural circles, has encouraged this redefinition of conjugal roles. The man, once freed of his mother, no longer has to play the ambiguous role of husband and son.

When living conditions are precarious, the roles tend to evolve in a more complex manner. In some cases, a matrifocal family may come to predominate, meaning a family unit in which the husband occupies a marginal position associated with the uncertainties of his economic condition (through lack of qualifications, inability to adapt, unstable employment and absenteeism) whereas his wife, if she can manage to bring home a regular income by working as a servant or carrying out regular work, can consolidate her position at her husband's expense. In other cases, the woman's situation reflects the precarious living conditions. Life is difficult in the shanty towns (*cuidades perdidas, barriadas, villas miseria*), where, as well as the absence of hygiene, undernourishment and insanitary lodgings and environment, there is constant insecurity. Promiscuity, frequent sexual relations between fathers and their daughters-in-law and rape induce women to risk their lives by undergoing abortions. A survey was conducted in 1977 in five large urban centres in Mexico which showed that 21 per cent of women living in the slums had had more than one abortion. Infant mortality there is still very high, and according to the same survey one woman in two has lost at least one child.

In such milieux, which are the most unprivileged of all, large families of between five and ten children are the rule, as is abortion as the brutal means of birth control. Large families form the basis of what Lewis (1961) has called the 'culture of poverty': they satisfy the husband's macho impulses (he won't use contraception), offer a refuge, however precarious, to abandoned women and intensify spiritual kinship ties through the *compadrazgo* system.

This migratory phenomenon has also entailed a break with traditional forms of behaviour associated with engagement (*noviazgo*) and proposals of marriage, which the colonial period had gradually established. Meeting other people is easy in town, in the factory or the residential quarter, and encounters between young people are simplified when their parents are far away and the watchful eye of the community has gone, rendering obsolete the old formal ways. In the towns, families have put an end to the exchange of gifts and food, which considerably reduces the expense and duration of *noviazgo*.

However, migration has not just had a reducing effect. It is significant in social terms that networks of sociability have been set up to facilitate contact between young people of the same village or the same ethnic group. Meetings are organized every Sunday in the big public parks (Chapultepec in Mexico), in the residential quarters or in places like the *coliseos* in Lima, a kind of popular theatre where people go to hear songs and watch country dances. Marriage is also acquiring a new ritual form, one adapted to urban conditions and involving a celebration spread over several days. In the same way, some old forms of behaviour are reaffirmed: comments are made about the flighty nature and infidelity of husbands chosen from outside the original village group, as well as about the clumsiness and laziness of 'foreign' wives.

Kinship occupies a considerable place in the migratory phenomenon which it structures and organizes. The decision to migrate is taken along with relatives, and it is in their company that the move to town is undertaken. Finally, it is with other relatives that a temporary home is arranged, as is the search for a place in the labour market. These town 'uncles' play a vital role when country people first come into contact with disconcerting town life. Kin retain an energetic role within the residential units which gather several dozen families together; they maintain close relationships of mutual assistance and reciprocity, and give them concrete form by helping new arrivals to buy a plot or build a house. However, integration into urban life and social advance tend to reduce opportunities for interaction between kin. Kinship is fading as less is expected from it.

At the end of the 1960s the migrants were hit by two associated phenomena; one was the impossibility of returning to the countryside, which had too many people and no employment prospects; the other was the exhaustion of the towns' absorption capacity, since their extraordinary growth had not been accompanied by proportional growth in industrialization and employment. Hence the stagnation (*rezago*) of unskilled migrants, who have become increasingly marginalized and have withdrawn into their ethnic solidarity and identity.

The last decades of the twentieth century have not only been marked by the pauperization of migrants to the towns; they also represent a profound upheaval in sexual roles as a result of political involvement, in certain circumstances, of women from indigenous rural backgrounds. This female militancy is amply illustrated by the domestic servants in Cuzco who have joined a union, by Rigoberta Menchu in Guatemala, and above all by Domitila, a Bolivian worker, in whose story we find themes which are typical of the way of life in peasant families. Domitila's mother died in labour, leaving six orphans behind her. Domitila, the eldest, cared for her brothers and sisters and managed the home, while their father, a guitar player, took to drink, neglected his work and let off steam in the evenings by beating his children. Young Domitila very soon got a job in the Siglo XX mine, where she met her future husband, a worker who, like her, had come from the country. The workers were driven by their difficult economic situation to form a union. In the course of a repressive operation conducted against the miners, the women decided to organize themselves as well, at first spontaneously and then pursuing a tighter strategy. This was how the housewives' committees were formed in 1961, which now exist in all the nationalized mines. The unionized women then had to conduct a dual struggle: against the forces of repression, in which they were seconded by the workers and university students; and against their own husbands who did not understand their wives' commitment and activity outside the family circle. In their struggle for the rights of miners these women thus came up against other women's groups, including the one for Christian women (which actually has a

Protestant affiliation), which defend the traditional functions of wives.

We cannot claim that the themes developed in these pages have exhausted the diversity of contemporary family situations in rural and urban circles, which would after all be an impossible task. To make up for this, our choice of topics does illustrate the fact that all the problems linked to the family, in Mexico as much as in the Andes, were already present or germinating in the Spanish period. Is not the Latin American family the dual product of religious cultural integration and colonial rule? Is it not also the fruit of the accumulated effects (and side-effects) of Westernization and modernization? From the sixteenth century Western models have been brought to bear on the populations of the American continent and their destiny to such an extent that the gap between the norm imposed from outside and Latin American reality has been growing ever since. While the sixteenth-century colony had inspired a model adapted more or less to its specific context, twentieth-century independent America simply imported a ready-made liberalism designed for other lands. As for the penetration by the media in the late twentieth century, America has been projected in representations and values which contrast grotesquely with everyday experience. The interest which all sectors of society take in radio and television programmes devised in North America but transposed for Latin American society is symptomatic of a new modification of family ideology and sexual morality which tends to 'normalize' social and cultural differences. Literature provides the best witness to this romanticized vision of the family and of sexual relations, since in Latin America authors such as Vargas Llosa and Manuel Puig still play an avant-garde role.

FOUR

The Long March of the Chinese Family

Michel Cartier

In the aftermath of the Taiping Rebellion of 1850, when the rulers of the Qing empire involved their country in the adventure of modernization, the loose administrative apparatus at their disposal was no longer able to contain a population of some 400 million people. They thus had to rely on intermediate structures. The period of reconstruction of the state known as the Tongzhi Restoration (1862–74) may be characterized as a phase of compromise with local gentry, which amounted to consecrating the role of relay as performed by the institution of the family.

Generally speaking, the imperial administration intervened in the affairs of the population through the medium of groups endowed with collective responsibility, which had been set up on the basis of land ownership or neighbourhood, or through the intermediary of gentry to whom powers had been delegated informally. The *baojia* or neighbourhood group charged with maintaining order since the disappearance of the *lijia* or groups with fiscal responsibility, constituted a purely formal organization, which took account neither of village solidarities nor of distinctions in wealth or status, and the people in charge (commoners), who were chosen especially for their skill in acting as buffers between the population and the authorities, had only limited autonomy and often only mediocre prestige. In the majority of cases, then, these people were from families which combined the possession of land and knowledge, given concrete form by the acquisition of the two first academic degrees, and thus found themselves guiding the populace, organizing the self-defence militia, raising special contributions and levying or managing assistance in the event of shortages. To the extent that this authority was exercised more within the context of clan structures than upon isolated individuals, it was the clan in its capacity as a supra-family institution with its own temples and grain stores, raising its own self-defence militia, which constituted the privileged intermediary between state and people.

Lineage villages or local solidarities

The Chinese territory in its immensity presents a great variety of situations. We therefore have to distinguish between several typical cases according to whether a small region or area is dominated by one or several great families. In actual fact, the model of lordship as a group of villages under the authority of a single clan with rights over the land is a relatively rare phenomenon. An institution which is especially widespread in the southern half of the country is the 'lineage village' which has attracted the attention of sociologists and anthropologists (Freedman, 1966; Baker, 1968). Although the phenomenon has not been studied as a whole, we know that many villages, in the north as much as the south of the country, are designated by toponyms of the type 'domain of family X' or 'village of family Y'. These are frequently inhabited by villagers who nearly all bear the surname of a single family and consider themselves to be the descendants of the founder. It is very likely that these villagers are descended from an agricultural establishment founded by the junior branch of a lineage, an impression confirmed by examining the sites, which are at the entrances to little valleys or on exposed slopes. Everything thus leads us to believe that we have here colonization or land-clearance villages, corresponding to an expansion of agricultural territory.

Opinions differ largely about the manner in which the initial situation was maintained. Were lineage villages family foundations which had been perpetuated, or were they the results of a more or less deliberate strategy for evicting foreign elements? It can indeed be observed that a village of this type is only seldom inhabited exclusively by villagers bearing the eponymous family name, but that in most of the cases studied, there was an appreciable proportion of representatives of other lineages. Observations made mostly in the southern provinces of Guangdong and Fujian tend to prove that lineage homogeneity is indeed secured by marginalizing, even brutally evicting, inhabitants who bore different names. Thus municipal decisions at Sheung Shui (New Territories, Hong Kong) were taken within the context of the assembly of the dominant clan, and 'external' elements were not allowed to build houses, take part in economic life or purchase land without the consent of the clan authorities. A recent survey conducted by researchers of Amoy University has shed light on various exclusion processes aimed at maintaining the members of dependent families in an inferior situation; the prohibition of marriage with members of the dominant clans, rules about their dwellings and clothing, confining the 'intruders' to activities like porterage which were not considered very 'honourable'. In short, maintaining homogeneity would have been both the result of a strategy of land ownership – constituting a clan estate with the purpose of covering the clan's general expenses and of letting it to the poorest members of the kin as a priority – and of discrimination against outsiders.

Of course this coincidence of clan and local institutions generated numerous conflicts. The southern mainland provinces, Taiwan and the New Territories of Hong Kong had long been the theatre of armed feuds between villages or federations of villages linked by common surnames, matrimonial alliances or the use of similar dialects. During the first half of the twentieth century, these manifestations of 'familialism' and parochialism were generally considered by political theorists and sociologists as defects inherent in Chinese society. These conflicts inhibited both the development of a genuine civic spirit and the constitution of a nation. The sociologist Fei Hsiao-T'ung had, in the course of a lecture series published only in Chinese, gone so far as to depict the society of his country as a series of concentric circles. In the centre is the clan or family, which groups persons linked by moral obligations. Around this kernel, the neighbourhood community could be defined as a solidarity group directed against the outside world. The other outer concentric circles would then correspond to the canton, the administrative units of district or prefecture type, and then the province. This diagram is complicated by the existence of dialect solidarities which do not completely match geographical or administrative divisions.

Where relations with the outside world are concerned, Chinese people will always give preference to the inner circle at the level in question. In other words, the family will be played off against the neighbourhood community, the latter against the canton, and the provincial or dialect affiliation against the nation. There is no shortage of examples of types of behaviour determined by interlocking solidarities. Just as many instances can be found in economic life, where activities tend to be monopolized by groups based on dialect or regional origin, as in political life, where local solidarities are frequently superimposed on partisan affiliations. We need only recall the classical case of the merchants of Huizhou, about whom a major series of documents exists. The region of Huizhou, in the upper valley of the Xin'anjiang, a river which feeds the mountain range lying to the south of Nankin, was until the sixteenth century a relatively poor

Imperial order, family order. The Dowager Empress sitting between the imperial couple. ANA, Paris.

zone. The richest families threw themselves rather late into selling plantation products (tea and lacquer) using dependants or servants as intermediaries to whom capital funds were entrusted. The 'merchants of Huizhou' gradually built up a network of business contacts scattered throughout the lower Yangzi valley, and they assumed control of the salt trade, pawnbroking and, later on, the export of green tea. There are many such examples. Family solidarities, frequently reinforced by various practices on the edge of legality, such as adopting children who had no kinship link with their adoptive parents, concluding engagements between children as yet unborn and arranging 'in-law' marriages, filled the lacunae in a commercial law, according to which an association was defined only in the form of a pledged loan. As it was, once outside their region of origin, the merchants could count on assistance from their 'country' (*tongxiang*), use the facilities offered by hotels (*huiguan*) which had been built to take in students and officials originally from the province or prefecture in question, and even solicit the protection of their representatives in the civil service. The constitution of such networks was not limited to trade. It can be found in the background of the creation of modern industrial enterprises as much as of overseas expansion, which set up real filiations characterized by common geographical origin and dialect, and specialized economic activity in south-east Asia during the colonial period, or more recently in America.

The revolt against the family

This familialism was denounced with particular vigour by revolutionary theorists at the end of the Empire and the beginning of the Republican period in that it prevented the constitution of a nation in the modern sense of the term. Attacks on the family began with a double revolt by women and young people who traditionally constituted the least privileged groups. The movement for the emancipation of women can be traced back to the second half of the nineteenth century. As we have already shown, women were everywhere the victims of a true form of marginalization in the sense that they had no access to land ownership, were excluded from most forms of work and had little education. Added to all this were the physical consequences of mutilating their feet, which limited their freedom of movement and ended by confining them to household duties, procreation and the education of small children.

The emancipation of women

The movement for the emancipation of girls appeared in the open ports in the south, where it chiefly involved the official and merchant classes most exposed to outside influences. It found a special echo in the diaspora, a largely half-caste society in which interethnic marriages were frequent and wives often enjoyed greater autonomy. Among the claims which came to the fore during the first years of the twentieth century should be mentioned the abolition of foot-binding, access to education, free choice of spouse and a more active participation in social and economic life. The emerging feminist movement found its martyr in the person of Qiu Jin (1875–1907), a young revolutionary woman who was executed in the aftermath of a failed plot (Gipoulon, 1976). Qiu Jin's fate is particularly representative. As the daughter of an official with advanced views, she escaped foot-binding, took part in sport and enjoyed riding. She was married relatively late, at the age of twenty-one, separated from her husband and in 1905 went to Japan, where she met other exiles. On her return to her family's province of origin, she taught in several schools and took part in clandestine revolutionary activities. She was arrested with several of her pupils the day after the provincial governor was assassinated.

The course which Qiu Jin followed – unbinding her feet, breaking up her arranged marriage, taking part in the movement for the education of girls and in revolutionary militancy – anticipated an evolution which would only very gradually reach other classes of society. Mutilating little girls' feet resulted from a deeply entrenched belief in the necessity of keeping women separate from the world of production. When, during the second half of the nineteenth century, the tea planters in Hunan province appealed for a female workforce to meet the sudden growth in demand, popular opinion, as relayed in local pamphlets, viewed the young girls 'with natural feet' who joined in the picking work as unruly hussies who were endangering the whole social order. The Japanese colonial administration only succeeded in abolishing this 'retrograde' custom by applying force. Societies for the abolition of foot-binding only really took off from 1900 onwards, and they had to wait until the 1920s for the movement to secure any significant results. Education for women progressed even more slowly, although the number of girls' schools certainly increased after 1900 with the support of the Dowager Empress Cixi, who had been won over late to the cause of modernization. In spite of official encouragement, however, the proportion of Chinese women who had received education was certainly not above 4 or 5 per cent, a rate scarcely higher than the traditional one. As for women's participation in the world of work, it remained restricted to a few occupations and jobs. While there certainly was a small number of women teachers, in most cases women's sphere of activity was confined to trade, brokerage or spinning and weaving work.

The Young People's Rebellion: the New Culture Movement

The Young People's Rebellion, which culminated in the Beijing Demonstration of 4 May 1919 marked the beginning of a movement of radical challenge directed in the first place against Confucian ideology as manifested by the authority of the patriarchal family. Traditional society did not value youth, which it regarded as the age of apprenticeship, and particularly of long-drawn-out studies to acquire academic titles in order to enter the civil service. The degree of competition engendered by the examination system meant that it was hard to obtain graduate or doctoral degrees before the age of twenty-five or thirty. When the imperial examinations were abolished in 1904 the effect was to increase young people's disarray. Apart from a few open ports where foreign schools, generally run by missionaries, dispensed modern instruction, it was a long time before the reform of education got under way. From then on, the shortest route to a higher education still in embryo form, and to the official posts to which it ensured access, was via a spell abroad, in Europe, America and especially Japan. Tens of thousands of young people were sent overseas with a summary apprenticeship in foreign languages as their only preparation. Studies pursued in this manner, and often under precarious conditions, emphasized the break between the student elite, which came from the ruling class, and national values. The world of scholarship students easily eluded the tentative supervision which the embassies tried to impose on it and constituted a cultural mix ideal for propagating subversive theories and modernist ideas. Numerous students joined revolutionary or reform groups in exile and took part in secret societies planning to overthrow the Manchu dynasty. The success of the 1911 Revolution appeared to inaugurate a rapid transformation of society. On their return to China, however, these foreign students found a situation which did not come up to expectation. While some of them secured the responsible positions to which they were entitled by their knowledge of Western technology or ideology, most of them experienced problems in adapting to an extremely fluid political situation. So they threw themselves into militancy, seeking to win to their cause young people who had not had the opportunity of leaving the national territory. The review *Xin qingnian* (Youth) was brought into being by Chen

Figure 2 *La Jeunesse* (Youth), the controversial review that introduced Marxist ideas

Duxiu, one of the 'foreign-returned', and by 1917 it was distinguished by its iconoclastic tone and political radicalism. Chen Duxiu and his friends advocated a sort of 'cultural revolution', characterized by their outright rejection of Confucianism. On 4 May 1919, the student youth of Beijing demonstrated against the capitulation by the delegates of the Republican government to the demands made by Japan at the discussions preceding the Treaty of Versailles. The unarmed procession of young people clashed with troops. The repression of the Beijing Demonstration gave the signal for a wave of protests and strikes which shook university and economic circles in most of the provincial cities.

Led by angry young people, the 'May Fourth Movement' relied on a relatively narrow social base of sons of landowners, officials or traditional literati – the educated fringe of Chinese society – but it had a great impact among senior school pupils throughout the country, for whom it provided a sort of counter-culture. Apart from its intransigent nationalism, which was mainly expressed in movements to boycott foreign goods and in often ill-defined revolutionary aspirations, the post May Fourth period was characterized above all by its vehement denunciation of family oppression. Autonomy for young people and freedom to love were the main themes of a popular literature which found its voice in a mass of politico-literary publications, sometimes ephemeral in nature. It is significant that one of the sensations of the period was the love marriage between Xu Zhimo, a young poet fresh from Cambridge, and May, a young society woman who had just left her husband to whom she had been married against her will. Ten years or so later, Pa Kin, on his return from a spell in France, made the confrontation between a young man and his family the subject of his novel *Family* (1931), one of that period's best-sellers. Rebellious lovers, whether unhappy or carefree, and young people who had broken with their families constituted the ubiquitous heroes of novels and collections of verse. Free choice of a partner did not necessarily bring happiness. Juansheng and Zijun, the protagonists of a novel published in 1925 by Lu Xun, proved incapable of living out their passion, whereas Shafei (Sophie), the heroine of the *Diary of Miss Sophie*, which immediately ensured Ding Ling her literary reputation, struggles with the torments of triangular love affairs. Indeed, the characters typical of this period were very often waverers easily overcome by society, and their authors mostly tell us about their failures and problems with life. From the early 1930s writers began to imitate Lu Xun by putting themselves at the service of politics and the Revolution, and their commitment took its cue from these Don Quixote-type conflicts with family and society.

One great stable feature of the family as an institution

These vehement attacks on the family, most particularly on the large communal family, which filled the literary works of the revolutionary period, should not conceal the actual social situation during the inter-war period. Surveys taken at the time and retrospective studies help us, in fact, to paint a more realistic picture of society and family in the 1920s and 1930s.

As in the Imperial period, the Chinese economy was still dominated by small agricultural enterprises, tiny farms run by families containing on average five persons. In 1953, the proportion of persons aged over sixty-five still did not exceed 5 per cent of the population. Parents thus soon disappeared, and the passage from one generation to the next occurred early on. The average farm was about 1 ha in size, with great variations between the provinces. Most families engaged in subsistence farming, supplemented by a few commercial crops and sometimes a few home crafts. The division between the sexes remained very marked; women seldom worked in the fields. Most peasants were too poor to be able to devote more than minimal time to the education of their children, who had to contribute as soon as they could to the family resources by gathering twigs and kindling for cooking and by taking the animals out to pasture. School attendance was consequently low and confined largely to boys. For the generations born before 1920, the proportion of illiterate and semi-literate persons in 1982 was in the order of 60 per cent for men and 95 per cent for women. Among the peasant population, the ratio rose to 64 per cent for men and 97 per cent for women, thus justifying Fei Hsiao-T'ung's remark, that 'the peasants live in a world without writing.' Furthermore, very few children continued beyond primary level. Less than 5 per cent of Chinese now over seventy have attended an institution of primary or secondary education. Young girls made up only 10 per cent of total numbers in the first cycle of the secondary school curriculum, but in the universities the average was almost one girl for every five male students.

Marriage and fertility

Marriage was still very much a family affair. Girls were considered economic burdens, and were often engaged to be married at puberty, with the marriage taking place between the ages of fourteen and eighteen. Account must nevertheless be taken of geographical and social variations. Generally the divide was not between town and country, but between social classes. Girls would leave their families at even younger ages if they came from humble backgrounds, since though the bride price increased with age, it only partly compensated for the expense of educating and supporting her. The custom known as 'child-brides' (*tongyangxi*), which consisted of entrusting a little girl about ten years old with the care of her future husband, a boy younger than herself, is mostly attested in the poor regions of the south. Paradoxically, early unions do not appear to have had any repercussions on the general level of fertility, which remained low at five children per woman. Several years often elapsed between the marriage ceremony and the birth of the first child, which took place on average when the mother was nineteen. This delay is clearly explained by the couple's lack of intimacy as a result of co-residence with the husband's parents. His young bride was no more than a servant (Wolf and Huang, 1980). A borderline situation was discovered in the southern province of Fujian by a survey conducted around 1950. The young brides of Hui'an district were only allowed to live with their husband's family after the birth of their first child, and local custom also set a maximum limit on the number of meetings permitted between the young couple. Thus the delay between the couple's marriage and their cohabitation generally stretched to between three and five years. This situation has been interpreted by Lin Huixiang as a relic of matriarchy, in which the girl's parents would refuse to allow her to take her place in her husband's family. It is clear that this practice reveals an exacerbation of the hostility which frequently characterized relations between allied families in the southern provinces. In this respect, it is not irrelevant that in Hui'an region women engaged in agricultural work.

Whatever the situation, allied families kept their distance. Marriage was necessarily concluded by resorting to match-makers. The high point of negotiations was the presentation of betrothal gifts, or the 'bride price', which marked the point of no return. The marriage ceremony proper was celebrated separately in both the bride's and her young husband's homes, entailing festivities which occasioned sumptuous expenditure and many exchanges of gifts. Contributions from the married couple's friends and acquaintance sometimes exceeded the entire expenditure taken on by the families (Cohen, 1976). Moreover, the girl's family could transfer movable goods for the young bride's benefit, which constituted a sort of dowry guaranteeing her position in her new family. Marriage thus remained an occasion for reaffirming a family's prestige, even though this might provoke competition between the husband and wife's kinsmen. The only notable concession to Western customs was the habit, which was spreading in the towns, of proceeding to 'presentations' at which a young marriageable girl could catch a glimpse of her intended husband and possibly refuse him.

The results of retrospective inquiries into fertility conducted in the 1980s show that women born before 1920 would have given birth on average to only five children. With the very heavy infant and child mortality prevalent at the time, this was only just enough to allow for generation renewal. Such results may seem surprising as the proportion of women aged between fifteen and forty-five in situations conducive to motherhood exceeded 80 per cent as a result of early marriage and the very low incidence of divorce. The number of sterile women or women with no descendants following the death of their children was lower than 7 per cent of all women, and very few women had given birth to ten or more children. Should this low level of fertility be considered a cultural characteristic or the consequence of a particularly troubled political situation? There is no doubt that the various calamities and civil and foreign wars which followed one after another almost without a break during the first half of the twentieth century had adverse effects on the population's standard of living. One must, however, point out that women born around 1920, who grew up in an atmosphere of war and revolution, have a fertility structure fairly similar to their mothers', which was subjected to surveys in the 1930s. We are probably dealing with a cultural phenomenon which combines the negative effects of prolonged lactation, well-anchored customs separating the sexes and, possibly to an equal extent, a strong incidence of acquired sterility.

There is still great uncertainty about the rhythm of demographic growth during the Republican period. While the final figure – 540 million in 1949 – seems from that time on to have been well established, the same does not apply to the starting point which varies, according to the estimates, between under 400 million and nearly 500 million inhabitants. This differential shows up our lack of information about the human costs of the sequels to the Taiping Rebellion and all those natural and human calamities which are generally referred to as the 'crisis of the nineteenth century'. Surveys conducted around 1930, a time of relative calm, revealed birth and death rates of 40 and 30 per 1,000 respectively, which would allow a natural growth in the order of 1 per cent, but it looks as if we should revise this latter figure downwards. Taking into account a life expectancy at birth in the neighbourhood of twenty-seven years, corresponding to a high level of infant and child mortality which decimated girls in particular since they were not tended as carefully as their brothers, we must reckon with a 50 per cent survival rate at the age of twenty. Reflections based on the classifications by age which were observed in the course of the 1953 and 1964 censuses, have led to a re-evaluation of the total number of births in the first half of the century. According to this, the population started off in 1900 at a level close to that before the nineteenth-century crisis – between 420 and 450 million inhabitants – and would have grown by 100 million in fifty years, that is an average annual growth rate of 5 per 1,000 or less.

If we take into account the considerable opportunities for absorbing the population surplus into the modern sector which was then developing, and into the internal colonization zones such as the northern frontier and Manchuria, we are entitled to speak about the quasi-stability of rural society. Nevertheless, there is certainly no question of denying or minimizing the problems to which rural populations were subjected as a result of the civil wars, the Japanese invasion and the imbalances resulting from an economic development centred on the coastal towns and a few industrialization zones. Peasants' living conditions are often described, and rightly so, as being on the edge of the unbearable. We must not underestimate the fact that traditional structures, the first being the family, were institutions of refuge capable of ensuring a minimum of protection to their members. Although to outside observers the family cell may appear wholly inegalitarian and bound by tradition, with its members living, to adopt a Chinese sociologist's vivid description, 'beneath the shadow of their ancestors', it was still the principal place for socialization. In this respect it serves as a palliative for the inadequacies of a distant state totally incapable of transmuting into a nation a people in the throes of a population explosion. In any case, in the same way as under the Empire, and doubtless for the same reasons, the family cell sets its own interests before those of the community. It feels itself to be an independent organism which ignores frontiers and political divides. This stability is certainly not unconnected with the failure of attempts at modernization imposed from above.

Attempts at reform

Confronted with the massive reality which rural China and its families presents, attempts by the state at reconstructing and renovating society, whether undertaken by the Republican government or its communist opponents, produced only poor results. Re-establishing a central authority proved to be a slow and difficult process. The usurpation of the revolution by the military leaders, who counted among the principal agents of an authoritarian Japanese type of modernization, ended in 1916 with the country splitting into *de facto* zones of influence. This was the period of the 'Warlords', a confused episode lasting about ten years during which the political class's whole attention was fixed on the continuing power struggles.

It was only at the end of the 1920s when one phase of the military reconquest was over that the Nationalist Party (*Kuomintang*) managed to establish its authority over a dozen or so provinces constituting the core of the 'useful country'. This victory was won at the price of allying with the reformist wing of the army and was paid for by breaking with the radicals and, in particular, the Communist Party, which for the time being was confined to a few marginal zones. It is still difficult to make an objective assessment of this period and of what the nationalist measures achieved, in so far as subsequent events, marked by the eviction of the Kuomintang and the victory of the Communist Party led by Mao Zedong, have completely distorted our perspective.

At the start of the 1930s, when the Nanking nationalist government appeared to have won, two totally divergent projects for reconstructing the state and reforming society were in competition. The nationalist model had been worked out in Westernized circles in the big cities, and it stressed modernization and progressive assimilation to Western civilization while postulating growing economic integration into world markets. The communist project had been tried out in the laboratory of the Soviet Republic of Jiangxi, a poor rural region, and drew on its revolutionary experience, while taking account of peasants' egalitarian aspirations. The two attempts were obviously not situated on the same map. The Nanking government's achievement was above all legislative; the action taken by the communist rebels was limited by a more or less hostile social environment. Furthermore, the contest took place beneath the constant threat of invasion and in a climate of siege brought about by economic blockade.

The Nanking legislators were not working in the abstract. Their work was based on numerous sociological and legal surveys and was orientated in two directions: reforming family law and redefining the concept of land ownership. Where the family was concerned, their objective was to reach a new concept of marriage, of relations between generations as well as greater autonomy for the individual. They also undertook to draw up an inventory of rights over land in order to clarify relations between landowners and farmers and to inaugurate a fairer tax system. This legislative action taken by the Nationalist government had very little real effect. The Nanking authorities, who controlled only a fraction of the national territory, were capable neither of instituting registration of birth and marriage nor of taking a census. The Civil Code promulgated in 1931 had only a theoretical bearing. In fact, it established Western-style relations between the various members of a family which were difficult to implement given, for instance, the absence of registration of marriages and of procedures for settling disputes over inheritance. This new form of marriage, defined by equality of the spouses and mutual consent, thus remained a dead letter for all except the more educated strata of the population. Collective weddings were celebrated in the towns in order to make different social classes aware of the civil nature of the institution. In the countryside, this process was prolonged by the 'New Life' movement, an attempt to provide the peasants with behavioural models and, in particular, to dissuade them from engaging in the wasteful expenditure occasioned by marriage and funeral celebrations. The reform of land ownership came up against almost insurmountable obstacles. In fact, surveys revealed not only very unequal distribution but above all an insuperable confusion of rights. Getting a new system of land ownership going as a preliminary to modernizing agriculture would involve identifying and compensating all the holders of rights, designating a legal landowner and fixing reasonable levels for rents and taxation. As in the domain of family law, the authorities were incapable of proceeding to a revision of their cadaster and limited themselves to issuing recommendations which were rarely translated into fact. From 1938 the Japanese advance drove back nationalist rule to the poorest western provinces, henceforth preventing any further serious attempts at reform.

The communist experience: from radicalism to compromise

The policies implemented by the Communist Party first of all in Jiangxi and then in the liberated north-western area, have been the subject of in-depth studies (Hua, 1981). However, we must not lose sight of the fact that they concerned marginal regions. In contrast to the nationalist authorities, the communists put their trust in the spontaneous aspirations of the people, which they channelled and organized. Their method, which was applied over and over again after the People's Government had been established, consisted of exposing conflicts to the light of day and then solving them in a atmosphere of crisis and psychodrama. Reforms thus hastily defined were subsequently put forward as models. A second original feature consisted of always tackling head-on economic reforms and transformations in relations between individuals. Each revolutionary advance, then, entailed a corresponding redefinition of the family.

In accordance with the analysis made by Mao Zedong and the Chinese

Marxist theorists, poor peasants and women were presented as the victims *par excellence* of the social order. By the end of the 1920s, the motor force behind the peasant movement was the Communist Party, with the result that it associated the liberation of tenants and agricultural workers with the emancipation of women. Seizing power in a village or a canton was invariably followed by 'settlements of account' in the interests of these two most exploited categories. The solutions proposed, on the other hand, varied according to the political situation. During the most radical phases of the struggle, the Communist Party did not shrink from extreme measures: eviction of the 'exploiting' element of the population, egalitarian distribution of land and liberation of women. In periods of union or political compromise, more moderate solutions were recommended: reducing rents and acting as conciliators in internal family disputes. The twenty-year history of the Civil War is characterized by such alternating hard-line phases and periods of compromise.

In the southern provinces of Hunan, Jiangxi and Fujian, where the communists' action developed from the 1920s onwards, they had to deal with more structured clan forms. The revolutionaries sided systematically with poor relatives against family authorities. Collective properties, such as lands held in common or foundations for supporting clan institutions which were generally farmed out to small tenants, were brought together into large holdings. The model of peasant society which influenced the rulers of the Soviet Republic of Jiangxi rounded up nuclear families within the framework of neighbourhood associations, thus breaking up former kinship solidarities. Women's liberation concerned the most alienated categories such as second wives or 'child-brides', who were particularly numerous in the south of the country. The strict separation of the sexes and marginalization of women consequent on the practice of virilocal marriage often exacerbated conflicts, which were then put to use during the phases of political take-over. It would however be mistaken to believe that the Communist Party was planning to implement a programme for overturning family relationships. Accusations of 'sharing wives', as complacently circulated by nationalist propaganda at the time, were totally unfounded. On the other hand, responsible elements from the urban intelligentsia certainly did entertain very liberated relations with female militants from their own circle. The schoolgirls or students with their 'short hair' who took part in revolutionary action at the time left a trail of scandal behind them, with the consequence that their political adversaries often treated them extremely brutally. The Communist Party, on the other hand, was careful to avoid any clash with peasant morality. The different laws promulgated by the Jiangxi Soviets in 1931 and 1934, and then by the Yan'an authorities in

1939 aimed above all at correcting excess and protecting women. Using terms close to those of the 1934 Civil Code, they abolished the various forms of union which resorted to constraint or money payments, and they raised the legal age of marriage to eighteen for girls and twenty for men. Their most radical provisions concerned betrothals, which lost their compulsory nature for the girl's family, compulsory registration of marriages with the aim of establishing the spouses' freedom of choice, and the introduction of divorce by mutual consent.

Driven out of its southern bases by a series of military operations, the communist leadership took refuge in 1935 in the 'frontier region of Shaan Gan Ning', a relatively deprived region where it tried to implement a policy inspired by the principles of the Soviet Republic of Jiangxi, with the brutal elimination of landowners and establishment of an egalitarian peasant society. The difficulties encountered among a population which was very different from that of Jiangxi, and above all the necessity for a united front against the Japanese, determined an about-turn in 1939, which led to the shelving of most of the reforms. Thus equality was temporarily abandoned in favour of lower land rents still guaranteeing the rights of landowners. On the level of the family and its customs, there was no longer any question of imposing a marriage reform which went against local customs such as polygamy in the Islamic section of the population or the temporary 'renting out' of wives. The 1939 version of the marriage law was thus more evasive than the text drafted five years earlier in Jiangxi. In practice, traditional forms of marriage were tolerated and the committees set up to regulate conflicts often advocated reconciliation in divorce suits. Emancipatory ideology certainly did continue to inspire official speech. One of the most famous works of literature of the time, *The Girl with White Hair*, tells the story of a young girl who has been assaulted by a tramp and joins the revolutionary camp. The episode of 8 March 1942, when the female novelist Ding Ling was subjected to fierce criticism for depicting the female condition in Yan'an in an article published in the party's official organ for 'Women's Day', finally revealed the disquiet caused by the wide gap between the emancipatory official line and a practice still under the heavy weight of tradition. The population under communist rule lived under a dual contradiction. Whereas the administrative organs set up by the party compromised with local customs and maintained a social order which was largely founded on respect for property and the authority of the family, the ruling faction had adapted to the liberation ethos inherited from the May Fourth Movement and its struggle. Among them, couples were formed at the whim of desire and affinity, with no legal sanction. Nevertheless, given the great imbalance between the sexes and the dominant position of men, women, and more particularly the young educated women from the 'white' areas, were objects of intense competition between members of the ruling group. The case of Mao Zedong, who repudiated his third wife He Zezhen, in order to live with Jian Qing, a young actress recently arrived from Shanghai, was in no way exceptional. The effect of this situation was to reduce women to the rank of objects and to confine them to relatively subaltern functions.

The communist leaders' revolutionary practices did not, any more than the legislation of the Nanking governments, have a profound impact on a mostly agrarian society which was driven back onto its own resources by the political conditions of the first half of the twentieth century, civil war and Japanese occupation. Curiously enough, the economic difficulties and exceptional privations to which the population was subjected between 1939 and 1949 do not appear to have left the demographic scars which one would expect. The 1953 census revealed, in fact, an age pyramid entirely lacking in indentations corresponding to hollow age groups. What was more, growth was maintained, even if at a slower rate. The fertility rate, as reconstituted for the 1940–9 period, wavered at around 5.3 children per woman, with slight dips in 1942 and 1944. Age at marriage varied little, but was in any case lower than the limits set by the different legislations. One can discern in 1953 a net surplus male population in age groups born during the most troubled period, which might point to a tendency to resort to infanticide, or at least to neglecting girl babies, but this phenomenon is more difficult to show on the two age pyramids for 1964 and 1982, and it could correspond to a registration bias. These few indicators thus lead us to think that the nation's survival was guaranteed in some manner by the maintenance of its ancient family and social structures.

Communist rule and the family

When the Communist Party came to power in 1949 after a long period of civil war, it put into action a threefold policy: socialist transformation of the economy, industrialization and social reform, with all its implications for the evolution of the family. For the first time since 1911, a central power was exercising its authority over the entire national territory while commanding the necessary means for radically reshaping society. The results of forty-five years of reform cannot be summed up simply by listing the measures adopted, and we must also try to evaluate the degree of society's response to legislative encouragement and take into account the unintended effects of this policy.

The 1950 marriage law figures among the very first reforms decided on by the People's Government. It is important to note that it began to be applied at the same time as the agrarian reform was being implemented, and that the combination of the two was not fortuitous, because what the rulers envisaged was nothing less than a radical remodelling of the peasantry. Basically, the 1950 law picked up various regulations made by the nationalist legislators and later relating to marriage in the 'liberated areas'. It thus restated the principle of union by mutual consent, the obligatory character of monogamy, equality between spouses and equal rights of divorce for husband and wife. In practical terms, it introduced official registration, banned intervention by match-makers and denied that the presentation of betrothal gifts had any binding force. The minimum age remained set at eighteen for girls and twenty for boys. Coming into effect simultaneously with the redistribution of land between peasant families, the marriage law promoted a new and often brutal reordering of rural society. It aimed in particular to correct and punish abuses and crimes committed by landowners and rich peasants, and was thus retrospective. The teams whose task it was to implement the agrarian reform were duplicated by groups investigating matrimonial situations whose objective was to get the victims themselves, wives who had been married against their will and concubines, to denounce illegal actions on the part of the exploiting classes. These investigations were often the occasion of confessions and summary justice. The application of the new legislation gave rise to a flood of divorces, generally in favour of wives who had been subjected to injustice. It also showed up the persistent nature of customs which were hard to reconcile with the spirit of the law but which could not be eradicated without attacking cherished customs. With regard to poor peasants, who were the main beneficiaries of the agrarian reform, the attitude adopted was first and foremost educative: rules on age at marriage and payment of betrothal gifts were for the time being ignored. Statistics based on recent surveys show that the average age of girls at marriage rose from 18.6 to 19.2 years between 1950 and 1957, but that many young girls still celebrated their marriage before the age of seventeen. Peasant habits were not to be modified in any fundamental way.

In the absence of precise studies it is difficult to assess the impact of agrarian reform on the lives of rural families. In terms of the 1950 law, a ceiling of ownership had been established, and rich families were forced without compensation to give up their excess land, which would then be shared out among poor families. Thus the society inaugurated by the agrarian reform was not properly egalitarian since it was impossible to round out any excessively small property by renting more land. During the years following the redistribution of the fields, a solution to these new inequalities was sought by constituting mutual assistance groups or co-operatives. Although traditional society had certainly known some forms of mutual assistance, these would generally have involved exchanging labour or services within the framework of kinship or neighbourhood solidarities. The mutual help which was called for in the early 1950s stressed class solidarity.

The breadth of the transformation in urban society is in contrast to the moderation of rural policies. Within a few years, large firms were nationalized, mixed-economy enterprises established, and workshops and small businesses regrouped into co-operatives. In practice, urban society was thus transformed into a society of wage workers in which the family ceased to play an economic role and became a mere unit of consumption. About 1950 some 20 million non-agricultural jobs supported an urban population of about 60 million. At that time, wage employment represented less than half the total. In 1957, when the transformation to a socialist economy had been completed, nearly 30 million wage jobs were counted. The private sector had practically disappeared. Important disparities remained in housing and disposable income per head of population, but overall it was the number of jobs which each family filled that determined its economic standing, especially after a drastic levelling of wages. From then on, though, access to employment was entirely controlled by the administration.

Viewed retrospectively, it is quite clear that the 1950s were characterized by a new phenomenon, the consequences of which escaped the rulers' attention at the time. This was the new rise in fertility, or rather a strong increase in the rate of reproduction linked to lower infant and child mortality. In absolute figures, the gain was a modest one because the fertility rate rose from 5.5 to a little over 6 per cent. When this is calculated in terms of survivors, it shows a spectacular advance. One woman's surviving children increased in number from three to five. The new rise in fertility was thus translated into a markedly more youthful population. The proportion of under-sixteens rose from 38 per cent in 1953 to 43 per cent at the 1964 census. On the other hand, taking into account the multiplication of non-agricultural jobs and the increased participation of women in productive work, the dependency level evolved favourably because the proportion of the working population rose from 36 to 38 per cent of the total. Nevertheless, by 1956 some economists were worrying about the predictable consequences of the changing dimension of the generations. The first campaign for limiting births was launched. At the same time, restricting the number of descendants was viewed as a means of liberating women and of making it easier to integrate them socially.

From people's communes to the Cultural Revolution

The country went through a troubled period from 1958 to 1961, which is considered with hindsight to have been a phase of madness, a moment when the 'wind of communism' blew over the land. The truly catastrophic consequences of the 'great leap forward', on the economic as much as on the social level, prohibit, among other things, any objective appraisal of the whole experience. Collective memory has retained from that time the remembrance of privation and famine. Furthermore the institution of people's communes was very quickly emptied of its social content to become a mere administrative level.

The idea of people's communes took shape in the spring of 1958, when the Chinese government tried to speed up the rhythm of economic development by raising the rate of growth combined with an unprecedented mobilization of the workforce. This meant that bringing about the disappearance of the family as a consumer unit came to the forefront as a formula for reducing production costs. This policy was tried out experimentally first of all on the peasantry, which was hastily organized into large units of several thousand or tens of thousands of people pooling their resources to constitute great agro-industrial enterprises. At first the strategic model was inspired by the experiences of millenarian rebellions. In its most radical form, the commune, called significantly a 'bridge to communism', imposed a strict separation of the sexes, with furniture and kitchen equipment owned in common, and a communal lifestyle involving the collective care of children and old people in nurseries and hospices. The family cell was thus thoroughly undermined as a unit for living and consuming.

These measures very quickly gave rise to strong passive resistance, provoked as much by people's dislike of communal living as by a very comprehensive reaction against the extreme hardship brought by the 'great leap forward'. When, in the course of 1959, the government planned extending the formula to the towns, the opposition was so great that it immediately had to retract. In reality, the national economy had been reduced to such chaos by the collapse of agricultural production and the crises which hit various sectors of industry and trade in succession, that the situation was not propitious for experimenting with new forms of social organization. Looking back over the years, the demographic statistics depict this period along the lines of a classic subsistence crisis. There was a spectacular rise in mortality and a drop in the birth rate which in 1960 fell below the death rate. The rural population which drew its main resources from agriculture was particularly hard hit. Many regions experienced famine and the most stricken villages were abandoned. Different forms of behaviour in town and country were noted: whereas among the peasants brides became notably younger, since families were no longer able to keep their daughters at home and tried to get rid of them early on, in towns the age of marriage tended to rise, as a result of the lower standard of living and insecurity about employment.

These communist experiments were abandoned from 1961. Important concessions were made to the peasants, who reorganized their lives within the framework of nuclear or extended families. Henceforth each home had its own plot of land, adjusted to the number of family members; houses and movable property were restored to their former owners and remuneration for collective agricultural work was paid to the heads of families. Nevertheless the family unit had only a limited role in the organization of production. Secondary activities and free markets were merely tolerated, and the peasants were reduced to the status of agricultural wage-earners working on farms of variable size, with large teams bringing together between fifty and a hundred households.

For most city-dwellers, their unit of work, whether factory, administrative unit or craft or commercial co-operative, does not correspond to the framework of their lives. Indeed, only the large administrative sectors and nationalized industries are capable of providing their employees and workers with collective lodgings and social services. On the other hand, living conditions for the urban population, which had been shielded from the crisis of the worst years, were overturned by the horrors of the Cultural Revolution.

The significance and the roots of this movement, which erupted in 1966 within an apparently favourable context, could be discussed at length. Was it a bid by the ageing Mao Zedong, anxious about his country's lapse into 'revisionism', to regain power? Was it a revolt by young people breaking with ways of life inherited from the 'old' society? Was it merely a struggle between factions? There is probably an element of truth in each of these interpretations. Unlike the 'great leap forward', the Cultural Revolution had no immediate economic end. Rather, it aimed at relaunching production by redefining social relations. Thus it was not so much the family, which had long since been deprived of its real economic functions, as the remnants of feudal and bourgeois attitudes and habits which were subjected to criticism and assault. Foreign observers were particularly taken aback by the Red Guards' violence, which characterized the most brutal phase of the struggle (1966–9). There is no doubt that young people were undergoing a crisis, aggravated by employment problems. By about 1965 the raising of school standards and the development of secondary education implemented for the past fifteen years had produced a whole new generation of 'educated young' in search of their first job. Opportunities, however, were limited, and the possession of a middle school certificate was no guarantee of a technical or administrative job. Furthermore, in order to enable a proportion of young people from the countryside to be absorbed into the modern sectors, it was necessary to bring the urban workforce to the country. Pupils in secondary schools were kept in uncertainty about their entry into professional life and were thus open to the promotion of a militant attitude directed against traditional values. The demonstrations, whether spontaneous or organized, of the young people's revolt were not directed against the family unit as a living and consumer space – there was no question of setting up communal ways of life – but they did attack the survival of privileges such as ownership of art objects, private libraries or expensive furniture, and adherence to styles of consumption which expressed social differences. Many well-off families thus preferred to take the initiative by ridding themselves, by selling or destroying, of objects which might symbolize any attempt to be different. The iconoclastic phase lasted only a short time, and as soon as things came under control again in 1969, the most radical groups were dissolved and many young people were sent to the countryside or to state farms in frontier regions for re-education. All in all, the movement of confrontation resulted in an egoistical withdrawal into the family group and, paradoxically, a revival of previous forms of behaviour.

It is necessary to distinguish between the urban part of the population, riven by interfactional struggles, and the peasantry, which on the whole kept itself apart from the convulsions of the Cultural Revolution. Urban society was affected by constraints resulting from the development of towns as well as by the practice of sending one out of every two adolescents to the countryside; nearly 20 million left for spells of three to seven years between 1966 and 1978. It was only after Mao Zedong's death in 1976 that it rediscovered its own lifestyle. The 1970s, when family planning was relaunched, were characterized by an extremely low birth rate which corresponded to some extent to 'emptying' the cities of their young people. The rural population, which represented more than 80 per cent of the entire population, seems to have been much less affected by the ups and downs of politics, although the restrictions on individual activities deprived many families of a significant part of their income. A slow evolution in behaviour can be observed. During the 1960s the fertility level remained at close to six. It might be expected that the distribution of income in kind according to family size, which made up the bulk of the peasants' resources, would act as an incentive to maintain a high birth rate, and the launch of the birth control policy, one

A family planning poster. The single child symbolizes a better life.
Comstock/Gerster.

element of which was 'late marriage' (from the age of twenty-five), had only a gradual effect. Fertility retained a clear lead over levels in the towns – in 1975 the figure was 3.9 children (1.8 in the towns) – whereas age at marriage rose only very slowly. The persistence of some customs, such as betrothal of girls at the age of thirteen or fourteen, and the presentation of substantial gifts to the family of the betrothed girl, is witness to the strong resistance of peasant forms of behaviour, which goes hand in hand with the survival of considerable inequality in education and employment. Indeed, it was not until the new generations of girls born after 1957 came onto the scene that the illiteracy rate fell below 40 per cent.

Decline or renewal of the family?

At the time when the 1982 census was taken, more than 97 per cent of the Chinese population were living in 221 million households. Around 60 per cent of households comprised at least five persons. By 1990 the number of homes had risen to 277 million; at an average of 4.1 persons each, they are slightly smaller than at the beginning of the 1980s. This evolution corresponds more to a slight reduction in the number of children than to any progress on the part of nuclear families. Recent figures show that the great majority of old persons, who are proportionally still few in number, live in vertical families comprising three or even four generations. They are generally supported by their children; indeed, few old people draw pensions or have sufficient income to live on their own. Although marriage now occurs perceptibly later than at the start of the 1970s, with the age at marriage now set at twenty-two for women, the tendency for it to rise has stopped. The proportion of unmarried adults is still very low. These few figures reveal the importance of the family institution as a life context, a place for consuming and, increasingly, a unit of production.

The trend towards decollectivization of agriculture started in 1979 and has restored economic autonomy to the rural families which constitute nearly three-quarters of the population. During the first period, land and animals were allotted to households according to family size, and in most cases this included the children; later on, people were left free to manage their lands as they wished and to combine secondary activities with agriculture so long as they sold a certain quantity of cereals or vegetable produce to the state at fixed prices. We are witnessing a strong trend towards social differentiation among rural families, some of which have

Table 3 Parameters of fertility: age at marriage and level of education

Generation	Proportion of illiterate women (%)	Median age at marriage	Fertility achieved (children)
1925	90	18	5.5
1930	85	18	5.7
1935	75	18	5.3
1940	60	19	4.5
1945	45	19	3.8
1950	40	20	3.0
1955	37	22	2.5

launched into industrial enterprises or services such as freight, which is revealed above all by a greatly diversified habitat, with the construction of private houses displaying their owners' wealth.

In the towns, where the state has long retained its monopoly over employment and the majority of people live on their wages or pensions, and where municipal councils and enterprises control housing, a similar evolution is taking place. The state sector (industry and administration) is no longer capable of absorbing all the young people entering the labour market. At the same time the flood of country people seeking to set themselves up illegally in town creates strong employment tensions. We are thus witnessing a boom in the private sector, which is matched by the appearance of an informal sector.

This renewal of the family is directly prejudicial to the implementation of the radical birth control programme which was intended from the mid-1980s to generalize the model of the single-child couple. As far as can be established, fertility rates were maintained at 1981 levels during the whole of the decade, at an average of 2.5 children per woman. Since 1986 the conjunction of two factors, the coming to reproductive age of the very large cohorts born during the 1960s, and the reduction in the age at marriage, has produced a rise in the birth rate which Chinese experts have called the 'third wave in the birth rate'. Population growth is still over 15 per cent per annum, and it is now clear that the predictions of population stagnation or reduction in the first decades of the twenty-first century are pure fiction. The conflict between the family and the state has, so to speak, been transferred from the field of the economy to the domain of reproduction. Although the single-child policy has been relatively well accepted in the towns, where the advent of a second child spells great problems for its parents – with the exception of marginal urban elements who engage happily in 'guerilla-type operations' for exceeding the fertility rate – it is very ill-received by the rural masses for whom social success is related to the size of their family, and especially to the presence of sons. The administrators of the birth control programme often resort to extreme brutality, inflicting fines on contraveners or forcing women to undergo abortions and even sterilization. The population normally reacts to coercive measures of this kind by a combination of passive resistance to the payment of fines, concealing 'excess' births and outbreaks of violence. It is clear that the pursuit of the single-child policy over several decades would imperil the institution of the family to such an extent that it would generate an inverted society, in which the number of descendants would diminish with every generation and kinship relations such as brother and sister, cousin, uncle and nephew would rapidly disappear.

FIVE

The Family: Instrument and Model of the Japanese Nation

Patrick Beillevaire

The return of the emperor (*tennô*) to the forefront of the political scene in 1868 marked the onset of modernity for Japan. Weakened internally by the inequities of feudal society and too irresolute to defend the nation's territorial integrity in the face of an immediate threat by colonial powers, the Shōgun government was obliged to resign under pressure from the armed partisans of the restoration of direct imperial power (*ôsei fukko*). The restoration of the emperor, called the 'Meiji Restoration' (*Meiji Ishin*), from the name of the era which then began (1868–1912), was merely the preliminary to a profound upheaval in institutions and society as a whole, an upheaval which for a brief interval enabled Japan to expand beyond its frontiers and to oppose Western countries not only on the economic but also on the military front.

After taking an initial oath in which the emperor promised to base his policy on 'public opinion' as expressed through assemblies, the new government entrusted an Imperial Council with the task of elaborating a constitution modelled on those of European nations. During the execution of the project, the influence of Germany proved decisive because the political system of that country gave preponderance to the monarchical principle. Ito Hirobumi, the prime minister and one of the most striking personalities of the period, played a major part in shaping it. Promulgated in 1889 (on 11 February, the date chosen to commemorate *kigensetsu*, the mythical foundation of the Empire by Emperor Jinmu in 660 BC) after lengthy preparatory work, and implemented in the following year, the so-called Meiji Constitution, *Meiji kenpô*, excluded the idea of the sovereignty of the people, thus approving the original autocratic style of a rule which had been shown to be stable over the two previous centuries. This constitution was entitled *Dai nihon teikoku kenpô*

(Constitution of the Empire of Japan). Presented as a gift from the emperor to his subjects, this charter laid down that sovereignty resided in the 'sacred' person of the emperor, the heir to a divine and eternal dynasty. Represented by a cabinet of ministers responsible to the emperor and not to the Diet, the executive power was clearly recognized as pre-eminent (the same applied to the armed forces). Despite the existence of parties, which had some influence on government decisions, popular representation in the Lower Chamber, which was anyway subjected to restrictions involving payment of the poll tax, played only a secondary role confined to the power of veto on the budget law.

Although the 1871 law on family registers (*Koseki hô*) merely sanctioned the customary subordination of the individual to the family unit, a series of different government measures also adopted in the early 1870s altered the feudal social order decisively. These included the abolition of the Confucian system of statutes (though leaving a residual distinction between nobles and commoners), recognition of freedom of movement, authorization for the sale of land (which had the effect of increasing disparity in rural areas), obligatory school attendance and the inauguration of national military service. With these structural transformations and the technological boom which accompanied them, there also went a far-reaching change in political and social thought. New words were created, others acquired new meanings in order to introduce Western notions about society (*shakai*) into the Japanese language, notions of liberty (*jiyû*), law (*kenri*) and even of family (*kazoku*), a term designating a group founded solely on the ties of blood and alliance as opposed to the traditional notion of house or *ie*. This was the age of 'opening up to Western civilization', *Bunmei kaika*, which was reflected in the towns by a mild obsession with Western customs, including dress and cookery.

But as the evolution of the Meiji system of government effectively demonstrates, the speed with which every sector set out to make good what was considered as its 'backwardness' compared with the West should not give the impression that the values and forms of behaviour inherited from the past were dissipated. In fact, in spite of the lively interest which European liberal politics initially aroused among the young intellectual elite of the time, the aim was that the adoption of foreign sciences and knowledge should be reconciled with preserving the Japanese soul; hence the slogan *wakon yôsai* (Japanese soul, Western technology; 'Japanese soul' is *Yamato damashii* in its *Volksgeist* meaning, or, for the premodern nationalist thinkers of the Kokugaku school, *Yamato gokoro*). To this end, the process of modernizing the country was matched, at the price of transfiguring history, with an ideological traditionalism wholly based on the dual concept of emperor and family.

The family and the construction of the modern state

The Meiji Civil Code

In order to achieve parity with Western nations, Japan had to follow their example by acquiring a system of penal and civil legislation. Preparatory work to this end started in 1870. The Japanese authorities were aware of the Napoleonic Code's prestige and reputation for universality, and so surrounded themselves with French legal advisers, including Georges Bousquet and especially Gustave Boissonade de Fontarabie, who spent nearly twenty years in Japan. Although it started off as a straightforward translation of the French model, the code project evolved draft by draft until it was less at variance with traditional concepts in matters of family organization and the transmission of property. This bias reflected the growing interest brought to bear on customary law, as evidenced by the publication over the years 1870–80 of several inventories of regional legal practices. As opposed to penal legislation, which was applied from 1882 and gave rise to no opposition, the Civil Code was subjected to increasingly lively attacks by conservative jurists who were keen to preserve the traditional family ethic. Two important figures in this trend, Hozumi Nobushige and his brother

A family of cake sellers, Tokyo, *c.*1875. Roger Viollet.

Hozumi Yatsuka, later dean of the Imperial University of Tokyo, both of whom were educated in the school of German legal history, played a preponderant role in establishing the cult of the emperor and spreading the concept of the state as a family (Minear, 1970).

The code was finally promulgated in 1890 and would have been applied in 1893 had the Diet not decided in the meantime to adjourn in order to proceed to a review. This report enabled whole sections dedicated to family law to be recast, and, in the final analysis, largely purified of any too individualistic *a prioris* in European law. The latter, on the other hand, continued to govern dispositions relating to property in the final version of the code, which came into effect in 1898.

Meiji minpô, the Meiji Civil Code as it is called nowadays, by recognizing the house or *ie* as subject to law, maintained the traditional point of view in which the house constituted the first and fundamental element of Japanese society. Consequently, individual identity continued to be defined principally by membership of a house and by inscription in a family register called *koseki* (the term and the practice go back to the previous age). The code also determined the moral primacy of the head of the house, *koshu*, over all the other members. His consent was required for the marriage of men under the age of thirty and for women less than twenty-five years old. In cases of disagreement, the code even granted him the possibility of securing the annulment of a marriage during the two years following its registration. Thus the head of the house had the sole power of deciding whether to admit new members and of excluding members who had been judged unworthy.

The wife, for her part, had no legal capacity to oppose the father's authority over his children. Although the code did make a few concessions to the principle of right to property, it stipulated that her personal property should be administered by her husband. This meant that she was entirely subject to decisions taken by her husband and his family. Furthermore, marriages were often only registered after a probationary period of a few months to allow the in-laws to assess the young wife's qualities and, possibly, to decide on a separation at the lowest possible cost. In divorce matters, two proceedings were available: mutual consent and judicial decision. Although in practice it was easier for a man to get a divorce (the most frequent reasons for divorce being the wife's alleged sterility or her unfaithfulness, while male adultery was not a sufficient reason), officially the wife too had the right to demand a divorce, for instance for cruelty or desertion by the husband. The code did not allow married men to engage in concubinage, but this ancient practice, which was briefly given official status just after the Meiji Restoration, had already been abolished in 1880.

In its chapter on inheritance, the code made a distinction between succession to the status of head of the house, *katoku sôzoku*, and the transmission of property, *isan sôzoku*. In the first case, boys took priority over girls and the eldest over the younger, which amounted in practice to male primogeniture. As the continuator of the family line, the inheritor was entrusted with the care of genealogical documents and the utensils for ancestor worship. The legal heir could only be excluded from the succession for a grave reason such as a physical or moral defect. Given that the perpetuation of the house was an obligatory duty, in the event of no male heir, provision had been made since time immemorial for the head to adopt a son-in-law (*muko yôshi*), or if he had no daughters, any male person capable of succeeding him. The adopted son and potential heir enjoyed the same advantages as a biological child, but he had first to renounce honouring his own ancestors and to assume the name of his adoptive father (patronyms were made obligatory in 1875). If the head of house died with no son or heir designate, the responsibility of naming a successor devolved on his father and mother or even on a family council (*kazoku kaigi*). Their choice would then fall, in order of preference, on his wife, if her husband had been adopted (in such cases the wife was known as *kajo*, 'daughter of the house'), on one of his brothers or sisters, and only then on his wife if she had come from another house, and finally on a nephew or niece. As may be seen, women were not excluded in law from the succession, but they always came after the men in the same degree of kinship.

The code stipulated that the successor could not receive less than half of the inherited property, with the other children's share depending on their father's will. Provision was also made, according to a customary practice, which was particularly common in the regions to the north of the country, for the younger children of both sexes to have the opportunity to found branch houses (*bunke*) to serve the needs of the family economy, while remaining dependent on the 'house of origin' (*honke*). However, the development of a market economy demanded that the family structure should not hinder an individual's initiative and responsibility. To this end, those compiling the code had dissociated a person's quality as member of a house from his individual right to property. Each individual was thus permitted to transmit equal shares to his descendants, whatever their sex or family membership, of such wealth as he had himself acquired. In order to take this individualistic per-spective into account, the new law on family registers laid down a personal identification system, distinct from that for family registers, called *mibun tôki* (register of the condition of persons).

On the whole this legislation kept faith, in many essential aspects, with the principles governing the traditional organization of the family, and most particularly that of the ancient military class (Samurai influence was even clearer after the code was revised in 1912). The most notable consequence of applying it was to stress the cultural unity of the country by extending the same more strictly Confucian family ethic to all classes and all regions. Until then, in fact, peasant customs had been based on varied rules which had generally been less constricting where the father's authority, the status of the bride and inheritance practices were concerned. Nevertheless, in spite of the determinedly conservative orientation of its provisions relating to the family, there is a case for saying that the Meiji Civil Code marked a clear break with the previous period by introducing a fundamentally new notion, that of right. Pre-Meiji Japanese culture was aware only of the principle of obligation, *giri*, the true cement of traditional society linking individuals together in a more or less asymmetrical but always enduring fashion. It proved necessary in any case to adopt a neologism, *kenri*, associating the idea of power, *ken*, with that of interest, *ri*, to render in Japanese the notion of right as borrowed from the West. There is evidence that this was the first stage of an individualistic social philosophy which could have imperilled the community values of loyalty and filial devotion which were characteristic of traditional Japanese society. This is why, right from the start, the conservative and already dominant discourse tended to interpret the notion of right, notably in the case of the person of the head of the house, as a power which was not inherent in the individual but was delegated to him by the state.

The family and nationalist ideology

The problems raised by the elaboration of the Civil Code, which echoed the divergent interpretations of the constitution, show that for many contemporaries the family could not be reduced to a mere component of civil society, but that, on the contrary, it remained the cornerstone of the social order. On this major point no discontinuity of principles can be observed between the previous society and the Meiji nation-state, but rather a strengthening effect brought about by promoting the policy and the necessary adoption of a constitutional and legislative apparatus. With the rise of national consciousness, family organization had been transformed from a spontaneous model, a sort of diffuse cultural canvas, which had supplied political as well as economic relations within feudal society with a significant part of their vocabulary and rules, into a well thought-out model, thanks to which it was possible to think in terms of both the unity of the country and the nature of relations between the imperial power and the people. When using the word 'model' here we should be wary of ambiguity. In fact, unlike traditionalist authors in nineteenth-century Europe, for the conservatives of the Meiji period, followed by the propagandists of martial nationalism, it was not a matter of establishing a simple analogy between family and state, but of affirming the basic identity of these two realities (Maruyama, 1979). This point of view was undoubtedly rendered explicit with the greatest force and concision by Hozumi Yatsuka in a corpus of articles which appeared in the 1890s and had a decisive influence on the ruling elite (Kôsaka, 1958). This author described the Japanese state as the product or, to be more exact, the extension of the family institution, and he claimed, conversely, that the latter was to be considered as nothing less than the 'state in microcosm'. Given that the origin of the nation was merged with that of the imperial house, the emperors' divine ancestors became those of the entire people; this homogeneity of Japanese society, which was both spiritual and racial, also justified considering filial piety (*kô*) as the basic manifestation of the loyalty (*chû*) of subjects to the imperial authority and state representatives. By honouring his ancestors each subject was perpetuating the links between the generations and thus ensuring the survival and harmony of the country. This theory of the state-family, *kazoku kokka*, led in the end to considering the family as the very matrix of the Nippon state and the source of its ethos (it should be observed that *kokka*, the state, an ancient term of Chinese origin, already included in its graphics the character for house associated with that for country; note too that the necessity of defining Japan as a nation equal to other powers led, under the influence of the German notion of *Volk*, to giving pre-eminence to the biological and racial dimension, which had hitherto not counted for much in popular culture, as much at state as at family level).

From the beginning of the Meiji period, the government had laid great importance on its system of school education, and in particular history teaching. From the 1880s onwards, and especially under the influence of Mori Arinori, who was appointed education minister in 1885, history became the principal instrument for the diffusion of a social philosophy based on the recognition of the supremacy of the state (*kokka shugi* or 'statism'). Mori's modernism had seemed in the eyes of some people to prejudice the spiritual tradition of the nation, and his assassination in 1889 led conservatives to desire a more direct intervention by the emperor. This gave rise to the publication in the following year of an imperial rescript on education (*Kyôiku chokugo*). This text, although still leaving room for divergent interpretations, implicitly thwarted the democratic aspirations which were defended above all by the Movement

for the Liberty and Rights of the People (*Jiyû minken undô*). Thus it
called on each person to deny himself and to work for the common good,
and held affection between relatives, filial piety, veneration for ancestors
and loyalty to the state to be indissociable virtues, which were inspired
within the Japanese people by the ancestors of the imperial house.

The rescript served as a basis for the compilation of schoolbooks for
moral education (*shûshin*). In the course of successive revisions, these
works departed from their initially cautious view of the creation of the
country by the imperial ancestors to an open exaltation of the divine
nature of the emperor, in direct line of descent from *Amaterasu-ô-mi-
kami* (the sacred person of the emperor was considered to be the very
incarnation of the state and not a mere 'organ of the state', a concept
which also had its partisans, the most famous of whom was Minobe
Tatsukichi, but who remained very much a minority). Since the Meiji
Constitution had recognized freedom of choice in matters of religion,
devotion to the emperor (*tennô sûhai*) did not officially come under
religious practice but under what can conveniently be called civic duty.

The imperial ideology, along the principle of the state-family, which is
summed up by the expression *tennô sei* or 'imperial rule', drew its
strength and novelty from assimilating the traditional respect due to the
imperial person, the source of all legitimacy but not the object of a
popular cult, with the veneration for family ancestors (*sosen sûhai*). The
emperor was described as a father (*kachô*, 'head of house') benevolently
guiding his people, and each individual family as a branch derived from
the imperial house (designated as the 'founding house of the people or the
nation', *kokumin sôka*). This doctrine was nourished by the oldest
myths, which were elevated to the rank of historical evidence and
symbolized the genius proper to the Japanese nation, its 'immutable
essence' or *kokutai* (*koku* meaning 'country' and *tai* 'body', 'substance'
or 'form'), as distinct from its 'governmental or political form', *seitai*. As
the army's influence over the government grew, an influence which
would prove decisive from 1930, the cult of the emperor was charged
with increasingly militaristic and patriotic connotations (an evolution
expressed by joining the words *aikoku* ('love for the fatherland') and
chûkun ('loyalty to the emperor') to form the slogan of the day: *Chûkun
aikoku*.

'Familialism' in business

Ideologically invested as the figure and essence of the state-nation, the
ideal type of the traditional family also served as a model for organizing
relations between workers and firms. Job security for part of the salaried

workers at least, unfailing faithfulness and devotion (*chûsei*) to the firm, remuneration according to seniority (which however did not exclude bonus payments for ability) and hierarchical independence based on the managers' cordial attitude (*onjô*) and the employees' sense of obligation (*giri*): such were the principal characteristics, well known because they are still in force, of a form of management which is qualified as 'familial' (*keiei kazokushugi* – the term 'paternalism' which is often used in translation, does not correspond to the literal sense of the Japanese expression; *onjô shugi*, or 'affectionism' is also used).

During the first phase of industrialization, two factors concurred to perpetuate earlier forms of behaviour within the new economic structures. On the one hand there was a waged workforce which had come straight from the countryside and was composed of peasants impoverished by agriculture, younger sons excluded from inheritance, and share-croppers with no chance of work, all of them ready to reproduce a community habitus which enhanced ties of dependence and assistance (Vogel, 1967); on the other hand, there was a deliberate strategy on the part of business managers, who were often of Samurai origin and were keen to ensure the loyalty of staff they had themselves trained.

The theory of the state-family as promoted by government circles, which went hand in hand with a rejection of utilitarian individualism, also contributed to shaping entrepreneurs' management concepts. Thus by the end of the nineteenth century some business leaders were drawing up veritable 'family charters', which would be solemnly read out to employees, exhorting them to pay almost filial respect to the management and to dedicate themselves entirely to their task, as much out of affection for the emperor as for the prosperity of the entire nation. Among the most active propagandists of the familial ideal, we should cite Goto Shinpei, director of the state railways when they were nationalized in 1906, who went round the country preaching to railwaymen about their membership of a 'single family' (*ichizoku*), and Yamaoka Juntaro, director of the Osaka Steelworks (which later became the Hitachi group), who spoke of the company in 1914 as a 'house' represented by its head, to whom the workers owed the same degree of solidarity among themselves and application to their work as the members of a family (Hirschmeier and Yui, 1981). After 1938, towards the end of the military phase when trade unions had been abolished, the Industrial Association for the Fatherland (*Sangyô hôkoku kai*) continued to preach the idea that each firm constituted a 'large family' with all the energy demanded by the urgent need to step up production.

In fact it was especially in the aftermath of the First World War, at the end of the Taishô period (1912–26), that the familialist form of management was brought into general use in the most important firms with the aim of preventing the growing ascendancy of Marxist-inspired trade unions over a worker population increasingly disposed to demonstrate its displeasure at the staggering price rises and concomitant stagnation in wages by flouting discipline or going on strike. Employers were induced to strengthen the links uniting the worker to the firm by giving him the material or financial help he needed throughout his life. The expression 'job for life' (*shûshin koyô*) takes on its full meaning when one knows that employment began on leaving school and that, although retirement started at fifty-five, average life expectancy for men during the 1930s was below forty-seven years.

We must not exaggerate the novelty, in Japan any more than other countries, of this transposition of family values into the economic field. Indeed it seems that it was the apprehension, in both meanings of the word, that the two elements might become disconnected that constituted the truly novel phenomenon of the time. Since time immemorial, the family unit known as *ie* had been modelled to meet the economic requirements of agriculture and commerce, so much so that its biological extension might seem to lack an innate coherence. Conversely, the hierarchical structures in the most varied fields of activity, political, economic and artistic, habitually took on the form of kinship relations of the parent–child, eldest–younger and principal house–branch house types, relations which, though fictional, still possessed the practical, moral and religious aspects of true kinship. This familial concept of relations between employers and employees was naturally maintained after the Meiji Restoration in small manufacturing and commercial firms, which were generally still operating in rural surroundings. Later, when industrialists deliberately chose to take charge of what is in the West considered to belong to the private sphere, sometimes going so far as to organize their employees' marriages by acting as intermediaries between the spouses, one might think that they were simply reproducing the role of godfather and employer (*oyakata*) which had formerly been played by the heads of dominant houses in rural communities towards their dependants (*kokata*, those of the 'rank of child'). In the same order of ideas, old-established firms such as Mitsui or Mitsubishi, which were constituted into trusts or *zaibatsu*, came to dominate the economy of the country and influence its political and military destiny. For a long time they too managed to maintain cohesion between their many business sectors by maintaining a familial style of management.

Because of this, the term *kazoku*, used in *kazoku shugi* (familialism), although recently created to mean 'family' in the restricted sense that it had acquired in the West in the nineteenth century, remained charged with connotations of the *ie*, especially because of the absence of differentiation between economic functions and interpersonal relations, which has been stressed above. It was against this background of social traditions and the problems of a national economy burdened by the effort to establish Japan as a colonial presence on the Asian mainland, and also in order to prevent unrest in a working class which, while still not very unionized, was calling on the authorities for better-regulated working conditions, that employers were able to promote the association of capital and labour (*kyôson kyôei*, 'live and prosper together') and get it accepted as the basis of social harmony. Although the conditions granted to some workers in large firms were advantageous, conditions were often far less favourable, both in wages and in the precarious terms of employment, for staff in middling or small firms which acted as their subcontractors (not to mention the semi-slave status of many young women).

Literary and academic vision of the family

It is equally necessary to refer briefly to the importance of the family as matter for reflection in literary and university circles. It was a recurrent theme with numerous novelists and essayists in the first decades of the twentieth century (I need only mention Tayama Katai, Shimazaki Tôson and Natusme Sôseki, who were all well-known novelists, and the critic Shimamura Hôgetsu). Guided by their concern for naturalism and a sometimes ambiguous bias to individualistic subjectivism, their works were marked by a critical tone which contrasted with the government's idealizing slogans. Their sensitive descriptions of the tensions and constraints working within family attachments testified, beyond the ageless reality of human egoism, to a slow but irreversible decline in the system of values bequeathed by the past but now incompatible with the new horizons opened up by modern urban life (Koyano, 1980).

Conversely, university research into the family by sociologists, ethnofolklorists, jurists and historians, in spite of its austerity, won acceptance for the official thesis of family life as the crucible of Japanese sociability. It was during the 1920s that a truly sociological study of the family began in Japan, notably with Toda Teizô's historical and statistical analyses. He was led, under the influence of formal German sociology, to view the family as a fluctuating entity made up of interacting individuals rather than as an institution. Because of this orientation, his work was criticized for its individualistic prejudice by ethnologists like Suzuki Eitarô, Aruga Kizaemon and Yanagita Kunio. While the research done by these authors is still extremely interesting on account of the wealth of material on which they based their findings, it was almost exclusively concentrated on the rural family. Among the principal ideas to emerge was the emphasis on the family unit within Japanese society, its character as an organic whole, the internalization of its norms by individuals and its function as a mediator between them and the group. What is more, they stressed the preponderant role of fictive kinship and neighbourhood relations in ensuring the cohesion of village communities. Yanagita considered that the organizational requirements of collective work constituted the primary reason for the Japanese household, thus explaining the relatively secondary importance of blood ties (Koyama, Morioka and Kumagai, 1981).

A fairly general feature of studies on the family before the Second World War, in which one cannot fail to see evidence of the spirit of the age, was to place undue emphasis on the strongly hierarchical family and community configurations in the north at the expense of the more associative and egalitarian forms to be found especially in the west and south. From the evolutionist point of view, shared by most authors at the time, the groups of houses designated by the generic term *dôzoku* ('same people'), in which several houses (*bunke*) were economically and ritually subject to their original mother house (*honke*), were regarded as more or less the archetypes of the Japanese 'familial system' (*ie seido, kazoku seido*; but it is true that the structures of large industrial groups partly reproduced this *dôzoku* model). Although this excessively unilateral point of view has since been challenged, in particular by Fukutake Tadashi, a specialist in rural sociology, it must be noted that it has even now far from lost all ideological credit.

The Civil Code of 1948

Capitulation in 1945 put an end to nearly four years of total war, leaving the country bled dry. More than 2.5 million civilians and servicemen had died, the economy was in ruins, and the people, who had never before been dominated by a foreign power, were experiencing a situation of general scarcity and a profound collapse of nationalist faith. A new constitution, a sort of charter for the rights of man, was worked out under the supervision of the Allied command. Adopted in November 1946, it came into force on 3 May 1947. Its first article designated the people as sovereign and limited the role of the emperor, who had already publicly denied his divine nature, to that of symbol of the Japanese state and the unity of the people. In the family, article 24 provided, out of respect for human dignity, for complete equality in law between men and women with regard to right to property, inheritance, choice of domicile and divorce; it stipulated that marriage rested on the consent of the spouses and that its maintenance depended on their mutual assistance. The new constitution thus legally abolished the old familial system.

Elsewhere it guaranteed the state's complete neutrality in the field of religion. There were to be no more organizational links between Shintô and political, administrative and educational activities. The revision of all history textbooks was rapidly undertaken in order to substitute factual reality for nationalist myths, lacunae and lies (but the national feast of the Founding of the State by Jinmu tennô was officially reinstated in 1967, and in 1979 it was decided to retain on calendars the use of the name of eras, or *nengô*, given since Meiji to the reign of each emperor, the present Heisei era having begun in 1989).

The Civil Code has been in operation since 1 January 1948 and conforms to the principles enshrined in the constitution. The reference to the *ie* has disappeared in favour of the rights of the individual. Each child of either sex is thus entitled to receive an equal share of the inheritance, and provision is made for leaving a third to the widow. While the code authorizes one of the heirs to continue the ancestral cult and to retain all the utensils related to it, all have the same obligation to provide for the needs of aged parents. A couple can choose to bear either the husband's or the wife's patronym (which makes it even easier to be succeeded by a son-in-law). Marriage is permitted from the age of eighteen for boys and sixteen for girls, but the consent of a parent is necessary before their legal coming of age, which is at twenty.

While retaining the use of the term *koseki*, the 1948 Civil Code transformed the family register into a civil state document, generally established at the time of marriage, and kept by the administration. The person heading the register, *hittosha*, is the one whose name the couple bears (the husband in most cases); after that come the names of his wife and children. Death and divorce are duly entered. Changing a name after divorce or annulment of adoption, and possibly after the decease of a spouse, results in a new entry in the register. Unmarried mothers and fathers are given their own register, and their names are crossed out in their parents'. It is also possible for any person on attaining legal majority to possess a personal register. The new *koseki* is thus restricted to the narrow framework of the nuclear family, meaning a maximum of two generations.

Family legislation provides four graduated procedures for divorce: mutual consent, arbitration by a tribunal with the agreement of all parties, court order if no appeal has been lodged within the space of two weeks, and finally judicial decree, which allows grounds of adultery, desertion of the marital home, mental cruelty, ill treatment and even serious and incurable mental illness. The family point of view which had prevailed with the previous Meiji Code, and which generally led to custody of children being allocated to their father, has disappeared.

The structural evolution of the population and the family

The demographic thrust

The Japanese population rose to 44 million inhabitants at the start of the twentieth century, and to 72 million by 1940. In 1990 it exceeded 122,300,000 inhabitants (Japanese nationals). If one leaves out the historical maximum annual growth rate of 3.5 per cent in the years immediately after the war (and an exceptional 2.8 per cent in 1950), its strongest annual growth rates came during the 1930s (1.5 per cent) and between 1971 and 1974 (1.4 per cent). This progression had dropped below 0.9 per cent by the end of the 1970s. Given that the population's net reproduction rate is below one per cent (0.62 per cent in 1989), generation renewal is no longer guaranteed, and the present rate of growth is explained only by the balance between births and deaths, which is still positive (a maximum figure of 139 million inhabitants towards the year 2015 is anticipated).

In the same way, the urban population living in towns of 50,000 inhabitants or more, which already made up 16 per cent of the total population in 1920, and 34.6 per cent in 1940, nowadays represents over 68 per cent (1980 figure, and only 56 per cent if only towns with at least 100,000 inhabitants are taken into account). It was in the years 1950–60 that migration to the great urban centres was at its height (during this period the population of the six most important towns grew by 50 per cent); in the following decade the process of expansion affected chiefly the middle-sized towns.

Compared with the general demographic evolution, the average size of hearths (*setai* or *shotai*, a unit which includes persons whether related or not) remained astonishingly stable during the whole of the first part of the twentieth century: the national average, which was 4.89 individuals per hearth in 1920, the year when censuses covering the entire country started, rose slightly to 5.03 in 1935 and then, after a drop to 4.85 in 1945, remained at 4.97 during the decade after the war. It was only between 1955 and 1960 that this figure began to drop regularly: to 4.54 in 1960, 3.69 in 1970 and 3.33 in 1980. It is worth remembering at this point that the estimated average size of households in the Edo period

(1600–1867) was around 5.0, or even slightly less, which reveals great stability over a period of three centuries. The slight rise observable during the decade 1945–55 was due to the very high birth rate after the war (33.6 per 1,000 in 1947, 23.7 per 1,000 in 1950), and to the lack of housing.

These figures are of course calculated for the whole of the territory, and although the same evolutionary tendency can be observed in the country and the towns, rural hearths counted on average 0.5 persons more than urban hearths (except during the period from 1945 to the early 1950s, when the gap reached almost one per cent). It must also be pointed out that there are still important regional variations, reflecting ancient variations in family organization. Thus the average size of hearths in the north-eastern region of Honshu, the main island, is still noticeably higher than in the the south-east of the archipelago (Gamo, 1981).

The foregoing figures should be rounded off by examining the changes in the composition of hearths. National censuses have shown that in a period of fifty years, from 1930 to 1980, the proportion of hearths comprising between one and four persons continued to increase, whereas that comprising five persons or more was declining. The clearest growth has been in hearths of only one person, whose proportion has grown from 15.1 per cent to 26.6 per cent. Conversely, the proportion of hearths numbering at least seven persons has fallen from 25.7 per cent to 3.4 per cent.

Families of the nuclear type (those made up of a married couple living alone or with unmarried children, or of one of the two parents with unmarried chidren) represented 54 per cent of the total number of hearths in 1920 and 59.6 per cent in 1955; by 1980 their proportion had reached 63.3 per cent. The gap between the 1955 and 1989 figures is even clearer if one takes into account only those hearths made up of related persons: in that case the proportion of nuclear families changes from 62 per cent to more than 75 per cent (the difference is explained by the considerable growth of hearths comprising only one person, which have been left out of this calculation). Regional variations in the proportion of nuclear families reveal the same contrast as that between the size of hearths in north-eastern and south-eastern Japan: thus in 1975, families of this type represented only 49.6 per cent of all hearths in the northern Yamagata province, but 67.5 per cent in the Kagoshima province at the southern end of Kyûshû Island.

The birth of the conjugal family

In spite of their radical character, the legislative reforms following the Second World War did not immediately modify the traditional picture of the family. In fact, it was not before the late 1950s that the notion of the nuclear family as the most widespread family form and the common norm impinged on Japanese public opinion, notably through the press. Many sociologists also began to take an interest in the phenomenon of the 'nuclearization of the family' (*kaku kazoku ka*), in order to analyse its effects on Japanese society, and the expression 'nuclear family' very quickly came to be employed in specialist reviews. However, its descriptive value seems debatable. Families of this type, as we have seen, were already in the majority in 1920: one can even suppose, taking account of estimates drawn up for the Edo period, that this had been the case for at least three centuries. Given that their numerical growth after 1945 was relatively modest, 'nuclearization' does not really represent a marked change in the composition of the family unit, but rather a shift in its centre of gravity from the relationship between the generations to that between the spouses. In other words, the nuclear family has generally ceased to be considered as a transitional phase in a process of development leading to the formation of an extended family of more than two generations. In this context then, it is preferable to speak of a 'conjugal nuclear family' or simply a 'conjugal family', while retaining a sufficiently neutral descriptive and functional meaning of 'conjugal' to avoid endowing conjugal relations in Japan with the same attributes as they possess in the West.

The modifications to Japanese vocabulary since 1945 testify to its new representation of the family, and to the evolution of relations within it. To start with, the term *ie*, 'house', which for the majority of Japanese no longer corresponds to a concrete reality, is disappearing from common speech. It has been replaced in official language and sociological terminology by the idea of hearth or household (*setai*, *shotai*, or *katei*). In consequence, the 'head' or 'master of the house' has himself become a 'head of household', *setai nushi*, with the same neutral connotation that this administrative designation has for us. While terms for parents cannot of course vary at the same pace as laws or political institutions, one can now frequently hear children calling their parents by the Western terms 'mummy' and 'daddy' instead of the traditional *otôsan* and *okâsan*: the onus of authority and obligation of deference which are attached to the Japanese words would explain, together with the attraction of customs from across the Pacific, why these terms are no longer applied in present-day family contexts. The disappearance of the *ie* and the diminished importance of parents-in-law have also deprived the expression *yome iri* ('the bride's entry') of its meaning, although it used to designate the marriage ceremony with a degree of realism, and it has been abandoned in favour of the more neutral term *kekkon*.

In statistical terms, what had been called a 'decline of the *ie*' corresponded to a very rapid reduction in the size of hearths, which shifted from 4.97 persons to 4.05 between 1955 and 1965, in other words a drop of about 18 per cent in ten years. However, the characteristic feature of this evolution has been not just its speed and the absence of resistance, but on the contrary the esteem for the conjugal family felt by Japanese people.

Different factors lie behind this. In the first place, one cannot discount the effects, recorded above, of the disappearance of the institutions which supported the traditional family, even though a certain notion of the Western family was popularized through the influence of American culture. Next, the rural exodus provoked by what we may call the 'high-growth economy' (from about 1955 to about 1973) brought about the dispersal of families and split up the generations. The appearance of the megalopolis and the widespread acceptance of an urban lifestyle also went hand in hand with growth in the numbers of wage-earners; thus the proportion of hearths which derived their living from wage labour moved from 49 per cent in 1955 to 60 per cent in 1965 (63.7 per cent in 1980), almost entirely at the expense of agricultural households, of which a steadily growing number now practise agriculture only part-time (almost two-thirds nowadays) (Miyajima and Beillevaire, 1983). Finally, the government-supported spread of birth control has favoured the ideal of the small family centred on the wife and children (the birth rate fell from 33.6 per 1,000 in 1947 to 18.1 per 1,000 in 1955).

However, when one examines family statistics in relation to the population structure by age, one gets a modified picture of the predominance of the conjugal model in contemporary Japanese society. The high birth rates of the 1930s and after the war led to a notable boom in the number of people in the generations which nowadays constitute the active population, and hence to a multiplication of new homes. When one takes this fact into account, it is interesting to observe that in 1980, 60 per cent of persons aged sixty-five and over were still living with one of their adult children, whether or not there were grandchildren. This percentage, although constantly falling, is still markedly higher than those in comparable Western societies.

On the other hand, there is a pronounced difference between hearths in the farming community and those in other professional categories: whereas 52.5 per cent of agricultural households sheltered three generations in 1977, the proportion was only 11.9 per cent of other families. The obvious reason for this gap, which basically reveals conflicting practices between town and country, relates to the very nature of agricultural hearths, which are not only family groups but also enterprises, generally small in size, whose survival depends on the selection of a single heir. The child thus singled out (nowadays he is still generally the eldest son) continues as formerly to co-reside with his parents: their withdrawal usually obliges the other children to give up agriculture, and often to migrate to the towns (this migratory movement was very intense between 1950 and 1970, and has led to a relative ageing of the rural population compared with that in towns). Although it is also common outside farming families for parents to favour one of their children in order to secure support in their old age, the division is generally less unequal, and co-residence is less systematic.

Consumer families and consumer society

The *denka bûmu* (the boom in electrical household appliances) at the end of the 1950s marked the arrival of the consumer society which during the following decade brought about a sort of ideological consecration of the conjugal family. To the accompaniment of promotional campaigns aimed at creating a new environment, happy homes, comfortable interiors and personal fulfilment have become the objects of special interest on the part of large industrial firms, the most famous advertisement slogan of all undoubtedly being *mai hômu shugi* ('my home-ism'), launched by the Matsushita Company. After the period of concerted efforts at rebuilding the country, private life was now presented as a commodity accessible to everyone. Access to it was nevertheless gradual; first there was the period of the 'Three Sacred Jewels', or *sanbo*: the refrigerator, the washing machine and the vacuum cleaner (the allusion is to the Three Sacred Jewels of Buddhism: the Buddha, the Law and the monks), followed a few years later by the 'three C's': car, colour television and cooler. The wave of triple slogans did not stop there, but with the 1970s and the move of fashion from material objects to matters of the heart, advertisement campaigns have acquired a real cultural marketing dimension, aiming at no less than the construction of tomorrow's world.

In 1965, 90 per cent of homes already owned at least one television; in 1982, the proportion had reached 98.9 per cent, and an estimated average of three hours a day were spent watching it. In spite of this, newspapers have retained an important place: 96.7 per cent of homes comprising two or more persons subscribed to at least one newspaper in 1981. If the *ie* could formerly have been described as a unit of production, it would be fair to say that the family home today has become a unit of consumption: from nursery to the age of maturity (advertising euphemism for retirement), its members are constantly being importuned by advertisements, which take up 43 per cent of newspaper space and 18 per cent of broadcasting time on all television channels.

The high-growth economy gave rise to a greater density of the urban network and to a reduction in the average size of dwellings, although these became more comfortable in the period, especially where sanitation is concerned. Successive government plans corrected the tendency to reduced size, and the average area of town dwellings rose to 66.2 square metres or 3.92 rooms in 1978 (the national average being 80.2 square metres or 4.25 rooms). However, rented lodgings are generally markedly below this average. In that same year, 40 per cent of dwellings were overpopulated. Many young couples with children have to put up with a *kichin apâto*, meaning one of those apartments built of standardized components, consisting ordinarily of only one or two rooms and a kitchenette. Most Japanese, however, still want to acquire a home of their own. Although in 1950 80 per cent of families owned their own home, the proportion later fell to below 50 per cent, climbing back to 60 per cent in 1978 thanks to the government's policy of encouraging the construction of housing. Owing to the inflation in land prices, households have found that housing constitutes a growing proportion of their debt, which is already considerable. The impossibility of meeting financial obligations, and recourse to loans at extortionate rates of interest from the flourishing *sarakin* (companies for 'loans to wage-earners') often lead to family dramas involving flight, murder or suicide, which are constantly reported in the press.

Role allocation

Although the wife has been emancipated from her in-laws' guardianship, she is still an 'indoors person' (*oku-san, ka-nai*), with almost exclusive organizational control over a little home world cluttered with bits of equipment, but so small in size that it is ill-adapted to the presence of children and their father together. The latter, however, is frequently away until late in the evening: more than 50 per cent of white-collar workers do not eat supper at home more than three or four times a week – the proportion rises to 60 per cent for the managerial classes. It is normal for the husband to hand all his earnings over to his wife, who is then responsible for giving him his pocket money and for managing the household.

For most women, the birth of the first child often still means stopping work. This renunciation is no longer obligatory, as it was before the war when the rules allowed employers to sack without compensation any women who turned thirty or decided to get married (the 'celibacy clause' was however retained in some firms until it was declared unconstitutional in 1966 in a case involving the Sumitomo firm). Employment legislation now provides for six weeks' maternity leave before and after giving birth. Nevertheless, the notorious lack of nurseries and kindergartens has obliged a considerable number of women to stop working, in spite of efforts to remedy the situation.

The opposition between male and female roles is very marked in modern families and in society as a whole; it is undoubtedly even more emphatic than in the earlier peasant communities. Typically, the man dedicates himself primarily to the firm which employs him and to maintaining relations with his colleagues, very often after working hours; the wife gives her time to housework and the children's upbringing. She is also committed to giving her husband a devoted welcome at all times. Although the leisure time spent together by the whole family is increasing, the conjugal relationship does not, in the main, appear to be more than an instrumental function related to the husband's professional needs (in spite of any initial idealization when the couple was formed).

Although a survey was conducted in 1982 which showed that 72 per cent of Japanese women, far more than in Western countries, feel various degrees of satisfaction with such a situation, the wife quite often compensates for her isolation by demonstrating an extreme form of maternal solicitude, which allows her to hope for fulfilment through her children's success at school. The remoteness of the father-figure and the excessive devotion of these *kyôiku mama*, mothers who give themselves body and soul to their children's upbringing, are themes frequently discussed in the popular media as well as in university textbooks. The mothers' manipulative attitude is also the consequence of an extremely competitive educational system (starting sometimes in kindergarten) which forces many children to pursue intensive courses of study outside normal school hours in order to have the best chances of getting through the entrance examinations to the most prestigious universities. Furthermore it is especially in this parallel training that the mother makes her authority felt. It has been shown in recent comparative studies that Japanese children spend more time doing homework than their counterparts in the West. The constant pressure to which they are subjected has been seen as the cause of the high occurrence of psychosomatic illness in these children. The educational system has also been blamed for the dramatic suicides by children, and by mothers with their children.

However, since the 1970s the phenomenon which most exercises public opinion is undoubtedly violence, including murder, practised by some schoolchildren against teachers or parents. Mothers are very much at the top of the list of victims of family violence (82.8 per cent), followed by fathers (21 per cent) and younger sisters (17.3 per cent). Statistics for murderers show that they are mainly eldest (83 per cent) or only sons (31 per cent) (see Kumagai's contribution in Koyama, Morioka and Kumagai, 1981).

Forming unions

A wife may resent her isolated situation all the more because of the marked contrast between the idealization of the conjugal relationship before marriage and the dreary routine of domesticity after it. There is a flourishing literature for young people filled with recipes for seduction and advice about achieving perfect love, which propagates the romantic vision of a couple's life freed from social constraints and with no other end than that of personal fulfilment. A whole promotional arsenal has been mobilized to signpost this progression to happiness with tangible signs generally derived from Western models. The marriage ceremony, which in the past was of only secondary importance, now involves considerable expenditure, met especially by the husband's family. In big towns it is often held in hotel rooms. Although the most common practice is still to have the union consecrated by a Shintô priest, the wedding day is now often padded out with a Christian rite independent of any doctrinal concerns (this is the object of negotiation). However, once the *uedingu* (wedding) rejoicings are over and the the couple have come back from their *hanemûnu* (honeymoon), the 'parenthesis' in their lives is soon over, and each spouse has to conform to the divergent social demands made of them.

Prior to 1945, only a few intellectuals had declared themselves in favour of marriage based on free commitment by the spouses. Since then, and especially since the 1960s, the *renai kekkon* or love match has come to be preferred by most young Japanese, rather than arranged marriages prepared by preliminary interviews or *o miai*. (The latter custom, though widely thought traditional, in fact came from the Samurai and merchant classes, and was only adopted by the rest of the population after Meiji.) In practice it is no longer easy to make a clear-cut distinction between the two modes of marriage. The idea that marriage, whatever the manner in which it is concluded, rests on a direct promise (*yakusoku*) between the man and woman is now widely prevalent. Arranged marriages do not exclude prior acquaintance between the young people, and in practice it is their opinion rather than the agreement between their families which determines the outcome of the relationship. Conversely, although the liaison in love matches is in principle formed without intervention by the families or a third party (the employer or a firm representative, for instance), its evolution can subsequently conform to various degrees of control by the families (including an inquiry into the future spouse's family origins). The difference thus depends on one's point of view or the general atmosphere. What is more, in spite of their generally favourable attitude to love matches, one can often hear students discussing the arbitrary nature of selection based on love: perhaps, they say, it is actually better to apply the criteria of reason from the start rather than be forced to find reasons later on.

Recently the mere observation that the number of divorces is fast rising has resulted in renewed interest in arranged marriages. Curiously enough, the divorce rate was very high in Japan during the Meiji period; between 1870 and 1890, it reached 2.8 per 1,000, a rate unknown in the West before the middle of the twentieth century. One hypothesis advanced to explain this high rate is that the strengthening of the patriarchal character of the *ie*, as a consequence of diffusing the Samurai family model, would have exacerbated tensions between brides and their in-laws. Whatever the reason, the frequency of divorce then regularly declined (except immediately after 1945) and settled at about 0.75 per 1,000 in 1960, before starting to climb gradually and reach 1.26 in 1988. It is interesting to note that divorce is sought 2.5 times more often by wives than by husbands. In spite of this, the condition of the divorced woman is still difficult to accept today and imposes a degree of marginalization on account of social disapproval.

The average age at marriage for men, as for women, has risen slightly in the course of the twentieth century and stands at twenty-eight and twenty-five respectively, with the the gap narrowing. The incidence of celibacy is still fairly low in Japanese society; by the age of thirty-four, the proportion of married men is 85 per cent, and 90 per cent for women.

Working women and contraception

The division of family roles seems to have been progressively challenged by the increasing length of time spent by women in professional life. There are two main reasons for this evolution: on the one hand, the growing number of girls taking up places in institutions of higher education (33 per cent in 1981, compared with 40.5 per cent of boys), and consequently acquiring better-qualified jobs which they are less prompt to leave after having a baby; on the other, as surveys by the ministry for health and social affairs indicate, many households are obliged to earn a second income in order to meet the financial burdens weighing on them. Thus the average age of working women has increased regularly over the last four decades: 23.8 in 1949, 29.8 in 1979 and 34.9 in 1980; almost two-thirds of them are now over thirty. Another clue to this evolution is the duration of uninterrupted employment, which grew during the same years from 3.6 years to 4.5 and then to 6.3 years. In 1981, when 47.7 per cent of women of working age were employed, 58 per cent were married: it would thus be incorrect to retain the image of an unmarried girl which has long been that of the working woman.

With the help of the rise in its standard of living, Japan has succeeded in mastering its demographic expansion since the war. Japanese couples make extensive use of contraceptive methods. Among these, the condom is top, followed by rhythm method combined with condoms and intra-uterine devices (Coleman, 1983). The government still applies the argument about the uncertain side-effects of oral contraceptives to oppose their sale, and they can only be prescribed for therapeutic reasons. In fact, only 8 per cent of women use them. The movement in favour of birth control began in the 1920s, predominantly with the aim of improving the condition of poorer women. From 1936 the government began to promote a pro-birth policy and soon proscribed the organizations offering contraceptive advice (the slogan at the time was *umeyô fuyaseyô*, 'procreate and increase the population'). Abortion was legalized in 1948, putting an end to the period of anarchy after the war. However, in the face of the dangers incurred by women, the law was revised in 1953. Since then, abortion can be practised legally only by a doctor, and only in cases when it is essential to safeguard the well-being of the mother or where there is economic hardship. Alongside the action taken by family planning associations, the government created centres for education in eugenics. Mastery of demographic growth and the substitution of contraception for abortion constituted the aims of the period. The maximum number of abortions seems to have been reached in 1955: officially, there were 1,170,143. The present number is about 700,000, but it could in reality be two or three times higher. One married woman in three claims to have had at least one abortion. But in spite of its everyday nature, abortion generally involves a feeling of guilt mingled with fear, with regard to the foetus (*mizugo*, meaning 'child of water', or 'child who does not see') thus condemned. This is testified to by the increasing popularity of the cult of Jizo, the *bodhisattva* who protects the spirits of foetuses, and it is the custom to dedicate a little statue of Jizo to the aborted baby.

The problem of old age

The nostalgia which Japanese citizens still feel when the village community they derive from is mentioned undoubtedly reflects the weakening of family solidarity. Marriages and funerals constitute the rare occasions when relations come together. Ancestor worship, although it has far from disappeared (nearly two-thirds of those questioned on the subject said that they cared about it), has nevertheless given way to an increasingly rudimentary practice. In extreme cases, the only observance practised by members of the younger generations is to keep a photo of their deceased parents, both the husband's and the wife's, on some sort of memorial ledge which serves as an altar (Smith, 1974).

The difficult situation of a growing number of old people is one of the most worrying consequences of these loosened family links, and several factors have converged to make this problem particularly acute in Japan. The population has aged very quickly: in 1950 only 5 per cent of people were aged sixty and over, but the proportion has now reached 10 per cent and will be 20 per cent by the year 2000 (a projection for 2015 predicts 18 per cent persons aged sixty-five and over). The synthetic fertility indicator, which stood at 3.6 births per woman in 1950 was down to 1.45 in 1993; the birth rate rose no higher than 10.8 per 1,000 in 1988). On the other hand, average life expectancy at birth has been considerably extended since the war: it is now seventy-three years for men and seventy-eight for women. Finally, there is the inadequacy of retirement pensions and a lack of establishments for caring for old people. Retirement still often starts at fifty-five, while pensions, which are normally too low to provide proper support, are only paid from sixty or sixty-five; thus many retired persons are obliged for a few years to take on jobs for which they are normally too highly qualified. Understandably enough, these conditions prompt demands for the retirement age to be raised to sixty or sixty-five.

Since 1973 persons aged over seventy have been entitled to free medical services; below this age the costs are covered by state and municipal insurance systems. In a society where the main duty of children, especially the eldest, is to care for the well-being of their aged parents, the idea of going to live in a retirement home is still viewed with dismay. Opinion polls have shown, however, that young people are becoming increasingly less willing to assist their parents and feel that this duty should be incumbent on society as a whole. Indeed, when parents do co-reside with a one-child household, this often involves no more than the juxtaposition of two conjugal families.

In the 1960s, when the Japanese economy had regained its level of productivity and begun to conquer international markets, the conjugal family was able to appear as the vector of a concern for individual autonomy, of a privatization (*shitekika*) of the individual, which would have broken with his traditional subordination (*shi, watakushi*) to the public sphere (*kô, ôyake*) assimilated to power. A society of citizens (*shimin*) in the pattern of Western democracies was to be born. It must be observed, without implying any sort of judgement, that such an ideological upheaval has not taken place.

However, the *ie* as a form of family organization certainly has almost completely disappeared, and in a way which there is every reason to believe is irreversible. Furthermore, outside the field of real kinship, the explicit reference to the family model and recourse to fictive kinship can be observed nowadays only in special areas like art schools, where the master is called *ie moto* (origin of the *ie*) by his journeymen, or in the underworld (*yakuza*).

Numerous authors, nevertheless, including sociologists, historians and economists, concur in seeing the permanent presence of the spirit and organizational principles proper to the *ie* in the general characteristics of large firms, in the strength of the vertical links and the stress laid on hierarchical distinctions, counteracting the potential tension between elements at the same level; and in the primacy of membership of the group over the differentiation of functions within it (Nakane, 1974). In the image of *oyabun-kobun* (fictive parent–child relations), the links uniting the manager to his subordinates, or (even more so) the old employee to the new one (*senpai* and *kôhai*), are still experienced as a personal and reciprocal undertaking which transcends the mere task to be accomplished. Modern firms thus appear as no less than a reincarnation of the family and community system of former times. Furthermore, these characteristics are found just as much in the way public administration functions as in political parties and universities, as if the whole of Japanese society had proceeded from the *ie* (Murakami, Kumon and Satô, 1979). For the psychiatrist Doi (1982), this propensity of the Japanese to identify with the group and its head has its origin in the dependence of the young child on his mother, for which the Japanese language is alone in providing a specific term, *amae*. Where Western mothers educate their children to feel autonomous and to be responsible for themselves very early on, Japanese mothers encourage them to accept the care and indulgence lavished on them. The dependent attitude thus engendered is seen as the source of a gratification which the adult seeks to rediscover among his colleagues and superiors at work (De Vos, 1984).

Whatever the merits of this psychological explanation, the values attached to the *ie*, once criticized for their feudal nature, are treated in current discourse, which is supported by economic success, as the basis of a future society which will be egalitarian, harmonious and achieving (in contrast with Western societies, which will be undermined by their insistence on the primary role of the individual). What emerges is that continuity does exist between this point of view and the theory of the state-family advocated before the war. In both cases, the *ie* is invested with the function of an overall model; however, a shift in emphasis has apparently taken place from the political to the economic level, and from loyalty to the national myth to the sole virtue of efficiency.

SIX

India: the Family, the State and Women

Roland Lardinois

A t the beginning of the nineteenth century, under British colonial rule which brought about the partial political unification of the country, Indian society entered the most important period of change in its history. Within a few decades, India, which had been linked to the world only by the great mainstreams of trade in the classical age, was forcefully integrated within a world economy dominated by British imperialism. The values propagated by the reformers and propagandists who accompanied the new masters were based on very Western ideas about reason and progress. Related ideas about equality and the recognition of individual rights were not new to India. However, what was new was the fact that these values were now produced by economic, social, political and ideological transformations exogenous to Indian society, deriving their legitimacy from the colonial powers. As demonstrated in volume I, the Hindu joint family, which is both a system of representation and a family grouping, and whose strength lies in its legitimacy and legality, meaning that it is founded in religion and law, had accommodated itself since medieval times to egalitarian and individualistic forces of division which sap its very foundations. By assimilating these values, the Indian intelligentsia, which constitutes a very active minority drawn from different social strata, attempts to explode these contradictions; in fact, it is to some extent still hemmed in by them, because the new world vision into which it attempts to integrate them is still basically Hindu.

From the beginning of the nineteenth century, everything was happening as though the forces of change were making an issue of the Indian family, for two groups of reasons at least. On the one hand, it was women and the place occupied by them within the family and society which lay – and still lie today – at the heart of the reforms and debates, as

Family planning propaganda, Nepal. Panos Pictures/Sean Sprague.

if everyone agreed in acknowledging very early on that economic and social mutations had to pass first of all through a change in the status of women. On the other hand, and more fundamentally, it was demographic growth – the result of an imbalance between a birth rate which has remained high and a death rate which has fallen by more than half within half a century – which have made fertility and family politics one of the important issues for the future of India. Consequently it is not surprising that the struggles around the Indian family have developed with increased intensity, starting with the colonial period in the legal and the religious fields, and continuing in contemporary India. Progressively, however, the issues of these struggles have been subordinated, in part at least, to those which were developing in the political field, initially around the themes of Gandhi's nationalism up to Independence, and since then around those of growth and development.

The family, the state and the law
(nineteenth–twentieth century)

The principal issues of the reform movement in the first half of the twentieth century were the cremation of widows and the social ostracism to which they were subjected, female infanticide, child marriage and the education of women confined in purdah. At the time, the moderate liberalism which set its mark on colonial administrative policy was exemplified in the person of William Bentinck, governor-general of India and architect of the struggle against suttee (cremation of widows) and girl infanticide. Very soon, however, the Indian liberal movement, which was closely linked to the general trend in favour of a Hindu renaissance as the expression of a new urban elite enriched by colonialism, produced ardent spokesmen in support of the modernization of India and the abolition of customs which many thought unworthy. Originally, this reform movement fitted all the better within the colonial framework in that its members owed their social rise and wealth to it. The birth of Indian nationalism at the end of the nineteenth century radicalized the issues at stake in the struggle. By intervening in an organic manner in the political field, by widening the debate to include the whole of the Hindu family code, women, hitherto passive objects of the reforms, now became their subjects.

Hindu renaissance and social reformism

The struggle against suttee and female infanticide   Several attempts to abolish the burning of widows were made before the advent of the British: Albuquerque forbade the rite in Goa in 1510 and, a few years later, Guru Sikh Amar Das did likewise, but without success. At the end of the eighteenth century, the Maratha rulers were generally hostile to the sacrifice, and it was banned in several states under their control. However, the rite continued to prevail in northern India, especially in Bengal, where the number of occasions when suttee was performed increased in the late eighteenth and early nineteenth centuries. As Nandy has demonstrated, this recrudescence did not develop among the poor peasants, but in the midst of the new Bengali urban elite, the *bhadralok*, who found in the ostentatious manifestation of the rite of suttee the sole pathetic means of reaffirming, in their eyes and those of others, their traditional cultural identity, thus demonstrating all the more clearly the crisis of conscience which had been provoked among these *nouveaux riches* by their rapid social rise (Nandy, 1980, pp. 1–31). The first British measures were marked by tolerance and sought to control the conditions surrounding the rite rather than to abolish it, thus contributing in fact to legitimizing it. The number of suttee performed only diminished progressively after 1829 when Bentinck promulgated a law banning it.

Whereas the immolation of widows was often performed in public and had long been known about, it was a long time before female infanticide

A Radja woman cremating herself after her husband's death. A manuscript illustrating Niccolo Mannucci, *Storia di Mogor* (1653–1708). Bibliothèque Nationale, Paris.

was discovered, because it was confined within the world of purdah, and the struggle against it proved difficult. In 1789, Jonathan Duncan established the evidence for this practice among the Rajput of Uttar Pradesh, its existence having already been suspected by European travellers. The first colonial surveys confirmed the extent of its prevalence: according to the region, the number of men per hundred women varied between 150 and 300 (Panigrahi, 1972, p. 66). In this case too, the British adopted prudent and flexible measures: the practice varied according to region and set at risk the matrimonial strategies of the dominant Ksatriya castes, which were often localized in the native states, over which colonial rule was only partially extended. By applying moral pressure and preventive measures (introduction of civil registration as a regulatory measure, the struggle against hypergamy and attempts to reduce the costs of marriage), the British secured some success, but it was only in 1870 that the Infanticide Act was passed. In any case, because the struggle against female infanticide fundamentally challenged the means of social reproduction of the groups concerned, its legal prohibition (as in the case of suttee) was necessary but not sufficient to suppress practices which were deeply rooted in mentalities. Even nowadays, they subsist under forms which are not always hidden or denied.

Westernization and neo-Hinduism   After half a century of colonial presence, the years 1820–30 were marked in Bengal by intense intellectual activity: numerous *sabha* (associations) and *samiti* (societies) were created, the English and vernacular press was developed as the great colleges were opened in Calcutta. In this period, Ram Mohan Roy (1772–1833) emerged as the most prominent representative of the Indian liberal and reformist trend. On his father's side he came from a literate bureaucratic family, and on his mother's from a family imbued with religious fervour, and he belonged, as did other Bengali *bhadralok* co-religionist, to the same *Rādi kulin* Brahman group, who adhered to a hypergamic matrimonial system and thus kept their women in an unenviable social situation (Mukherjee, in Allen and Mukherjee, 1982, pp. 155–78). Ram Mohan Roy founded the Atmiya Sabha in 1815, the first society for combating the rite of suttee, and in 1828 Brahmo Samaj, a theist movement strongly tinged with Christian morality whose reformist impact extended to the religious and social domains. By publishing pamphlets and articles in the press, and engaging in numerous debates and petitions, Ram Mohan Roy and his friends confronted public opinion with the situation of women in the family and society with all the more passion and contradiction in that their personal lives were involved: they campaigned against widow sacrifice, child marriage and polygamy, they fought for the reform of women's inheritance and succession rights and they became the apostles of female education. This was the period when numerous *bhadralok* began to educate their wives, seeking to find in a new definition of conjugal roles and family morality an answer to the Westernization of their ways of thinking (S. N. Mukherjee, 1970; Borthwick in Allen and Mukherjee, 1982, pp. 104–34). Remarriage for widows became, under the impetus provided by Isvarachandra Viyasagar (1820–91), the object of a victorious campaign ending in the 1856 Act. Paradoxically, however, this law, as with others which touched personal status and inheritance rights, often went against recognized legal customs and contributed, in fact, to making a Brahman model widely known (Carroll, 1983). In 1872, the Special Marriage Act legalizing intercaste unions was the personal achievement of Keshub Chandra Sen (1838–84), leader of the New Brahmo Samaj of India.

Although Ram Mohan Roy's liberal reformism had never possessed the radical character of Henry Derozio's Young Bengal Movement (1809–31), by attacking the family institution, it could not fail to engage head-on with the adherents of orthodoxy, who formed the Dharma Sabha movement around Radhakanta Deb and campaigned in vain to get the prohibition of the suttee rite lifted. However, they too, by actively participating in the development of English education, for girls as well as boys, contributed to the diffusion of the spirit of reform.

From the 1880s, the movement spread over all India (albeit more in the north than the south) by becoming rooted in the distinctive social and cultural character of each region. In the province of Bombay, where Western influence was long established and deeply entrenched, M. G. Ranade (1852–1901) was one of the founders of Prārthanā Samaj, a movement aimed at improving the lot of widows and intercaste marriages. Lastly, Dayananda Saraswati founded Arya Samaj in 1875, a movement centred on the Punjab, which undertook to reconvert the adherents of other religions to Hinduism. This militant and nationalistic *sannyāsi* rejected the use of English and preached the return to Vedic sources, purified of the evils of Brahman orthodoxy: integrating the social reformism of Brahmo Samaj, he turned the struggle against the caste system, ancestor worship and child marriage into the slogans of the movement, which gained a far larger audience than its predecessors. Even so, all these neo-Hindu currents were limited to the new educated urban elites, and had no effect on the everyday practices of popular Hinduism. However, one must not underestimate the importance of their contribution to rousing social and political awareness. Many of the great female figures to emerge in the struggle at the end of the nineteenth century and early in the twentieth were its first inheritors.

The reform of family law

The foundation in 1887 of the National Social Conference, an offshoot of the Indian National Congress, which had held its first session in 1885, marked the advent of the reform movement in its national and political phase, as well as respecting the division between its political and social objectives. From then on, the reform of the legal foundations of the traditional Indian family could not be dissociated from the struggle for national independence, to which it was progressively subordinated.

The women's movement and the struggle for Independence

Whereas the history of Hinduism can take pride in its tradition of famous holy women and poetesses, the first associations to campaign for women were led and dominated by men. By the end of the nineteenth century missionaries were taking young Christian girls into their schools. It was, however, above all the movement supporting widows which enabled the latter to enter public life by becoming teachers and running homes for taking in young widows, as in the exemplary cases of Pandita Ramabai in Poona (Maharashtra) and Subbulakshmi (widowed at the age of eleven) in the Tamil country. During the same period, one of the most ardent advocates of the movement, Viresalingam Pantulu (a Brahman from Andhra) founded the Madras Association for Social Reform in 1892.

Early in the twentieth century, feminist ideas were being spread by the words and actions of a few women who had close links with the Indian National Congress. Annie Besant came to India in 1893, after being the victim of a trial in Great Britain on account of her birth control campaign. On becoming President of the Madras-based Theosophical Society in 1907, she used her position to popularize the political and social ideas of the Congress Party, of which she became president in 1917. During this period, the annual sessions of the National Social Congress provided intellectual Indian women with a privileged meeting place and a platform. The maharani of Baroda, Muthulaksami Reddi, and above all the poet Sarojini Naidu were its main spokeswomen. Though her mother tongue was Bengali, Naidu wrote in English; at the age of nineteen she married a man of the Naidu caste (originally Telugu) after spending some years abroad in London and Cambridge. Her great artistic sensibility and eloquent lyricism made her the unchallenged minstrel of the feminist and nationalist cause until her death in 1949.

At first these spokeswomen for the feminist movement were content to advocate the social promotion of women by emphasizing their image as exemplary spouses and mothers in the traditional family. This ideology still coloured the first writings of the women's organizations formed in the 1920s. Annie Besant founded the Women's Indian Association in 1917; in 1925 the National Council of Women in India opened in Bombay as the Indian branch of the International Council of Women; in 1927, finally, thanks to efforts by Margaret Cousins and her friends, the All-India Women's Conference was set up. Between 1930 and 1940 this last organization, which forged special links with the Congress Party and its political leaders, developed more than 100 centres throughout the country, and with its newspaper, *Roshni*, became the most powerful women's movement. In 1934, Renuka Ray presided over an Indian Women's National Day and demanded the creation of a committee to examine women's situation in law. The question was put before the Committee of National Planning in 1939–40, when its president was Jawaharlal Nehru. From then on, it was no longer so much a matter of promoting women as of forcing through equal rights with men by fighting for a revision of the traditional legal basis of the Hindu family.

The Hindu family code

Around the 1880s, the missionary movements and members of Brahmo Samaj were putting pressure on the government of Bengal to reform the practice of child marriage. The promulgation of the Age of Consent Act in 1891, which introduced a lower limit on the age of marriage, produced a hostile reaction from Christians (calling themselves Hindu Christians) as much as from orthodox elements of the reform movement, which were opposed to any intervention by the state in regulating Hindu religious practices (Oddie, 1979, pp. 75–109).

It was, however, in the 1920s that the most important struggle was started. The initiative for reform projects is often credited to a few liberals from the anglicized urban classes, who filled the liberal professions and chaired the new legislative councils established in the provinces and at central level by the Montagu–Chelmsford Reform (1919). The Child Marriage Restraint Act, known by its author H. B. Sarda's name, was voted through in 1929 after several years of acrimonious debate. It set the legal age of marriage at fourteen for girls and eighteen for boys. The adherents of the strictest orthodox form of Hinduism felt deeply wounded in their honour and religious convictions at no longer being able (legally) to marry young girls when they reached puberty. The six-month interval between the passing of the Act and its implementation was used by many communities to celebrate hasty child marriages.

Between 1928 and 1939, H. S. Gour and G. V. Deshmukh, among others, joined their efforts to H. B. Sarda's in an attempt to reform women's inheritance rights and to legalize the dissolution of marriage. In 1937 the Hindu Women's Right to Property Act was passed, which granted Hindu widows a limited share in the family property, whether divided or not, along the lines proposed by the Mitaksara school of law. Opposition to this, however, remained keen, and its success was limited. Early in the 1930s the native states of Mysore and Baroda undertook a wholesale reform of the Hindu code, and in 1937 Baroda legalized divorce in its Hindu Nibandha Baroda Act, under the direct influence of the English law of the same year.

In 1941–4, the government constituted a committee of jurists under the chairmanship of B. N. Rau, who was finally given the task of proposing a wholesale and coherent reform of the Hindu legal code. After an impassioned debate, the new Hindu Code was finally adopted by Parliament after Independence in 1954–6. It was split into five separate Acts so as to weaken opposition, and was subsequently completed by means of amendments. The legal age of marriage was brought forward to fifteen for women (the 1976 amendment made it eighteen, and twenty-one for men); divorce was legalized and polygamy prohibited; lastly, women acquired the right to an equal share of the inheritance (Everett, 1981, pp. 141–89).

In little more than a century and a half of struggle and reform, India had acquired a set of laws which challenged the legal foundations of the Hindu joint family, although the latter had always been recognized in law. Nevertheless, some agreed that this reform did not meet the real needs of the vast majority of the population, and that in many respects it remained a dead letter. Only the most Westernized urban sections of the dominant groups (for whom English was progressively becoming their mother tongue) had the social and cultural means to make use of a reform which had in the first place been conceived by and for themselves: 'Education of the nation . . . through concessions to the needs of a small but vocal minority of it!', as the jurist J. D. M. Derrett exclaimed bitterly (1978, p. 193). Nevertheless, in the first half of the twentieth century, women did enter social and political life by giving massive support to the independence movement. In this period, however, women had not so much taken on public life as made it an extension of their private spheres: the social opening up of the female world has happened on the metaphorical model of the extended family (Minault, 1981, pp. 3–18). 'Politicization was interiorised as a special form of sacrifice in an essentially religious process' (Sarkar, 1984, p. 101). In other words, the change was still being expressed in the language of tradition.

From village to city: undivided families and family networks

If the gap between the formal legal reforms and the reality of the Indian family is still deep today, should the conclusion be drawn that the latter has not evolved over two centuries? The changes affecting the size and structure of family groups seem to be the results of contradictory historical forces: the constraints of population growth tend to keep together households which otherwise would have been encouraged by economic and social changes to become autonomous. Because, however, the Hindu joint family is not defined by its residential functions, the fact that the family units which make it up may be dissociated in spatial terms does not mean that this family form is about to disappear. We must therefore inquire into the evolution of the functions it fulfils for its members – the possible impoverishment of its symbolic functions but, also, the appearance of new functions – as much as the changes to the mode of relations maintained with it by its representatives.

Non-division and segmentation: disequilibrium and rupture

The disintegration of ancient structures The British imposed their rule in India through the use of military force and by smashing any resistance from local sovereigns. They gained control of the country and its people by securing the submission of its rulers, the disarmament of their troops and the subordination of ancient solidarities to the new masters. For the military aristocracies, the ideal types of which are exemplified by the Coorg and Nayar, these shattering events were all the more rapid and brutal in that they affected the very basis of these groups' conditions for reproduction. If their personal relations of subordination and dependence, which provided the pattern for family relations, fell into disuse, would the family be able to keep going under its old forms for much longer?

The British annexation of Coorg province in 1834 and its integration into the Empire some twenty years later marked the end of Coorg military supremacy and the progressive disintegration of the patrilinear and patrilocal family, the *okka*. Landed property, which was traditionally held jointly by the family group, came into competition with individual grants of land exempt from all taxation which the British were distributing to soldiers in recognition of their services in suppressing the Canara Rebellion in 1837. Simultaneously, the abolition of slavery released a workforce seeking employment in the new coffee plantations which were rapidly expanding and competing with the traditional rice crops. The appearance of land as private property and as a commodity, and the flow of money and labour to the plantations sapped the foundations of the *okka*. Individual interests prevailed over collective interests, favouring the irreversible division of the family group: 'These individual enterprises seem to be the natural transition of an impending general social reform – the breaking up of the great houses and the independent establishment of each married couple residing near their own paddyfield and eating the fruit of their own labour', as a British observer wrote around 1870 (quoted by Srinivas, 1978, pp. 18–19).

An analogous process was taking place among the matrilinear groups in Kerala. When the armies of the Malabar, Cochin and Travancore provinces were disbanded (1792–1809) and the Nayar returned in massive numbers to their villages, they brought with them the germs of the disintegration of the matrilinear and matrilocal system called *tarvad*. Here too, economic changes proved decisive, albeit with many variations according to regional and social circumstances (Fuller, 1976, pp. 123–50). The legalization of the property market in the 1860s, the extremely rapid development of a commercial economy (centred on the coconut and its derivatives), and finally the population growth which, although real, is disputed, contributed to splitting up family groups and dividing formerly indivisible landed inheritance. In Travancore, this led to the pauperization of the Nayar, who resold their lands to Christian Syrian traders, then at the height of their prosperity, whereas in central Kerala their lands were bought back by those Nayar who had managed to change over to the new and expanding liberal professions. Irrespective of whether the economic consequences were positive or negative, what we are seeing is the emergence of households recentred on the husband to the detriment of the traditional matrilinear group. By the end of the nineteenth century, the Nayar were in such an economic and social crisis that, rightly or wrongly (and often under the influence of European ideas) their criticism was turned against the matrilinear institution of *tarvad*, as summed up in the report by the Malabar Marriage Commission, published in 1891. In 1896 the Malabar Marriage Act, which recognized *sambandham* unions (secondary marriages in the traditional system) as the only legal form of marriage, sanctioned the end of unions with Nambudiri Brahmans and opened the way to nearly fifty years of legal reform dedicated to the disintegration of this family institution.

Nevertheless, in mid-twentieth-century Kerala, villages could often be found in which nearly 70 per cent of households were of the extended type: fifteen years on, however, this group represented only 39 per cent.

By then matrilinear ideology had been considerably weakened to the advantage of a stronger relationship among the allies of the patrilinear group. If, about 1950, M. N. Srinivas was still able to observe a few *okka* among the Coorg, albeit in degraded form, these, like *tarvad*, were now no more than survivals of the former regime.

Demographic growth, land and family The modifications introduced to the demographic system of the Indian population by the colonial administration contributed to challenging the economic foundations of the peasant family. On the one hand, India has passed within about a century from a demographic system dominated by acute crises to a system of latent crises of diminishing intensity, within a context of demographic growth which has been in the order of 1.5 to 2 per cent per annum since 1930–40. However, it must be borne in mind that acute crises, though exceptional, are ever-present in the mentality of the population, as they form part of the recent history of the Indian subcontinent, with a sufficient reminder in the Bangladeshi famine in the 1970s. On the other hand, the inheritance system, involving egalitarian or preferential division of the land between heirs, and the fall in the death rate resulting in an increased number of male children surviving to adulthood, encouraged a trend to fragmentation of the landed inheritance with each new generation. This fact can be observed everywhere in India where the figures permit, at least since the second half of the nineteenth century (see especially Gadgil, 1971, pp. 165–7). At Vilyatpur in the Punjab, micro-properties smaller than 0.8 ha in size, which represented 7 per cent of all properties in 1848, constituted 44 per cent in 1968. During the same period, nuclear households, which totalled 35 per cent of all households in the mid-nineteenth century, reached 55 per cent of the total in 1968 (Kessinger, 1975). Agrarian reform and progressive legislation by the state, which have favoured access to landed property for social groups traditionally excluded from it, have contributed in varying ways, depending on the region, to increasing population pressure on the land.

Although there is no straightforward correlation between the fragmentation of landed property and population growth, it may be imagined that in periods of competition for land, the dominant castes could only intensify their strategies for controlling possession of land by strengthening non-division, negotiating marriage alliances, limiting their fertility or, more likely, by using a combination of all three methods as well as others, making large families concomitant with large farms. For the most deprived elements, however, the first function of the family is to ensure the support and biological reproduction of the group's members. In its extended form, the family often provides a last economic and social resort, allowing its members to survive by maintaining their little plot of farmland which is permanently under threat of disappearance at, and often below, a minimal threshold of viability (under strictly demographic aspects, cf. Mahadevan, 1979). In these two situations, one would also have to take account of the differential symbolic functions of land which strengthen the cohesion of the group: the affirmation of the historically dominant position of the landed castes or the means for some family groups belonging to low castes to raise their status by subjecting their values and practices to a process of sanskritization. Thus, for instance, in a village in the semi-deltaic lowlands of coastal Andhra, among the dominant Kamma caste, the joint family constitutes the means of a real capitalization of landed property: whereas the average holding for a landowning household is 3.8 ha in the case of small households, it grows to 5.6 ha in the case of enlarged families and to nearly 8 ha for multiple households containing on average eight persons. Among agricultural workers, the correlation is much less clear-cut: a single household owns on average no more than 0.6 ha, and a multiple household varying in size between six and seven persons has only 1.2 ha (Lardinois, 1977, pp. 409–20).

In India today, nearly 80 per cent of those households defined in the censuses as one unit of residence and consumption are nuclear in type (Dandekar and Unde, 1961). By turning land into a rare possession, access to which depends on the social status of peasant family groups, population growth has forced these groups to redefine their reproduction strategies within an economic and social environment which has profoundly changed since the colonial period. Non-division, which is one of the means available to the group, is given different meanings according to the particular contexts in which it is shaped. Under these conditions, when one is aware of the sociological and historical foundations of the Hindu joint family (see vol. I, ch. 15), one understands that the family structures observed in contemporary India are the result of an aggregate of contradictory forces which can only produce an extemely confused picture when one tries to reduce them to a purely formal model (Kolenda, 1968).

Urban families: making good use of relatives

In W. J. Goode's classic comparative study of the evolution of the family in the early 1960s, the author clearly discerned a shift in the Indian family towards the conjugal model, the corollary of a weakening of kinship links within the extended family. He conceded, however, that it was difficult to measure the extent of this change, and even more so to attribute it to the industrialization of the country, which was weak then as now, or to urbanization, which is as old as Indian civilization – 75 per cent of the population was still living in rural areas in 1981 (Goode, 1970, pp. 203–69). Just how ambiguous his assessment is becomes clear when it is shown that the principles of caste and kinship, on which are based the fluctuating links between family groups within joint families, create a continuous structure of Indian society between country and town.

Trade and the spirit of enterprise In order to understand the evolution of family structures under the impact of contemporary economic developments, we should study the traditional trading communities, which are particularly interesting: they are present in the most varied sectors of the economy, a fact which initially never fails to surprise if one is aware of their reputation for religious orthodoxy. Among the merchant (*baniyā*) or moneylending (*mahājan*) castes, the joint family is frequently the dominant model. In a rural township in Uttar Pradesh which has been studied by Robin Fox, such families represent 47 per cent of the total and include 64 per cent of the population (Fox, 1969, pp. 168–81). In the port of Mahuva in Saurashtra (north of Bombay), an old small trading town which is as rural as it is urban, the proportion of joint families was 58 per cent, according to I. P. Desai in the early 1960s (1964, pp. 40–62). It was still the extended family which predominated among the Aggarwal merchant caste studied in Delhi during the same period by Gore (1968). In every case, whether the type of enterprise is commercial, proto-industrial (processing food grains, manufacturing stainless steel cooking utensils, etc.) or a combination of both, it is generally a family concern. Fox notes that of 567 enterprises observed, only one had avoided this model; instances of associations were not more than 6 per cent of the cases, and the majority of partners were in fact members of the kinship group closest to the joint family. In the small family enterprises which have been observed at village or township level, it is rare to find an economic distinction between the sphere of family expenses and those of income or production (as in the case of the peasant family). Although the spirit of calculation is far from absent, these small units function more by maximizing their human potential than their economic capital, although concurrent use of the two is far from excluded: in the same family a man can be both merchant and moneylender, as well as holding a prosperous farm entrusted to his eldest son, while a brother of the head of the family runs a factory for de-hulling paddy. As J.-L. Chambard noted, in these small family units, there is 'a

rational utilization of the capacities of each one in the interest of all'
(1974, pp. 48–51). The same remarks can be applied to the Tamil
Muslim merchants in the Madras region (Mines, 1973, pp. 297–317).

For these communities, however, both village and market town are
often no more than the final links in a larger organization, on a regional
or provincial scale, based on family networks which have been kept alive
by matrimonial alliances. In almost every case, the traditionally dominant trading groups had constituted these networks well before the
colonial period. In the nineteenth century, however, the development of a
market economy and India's integration, under British rule, into economic exchange on a global scale enabled these communities to extend
their networks considerably. The Nattukottai Chettiar of southern India
are a typical example of this. As traditional bankers involved in the
textile and rice trade, they had developed a regional system of branch
houses, based on caste and kinship links, to which they would send their
children for their apprenticeships. If their first profits proved adequate,
the children would then be brought in as partners or allowed to set up
their own agency. By the beginning of the twentieth century, these
kinship networks, based on the economic and symbolic unit of the joint
family, stretched beyond southern India and Ceylon to the countries of
south-east Asia: Burma, Indochina and Malaya.

This often resulted in breaking up the family group and separating the
members of its units: wives would remain in their village of birth with a
few relatives, leading very orthodox lives in sumptuous houses built in
the 1930s when these families were at the height of their power, while
their men were living in concubinage with native women in the countries
where they were resident, leaving them and their illegitimate descendants
a few fields before they returned to India. This situation persisted until
the Second World War and the economic and political crisis which
followed the decolonization of Burma. The Nattukottai Chettiar were
then forced to pull back into southern India, where they still held a
dominant position in banking and the textile industry. Nevertheless, their
family networks are perhaps no longer as forceful and dense as those
which H. Stern observed in a merchant caste in Rajasthan (the Oswal,
known by the name Marwari), whose ramifications, though centred on
north-western India, also reach to the south. Among this caste, whose
activities stretch to the commercial, industrial and financial spheres,

> the most powerful families which control the big groups . . . get their
> relatives and in-laws to manage the production, putting them in respons-
> ible jobs . . . they organize the distribution of products by means of
> exclusive contractual relations established with families which have often

given them daughters in marriage and which operate in the commodity markets and the big national markets, the regional agencies (wholesale) and local commerce (wholesale trade and retail); and within this network of commercial distribution, it is often the eldest branch of a lineage which entrusts lower rung management and profits to a junior lineage ... (Stern, 1982, p. 140)

Employees and workers: kinship, kin and neighbourhood

Whereas the study of merchant communities allows us to challenge the false tendency to oppose town and countryside, modernity and tradition, we should also question the transformations which affect the modes of family organization and the values of social groups with access to urban life. One of the first principles of differentiation among these groups is the antiquity of their access to the urban way of life, which itself depended on the degree of proximity to the centres of power enjoyed by these groups before and after the colonial conquest. In the nineteenth century, it was these high castes, which had traditionally had access to education and to public service prior to the British presence, which were drawn to the presidencies and filled the new intellectual professions: Tamil Brahmans from Tanjore and Tirunelveli, for instance, who migrated to Madras, or the Kayastha and Vaidya, who set up in Calcutta and became the representatives of the Indian National Movement. As S. N. Mukherjee has recorded in the case of Bengal, these groups were differentiated by the modalities of their urbanization process and the rapidity with which they assimilated the values and modes of urban life. From the end of the eighteenth century, the *bhadralok* group had transformed its temporary residences in Calcutta (*basa*) into permanent residences (*bari*), whereas many other castes continued for a long time to divide their lives between town and their village of birth, where a part of the family group remained and the important life-cycle ceremonies were celebrated (1979, p. 45). The same phenomenon can still be observed nowadays among the Brahmans in Madras and, above all, the Nattukottai Chettiar, who are finding it increasingly expensive to maintain their empty houses of birth all year round, opening them only to celebrate marriages.

There are clearly great problems in characterizing the family models of social groups as heterogeneous as those of the working classes, which are extremely diversified both in their practices and interests, and in their ways of thinking. Heuzé writes that 'no statistical study allows us to characterize the worker family specifically from the point of view of its typology (extended or nuclear family), its practice in intermarriage or birth control. The workers behave either like the middle classes, to which they attach themselves if they achieve status, or like poor peasants and the sub-proletariat among whom they live if they are deprived of status' (1982, p. 200). Among the different groups which are collectively grouped as the middle classes, the conjugal family is by and large dominant: it includes 85–90 per cent of the households of minor civil servants, which were studied by S. Vatuk in the mid-1960s in the town of Meerut in northern India, 80 per cent of households of workers employed in the machine shops at Howrah near Calcutta, and every family in the case of workers in the model steel factury at Jamshedpur, in the state of Bihar, where the nuclear configuration has been imposed by the way the workers' dwellings have been designed, the plan being inspired by the notion that the extended family presents an obstacle to modern industrial development. Nevertheless enlarged families could amount to 40 per cent of households among the Howrah entrepreneurs, whose workshops are often jointly managed by a family group (Vatuk, 1972; Owens, 1971, pp. 223–50; Ames, 1973, pp. 107–31). In these situations, the family groups living in town almost always retain their shares in the ancestral property, which continues to be farmed by other members of the family from whom they receive the produce. In exchange, and within the limits of incomes which are always low, the urban members share in the expenses of maintaining the family home and the temples of their lineage, making financial contributions at the rituals, which always present an opportunity to return to their native countryside.

Do caste and kinship, which structure the traditional Indian family in town as in the country, enjoy the same importance among these social groups? It is extremely difficult to provide an overall reply on this point because studies of the family and kinship in the towns are rare in spite of the existence of an abundant literature on the theme of 'the Indian family in transition'. We will take a detailed look at S. Vatuk's works, mentioned earlier, on two quarters (*mohallā*) in Meerut (Ganeshnagar and Kalyanpuri), a small administrative centre and market town on the Ganges plain, which numbered 280,000 inhabitants in 1961. These two quarters were built from 1930 onwards, and are inhabited by a socially homogeneous population, consisting of high-caste Brahmans and Baniya of rural origin, with a high level of education and strong recognition of academic qualifications and values, most of whom occupy administrative positions as civil servants, teachers, clerks and the like. In Ganeshnagar, 44 per cent own their own dwelling, but overpopulation means that each family can have no more than two rooms. Although the great majority of family groups are nuclear in type, they are inserted into kinship groups which function as networks.

For first-generation migrants, these networks provide a preferential link with their village of origin and serve to guide individual migrations from the country to the town: for second-generation migrants, these networks, which in Meerut stretch beyond their *mohallā*, provide the necessary intermediate contacts for forming matrimonial alliances. When a couple sets up in Meerut, as a result of migration or marriage, it founds a new house and household, which, because it is a neolocal residence, introduces a modification to their kinship relations, attitudes and behaviour. If, by migrating, the woman ends up far away from her native village, she is nevertheless not integrated into her husband's kin as strictly as she would have been formerly, and though the purdah system is still present, it is now much less rigid. For second-generation migrants, and particularly those who remain in their quarter of origin after marriage, their neolocal residence introduces a third centre of reference to the kinship. Wives, who are no longer cut off from their families of origin, now maintain closer relations with them, which are marked by a strengthening in the mother–daughter relationship. Although the *mohallā* is the birthplace of some wives the fact that their husbands live there does not make them *ghar jamai* (equivalent to sons in the wife's family). The proximity of the two family groups around the new couple and the increased frequency of exchanges have introduced a softening in the wife's favour of the traditional asymmetrical relations between donor and taker groups. In this patrilinear society, changing a patrilocal (or patri-virilocal) residence for a neolocal and urban residence carries the seeds of the development of a bilateral tendency in the kinship (Vatuk, 1972, pp. 140–8).

While exchanges within family networks always provide privileged occasions for meeting, they are in competition with neighbourhood relations in which the affinities of ethos of a homogeneous fraction of the urban lower middle classes are not negated by a unit of high-status caste values: a landowners' association will emerge particularly to celebrate Holi, the feast of spring, and women, who on the whole are engaged solely in domestic activities, come together for collective readings of the *Ramayana* and for devotional singing sessions. The general impression given is that the Indian family has, by modifying, retained the ability to preserve its values, or, as E. Sapir more precisely notes, 'the different degrees of conservatism in regard to custom' vary in the behaviour of a single individual because of the different types of social participation into which he enters' (*Encyclopedia of the Social Sciences*, vol. IV, p. 661). Outside the family, men, whether in office or factory, are attached to the values of the modern world, while delegating to their wives the function of guardians of traditions to which they still submit within the family sphere (for a similar observation among the big industrial bosses in

Madras see Singer, 1968). Under these conditions, it is clear that the situation of women lies at the very heart of the struggles whose issue is the family.

Women at stake: family, status and power

In one sense, the ambivalent position of women which can be observed today in Indian families and society is one of the constant features of their history, at least since the medieval period, as summed up for the literate world by the *Brhad-Āranyaka-Upanishad*: 'At that time, Yajnavalkya had two wives, Maitreyi and Katyayani. Maitreyi was learned in the knowledge of sacred matters, whereas Katyayani kept to the ordinary sphere of women.' According to the point of view one prefers, the history of Indian women can be read up to our times as a long struggle for emancipation (Thapar in Jain, 1975, pp. 5–17) or as a long deterioration of their condition and status since the mythical golden age of the Vedic period (Altekar, 1959, p. 359). Since the 1930s, India's population growth and economic development have contributed to putting women at the heart of struggles over the control of the family's reproductive function, whether by the state, which tries to regulate fertility and the conditions of biological reproduction, or by social groups which attempt, often by manipulating in dramatic ways women's access to the marriage market, to master their strategies of social reproduction in a period when their statutory position is in general crisis.

Women, families and work

The development of an unskilled workforce   At the start of the twentieth century almost the entire female population could neither read nor write. In 1981, 25 per cent of women were literate, compared to about one in two men. The gap between the sexes, which was 9 per cent in 1901, was 22 per cent in 1981. During the same period, although the number of women entering working life has increased in absolute terms, in terms of the entire female population, it amounted, according to the censuses, to almost 34 per cent in 1901, 28 per cent in 1961, but only about 12 per cent in the 1980s. The total working population, which numbered only a third of all women until 1961, now stands at somewhere between 15 and 20 per cent (*Towards Equality*, 1974, pp. 148–233). This fall in female employment during the last forty years lies at the centre of the muddled speculation which is growing up about the deterioration of the female condition in contemporary India. How-

INDIAN EXPRESS
(SUNDAY EDITION)

Express Magazine

Early in the morning of July 11, 1977, the rural quiet of Ghemo in U.P. was shattered by chilling screams. The neighbourhood was soon alive with people clamouring for attention outside the sarpanch's 'haveli'. Quite suddenly, he appeared on his balcony, his rifle trained at the crowd below. "Disperse, I say. If anybody dares to enter, he'll not see the dawn." The pallor of that dawn soon faded into morning. It shed light on the charred remains of Kanta, her teeth exposed in a macabre smile. There was breath in her body, a large number of villagers swear, when the bier set out for the cremation ground at 11 a.m. Kanta finally died on the funeral pyre. Her case still languishes in the Sessions Court of District Mainpuri, U.P. — one of the increasing numbers of 'dowry deaths' in the country — and is likely to be abandoned for want of evidence.

Is dowry a natural law? Why is it so durable? Are young women really dying because of dowry or are there other factors? Who gets burnt — strong or submissive girls? Using vignettes drawn from 38 genuine cases of unnatural deaths, reportedly due to harassment over dowry, the author attempts a deeper understanding of this issue.

WHY DOWRY SPELLS DEATH

Are we really against dowry?

THE dowry system cannot be rooted out of our society by legislation or any government ... because the malaise is not one th...

Need for anti-dowry drive

ONE of the burning problems of our society is dowry. Not a day passes without cases ... married brides ...

Doing away with dowry

GOING by newspaper headlines, there is ... let-up in the number of ... young brides beca...

188 women died of burns in Delhi in just six months

NEW DELHI, March 7.

In just six months from August last year to January this year 188 women died of burns in the capital, Mr P. Venkatasubbiah, Minister of State for Home, said in the Lok Sabha today.

In the same period, 90 women committed suicide and eight more died because of beating, he told Mrs Pramila Dandavate and Mr Subash Chandra Bose Allgu.

On the basis of complaints 23 suicide cases, 41 cases of burning and eight of beating have been registered.

Replying to Mr N. C. Parashar, he said there had been a marginal increase in crimes of murder and rape in Delhi between 1982 and 1983. There were 247 cases of murder and 83 cases of rape last year as against 240 and 71 in the previous year.

... The Home Minister, Mr P. C. Sethi and Mr Venkatasubbiah told the House that an inquiry had been ordered into police apathy ...

In-laws cause of more suicides

NEW DELHI, April 26 (PTI).

"Quarrels with parents-in-law" was the second major cause of suicides in the country, accounting for 9.3 per cent of a total of 40,297 such deaths during 1978.

The major cause of suicides during 1978 was "dreadful diseases" which accounted for about 17 per cent of total suicide cases.

"Love affairs" and "quarrel with spouse" were the other important causes taking a toll of 5.8 per cent and 5.7 per cent respectively.

... age group 18-30 years (41.7 per cent) and minimum (13.1 per cent) were committed by the persons of above 50 years of age.

Persons below 18 years of age accounted for 18.8 per cent of total suicide cases and persons belonging to the age group 30 to 50 year accounted for 29.4 per cent of the total suicide cases reported during 1978.

The age-wise pattern of suicides during 1978 was almost the same for states, Union Territories and metropolitan cities as a whole.

Figure 3 The Indian press contributes to the debate by making its readers more aware of the social problems raised by dowry. Pages from *Indian Express, Hindu, India Today, Beautiful Working Woman* and *Femina*.

ever, the poor quality of the data (due among other factors to variations in the definitions employed) leads many authors seriously to question the size and even the reality of this drop. It will be observed that a proportion of 25–30 per cent of working women is comparable to that noted in European countries between the mid-nineteenth and mid-twentieth centuries. Furthermore, Indian women in employment are not a recent fact linked to the recognition of their civic and political rights from the end of

FEMINA:COMMENT

OUR FIGHT GOES ON...

It is imperative that the amendments proposed by several women's organisations are incorporated in the Dowry Bill, says SHRABANI BASU. Only then, will every bride feel safe in her new home. And only then will her scheming in-laws be caught in their own web of greed and deceit

THE monsoon session of Parliament has begun. And a lot of changes are on the cards.

While the much required Dowry Prohibition (Amendment) Bill was squeezed into the agenda in the previous session—it is likely to come up again for discussion this time.

Yet many of the important suggestions put forward by the Joint Select Committee and the Law Commission have been ignored in the Amendment Bill.

Seven women's organisations in Delhi along with the People's Union for Civil Liberties and the People's Union for Democratic Rights held a series of meetings to chalk out the inconsistencies and drawbacks in the Dowry Amendment Bill.

The very definition of dowry as offered by the Amendment Bill was disappointing. The 1961 Act defined dowry as "any property or valuable security given or agreed to be given either directly or indirectly—by any party to marriage to the other party to the marriage: or by the parents of either party or by any other person, at or before or after the marriage as consideration for the marriage of the said parties."

The Joint Select Committee demanded that the words "as consideration for the marriage" be deleted, as it was ambiguous and ignored the fact that pressures could be applied for reasons shown to be other than marriage.

The Amendment Bill of 1984 however merely substituted the words to "in connection with marriage."

The women's organisations agreed jointly that it should apply to mean "before, during and after the marriage" to give greater clarity and protection to the bride.

They also felt that the definition of dowry should be extended to mean "money demanded or taken" as opposed to the Amendment Bill which says only "money demanded".

Former professor of law at Delhi University, Dr. Lotika Sarkar pointed out that the present Bill left many things vague and thus dowry takers could escape by finding some loopholes in the law.

The organisations have pointed out that the "excellent" recommendations made by the Joint Select Committee of Parliament to introduce ceilings on marriage expenses as an essential part of the strategy to eradicate dowry have been altogether ignored in the Amendment Bill. The Select Committee had suggested a ceiling of expenses on the bride's side to be not more than Rs 3,000 or seven per cent of the family income from all sources for the year before the marriage. The women's groups feel that this should be extended further and the

Figure 4 A page from *Femina*

the nineteenth century, or to the development of new values related to their emancipation and independence. Finally, it is quite possible, and even probable, that female employment has fallen in India, whatever the value of the data.

In the great majority of cases, female employment in the countryside is typified by women from middling or poor peasant groups and, in the towns, by women belonging to the least privileged classes. In 1961, 31 per cent of working women were employed in the primary sector, 15 per cent in industry and 11 per cent in the tertiary sector; in 1981, these proportions were in the order of 82 per cent, 7 per cent and 11 per cent respectively. However, over the last fifty years, economic development and the introduction of modern technology have progressively squeezed women out of skilled jobs. The fall in female employment in the industrial sector is firstly the result of a decline in domestic crafts: weaving, de-hulling paddy, processing oil, tanning and manufacturing cigarettes. However, it is also the result of an evolution in the recruitment of the industrial workforce. In the Bombay textile industry, the pioneering days when workers were taken on according to family solidarities and caste gave way in the 1920s and 1930s to a period of labour rationalization which was accompanied by giving the worker family a new framework and definition. Although the majority of women engaged in this work were heads of families, widows or divorcees with children to care for, we can see the emergence of the notion of a male working wage centred on the conjugal family, which relegates female salaries to a supporting role. The prohibition of night work for women and children after 1911, and the appearance of social laws protecting pregnancy in 1929, contributed to keeping women out of factories and to defining a new morality for worker families based on their function in the reproduction of the workforce under the increased control of the state and enterprises (Kumar, 1983). In rural areas, when small factories employing a mainly male workforce take over work such as processing cereals or de-hulling paddy, the consequences for family economies are often dramatic. This evolution is suppressing not only one source of employment for women but also a source of income which has almost always been paid in kind, and which they have been able to dispose of freely (M. Mukherjee, 1983). The commercialization of these products is also being transformed. Thus it is clear that the stagnation of the female workforce employed in the tertiary sector and its increase in the primary sector mask profound and drastic internal changes. Between 1951 and 1971, the number in absolute terms of women defined as farmers or small-holders has diminished by half: in 1981 they represented only 30 per cent

Women are an important part of the workforce in the construction
industry. Christine Osbourne.

of working women, whereas 52 per cent were employed as waged agricultural workers.

Although several factors concur objectively in lowering the rate of female participation in working life, one can in fact observe a shift on the part of the female workforce into the unorganized sector, estimated by economists to represent 90 per cent of all workers – and a concentration into the most irregular and unskilled forms of employment, which have every likelihood of not being taken into account in official surveys. In spite of the transformations affecting the labour market and the structure of employment, the basically rural economic work done by women is still dominated by the requirements of family life. With the constraints of population growth and the break-up of farms, it is increasingly difficult to support a family when additional income from home crafts can no longer be relied on. Women are thus induced to extend their labour, often working in teams, into seasonal or permanent jobs, full- or part-time: planting out rice, weeding, harvesting, winnowing, as well as heavy labour in demolition and construction work, which often involves migrating between town and the countryside for several months in the year. It is clear that the logic underlying these forms of behaviour has nothing to do with the diffusion of any kind of modern ideology. Quite the contrary: it can only be understood within the extension of traditional values and behaviour which produce, within a complex economic social environment, modes of adapting to an increasingly diversified labour market.

Marriage, status and work: conflicting values   While the distinction between rural and urban surroundings is a discriminating factor in female employment, the second criterion to be taken into account is their married status: in the countryside 50 per cent of married women were working in 1961, compared to only 13.5 per cent in towns (Visaria, 1983). In order to understand how the ratio of female employment varies according to class (or caste) over time, we must take account of the economic, social and statutory position of these groups as well as the direction in which their social trajectories are moving. In rural surroundings, productive labour, especially in its waged forms, is characteristic only of the small landowning peasants, tenants and the landless poor. Among the big landowners (in Thakur in northern India, Kamma in coastal Andhra and Vellala in the Tamil country), male employment is limited to supervising and allotting agricultural work, as is female work in the domestic sphere, though this varies according to family. In this society, based on hierarchy and inequality, there are, as a matter of principle, always persons inferior to oneself to perform tasks which are considered all the more impure in that they involve practical and material work; raising oneself into the sphere of social and statutory positions thus means freeing oneself from these forms of work by increasing the number of one's dependants, to whom they can be delegated. Among the complex processes of social mobility which affect family groups in the middle-ranking and lower castes, and which are encapsulated in M. N. Srinivas's word 'sanskritization' (Srinavas and Ramaswamy, 1977; for a criticism of this notion, see Dumont, 1979), we may include the move to give up female work, firstly outside the household, which always constitutes the most obvious sign of a rise in status 'because women in particular, find high status inconsistent with even extra-mural movement, with the result that upward mobility leads to their "immure-ment" (Srinavas, 1966). It is thus clear that enclosing women can only reinforce their function as the guardians of home values, meaning the purity of the house and its members. When these family cults are practised among relatively high-status castes, very often in order to satisfy worldly interests, to conceive a child or find a cure, or to bring success and prosperity to an enterprise, it is first and foremost the women's business. The men provide the material conditions for the rituals by paying for them and often taking part, but they do not always seem to be really involved. In the great Indian cities, these forms of behaviour can exist among the same family groups alongside Western consumer practices, whose rapid dissemination can only be explained by the fact that they are integrated into a system of traditional family values: this applies to television, and above all to the recent and rapid develop-ment of videos, the use of which in these groups strengthens the 'enclosure' of women within the family world.

Nevertheless, there is a world of difference between high-caste rural women and others, themselves derived from the highest castes, in the upper echelons of the urban classes, whose work makes them participate in the values of the Western world. However, although 40 per cent of women in the towns are literate, only about 1 per cent have a university degree and, of every 100 in employment, sixty-five are teachers, fifty at elementary level, fifteen occupy subordinate positions as employees, and twenty practise a liberal profession. By turning a regular salaried job, based on the possession of an academic qualification, however minor, into a legitimate and valued activity outside the home, these groups are trying to impose a new definition of the accomplished woman. This explains their importance in ideological terms, quite out of proportion to their numbers in Indian society, which are still restricted. The new representation, among others, is imposed by means of the development of an English-language women's press, which competes with the traditional women's newspapers in Indian languages and deals with the condition of women doctors, managers of firms or artists (the best example being the magazine *Beautiful Working Woman*). Although women's access to education, all the more probable in town, is a necessary condition of obtaining these new forms of employment, it is never a sufficient condition. Everything depends on the logic according to which the educational capital which they possess has been constituted and used, and which is of value both on the labour market and on the marriage market.

Families, powers and social controls

Marriage market and dowry: a statutory crisis In the last fifty years, the institution of marriage has undergone a profound crisis, manifested by the extension and intensification of the practice of dowry among social groups which had until recently been little if at all concerned with it. Nowadays the problem has become so acute that it often assumes tragic forms. The dowry, the economic importance of which is out of proportion to families' average incomes, puts the young bride in an unbearable position: caught between her in-laws' pressing demands and her parents' financial inability to satisfy them, which is often the case, she is sometimes driven to an accidental or criminal death, burnt alive by her husband in punishment for her inadequate dowry. In 1983, nearly 700 cases were officially notified in Delhi alone, and resulted in judicial proceedings. In the absence of detailed studies, we will try to isolate the problem by tackling some important questions.

In the whole of India, the average age at first marriage, which was twenty-one for men and thirteen for women in 1891–1901, shifted to about twenty-three and seventeen respectively in 1961–71; the age gap between spouses had thus been reduced from eight to five years. Nevertheless, as S. N. Agarwala (1977) has demonstrated, the rise in the age of marriage for women masks a relative stability in the average age at which the spouses co-reside, which is the result of reducing the interval between marriage and cohabitation. Nowadays, women marry and begin to cohabit with their spouse on average four to five years after puberty. In town, the average age at first marriage is a little over twenty-four for men and nineteen for women.

What are the consequences for the family and kin of the changes which are expressed by this rise in the age of marriage? It must be pointed out first of all that it is not pertinent to set one form of traditional, endogamous and preferential marriage against a so-called modern form based on the elective affinities of spouses who belong to different castes or communities, even though some intercaste marriages can be observed, following the logic of social homogamy, among the Westernized parts of the ruling classes. Today as in the past, marriage remains subject to control by the family group in its widest sense.

As pointed out above, the most profound crisis lies in the extension of the practice of dowry, especially in northern India, and its extension in southern India to what are generally low-status groups which normally practise payment in the opposite direction, since bride price is still in fashion. When dowry is discussed, what is meant are the presents in cash or kind from the bride's parents to their son-in-law or his family. On the one hand, these payments constitute no more than part of the expenses incurred on the occasion of a marriage. On the other hand, by the use of these terms the presents given on the occasion of specific alliances are isolated within a series of reversible or directional exchanges spread out over time. If one sets them within the whole cycle of payments, it is probable that the evolution is not as straightforward as the current formula suggests (Dumont, 1975, pp. 7–83; see also Tambiah in Goody and Tambiah, 1973, pp. 59–169). Nevertheless, this does not affect the special feature of dowry, that it is an asymmetrical and specific payment, which will not revert increased in value, at least in the same form.

What is the role played by demographic growth in these changes in the marriage market? According to J. C. Caldwell (Caldwell et al., 1983), the fall in mortality and rapid rise in population since the 1920s have been determining factors. Between 1930 and 1970, they claim that the ratio of offer to demand on the marriage market was inverted: the number of women in marriageable age groups between ten and nineteen years old, which had initially been deficient, grew until it was surplus to the number of men aged between twenty and twenty-nine; this would explain the spread of the dowry phenomenon. However, this mechanical determinant is not very convincing. In the first place, the demographic evidence is not as clear-cut; the proportion of surplus women in the age groups under discussion was relatively stable at between 7 to 10 per cent between 1901 and 1961 (I base this on the only homogeneous source available for the whole of India for this period: S. Mukherjee, 1976, p. 65); it was only in 1971 and 1981 that the census data revealed a 30 per cent surplus of women. Secondly, although the practice of dowry is not mentioned in the *smrti* texts, it appears in the medieval period among the Rajput (*ksatriya*), for whom it is supposed to have become a scourge in the thirteenth and fourteenth centuries (Altekar, 1959, pp. 68–72). Furthermore it has been observed that in this case, it was linked to inequality of status and accompanied forms of hypergamic marriage among groups deficient in women. The appearance of dowry in northern India is perhaps linked to Muslim influence. However, we must still take account of the historical and sociological reasons for its development in the Hindu world. In this context, two facts are often cited either to confuse them with dowry or to legitimize it: *stridhana* and *kanyādāna* ideology. *Stridhana* represents the property received by the woman in compensation for her exclusion from the inheritance, and in principle is transmitted through the female line. Can dowry be reduced to the category of *stridhana*?

In our days, if we make a breakdown of the expenses involved in a marriage, the dowry is distinguished from the actual property given to the woman, such as her jewels, which may be more valuable anyway. By referring to the ideology of the gift of the young girl to the Brahman, it is shown that dowry is assimilated to the symbolic payment of *daksina*. This ideology is present in the hypergamic model of marriage, for which the association between the Nayar and the Nambudiri provides an exemplary instance. What has been observed in their case is that dowry has developed as a corollary of the general spread of hypergamy in its secular forms: status is no longer defined simply within its traditional ritual component but also according to income, education and, in short, to class. The reinterpretation of this transformation within the logic of *kanyādāna* serves at the same time to legitimize the change. In southern India too, and in Madras in particular, the practice of dowry developed in the 1930s firstly among the Brahman community which enjoyed early access to European education and salaried employment in the public sector.

Thus the delay in male nuptiality was a result of the advance of education. But, given that marriages always occur within a precise caste context and that the age gap between spouses is still high, women have also been obliged to delay their nuptiality. The ensuing free time before coming onto the marriage market is filled by prolonging school attendance, which has become necessary to allow the girl to acquire the indispensable educational and cultural capital (apprenticeship in singing and dancing) which she needs, both to adjust to the higher educational level of her potential spouse and to compensate for her loss in status occasioned by prolonging her unmarried state beyond puberty. The spread of liberal and reformist values from the West has only served to reinforce this tendency by legitimizing it. It can thus be seen that for women, access to education must firstly be understood within the functional logic of the marriage market. The case is clear-cut for the middling and lower castes where academic levels for both sexes are low; too high an educational level for a woman could be a disadvantage when looking for a husband of the same caste who must have attained an even higher level. If the search for the right kind of party to achieve a hypergamic marriage drags on, the woman could be forced to enter the labour market temporarily (or longer), often in order to contribute to her own dowry.

What we want simply to suggest here, as Dumont has shown in the case of the Nayar, is that in order to understand the institution of marriage within its past and present forms, we need to consider the general economy of the material and symbolic exchanges between the groups. The rapid development of a commercial economy which affects the castes in different ways, population growth and heightened pressure on land have shaken the caste system and the way it functions to its foundations. Status now depends not only on ritual purity but on level of education, form of employment, income and, in short, class position. It is logical that this crisis of status identity should crystallize in the institution of marriage, because status is always upheld by men and it is by forming new alliances with women, often at a heavy price, that groups can hope to improve it.

Fertility as a social issue   At the end of the nineteenth century when censuses were first established, the appearance of official statistics contributed to the new awareness of population problems on the part of Indian public opinion, meaning in fact representative groups, such as civil servants, militant nationalists and doctors. The intensity of the debates sparked off in every decade about how to interpret the growth rate between censuses and the corollary evidence about fertility and death rates shows, despite the poor quality of the data, the importance of the social and political issues which population growth and the fertility of Indian women have become.

The birth rate, which probably increased in the 1950s, has fallen slowly but surely since that period. It was about 45 per 1,000 at mid-century, 40 per 1,000 around 1970, and about 1990 in the order of 30 per 1,000 (Jain and Adlakha, 1982). The rise observed after independence is thought to be the result of a reduction in both the traditional period of sexual abstinence after giving birth and in the breast-feeding stage. This rationale presupposes a modification in individual relations within families: less control by the older generation over the sexuality of married children living within joint families, and a weakening within couples of traditional family morality in this matter (Caldwell et al., 1984, pp. 187–207). Nevertheless, the most important evolution over the past fifty years has been the drop in the death rate: the gross mortality rate, which was above 30 per 1,000 about 1950, is thought to have been just above 10 per 1,000 in the 1990s. Above all, however, it is the consequences of the decline in infant mortality which matters: from a level above 250 per 1,000 at the start of the twentieth century, it is at present about 80 per 1,000 and often less in southern India (Chandrasekhar, 1972). However, the excessively high death rate for females in the first years of childhood and early adulthood is still significant, particularly in northern India where the sex ratio in the 1981 census came to between 110 and 115 men per 100 women. Specialized medical help is less often resorted to when young girls are ill, they tend to be given a lower-calorie diet within the family, and the dangers which they incur in childbirth during the years of fertility are factors, among others, which account for variations in the death rate according to sex, and witness to differentiated forms of behaviour towards children (Miller, 1981).

In any case, among the most privileged social groups in town and country, the fall in infant mortality and a lower fertility rate within an economic and social environment which has itself been profoundly transformed, have served to reverse the direction of economic exchange between generations and to alter the position of the child; the latter was perceived in the past as wealth-producing capital (work, insurance, etc.) but is nowadays considered an expense. As J. C. Caldwell writes, his net economic value has altered, entailing a consequential fall in fertility. However, we must be careful not to attribute this situation, about which little is known, to all social groups and to the whole of the Indian subcontinent (for a criticism of Caldwell's thesis, see especially Cain, 1982). What role has been played by the family planning policy implemented by the government in the decline in fertility which has begun in India, in ways varying with class and region?

Until 1947, the birth control movement merged with the struggle for national independence and the reform of family law. From the 1920s, and influenced by trends in Europe, specialized clinics, public and private, opened in Bombay and Bangalore, and a birth control society was started in Madras in 1928. During this first phase, the spread of ideas and techniques was limited to the most Westernized intellectual elements in nationalist circles. After independence and especially in the 1960s, when international organizations and the United States started to intervene urgently, India acquired the material and financial means to conduct a vast policy of education in matters of birth prevention based on persuasion and incentives: family planning services were to provide the Indian peasant masses with the means (to which they were supposed to aspire) of controlling their fertility.

At the start of the 1970s this policy was embodied in huge campaigns for male sterilization at an annual rate of 2–3 million vasectomies performed publicly in a carnival atmosphere, at which rewards in kind and money would be distributed. This policy reached its peak during the state of emergency decreed in 1975–7. A series of measures, mostly coercive, were taken in education (initiation into population problems), public and political life (representation by the federal states at central level and financial grants allocated up to 2001 on the basis of the 1971 population), as much as individuals (abolition of bonuses for civil servants with more than two children, quotas of obligatory sterilizations etc.). In fact, with more than 8 million operations performed, sterilizations reached record numbers in 1976–7. However, the policy of depending on voluntary compliance turned into state use of brute force, revealing that the gentle persuasion on which it claimed to be based was no more than a cunningly manufactured myth (Vicziany, 1982). As Thomas has observed, the public riots would perhaps not have been so violent had this policy not revived the ubiquitous fear of castration which underpins Ghandi-ism and its fantastical economic theories (Thomas, 1979, pp. 111–30). Since the 1980s, family planning policy has reverted to euphemism in publicizing its aims: it no longer refers to birth control but to the well-being of the family.

Has it failed or succeeded? Careful study of the data published for the whole of India reveals that the population touched by the campaigns belonged chiefly to the most economically deprived strata, illiterates with no knowledge of birth control techniques. Sterilization, carried out by force, or with the lure of momentary gain, was undergone by individuals without bringing about any change in their material conditions of life or to the system of values which determine their practices in the realm of fertility. As an instant and irreversible operation, it contrasts with the use of other contraceptive techniques which allow the better-off elements of the population, which tend to be educated, urban and upwardly mobile, firstly to space out and then to limit the number of births. It is clear that there is no straightforward relation between a lowered fertility rate – for which the data are poorly differentiated for time and social group – and the establishment of a family policy which can only be received differently by different social groups. The rise in the age of marriage for women and the reduction in the age gap between spouses, as much as the rise in their level of education, make it more difficult to subordinate new couples within complex families, and can only tend to increase communication between husband and wife about the problems of birth control. However, it is illusory to believe that the key to the lowered fertility rate is to be found in the development of education for the masses, and in an increase in the marginal expense of the child which this entails (which does not mean that this education is not desirable). Rare indeed are the studies which attempt to understand, in socially differentiated ways, the dual play of economic determinants and the implicit value systems which establish fertility patterns. While the decision to have a child depends on the objective expense involved as well as the subjectively perceived expense, it also depends on the value put on the number of children. The wish for a son, the fear of sterility and the cults at the temples of goddesses to exorcize this fear as well as the open or veiled disapproval to which single and childless women, spinsters and divorcees, are subjected, remind us every day of the strength of the feeling for childhood and family which lies at the heart of Hinduism. If contemporary evolution can only accelerate the constrained fall in the birth rate which has taken place, we still need to understand how the voluntary birth rate is evolving.

The Hindu joint family is one of the most enduring customs mentioned by E. Sapir, those 'which either correspond to so basic a human need that they cannot well be seriously changed or else are of such a nature that they can easily be functionally reinterpreted' (*Encyclopedia of Social Sciences*, 1967, vol. IV, p. 660). The ontological notion of debt which lies at the centre of its representations fixes the continuity of relations between father and son, between living and dead, and gives its members the sense of belonging to a world ruled by values. However, this does not mean that the institution has been maintained unaltered. The size and structure of the joint family, which is primarily defined as a theoretical family grouping, depend on its ability, as a practical group, to integrate within a community of economic and symbolic interests each of the family units which make it up. While the rise of egalitarian and individualistic forces which tend to produce nuclear families is not a modern fact, much less a contemporary one – although in our day they have increased in intensity for reasons which are as much economic as ideological – it is clear that the emergence of the conjugal family centred on the couple does not have the radical character which is attributed to it today, and all the more readily in that some groups have an objective and subjective interest in its appearance. On the contrary, we are witnessing both a redefinition of the forms of the joint family and a progressive modification to the modes of participation maintained by its individual members with it, and a reinterpretation of its functions. The differentiated social trajectories of its members, the less direct and intense relations which they establish among themselves and the curtailing of family rituals are perhaps signs of changes which are more profound nowadays. However, because it is founded in traditional law and, above all, in the religion which provides the majority of Hindus with their only structured representation of the world, the traditional joint family finds in these two elements its best guarantee of durability.

SEVEN

Africa: the Family at the Crossroads

Jean-Pierre Dozon

A frica (meaning sub-Saharan Africa) is special in possessing not only the features of a typically underdeveloped world or, to adopt fashionable terminology, a developmentally sick world, but also the much more attractive and in many respects exotic ones of a continent endowed with fabulous treasures, which can help us to a better understanding of how mankind has evolved and of the many different ways to organize social life and invent rules and symbolic systems for ensuring its lasting cohesion. Recent discoveries by palaeontologists have designated Africa as the cradle of mankind, or rather as a particularly favourable site for carrying out the various stages in the process of becoming man. For their part, ethnologists have observed or reconstructed a very wide range of social forms, from bands of hunter-gatherers to so-called traditional states (an expression which merely distinguishes between states formed prior to colonization and the present 'nation-states') passing via a whole series of societies, with no separate centralized ruling apparatus, which were structured according to criteria of sex, age and status on the basis of kinship groups and alliance relations. From this point of view, Africa constitutes a very special terrain for anthropology in general. It is here that anthropology can satisfy its bent for drawing comparisons, i.e. confronting different social and political systems in order to discern invariables and possible sociological laws. However, it is just as possible to inquire into the origins of social institutions, to research for instance into the historical conditions and circumstances which have determined the emergence of a particular family institution or form of state.

There is apparently nothing contradictory about these two pictures of an Africa which is both poor in the economic domain and rich in the cultural sense. Is not underdevelopment the allegedly negative side of an

Village life, Gambia. Christine Osbourne.

African reality which has been able, in spite of European colonization and the creation of nation-states, to keep a hold on its points of reference and its traditional ways of life? Do not those aspects which fascinate anthropologists, and which indirectly justify the West's exotic view of the continent, become in the eyes of developers – a term indicating the agents of development at all levels – and, to a certain extent, in those of African politicians, impediments to change and socio-cultural obstacles? Are not the repeated failures of attempts to improve rural conditions, and the difficulties experienced by states seeking legitimacy and stability, derived from archaic features which are still in existence and of particular features which do not always succumb to universalizing injunctions on the part of the economy and politics? These are questions which have given rise to a dilemma and have induced some people to rethink the manner in which black Africa can be developed, to argue against practices which aim at destructuring African societies the better to submit them to the imperatives of a commercial economy and productivity. It is true that such revisions, which are shown in a new regard for local and traditional ways, have come at a time of crisis when the West is uncertain about its own future, when the idea of progress which it has promoted and which it represents is attacked by doubt and scepticism. Africa thus comes much closer, and there is an element of historical morality in the way the West, having subdued and colonized Africa, is now tussling with problems about its own identity; the West is rediscovering its traditions, valuing specific cultural and local features, and some are proposing cures in economic and social matters which are similar to the alternative solutions proposed in Africa and more generally in the Third World.

The age of administrators and ethnologists

In this field of discussion and representations relative to Africa, where intellectual and scientific interests, economic and ideological issues and developmental problems converge, the family occupies a special place. First of all, as an object of knowledge, the institution of the family in its extremely varied forms has absorbed a great part of Africanist research. French ethnology and especially English anthropology have in fact recognized in it one of the 'treasures' which Africa has contributed to the sum of knowledge. In a famous book which appeared in 1950 under the title *African Systems of Kinship and Marriage*, A. R. Radcliffe-Brown wrote with regard to the family: 'In order to understand any aspect of the social life of the African population, whether economic, political or religious, it is essential to possess a profound knowledge of its family and matrimonial organisation . . .' Further on he says: 'It must be hoped that the present work will be read not only by ethnologists, but also by some of those who have the duty of elaborating or carrying out colonial administration on the African continent.'

These propositions, set out in the form of a programme, are interesting for a variety of reasons: in the first instance, in order to understand Africa, that is to say, to penetrate its very essence, it is not enough to hold on to the three registers which in our own Western traditions define all social reality in economic, political and religious terms, registers which exhaust all functions and intentions. One must aim deeper at their common substratum, the family and matrimonial organization, which informs all of them and allows each one to relate to the other two. This is how Radcliffe-Brown had clearly proclaimed the fundamental role played by the study of the family and more generally of kinship in the analysis of African societies. It is a role which has been called 'pluri-functional' by Maurice Godelier (1973) because it is a constituent of the order of things and can metamorphose into economic structures as much as into religious systems. But Radcliffe-Brown has more to say: he defines his position more precisely by adding that such an approach to African societies involved not only fellow anthropologists and the scientific community but also his compatriots who have the job of administering them. According to him, the colonial authorities had everything to gain from taking an interest in family systems, because knowing about them and taking them into account was essential to their ability to provide a better-adjusted and more harmonious administration for these societies. The object of knowledge has virtually become a practical object.

Thus, in the work of a great British anthropologist, may be discovered a wholly decisive way of thinking about Africa. Understanding African societies requires aiming at their heart, meaning family institutions, and taking account of socio-cultural variations involves as a priority studying the symbolic and practical procedures which underlie these institutions and allow one to identify and classify each society, each ethnic group, at a stroke; to state that a particular population is patrilinear is tantamount to formulating a basic proposition, in this case recognizing in it an inherent feature which defines it as a wholly distinct subject.

We should now take the measure of this method of identification. Our first remark is that its wholesale nature means that it provides a good legitimization for a concept frequently applied to black Africa, to wit that of a traditional society. Over and above particular configurations and specific ethnic features, Africa can easily be defined in these terms, since family systems of whatever kind also constitute privileged frameworks for the enunciation and transmission of traditions. In other terms, if Africa presents itself to us as a continent under slow evolution, where traditional ways of life and thought persist in many places, it is because the family systems at the heart of its societies, with all that they imply in terms of laws, obligations and representations, seem to continue to mark and control individual and collective destinies. *A contrario*, the many manifest signs of modernity which can be perceived (nation-states, urbanization, new social stratification, etc.) can only be properly evaluated by taking a close look at the evolution of family institutions. Indeed, everything seems to turn around it as if, on the basis of the diagnosis which could be brought to bear on this evolution, one were in a position to conclude that profound social changes have occurred in black Africa, or conversely, that the weight of traditional structures is still dominant; and so much so that the signs of modernity are perhaps mere show, that in spite of the visible and detectable transformations, they can always be accompanied by ancient logics, and family codes can find in them new fields for extension. This question has taken a central place in the Africanist research developed in the 1960s during the late stages of decolonization.

It is particularly in France that precisely these lines of research have revealed subtle and ambiguous relations between modernity and tradition. They have been inspired by the sociologist G. Balandier, whose ethnological research stood out clearly in the 1950s because of its excessive tendency to view black Africa merely as a collection of traditional societies, and to forget that it had been conquered and subdued by Europe, and that colonization had created new situations which brought about social transformations. Such research has been carried out within the framework of what have been called 'ethnic monographs' (meaning the simultaneously ethnological and sociological study, on the basis of a sample of villages, of a society whose members acknowledge a common identity), which have emphasized the study of social changes and disruptions since colonization, while trying to identify any permanent features. Family institutions have most of the time been at the centre of these monographs, as the central criterion by which finally to evaluate the impact of colonization, the market economy and more recently the effects of development on a particular ethnic group; very often too, in spite of their partial destruction, these institutions turn out to be still effective, with their modes of filiation, matrimonial rules and practices (prohibited marriages, preferential alliances, dowry, polygamy, etc.) still more or less at work, thus relativizing the changes which can be perceived elsewhere.

Our second remark is that this organic involvement or mirror play between African societies and family systems does not simply belong to the order of things but also to a certain type of representation whose origins go back to the very beginning of European colonization. Radcliffe-Brown, as we saw above, made acquaintance with family systems the preliminary to any in-depth approach to African societies, and in doing so he traced the boundary of this special field of ethnological research. This sort of research has to be understood here in its most literal sense, as a science that treats of ethnic groups; while it is certainly destined to emerge from the study of particular cases in order to compare these family systems with one another and to 'discover a small number of general principles, touching their common structure' (1950) (a form of comparison which can be extended to other cultural spheres), it is primarily a manner of recognizing and classifying ethnic groups.

Even before the ethnologists, colonial administrators had already applied these organizational principles, classifying populations and above all identifying those territories and names about which there could be no doubt. They thus had to develop an interest in languages, customs and native practices, and to improvise linguistic or ethnographic skills for purposes of administration and colonial policy. Although he implicitly judged this production of knowledge superficial, Radcliffe-Brown, by designating family and matrimonial systems as the substantial reality of African populations, reproduced and in some respects reinforced the previous identification procedures. This is why he could link scientific and practical matters by making ethnology the indispensable complement to a good administration of the colonies.

In other words, the recognition of family institutions as the best means of penetrating African societies, however legitimate it might be, was inscribed into a tradition which the colonial state in its quality as a system of thought and action had itself set up. In fact it has frequently been thought that Africa is an ethnic mosaic, and that by saying so one touches its essence, its authentic nature, or that such a picture refers back to its pre-colonial reality. This belief is largely incorrect. It is much more the case that colonization has fixed and crystallized African societies under the ethnic label, having identified and mapped them according to its administrative and economic requirements. We are aware nowadays that a number of ethnic entities had no real equivalents in the pre-colonial world, or rather that the societies which are supposed to correspond to them do not identify with the names and territories assigned to them; that other modes of collective identification and social integration were at work following historical circumstances of a political (construction or expansion of a state), economic (regional specialization,

commercial networks) or simply social order (displacement of populations, migrations involving a change of identity). What is more, it is often
where groups characterized solely by their family systems are concerned
(as opposed to those which also have a political system) that the notion
of ethnic group is particularly problematic; the collective identity, which
seldom overlapped with the tribal or clan framework, was liable to
variations; it could change at the whim of the break-up and dispersal of
its residential and family units, the aggregation of groups and individuals

The French colonies explored by Brazza. Engraving by Dascher, from
Congo Français. Bibliothèque Nationale, Paris.

of different origins, and the emergence of new social spaces.

Such a criticism of the notion of ethnicity does not really challenge the idea that the study of family systems is indispensable to any under-standing of African societies. It simply serves to relativize its impact, by showing that what passes for in-depth knowledge of these societies reveals at the same time the presence of a third party, that of the administrations and states which identify and classify, mingling learned discourse with practical ends. It could be asked whether it is possible to refer unequivocally to the Bambara kinship system (an ethnic group in Mali), when it has just about been proved that the 'Bambara' population was only recognized and identified under this ethnonym following a quasi-legal decision in 1912 by Maurice Delafosse, an administrator who was both linguist and ethnographer, and that the term (*bambana*, to be precise) had certainly been known before, but was employed according to a whole range of uses and connotations, and designated, depending on speaker and historical period, an assortment of groups, which might not even share the same language or kinship system (Bazin, 1985).

All this certainly deserves to be developed further, but these few reflections on Radcliffe-Brown's thesis lead us to consider other registers in which the problem of the family in black Africa occupies a central and strategic position, revealing all the more clearly the practical and ideological issues which underlie it.

Such is the strange and ambiguous image of a black Africa which both fascinates for its traditional mentalities and structures, and arouses unease and perplexity over its development, or misdevelopment.

Family systems and misdevelopment

For a whole period (roughly the decade 1960–70), it was usual to establish a cause-and-effect relationship between the two phenomena and to believe that black Africa's present situation was comparable to that of the West a few centuries beforehand. This is why breaks with traditional society were encouraged, and modern, innovatory atti-tudes and individual forms of behaviour suitable for taking the initiative were promoted. However, the traditional society thus targeted largely identified family structures with coextensions of the social field; it is within extended families that tradition is transmitted and conformist attitudes and patterns of thought hostile to innovation are perpetuated, as was established by a developmental sociologist during those years (Hozelitz, 1960). From this point of view, development is easily per-ceived as a process which breaks down socio-cultural obstacles and casts disturbances and deviations from the norm into a world apparently unaware of history and progress.

However, this Promethean enterprise soon gave way to disillusion. The sum of developmental operations is generally considered negative; some even acknowledge that the situation is going from bad to worse, that the actions undertaken have on the whole only served to accentuate under-development and prolong its existence. This is why recent years have seen important re-evaluations. Rather than wanting to break up ancient structures at all costs and introduce products or techniques which encourage the emergence of economic and rational comportments, should we not build on them? This is turning the argument on its head: instead of discrediting African rural societies, which are inherently incapable of innovation, it recognizes and esteems them. Although the issue is still that of improving the *status quo* (in the nutritional, sanitary and social fields), the solutions proposed must be compatible with the internal logics of these societies and be received by them without causing any great upheaval. With everything turned on its head, family institutions once again occupy a special position; they confer on each society its particular tonality, and it is these institutions which in the first instance must take charge of technological improvements and integrate them without compromising their own coherence. 'Local' or 'community' development and 'eco-development' are alternative notions and solutions whose aim is to improve, but in such a manner that African societies can preserve a considerable part of their traditions, cultural values and knowledge, all of which are transmitted from generation to generation and take on meaning within village and family collective groups.

Thus, forty years on, we have come very close to Radcliffe-Brown's postulates. Africa's destiny and ability to develop are seemingly being played out not in problematical nation-states, or in costly and in the end ineffectual operations, but within its multiple micro-societies which still possess treasures and knowledge, of which its family systems are both the paradigm and the means of transmission.

This insistent reference to the family is not the preserve of ethnology and certain spheres of development. It is also the creation of political power; among the crowd of independent nations several great African leaders, notably Léopold Senghor, Kwame Nkrumah and Julius Nyerere, elaborated doctrines which come fairly close to an 'African socialism'. Indeed, according to what they proclaimed and wrote, Africa's very being is socialist; this primary quality has been inscribed from earliest times into traditional society, and most particularly into the African family. Nyerere is the man who expressed this idea best in the form of a postulate: 'The foundation and the aim of African socialism is the extended family.' Nkrumah put forward the notion of 'communalism' as the abstract equivalent of traditional society whose characteristics constitute the organizational principles of the modern and socialist African nation. This manner of living in families since time immemorial, in an egalitarian and binding mode, takes on a democratic character for the former head of the state of Ghana, which the contemporary state must reaffirm and make its own.

It cannot be said often enough that we are dealing here with ideologies, meaning spoken concepts which do not correspond to the way things really are, and whose purpose is simply to be believed and to get accepted. For Nkrumah, 'communalism' was a mobilizing concept aimed at motivating the Ghanaian people and creating a national consensus (Nkrumah is also the father of a movement called 'consciencism'); Nyerere's doctrine of African socialism in fact forms the basis of Tanzanian economic development, actually a rural development baptized *ujamaa* (the Swahili word for 'extended family', 'mutual help' and 'community'), whose objective is to create a network of villages based on sharing all economic and social activities in common.

Beneath these words, these ideologies, can be glimpsed two basic motivations: to legitimize the power of the state and the policy of development advocated by it; and to establish this legitimacy by setting up markers in relation to the West and the former colonial powers. Capitalism and Marxism were thus superseded by affirming the existence of an African socialism inherent in traditional structures and mentalities.

In view of this, the family does seem to be at the crossroads of the African world; ethnologists, developers and heads of state all agree that family systems represent its substratum and specificity; all turn it into an issue, as though a typically African modernity were to rise up from the systems and traditions which they delineate. It is obvious that one person's theories are not the equivalent of another's. The ethnologist pays particular attention to diversity and complexity and cannot accept this manner of reducing African systems to a single extended family; he is undoubtedly sometimes sceptical about the developers' enterprises, even when they appeal to his knowledge. As it is, however, by making it his special object of study, he is participating in this wholesale representation of an Africa still largely dominated by its traditional structures and values.

The gap between this representation and the reality of things has yet to be measured. Thus it is suitable to give a more precise content to these family and matrimonial systems, to put them back within the context of social organizations for which they provide the frame and whose particular determinations they experience in accordance with historical circumstances and evolutions.

Familial frameworks of 'traditional' African societies

African familial systems are characterized by the diversity of their modes of filiation, which are patrilineal, matrilineal or bilineal as the case may be, so that every individual is included within a framework which links him to others via genealogical connections: he belongs either to his father's group or to his mother's (or to both according to different modalities). Such lines of descent derive from the collective group and produce what are called lineages (patrilineage, matrilineage), meaning collections of men and women descended either through the agnatic or the uterine line, from one ancestor or ancestress (see the chapter by Françoise Zonabend in volume I).

In the same way, African matrimonial systems differ from one society to the next, but most are familiar with monogamy, if only on account of the sex ratio within the population. However, polygyny (polyandry being fairly rare in Africa) is indisputably esteemed; it is part of a representation in which multiplicity of spouses and descendants is both a source of wealth and a sign of power. For this very reason it is not practised by all, providing instead a privileged arena for social competition and differentiation.

Within the context of a study of familial transformations, it is all the more important to bear these traits in mind in that a number of traditional African societies are organized on the quasi-exclusive basis of kinship. They are currently known as 'stateless' societies, but they do not exhaust the range of social formations in traditional black Africa, state societies being at least as numerous; but they offer the advantage of displaying a logic proper to familial and matrimonial structures, and of being not totally foreign to state societies, since most of these contain similar structures.

Stateless societies are known more positively as 'lineage societies', in the sense that their organization rests in the first place on a framework of filiation groups. The model of these societies was provided by P. and L. Bohannan in connection with the Tiv of Nigeria (1953). This population totals about a million; it follows the rule of patrilineal descent, with the special feature of being included in a single genealogical chart and of being governed by a pyramidal structure formed by a process of segmentation. Starting with one ancestor of reference, a 'primitive' group took form, which segmented as it grew, and gave birth to several patrilineages which became autonomous by moving to their own habitat; these in turn gave rise to new segments and new lineages and so on. This formal process was accompanied by conquests and occupations in terms of space, so that the lineage groupings are assimilated to territorial units, which, strung together, make up the Tiv country.

In order to describe this type of society we need to resort to notions other than those of lineage. For, beyond the descent group proper which generally includes between 100 and 200 individuals linked by a common real ancestor, its poly-segmentary structure involves levels of interlineage connections. This is how we come to speak of clans (patriclans and matriclans) to designate a collection of lineages which acknowledge common descent but are not able to establish precise genealogical links, and can only refer to their common ancestor in a mythical mode (in this sense all Tiv are in the final analysis related through the agnatic line; but this representation merely conforms to the very basis of their social organization).

The notion of tribe is used in much the same way; it is often equivalent to the notion of clan, but introduces a particular dimension, that of territory; the tribe in fact occupies a space over which are distributed residential units themselves made up of lineages. E. E. Evans-Pritchard (1968) in his famous book on the Nuer in Sudan (the Nuer also have a lineage society, but their territorial and political system does not entirely match their lineage system), provided the most complete range of notions accounting for this system of encapsulation into lineages; on the basis of the reference lineage (the sole concrete form of grouping) known as minimal, he distinguishes minor, major and maximal lineages. On some occasions, several minimal lineages co-operate, for which they no longer refer to their respective ancestors, but go back to a more distant ancestor common to them all; they thus form a minor lineage. An identical procedure can be adopted by entities at a higher level.

The tribe often constitutes a space for preferential alliance relationships, with the clan or the major and maximal lineages sometimes proceeding to marriage exchanges among themselves. This is very understandable because, as the process of segmentation proceeds, territorial units form which to some extent deconstruct the original filiation ties and socialize relations between groups, notably on the matrimonial level. In this respect, we must emphasize an important fact. Lineage societies are often warrior societies; in this type of social organization war is essentially an internal phenomenon involving protagonists who share a common origin, at representational level at least. This is why war is closely linked to the question of marriage: it is precisely those groups in confrontation which are capable of exchanging wives; better still, war releases them from ties which had formerly united them, thus making alliance possible.

In lineage societies, the union between a man and a woman is derived from a social logic which shows up not so much individuals as filiation groups; one particular lineage will give a wife to another such. The logic thus created between the donor and the receiving group has an asymmetrical bias, which can be compensated for by an almost immediate reciprocity, thus inaugurating the straightforward exchange of sisters. This practice is attested among some populations, but seems to present an archaic solution to the problem of marriage, as though its very straightforwardness were ill-adapted to the development and expansion of lineage structures. It is more a case of African societies acknowledging this asymmetry and inventing, in order to establish reciprocity, what is known as bride-wealth; this underlines very precisely the fact that the donor group loses a woman and that, thanks to her and through her husband's intervention, 'the receiver group will be able to swell its ranks' with new progeny.

In spite of its common nature, bride-wealth varies in degree from one society to another. It is often the case that matrilineal systems involve only slight bride-wealth, for instance labour services rendered by the son-in-law to his future parents-in-law, accompanied by a few symbolic commodities. This is explained by the workings of preferential marriages, which occur frequently in these systems. The allied families are already relatives, and consequently the debt incurred by the receivers to the donors remains within a tight familial circle; the workings of the matrilinear system itself are another factor, since the woman, by transmitting her descent ties, has a wider margin of manoeuvre than in a patrilineal system, and divorces readily (the Baoulé on the Ivory Coast provide a fair illustration of this instance – see P. and M. Étienne, 1971).

Within patrilineal societies bride-wealth undeniably occupies a central position; in fact, a whole collection of commodities (prestigious objects, livestock, cloths, etc.) circulate between lineages in an inverse direction to the flow of women, and are the object of negotiations and payments which commence very early on in the lives of future spouses. Such practices, which favour accumulation strategies, are well explained by the general way in which these societies function. Lineages are often bound by a logic of prohibition, and each develops its matrimonial policy and diversifies its alliances on its own account; with this aim, the marriage goods it receives from one group will enable it (as opposed to the exchange of sisters) to negotiate a marriage for one of its members with another descent group. Furthermore, with regard to some matrilineal societies, it has been shown by ethnologists that some groups within them were negotiating matrimonial alliances with their patrilineal neigh-bours and paying them bride-wealth in accordance with the rules. This is the case notably with the Alladian on the Ivory Coast, who were studied by Marc Augé (1975). The interesting feature of this kind of marriage strategy can be formulated thus: taking account of the disharmony between a uterine rule of descent and a rule of patrilocal residence, the son is destined to leave his matrilineage or his father's segment of matrilineage to go and live within his maternal uncle's matrilineage as soon as he succeeds him. By 'dowering' women from a patrilineal society, matrilineages definitively retain their progeny and thus acquire greater autonomy. This example sheds light on the flexibility with which descent groups function.

In the same way, in patrilineal systems the scope of maternal kinship is very considerable. Marriage prohibitions covering the mother's lineage, the maternal grandmother's, and so on, while certainly constituting a negative rule, simultaneously create the conditions for a 'complementary filiation' (to adopt the term formulated by Meyer-Fortes, a British anthropologist, in 1953). For Ego, such lineages figure in his kindred (meaning the sum of his relatives of all lines combined), and through their intervention he can sometimes demarcate himself from his own descent group, and even separate from it by going to live with his maternal uncle, thus joining his mother's lineage.

Whatever the descent line in force, each kinship system is affected by varying degrees of bilaterality, or evolves into 'virtual cognatism' (Augé, 1975, p. 67), allowing the other line to act as a counterweight and to be at the origin of individual or collective strategies. This point deserves all the greater emphasis in that it accords with certain criticisms formulated earlier. These concerned, it will be recalled, the mode of identifying an ethnic group by starting with its kinship system, which seems to represent the 'royal route', involving an in-depth knowledge of African societies. Now lineage systems are not necessarily homogeneous, and they adapt easily to local conditions. In a particular region the recognition of two lines can be a substitute for counting only a single line, as in the case of the Bété on the Ivory Coast (Dozon, 1985), with whom several tribes, although practising patrilineal filiation like their neighbours, are redis-tributed into vast matriclans. We should not see this as a contradiction but as a local arrangement, which must be dealt with as such. There are even more disparate situations, as with the Senoufo (whose territory is distributed between the Ivory Coast and Mali), among whom some groups are patrilineal and some matrilineal.

These observations suggest that familial institutions, especially lineage structures, are evolving and being transformed or manipulated according to local circumstances and issues; and that symbolic labour is itself linked to social practices which cannot be reduced to the rules of kinship. Thus the alliance strategies (with foreign women) adopted in the nineteenth century by some Alladian matrilineages can be explained in terms of their chiefs' desire to accumulate dependants in order to exploit and commercialize their palm nut oil. These corporate groups or lineages are perhaps also primarily economic, politico-legal and religious units, in which all the facets of social activity in its widest sense are developed.

Apart from the transmission of goods (notably marriage goods), lineages can concentrate on the exploitation of a crop-growing terrain or on stockraising; they can engage in hunting; they may observe this or that dietary prohibition or identify with a particular religious entity; thus they appear as descent groups, meaning discrete social units generally designated by a name of their own. Patrilineal societies provide the best illustration of this approach to lineage groups. Thus, with the Bété and the Dida on the Ivory Coast, their patrilineage before colonization was a hunting group, identifying with its great net, which represented both its unity and its autonomy. At each segmentation, this net, which was endowed with anthropomorphic properties, would be divided to symbolize the intralineal split. Furthermore, the larger units like tribes, clans, maximal or major lineages, etc., only occasionally formed 'corporate groups' at funerals, special rites or important warrior conflicts, when related lineages would assemble in a clan to confront, for instance, a neighbouring clan.

Although sexual differentiation (see Zonabend in volume I) constituted the preferential prop of kinship organization (as evidenced by the choice of a particular descent line), it also gave rise to a division of tasks and activities between men and women. Almost everywhere in Africa, societies have thought up (depending on the constraints of their surroundings and on their economic situation) a sexual division of labour, which can vary considerably in content from one society to the next; for instance, in places where agricultural work is predominant, the products and appropriate farming tasks are divided between the sexes. Elsewhere, men are little involved in agriculture, which is the preserve of women, and dedicate themselves principally to hunting and warrior activities. Although this division may be based *a priori* on merely technical or practical considerations, it is often evidence of male domination.

It would certainly be unwise to proclaim a general law under which African societies everywhere would function around the same unequal relationship between men and women; it may simply be observed through anthropological literature that practices held in esteem by these societies are appropriated by men, and that women's work, often unspectacular in nature such as housework, represents tasks of a particularly time-consuming and restrictive nature. It is on this basis of the sexual division of labour that lineage societies organize their various kinds of productive work and elaborate further divisions and different relations between individuals or groups of individuals.

In this respect, it is important that the work done by anthropologists should have exposed the unequal relations proper to this lineage world which give the lie to any presentation of African societies as having been egalitarian and unoppressive. Such notions are largely derived from the myth of the noble savage propagated by Rousseau, which has been taken up and manipulated by a few developers and heads of state. Apart from male–female relations, other inegalitarian relations preside over the organization of lineage societies. Within descent groups, certain individuals control all social relations (notably marriage exchanges) and submit the rest to varying degrees of dependence. These individuals are called elders, though the term does not necessarily refer to biological age, since elders are not always the oldest, and junior status can be perpetuated for the whole of a man's life. It is these elders especially who practise polygyny and restore the demographic balance between the sexes by delaying the age of marriage for their dependants (in many lineage societies no one may marry before twenty-five or thirty). They too organize economic work, profit from younger sons' labour, recruit captives, meaning a category of individuals who are generally purchased from other groups and over whom society exercises an even greater control than over younger sons (captives known as house captives vary in number from one society to another, but they exist in most cases). The elders of the Alladian matrilineages on the Ivory Coast were not content with dowering foreign women, they would buy in captives, marry them and thus have entire disposal over their progeny.

These various inegalitarian relations demonstrate that kinship bonds constitute procedures for incorporating and submitting individuals to the logic of a power which, while definitely symbolic in nature, is also held in very concrete form by privileged actors, the elders, who control the principal forces at work in the lineage system.

This enables us to understand why, in a fair number of societies, lineages are not simply made up of the descendants of one or the same ancestor. They are supplemented not only by captives and relatives derived from other lineages (for instance, uterine nephews in the patrilinear system), but also individuals who have been adopted or affiliated and who, like the others, are bound to respect lineage exogamy; such practices are evidence of the ability of descent groups, under the rod of their elders, to increase their population potential and swell the number of their dependants in accordance with economic issues and political strategies.

Although Africa is easily represented in terms of its familial institutions, magic and witchcraft present a further and equally widespread aspect. These two phenomena are closely linked. It is in fact at the very heart of familial institutions, within descent groups in particular, that the practices and language of witchcraft, with suspicions and accusations of 'double' murder (double meaning here that it is not an actual murder but a symbolic act of violence produced by non-physical means), the manipulation of protective objects and ordeals, are all the more intense. It is between close relatives in filiation terms that suspicion and defiance are manifested the most, and that sickness and death acquire immediate meaning in the language of witchcraft. This intralineal violence is significant in more than one sense. On the one hand, it shows that descent groups are riven by rivalries, violence and conflict, and that asymmetrical relations and the inequalities which operate in them are both challenged and legitimized by belief in witchcraft; the holding of power, or accession to the position of elder, denotes a person's capacity to be neither victim nor accused, in short to embody the face of power. On the other hand, this violence represents a wholly efficient means of social integration and control: being inherent to lineage structures, it reduces the natural order (sickness and death) to the social order and forces each person to interpret the vicissitudes of his life according to his descent group's code and intrigues.

The foregoing brief analyses of African familial systems have left the problem of the continent's history largely in the shade. It cannot be supposed that lineage societies were not, well before colonization, the product of historical processes or particular economic circumstances. The compilation of African history comes up against an apparently insurmountable obstacle; the near-absence of written documentation. The oral traditions on which anthropology relies to decipher kinship and alliance systems, although they describe a certain framework in time (notably through the medium of genealogies), do not seem to be viable as objective historical sources. Such traditions do not tell us about the real genesis of familial systems, but rather the manner in which people identified with them and produced a historical account which conformed to their symbolic order. From this point of view, the Tiv society mentioned earlier is exemplary. It is based on a representation of its origins which in fact replicates its lineage and poly-segmentary structure, being a sort of genealogical charter which includes the whole corpus of local groups.

By declaring that it is difficult or impossible to write a history of familial institutions in black Africa, ethnology is constructing a specific object, the traditional society which has all the attributes of a substance, of a reified world, about which it is enough to know a bit here and a bit there about its internal structure in order to allow the developer or the head of state to act or lean on it. Ethnology freezes societies into ethnic groups which appear to have always borne the same name, and, faced with the difficulties presented by historical research, it declares all too easily that African societies, most particularly lineage societies, are deprived of history or dedicated to reproducing themselves in an eternally identical manner. Too easily, in fact, because we do after all have written documents. Black Africa has been visited by Europeans since the fifteenth century; commercial activities, especially the slave trade, conducted by the English, French, Germans and Portuguese, have left behind numerous archives which sometimes provide precious information about the coastal populations. Furthermore, we have documents, narratives in Arabic relative to the Sahel part of black Africa; although dealing with a socio-cultural environment which has evolved for many centuries within the framework of state systems (the famous states of Sudan) they nevertheless all contain information about the relations which were maintained by lineage structures and the political apparatus.

What is more, it is not certain that oral traditions were entirely subject to symbolic systems. Within a single society, they often present contradictory accounts, versions which apply to particular groups but are challenged by others. When ethnologists come across such cases, they have trouble interpreting them and finding the correct version within the range of available narratives. The problem, however, is not so much that of establishing historical truth but of recognizing in the diversity of traditions the expression of differential processes, of historical events and crises. The fact that a lineage society is in one case frankly patrilineal and in another closer to a double system is not due to purely arbitrary symbolism; it can be explained by particular circumstances, traces of which have been preserved by the traditions in their own way. The latter can be filled out and interpreted by operating, whenever possible, a pendulum movement between oral traditions and written documents, and by appealing to other disciplines, such as linguistics and archaeology. By multiplying the sources in this way and using new ways of inquiring into oral traditions, writing the history of lineage societies should no longer present an impossible task.

The time of observable metamorphoses

The preceding analyses apply to what is generally called traditional society, but, taking account of the reservations and comments made above, it would undoubtedly be better to speak of pre-colonial societies. Indeed, the family and marriage systems have been presented within a context freely acknowledged to be imprecise, but which merely serves to suggest a period prior to colonization and the possibility of writing its history in spite of the difficulties involved. Seen from this perspective, the European powers' entrance onto the stage in the late nineteenth century can perfectly well be conceived as a particular historical circumstance. After all, when set within the long-term scale, colonial activity in black Africa (leaving aside the old trading relations which were started in the fifteenth century by the Portuguese) has apart from a few exceptions (South Africa is not considered here) covered no more than a relatively brief period of a few decades. It is thus not illegitimate to think that the advent of independent states was accompanied by the end of a historical period comparable, from the point of view of social transformations, to previous periods (for instance the fifteenth and eighteenth centuries when numerous African states were constructed). Although we must bear this line of argument in mind, it cannot be taken to a conclusion. The European colonizations inaugurated a period which did not end with the 1950s, and which persisted via the construction of the nation-states, and in many cases via the development of relations with the former colonial powers, notably on the economic level. Also, some of the processes which developed under colonial rule have become more clearly defined, reaching irreversible thresholds; phenomena as important as urbanization and school education cannot be considered provisional.

A second aspect distinguishes the colonial period from all others: the transformations, effected wholesale since the beginning of the twentieth century, which have been the subject of much attention from the European authorities. The socio-cultural worlds which they discovered and subsequently, often after subduing them by force, administered within the framework of development policies, seemed to them incongruous on many levels: polygamy, bride price, belief in witchcraft and paganism in general (which they called animism or fetishism) appeared as reflections in reverse of their own image, signs and proofs of a savage or primitive state which they had to combat (Christian missions often formed the spearheads of this fight). Thus the authorities observed the evolution of these societies, in order to measure the effects of their own actions and to distinguish between the populations according to their greater or lesser aptitude for progress. We must observe in this respect that strict lineage societies have generally been the object of the fiercest criticism and of particularly derogatory comments: thought 'anarchic', in that they gave rise to their single familial and village organizations and their unique form of fetishism, these societies mobilized the colonial authorities, all the more in that they had often put up strong resistance to the European conquerors, showing that in spite of their apparently anarchic dispersion they were capable of establishing some kind of unity through tribes, clans and other forms of lineage gatherings. 'Direct rule', as it was called, was imposed precisely on lineage societies. The colonial authorities cobbled together a native chieftaincy from disparate elements and, with its connivance, adopted draconian measures of control, often in levying workforces for development projects.

Stratified societies or those with state systems were held in greater esteem, and the colonial authorities relied on their chiefs and sovereigns to get their policy applied, though this indirect administration sometimes resorted to intrigue and occasional forcible intervention to impose a particular chief.

The colonial administrations produced extensive records; numerous reports were compiled, practices and customs listed and their evolution measured over time; ethnography and, to a certain extent, historiography thus made their massive entrance onto the African stage, bringing witnesses to the permanent aspects of social and familial institutions, as well as to their transformations. With regard to the preceding periods, such an irruption of 'graphic reason' (Goody, 1979) constituted an unprecedented fact: it inaugurated the age of observable metamorphoses and of the frequently subtle relations between tradition and modernity.

On the level of social change, European colonization had paradoxical results. On the one hand, it provoked splits and crises in the ancient order of things; on the other, it gave rise, often deliberately, to forms of social reproduction. In spite of their declarations of intent regarding a faster evolution of African societies, the colonial societies were in reality content with a slower process, satisfied with the economic advantages they were extracting from them. Let us take a closer look at this dual trend.

The colonial conquests shattered African societies, and their social and economic practices became unviable or were wiped out by the constraining measures adopted by administrations. Whole networks of exchange and trade were smashed. Lineage societies such as those along the Ivory Coast had to abandon activities which they held in great esteem, such as war and collective hunting with nets. Their segmentary practices, which had involved considerable mobility in the groups, disappeared along with the organization of fixed village networks controlled by local administrations. Thus African societies, under the impact of colonization, faced profound crises which touched whole sections of their socio-economic organization. What happened, more precisely, to their family and marriage systems?

We will tackle this problem from the angle of social relations within lineages by referring to the Fang of Gabon who were studied by Balandier (1955). In the manner of many lineage societies, which were subjected to conscription of their workforce for public works or use by private concerns, the Fang, on being harried by the administration, sent their unmarried young to work far away from home in the European concessions. Although this migration to wage employment had an obvious economic interest, it also represented a general policy issue for the colonial authorities, in that it involved a break with the traditional social organization which was judged archaic and incapable of adapting to the 'benefits' of civilization. These migrations were apparently successful; a fair number of the young migrants, who were in fact younger sons in their place of origin, discovered 'new ideas' (a colonial expression) where they came into contact with Europeans or other peoples. Furthermore, although they were subjected to particularly bad working conditions, and many died, these young people acquired some independence and envisaged emancipating themselves from their elders' control. However, their new ideas very soon came up against the very concrete problem of marriage. It was precisely in this crucial matter that colonial strategy had unexpected results. In fact, the Fang patrilineal society underwent a clear transformation in the way bride-wealth functioned; money was substituted for the goods which had previously circulated between descent groups, but, far from diminishing its importance, it created an inflationary process; bride-wealth had become expensive, and by the same process women appeared as commodities to be employed as profitably as possible. The money obtained by means of a daughter's or sister's bride-wealth was no longer used to pay for a son's or dependant's marriage but was disbursed for other purposes.

Although the migration of young men should have brought about a break in the lineage system, the latter was instead strengthened by translating bride-wealth into monetary terms. Faced with this situation, young men were either forced to wait until their elders were disposed to 'pay' for a wife for them (often with their own money earned elsewhere) or until they themselves had amassed enough money to pay the bride price. In every instance, this commercial logic favoured polygyny on the part of elders and augmented the relative weight of monogamy. Thus the lineage system was somewhat modified, but not in the sense the colonizers wanted. In any case, by accentuating social inequities, it came up against new tensions between elders and younger sons, and between men and women, who did not accept their new role as commodities.

The evolution of Fang society during the preliminary colonial period is wholly typical, in that similar processes can be observed in other regions of Africa with only a few variations. On the Ivory Coast, among the lineage populations mentioned above such as the Bété, Dida and Gouro peoples, the members of the administrative chiefdoms set up by the colonial authorities took advantage of their new political power (profiting notably from a commission on the taxes raised by them from the people they administered) to practise a sort of polygyny which had nothing in common with anything prior to colonization. Some had as many as two or three dozen wives. Their bride-wealth, as with the Fang, became increasingly expensive once money was introduced into the marriage circuits.

Where the Punu and the Kuni of Congo-Brazzaville are concerned, P. P. Rey (1971) has worked on a more theoretical interpretation of these new lineage logics. According to him, the colonial powers deliberately allied with the 'ruling class' (in this instance, the elders of these two societies) the better to exploit the large population of younger sons. The elders somehow carried out the work of social control and repression which the administration did not succeed in applying directly. In this particular case, the administration seems to have made a choice, preferring economic development to the struggle against the lineage system and polygynic practices.

We saw earlier how descent groups and beliefs in witchcraft were closely linked, structuring a language through which both social control and intralineal rivalries were expressed. Far from fading out with the advent of colonization, this language was amplified; this phenomenon can easily be explained in the light of our previous examples. Lineage societies engendered contradictions between different social categories (elders and younger sons, men and women), and those who secured dominant positions (notably chiefs appointed by the administration) were much resented.

All of this was translated into the language of witchcraft; frequently abortive attempts by younger sons to emancipate themselves from their elders' control gave free rein to its interpretative codes. Fathers, uncles and eldest sons were rumoured to be able to act from a distance and provoke failure, illness and death (which corresponded to objective facts, for many colonies experienced a significant increase in their morbidity and mortality through epidemics and poor working conditions). Such an extension of witchcraft left the colonial administrations powerless, although they tended to substitute their own jurisdictions for traditional ordeals. In this respect, the initiative reverted to the colonized people themselves in an effort to throttle the increasingly ubiquitous witchcraft; in some regions persons imbued with varying degrees of Christianity and feeling a prophetic mission created cults and new churches (termed syncretic on account of the mixture of paganism and Christianity promulgated by them) expressly to fight witchcraft and fetishes. Most of these movements appeared early in the twentieth century, and not only do they still exist but they have multiplied, thus witnessing to the lineage system's grip on contemporary black Africa and to its inherent contradictions. In spite of the profound crisis which affected African societies, European colonization gave rise to a renewal and even an amplification of some of their beliefs and institutions; the lineage system, although deprived of its socio-economic props, to some extent contracted within itself by radicalizing its internal logics; although it was henceforth 'worked' by processes and transformations which appeared to undermine it, at any rate in the long term, its ability to manage or manipulate them does not seem to be compromised so long as it can retain its mastery over their meaning and interpretation.

Whatever the colonial authorities thought about this paradoxical situation, they were induced to make a virtue of necessity and to reckon that the evolution of mentalities is a long-term process which does not respond to force and constraint. In any case, their priority (after an initial phase when an administrative network was established and, in some regions, native resistance was repressed by violent means) consisted of developing the colonies, notably by introducing crops for export. In this new economic situation, they found their firmest support in family institutions and more generally in lineage and village communities. In fact, in those places where the colonial administrations had been able to take advantage of a success, where within a few years whole populations had effectively dedicated themselves to cultivating commercial produce, the resort to constraint (which was freely used) proved far less effective than the manner in which local societies were able to appropriate this commercial agriculture.

In these circumstances, their efficiency was due to lineage structures, to familial systems which, as they were being transformed and were generating new social differentiations, still managed to reproduce themselves and to adjust their rules and procedures to new economic data. In this regard, plantation economics based on the cultivation of coffee and cocoa, which were developed in Ghana (from the nineteenth century), in Togo, Cameroon, Gabon, the Ivory Coast and the Congo provide very good illustrations. In the forest zones of the Ivory Coast and Cameroon, ethnologists and sociologists first of all observed a definite upheaval in the lineage organization or, more precisely, its disintegration in favour of restricted families. With the disappearance of pre-colonial socio-economic activities, and with the expansion of tree cultivation, matrilineages and patrilineages ceased being corporate groups; forms of co-operation which had once animated the descent groups now gave way to a process of individualization; each member of a lineage became a wholly separate planter and cultivated his own plots of land with his wife or wives, his children and possibly a close collateral, turning land into private property, as opposed to the former land system in which land was owned collectively and was the object of individual rights of use.

The same ethnologists also observed an evolution in hierarchies and statutory differences. As we have seen, lineage groups were organized on the basis of unequal social relations, notably between elders and younger sons, between free men and captives; now the dominated elements were able to use this individualizing process to win economic autonomy for themselves by becoming planters and chiefs of family enterprises.

In any case, as a counterpoint to this first picture, a second picture enables us to discover permanent aspects, or rather adaptations for safeguarding certain fundamental features of lineage organization. Although confronted with emancipatory tendencies on the part of their dependants, the elders did not relinquish their control over matrimonial alliances. Within patrilineal societies, they continued to increase the bride price, thus forcing captives and younger sons to work for them in return for a promise to pay bride-wealth for them or to hand over the equivalent in cash to enable them to arrange a marriage with the elder of another lineage. The end result worked to the elders' advantage: the money which they manipulated by determining bride-wealth and the labour dues which they demanded allowed them to carve out, in their own right, larger plantations than those of their dependants, and thus to start a cumulative process of social differentiation. Even in matrilineal societies where bride-wealth was still low, the moral pressure and social controls applied were so strong that dependants would consent to the same obligations.

Finally, the strength of the lineage system lies in the fact that although it has become the site of numerous conflicts, strategies and counter-strategies, at the same time it tolerates the progressive emancipation of one lot of people and the prerogatives of another; and manages to maintain these contradictory processes within a symbolically coherent framework. On this precisely symbolic terrain, lineage societies, while evolving within the framework of commercial relations on the part of private appropriations around restricted families, have been able to manage the old and the new without any radical split. More particularly, after the first impact of colonial penetration, these societies converted to a plantation economy by adapting their rules to it.

On the whole, control over marriage matters was maintained, especially at the level of bride-wealth and fundamental prohibitions of marriage. Modes of property devolution were somewhat modified, but within fairly narrow margins. In patrilineal societies, logic demanded that the transmission of inheritance should follow a collateral line (from the eldest son to the second, and so on), but the importance which was henceforth granted to restricted families as units of production inflected this horizontal rule into a mode of vertical transmission (father to son); in any case, between respect for tradition and submission to new realities, there is room for compromise solutions: thus the father can bequeath his plantation to his son either in his will or while still alive, but the rest of his property will devolve to his 'legitimate' heir. In the same way, in matrilineal systems, the plantation economy accentuates tendencies to bilaterality; for instance, among the Attié on the Ivory Coast who were studied by Marguerite Dupire (1960), the son inherits his father's plantations, generally bequeathed to him in a will, but prestige items remain within the father's matrilineage. It is interesting to note the correspondence between plantation bequests and recourse to the written word, the will, which is a sign of a real or novel transformation, and at the same time to observe the transmission of traditional property which is satisfactorily managed by the oral process. One could multiply these instances of social reproduction by recalling the great significance of belief in witchcraft which constitutes one of the pivots of social control. We could also mention the role of funerals and ritual feasts; the latter, in the absence of any other mode for actualizing the lineage system (segmentation, war, etc.) are overinvested with customary practices; in them, the order and distribution of tribes and clans are rehearsed, and lineages and complementary filiation confront one another.

Generally speaking, plantation economics, which are taken as the model of colonial rule and the submission of African societies (destructured by the spread of commercial relations) to the iron laws of world capitalism, only developed thanks to the relative maintenance of lineage structures; the 'fetishes' of money, property and trading commodities in general have certainly penetrated them, and have sometimes got a grip on their workings, but they have also been lost on contact with other values. The wealthy planter would not be able to accumulate money without being polygamous, and the full measure of his wealth could not be taken without being tested within the lineage system or being partly redistributed and 'placed' in a network of relations, in symbolic circuits in which the person who possesses wealth acquires additional prestige and power.

The colonial administrations had to put up with this evolution, although they certainly frequently expressed disappointment at the slowness of the process and at the perpetuation of social logics which seemed to undermine their 'civilizing work'. Was it not, however, more profitable to register and reckon up the tonnage of commodities and to forget the conditions under which they were produced? After all, had it been necessary for the colonial states really to destroy the lineage systems, this would have required not only a despotic will in every instance (a will which showed itself in other circumstances but, more particularly, material and human means which their capitals were not prepared to supply. Finally, lineage structures and family institutions allowed them to 'function thriftily', for it was these that took charge of production and producers, and which ensured social reproduction in its widest sense.

With these first analyses, the idea that the colonial period constituted only a special historical situation is not wholly improbable. During this period family structures linked together changes and permanent features, as they must have done previously in different political and socio-economic contexts. Certain processes or phenomena, however, oblige us to correct this view: over the years the lineage systems have become involved in novel situations, in the general shift of new social relations in which they underwent clear reorientations or clear transformations. These processes and transformations emerged during the colonial period, but they only assumed their true breadth after independence and constitute the favourite themes of present-day sociology in black Africa. We will give our attention mainly to three of these.

The first concerns women. We have seen the great importance of the relationship between men and women in the constitution of kinship systems and in the division of work which each sex performs. We have also shown how colonization and the development of commercial economies relaunched lineage organizations while modifying certain elements. In many African societies, this evolution made the position of women harder. Apart from the monetization of bride-wealth it is above all on the level of work that the inequality between the sexes has become increasingly obvious. Within the framework, notably, of plantation economies, they amass a maximum number of tasks; domestic work and raising livestock as well as taking part in shrub cultivation (coffee, cocoa); in the latter case, men form the management as heads of cultivation, which relegates women to a position of near-employees (evidenced notably by forms of remuneration in kind or money at the end of each harvest). This exploitation of the female workforce is loaded with contradictions; it lies behind the many divorces which make the marriage bond seem fragile. Over and above relations between spouses, what has progressively emerged is nothing less than a wholesale rift between men and women. Thus, at the end of the 1950s among the Bamiléké in Cameroon, the women collectively destroyed the coffee plantations (Bisilliat and Fieloux, 1983); here and there genuine strikes can be observed, notably involving the refusal to prepare meals for men. Some societies had to tackle very early on, meaning at the onset of colonization, their 'dangerous half' (to use the expression of Balandier, 1974); this was notably the case with the Baoulé on the Ivory Coast, whose women, who already possessed considerable room for manoeuvre before the French settled there, increased their autonomy by marrying men from other ethnic groups (sometimes whites) and migrating to the urban centres where they engaged in a variety of trades.

Generally speaking, these processes or attempts at female emancipation are of recent date. Women had first of all to experience the expansion of commercial crops in order for their daughters or granddaughters (often school-educated) to refuse to stay on, leaving the village circle instead. From then on the migration of women to the towns has constituted a major phenomenon in black Africa; they are in fact engaged

Senegal street scene. Migration to the towns helps the emancipation of women, but indigenous costumes continue alongside European fashions. Peter Saunders.

in challenging the lineage system, and tradition in general, by acting directly on the logic of matrimonial exchanges, compromising marriage opportunities for country people and at the same stroke intensifying the male exodus. This emancipation through migration has its negative counterparts. For, apart from the fact that it sometimes ends in prostitution, access to the urban world does not necessarily confer on women a better position than the one they have within the lineage system; they are often confined to low-grade jobs and to domestic work just as demeaning as in rural surroundings. However, the movement is well entrenched and leads to sharp confrontations between the sexes (Vidal, 1978), with a growth in separations and divorces and a defiant attitude to marriage, the formation of free unions and ephemeral relationships, and rejection of motherhood involving the use of contraceptives and abortion. While their refusal to marry forces many young women to turn to their own networks for help and to find a measure of security with a relative, some become even more marginalized and set up their own solidarity groups.

School education constitutes the second important phenomenon. The process was started during the colonial period, notably by Catholic and Protestant missions, and since independence has continued to grow in scope and to contribute to the flow of migration to the towns, as well as representing the most efficient means of social advance. It is identified with the state not only because the latter has made it compulsory more or less everywhere, but also because the state is the main provider of employment to school-leavers. Being a particularly complex phenomenon, it presents African public authorities with difficult problems of finance and educational policies (which are often inadequately adapted to local realities and to the imperatives of national development). School education also reveals the subtle relationships between tradition and modernity at family level.

Between these two poles one can in fact observe a curious contradiction. On the one side there is the apparently rapid tendency to the dissolution of the traditional rural milieux. Attending school (except in Islamicized societies where Quranic schools are often in direct competition) virtually implies a split, and gives rise to aspirations to escape from lineage obligations and beliefs, and to a mode of individualization which opens access to social groups in which the weight of tradition has diminished even further (and where class interests such as those of privileged strata of the civil service are forged). In a spectacular process of speeded-up history, it has often taken no more than two or three generations to enable an individual whose grandfather witnessed the arrival of the Europeans, and whose father saw the development of commercial agriculture, to become a top civil servant. This model of social mobility which covers the colonial period and the early years of independence, is now being throttled by the existence of ruling classes who block access to their own sphere. However, it goes on functioning all the same, justifying the process of disengagement from the rural world. In this respect, the many educational failures and high unemployment levels are revealing. Instead of encouraging people to return to their villages, they very often engender marginal forms of existence, particularly in urban surroundings where many school drop-outs live by their wits or from small trades.

On the other hand, one can spot contradictory tendencies in which school, precisely because it is a carrier of social change, represents an issue which mobilizes lineage and kinship networks, while revealing the dominant position of restricted families. For many lineage societies (especially in regions with plantation economies), school education confirms the existence of disintegration processes within descent groups which first started at the onset of colonization; generally the restricted families are responsible for this and bear the burden. Imbued with the model of success via school, families often overrate the obligation which devolves on them of ensuring their children's education, by sending some of them (boys and girls) to private schools, thus correcting the low possibility of being accepted into a state school. Such dynamism, however destructuring its effect on the lineage world, is applied within its framework; it intervenes as an element of rivalry and competition between family units; each one sends its children to school, albeit under the others' watchful eyes, with the result that their academic failures and successes take on meaning within the symbolism of their lineage. Gibbal (1974) has shown how schoolboys on the Ivory Coast interpret their academic failures in terms of witchcraft and accuse or suspect particular members of their lineage of having brought harmful influences to bear on them.

School education is thus particularly revealing; it stresses the autonomization strategies used by families, but the lineage environment in which they continue to evolve compromises them by investing the school with its ideology and interpretations.

Some of these strategies serve to show the nature of the struggle in which lineage structures and restricted families are engaged. In order to find solutions to school problems, they approach relatives from descent groups other than their own, as though mutual assistance were only accepted and acceptable outside the strict sphere of the lineage. There is an interesting reorientation of family systems in all this, generally linked to urbanization; that is to say, a clear tendency to value 'complementary filiation' networks and to constitute a familial solidarity which avoids intralineal rivalries.

Town life and urbanization illustrate still further these processes of social transformation in black Africa in which traditions are simultaneously compromised and reinvented. As with school education, urbanization as a mass phenomenon is recent in black Africa and goes back for the main part to independence (though the towns themselves are older, generally going back to the colonial period and sometimes even earlier). It is of course linked to the inauguration of states, the creation of public services and the implementation of development policies which, although they principally address rural conditions, at the same time give rise to migrations to the cities. There are several reasons for this: school education, the contradictions inherent in local societies (female migrations are exemplary in this respect), opportunities for paid work, and especially the attraction of the urban environment as an alternative to the village way of life. It is also linked, under the most spectacular forms of great urban concentrations, to extensive migratory movements between states, which reveal the gulfs between their differing development and economic potential. Nearly half of the population of Abidjan, which has one of the highest growth rates in the whole of Africa (10 per cent) is made up of people who do not come not from the Ivory Coast (Burkinese, Ghanaians, Malians, Senegalese, Europeans, Lebanese, etc.).

In its different ways the urban phenomenon is the antithesis to the rural and traditional world. It organizes new social relations by dispersing and redistributing individuals and groups among differentiated socioprofessional spheres (place of work, dwelling-place) according to criteria of a socio-economic or socio-professional order. It arranges new modes of social distinction and gives rise to novel forms of collective consciousness, according to the group or social class to which people belong.

With these processes and these very real breaks with the traditional world, one might expect kinship systems finally to disintegrate and leave the way clear for nuclear families, monogamy and strictly private universes modelled on Western manners. In fact, matters are much more complex, and although real transformations are occurring in urban environments, they do not necessarily lead to this family model. The first consideration is that in spite of the migrations and the excessive growth of some capital cities, rural life is still predominant in black Africa. The continent's very low rate of industrialization limits the rural exodus, while agriculture is still generally the main economic activity. Furthermore, urbanization is a recent phenomenon; the majority of the population have not been city-dwellers for longer than the last one or two generations. These are factors which require the urban environment to be analysed in relation to rural societies. They do not really contrast a modern reality with a traditional world, but on the contrary weave organic connections between the two polarities. After all, rural life, and lineage structures in particular, have already been modified; since the colonial period they have turned to the practices and strategies of restricted families, and the world of the cities and paid work increases tendencies to autonomy. School education is fully representative of this. Yet as we have seen, the lineage system still forms the framework for these processes; it is somehow accountable for each one's evolution, for their failures as for their successes.

This is why city-dwellers, though far removed from their place of origin, do not escape or try to shirk their lineage obligations. They participate notably in funerals, giving added *éclat* to these special events at which lineage systems are still actualized. Furthermore, city-dwellers frequently organize themselves in town into associations or mutual aid societies in order to meet various requests from their place of origin, or to intervene in disputes which it has failed to settle. To this extent, relations between city-dwellers and lineage milieux are imbued as much with respect as with suspicion. While they seldom shirk their traditional obligations, they tend instead to be evasive or to seek compromises with other types of pressure (regular financial assistance, for instance). This involves a subtle game which allows them to keep their distance, but within certain limits; city-dwellers (even when they have detached themselves) are not protected from interpretations which confer on lineage systems their astonishing ideological vigour. Belief in witchcraft has penetrated the world of school, and more generally won over the urban world as well. For many city-dwellers, their environment, far from offering security, is more the source of difficulties and failures (loss of work, conjugal problems, etc.). One possibility is to blame the world: the wealthy, the state, underdevelopment, even oneself, but attempts at finding an interpretation will often dwell on attempts to decipher the lineage code, which is capable of giving instant meaning to the misfortunes and misery in life.

As a counterpart to the relations which the urban environment keeps with the rural, town life produces family practices which effectively break away from the lineage system. People in town often do not reconstitute their descent groups; related families are separated in space, and each evolves in different ways according to its economic standing or membership of a particular social grouping. Members of the same lineage or even clan maintain relations, but, as we saw above, more to meet the requirements of their village milieu than to reproduce the lineage model. In any case, the great majority of these families do not correspond to the nuclear family: although they tend to limit the number of their members, they do not achieve the elementary level of a couple and their children. The more exact term defining them is 'composite and extended family household', in the modern rather than the traditional sense. Studies conducted in the towns show two or more nuclear families living under one roof, or one nuclear family along with several people somehow related to a member of the family (or some other combination with similar features). The morphology of urban family units certainly varies in accordance with particular obligations (taking care of schoolchildren for instance), but also according to all sorts of choices, affinities and interests. Marie (1984) conducted a study in Lomé (Togo) in which he stressed that although many such extended family households originated from patrilineal families, they have been constituted on the basis of mainly uterine relations, as though the latter, unlike agnatic structures, did indeed create solidarity. In Abidjan, Gibbal (1974) showed that the morphology of family groups was not linked to traditional kinship structures, but varied irrespective of whether the head of the household belonged to a patrilineal or a matrilineal society.

Furthermore, town life multiplies opportunities for interethnic marriages, which have the effect of contrasting symbolic registers and of adapting this type of family unit to the obligations and kinship relations of each spouse. Thus the urban environment generates original and novel family units, which simultaneously draw on their kinship networks and adjust them following formulae of 'variable geometry' which do not reproduce a strict lineage order but are the product of a compromise between tendencies to 'restriction' and the demands of effective solidarities.

These family innovations only make sense when related to the more general situation of African countries, to the processes, social relations and contradictions which animate the societies as a whole.

First of all, urbanization is an ongoing phenomenon and, although limited by agricultural employment, the rural exodus is swelling and swamping the job opportunities offered by the state and business. Thus there is considerable unemployment in black Africa, and school provides the only means of concealing its extent or delaying its impact. Under such conditions, urban families function as structures providing accommodation and social security; they contain any potential marginalizations (which become wholly real in cities like Abidjan or Lagos) by ensuring the minimum necessary for survival. However, such families also create outlets in their own way; some of their members (especially the young) are only given board and lodging in exchange for work and many kinds of services. While they certainly provide a welcome, like an employer, they dismiss any who do not perform their tasks. This is why, whenever they hold forth on the reality of their family life, city-dwellers veer between denouncing its parasitical side and appreciating the advantage which they perhaps derive from it. Furthermore, these urban families sometimes possess real economic strength; either because they control a craft manufacture, run a business or a small firm, or because they are engaged in market-gardening in the town's outskirts or in land deals.

Over and above these objective functions, however, urban families fit into a wider framework of relationships, into whole sets of social stratifications which both reinforce and relativize some of their characteristics. First and foremost, family solidarity tends to spread across the whole of the social body through the different strata of society; it necessitates redistribution and creates situations involving co-residence by people of very different socio-economic status. However, this trend is limited and even countered by the practices adopted by the prosperous classes in an attempt to delineate their differences by restricting their family world even further, frequently by practising monogamy (apart from reverting to polygamy in the form of extramarital relationships) and marriages outside any traditional framework (interethnic marriages in the wider sense, denoting straightforward affinities or class interests).

These social practices on the part of the prosperous classes, the 'national middle classes' (practices which do not at all exclude certain types of relations with their circle of origin) enable us to pinpoint more precisely the kin's influence in an urban environment. The city-dwellers who undergo this influence or discover some sort of socio-economic rationality in it mainly belong to the intermediate social classes, those with regular incomes and stable dwellings, but not in a position to adopt or imitate the practices of the prosperous classes.

The most deprived social categories come closer to the nuclear family than to the composite family household (Antoine and Guillaume, 1984). These categories are in direct contrast to the prosperous classes, and tend rather to flee their kin and sometimes even the married state, so that their ranks include a high percentage of unmarried people.

The overall impression is that family solidarity is being concentrated at the node of urban social stratification, traversing it up to the point where other practices and family strategies operate. This observation invites the conclusion that the determining factors behind urban families and their morphology are less a function of obligations linked to tradition than of socio-economic conditions: a poor city-dweller who patently has no prospects is not appealed to by his kinship network.

Matrimonial relations fall within the same analytical plan. Although monogamy is present in every social class, polygyny retains its prerogatives among the urban middle classes who are evolving within relatively stable economic conditions. As a counterpoint, the conjugal problems and separations mentioned above seem mainly to affect monogamous households; whatever the causes (rejection of polygyny, misunderstandings, poor living conditions), this matrimonial instability makes for new features in urban families, for instance taking in a sister, a niece or a cousin.

The destinies of the family in the nation-building process

At one remove from the official discourse and the representations referred to above, the African family is standing in a very real sense at a crossroads with several roads leading off. The first weaves its way through a rural world which has clearly retained the imprint of lineage systems in spite of notable transformations. The second runs through the world of towns, and, although connected to the first, has discovered whole series of novel and less structured families, whose evolution is a sort of compromise between respect for tradition and the socio-economic necessities of the present age. The third, finally, climbs those giddy heights where the prosperous classes and the governments seem to be setting themselves up on the model of family practices conforming more or less to Western manners. This diversity describes the overall situation in African countries fairly well: in the course of their development they are still closely dependent on their agriculture while promoting new aspirations and social stratifications which begin among their politicians. The urban world lies at the crossroads where these two tendencies meet; the families which they create adapt to contradictions by producing frequently efficient responses to all sorts of problems (unemployment, housing, education, etc.). This is tantamount to saying that the destinies of the family are largely determined or informed by the overall evolution of African societies. The rise in poverty and the onset of lasting underdevelopment (as in some countries of the Sahel) can serve to strengthen family solidarities and crystallize inequities; it can multiply the number of people with no families and the urban marginal elements, and give rise to a return or a temporary retreat to the countryside, and thus give back some of their vitality to traditional values.

Nevertheless, faced with these fluctuating realities, the African states are not content to embody social success or to articulate new family models by forming ruling classes. As founders of nations, it is incumbent on them everywhere to represent public authority by leglislating for the family organization, notably by codifying it. This is how the family codes were drawn up in the wake of each state's independence. Some have clearly been inspired by Western law, such as the Ivory Coast Code, which prohibited bride-wealth and polygyny in 1964, thus conferring on the nuclear family a determining role in the nation-building process. The Mali Code (1962) permits up to four wives, but encourages the monogamy option; the Senegalese Code (1972) does likewise, but limits the number of wives to three and insists on an initial choice between monogamy and polygamy. African laws thus vary from one country to another, but such differences are still largely formal in that they all share the common feature of not being widely applied, or alternatively not being enforced by penal sanctions. On the Ivory Coast, bride-wealth and polygyny are still practised, and it is likely that legal proceedings would be greeted with surprise and ridicule. Yet legislation of this kind is not useless from the states' point of view, for it provides the people with laws to respect and resort to, even if only as points of reference, when they give up traditional practices. In this way, unlike Western public law, which often lags behind the morality of the day the African states are anticipating evolutions, or rather appearing as advocates of development by rechannelling those tendencies which approximate their laws most closely.

This is why, in so considerable a domain as the inheritance of property, modern laws rarely contradict customary rules. In the countryside, where lineage systems retain some vitality, they are content to recognize such evolutions as are occurring and, in the case of litigation which is not settled in the customary tribunals, they try to find compromise solutions without retracting. For instance, the tendency to transmit inheritance from father to son, which as we saw has been very marked since the development of market economies (in patrilineal systems as much as in matrilineal), is becoming increasingly confirmed in law; however, it is coming to the fore only because it is already the result of previous compromises, which admit a particular mode of devolution but acknowledge the right of 'legitimate' heirs to claim the more traditional property.

Generally speaking, African legislation tends only to apply to new situations, to social relations which clearly elude the constraints of lineage systems, most particularly in the towns, where families often have access to new forms of ownership (commercial capital, lodgings, etc.), where divorce is on the increase, as are claims by women to inheritance and child custody (in lineage systems, women inherit little or nothing; instead, they sometimes form part of the inheritance, with a man's widow passing to his brother). However, legal proceedings are only effective if those men and women who resort to them have previously recognized the state as the guarantor of their marriage, property and right to bequeath it. These are all far from common things. Although African legislation grants women more rights than they had within lineage structures, the exercise of these rights by women depends on the legal nature of their marriage and on their ability to enforce them in the course of their conjugal and family lives.

Like mirror play, public law only really applies to the social classes which are most likely to use it, those which are evolving in relative modernity. For the others, the contacts between the law and family practices involve a patchwork of legal practice and a jurisprudence which views customary rights and usage with great tolerance.

Over and above these legal questions, relations between states and societies, and between states and family worlds, require a more sociological approach. The problem of political power in black Africa is not simply legislative and juridical. It still has to establish a proper legitimacy: the preponderant position occupied by the state in the process of national development and construction has to gain acceptance and justification. We have seen how some heads of state tried to solve the problem by relying explicitly on the values of traditional society, particularly the 'extended family'. Without resorting to such ideologies (authenticity, communalism, etc.), other leaders and other regimes manipulate family and traditional registers in their own way. Kinship is regularly used as a metaphor for politics. Thus the single party, which has been presented in many African countries as the condition and guarantee of national unity, is also symbolized as a vast family in which business and conflicts are regulated in a sociable atmosphere under the authority of its elder.

However, without requiring any official line or ideology, the real practices of political administrations and ruling classes infiltrate the convolutions of local societies and family networks. Although they tend to avoid the constraints of the composite family household, they are still seeking legitimacy and social bases. Strategies for gaining power and struggles for influence travel along the paths of tradition. No one can gain a position of lasting importance without occupying a position in his lineage, his clan or his tribe, without exploiting his noble or distinguished origins, manipulating his genealogy or even concealing slave ancestors, and without taking part, indirectly at least, in the destinies of his village of birth and acting as its spokesman.

In short, whether on the official stage of power or in its corridors, in ideological or practical terms, lineage and village background and kinship networks constitute poles of reference to which the state and ruling groups can resort to establish and legitimize their social position (this is denounced by military *coups d'état* precisely because they view it as clientelism and nepotism). Taking account of these organic links between the rural milieu and the machinery of state, it is fairly easy to understand why opportunities for implementing African legislation are still very restricted.

In its own way, the question of Islam illustrates these organic links between states and societies in black Africa. The Muslim religion has been penetrating sub-Saharan regions since about the tenth century by a variety of means: conquest, trading networks, conversion of warrior aristocracies and holy wars (*jihad*). It has settled basically in the Sudanese zone, and its spread is closely linked to the construction, expansion and subsequent disappearance of prestigious empires and kingdoms (Nicolas, 1981). More recently, however, it has been winning ground further south, towards the coastal countries. It is generally agreed that Islam has been able to adjust to African family and marriage systems fairly well by adding to them without modifying their internal logic in any deep sense. It is agreed too that it has become a black Islam (Monteil, 1971), notably because the Quran's precepts and regulations coincide with the most widespread rules governing the way pre-colonial African societies functioned. Polygyny (up to four wives), bride-wealth, the inferior status of women, certain prohibitions of alliance, certain preferential marriages, slavery and the lineage, the clan (Quranic laws favour the agnatic line, but they do not appear to have constituted obstacles to the Islamization of matrilineal societies) are meeting-points which explain, over and beyond forcible conversions and holy wars, the spread of Islam in black Africa.

The modern states which have been most affected by the spread of Islam, such as Senegal, Mali and Niger, have elaborated family codes which acknowledge the traditional secular dimension of Islam; evidence of this is provided by the Mali and Senegal Codes which do not prohibit bride-wealth and legalize polygyny within the limits set by the Quran. In this, they have no doubt found an equitable compromise between the necessity of asserting their role as public authorities and permitting certain precepts in Islamic Law. Islam has a further role in these states. In the countries of the Sahel, it occupies important positions of power, notably through brotherhoods, sects and the business classes which weave complex and close links with the administrative and political spheres, to the point where it is often difficult to decide which of the two, state or religion, is commanding and using the other. When one knows that these same countries are the poorest and least 'advanced' in black Africa, and that their governments are barely distinguishable from

mechanisms of power appropriated by a few privileged sectors, it may
well be asked whether Islam is occupying an increasingly dominant
position, as is notably the case in Niger, or whether it offers an overall
alternative to the Sahel's problems, by operating a sort of return not only
to its own religious values, but to the values of those peasant societies
whose lives it has shared for centuries. As the embodiment of both power
and tradition, Islam can operate within its own code, the Quran, and at
the same time perpetuate the form of local societies, thus revitalizing the
ancient family orders.

EIGHT

The Arab World: the Family as Fortress

Philippe Fargues

The traditional Arab city has given the Arab family the image which is most readily associated with it. In the city, each house resembles a fortress, protected from external attack by its blind walls. It can be penetrated only from an internal courtyard, in which all forms of communication become transparent.

This style of architecture is becoming increasingly less respected in modern towns, where house fronts are opening up and the rate of growth has led to more precarious ways of living which prevent families from persisting in their isolation. Have the rules which determined marriage and allotted roles within the family evolved in a parallel manner?

The division between the male and female spheres forms the keystone of this family structure, which is why we will inquire particularly into the situation of women. Indeed, it is in this area that we must seek the signs of an evolution.

We will restrict ourselves to those societies between the Euphrates and the Atlas mountains whose cultures have been unified by the Arab language (Berque, 1985); these are the countries where Arabic is both the official and the spoken language, the member states of the Arab League, minus Djibouti and Somalia.

Marriage: a family affair

'God created male and female that we might understand his purpose: one cannot escape marriage!' exclaims Oumm Hamida in a fine novel by Naguib Mahfouz called *Passage des miracles* (1983). In fact, marriage is almost universal among the Arabs: 97 per cent of men and women contract at least one in the course of their lives. Chance alone is not sufficient to marry everyone, even when the number of encounters is multiplied (Le Bras, 1985). If Arab society succeeds in doing so, it is because it devotes particular energy to the purpose.

Oumm Hamida is a professional marriage-broker. The underlying rationale is that Arab tradition has attached rigid norms to the formation of couples: the man is predestined to marry the daughter of his paternal uncle. However, as soon as demographic conditions prevent every couple from being constituted by tradition, individuals are, so to speak, caught short. This is indeed what happens in the melting-pot of the working-class quarter of Cairo where our marriage-broker holds sway: family clans have been dispersed by the rural exodus, condemning male cousins not even to know of their promised girl cousins' existence. It is to be expected that at least one of the two norms which had hitherto coexisted, the universality of marriage and patrilineage endogamy, would give way before the onslaught of modernity.

Unequal marriage: the power of age, the power of dowry

As far as can be judged, marriage is still universal. The proportion of permanent celibates aged fifty is almost nil; it is in the order of 3 per cent among seventy-year-olds, men as well as women. The results of the latest population counts reveal a uniformly intense nuptiality from Mauritania to Iraq, without notable regional variations. The percentage of persons to have contracted at least one marriage before the age of fifty varies in the case of men between 96.2 (Egypt, 1976) and 98.6 (Libya, 1973), and in the case of women between 96.2 (Egypt) and 99.5 (Libya). Lebanon, however, constitutes the exception: before the Civil War, at any rate, people married less there than in other countries, and, uniquely among these countries, slightly fewer women than men got married (93.1 per cent versus 94.3 per cent). Beirut society was alone in granting women a social status which was not based on their family role. Furthermore the divide was more between Beirut and the rest of Lebanon than between Lebanon and the other countries.

The processes which led to marriage being so common are completely distinct as between men and women. The husband's absolute authority over his Arab family is a corollary of the age difference between spouses. The man marries a woman ten years his junior. This presents a simple accounting problem. If women marry at eighteen and men at twenty-eight, the sexual balance in the population of an age to live in couples is distorted. There are more women aged eighteen and over than there are men aged twenty-eight and over, all the more so in that men are more affected by the death rate. If each man were to marry only once, many women would be left out of the count. In order to marry off every woman and at the same time to base male authority on the age difference between spouses, Arab societies have invented repudiation. We will see what a vital role divorce plays in regulating the Arab marriage market.

With women, early age at marriage varies from one country to another. In Bedouin societies and those which have recently become sedentary women marry youngest, on average at fifteen in Mauritania in the 1970s (EMF). At the other extreme, the average age of marriage for women in countries which have been urbanized longest is scarcely lower than that of European women; twenty-three years in Lebanon (1970 survey) and twenty-two in Egypt (1976 census). Concern about limiting population has resulted in the legal age of marriage being raised by recent legislation, for instance to eighteen for Algerian women (1984 Family Code).

Marriage for men, on the other hand, occurs uniformly at a late age, from an average age of twenty-six in Mauritania and twenty-nine in Lebanon and Egypt. The consequent age gap between spouses is itself fairly widely variable: eleven years in Mauritania, ten in Sudan, seven in Egypt and five in Lebanon. It is rare for husband and wife to be close in age. The age gap between them is five years or more in 71 per cent of marriages in Egypt, and 77 per cent in Tunisia and Jordan (United Nations, 1984). It is ten years or more in 35 per cent of cases in Egypt, 41 per cent in Tunisia and 37 per cent in Jordan.

The late age for men at first marriage cannot be dissociated from the custom of dowry, which is still universal. Dowry is the price men pay to marry. Paid to his bride or to her father, it can come to a considerable amount, several months or even several years of the average city-dweller's income. The 'ordinary' explanation is the one which is provided spontaneously by every man who is obliged to work many years in order to accumulate the *peculium* enabling him to dower his future spouse: it is the obligatory nature of dowry which drives him to delay his marriage. However, the reverse argument could well apply. A dowry is required so that marriage can be delayed. In order to keep patriarchal structures alive, the husband must dominate his spouse by his greater age. The cost of marriage, by preventing it from taking place too soon, appears in the guise of a powerful regulatory mechanism. Furthermore it gives coherence to the husband's power, by reinforcing the authority his age gives him with the power he derives as creditor.

However, it is not enough to guarantee the family's power over the women it has appropriated. Society has also to make sure that all women are thus appropriated by families. This is where the second regulatory mechanism intervenes: the practice of repudiation.

Two rivals: repudiation and polygamy

In European societies, the rise in the divorce rate during the second half of the twentieth century has often been interpreted as a challenge to traditional family forms. In many Arab societies, the incidence of divorce has long been as frequent as in France since the 1980s. But divorce has an opposite meaning among the Arabs: it is the method by which the family institution is perpetuated in one of its foundations, the universality of marriage.

In order to meet the sexual imbalance in the number of marriageable persons which is implicit in the husband's greater age, one man must marry several wives, either simultaneously (polygamy is the solution adopted in black African societies) or successively, by repudiation, as in Arab societies. The custom obeys an elementary arithmetic: given that there are ten women to every seven men and that celibacy is not allowed, of the three women who are no longer married, one has been repudiated and the other two are widows. These last two are the oldest, ensuring that in every couple, the man's superiority due to age is well respected. This mechanism is well illustrated by the Mauritanian age pyramid (Arab-Berber population, figure 5) in which the shaded areas representing the non-celibate population are broader on the women's side than on the men's. This diagram also shows that it is due to the almost exclusively female population of widowed or divorced persons, which increases in

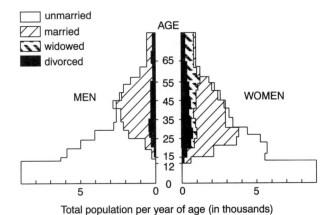

Figure 5   Sex/age distribution of marital status in Mauritania, 1977

proportion with age, that one can obtain an almost equal overall number of married persons for both sexes, while retaining a population in a state of union in which women are younger than men.

An identical pattern can be found, with minor variations, throughout the Arab world (table 4). In an adult population in which women are slightly preponderant (92 men per 100 women aged fifteen years and over in Egypt, for instance), celibates are predominantly male: between 132 and 177 men per 100 women depending on the country (compared with 120 in France). Married persons are almost equal in number: 91–9 men per 100 women. Widowed and divorced persons are above all women; there are only between 7 and 17 widowers per 100 widows (20 in France) and between 17 and 48 divorced men per 100 divorced women (66 in France).

Men and women thus experience very different marital histories. The Mauritanian age pyramid shows these differences in a country of pronounced marital instability. A man aged around twenty has nine chances out of ten of being still unmarried. He has none at all of being widowed or divorced. At the same age, more than half the women are married. One in six has already been divorced. At the age of sixty, nearly all men are still married. There are still almost no widowers or divorced men. At the same age age, three women in ten are still married and living in union, two others are divorced and five are widowed.

Thirty years after their first marriage, between a third and two-thirds of women have seen it dissolved by widowhood or divorce, with a variable probability for the two events (see table 5). If in spite of everything, divorced women are not legion, it is because their chances of remarriage are proportional to the ease with which they are repudiated. By the thirtieth anniversary of their first marriage, 29 per cent of Mauritanian women have been married twice, 13 per cent three times and 11 per cent four times or more. That makes an average of 1.9 marriages per woman. Mauritania presents, it is true, an extreme form of matrimonial circulation among Arabs.

In order for repudiation to exercise its regulatory function properly, the remarriage itself must be unequal. If each man to be 'freed' by repudiating his spouse were to remarry a repudiated wife, the effect of the operation would be nil. To prevent this, it is necessary for divorced men to remarry repudiated wives and spinsters in alternation. The implication is that divorced women have fewer chances of remarrying and will have to wait longer than men to do so.

Before going into more detail about repudiation, we should analyse the other solution for marrying off all women, which the Arabs have not really retained, in spite of making them marry men older than them-

Table 4 Number of men per 100 women in each marital category

Country		Celibate		Non-celibate		
			Total	married	widowed	divorced
Algeria	(1977)	159	75	91	10	26
Egypt	(1976)	132	82	99	12	32
Jordan	(1964)	147	80	92	16	45
Morocco	(1971)	146	77	94	12	38
Mauritania	(1977)*	176	73	95	7	17
Syria	(1970)	177	83	94	17	48
Tunisia	(1975)	146	84	96	17	36
(France)	(1982)	(120)	(86)	(102)	(26)	(66)

*Nomad population plus population of Nouakchott, i.e. almost the entire Arab-Berber population.

Table 5 The outcomes of women's first marriages after thirty years

| | | Percentage of dissolved marriages | | | Remarriages per 100 dissolved marriages |
	Total	Widowhood	Divorce	
Egypt	(1980)	37.2	23.3	13.9	57
Jordan	(1976)	24.9	16.7	6.1	43
Morocco	(1980)	41.8	18.4	23.5	71
Mauritania	(1981)	64.7	19.3	45.3	83
Sudan	(1979)	35.2	17.8	17.4	58
Syria	(1978)	24.8	18.5	6.3	44
Tunisia	(1978)	27.4	17.9	9.5	56
Yemen	(1979)	39.7	15.5	24.3	81

Source: National surveys of fertility rates.

selves, namely polygamy. Islam, as we know, allows men to have four legitimate wives. With the exception of Tunisia since 1957, all the Arab countries recognize the legitimacy of polygamous marriages. The recent Algerian Family Code, for instance, simply reasserts Quranic Law in this domain. Nevertheless polygamy could well join the harem along with the whole panoply of images of the medieval Orient conjured up by the *Arabian Nights*. Polygamy is marginal in the contemporary Arab world, even in the Gulf Emirates, though the claim is often made that this is due to modern living conditions. The monetarization of all economic relations and the cramped space of town dwellings are said to be some of the factors which prevent husbands from respecting the Quranic prescription of perfect equity towards their different wives. They say that they are monogamous by constraint.

Implicit in this analysis is the notion that there was once a time when polygamy had been the rule. This may be true. It is also possible that Arab polygamy impressed Western minds, in spite of being relatively rare in practice. There are no documents to show that it ever achieved a breadth comparable to that encountered in West Africa nowadays, where the proportion of women with at least one co-spouse can be as high as 50 per cent. Furthermore, it is in the two Arab countries which have penetrated the world of black Africa that polygamy occurs most frequently. Thirteen per cent of Mauritanian women live in polygamous union (EMF). Among the Hassania-speaking Arab women there, however, no more than 3 per cent are in this situation. In northern Sudan the average proportions are higher; they increase regularly with age, rising from 11 per cent in the case of women below twenty-five to 21 per cent for those aged thirty-five and more (EMF). However, this Sudanese survey fails to specify the linguistic groups involved, so that it is not possible to tell whether Arabs differ from black African ethnic groups by engaging more generally in monogamy. In all other Arab countries, polygamy represents less than 5 per cent of all unions.

In Syria for instance (1970 census), 3.7 per cent of married men are in polygamous union, in which case they generally have two wives (3.3 per cent), seldom three (0.2 per cent) and four only exceptionally (0.02 per cent). Polygamy occurs slightly more frequently in the countryside (4.6 per cent) than in the towns, where however it has not totally disappeared (2.4 per cent). The two professional categories to engage in it most often are agriculturalists (5.2 per cent) and shopkeepers (3.5 per cent). It is a corollary of a low level of education and practically never occurs with men who have been to university (0.9 per cent). The low social origins of polygamous men clearly indicate, not that they are the modern heirs of the harem and its splendours, but rather the heirs of the labouring classes for whom a large family guaranteed plenty of workers; 56 per cent of them are self-employed. The same category represents only 34 per cent of monogamous men.

Does this allow one to predict that polygamy is about to become extinct? That it will gradually reduce with the spread of waged work and education? The answer cannot be found by examining the way the proportion of polygamous men grows according to age (see figure 6). The fact that polygamy is practically non-existent before the age of thirty, and that it increases regularly up to the age of fifty, is due in the first place to the fact that a man has to be old to be polygamous, if only to meet the expense involved. Is it also the result of a degree of disaffection with this type of union on the part of younger generations, those aged under thirty in 1970? The remarkable steadiness of this proportion in the case of the over-fifties gives the impression that there was simply no onset of an evolution prior to the generations born around 1915–20, that is, until the recent past.

Although the arrival of a co-spouse in fact presents a fairly limited threat to the modern Arab wife, this does not guarantee the security of her marriage. The latter is an unstable institution, a prey to divorce, which has a higher probability than in most societies. In several Arab countries, the number of divorces registered every year represents between 20 and 25 per cent of all marriages celebrated in the same year (see table 5). To achieve a comparable level in 1978, the French divorce rate would have had to increase by a factor of three over its 1963 level,

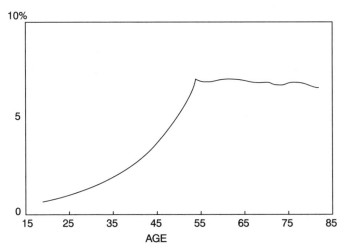

Figure 6 Percentage of polygamous unions according to husband's age (Syria, 1970)

both by raising the number of divorces and by reducing the number of marriages. In the Arab world, on the contrary, the phenomenon is stable. Divorce is a well-established tradition.

The procedure for divorce is generally speedy and continues to be the husband's prerogative. The evolution towards less inequity between the sexes is very tentative. When the Family Code was being debated in Algeria, the initial draft (1981) included the following formula: 'Divorce is the exclusive faculty of the husband.' The text finally adopted (1984) was amended to 'Divorce intervenes through the will of the husband or at the request of the wife' (Vandevelde, 1985). Two steps forward can be followed by one step backwards, as was the case in Egypt. The *Jihane el Sadat* Law on individual status granted women the right, among others, of demanding divorce from their husbands if the latter had just taken a co-spouse. This law was annulled in May 1985 by the Constitutional High Court under pressure from Muslim fundamentalists, who considered it contrary to the divine order. Two months later, Parliament had to overturn this annulment by passing a law similar to the 1979 law.

Arab divorce is peculiar not only in its procedure but also in the point at which it occurs in people's lives. It is extremely early. Generally speaking, three-quarters of divorces have occurred before the fifth marriage anniversary (in France the figure is under a quarter, see table 6). In most cases they dissolve an infertile marriage and, of course, infertility is largely implied by this speed. The converse relation for divorces after more than five years of marriage, although statistically in the minority, is extremely significant: it is the almost automatic sanction for an infertile marriage. We are here at the heart of its function.

Basically, repudiation is an ancestral mechanism for maximizing the reproductive potential of society, inherited from Bedouin societies for which it constituted one way of responding to their isolated situation. The inegalitarian nature of repudiation is derived from the demographic constraints imposed by patriarchal authority; it authorizes matrimonial circulation, thus enabling sterility to be eliminated by means of successive trials. City-dwellers have robbed it of its original function and have turned it into an instrument which the husband uses for increasing his authority over his wife. This increases the power of the family as a whole, because any children born prior to the divorce contribute to the strength of their father's family.

Marriage norms are the rules fixed by society to ensure its survival under a given set of reproductive conditions. The quantitative characteristics which we have just reviewed reflect circumstances which have evolved with increasing speed during the last few generations. In spite of the inertia which every social institution exerts against change, one of

Table 6 Recent evolution of divorce: its early occurrence in marriage, and children involved

Country	Number of divorces per 100 marriages		Percentage of divorces occurring before		Children born to the marriage prior to divorce	
	1963	1978	1st anniversary	5th anniversary	Childless percentage	Average no. of children
Egypt	21.6	20.8	31.7	75.8	74.3	0.5
Jordan	12.8	19.8	18.1	74.3	67.0	0.9
Libya	25.7	26.0	—	—	—	—
Syria	10.5	6.4	25.1	71.5	67.8	0.6
Tunisia	14.4	15.0	14.2	62.7	—	—
(France)	(8.9)	(23.2)	(0.4)	(18.9)	(25.1)	(1.5)

Source: United Nations, *Annuaire démographique 1982* (New York, 1984).

these rules is nowadays undergoing a clear evolution: the age of women at marriage is rising.

The extremely early age of marriage for girls is derived from precise endogamous rules which used to guarantee the cohesion of the group. Given that the person the girl must marry has been known since her birth, the age at which she is married is not significant, even when this occurs before puberty. The younger she is married, the more the clan is reassured that the norms have been respected, even when it seems that the primary function of marriage, which is to procreate, is undermined. Procreation, of course, must await puberty. An opinion poll taken in the late 1960s in Algeria has been interpreted as a prediction that these norms will soon be challenged. When questioned about the best age for girls at marriage, 85 per cent of men, as opposed to only 64 per cent of women, gave an age below twenty. Among the literate proportion of the population, 33 per cent of men but 69 per cent of women advocated marriage after the age of twenty (AARDES, 1970). Their answers to other questions showed clearly that women were keener to free themselves of these norms than men were to let them do so.

Cousins and spouses

Arab society practically never leaves any opening to chance. While the West has developed balls and social occasions with a code of 'fortuitous' encounters to encourage the formation of couples, there is nothing comparable among the Arabs. It is quite possible for a woman to meet no one but blood relatives in her entire life. Her whole world is arranged to exclude strangers. Her marriage is concluded with a close relative, if possible with the son of her paternal uncle, or with the uncle himself, in any case with a member of the family.

Much has been written about endogamy among the Arabs, and their society prescribes a practice which many others prohibit as incest. Marriage between parallel cousins is forced to the extent that in many places the son of the paternal uncle enjoys a full right of veto over any other marriage his cousin may contract (Berque, 1969).

This sort of 'obligatory incest' has been inherited from pre-Islamic Bedouin society (Tillion, 1983) where it was undoubtedly imposed by its nomadic isolation in the desert. However, we will not venture into the labyrinth of contradictory explanations which anthropologists have produced, but will content ourselves with underlining the extraordinary power conferred on the kin by the practice of selecting alliances within the lineage, creating an identity of alliance and descent groups. More than anything else, this system intensifies family relations (Khuri, 1970) to the detriment of relations outside the lineage.

It consolidates the economic foundations of the patrilineage by making sure that inheritance is retained. When Islam recognized the right of women to inherit their father's property, it was going against the pre-Islamic Arab custom of disinheriting women. In doing so, it opened a 'breach in the traditional system of the circulation of wealth ... Arab societies have never accepted this' (Bouhdiba, 1975, p. 137). Far from doing so, these societies have guaranteed the preservation of their family inheritance by disregarding Islam and disinheriting women in a fairly systematic manner, which amounts to limiting the wealth allowed to circulate with wives to their dowry alone, and to restricting the circulation of women to within their patrilineage. 'Women will circulate on their own; property will not follow them', commented Bouhdiba (1975, p. 139), who went on to quote a Tunisian proverb illustrating the frontiers which dowry is not readily allowed to cross: 'Why water the jujube tree? The olive tree has prior claim to the water!' Endogamy is not practised solely by the Muslims in Arab societies but can also be found, albeit in less intense form, among the Christian communities of the East.

The tendency to glorify Bedouin tradition means that the norm of the family as a unique social world, the ideal of 'living among one's own' (Tillion, 1983), has been transported into the towns. It has contributed to giving towns their familiar profile – blind walls, windows screened by *mashrabiyya* and veiled women – which is paradoxically so contrary to that of a Bedouin camp.

The Bedouin group has no need to hide its women from its own clansmen. Isolated from other tribes, these women moved about freely within the whole of their available world, which the the desert reduced to the members of their clan. In town, on the other hand, the limited space imposes tighter groupings, which entail the risk of mingling juxtaposed clans. In order to retain tribal customs, and in particular endogamy, two barriers have been raised, the one around the family being the house with its concealing and impenetrable outside walls, and the other around the woman, whose veil allows her to move in the midst of other clans while remaining within her own. In villages, which are half-way posts between camp and town life, opportunities for encounters between the sexes are reduced; women have their routes, or their hours for going out, which are not the same as the men's. According to Bouhdiba, this is how cousinage leads to 'the real social exclusion of women, accentuates sexual division and de-realizes women' (1975, p. 140). The way in which urbanization, far from liberating women, has given rise to novel forms of alienation, is a peculiarity of the Arab world.

In the most current modern Arab terminology, *'amm* still means both father-in-law and paternal uncle, and the latter is universally distinguished from the maternal uncle, or *khâl*. Is this simply a matter of linguistic inertia, or is it because the practice of marrying parallel patrilateral cousins is still flourishing? Various observers have noted that, whenever possible, it remains systematic. Although the available data on the subject are rare and fragmentary (table 7), they suggest that an evolution is taking shape.

1 Marriage between parallel cousins continues as a dominant marriage form between relatives only among the Shiites of Shatt al-Arab in Iraq. What is more, the data for this are unreliable and not up to date. In Damascus, and especially in Beirut in the 1960s, on the other hand, it has become a residual form (1 per cent of cases among Sunni in Beirut, 3.5 per cent among Maronites).

2 Marriage between relatives seems to occur slightly more frequently among Muslims than among Christians. The explanation for this lies not so much in religion but in the Christians' greater degree of urbanization.

3 Among city-dwellers, marriage between relatives has become a minority practice, which was not the case fifty years ago. This evolution is concomitant with that of the town itself. Although, in the first stage of urbanization, the population derived from the rural exodus tended to form groupings on the basis of family, the very process of passing from country to town made it difficult for the members of a lineage to become acquainted, and the mixing that resulted favoured interchange between different families. The perfect accord between architecture and clan endogamy which used to reign in the traditional city has not been broken only by the windows which pierce modern house fronts. The family itself has begun to open up.

4 Modern education does not favour marriage between relatives; it encourages women in their aspirations to autonomy and delays the age at which they marry. As women draw closer in age to the generation of their future spouses, their authority within the couple increases, whereas 'preferential' marriage within the patrilineage is the corollary of absolute authority on the husband's side.

These few comments are surely not enough to allow us to predict the near demise of this ancient custom, but as 'preferential' marriage represents at best only one case in every three, and generally less than one in every five, it is the non-prescribed marriage which has become the more usual form of union, since it unites two out of every three couples.

Table 7 Distribution of marriages according to degree of kinship between spouses (%)

Type of marriage	Lebanon (1971) (1)									Rural marriages 1900–1970 (2)		Sunnis (3) Damascus		Sunnis (3) Beirut		Shiites 1960 (3)		
Relatives:	34	—	—	—	—	—	—	—	—	51	27	41	29	50	12	60	—	67
parallel cousins	17	22	15	21	25	21	10	12	6	38	13	11	6	15	1	20	11	33
otherwise related	17	—	—	—	—	—	—	—	—	13	14	30	23	35	11	40	—	33
Non-kin	66	—	—	—	—	—	—	—	—	49	73	59	71	50	88	40	—	33

Sources:

(1) *La Famille au Liban (Al'Usra fī Lubnān)*, opinion poll survey, June 1971, conducted by the Lebanese Family Planning Office (Beirut, 1974).

(2) R. Cresswell, 'Lineage Endogamy among Maronite Mountaineers', in J. G. Peristiany, *Mediterranean Family Structures* (Cambridge, 1976), pp. 101–14.

(3) Prothro and Diab, quoted by S. Nasr, 'Formations sociales traditionelles et sociétés urbaines du Proche-Orient', in *La Ville arabe dans l'Islam* (Paris, 1982), pp. 357–84.

(4) A. Zghal, 'Système de parenté et système coopératif dans les campagnes tunisiennes', *Revue tunisienne des sciences sociales*, no. 11 (Tunis, 1967).

In order to function properly, the endogamic rule relies on two demographic conditions. Each individual has to have numerous kin, in order to increase his chances of securing a potential wife within it, which presumes a high rate of fertility. Furthermore, his kin must not be too dispersed in space, so that any two individuals capable of marrying each other have a good chance of meeting. This implies that there are no migrations. If migration does occur, it must involve the displacement of an extended kinship group, and not any individual centrifugal mobility. In the next section we will see that, while the kin remain numerous, they are now often dispersed. The geographic mobility of the twentieth century has speeded up the transformation of marriage norms.

The marriage market has crossed the bounds of the family circle. Does this mean that the family has surrendered all its prerogatives over the formation of the couple? Or does it continue to control the workings of chance by negotiating arranged marriages? 'The young girl stood beside her betrothed, covered from head to foot in a veil of red gauze embroidered in gold. The priest lifted the veil for a moment and the young man was able for the first time to glimpse the one to whom he was binding himself for life.' This description of a Christian wedding at Deir el-Qamar was recorded by Lamartine in his *Voyage en Orient*, and it is not very different from the theme which is so dear to Egyptian cinema: that of the conflict which ensues when love and family make different choices.

We have very little objective information about the extent of family intervention in the choice of spouse. A survey of Sunni marriages in Beirut and Damascus (see table 8) shows that families continue to intervene in the majority of cases, but that this intervention tends to be attenuated. It is now most unusual for the spouses to meet for the first time at their wedding. In both Beirut and Damascus, marriage is less a family affair nowadays than forty years ago. If these findings could be applied to Arab towns in general, it would mean that arrangements between families have not replaced endogamy in order to preserve the family inheritance.

As endogamy disappears, dowry effectually takes this inheritance outside the lineage. It might be thought that once the rule of endogamy had become impracticable in the modern world, families would try to replace it by means of arranged marriages, in order to control the new circulation of inheritance. However, this does not seem to be the case, since there is no evidence of any growth in arrangements between families concomitant with the decline of marriages within the lineage.

Some explanation for this may be found in the answers given by Algerians when questioned about the best marriage they could envisage for their daughters and sons. Only a minority were still in favour of arranged marriages without the agreement of the future spouses. On the other hand only a minority were in favour of freedom of choice in the matter of a spouse without the parents' agreement. This has all the signs of a transition. Although women seem to have advanced further in this transition, since they voice slightly less traditional opinions than men, especially in the better-educated sections of society (the professional classes), they (including the educated group) have a more traditional attitude towards their daughters than their sons. Alongside this lineage endogamy which is undergoing a rapid regression, there is a further form

Table 8 Family intervention in the formation of couples: reality and aspiration

Sunnis in Beirut and Damascus

		Marriages arranged by the parents %	Wives who had not seen their husband prior to	
			betrothal %	marriage %
Damascus	1930	96	67	56
	1960	64	30	5
Beirut	1930	85	29	9
	1960	55	17	4

Algeria, 1970

	Men		Women	
Opinions given as to the best marriage	Total %	Professional classes %	Total %	Professional classes %
Marriage of a daughter				
arranged by her parents	24	3	22	0
arranged with the girl's agreement	63	59	59	45
free choice by the girl	12	38	18	55
Marriage of a son				
arranged by his parents	15	3	19	0
arranged with the son's agreement	67	52	54	35
free choice by the son	17	45	26	65

Sources: E. T. Prothro and L. N. Diab, 'Changing Family Patterns in the Arab East' (American University of Beirut, 1974) (quoted by S. Nasr, see table 7); Algerian Society for Demographic, Economic and Social Research, *Enquête socio-démographique*, vol. IV: *Rôles assignés aux hommes et aux femmes* (Algiers, 1970).

of endogamy whose evolution is recent and hard to distinguish: this is religious endogamy. As we know, Islam holds on to its daughters by prohibiting marriage with non-Muslims. 'The Muslim girl may not marry a non-Muslim', states article 31 of the Algerian Family Code (1984). Islam has no need of a symmetrical prohibition to hold on to its sons. The legal authority of the husband over his wife automatically results in the woman converting to Islam through the mere fact of marrying a Muslim. Multi-religious societies such as Egypt and Lebanon have introduced a whole series of exceptions to this rule. In these countries mixed marriages are practised both ways, although Muslim families generally disapprove of their daughters marrying Christian men. The Lebanese administration does not make these kinds of marriage easy. By registering only those marriages which are transmitted by religious or consular authorities, they oblige candidates for mixed Christian–Muslim marriages to marry abroad. Cyprus has thus been host to many a Lebanese wedding.

Extended families and nuclear households

Have these current mutations in the way couples are formed sounded the knell of the extended patriarchal family and the advent of a nuclear model? Some recent population counts have provided interesting information about the composition of households. However, the lack of points of comparison in the past means that we will not be able deduce any signs of a trend from them.

In Egypt (see table 9), the nuclear family (a couple with or without unmarried children) represents half of all households, slightly more so in town and rather less in the countryside, where the extended family is dominant. The most frequently occurring form of extended family (20

Table 9   Egypt (1976) Distribution of households according to type (%)

Type of household	Countryside	Towns
Single individual	1.0	1.3
Restricted nuclear family (1)	44.5	56.1
Extended family (2)	51.0	39.1
With no kinship bond	3.5	3.4

(1) A couple with no children, or a couple (or the surviving member) with unmarried children.

(2) A couple (or the surviving member) and married children or a couple (or the surviving member) and the parents of one spouse with or without children, whether married or unmarried.

Source: 1976 census of the population and habitat.

per cent of urban households, 27 per cent of country households) involves the co-residence of at least three generations: a couple with married children and the parents of one of the spouses. When described in this way, the composition of the household does not suggest that the generations are organized along hierarchical and patriarchal lines, because the head of the household is the man belonging to the intermediate generation. Both in Egypt and in many other countries, the explanation for the co-residence of several family units is found in the shortage of accommodation in towns and, in the countryside, in the persistence of the family cell as a unit of production.

In Syria (1970), the nuclear model may be rather more widespread, depending on whether the census definitions are comparable to those in the Egyptian census. Seventy-two per cent of households consist of a single family unit, 13 per cent of two or more. Among households which include several units, the rule is that the head of the family accommodates his daughter-in-law (9.2 per cent of rural households and 5.6 per cent of urban). The son-in-law is accommodated only exceptionally, in 0.2 per cent of rural households and 0.5 per cent in town. This last percentage shows that, while uxorilocality may be firmly relegated to the countryside, the shortage of living space in the towns can force a young city couple to resort to it. In Kuwait (1980, excluding foreigners) the households are split up into 64 per cent with a single family unit, 25 per cent with two units, 8 per cent with three and 3 per cent with four or more, with 97 per cent of the latter comprising more than fifteen persons.

In any case, statistics for households according to the number of family units tend to overestimate the position of the restricted family. The mononuclear family is an obligatory phase in the life cycle of an extended family, in every case where the husband's parents have died before his eldest son has married.

As we know, the concept of household is closely linked to the unit of residence, and the extended family can function as a real group without involving co-residence by all its members. The predominance of the restricted family in these groupings constitutes a form of nuclearization for the Arab family. Nevertheless such a family has a very specific character in relation to other nuclear models, both from the point of view of its size and rate of reproduction and from the point of view of the distribution of roles within it and its function in society.

Family domains

Widening the circle

Marriage inaugurates sexual activity on the woman's side, since the threat hanging over premarital relations is so effective that it never fails to act as a deterrent. The men of the family enjoy absolute power when it comes to ensuring respect for the virginity of their unmarried sisters and daughters; from one end of the Arab world to the other, the law grants benevolent absolution to murder for breaches of honour. Such practices are current among Christians as well as Muslims. Murder avenges not only adultery but also premarital relations, in which case the brother is judge, even when junior to his sister.

The only objective criterion available to us for measuring the incidence of premarital sexual activity is provided by the data for illegitimate births and premarital conceptions. Arab societies are possibly the only ones in the world which repress illegitimacy to the extent that it is statistically nil (see table 10). Mauritania is the only Arab country where the children born prior to marriage, albeit a very small proportion of total births, form a statistically significant category (2.7 per cent of first births, six times less than in France, for instance). Although the survey does not record their ethnic distribution, it is very probable that the majority of these births are Poular or Soninké (African ethnic groups), and that the Arab ones are few and far between.

It is possible that the prohibition of premarital sexual relations is relaxed when a marriage is about to be concluded, in North Africa at least. The proportion of first births to occur less than seven months after marriage, which implies that conception occurred prenuptially, may indicate a degree of tolerance. While this may be the case, this proportion

Table 10 Distribution of the intervals between marriage and birth of the first child (%), *c.*1970–80

Country	Negative interval	0–7 months	8 months or more
Egypt	0	0.8	99.2
Morocco	0	11.4	88.6
Mauritania	2.7	4.5	92.8
Sudan	0	6.1	93.3
Syria	0	0.5	99.5
Tunisia	0	1.9	98.1

Source: EMF.

has to be interpreted cautiously, given the difficulties involved in measuring precisely the interlude between marriage and first birth in the course of retrospective population surveys.

Once her sexual activity has been solemnly inaugurated by marriage, the woman dedicates the rest of her fertile existence to increasing her family. Hers is a numerous progeny: taking all marital situations together, she gives birth to an average of seven children. In the case of a woman whose first marriage took place before she was twenty and was not dissolved before her fiftieth birthday, this corresponds to an average progeny of eight to ten children: 9.1 in Yemen and 9.4 in Syria, for example. This is not the maximum possible progeny, because every human society sets limits to the natural procreative capacity of women, but it is the highest in the world, alongside that of African women (table 11).

The motives underlying these high fertility levels in the Arab world are mainly the same as those which have been abundantly described in other societies. First of all, the procreation of a numerous progeny is the expression of an economic and social rationale, based on the very high mortality which affected Arab peoples until the early twentieth century. Death took one in every three new-born children before its fifth birthday, and a second died before reaching the age of fifty. Given that only one

Table 11 Average final number of children per woman

	1950	*1980*
Algeria	7.3	7.2
Egypt	7.1	5.3
Iraq	7.2	7.0
Jordan	7.2	7.3
Kuwait	7.3	6.6
Lebanon	5.7	4.3
Mauritania	6.7	6.9
Morocco	7.2	5.9
Sudan	6.7	6.7
Syria	7.1	7.5
Tunisia	6.9	5.1
Yemen	—	8.5
All developing countries	6.2	4.6

Sources: United Nations, *World Population Prospects* (New York, 1985); Egypt, Yemen and Morocco: EMF.

Note: These tables do not include countries with a lower birth rate which are dominated by an immigrant population (viz. Bahrain, United Arab Emirates, Qatar) or countries whose fertility figures are not based on reliable sources (Saudi Arabia, Libya, Oman, South Yemen).

child in two is a boy, no fewer than six children had to be born to allow one male child to survive his fiftieth year and to ensure the reproduction of the patrilineage.

Furthermore, in a world where men restricted women's work to the domestic sphere, the same unconscious calculation led them to procreate at least six children in order to ensure that one male child survived to supply his parents' needs when they were too old for productive work. The search for security in old age was only one aspect of this economic rationale. Putting the children to work was another, given that even very young children could earn more by working than it costs to keep them. In economies where the family is the unit of production, the contribution made by children to the workforce is a powerful inducement to achieve a high fertility rate.

Nowadays this economic argument is less pressing than in the recent past. The death rate has already fallen markedly and has invalidated the calculation which justifies the procreation of large families. The number of children in every ten born who survive to fifty has risen from three to eight. Whereas in the past six children were required to safeguard posterity, nowadays the task is fulfilled just as well by three (in terms of statistical averages).

Individual forms of behaviour do not, it is true, obey the logic of statistics. They are much more likely to adjust to economic considerations. Although the profits derived from child labour possibly constitute a less general incentive than previously, the search for security in old age is just as vigorous. Indeed, only a privileged minority of citizens are actually cared for by the community. We know, for instance, from the Egyptian fertility survey in 1980 that children are still deemed to become 'useful' at a very young age, at 9.9 in the case of girls and at 11.5 in the case of boys. In the countryside, the majority still wish to live with their children and to derive financial support from them in their old age (64 per cent of those questioned), but in town this applies to only 22 per cent.

Although an average of seven children per woman constitutes a very prolific issue, it represents only half the maximum possible. There are two sorts of mechanisms which all societies have always used to control the number of their descendants: limiting the duration of conjugal life and extending the interval between successive births.

We have seen above what happens to the first mechanism: if Arab societies resort to it at all, it is only within narrow bounds. In fact, the early age of marriage for girls guarantees them the longest possible reproductive life. While repudiation certainly contributes to reducing its length, remarriage attenuates the effect on fertility and occurs all the more frequently when repudiation is practised more easily.

In fact, this gap between practice and the maximum procreation possible is explained mainly in terms of the spacing out of births. Breast-feeding is known to prolong *post partum* infertility and provides the principal means to this end; indeed, breast-feeding is particularly pro-longed and is sometimes made into a legal requirement: 'The wife is obliged to breast-feed her progeny if she is capable of so doing,' enjoins the 1984 Algerian Family Code. By the end of the 1970s, Arab mothers were still breast-feeding their babies for an average of eighteen months after birth, rather less in Syria and Tunisia (fourteen months) and rather more in poorer countries (eighteen months in Mauritania, twenty in Egypt) (EMF).

Spacing out births by means of extended breast-feeding is not prim-arily aimed at reducing the number of children born to a woman but at increasing the chances of survival for those babies already born. It is a paradox worth stressing that the primary effect of limiting births by spacing them out is to increase the size of the surviving family.

One characteristic of the Arab family must be stressed: its preference for boys. With the Arabs, female inferiority begins at birth. Girls are less often wanted than boys, especially for the first birth, and they undoubt-edly enjoy less attention. All this is revealed by a phenomenon which is as common in Arab societies as it is exceptional in other contemporary societies: the higher mortality rate for young girls (see table 12).

The Egyptian figures, for instance, are eloquent: during the first month of life, the baby still comes under the protection which was transmitted to the foetus from its mother regardless of sex; little boys die more often (62 per 1,000) than little girls (56 per 1,000), which appears to be a

Table 12   Higher mortality rates for young girls in Arab countries, *c.*1975–80 (deaths per 1,000)

	0–1 year		2–5 years	
	Boys	*Girls*	*Boys*	*Girls*
Egypt	131	134	63	73
Jordan	64	75	26	29
Mauritania	99	83	102	93
Morocco	91	91	44	60
Sudan	90	86	71	68
Syria	59	72	22	25
Tunisia	81	74	25	31
Yemen	166	156	87	93

Source: National fertility surveys; data derived from the mothers' reproductive histories.

natural law. Once past the first month, the effects of nature are superseded by the child's environment and its parents' actions. This is when little boys start to die less than girls (69 per 1,000 between one and twelve months, as opposed to 79 per 1,000). In all likelihood, this is because boys are protected more carefully than girls. After the age of five, the mother's protection is less decisive in ensuring the child's survival. Once this element of sexual differentiation has gone, nature resumes its rights, and girls once again die less frequently than boys. Although nature favours girls, this biological inequality has been more than compensated for by the preferential care given to boys. This peculiar cultural trait (Tabutin, 1976; Bchir, 1983) is encountered outside the Arab world only in parts of India and Pakistan, and it disappears in the two Arab countries abutting onto black Africa: Sudan and Mauritania.

Large families: rules and exceptions

What does the future hold for the large family? In the mid-1980s, the Arab world, alongside black Africa, was the last bastion of resistance to birth control. Whereas very high fertility levels first began to dip in southeast Asia ten or twenty years before tropical Latin America in the 1970s, such a movement has been very faint indeed in North Africa and the Middle East. This delay of a few decades has been enough to change the balance of world population. It is as though families here, more than elsewhere, had made the political ambitions of their states their own.

Let us return to table 11. Between 1950 and 1980, the number of children per woman dropped perceptibly only in Egypt and Tunisia. Along with Lebanon, these are the only Arab countries in which women give birth to less than six children on average. Everywhere else, the number has been static or even risen slightly (Jordan, Syria).

Let us begin with a word about this rise. It is in all likelihood ephemeral. It is derived on the one hand from an improvement in sanitary conditions and a more efficient supervision of pregnancies; the proportion of conceptions not resulting in a live birth has diminished through a drop in intrauterine mortality. It is also due to a recent reduction in the breast-feeding period, which would tend to shorten the intervals between births. It denotes, not a change in the size of families, but on the contrary, the maintenance of traditional behaviour in conditions which are evolving rapidly.

An explanation is also required for the Egyptian and Tunisian cases. The perceptible drop in the average number of children which has been observed there (−1.8 in Egypt and −1.3 in Tunisia) is not unrelated to the considerable financial support which both countries have given to family planning programmes, which they are alone in the Arab world in having officially put into operation, both in the same year (1964). This drop is minute in relation to the financial resources involved, and testifies to the resistance of Arab families to any attempts at limiting their size.

However, it does seem that a minority of families in all the Arab countries are already keen to reduce their size. Modern contraceptive aids are not as readily available in every country as they have been since 1964 in Egypt and Tunisia, or were not at the time when the surveys were conducted, although they may have become so since, in Algeria for instance. The reduction in the number of descendants which has been observed in both these countries could thus correspond to the average number of children whose conception, given the absence of legal contraceptive methods, could until now not be avoided in the other countries. This interpretation restores a degree of homogeneity to family norms in the Arab world.

Such diversity as does exist is manifested within each country, according to criteria which are common to them all. The very high average fertility levels are not derived from the absence of population categories which advocate the two- or three-child family, but from the fact that such categories are still very much in the minority. In table 13, I provide a sample of the profuse data now available to cast light on these processes.

Towns are less fertile than the countryside. They are all the less so the longer their inhabitants have been city-dwellers. Thus, Cairo, which absorbs the bulk of the rural exodus from the Nile valley, is more fertile than Alexandria, an ancient city with fewer attractions for countryfolk. The same differentiation can be found in other countries, Morocco for instance, where the overall fertility rate in small towns is 5.0 children per woman, whereas in big towns it is 4.2. Paradoxically, the same reality is expressed by the fertility rates for Mauritanian women, which are

Table 13 Differential criteria for the final number of children per woman

Egypt, 1980		Lebanon, 1981		Morocco, 1980			
				Standard of living		Education	
Alexandria	3.1	Christians and Druze	3.6	well-off	3.7	secondary	4.2
Cairo	4.1	Sunnis	5.2	average	4.5	primary	4.6
Upper Egypt (rural pop.)	6.3	Shiites	6.6	poor	6.7	illiterates	6.4

Source: Egypt and Morocco: EMF, 1983 and 1984; Lebanon: OLPF, 1974.

identical in Nouakchott and the rest of the country. In the 1970s, the flood of refugees from the droughts made Nouakchott grow too quickly to allow the attitudes which were observed in the 1980 survey to develop an urban typology.

In all those Arab countries for which this type of data exists, it may also be observed that the poor are more prolific than the rich, and that a rise in the level of education is accompanied by a reduction in family size. Demographers are inclined to think that the second variable determines the whole process. By raising their level of education, women develop aspirations outside the family. Their relations with their husbands tend to balance out. They procreate less. Just as the most educated women are found in towns, so too are the less numerous families found there.

Can this explanation be applied without further ado to the Christian communities among which, in Lebanon at least, a more marked dip in fertility levels has been observed? Religion may have an indirect effect on family size because the social composition of the population varies from one religious community to another. The lower fertility levels among Christians would thus primarily reflect the greater incidence of social groups with a low rate of fertility among Christians. At the same time, however, religion can have a direct effect if the different religious doctrines articulate different norms in family matters. Christianity frowns on the sexual act when its purpose is not procreation. It constitutes an indirect incitement to procreate. Islam, for its part, values sexual enjoyment and makes procreation into a divine requirement. While the Christian's faith incites him indirectly to procreate, the Muslim's obliges him to do so.

Chamie concludes his minutely detailed examination of the rare data on the subject by opting in favour of an interactive mechanism (1981), in which education plays the central role. Education is unequally apportioned between Muslims and Christians, since the latter enjoy on average a superior social position, which gives them privileged access to schools. We have seen the effect education has on fertility. Added to this is the conditional effect of religion, since schooling determines the degree of freedom enjoyed by individuals in interpreting religious doctrine. Given that Islam esteems the procreation of many children in a more explicit fashion than Christianity, religion would have an effect on women with a low educational level, who are more fertile if they are Muslim, but not on better-educated women, who are in fact observed to behave in the same way in both communities. This micro-sociological explanation fails almost entirely to address the question which historians will soon be asking: why is it the Christians of the Middle East, a minority in Arab society, rather than the Muslims, that have abandoned attempts to maximize the size of their clan? Is there any coherence between this behaviour on the part of Lebanese Christians and the revival of their irredentism?

It is very difficult to penetrate the intimacy shared by a couple. Nevertheless the Egyptian inquiry into fertility (EMF) has contributed a few suggestive findings. In it men and women were questioned separately about whether they had discussed the size of their family as a couple. The response was positive in 39 per cent of cases. The variability of the positive responses matches almost perfectly the real size of families: 60 per cent in the towns of Lower Egypt, 57 per cent in Cairo and 20 per cent in rural Upper Egypt; from 77 per cent among city women with secondary or higher education to 20 per cent among rural illiterate women; 35 per cent in urban households with monthly incomes of less than 20 Egyptian pounds as opposed to 69 per cent in those with incomes of 80 pounds or more, etc. Thus the size of the family has become subject to individual choice. This movement, albeit still tentative, gives the impression that the very large family is a norm which is now being challenged.

Family: the woman's work; work: the man's world

The sexual division of roles is strict: all the tasks performed in the home are assigned to women, whereas men have the exclusive prerogative of all work of a non-domestic nature.

The stages in a woman's reproductive life are modulated in accordance with her successive roles within the family. When she marries, she breaks with her family of origin. She quits the protection of her father, or her eldest brother if her father is dead, and submits to her husband's protection. Unless she is repudiated, she will owe allegiance to her husband's family until she dies. Once widowed, she will come under the protection of her own eldest son. During the whole of her life, she will never, or almost never, be consulted on any decisions which involve her family with the outside world. On the other hand, she will be increasingly able to intervene in family decisions as she grows older, and following her successive births. The procreation of her first child, especially the first boy, constitutes a first decisive phase in the wife's gradual ascent up the power scale. However, her household duties will only be alleviated when her first son marries, bringing her a daughter-in-law. This contributes a further element to her life cycle, since this type of household effectively changes a woman's family role. So long as mother-in-law and daughter-in-law co-reside in an extended family, the latter is relegated to the bottom of the power scale. However, she acquires a degree of autonomy when the family becomes nuclear.

Employment statistics are unanimous in revealing the low participation of women in economic employment, or in work recognized as such, in modern Arab cities. Whereas 35 per cent of women of all ages are engaged in economic work throughout the world, in Arab countries the proportion lies below 10 per cent, and often below 5 per cent. It is 3.5 per cent in Algeria (1977), 3 per cent in Libya (1973), 4.8 per cent in Kuwait (1980), 5.3 per cent in Syria (1970) and 5.5 per cent in Egypt (1976), etc. Of these working women, the proportion representing unpaid family workers is itself high (38.3 per cent in Syria for instance).

It might be thought that this was an ineluctable consequence of the high birth rate, as a result of which women are gradually prevented by their high number of pregnancies from engaging in any work other than that of bringing up their children. Were this hypothesis correct, the proportion of working women would 'normally' be high among younger women and would only decrease in inverse proportion to their increasing families. However, this is not the case. Although a drop in employment can be observed (see figure 7), this starts from a very low maximum level. A mere 10 per cent of women between the ages of twenty-five and twenty-nine are in employment, a phenomenon which is not solely derived from the numerous births women undergo.

It is a truism that the classical tools for evaluating economic work are particularly ill-adapted for establishing correctly the contribution of women. They take account of neither the productive contribution made by domestic work, nor of the economic nature of a whole range of female production in the home, generally for consumption by the family. The few 'time-budget' surveys to have been conducted in Arab countries show what an essential role women play in the agricultural economy: growing food crops and carrying water are generally the preserve of women.

Although it would certainly be useful to review the concepts employed in the inquiries in order to take better stock of women's effective contribution to economic production (Zurayk, 1985), it is of little import here that the statistics are deficient in economic terms. For sociologists, the way in which female work is consistently undervalued in all the surveys conducted in the Arab world can be considered a significant social trait in itself. It reveals the enclosed life of women, the overwhelming majority of whom carry out their work wholly within the narrow confines of their family group.

Male employment, on the other hand, reveals the opposite picture, one which presents a classical view of the Third World. Work begins at a very

North-east of Aleppo, in Syria. The tiny dwellings force women, as in this case, to share a room with their daughters and young sons.

Philippe Fargues

Proportion in employment (%)

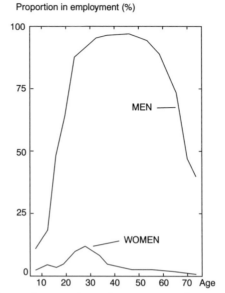

Figure 7   Incidence of economic employment, according to sex and age, in Egypt (1976)

early age: 15 per cent of boys aged between six and ten are already employed in a trade in Egypt. It is extended particularly late, and is often interrupted only by death; among seventy-year-old men, one in two is still working. Families mobilize their entire available workforce, in the towns as well, despite high unemployment, because their work is needed to enable them to live. However, this need is not sufficiently imperious to require family groups to contravene the rule which impels them to guard their women by restricting their movements to the home.

Urbanization does not in itself appear to bring about any profound changes. On the contrary, the divide between the traditional roles of men and women is more clear-cut in town. However, it is also in town that certain agents of change develop best, particularly those represented by contact with different societies and by the emancipation of women through school.

A first opening: emigration

Contact with different societies has followed a multitude of paths, from the direct but limited course pursued in the colonial period to the daily penetration of the West into the heart of the family through the media. I shall refer here to a specific form of contact, emigration, and to its repercussions on the Arab family.

Since the 1960s, the Arab world has been traversed by two great streams of migration: from the Maghreb to Europe (a total 1.7 million North Africans were resident in western Europe in 1985); and from the non-petroleum-exporting countries in the Middle East (Egypt, Yemen, Jordan, Syria and Lebanon) to the oil-rich countries of the Arabian peninsula as well as to Iraq and Libya (between 3 and 4 million emigrants in 1985).

The ensuing changes affecting the society of departure are complex indeed (see *Annuaire de l'Afrique du Nord*, 1981; Fargues, 1980). However, this is not the place to discuss the many connections between emigration and family, such as the role played by the kin in migratory networks and in determining the type of base in the host countries, or the role played by the family situation in deciding whether to migrate, etc. Instead, we will concentrate on what is for us the important aspect, namely the impact of emigration on family structures.

First of all, emigration sets a process of acculturation in operation. It conveys new attitudes which penetrate the society of departure through the contacts maintained with it by the emigrant, particularly when he comes home. This acculturation process is revealed, for instance, by the architectural forms he brings back with him. The savings he sends home from abroad are primarily invested in property. From Morocco to Yemen, the emigrant's house can be recognized by its borrowings from the West, not only by its openings onto the outside, but also by the way things are arranged inside (CIEM, 1984). The acculturation thus effected is certainly more radical to the west, where North African emigration is directed towards Europe, than to the east, where people emigrate to other Arab countries whose family traditions are even stronger than in their own country of departure. However, Egyptian emigrants too can bring home 'Western' values, even from Saudi Arabia. Their aspirations are transformed in line with their rising power of purchase. They adopt certain specifically Western forms of consumption in connection with their dwelling, their clothing, etc., which can have a perceptibly distorting effect on traditional norms.

Alongside this confrontation with the outside world, emigration involves the family in a purely internal dynamic process. The reference here is not to the social rise which often results from realizing their savings. Although this can speed up some transformation processes, especially when accompanied by new aspirations for the children, which lead to girls attending school, the evolutions involved are necessarily slow. We shall look instead at the way the husband's emigration forces his wife to break with traditional roles when he emigrates on his own, as is customary.

This, for instance, is what happened in a village of the Nile valley close to Cairo (Taylor, 1984). The departure of the head of the family immediately presented the problem of who was to replace him. Who would now be in authority? His wife or a protector to whom he confided this responsibility, generally his brother or father? It all depended on which stage in the wife's life cycle had been reached when her husband emigrated.

If it happened prior to the birth of her first child, it weakened the wife's position, and in this case she was always taken in by the emigrant's parents. The man entrusted with her protection managed the savings sent home from abroad. To make matters worse, her husband was no longer there to calm down quarrels between mother and daughter-in-law. The latter lost the leisure to visit her own family, lest anyone should interpret such a gesture as a demonstration of ill-will on her part towards her husband's family. When the wife was the mother of young children, but lived within the extended family, the emigrant never failed to mention what share of the funds he sent home was for her and her children, thus securing some improvement in her material position. However, it was only when she lived on her own with the couple's children and without protectors that she too derived a new power from her husband's emigration. This was when novel attitudes appeared, of which the one with the most future was undoubtedly the new ambition which the wife entertained for her own daughters once she herself had been liberated from her husband. She sent them to school and kept them there significantly longer than all the other types of family did.

The second opening: school

Boys and girls do not start life with equal rights. After their inequality in the face of death, girls will have to face inequality with regard to school. Among adults, the proportion of illiterates is often twice as high in the case of women as among men (see table 14). Indeed, there are many countries where nine out of ten women are unable to read. Given that the Arabs' system of marriage and subsequent family life depends entirely on the seclusion of their women, this is inculcated in them from childhood.

School is not designed for little girls, being set in the world outside the family. School is reserved for boys, since it dispenses instruction which could weaken the traditional hierarchies based on sex and age by introducing a hierarchy based on knowledge.

However, the present situation is far from being permanent. Fifty years

Table 14   Proportion of illiterate persons aged fifteen and over, according to
sex

Country		Men	Women
Algeria	1987	36.6	64.4
Bahrain	1981	25.2	48.1
Egypt	1986	41.6	67.2
Jordan	1991	9.2	24.9
Kuwait*	1985	21.8	31.2
Libya	1984	23.1	57.7
Morocco	1982	56.3	82.5
North Yemen	1970	82.4	98.5
South Yemen	1980	52.3	92.1
Syria	1981	26.4	63.0
Tunisia	1989	30.8	54.8

* Excluding foreigners.
Source: UNESCO Statistical Yearbook, 1994 (figures for Bahrain, North and South
Yemen from 1984 edn).

ago, the men and women of the Arab world were almost equal in this
respect, since illiteracy was their common lot. During the second third of
the twentieth century, schooling developed rapidly, with varying degrees
of speed, depending on the country (fast in Lebanon and Palestinian
areas, slowly in Libya, Morocco and Yemen). Boys were the first to
benefit. The inequality that exists between the adults of today is that
which existed between the children of the past.

The last twenty years have seen the girls catching up. Although girls
still had unequal educational opportunities in 1960, these are rapidly
being made good, not only at primary but also at secondary level and
especially in higher education. Between 1960 and 1980, the number of
girls aged between eighteen and twenty-three attending institutions of
higher education multiplied by eight throughout the Arab countries,
while the number of boys multiplied only by three (see table 15). This

Table 15   School registration levels (percentages)

Age		Arab countries		World	
		Boys	Girls	Boys	Girls
6–11 years	1960	50.5	28.2	68.3	55.6
	1980	76.2	56.9	79.5	68.1
12–17 years	1960	25.6	9.8	42.9	33.6
	1980	53.6	33.5	54.8	46.4
18–23 years	1960	6.4	1.3	10.2	5.5
	1980	20.6	10.6	20.2	15.2

educational inequality between the generations can disrupt parent–child relations, especially when the daughter is better educated than her father (Bouhdiba, 1967).

It was not only girls who were catching up with boys during the 1970s, but the whole Arab world was involved in a spectacular catching-up process with the rest of the world. Indeed, it is very likely that the difference between male and female education has already peaked and will soon diminish, if it has not already started to do so.

In Jordan, the spread of education has been so rapid that its whole history can be traced in a single census (see figure 8). The generations born at the beginning of the twentieth century, those aged over seventy in the 1979 census, included a high proportion of illiterates distributed equally between the sexes. Opportunities for attending school had been almost as limited for men as for women. The generations born between 1910 and 1935 had experienced growing differentiation between the sexes. Only boys benefited from the expansion of schooling; the male graph dips while the female line hardly goes down. The generations born between 1935 and 1960, on the other hand, witnessed the gradual diminution of these sexual inequalities; the lines draw closer together. The situation for the generation born after 1960, almost at the end of this catching-up phase, is once again one of near-equality, but this time the proportion of illiterates is practically nil. Although Jordan is definitely ahead of the rest of the Arab world, it is so by only a few years. The evolution which we have observed there has every chance of being reproduced in other countries.

The most educated women are still at an age when they have no claim

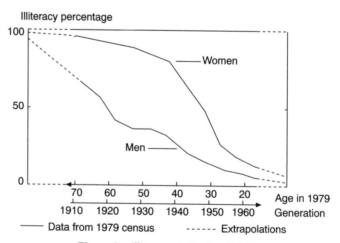

Figure 8   Illiteracy in Jordan (1979)

A woman reading a newspaper in Tunis. Women are only allowed out on condition they wear the veil.

to any power of decision in the family, irrespective of sex, since they are under twenty years of age. This situation is one that cannot last. However, its corollary is that power resides with those generations which experienced the greatest inequality between men and women. These people are aged over sixty and thus will soon have given way to their juniors. Ensuing generations will be increasingly egalitarian. When one considers that some delay must occur between the acquisition of knowledge and the recognition of a status of authority associated with this knowledge, one is forced to predict that the changes to come will prove far more decisive than those which have already been witnessed among a minority of city-dwellers.

As in all contemporary societies, the family is but one social group among others to which an individual can belong. These include the groups which are first formed at school and subsequently at work or in politics, in a residential area or in leisure activities. Until now, none of these groups has competed seriously with the family. On the contrary, the latter's functions continue to impinge on their territory. Several countries in the Arabian peninsula, for instance, still confuse the family with the state. The civil war in Lebanon demonstrated the extent to which descent can determine the political and military choices individuals make.

If it turns out that families really are dwindling in size, this will contribute to precipitating developments which we can barely glimpse at present. With the diminution in the number of kin, the diversity of contacts between relatives and of the functions assumed by the family will necessarily be increasingly impoverished. The family's preponderance over other groupings will thus lose some of its absolute character. As their family world grows narrower, women will have more compelling reasons for stepping outside it.

More and more veiled women are to be seen on the streets of Cairo, Tunis and even Damascus, even in the universities. Western observers never fail to ascribe the renewal of this form of exclusion for women to the growing influence of Islamic fundamentalism. Is this interpretation correct? The veil is not worn indoors; it is worn for going out. Perhaps one now comes across so many simply because the women who formerly never went out have today come outside into the streets.

PART III

The Western World: Industrialization and Urbanization

NINE

The Industrial Revolution: from Proletariat to Bourgeoisie

Martine Segalen

It is industrialization rather than the Industrial Revolution that should be credited with the changes which affected the family institution. The term 'Industrial Revolution' is in fact static, designating a starting point, which was selected as a historical and economic convention to describe the technical changes which gradually affected the whole economic evolution and social relations in the principal countries of Europe. The term 'industrialization' refers to a dynamic process of transformation in which the family institution was not always the passively affected party but rather figured as a site of reaction and resistance or as a close constituent of industrial dynamism.

As research into the relations between industrialization, urbanization and family changes multiplies, it reveals the plurality of the situations and configurations involved. The very fact that this process took place in contexts as diverse as nations, types of industry and population movements, to cite but a few of this complex phenomenon's variables, makes it impossible to put forward a hypothesis to account overall for the upheavals in the family institution caused by the technical and economic changes lumped together under the term 'industrialization'. The only theories of social change that exist are 'partial and local' (Boudon, 1984, p. 220) and the one which claims that industrialization exploded the 'traditional family' is no longer valid. Nowadays the consensus is that the relations between family, industrial and urban changes are neither straightforward nor linear: it is useless to look for single causes, and caution is needed in considering causal series. By acknowledging that it is impossible to support a general theory identifying the change with the strengthening of state control, one is led, contrary to certain propositions of Foucault (1977, 1980) and Joseph and Fritsch (1977), to bring to the fore the strength of the family as an institution. The family is not simply an object acted on by the harsh laws of economic and social forces, but rather a site of resistance capable of adapting to different situations. Even under the worst conditions imposed by industrialization, people tried to discover strategies adapted to their interests; these were often set within the family framework.

Several models of industrialization

There is no agreement among historians as to when the Industrial Revolution took place and how it should be defined. Following Rioux (1971), we can contrast the opposing theories that emphasize respectively the technical aspect and the development of capital. The first discusses access to new sources of energy, coal and steam, followed by electricity and the internal combustion engine, with a third revolution taking place in our own time – the microchip revolution. Some think that these technical developments were part of an accelerated trend, which first made itself felt at the beginning of the eighteenth century; others

The interior of a Lyons silkworker's home. Engraving from the first half of the nineteenth century. Paris, Bibliothèque des Arts Décoratifs. Photo: J. L. Charmet.

think of it as a break with the past. The opposing view stresses the accumulation of inherited property and the liberation of capital wealth as allowing a true form of capitalism to emerge, with funds for investment in industry. Whatever the virtues of these different interpretations, the considerable increase in production was linked to more than one factor: specialization of labour, use of machines, continuous technical progress, mobilization of capital with a view to profit, and a clear distinction between a bourgeoisie which owned the means of production and a wage-earning class. Vast numbers of the latter went to find work in the newly created industries, having been caught up in the whirlwind of the Agrarian Revolution which all authors agree took place alongside the Industrial Revolution, even preceding it and making it possible. Britain was the first nation to provide an example with the enclosures, when the common lands passed into the hands of private landowners who enclosed them and turned them into pasture for sheep. Peasants' dwellings were demolished and country people forced to seek employment elsewhere. At the same time, agricultural productivity rose markedly, which is not contrary to the trend described above, thus freeing a further supply of manual workers.

The Industrial Revolution was born in England more than 100 years before the French variant. Its precocious nature is explained by a complex group of factors: the sudden and strong population growth at the end of the eighteenth and beginning of the nineteenth centuries, the development of markets, the presence of coal and iron, a humid climate favourable to the cotton industry, and the existence of a workforce which, as Polanyi explains (1983, p. 68), became available as a result of the revolution in agriculture. The first industrial take-off had a cumulative effect, constantly bringing new workers to the industrial centres as migration from the countryside rose. Industries were grafted onto urban areas, which grew at brutal rates but were incapable of absorbing the masses of workers leaving the countryside; England thus presents an exaggerated model of the destructuring of social life in general, and family life in particular, at the beginning of industrialization.

Although demographic factors cannot be made into the sole cause of these transformations, we can be sure that the French model, which differs from the English, can be attributed in part to the exceptional French population curve, which was unique in Europe in featuring slower growth from the end of the eighteenth century.

In France, low population growth and the gradual rate of urbanization favoured the survival of local and regional markets and of craft manufacture of products with a reputation for quality and a high level of finish (Sewell, 1983, pp. 209–11). Although gross production per head of population was not lower in France than in England, the take-off there occurred in a context dominated by the rural world, and in a very decentralized urban network with long craft traditions. Thus France experienced a process of industrialization which was both much less brutal than in England and much less expensive on the social and human level.

Finally, these new industries produced different family structures and relationships, depending on whether they were based on a predominantly male or female workforce. The textile industries were basically run with female workers, which had the effect of disorganizing family relations and abolishing traditional and exclusively female spheres of knowledge; those industries which were predominantly masculine had less disastrous consequences on the organization of the family. England's rise was based on a predominantly female industry, whereas Germany's was based on its developing mines from the eighteenth century and then, bypassing the cotton phase of industrial development, on its steel industry and chemical production.

Instead of growing out of private initiatives, industrial development in Italy and the United States appeared in original forms stimulated by the state. In the United States, furthermore, industrialization and urbanization were accompanied by vast population movements, successive waves of immigrants from western and central Europe bearing with them their cultural and notably their family models, giving rise to as many models of industrial processes, family evolution and family types. Nevertheless, but at different stages over time, the same causes produced the same effects. As Rioux writes, there can be no industrial development without a profound restructuring of social relations; capitalism is marked by a split into social classes, each with its own particular models and family comportments, which may be antagonistic but which interact. This feature is common to all countries which experience industrial growth. Industrial society comes to birth accompanied by the appearance of a variety of working-class families, alongside a mosaic of so-called middle class or bourgeois families, from lowly clerical workers to the great business and landowning bourgeoisie.

To sum up, before the Industrial Revolution there existed a peasantry which possessed a variety of family models – all, however, organized in relation to modes of exploitation, types of agricultural activity and inheritance practices – alongside a small proportion of aristocratic and bourgeois families. After the Industrial Revolution, and for a relatively short period ending with the emergence of a uniform family model (a temporary model, judging by more recent periods), a great variety of family types emerged, as diverse as the hierarchies of work, the constraints of production and the social categories, all of which evade static classification on account of the constant and complex processes of social mobility.

It would be artificial to describe these various family models separately from the material conditions which provided their means of existence. On the contrary, by analysing this concrete framework, we can avoid the tendency to view people merely as puppets jerked along at the whim of events over which they had no control. Such a view takes no account of the family institution's formidable ability to resist and adapt, the most obvious proof of which is provided by its demographic behaviour. Indeed, the tendency to consider its high fertility rate as evidence of immorality, fecklessness or 'savageness' on the part of the working class is nonsense. On the contrary, this level of fertility involved a strategy which made sense at a given point in the process of industrialization. In the same way, the adoption of contraception resulted from a conscious will to adapt to the new social and economic conditions which resulted when industrial production had been developed. This well-known example illustrates the way families were able to adapt, even during the harshest periods of capitalist domination. The multiple functions of kinship networks provide a further illustration of the family's ability to resist.

Proto-industry: transformations of the family

Industry did not begin with the Industrial Revolution. In the countries of Europe there existed a dispersed rural industry located close to sources of energy like rivers and mines. A small number of workers would gather in workshops, operating in small units of production. The worker was not cut off from working in the fields, and pluri-activity was the rule. Such semi-worker and semi-rural households still belonged to their place of origin, forming part of the local community and participating in its traditional culture. Family structures and roles had continuity within a wholly rural context.

As a worker family still country-based and perpetuating the craftsmen and manufacturers of the *ancien régime*, the proto-industrial family did not disappear with the advent of large-scale industry but formed its necessary complement, whose degree of development varied from one industrial sector and country to another. At the beginning of industrialization, the industrial entrepreneur could not meet the growth in demand from his factories. He would distribute the necessary primary material about the countryside, among peasant craftsmen working in a family context, and later collect the finished products. Even in England until the

1840s, large quantities of industrial production came out of family workshops. Towns like Manchester and Liverpool were more like commercial crossroads linking a network of villages dominated by manufacturing production than large industrial cities. Indeed, the real launch of English industry was marked by the large-scale exploitation of coal, iron and steel, associated with the rapid development of towns.

In the proto-industrial system, commonly called the sweating system, the outworker was dependent on his contractor, who acted as the inter-mediary between the supplier of primary materials and the factory which bought the finished or semi-finished goods. Can the rural worker be viewed as representing an economy based simultaneously on two resources, land and outwork? This is unlikely, because such peasant workers drew the main part of their income from working at home for very low and insecure wages. They were obliged to work long hours all day, involving their wives and children in the common task. Whenever there was a fall in demand due to overproduction, the outworkers were the first to lose orders. This intensive system of exploitation did at least have the

A Lancashire Workingman, who now lives, "rent free," in his "own home."

The model English working man: thanks to his savings he is now the proud owner of his own house. Nineteenth-century engraving. Mansell Collection.

advantage of not disrupting the domestic group. As with the peasant household, the proto-industrial domestic group identified, possibly to an even greater degree, with a unit of production in which every viable contribution, from the youngest to the oldest member, was made use of.

Thus it is not surprising that multiple households involving the co-residence of several related couples, married brothers, ascendants and nephews, persisted in the proto-industrial family, since the underlying stategy involved assembling as many hands as possible to increase production. Leboutte (1983) has studied the lower Meuse valley, where artisan households lived by working for the powerful arms-manufacturing industry in Liège. Each house had a little forge attached to it, and the whole family was employed in the work. Unlike poor peasant households, which often placed their children in service with other houses at a fairly young age, these kept their adolescent and even adult children at home to compensate for the low wages. Maintaining this sort of 'large' family was one way of spreading poverty over the greatest number of people.

The weaving industry exemplifies the way family workshops persisted, scattered over the countryside, conjointly with the central unit of production, both in the Lyons region and in northern France. Lequin (1977, pp. 15–18) states that there were 20,000 peasant workers in upper Vivarais, Vercors and the Dauphiné, producing *ratines* and *cadis* (woollen cloths); canvas was woven in the family workshops of Voiron. Even the forms of production commonly called industrial came, in the second half of the nineteenth century, out of workshops which turned workers into 'proletarian proprietors'. The whole family workforce was set to work; the worker was subjected to the economics of international trade, and very harshly. However, he did own, in part at least, his means of production and could sometimes employ a few journeymen (Lequin, 1977, p. 44). An identical system was adopted in northern France. The factories of Amiens were based on weaving done in workshops scattered around the neighbouring countryside as far as 40 km to the south, which spread, as Pierrard (1976) tells us, the manufacture of cotton velvet, Utrecht velvet for furnishings and satin for shoes among 40,000 workers who derived a living from this uncertain form of employment.

Industrialization in the countryside thus prolonged traditional family structures, preserved links of dependency between the generations and maintained the power of mutual-help networks provided by kin and neighbourhood, as well as extending the frameworks which structured village values and customs to include workers. However, this mode of production introduced a new social form to the roles within the household: the distribution of work between the sexes was no longer respected as it was in the unit of agricultural production. Husband and wife were both chained to their trade for twelve or fourteen hours a day, or even longer. In the case of industries dominated by female labour, a real reversal of roles occurred. In Dauphiné, where the women did piecework for the glove industry, the husband made the soup and looked after the children so as to allow his wife more time for her work. It would sometimes be incumbent on the wife to maintain relations with the middleman who supplied the workforce and paid for the finished pieces. On her would fall the task of negotiating prices, which was often done in the café. Compared with the way the rural agricultural world was organized, this really was the world turned upside down, with the men staying at home and the women going out.

The way marriages were formed among proto-industrial workers also showed specific features. First, the age at marriage rose because parents tried to keep young adults at home as long as possible on account of their work contribution, which was highly valued. Second, marriages were marked by a very strong socio-professional endogamy. In villages which included weavers and cultivators, each group closed in on itself. This is understandable in the case of agriculturalists, but seems less obvious in the case of weavers. Nevertheless, setting up as husband and wife presupposed ownership of the tools of production, one or two looms, and possession of a skill which a peasant girl would know nothing of. Thus endogamy levels among weavers and other worker categories were very high.

This way of living was also accompanied by a very high level of fertility; children represented a burden for only a brief period since they were productive by the age of seven. Thus David Levine (1983) estimates that until 1850, the greater part of industrial growth in England must be attributed to the practice of putting women and children to work in family workshops; this period coincides precisely with the explosive demographic thrust referred to above.

All such households had their share of poverty and lengthy working hours, and all commanded a contribution from all hands in the home, from the smallest to the oldest member strong enough to work. Even so, their wages dwindled steadily, gradually forcing these rural craftsmen to take the road to the city and work in factories. Their departure corresponded with a new phase of industrialization linked to the development of the heavy industries, coal, iron and steel, which required a concentration of labour in the places of production. This phase occurred earlier and more brutally in England than in France. Furthermore, in the latter country, the existence of old urban corporations slowed down the development of an urban proletariat, as Sewell explains

(1983, pp. 213–15). In the textile industry, the craftsmen remained the dominant sector of the urban working class during almost the whole of the nineteenth century. In the same way, in the mechanical engineering sector a new category of prosperous craftsmen was created who preferred to use the title conferred on them by their qualification, like locksmith or coppersmith, rather than the vague modern title of mechanic. There were as many models of industrialization as there were patterns of working-class family.

Factory workers: with or without the family?

While it is possible to summarize the model of family organization linked to proto-industrialization throughout Europe and North America, it is difficult to do the same for the workers employed in factories and living in towns. Their conditions of production, work sectors, wage levels and housing conditions were all so varied that their family patterns were equally different. Nevertheless, there seems to have been a clear correlation between pay levels and a worker's degree of 'familialization'. The higher his wage and the better his living conditions, the more the worker was settled and stabilized within a family context. Let us take Marseille as our example, since it has been thoroughly studied by William Sewell (1971). In the mid-nineteenth century, half of all its industrial production came from factories, mainly mechanical construction in association with the port and oil factories. The workers' social, familial and political attitudes varied according to whether they were in skilled or unskilled employment. Unskilled workers were generally unmarried and mobile; qualified workers were stable and married. Among the latter, William Sewell distinguishes the 'qualified and closed' trades within which endogamy was strong and transmission of the trade from father to son played an important part. These were the masons, coopers, tanners and shipbuilding workers, who also shared a specific form of sociability, meeting on Sundays in the *cabanon*, their fishing hut on the shore which was the setting of these artisans' social life. Their trades were closed in on themselves and hostile to immigrants; they had powerful structures and secured much higher wages than workers in 'open' trades like joiners, cobblers, metalworkers and painters. Their group was centred less on the family and more on a masculine form of sociability in the context of the *guinguette* (café), which produced the contingents of socialist and democratic workers.

In towns and factories, the workers' family situations were as various as their wage and qualification levels. The further down the wage scale, the harder the worker's condition became. Cottage industry had at least allowed the worker to survive with the support of his garden and his common grazing rights. Deprived of this prop and projected into a town which was often no more than an agglomeration of factory chimneys, and had sprung up without any housing infrastructure for the workers, the latter had no defence at all against the effects of the first age of capitalism. Authors like Hobsbawm and Polanyi cannot find words harsh enough to describe the situation: Polanyi writes of the social and material swamp of hovels; Hobsbawm sees the economy as organized in a permanent conspiracy to keep the labouring classes' standard of living down (1962, p. 1050).

The onset of capitalism necessitated low wages and an unqualified workforce: the factory was buying, at the lowest possible price, the labour of a large workforce required to perform the same repetitive actions, which often needed no physical strength – hence the recourse to female and child employment.

In Lille, Roubaix, Manchester, Liverpool and Essen alike, the problem of worker housing in the mid-nineteenth century appears as a blight on this period of industrial take-off. The first town planners and the town councils themselves were unable to manage the influx of workers who

English working-class family living in one room, early twentieth century.

came to find mass employment in the newly erected factories. Where could they live? Private speculators responded to the question by hastily running up cheap dwellings on open spaces in the towns. These were often insanitary, cramped lodgings chock-a-block with families, who found the rent a heavy burden on their finances. Every space, from cellar to attic, would be filled. In Victorian England in 1840, according to J. P. Navaillès, 14,960 of the 240,000 inhabitants in Manchester were permanently lodged in cellars, and in Liverpool almost 20 per cent of the population, a large proportion of which was of Irish extraction, lived somehow underground (1983, pp. 32–3).

The same causes produced the same effects in the working-class towns of France, where philanthropists discovered to their horror single scantily furnished rooms where people piled in together to be born, to eat, sleep, make love and die. At Thann, in the Kattenbach district, father, mother, daughter and son-in-law all lived together in two small rooms with four children; access to their dwelling was via the door to a piggery (Duveau, 1946, pp. 352–3). Next door, two brothers with their wives and six children, ten persons altogether, shared a room 3 m by 5 m in size. If the workers did not live in the town outskirts close to the factories, which were themselves built on the edges of towns, they would occupy the town centres, which had been deserted by more prosperous families in their flight to other residential areas. Houses intended for a single family would be occupied by fifty to sixty people, who could only thus afford the rent.

These dwellings were often closed in on themselves, as in the *fort* system in Lille, the *courées* of Roubaix, the *corons* at the collieries, and the courts in Liverpool, Birmingham and Wolverhampton. In 1869, 36 per cent of households in Roubaix lodged in *courées* which, as Pierre Pierrard (1976, p. 58) stresses, had been built on the rural edge of the town but were engulfed by its growth. The Roubaix suburbs devoured the countryside, and the workers lost their little gardens. Thus one hardship suffered by working-class families was their chronic lack of space, which is so necessary to family relations. Indeed, rents were so high that such families would be induced to take on a lodger by subletting a mattress behind a curtain, which symbolized isolation and privacy. In the Roubaix *fort* Frasé, a woman with five children paid 5 francs a month as rent and sublet the recess under the stairs for 75 centimes: at the time, the architects explained that they did not make their dwellings any bigger precisely in order to prevent such practices. In spite of the tiny size of these dwellings, working conditions often imposed co-residence on different generations of the family, so that far from nuclearizing the family, as was claimed forty years ago, industrial-ization relied on the extended family, which was capable of providing a

London slums – all neighbourhood children. Mary Evans Picture Library.

certain number of basic services, in the absence of any collective provision of social assistance.

In the Lancashire cotton towns in the mid-nineteenth century, Michael Anderson has shown that co-residence between young couples and elderly parents was more widespread than in the neighbouring country villages (1972, p. 229). The women worked while the grandmothers cared for their children. On the other hand, in places where metal-working or mining industries dominated, the households tended to be nuclear, with the wife staying at home. In Detroit, in 1900, extended or multiple families still numbered 17 per cent among black families and nearly 16 per cent among Canadians from England and Ireland. The proportion of American families of British origin was similar, but they would take in young lodgers, unmarried workers, which enabled them to make ends meet every month without sending their children to the factory (Zunz, 1983, pp. 213–14).

The lack of space meant that this sort of co-residence was endured rather than desired. Although farms in the countryside could also be very small, the fields and communal spaces provided peasants and rural workers with an outlet. In the towns, however, workers moved between workshop and domestic space, and the first town planners were so aware of their need that they created 'green spaces' in the midst of the towns. In 1850 parks and promenades were opened in Manchester with the aim, as Navaillès points out (1983, p. 22), as much of providing the workers with a distraction, conducive to morality and family well-being, as with a moiety of fresh air.

Working conditions and family life cycle

The foregoing examples cast some doubt on the claim that family feeling among workers was attenuated, which nineteenth-century philanthropists made part of their concern about the 'immorality' of the working classes. Less biased observers like Victor Hugo discovered the worker slums of Lille with horror, and acknowledged that the material conditions of existence in such places prevented any form of family feeling from flourishing, since they made it impossible to exercise traditional family roles and distorted the social customs of families in peasant society or during the proto-industrial period.

In those days the family had been a place of apprenticeship where cultural skills were transmitted; the child learnt from his father and grandfather techniques which changed only very slowly. However, the advent of machines removed the need for family apprenticeship: they did not even require physical strength; it was enough to supervise and feed them. People learnt their trades on the job and in the workshop, without needing their elders' knowledge.

The traditional roles of husband and wife had been challenged in the proto-industrial family when wives went out and settled transactions with their merchant suppliers. In working-class families, too, the vertical relationship between generations was disrupted. The father no longer had knowledge or patrimony to transmit, from which he had previously derived the basis of his authority: he arranged his child's work, saw his suffering and could do nothing to remedy it. This inversion of roles could assume extreme forms, as when the father was unemployed and the wages were brought home by his child who was able to keep his job. Furthermore, domestic skills relating to the care of babies and sick children, household duties and the preparation of meals, were forgotten. Harassed wives now had no time or energy for cooking. What was the point of maintaining a dwelling which was no more than a sleeping-place, and how could this be afforded when there was no room even for the basic necessities? Working-class women had the reputation of not knowing how to cook, and of putting a 'little something to make it sleep' in the baby's bottle. Such features show the process of proletarianization, in which women and children were forced out to work because wages were so low. This set up a sort of vicious circle, for instance in the textile industry: wages here were far lower than those paid in the mines or steel industries, since a female workforce was required and women could be paid less. According to Pierrard (1976, p. 143), in 1856 the cotton and silk mills in Lille employed 12,939 men and 12,792 women, working from Monday to Saturday from 5.30 a.m. to 8 p.m., 300 days a year. Children's wages, however low, often made all the difference between a balanced family income and hardship. In France, the law of 22 March 1841 banned child employment under the age of eight; between eight and twelve, children were not to work more than eight hours a day in the factory, and between twelve and sixteen, not more than twelve hours. This law was frequently contravened, and it was not until 1874 that the minimum age for admission into factories was raised to twelve and the length of the working day for children was limited to six hours. In fact, it was only Jules Ferry's school attendance laws which succeeded in limiting children's working hours (Sandrin, 1982).

Being small, children were particularly useful in mines and textile factories, where they could slide under the machines while they were still running, to retie broken threads and gather waste cotton; all these jobs were performed on their stomachs or backs (Sandrin, 1982, p. 112). Indeed, these children's wages were so important that they account for fertility levels among workers. The large family, and thus the non-adoption of contraception, constituted workers' response to the conditions of proletarianization during the first phase of capitalism.

The wages earned by father, mother and children were pooled in one income which over the years followed a cycle in which periods of relative prosperity alternated with periods of hardship. When the children were young and their mother found working difficult, the income was often inadequate. At Roubaix in 1862, one household was able to enhance its finances by putting all five members (father, mother and three children) out to work: their total wages amounted to 1,150 francs and their outgoings to 1,000 francs (Pierrard, 1976, p. 143). However, as their children grew up and left home, the parents' income fell, although their expenses, notably the rent, remained constant. Towards the end of their family life cycle, the parents faced difficulties which got worse as they grew older and more infirm, in a system devoid of any form of social safety net.

More often than not, family budgets would be in deficit, as was that of the Mulhouse dyer who was working along with four of his five children in 1858: their resources came to 104 francs and their rent to 8.50 francs: they spent 87.25 francs on food, 21 francs on heating and maintenance; their total outgoings came to 116.75 francs, with a deficit of 12.75 francs

(Sandrin, 1982, p. 135). In 1857 in Lille, 16,688 destitute persons were counted from among 78,641 inhabitants; 4,000 families were regularly succoured by the alms office. At Manchester in 1842, one quarter of the population resorted to middle-class charity (Hobsbawm, 1962, p. 1059). It is in this context that worker 'immorality' must be placed, the most tangible signs of which were, according to observers, the rise of concubinage and illegitimacy.

It is simplistic to link working-class families with concubinage. Certainly the poorest elements were less likely to marry, such as immigrant workers without the means to pay for the administrative formalities necessary for marriage. However, although one might expect to find the highest percentage of legitimate couples among workers enjoying adequate wages, it can be observed that more prosperous men sometimes delayed marriage in the hope of marrying a girl from a social category they considered superior and thus achieving upward mobility, whereas there was nothing to prevent a young proletarian from marrying very young in order to pool his and his wife's wages. Women who got involved in illegitimate unions paid a specially high social price if the relationship broke down; workers who abandoned their partners were often condemning them to prostitution. Among the poorest Italian households in Florence at the beginning of the nineteenth century, a large number of women were heads of family; these were families which had become matricentral out of poverty, as often happens nowadays in the least privileged groups in society.

Illegitimacy was linked to proletarianization. At Mulhouse, according to Jean Sandrin, half of the weavers' children were born outside wedlock, whereas in the case of foremen's children, the proportion was only one in forty (1982, p. 156). The proportion of marriages increased steadily up the wages and qualifications ladder, and was often characterized by socio-professional endogamy. In the United States this was matched by a very stong ethnic endogamy: thus in Detroit, which Olivier Zunz has studied, it was all the more pronounced in that the ethnic groups were more concentrated in geographical terms. Of married Germans in the United States 78.4 per cent had married German women or women born in the US of German parents; 86 per cent of Polish marriages and 72 per cent of Russian ones were contracted within their own ethnic communities. Semi-skilled and unskilled workers were mainly recruited from among these nationalities. As these people rose up the qualifications ladder, they adopted exogamic practices, notably in the case of Americans, English and French Canadians. Irish and Polish white-collar workers, however, were still strongly influenced by their own cultures, and endogamy was as prevalent with them as in the working class (Zunz, 1983, p. 209).

The working-class family: strategies and resistance

However great the disintegration brought on by the psychological and moral impoverishment consequent to the conditions of production and low wages, the working-class family resisted, and provided the household with a framework and kinship networks. The domestic group continued to be the place where family strategy was determined, and kinship networks continued to fulfil many social functions. In spite of the very narrow margin of choice and action available to them, the decisions taken by working-class households had a general impact on the way industrialization and capitalism evolved in the course of history. The above example of the Marseille workers demonstrates the interrelation between family structures and degree of involvement in politics and union activity. The people who promoted worker housing and allotments were well aware that the time which men devoted to their homes and to gardening was time that would otherwise be spent in cafés and collective action, whether trade union or political in nature. The decisions taken by families about whether to maintain their level of fertility or to adopt birth control had indirect but perceptible effects on employment levels. In the textile industries in France, England and the northern United States, workers had struggled to retain their family frameworks within the factories, so that the unit of father, mother and children could be reconstituted in the workshops. Thus Hareven (1977, p. 196) has shown that in the Amoskeag textile factory in Manchester, New Hampshire the workshops were set up on simultaneously ethnic and familial bases.

Far from losing all functional attributes, kinship networks often eased the process of gaining employment in firms. In the English cotton industry, the first trade unions called on their members to secure the exclusive support of their own sons, brothers and nephews. The workshop could thus revert to being the place where families transmitted their technical skills from father to son. In the large firms in the Paris region such as the Papeteries de la Seine at Nanterre, which had a good reputation as employers and offered high wages, it was not rare for entire families extending over several generations to be employed and, with worker housing close to the factory, the workers' children would strengthen the integration between housing, family and work by contracting endogamous marriages. It is well known that kinship networks played an active role in welcoming the newly arrived provincial migrant, finding him somewhere to live and facilitating as far as possible his integration into the town. What these networks of worker kinsmen had lost through geographical mobility was their role as holders of local power, and sometimes their function as a means of social identification at local level. Thus the family framework was not rejected by the working class, which simply repudiated the middle-class values that philanthropists and industrialists were seeking to give it.

The family as a bourgeois ideal

As a direct product of capitalism, the division between social classes with different ways of living, values and attitudes was accentuated in the nineteenth century.

The diversity of working-class families was paralleled by a mosaic of bourgeois families; there were many kinds of bourgeoisie, from the upper to the lower middle classes, differing from one income level and one country to another. They all, however, shared an ideology which unified them over and above their material distinctions, by placing at the centre of their values a family model which played a considerable social role during the nineteenth century, both within domestic groups and kinship networks.

The family lay at the heart of the bourgeois pattern and was defined as the place of order, the conveyor of a powerful normative model, every discrepancy from which was considered a dangerous form of social deviance. In this crucible were refined the values necessary for individual achievement, the fruit of moral virtues which had been inculcated in the course of a long process of socialization.

Although not all middle-class families were the families of industrialists, the latter provided an archetypal image for this new class which specifically aimed at providing a model for its workers. Whether the families involved lived in northern, eastern or central France, both husband and wife together occupied an important position at the onset of industrialization. The corporate name adopted by firms often combined two family names because the marriage had been the occasion for the association of two sources of capital and two forces of energy in the business. In this sense, the anecdote about Pauline Motte-Brédard, the founder of the powerful Motte tribe, who gave out the day's work to her workers on her wedding morning with orange blossom in her hair, is revealing (Pierrard, 1976, p. 160). The expression 'family business' says it all: the kin provided the technical knowledge, the commercial outlets and the capital.

Take the case of a cotton firm at Héricourt on the edge of the Vosges: six generations of the same kin succeeded one another at its head; these were the Méquillet-Noblot family studied by Fohlen (1955). Like many industrialist families, they did not practise birth control. Their children did not represent a growing burden with each generation; on the contrary they constituted a solid network of social and commercial relations as well as a means of acquiring and renewing technical abilities. Industrial transactions were facilitated by maintaining an active correspondence between the branches of the family. The Méquillet in Paris gave their Héricourt relatives advice, and facilitated their banking operations in the capital. The Méquillet in Le Havre supplied the factory with cotton. They set their sons up in Colmar and Strasbourg with the task of recruiting qualified workers. Thanks to this very considerable family assistance, the firm was able to grow from workshop status in 1811 into a large enterprise which by 1855 had a mill in Chevret, along with worker dwellings called *casernes* with a schoolroom, and a unit at Héricourt which included printing, dyeing and drying shops and storage, as well as hand and machine looms and a hemp mill. Following the proto-industrial pattern described above, the factory gave out making-up work in the

Group portrait of a bourgeois family. Maude Royden with her brothers and sisters, *c.*1887. Mary Evans Picture Library.

surrounding countryside until 1870. The firm's own capital resources were considerable, and in 1860 it was able to supply 100,000 francs of its own money to buy a new plant.

In the same way, in the middle classes, the family was fundamental to running a business. Faure's study of the Parisian grocery trade in the nineteenth century (1979) has shown how both spouses had to work and how important the wife's dowry was, since, combined with a loan, it formed the firm's initial capital. He points out that these funds circulated along family networks, thus to some extent bringing peasant wealth into urban trade. Although large groceries were transmitted from father to son, great social mobility reigned in small shops where the children were committed to different fates. Leaving commerce was the surest way of rising socially, in the civil service or one of the liberal professions. Marriage marked the establishment of a bourgeois family. It was the subject of complicated inheritance strategies, similar to those of wealthy peasants who joined their patrimonies together at their children's

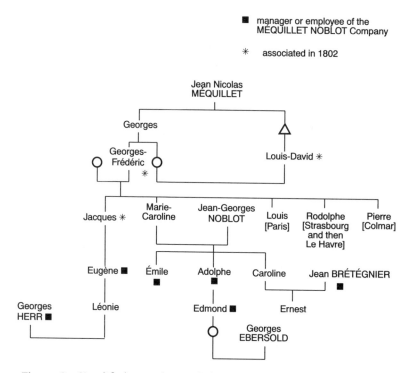

Figure 9 Simplified genealogy of the Méquillet-Noblot family (after Fohlen, 1955)

marriage. The wife's dowry was important in providing the young couple with the means to set up home together.

Although bourgeois women were often involved in the production process in the first period of capitalism, they later withdrew from it to devote themselves to raising their children and furthering social relations. This withdrawal of bourgeois women from commercial life became more marked as society diversified, with the growth of the civil service class and the development of the liberal professions. Women were at the centre of the family mechanism and were valued as mothers, a role whose virtues the nineteenth century emphasized. Such wives often performed their maternal and domestic tasks with the help of servants, whose numbers, varying with the family's income could include a nurserymaid, lady's maid, butler and cook. The bourgeoisie defined itself by the presence of this domestic staff; we know of households which stinted on everything (including the maid's food) to ensure that they had servants.

Once housework was performed by paid servants it became devalued. Whereas in peasant families such routine household tasks were part of the general process of production, as they were to a lesser extent in worker families where the provision of food and clean laundry was still vitally important, they were now devalued in relation to paid employment and regarded differently. The workshop and office were places where considerable profits were derived from productivity; housework was relegated to secondary status. However, it did provide a point of contact for bourgeois and working-class ideologies in the late nineteenth century, when wages were rising and a campaign developed for the return of working-class wives to their homes, just like bourgeois wives.

Between middle and working class: welfare housing

Philanthropists and industrialists became aware of the human wastage wrought during the first period of industrialization. Their first attempts at stabilizing the working classes were directed towards its 'familialization', associated with improved material conditions, notably decent housing. Although some individuals in this field may have been partly concerned to develop their own business or to pursue moral aims, they were very successful in meeting some working-class aspirations.

In the course of relieving poverty, the philanthropists wanted to moralize by bringing families together and limiting the number of abandoned children, which had risen considerably during the second half of the nineteenth century. Victorian philanthropists in England tried to find an answer to the working-class housing crisis by promoting the construction of blocks of flats financed by loans at 5 per cent interest –

HOMELAND.

Childhood, happiest stage of life!
Free from care, and free from strife.
Time, when all that meets the view
Brings its joy; for all is new.

The conjugal family: a postcard ideal? Mary Evans Picture Library.

hence the term 'philanthropy at 5 per cent' (Navaillès, 1982–3). These collective blocks of flats were governed by regulations which made them more like military barracks than places for family intimacy and freedom; their inhabitants were forbidden to keep animals, paint or paper the walls or insert nails, in short anything that could contribute to making their space a bit more personal. Individuals were subjected to a strictly regulated way of life, notably with regard to 'the demon drink'; tenants were set to spy on each other and report infringements of the rules. Some of these dwellings bore the inscription 'Model Houses for Families', carved on the pediment above the entrance, which had a repellent effect because it reminded people of repressive institutions such as workhouses. Workers did not like dwellings of this sort at all, and there were in any case far too few of them to keep up with the growth of the urban populations.

Although derived from the same ideology, such philanthropic housing should not be confused with the worker housing provided by firms. The latter was undeniably successful and constituted a considerable improvement on the urban dwellings which workers had otherwise to endure. By offering his workers a house on an estate near the factory, and one more comfortable than was available in town, the industrialist was trying to settle his workforce, to ensure its loyalty and regular working habits. At Le Creusot, Schneider housed 700 domestic groups, i.e. about 2,800 persons around 1867, who rented their houses for between 40 and 50 francs a year. Housing estates were rising between Mulhouse and Dornach, built by Dollfuss and the Koechlins; the chocolate-maker Menier let out flats at Noisiel to his workers (Duveau, 1946, pp. 360–5). In exchange for this marked improvement to their living conditions, working-class families had to accept supervision and a moral and religious framework. The workers were thus provided with a context in which they were paid and housed by their firm from cradle to grave. Their children were cared for and sometimes educated, and then employed in their turn in the local work process.

Gardens for workers enjoyed the same success; as well as providing balanced meals they also appreciably supplemented family incomes. In country and town alike, the vegetable patch was now no longer tended by women but by men. From the point of view of the employer who developed them, worker allotments had many advantages, material as well as symbolic, as Portet (1978) has shown. These gardens contributed to settling men in their homes; they had to be square in order to make the most of the available space, and the serried rows of vegetables and fruit bushes echoed a degree of regimentation in the workers' lives. Order, cleanliness and care were virtues which it was hoped they would inculcate in working-class families. By again drawing close to nature and the land, fathers and sons could work together, with the younger learning gardening methods and skills from the elder, as formerly in the countryside. Thus the garden also had an instructional function: within it was embedded a real educational project aimed at the children, through whom working-class families, the philanthropists hoped, would find their redemption.

A *single family model: the enhanced value of being at home*

Michel Foucault has shown that towards the end of the nineteenth century, the Church, state, employers and benevolent societies were all urging the restructuring of worker ways of life around a family model which conformed to norms derived from the middle class. Notably, the sexual division of tasks and greater attention to children and the home were involved. Although imposed by the ruling classes, such norms met with a favourable response on the part of workers, who were keen to secure material and physical well-being for their children and to enable their wives to leave the workshop and devote themselves to the home. The declarations of militant members of the French trade union movement during and after the First World War (quoted by Robert, 1981, pp. 58–9) are quite explicit on this point: 'The introduction of a systematic female workforce is absolutely opposed to the maintenance and existence of home and family' (Comité fédéral national des métaux, September 1917); 'The woman's natural place is at home, and forcing her into workshop employment incurs the destruction of the family' (Bureau national de la Confédération générale du travail, 1919).

> In a society which should be well-ordered . . . woman, man's consort, is firstly made for bearing children, and then for washing them, keeping her home in a state of cleanliness, educating her little one, instructing herself by instructing him and rendering her companion's existence as happy as possible by making him forget the monstrous exploitation of which he is a victim. In our view, this is her social role. (Syndicat général des industries chimiques, 1920)

It may be noted that this ideology was not derived from the adoption of middle-class values. It differs from them notably in its insistence on the free nature of the man's attachment to his consort, and in its implied recognition of cohabitation without marriage. In practice however, it approximates to middle-class models in being centred on the child. Workers' demands for higher wages were often based on the argument that these would allow their wives to escape factory work and stay at home to take better care of their children. By the beginning of the twentieth century, the working class could adopt contraceptive strategies, and their children were less numerous, better cared for, better educated and the objects of intense emotional investment because, in the end, it was through them that the whole family would achieve its social advance.

The early twentieth century and the period after the First World War witnessed the emergence of a middle-class culture which had been made possible by higher wages, which insisted on the separation of public and private spheres and the value of well-kept 'interiors'. This culture was taken furthest in Britain and Scandinavia, where it is summed up by the motto 'Home sweet home', for which there is no French equivalent. Home is the household interior, an overdecorated and embellished space held in the highest value. Being the woman's realm, a considerable part of her energy and time is invested in it. A whole series of specialist publications sprang up to advise woman about achieving personal fulfilment through decorating, embroidery, etc. The English and Americans even minted a new term 'home-making', which designated every activity intended for the home. Löfgren (1984, p. 460) has shown that in Sweden, between the 1880s and 1920s, the new family ideology coming from the middle class revolved around the notion of home as a private sphere, the couple formed by love, and the insistence on bringing up their children. This model was slowly imposed on working-class families which had previously experienced a marked division between the sexes, with male sociability organized around drinking, and female neighbourhood solidarity playing a considerable role on its side. The emergence of the idea of home, the care of which was entrusted to the wife, was based not solely on a technical division of tasks. Being at home was invested with all the virtues, as opposed to the outside world, which epitomized human and social disorder:

Private sphere	Public sphere
home	outside world
leisure time	working time
family	non-family relations
personal and intimate relationships	impersonal and anonymous relationships
proximity	distance
legitimate love and sexuality	illegitimate sexuality
feeling and irrationality	rationality and efficiency
morality	immorality

warmth, light and softness	
harmony and wholeness	division and dissonance
natural and sincere life	artificial and affected life

It may well be thought that this ideological opposition is still relevant, reflected in such frequently heard terms as the 'bastion of the family', the family as a 'refuge' and 'stronghold'.

Mutation of family structures: a phenomenon on a European scale

The transformations to the family outlined above have shown how complex is the way economic, cultural and social changes are inter-related. All Western countries have with varying degrees of brutality and precocity made the passage from an economy based on an agrarian civilization to an industrial economy supported by different political and ideological systems. In the mid-twentieth century, however, they all shared some common features relating to the organization of society, and notably to their system of family, characterized by a family group generally nuclear in structure integrated in a bilateral kinship network with versatile functions. If, unlike the societies generally studied by ethnologists, the European urban family is no longer the dominant institution around which the other spheres of society are organized, its adaptability as an organization and its dominant position in the process of social reproduction still give it considerable implicit power. Evidence of its importance is found in the way family policies are implemented at state level, and in the attempts to control and integrate families classed by social workers as deviant.

One characteristic proper to these European families during the post-war period is the normative weight of a single family model, any departure from which is deviance, whether it is single motherhood, divorce or concubinage. Viewing the family through the demographic data which describe it, one notices that until the 1970s, the model was characterized by the spouses' youth at marriage, by the number of children sufficient to ensure generation renewal and by a relatively low rate of divorce. The middle classes' model was a fusion of bourgeois ideology with the new aspirations of the working classes; it revolved around the enhanced value of the 'conjugal family' and seemed to dominate the whole of Europe. Since the 1970s, however, the families of Europe have experienced relatively parallel evolutions, which may be discerned in population statistics, which are nowadays of such high quality that international comparisons can be drawn. Although these curves do not in themselves hold any answers, they serve to indicate new familial models. The most remarkable thing about them is that these changes affect countries with different cultures, traditions, religions and political systems almost simultaneously.

Demographic transformations

First of all, formal marriage is declining in all the countries of western Europe and North America. The synthetic indices of nuptiality show a regular drop in marriages after 1970. Since 1985, the situation has been relatively stable in western Europe, with a slight tendency to increase in Belgium, the Netherlands, Norway and France. In the United States nuptiality dropped, but remains at levels superior to those of Europe (see table 16).

Irrespective of the age structure in each country (and it is clear that marriages are more numerous when the younger age groups are better represented), a marked drop in the number of legally recognized marriages has taken place. This has been particularly acute in the Scandinavian countries and notably in Denmark, where the tendency for couples to live together outside marriage is growing to the point that in some age groups unmarried couples outnumber the married.

The drop in the marriage rate has been accompanied by a rise in the number of divorces. Here too an astonishingly parallel pattern may be observed, since it is around the years 1963–4 that the number of divorces in all the countries of Europe rose very perceptibly, although these same countries still had legislation which made divorce the sanction for family breakdown, accompanied by a procedure making it complicated and difficult (see table 17). In Sweden one marriage in every two to three is ended by divorce, as in the United States. In Denmark the proportion is one in three, as in Britain. The divorce rate in France was only a little lower in the 1990s, affecting 30 per cent of all marriages.

Divorce is thus more widespread, and new in type, in that most petitions are now presented by young couples, often only a few years after their wedding.

It is difficult to deduce very significant differences on this point, given that we do not yet have the necessary perspective to understand such a sensitive phenomenon. The rate of remarriage for divorced persons in France is between 70 and 80 per cent, which is less frequent than in Britain or the USA. On the one hand, figures from the late 1980s indicate that the rate of remarriage following divorce is slowing down in France as in other Western countries, which shows that cohabitation is gaining ground even among not-so-young adults. Although marriages are less frequent and divorces more numerous, the couple as such has not been rejected, as the figures quoted above might lead one to suppose. The couple is simply more precarious and is being tried out in informal cohabitation formulae.

It is nowadays very common for a young couple to set up together prior to their legal marriage or as a substitute for it. Although cohabitation was formerly stigmatized by the pejorative terms concubinage and 'living in sin' and was generally associated with the working classes (although this is an ideological point of view because, as stated above, there was not always a correlation), it is nowadays accepted. The practice has spread in different ways. In France it was generally childless until the late 1970s, with the cohabitants celebrating their wedding when a baby

Table 16   Nuptiality index (first marriages per 1,000 unmarried people)

		1965	*1970*	*1975*	*1980*	*1985*	*1989*	*1990*	*1991*
Belgium	M	992	966	854	746	620	659	676	633
	F	1002	981	888	775	650	708	727	681
Canada	M	993	977	835	698	615	642	631	—
	F	910	921	812	695	638	675	674	—
Denmark	M	1026	752	621	491	538	555	562	555
	F	984	799	661	532	572	590	596	587
France	M	1013	915	822	689	531	540	551	537
	F	993	919	858	706	540	556	563	548
Germany									
(former West)	M	913	896	734	644	585	595	593	518
	F	1102	974	764	656	598	630		
(former East)	M	858	969	901	789	701	685	639	563
	F	1037	985	920	812	739	759		
Italy	M	998	1017	894	764	680	680	651	—
	F	1024	1007	931	765	695	670	670	—
Netherlands	M	1131	1012	775	660	555	590	619	603
	F	1132	1063	831	683	574	624	657	641
Norway	M	921	922	755	615	532	494	521	—
	F	872	956	794	648	562	521	551	490
Portugal	M	1105	1187	1450	840	765	795	806	811
	F	1008	1102	1309	878	787	822	838	843
Spain	M	1008	1030	949	749	640	670	662	—
	F	982	1003	1024	735	630	680	650	—
Sweden	M	986	584	566	486	490	411	524	473
	F	957	624	628	525	525	508	557	503
UK (England & Wales)	M	1038	1009	840	750	650	629	—	—
	F	1002	1040	870	761	656	644	—	—
United States	M	1061	1068	827	806	751	—	—	—
	F	948	970	824	808	776	—	—	—

Source: see table 18.

Table 17 Synthetic index of divortiality (divorces per 100 marriages)

	1955	1965	1970	1975	1980	1985	1990
Denmark	18.5	18.2	25.1	36.7	39.3	45.2	44.0
France	9.8	10.7	12.0	15.6	22.2	30.4	31.5
Germany							
(former West)	—	—	12.2	23.4	22.7	30.2	29.2
(former East)	—	—	—	28.8	32.3	38.3	22.3
Great Britain	7.4	10.7	16.1	32.1	39.3	43.8	41.7
Netherlands	7.2	7.2	11.0	20.0	25.7	34.4	28.1
Norway	8.0	10.2	13.4	20.7	25.1	32.6	42.9
Sweden	16.0	17.8	23.4	50.0	42.2	45.5	44.1
Switzerland	12.6	12.7	15.5	20.9	27.3	28.7	33.0

Source: see table 18.

was on the way. In other countries, however, the birth of children does not in fact lead to legitimation of the union, so that illegitimacy statistics reflect differences between local definitions of marriage rather than deviant practices.

Although the extramarital birth rate rose most spectacularly in Sweden and Denmark to reach around 50 per cent, countries like France have registered a rapid rise only since 1977 (9 per cent in 1978, 21.9 per cent in 1986 and 26.3 per cent in 1989). Hence, in Sweden and Denmark, the first birth outside marriage does not seem to be the natural precursor to marriage, as far as the couple's own intentions are concerned. Nevertheless, we can point out that seven in every ten cohabitants end by getting married. There is no way of knowing whether the Scandinavian model represents the final phase in an inevitable evolution or simply an original model.

Fertility trends in all European countries have, on the other hand, been closely similar, also serving to modify the marriage model established in the period between 1940 and 1970. Legal marriage is becoming less and less frequent, divorce is spreading, and a temporary or lasting cohabitation phase is now accepted; to these transformations relating to the couple must be added the reduction in the family's size, meaning in the number of children per couple. Another curious feature is that the downward trend in fertility rates has evolved in the same way in all the countries of Europe. Irrespective of the political system and the dominant Christian denomination, whether Catholic or Protestant, irrespective too of the policies implemented by the various states, family fertility levels have been observed to drop in every country. France, England, Austria, Switzerland and West Germany experienced birth rates (calculated by the ratio between the number of births according to the mother's age and the female population of reproductive age) of over two children per woman in 1971; in 1990, these levels had largely fallen to below 1.8 (with the exception of Sweden, where the rate seems on the rise again). The Mediterranean countries, which underwent their demographic revolution later and which had fairly high birth rates thirty years ago, have seen their levels plummet, now accounting for the lowest of Europe: in 1990, they settled at 1.27 in Italy and 1.33 in Spain. In the former communist countries of Europe, fertility has also plummeted, though staying fairly high in Poland and the former Czechoslovakia.

Demographers are in general agreement that it is not children as such that are rejected, but excessively numerous sibling groups; the limit is set at about two children, with great regional variations in every country. In Italy, for instance, the northern regions such as Piedmont, Liguria, Emilia-Romagna and Tuscany have not been able to ensure generation renewal since the 1930s, and demographic growth is basically effected by the southern regions.

This drop in fertility in the European countries presents considerable problems for their governments, which feel quite rightly that they are responsible for their nation's future. The alarm which this elicits illustrates the way individual and collective concerns are connected, with the family as one of the points of intersection.

While this ineluctable tendency to a falling birth rate would appear to have to proceed in accordance with population forecasts, some of the most recent indicators tell a different story. Although the very rapid fall is certainly continuing in the case of the Mediterranean countries, some countries in northern Europe are experiencing a revival of fertility. In Sweden, the index has been above two children since 1989 and a similar renewal has been noted in Norway, Denmark and Luxemburg. The causes lie in fertility levels higher than expected among older women, together with the renewed birth rate among the younger ones.

Indeed, the stabilizing divorce rates and the slight rise in the birth and marriage rates, could give the impression that family models in Europe are in the process of stabilizing, after thirty years of disruption.

When all the facts about the family that emerge from quantitative data on birth and divorce rates, illegitimacy and fertility in Europe and North America are taken together, they point to profound social trends. First among these are the transformations affecting the status of women.

Table 18 Synthetic fertility index (average number of live births per woman)

	1965	1970	1975	1980	1985	1989	1990	1991	1992
Australia	2.97	2.85	2.14	1.89	1.89	1.85	1.90	1.85	1.89
Austria	2.70	2.29	1.83	1.65	1.47	1.45	1.45	1.50	1.50
Belgium	2.62	2.25	1.74	1.68	1.51	1.58	1.62	1.57	1.56
Bulgaria	2.07	2.18	2.23	2.05	1.95	1.88	1.74	1.57	1.47
Canada	3.16	2.34	1.87	1.74	1.67	1.77	1.83	—	—
Czechoslovakia	2.37	2.07	2.43	2.16	2.07	1.95	1.96	1.92	—
Denmark	2.61	1.95	1.92	1.55	1.45	1.62	1.67	1.68	1.77
Finland	2.47	1.83	1.68	1.63	1.64	1.71	1.80	1.80	1.86
France	2.84	2.47	1.93	1.95	1.81	1.79	1.78	1.77	1.73
Germany	2.50	2.03	1.48	1.56	1.37	1.42	1.46	1.33	1.30
(former West)	2.51	1.99	1.45	1.45	1.28	1.39	1.48	1.42	1.40
(former East)	2.49	2.19	1.54	1.94	1.74	1.58	1.41	0.98	0.83
Greece	2.32	2.43	2.33	2.21	1.68	1.44	1.43	1.40	1.41
Hungary	1.82	1.98	2.35	1.91	1.83	1.80	1.87	1.87	1.80
Iceland	3.71	2.79	2.65	2.48	1.93	2.20	2.31	2.18	2.22
Ireland	4.03	3.93	3.40	3.23	2.47	2.12	2.18	2.18	2.11
Israel	3.99	3.97	3.67	3.14	3.12	3.03	3.02	2.91	—
Italy	2.66	2.42	2.20	1.64	1.39	1.29	1.27	1.27	1.26
Japan	2.14	2.13	1.91	1.75	1.76	1.59	1.54	—	—
Luxemburg	2.42	1.98	1.55	1.50	1.38	1.52	1.62	1.60	1.65
Netherlands	3.04	2.57	1.66	1.60	1.51	1.55	1.62	1.61	1.59
New Zealand	3.54	3.17	2.37	2.03	1.93	2.12	2.18	2.16	—
Norway	2.93	2.50	1.98	1.73	1.63	1.89	1.93	1.92	1.88
Poland	2.52	2.20	2.27	2.26	2.33	2.09	2.05	2.06	1.92
Portugal	3.14	2.83	2.62	2.19	1.70	1.50	1.50	1.50	1.48
Romania	1.91	2.89	2.60	2.42	2.31	2.20	1.83	1.60	—
Russia	2.12	1.99	1.97	1.87	2.11	2.01	1.89	1.74	1.55
Spain	2.94	2.85	2.79	2.20	1.63	1.36	1.33	1.28	1.23
Sweden	2.42	1.92	1.77	1.68	1.73	2.02	2.14	2.12	2.09
Switzerland	2.61	2.10	1.61	1.55	1.51	1.56	1.59	1.61	—
United Kingdom	2.89	2.43	1.90	1.89	1.79	1.79	1.84	1.82	1.80
England & Wales	2.85	2.40	1.77	1.88	1.78	1.80	1.84	1.82	—
Scotland	3.00	2.57	1.90	1.84	1.71	1.66	1.67	1.70	—
Northern Ireland	—	3.25	2.67	2.78	2.44	2.23	2.26	2.18	—
United States	2.91	2.48	1.77	1.82	1.84	2.01	2.08	2.07	2.08

Source (and tables 16–18): Catherine de Guibert-Lantoine and Alain Monnier, 'Conjoncture démographique', *Population* 4 (1993), 4, 1060–3.

Changes to the condition of women

The 1970s were marked by a renewal in female employment in all the countries of Europe. There was nothing new in this; we have seen how important women were to the worker production process. What was new was the entry onto the labour market of women from those middle classes who had previously stayed at home, over a period which can now be seen as belonging to the past, devoting themselves to their domestic interiors and their children. A whole complicated body of medical, social, economic and cultural factors has led women to seek employment outside the home and on a permanent basis.

This feminist awakening was made possible first of all by medical advances in all areas relating to female physiology. Perinatal mortality and the incidence of all specifically female illnesses have been greatly reduced, and women have been able to free themselves from what was considered their bodies' natural curse. Through contraception they could avoid excessive pregnancies, while medical progress limited infant mortality. It was now no longer necessary to put six children into the world to ensure that at least two would reach adulthood. Nowadays this seems so obvious and natural that one forgets that it has only very recently come about, over the past forty years or so, and that some disparities survive, depending on region, social class and country.

As well as benefiting from medical advances relating to their physiology, girls also won the right to a better education, which gradually became identical to boys'. They gained access to universities, acquired degrees and wanted to use them on the labour market. At the same time the economic boom of the post-war years, the relative fall in the price of consumer goods and the multiplication of household aids made housework less of a burden. During the 1970s, it became more economic to buy jam than to make it oneself, and to buy clothes rather than sew them. It was more worthwhile to work outside, all the more so since household tasks had been implicitly devalued, though not in the countryside, where work in the kitchen and upkeep of the home were included in the productive process. In the working classes, a division was set up between the two spheres, which often turned female domestic work into the necessary complement to male productive labour.

It was the emergence of a bourgeois model which devalued housework by handing it over to paid employees. Since then women have aspired to enter the world of work, with the novel feature that, since 1970, they intend to keep on working even after they have had children. The economic transformations which took place in post-war society created a situation which called for a female workforce, as Commaille has pointed

Table 19 Percentage of men and women employed in the service sector (in relation to agricultural and industrial sectors) in 1988

	GB	IRL	HOL	DK	BEL	GER	FR	IT	LUX
Men	53	45	58	55	56	55	52	53	56
Women	80	76	85	81	81	88	76	67	88

Source: *Enquête sur les forces de travail, 1988*, Eurostat, Luxemburg, Office des publications officielles des Communautés européennes, 1990.

out (1983, pp. 71–2). This included the development of the tertiary sector, administrative services, banks and insurance companies, at the same time as the growth of market services in the spheres of health, leisure, culture, etc. This largely explains the new salaried sector, recruiting women who would not have worked in preceding generations. The phenomenon developed concurrently throughout western Europe (see table 19).

Although women with children were the first victims of the economic crisis in the late 1970s and early 1980s, they have continued to make progress on the labour market. In France, 75 per cent of women aged between twenty-five and forty-nine with one child, and 70 per cent of women with two children, were working in 1988. However, it must be pointed out that the structure of female employment varies considerably from one country to the next in Europe, with part-time employment particularly well developed in the Scandinavian countries and Britain (about 45 per cent of working women), as opposed to in France (only 22 per cent).

The rise in female employment has clearly challenged the model of the couple. This can hardly now be called traditional, since, as we have seen, it has become dated and can be seen as resulting from the rise of the

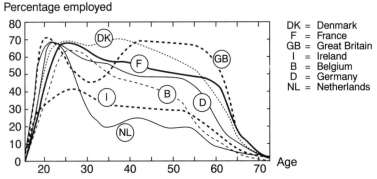

Figure 10 Percentage of women in employment in seven states of the EEC (1977)
Source: *Population et sociétés* (January 1983), 165

middle classes, embodying a model fused together from bourgeois and worker models. Female employment entails a degree of autonomy never previously experienced by women, because each individual draws her own wages. Even in prosperous bourgeois families, the inheritance brought in by the wife as dowry was not left in her hands: her husband would manage it. Paid employment, unlike revenues of an agricultural or workshop nature which devolve on the household as a whole, gives a woman the opportunity to stop living as part of a couple if she finds this unsatisfactory, just as it allows her to live a single life, because her pay provides her livelihood and gives her social status. Combined with the physical and chemical contraceptives which now enable women to control their fertility for the first time in history, employment has overturned the traditional image of the wife as subject to the double domination of her husband, who was not only the provider but, with traditional techniques of birth control, also had control over the conception of their children.

The couple has thus been profoundly transformed, being now based on a romantic ideal of love and, once freed of the economic constraints which used to weigh on the formation of unions, it has become the symbol of the individual liberty enjoyed by Western societies. A man and a woman develop a close relationship and decide to share their living space for an indefinite length of time. Cohabitation, and marriage too now that it is no longer so difficult to get a divorce, sets up couples for an unspecified duration; indeed, it may be for very long, but this is not part of the plan when the couple is constituted. Instead of getting married for life, people set up home together or get married for a period, during which each member will be able to pursue an individual agenda. When the couple appears to be drawing apart it breaks up, since to keep it together would smack of betrayal or hypocrisy.

This unstable family group is much smaller than its peasant, worker or bourgeois counterparts 100 years ago. It constitutes a small cell formed around one or two children, who are necessarily exposed to a very different form of socialization from that experienced in those sibling groups where the eldest children look after the younger ones. Such children shared a degree of affectivity and interaction which compensated for the reduced attention which the parents could pay each individual child. Limiting fertility does not mean that children are rejected, but that family life is programmed to suit the parents, not the child; the family's centre has now shifted from the child to the parents. Nowadays births are planned to fit in with the mother's job and the vicissitudes of her career, whereas formerly the woman would adjust her periods of employment according to when her children were born. Thus relations within the couple have been profoundly challenged in Western societies by the economic, social and cultural transformations of the last forty years, notably those affecting the status of women. Is this tantamount to saying that the family as an institution has been rejected?

New relations between the generations

We tend far too often to restrict the statistical study of the family to facts relating to marriage and birth rates. The immense changes in mortality have also disrupted the age structure, with consequences for relations between the generations. Life expectancy in the eighteenth century stood at around thirty-five or forty years; in 1992, it was about 81.3 for women and 73.1 for men. In the eighteenth century, the average person had lost both father and mother by the age of 29.5, whereas nowadays this does not occur before the age of fifty-five on average. The first consequence of this demographic revolution is that our time is witnessing the emergence of a new age group: adolescence. The effect of prolonging school education and allowing mass entry to universities, combined with difficulties in entering the labour market, has been to isolate an age group, which while more or less adult in psychological terms, is financially dependent. The internal complications inherent to this age group explain its 'crisis', which is to some extent expressed through an adolescent culture, pinpointed as a safe market for sales of drink, clothes and cassettes.

This longer life expectancy has also modified relations between the generations. There is a general tendency to refer to earlier families as large, with several generations co-residing under one roof, where property, knowledge and authority were held by the grandfather. However, the probability of having grandparents is far greater today than it was a century or two ago. Although the nuclear family model was gradually imposed on the Western world, the existence of elderly parents now makes interaction between the generations much more likely than in past centuries.

Not only are old people more numerous but they reach retirement age in good health and want to be active: hence the invention of the 'third age'. The first consequence is that the transmission of inheritance has been radically transformed; it no longer takes place, as it used to, as a single transaction at the parents' demise, but is spread over time. If a son nowadays were able to secure his inheritance only after his father's death, he would have to wait almost until his own retirement to set himself up. The transmission of property is organized in a much more flexible way throughout the family life cycle, with parents helping their children when they get married, even when they set up home without marrying, and subsequently at successive births. Furthermore, this older generation, which survives its own children's marriages by an average of twenty-five years, provides the younger generation with active support, which is returned with interest. All the studies conducted on European families reveal the importance of family assistance and the closeness of relations between married parents and their children. This help and these affective relations persist even in the case of unstable and informally established couples. This means that if the couple is in crisis the family, as an institution which unites the generations, is sturdy. Cohabitation, divorce and extramarital births have ceased to be deviant forms, and have been integrated in the whole process of family relationships. Even when the generations are separated physically, modern means of communication like the telephone and rapid transport allow close bonds to continue.

The functional aspect of these family networks covers the whole range from affective to social. In those contexts where close links exist between town and country, a great quantity of goods, services and information circulates along such networks, which can have decisive effects on the life of the couple.

Such, rapidly and perforce summarily outlined, are the broad features of the families of Europe and North America. There is an element of risk in pinpointing common characteristics, given the considerable variations in this large geographical context. Taking the social categories first (peasant, worker or bourgeois families), and then the occupational ones (workers, employees, management, etc.), we see that the first groupings do not match the second. Since also each country has its own definition of middle class, the distribution into occupational groups varies between countries, and since alongside the native populations (themselves often derived from former waves of immigration) there exist populations with other origins, which differ according to the state (Indians in Britain, North Africans in France, Greeks and Turks in Germany, etc.), it is clear that we must be alert to the diversity of families throughout the countries of Europe, even if they are only variants on an overall model.

The diversity of Western families

The term 'family' is derived from the Latin word *familia* which originally designated the body of *famuli*, or servants living in the same home (Benveniste, 1969, p. 358). However, this original content was gradually lost and the term came to designate the community of husband and wife, master and slave (ibid., p. 310). At this stage, 'family' implied the dual notion of kinship and shared residence, just as the term 'house' did.

Nowadays 'family' is still a polysemic term covering a whole range of contents which vary according to current speech and country. The fact that this term has become commonplace, at the expense of 'kin', is explained by its flexibility, which enables its semantic content to evolve. During an inquiry on the theme of the institution's crisis, one interviewee replied: 'La famille va mal, mais ma famille va bien' (the family is in trouble, but my family is doing well). By stressing the first syllable in the first *famille*, he distinguished the institution as a whole from his own kinship group, with which he identified in the second part of his reply.

The polysemic nature of the term is organized around a dialectic of exclusion and inclusion, which is tied up with the problem of co-residence. Nowadays live-in servants are no longer considered part of the family, which has thus rejected non-kin and is reluctant to include relatives by marriage alongside blood relatives. The expression 'to enter a family through marriage' used to be employed very much in this restrictive sense. When widened to accept both relatives and in-laws, the term excludes the notion of a shared residence. However, this may be reintroduced when the notion of generation is brought into the use of the term 'family', and when it designates children in relation to their parents, as in the case of the administrative term 'numerous family'.

Family, famille *and* Familie

If one and the same term can be used in many different ways within one language, it is clear that care is needed when looking at its counterpart in a different European language. Thus 'family' for North Americans designates the parental couple and its children, in other words the last meaning given above. An American will show a photograph of his children and call them 'my family' and, when the latter have left home, he will say, 'My family is gone.' The expression *parents*, which can be extended in French to include in-laws and blood relatives, is reserved in English for mothers and fathers, and its broader sense as used by French people is better translated by the word *kin*.

Do people know that the German use of the term *Familie* was borrowed from the French and only spread in the eighteenth century to designate the community of parents and children, with connotations of intimacy and affectivity? Earlier, the term *Haus* had referred both to the dwelling and to the corresponding social group occupying it (Mitterauer and Sieder, 1982, p. 6).

These differences of vocabulary are related to the different degrees to which kin are included within the family framework, and especially to the varying density of those kinship relations which exist in addition to relations between parents and their married children, and which are attested in all the countries of Europe and North America. On the other hand, the frequency and nature of interrelations with other members of the kin change, so that the thesis about the nuclearization of the family really seems to make more sense for some countries than for others, on condition of course that the two generations of parents and married children are included in this nuclear family. International comparisons are not easy in this domain because the study of familial relations is often limited *a priori* to that of these two generations, which immediately excludes the possibility of observing interaction with other members of the kin. Nevertheless, it does seem that the countries whose industrialization progressed relatively slowly, and which have a long rural history behind them, experience lively activity on the kinship level, and that this is far less the case in Britain, which was subjected to a more brutal process of industrialization and urbanization.

Different legislations and policies

Although there has been relative concomitance in the great legislative decisions taken in Europe supporting and favouring the birth of a new family model, it is nonetheless the case that great differences can be observed between one country and another where the law and relations between state and family are concerned. For instance, in France the law insists that property be divided on an equal basis between all the children, whereas in Britain and the United States, testators have free choice.

The relations between state and family can also vary according to the political philosophy prevailing in each state: they are characterized by the different degrees of state intervention in a sphere which is deemed private. Most policies have some sort of repercussion on the organization of the family: this may be indirect, as in the case of employment, or aimed precisely at the family, as in the case of housing policies.

One problem common to all the states of Europe and North America is the drop in the fertility rate. Some countries like Hungary and Romania did not shrink from imposing restrictions on abortion in 1974, which produced a temporary peak in the birth rate, followed by a drop (although Hungary has one of the highest birth rates in Europe). Thus pro-birth policies in eastern Europe have proved relatively effective, although it is often difficult to discern whether government measures or traditional attitudes on the part of couples have proved the more

compelling. Other countries have preferred to offer financial inducements, which have not been very effective.

The extent to which people resort to what is known as the welfare state
has also contributed to the modification of family relations. In France
social security policies have, in the name of the protection of children,
been directed above all at the least privileged families, and through them
at children: sociologists are inclined to analyse such policies in terms of
state control, dispossession and normalization. However there is a
dialectical relationship between the power of families and the power of
the state, evidenced by the resistance to pro-birth policies. In spite of
inducements, or because these fail to take account of couples' and
individuals' real motivations, governments have not succeeded in raising
fertility levels. Some have pushed social support to an extreme, as in
Sweden where all sorts of benefits were available until the early 1990s as
a substitute for what would have been provided through private initiative
within the domestic group or family network. Whether in consequence of
state encouragement or the emergence of new attitudes, fertility rates in
northern European countries have increased since 1985, in Sweden for
instance from 1.61 in 1983 to 2.14 in 1990, but it is difficult to say
whether these increases reflect basic trends or only cohort effects.

This is where the paradox of the interventionist state, the welfare state,
can be seen to develop. It is because of an alleged crisis of the family that
social programmes have been developed in the education, housing and
health sectors, which have contributed in some way to divest the family
of its traditional roles. In reality, the family has continued to occupy all
these domains, for instance by paying particular care to the type of
education its children receive or by increasing its use of medical services,
etc. Thus the welfare state has in the last analysis not deprived the family
of its former tasks.

When, in more recent years, recession forced the state to revise its
social programmes, a heightened revival of family functions has been
observed. It is difficult to evaluate the importance of the sector known as
the 'informal' or 'underground' economy, but we know it to be considerable in Italy and France. It consists of undeclared work which provides
resources in addition to those derived from regular work and unemployment benefits. This economy travels along informal networks, which are
often familial. Thus one of the perverse effects of the crisis in the welfare
state has been to encourage local initiative, community life and all sorts
of informal networks, and enable individuals to resume control of their
own destinies.

It is not totally fortuitous that sociologists are nowadays rediscovering
kinship networks within the Western family. Between 1950 and 1970

sociology postulated *a priori* that such networks were characteristic of the 'exotic' societies studied by social anthropologists. Nowadays the recession and its aftermath have forced them to acknowledge that, in the family context, the 'exotic' is in our midst.

TEN

Love and Liberty: the Contemporary American Family

Hervé Varenne

Papers about the American family typically start with a paragraph like the following:

> The American family has, in the past generation or more, been undergoing a profound process of change. There has been much difference of opinion among social scientists, as well as among others concerned, as to the interpretation of these changes. Some have cited facts such as the high rates of divorce, the changes in the older sex morality . . . as evidence of a trend to disorganization in an absolute sense. Such considerations as these have in turn often been linked with what has sometimes been called the 'loss of function' of the family. (Parsons, 1955, p. 3)

This particular passage dates from the opening years of the 1950s which, in the collective imagination of American social science, as popularized in countless books, movies, television series and newspaper commentaries, represents the classical decade of a real America that does not exist any more, indeed should not exist. The 1950s are the dream that is a nightmare, a pretext for ideological pronouncements that reveal much about the current situation. This is particularly true around family issues, from divorce laws to abortion regulations, from disputes about the distribution of condoms in schools to discussions about what authority to give social workers and others in ferreting out child abuse, etc. At one extreme, 'liberals' say that things are changing, this is good and policies must adapt. At the other extreme, 'conservatives' say that things are changing for the worse, and policies must reconstruct what has been destroyed. There is no consensus about the value of what has been happening, or about the policies to be developed. Indeed some 'liberals' are 'conservative' on some issues, and vice versa. There is however some agreement about certain facts, and, most importantly, about what is in dispute: in brief, a majority of the population of the United States has now experienced divorce, either through having been through one or through having been brought up in post-divorce families. A large proportion of the population, particularly among the poor, has never experienced living in a household made up of a father, mother and natural children. A vocal minority of the population, especially among homosexuals, demand the privileges accorded to families for their own intimate arrangements. These matters are inescapable, and it sometimes seems that the only questions worth asking should have the following shape: are these developments a good thing? A bad thing? For the adults involved? For the children? Such questions cannot be ignored, but they are not the fundamental ones for understanding what is special about the conditions of family life in the United States, that is, about 'the American family'.

The questions raised by the policy debates appear to allow for an objective answer which could then become the basis for action, and there are many who try to answer them, particularly in sociology and psychology. Others, like myself, wonder about the very source of the questions. What makes them compelling? How are they related to other matters? These questions are clearly of a different order, and they may appear not to have the same urgency and to reflect a detached attitude. I look at the American family as an anthropologist, as a professional outsider who has lived for many years in the United States, but was not born or raised there. There is every reason to believe, however, that much is to be gained by taking a broad cross-cultural view that emphasizes relationships between what may otherwise appear disparate and contradictory facts.

The family and 'family values', are areas of acrimonious debate in the United States. Before these debates can be outlined, along with some indication of why they are so acrimonious, one must first sketch the general principles that structure the American family. Only then can one take an informed moral stance. The presentation will proceed in three steps. First, there is an outline of the ideological foundations of American kinship, proceeding from the central symbols of the 'love in freedom' that justifies relationships and marriages. The act of love eventually leads to children whom parents must also love, but not with the same love that unites them, for eventually parents must let their children go free. In a second step, this chapter touches upon some of the problematic familial experiences that reveal both the power of the ideology and its limitations. There is an American way to divorce, as there is one to the framing of the relationship between parents and adolescents, or to the migration to

Florida or Arizona at retirement. Each of these complex events in the life cycle of the individuals and groups concerned is articulated around the general symbols of love and freedom, but involves different protagonists with different impacts on their lives and those around them. In a third step, the chapter concentrates on the specific difficulties that people in the United States face as they struggle with American culture.

The symbolic framework

Love

In an influential book David Schneider (1980) once summarized the structure of American kinship through three symbols: love, sexual intercourse and blood. Sexual intercourse is the mediating symbol. It concretizes the loving bond between a man and a woman, and, through procreation, establishes the special bond between parents and their natural children. Love, however, is what the family is all about. It is the core symbol around which all others revolve. It is not the passionate love of tragic romances, but the life force at the basis of all new social units: not only families, but also clubs, religious congregations, utopian communities, etc. The famous conservative slogan of the 1960s was so powerful because it played on the symbol: 'America, love it or leave it.' Better to move away than to give superficial adherence to a political system that one does not 'love', that is, a political system about which one is not convinced that it represents what is the best in the world. This slogan was controversial in the political sphere, but it remains at the core of the institutional and interpersonal politics of family life: better to divorce than to remain married when love is gone.

Thirty years later, the pattern of these symbols may have shifted, though perhaps less than it appears. Certainly, it is more and more difficult for conservative forces to argue that families must necessarily be founded in a sexuality linked to the possibility of biological reproduction. Sexuality, it has now been argued with overwhelming political success, is less about reproduction than about pleasure and love. Thus, and this is somewhat new but closely linked to the ideological evaluation that made contraception common sense, the gender of the participants should be considered a secondary, contingent matter, both in matters of sexual pleasure and in married love. Still, a distinction is maintained: pleasure is not the foundation of what remains a special state, that of 'family'. As it may have been for the past two centuries in the middle classes of Europe and America, the foundation of the family is love, a love expressed through a sexuality purified from reproductive considerations. On this basis homosexual couples, after they have publicly declared their commitment to each other – for example through 'certificates of domestic partnership' as they are known in New York City – should be entitled to all the privileges accorded by the American state to those who are married. Indeed there is a drive to push through the courts a constitutional purge of all mention of sex from regulations relating to marriage. Some think of this as an 'extension' of the concept of family to 'alternative' forms. Others, more accurately, think of the discussion as one that touches the very foundational metaphors that justify not only family life but political citizenship itself. This is too important a movement in American ideology for it not to be explored further before we move to examine its practical consequences and the difficulties which it produces.

The constitution of the couple: freedom, community and solidarity

Love symbolizes what unites people, or, more specifically, fully self-constituted free 'individuals', in a new social entity. This entity had no existence until they came together and committed themselves to pursuing the same goals in what Schneider called a kind of 'diffuse and enduring solidarity', that is one that is bounded neither by contractual limits (as relationships between employers and employees should be), nor by a specified time frame (even in an age of divorce most marriage vows still say 'till death do us part'). The entity of committed partners is more than that formed by a couple together for a few days or weeks of pleasure, it is a 'community' – a unity with others bounded by the personal involvement that first brought the people together.

The history of such a community ideology in the United States is a long one. What was made when English puritans founded villages in the seventeenth century after their transatlantic journey still echoes in a radically amplified manner when new groups emerge, establish their identity and claim their right to a space within the social matrix. In the earliest of American communities, a group of men and women got together and agreed to a set of principles that would rule their association. These principles were set down in great detail in a covenant. Being drawn up by small groups independently of each other, these founding documents differed somewhat, in both theological and economic terms. They were in fact the subject of constant dispute and amendment. These disputes led some to leave, sometimes under threat of violence. After 300 years, conditions have radically changed, but many groups continue to use the model more or less explicitly. In the 1960s many discontented people created what they called 'communes', and moved geographically to some place where they hoped not to be disturbed. Few communes survived, but new ones keep being established, though they are now most often regarded with suspicion by a public that fears 'sects'. More common are groups of people coming together to establish part-communities. It is not so rare, for example, to see a group of parents create a co-operative school based on educational principles different from those they find in neighbouring schools.

In the modern world, it may in fact be families, or family-like arrangements, that best allow for the realization of the community model on which America was founded. Not that many couples write explicit covenants when they get together. Certain members of the liberal intelligentsia do have very clear ideas about the political principles which organize their common life, and they may refer to them explicitly when sorting out such practical problems as who is to take out the garbage, who is to do the dishes or stay at home with the children. They may even draw up an actual contract – as the wealthy generally do, particularly on their second and subsequent marriages. Most couples find such contracts unpalatable, perhaps because marriage is precisely not a contractual matter. They will however negotiate who is going to do what; this may vary considerably from one couple to the next, and from one period in a couple's life to another. The results of these negotiations are the basis of the uniqueness of the couple, and act out practically the love which husband and wife thereby institutionalize – until such time as one of the partners reopens the negotiations, as a possible prelude to the breaking of the community. Love does not abolish freedom. In marriage one does not really 'give' oneself to the other – as the image may be elsewhere or 'elsewhen' in the Euro-American world. In marriage one 'shares' a self that remains one's own. Love, being about freedom, is also about separation. Marriage is about divorce.

Parents and children: the movement towards freedom

The ideological representation of the parental role is quite simple: parents are just as free to decide how to raise their children as they were when they decided to get married. This freedom, however, has an absolute limit: parents cannot make the choices which children can make for themselves, and the state is entitled, indeed required, to ensure that parents do not overstep this most subtle of boundaries. Parents enjoyed a freedom in the past for which they are now paying with the freedom they must give to their own children.

Anthropologists, of course, approach 'freedom' as a contingent symbol that arose through a process of historical evolution, and of freedom 'displays' as cultural practices that must be taught. It is not enough to be free, or to leave the other free. It is also necessary to teach what is involved in putting this freedom into effect. As much research in early interaction has shown, the first conversations between a mother and her child centre around what the infant 'wants' to eat, what clothes he would 'prefer' to wear. The questions are asked as if the mother expected that the child will choose something different from what the mother would have chosen. As child-rearing manuals emphasize, at birth the child is already a unique individual with a distinct personality which the mother must nurture so that it can develop 'according to its own desires'. These desires are not those of the parents, who must search for the signs that reveal the child's personality, and be careful not to mistake their wishes for his. Not surprisingly, the child soon responds in kind. The first grammatical constructions he learns centre around expressions of choice made in spite of and against parental choices.

A child's freedom is only fully established when he can make a community of friends for himself. To be legitimate, this community or 'peer group' must bring together a number of persons chosen among those known by the child independently of his parents. They will be drawn from school or neighbourhood. This group will be more central than cousins and other relatives, and will become the privileged setting for the rites that mark the various passages from childhood through adolescence. Baptism, First Communion and other religious rituals, even when they are celebrated, are rarely major family events, except in some ethnic enclaves. The major American rites are birthday parties and the graduations that mark the passage from one school level to another. One can thus see mothers celebrate the first birthday of their baby with the mothers of other babies of the same age. In a sense these babies are the baby's own community. As the child grows, he will impose a list of friends and the parents move to the periphery.

It has often been said that, in American families, the child is king. Critics have sometimes said that children in the middle classes of the United States can be quite isolated as parents shuttle them to the side to make room for their own interests while using the need to preserve the child's own freedom as a hypocritical rationalization. Taking all this into account, it would be more accurate to say that the child is a stranger, a respected guest to be taken care of. The fact that the child is not really a stranger in his family only makes the situation more tense. The child has not chosen his parents, and he was not a party to the negotiations which formed the conjugal community. He will probably not be either an active participant in the other negotiations that may lead to the break-up of this community. One might say that the child does not have a legitimate position within the family made by his parents. The child is not king, he is Other and will be independent.

The family after the departure of the children

The departure of the children to college, marriage, work and separate residence begins a period said to be difficult for the couple. Even if procreation is not quite considered the 'reason why' people get married, questions like 'When will you start your family?' or 'What will you do now that your family has left you?' are still asked of couples before they start raising children, and as their children move away to college and the world of work. Love is not about procreation, but the distinction between a purely lustful relationship and a loving one is a subtle one that children help resolve. After the children have gone, does the couple still form a family? The question may not arise literally, but it underlies a whole set of practices that constitute the specificity of the American pattern. In the best of all American worlds, parents and adult children who are now fully free actors renew the temporary links which united them. Parents and children are now equal and may establish a kind of community of shared interests as friends. Whether this does or does not happen, the next stage in the domestic cycle institutionalizes the separation of the generations. Parents try, and generally succeed, in making a new life for themselves, often after a migration to sunnier climes – towards a new America that is fully their own.

These structures are not merely symbolic; they are also practical. For many years now, a new type of real estate development has appeared both in the Sun Belt and in suburbs: condominiums arranged around an appropriately named 'community centre' with pool, tennis court and various spaces to hold meetings and parties. One of the things that makes this phenomenon interesting is the rules of ownership – actual covenants – which specify who can buy (only people over fifty-five without children, for example), what they can do with their property and perhaps even what will be the style of the community life. Children may come for brief visits but they may not reside there. Thus one can inherit the value of the property but not the physical property itself which thus cannot become the symbol of the continuity of a family. Indeed, to buy this condominium, the parents will probably have sold the house in which the children were raised. This house was not itself either the symbol of a lineage, for the rupture had already been consummated in the previous generation, since the parents did not themselves inherit a house that could have rooted their memory in geographical space. Nothing had ever obliged them to go for holidays at their own parents' or grandparents' homes, in the provinces, the countryside or even 'the old country'. There is no pressure on the parents to consider retiring where they were born. Any attempt to preserve a lineage is thus broken at each generation. Some among the very rich may attempt to control their children through the establishment of trust funds and the like, but this is tolerated rather than encouraged by the institutional system. No aspect of a family transcending the unit made by the marrying couple is recognized in legal documents: parents are not obliged in any way to leave any part of their estate to their children and may disinherit them. Once children have turned adult, the state loses all interest in the relationship between them and their parents. Love (and thus indifference, if not hostility) can now prevail.

Ideological contradictions

The ideological framework which I outlined must not be mistaken for a statement of statistical averages, or even for a hypothesis about what some people believe. Middle-class families, perhaps more than the families of any other social class, or than those of recent immigrants, may have more success displaying themselves so that they 'look like' the mythical image. It remains the case that constructing such an image is not easy. It requires a certain level of financial resources that many, in poverty or close to it, cannot achieve. One must be steadily employed; one must be able to afford what is significantly known as a 'one-family home' in an area where one can pay the taxes that ensure a good school for one's children, etc. When some of this is not possible, accommodations must be made, and the result may be kin relationships that are quite distinct from the image. This will be discussed in the final major section of the chapter. At this stage, I focus on practical, indeed existential, problems that America presents to the most committed conservative. There are many instances when the prescriptions of the ideology must necessarily reveal themselves to be in conflict with each other. It is ideologically clear, for example, that parents have the authority to organize the education of their children. This has to do with parental independence from the state. Conversely however, the state must prevent the parent from interfering with the child's own freedom. This battle continues to be fought all over the United States on issues of sex education, parental notification of daughters' abortions, etc. Ideologically, both father and mother are equally responsible, biologically and financially, in the development of their child; legal precedent through the abortion fights appears to have established that the father has very limited rights until the actual birth of the child. This has to do with the 'privacy', that is the radical individual freedom, of the mother, a freedom that may be limited by the love she may feel for the man involved, but not by the biological, 'blood' link that everyone recognizes between the father and the unborn child. This section approaches certain classical problems in American family life as directly produced by the ideological structure.

Independence

In an ideal-typical American family, the growing child has soon affirmed a marked difference in his tastes (music, clothing, hobbies, etc.), but also and above all in his social relationships. These acts of choice are proper and legitimate, but they are rarely easy, whether for himself or for his parents – even though the latter have taught him the need for such choices. And yet, at the crucial moment in his development, the 'teen-age' years, when the child begins to assume his individuality, freedom and independence, the process that actualizes the ideological model creates deeply felt tensions that have attained mythical proportions.

One of the most interesting of the things about those puritan communities of the seventeenth century mentioned earlier was the controversy that arose when the first generation started dying and their children could not quite affirm their own salvation, and thereby become full members and legitimate leaders in what had never quite been 'their' church and community. This was not a 'generation gap' as the phrase was used in the 1960s, but it may have been the first instance of a problem that remains: if children are free, and if adherence to a community must spring from independent evaluation, what are parents and children to do when the latter come of age? In the seventeenth century, the debates had a strictly theological cast while the models for everyday life in families remained European. In the eighteenth century, the question of independence took a political character. Later, with the explosion of industrial capitalism in the north-east, the opening of the frontier in the west, and other possibilities for social mobility, an economic twist was added to the problematics of freedom. The slogan of the time was the famous 'go west, young man!', to prosper far from one's family and all the other ties that keep a person in place. The 'self-made man' is above all the man who has not inherited anything from his parents. By the end of the nineteenth century, the situation had changed. One could no longer escape the products of unrestrained capitalism. One had to worry about the impact of the massive immigration of populations that appeared more and more different from the earlier ones. From 1900 to 1950, a great debate raged to redefine the place of independence in economic and social matters. Labour unions were accepted, or at least tolerated, a national retirement system was started and Franklin Roosevelt made it politically possible for the state to become directly involved in the economic life of the country.

In spite of these transformations, independence remained the foundation of sociability. One can understand for example the theories of education that sprang up around the work of the great American philosopher John Dewey as an attempt to rethink independence as requiring less a physical than a psychological escape. As the frontier closed, this may have been necessary to preserve a mechanism to realize the ideology. This evolved in an altogether Baroque manner through the popularization of Freudian ideas and the development of clinical and counselling psychology. The intelligentsia of the United States no longer debate divine predestination, but there is much concern with the definition of mental health. A true adult is a person who is 'free' from 'unhealthy' dependencies. Many of these theories affirm that nothing is worse for children than too great a psychological dependence on their parents, and much energy is spent in therapists' offices achieving a separation that a few argue actually goes against the grain of experience, and perhaps even common sense. The recent explosion of concern with child abuse and incest may be seen in the same light: the exercise of parental authority over children is always suspect. A child must make himself.

Such doctrines, particularly as they are inscribed in laws and regulations allowing state institutions to intervene in the household, make an extremely powerful network of constraints. Neighbours, school, church, innumerable professionals, all contribute to the construction of a graven image of 'the family' with which each family must live. Many of these specialists agree among themselves in affirming that the solution to most problems between the generations lies in a greater separation and even in the destruction of these linkages, and then they help their clients actually to realize this separation. In fact, the very persistence of such diagnostics reveals the strength of the familial links, not only among recent immigrants who may not yet be fully aware of the American ideological framework, but even among the most 'typical' of Americans. Thus, the disturbed young man who tried to murder President Reagan in 1982 was the product of a conservative upper middle-class family. His family went against their own feelings as they accepted the advice of a psychiatrist who thought he could be cured if he was expelled from the family circle in order to be independent, and so they literally rejected him.

Everyday-life dramas are rarely so intense. They are deep nonetheless, for there is always a tension between the ideology of independence and its ritual requirements, and day-to-day family relations. In general, American children, like children everywhere, are comfortable at home. But the scene of the car heavily laden with the miscellaneous stuff a child takes as he moves out of his parents' household is a scene which most Americans will play several times, as children and as parents. It is a scene that is placed under the symbolism of negative love, of divorce.

Divorce

On 4 July 1776 was proclaimed what is very significantly called a Declaration of Independence, which established the United States among the nations of the world. This declaration begins with these words:

> When in the Course of human events, it becomes necessary for one people to dissolve the political bonds which have connected them with another, and to assume among the powers of the earth, the separate and equal station to which the Laws of Nature and of Nature's God entitle them, a decent respect to the opinions of mankind requires that they should declare the causes which impel them to the separation.

One can recognize in these lines the great themes of individualism. The declaration has many of the features of a creation myth told as a triumphant divorce that puts an end to illegitimate dependency, and allows each party to affirm itself in separation and equality. The apologists of divorce picked these arguments up in the middle of the twentieth century when the laws ruling marriage were changed. In the current perspective, divorce is a liberation from a union that was never more than a political act. Divorce is not the sign of a disorganization of American culture. One could say, on the contrary, that it is the sacred act which constitutes America. First, children must divorce their parents. Only then can they marry. For many this first marriage itself is suspect, particularly if it is contracted when the couple is relatively young, 'immature', and the partners are not quite able to discern their true selves. An adult divorce, or the break-up of one or more lasting 'relationships' that have not been formalized, may be actual prerequisites to a fully legitimate, adult, free and independent marriage.

This is simple only in the ideological realm. In everyday life, the experience of separation after enduring intimacy is one of repeated loss, grief and disorientation necessitating major repairs. A whole class of professionals has in fact appeared to help with difficulties that do not have to do with any hostility to divorce. In the middle classes, divorce has

Table 20   Marriage and divorce rate

	Marriages (per 1,000)	Divorces (per 1,000)
1950	11.1	2.6
1955	9.3	2.3
1960	8.5	2.2
1965	9.3	2.5
1970	10.6	3.5
1975	10.0	4.8
1980	10.6	5.2
1985	10.1	5.0
1988	9.7	4.7

Source: US Bureau of the Census, Statistical Abstract of the United States: 1992.

become so commonplace that it forms the context of those who have not divorced. In many schools, the children of divorced families are now the majority. Two recent presidents (Ford and Reagan) were divorced, and so are many of the most powerful politicians. Divorce is ordinary, and the difficulties that accompany it must thus be the product of the ways in which it is constructed by all those involved.

In ideology and law, divorce is made to be something that happens between two persons, and to result in the severance of a relationship. In everyday life, marriage always involves a large number of consociates, and divorce, particularly when children have been born, is only a step in a relationship that, to all intents and purposes, will not be dissolved. Minimally, one of the ex-spouses will have to pay child support (and the other may have to go to court repeatedly to get the money); the ex-spouses will commonly have to accommodate their new lives to visiting rights; in cases of joint custody, the negotiations may be a daily matter. Sociologically, divorce should thus be understood as transformation rather than severance of a relationship. Paradoxically, one may never be so united with an ex-spouse as after the divorce, when it may become necessary to juggle two sets of in-laws, four sets of grandparents and two

Table 21   Marital status of the population (percentages)

	Single	Married	Divorced	Widowed
1950	22.8	67.0	1.9	8.3
1960	22.0	67.3	2.3	8.4
1970	16.2	71.7	3.2	8.9
1980	20.3	65.5	6.2	8.0
1990	22.2	61.9	8.3	7.6

Source: US Bureau of the Census, Statistical Abstract of the United States: 1992.

or three sets of half-siblings of very different ages. Marriages may not last, but the ties of divorce are for ever: they cannot be broken – perhaps because the state is much more active in regulating relationships between ex-spouses than it was before the marriage when the couple could claim a right to privacy that is abolished in divorce.

Evidence is accumulating that post-divorce arrangements are universally difficult. There are tales of successful divorces, but they are rare. Economic struggles are common, particularly for women who often end up quite impoverished if the divorce is acrimonious and the ex-spouse refuses to pay child support. There are emotional difficulties for grandparents, and sometimes even parents, who, because of the vagaries of custodial arrangements and the mobility of the population, lose any realistic access to the children. Above all, there is extensive evidence that children suffer during and after most divorces. There is no solid evidence that, in the long run, they do not adapt to what many of their peers also go through. But there is still a paradox here, given a culture that represents itself as particularly concerned with the needs of children. In fact children are only secondary parties to their parents' divorce: they have no right or claim, legal or customary, on the marriage.

The division of family labour

The great sociologist Talcott Parsons, in the paper mentioned earlier, gave an intellectual sanction for what became known as *the* American family to the American imagination, that later reacted against it. It was the dream for which soldiers were told they were fighting during the Second World War: a house in a suburb which a man leaves every morning of the week to go to work, by which he supports a wife who stays at home to raise a small number of children, all in the hope that the two of them will then retire on the fruits of their hard work. In both scholarly and popular imagination this division of labour was both natural and something to be achieved through legislation when conditions, whether because of poverty or older cultural patterns, were hostile. In earlier generations many women had worked outside the home, and many more did so during the war. But such situations were said to be socially unfortunate and psychologically unhealthy. For 100 years, trade unions had fought to take women out of the workforce so that all could enjoy an ideal that few had been able to afford. By the 1950s, it seemed that the American economy could produce this situation. It turned out that it could not, and that most adults must work outside the home.

Starting in the 1960s under the impetus of early feminism, and gaining strength since, ideological and economic contexts have radically changed. Women have rejoined the workforce. The modern image of the couple is one of individual workers joining together, with both participating equally in everything. There is no division of labour; all tasks are shared. This can be interpreted as an expansion of the foundational individualism which Parsonian sociology (and some recent psychological theorizing) contravened when it postulated an innate difference between men and women, thereby justifying their differing positions within the family: women were nurturant while men were not; men were particularly well designed to enter the public sphere while women were not. In a democracy based on absolute equality of similarly endowed entities, inequality must be explained through reference to postulated differences in endowment. The feminist argument that was radically successful in the courts and Congress stressed that differences in endowment may exist between abstract individuals, but not necessarily between sexes. Some human beings may not be able to do X or Y, but their right to do X or Y should be determined independently of any consideration of their sex. On this basis, more and more traditionally based male occupations were opened to women, including, recently, fighting combat missions in the military.

Two difficulties have not been resolved. They may even have been exacerbated. One is focused at the interpersonal level, in the midst of families at home. The other is focused at the national political level and may not be quite consequential: the conservative backlash against feminism reveals itself as not quite strong enough to reverse administrative evolution. Various figures, Phyllis Schaffly in the early 1980s, Dan Quayle ten years later, may make a name for themselves by emphasizing what was positive in the older models – generally by pointing to the difficulties contemporary children may have because of familial disruption, and the impact of their behaviour on other arenas of social life. Generally these figures fade away and the polity continues its move towards a greater integration of women in the world of work and political leadership. As feminists will point out when they talk about 'glass ceilings' and the like, there is still some way to go, but the distance already covered is extensive.

At the interpersonal level the situation is murkier. Men, in brief, demonstrate no particular desire to share in the world of the home, and all surveys of their participation in household chores and child-rearing routines confirm that the movement is very slow. At work, the state may regulate relationships, but at home and 'in love', a man and a woman are alone, conducting difficult negotiations according to shifting principles. In spite of all that has been said on the equality that should be established between spouses, it thus seems that, even when the wife works outside

the home, she is the one who directs familial tasks and performs more of
them than her husband, particularly when they concern children. She is
the one who takes the children to the paediatrician, who talks to
teachers, who organizes birthday parties. American women cannot be
said to be 'housewives' any more, but they are not quite free from the
house either.

Questions of authority

In America, no class or generation has any legitimate authority over
another. Nothing may be more foreign than Chinese strictures about
filial piety and the necessary respect which the young owe the old. There
is no doubt however that, through the simple mechanisms of differential
maturity and economic dependence, parents in the United States exercise
over their children a definite, though often specifically hidden, power.
Most parents have very definite ideas about the future they wish for their
children, and, given the necessary economic resources, they implement
their plans. American parents may not control the marriage choices of
their children. Neither can they directly control their career choices.
These are the absolute prerogative of the adult child, and there is little
that parents can do, even if they actively desire to resist the ideology,
whether on moral grounds or because they are recent immigrants from
other lands.

Parental control thus realizes itself indirectly, primarily through residential decisions that in fact proceed from an educational rationale, and
are dependent on economic status. On marriage, or at the time of a
decision to go beyond a temporary 'relationship', an American couple, it
is well known, establishes a new residence rarely related to the residence
of either of their parents. The choice of the location of the residence
depends on a compromise between what the couple can afford and their
perception of the quality of the schools in the town considered. By
carefully choosing their residence, parents thus control the set of people
among whom their children will start exploring matrimonial possibilities
through dating and other mechanisms. Indirectly they control where
their children may attend college, and thus their class position and
marital choices.

This control is quite indirect however. It is clear that, statistically
speaking, a good school district, or a prestigious private school, increases
the probability that a child will succeed. But neither ensures it, and one
can understand the anxiety of parents during the adolescence of their
children. What made the 1960s such a dramatic period for so many
middle-class families was the apparent demonstration that the 'children

of privilege' could consider renouncing what their parents had struggled so hard to give them. In the end, very few children actually renounced their privileges. But taking adolescents through school and college applications remains a painful process. Not all children do well in good schools. Teachers and others continually wave the flag of educational failure, or simply of educational mediocrity (not being admitted at Harvard is generally talked about as 'failing' to get into Harvard). Nothing here is experienced as easy.

Statistically – rather than experientially – the middle class reproduces itself in the United States as elsewhere. This demonstration remains a challenge to American ideology. Many cultures, like traditional India, place what Euro-America sees as social inequalities at the very centre of their ideology. In America the situation is quite different: any demonstration of group inequality not based on the talents or achievements of individuals becomes a scandal to be remedied through the strengthening of laws and regulations enforcing democracy. The disputes remain acrimonious even as some of the most glaring are apparently resolved. It is almost forty years since the Supreme Court outlawed school segregation, but in urban areas schools remain segregated, mostly because of residential patterns that are themselves the result of familial choices boosted both by ideological and economic structures. The bussing of children across district lines seemed a plausible solution for a while, but the idea does not seem to make much sense any more. Reformers are pushing instead for a revision of the tax systems that allow certain schools to have access to much more money than others. Others are pushing experiments where entire poor families are moved from inner cities to suburbs. None of these policies however touch the underlying structures that centre on parental freedom, and on schools as the mediating institution in social reproduction.

Diversity in everyday life practices

While the everyday life of American families cannot be understood apart from its institutional and ideological contexts, it is also constructed in an economic context which imposes other constraints. Still, the two contexts are really only one. A great part of the energy used in everyday life is spent in an attempt to put ideology into practice. The mother who asks her infant which of three types of mashed vegetables he 'prefers' must find these on the shelves of her supermarket. The industrial production of the country must be so organized as to place them on these shelves, and the mother must be given the economic wherewithal to buy them. In general, the realization of independence requires the economic means which allow the children to reside apart from their parents. This residence must be, if possible, the private property of the couple. If the wife stays at home, the husband must find an income that will allow two adults to survive 'independently', that is, without help from parents, friends or neighbours. Seventeen years later, this same couple will have to help the child express his own independence through such things as sending him to attend a university so distant that he cannot continue to reside at home, and major financial sacrifices will have to be made. Even the less well-off may put aside money for many years and even get into debt so that their children can go away to college. An anthropologist may see in this situation an example of early distribution of inheritance. It is also admitted that, even when the parents are comfortable financially, children should earn some money very early, and thereby begin to establish their independence. Thus, starting at thirteen, many young girls spend several hours a week taking care of the children of neighbours, and many boys distribute local newspapers. From sixteen, many adolescents work in restaurants and factories during weekends and holidays. All that can prevent a family who wish to look normal from living this model is thus a challenge.

Middle-class difficulties

Two situations are critical. For the children's independence to be effective they must find employment and housing. Depending on the economic situation of the country, this may be difficult to accomplish, and there have been times when adult children had to continue living at home. In the 1980s, when both the price of housing and interest rates were at their highest, it was common to read about the drama of young adults having to move back with their parents because they could not afford to symbolize their independence. The macro-economic forces that lowered interest rates in the early 1990s and allowed for a resurgence of the construction industry may reverse these trends, though some continue to talk about 'downward mobility' and the possible inability of the current generation to attain the level of comfort experienced by their parents.

At the other end of a family's career, the relationship between aged parents and their children is marked by similar problems. Above all, it is necessary to preserve reciprocal independence. Parents cannot be directly dependent on their children, and this is partly why, over the past sixty years, the social security system was created and continually reinforced. Despite this, Senator Goldwater, Republican candidate to the presidency, campaigned against it in the 1960s in the name of individual responsibility. For conservative Republicans, it seemed just that one should be poor in one's old age if one had not been careful during one's active life. As late as 1981, President Reagan attempted to limit benefits. He failed, in great part because the Republican electorate, an electorate that included many older people, made it clear that social security was not to be touched: actual independence is more important than intellectual discussions about 'responsibility'. Eventually the system was strengthened, and the taxes paid by younger Americans were increased significantly. In recent years the debate has focused on this burden: children may not have to support their own parents directly, but they are required to support the elderly in general. This is becoming an onerous task that threatens their own ability to exercise their freedom to produce an appropriate family.

Family networks in the working class

In its logic, the American kinship system is a-linear in so far as no mechanism allows for the institutionalization of a lineage. It is also intensely nuclear in so far as it radically devalues the extension of the household to include other relatives. It is not so much that parents and children do not maintain ties. These can be quite strong. It is, rather, that, in a juridical framework which ignores these ties, they must be actively constructed. Each household must maintain a body of familial lore through telephone calls, requests for help, exchange of pictures, reunions specifically designed to bring the family together (rather than the celebration of a rite of passage), etc. Certain households are parts of 'family clubs' that bring together possibly hundreds of people descended from the same couple. These groupings rarely become practically relevant in the everyday life of a middle-class family. There is evidence, however, that they can become much tighter when economic conditions get difficult. I have already mentioned the temporary extension of the middle-class household when adult children cannot get jobs. Such extensions are quite general among those who are perennially at the edge of economic disaster, the poor and the nearly (or working) poor, particularly in urban neighbourhoods.

There, family networks are activated that can associate many people dispersed over the whole country. Many black families have two centres of gravity, one in a large northern urban centre, and another in a rural district of the south where grandparents, and perhaps some of the adult children, are ready to take care of some of the grandchildren when the parents find themselves in trouble or even simply when they decide to shield their children from the influence of urban schools. In the urban centres themselves, similar kinds of networks organize themselves among parents and neighbours and they fulfil the same functions when unemployment, sickness, addiction, jail, etc. incapacitate parents. In these conditions it is not rare for a child to be informally adopted by an aunt or grandmother for months, even years. Until recently this was an underground pattern which welfare policy is now taking into account. These types of organizations can also be found among the poor southern whites who also find themselves obliged to migrate to the northern urban centres. European migrants generally were not able to build urban/rural networks, as they could sometimes do in Europe. The Irish, Italians and Poles had to settle first in large cities where they constituted for many years the reserve of cheap labour on which was built the economic success of the United States. The person who had just arrived had to construct a family separately from any network. The children of this generation experienced something very different: intense familial networks in tight neighbourhoods that had soon developed, and that helped with survival when conditions got worse – as they regularly did. Economic depressions and wars bring people together. Prosperity loosens ties. Thus, little by little, Irish, Italians, Poles and others moved to the suburbs where they are now mostly found. Through this process, America reconstructed itself.

European immigrant family. Hulton Deutsch.

Poverty and matrilinearity

This last generalization remains controversial as some argue vocally about the continuing relevance of alternative cultures that would be a deliberate challenge to the apparent hegemony of the middle classes. I have touched briefly on the issue of familial fostering, particularly among the black poor, through which aunts and grandparents take care of children for extended periods – a pattern that some would trace to West African traditions. The tendency of black families in poverty towards matrilinearity is sometimes used as another instance. Finally, there is much talk about the persistence of foreign patterns brought by not-so-recent immigrants perpetuating themselves in various ghettos. I expand on this in the next section.

Matrilinearity in the Euro-American kinship system appears to contradict both American institutional bilinearity and traditional patrilinearity (still alive in the transmission of family names). It has however been described as evolving quite regularly under conditions of economic stress, in England for example. This may prove to be related to the peculiar relationship between parents and children which a fundamentally nuclear kinship system fosters. As mentioned earlier, direct intergenerational links are deinstitutionalized, but they are not thereby radically broken. It is just that they must be locally maintained through such activities as keeping track of birthdays, anniversaries and genealogical ties, not to mention the exact relationship of children in a multiply divorced couple. Greetings cards must be exchanged, telephone calls made and family news and gossip disseminated. As far back as we have records for the United States, this seems to have been a female activity: women keep track of the extended family, including that of their husbands. Not surprisingly, in case of emergencies that cannot be handled through the resources of the household, the first relatives to be called will be on the woman's side. It is still more likely for mothers rather than fathers to be given custody of children after a divorce. Since *Roe* v. *Wade*, legal development has established the absolute right of women on unborn children, and may thus reinforce implicit matrilinearity. A mostly invisible fault line separates the father from the mother–child set. In case of 'family quake', the break will take place there rather than elsewhere. The result is something that looks like the family of American nightmares: the 'mother-headed family' from which the father is absent.

Poor blacks, and also immigrants from Latin America, have always been the victims of the economic conditions which make it difficult to maintain a couple together. One of the most famous and contested

436 Hervé Varenne

Table 22 Female family householders with no spouse present (rounded percentage of all families)

	White	Black
1960	8	21
1970	9	28
1980	12	40
1990	13	44

Source: US Bureau of the Census, Statistical Abstract of the United States: 1992.

pronouncements in American sociology is that written by Senator Daniel Patrick Moynihan, then professor at Harvard, later counsellor to President Richard Nixon:

> At the heart of the deterioration of the fabric of Negro society is the deterioration of the Negro family. It is the fundamental source of the weakness of the Negro community at the present time . . . The white family has achieved a high degree of stability and is maintaining that stability. By contrast, the family structure of lower-class Negroes is highly unstable, and in many urban centers is approaching complete breakdown. (Moynihan, 1967 [1965], p. 5)

Despite such calls for action, statistics reveal that the number of households headed by a woman continues to increase. From 1960 to 1990, the number of these households has gone from 8 to 13 per cent among whites, and from 21 to 44 per cent among blacks. One must point out however that what the census counts as a single woman is rarely alone living by herself with one or two children in urban isolation. A young mother will most probably live with her mother (or even her grandmother) and several of her brothers, sisters and cousins. This familial group is generally inserted in an extended network of kin who, to a certain extent, will help. These families then take a certain genealogical

Table 23 Rate of births to unmarried mothers (per cent of total)

	White	Black
1950	2	19
1960	2	22
1965	4	26
1970	6	38
1975	7	49
1980	11	55
1985	15	60
1990	19	64

Source: US Bureau of the Census, Statistical Abstract of the United States: 1992.

depth that is all the stronger when grandmothers and great-grandmothers are themselves relatively young and do not have resident husbands or companions.

The increase in the number of black female heads of households has been accompanied by an increase in adolescent sexual activity and in the number of teenage mothers. These rates continue to increase. Some have tried to explain this increase by hypothesizing a cultural difference between blacks and whites, suggesting that blacks accept such conduct while whites frown on it. In fact, black parents know that a young girl who becomes a mother condemns herself to a life among the poorest. But they are poor themselves, and are often the 'illegitimate' children of a temporary relationship between their mother and a father many do not know. Most will not reject this girl. They may hope for the boy to remain involved with his child without counting on it, and they will not be surprised by a separation. He may himself have children in various households whom he does not regularly support. Later, when the girl reaches her middle twenties she may get into longer-lasting relationships. Some of these may lead to marriage.

From a formal point of view, the picture that emerges is quite different from that of a middle-class family, but this is somewhat misleading, particularly if one discounts the effects of poverty and pays attention to an ideology that may in fact be even more radically individualized than that of the middle classes. What is sure is that the situation is too explosively political to allow for a sorting out of possibilities according to any canon of objectivity. One may say that, even if they do not marry as often as other groups, blacks in poverty do have powerfully structured families. What this structure is remains a murkier matter. In fact no one knows for sure the exact ratios of long-lasting relationships in which adults take extensive care of their children. There is an institutional fact which must make us doubt the accuracy of current statistics about household organization: there is no system in the United States directly to help families with children (on the model of the *allocations familiales* in France) and welfare is given easily only to households where there are 'dependent children' and no resident husband. There is thus no incentive to formalize a relationship that may still be real. Social workers who should report these situations often do not. What is more, the family of a young pregnant girl has no incentive to marry the father. The welfare money she receives can be merged in the family budget. It can also be used by the daughter herself to establish a separate residence if she is in conflict with her mother, or if this mother is herself a drug addict or otherwise unfit.

All this indicates that the increase in out-of-wedlock and teenage births is not only the product of a pleasure-oriented sexuality. If this were the only issue, the wide availability of contraceptives would have lowered the rate – as many expected it would. It is clear now that years of explicit sex education will not make teenagers use contraceptives when childbearing is socially advantageous. For poor adolescents, fathering or mothering a child is a sign that one has become an adult, and thus entitled to the privileges of independence. It is only for young middle-class whites that one can speak of an orientation towards eroticism, even though, there too, the ideology is that of the love which must come before desire. In any case, only a tendentious interpretation of limited statistics can allow one to speak of 'disorganization' to explain the absence of formal husbands in many households. Finally, care must be taken when generalizing statistics and ethnographies of life among the very poor. There is no doubt that, among blacks as among whites, as soon as material conditions allow, families take a decidedly middle-class shape.

Ethnic traditions

Some scholars insist that aspects of African traditions survive among blacks. Still, it has been more than 150 years since the last African crossed the Atlantic in a slave ship. Blacks are, along with the British, among those who have the longest history in America. The rest of the population is descended from people who made the crossing from Europe in the past century, and the extent of the differences that survive after three or four generations is quite limited. New immigrants are now coming heavily from the Middle East and Asia, and the debates about cultural clashes and a fragmented future have heated up again. These newcomers bring with them familial forms initially very different from European and American traditions. How far, and for how long will material and ideological conditions allow for the maintenance and reproduction of these forms? This is a classical question in the United States that has been essentially answered, as far as European immigrants were concerned: great-grandchildren identify with an ethnic label even when they have forgotten their ancestors' migration experiences, but their everyday behaviour is not very different from that of those who identify with other labels. Thus there are many contexts when people will not say that they are 'Americans', but rather that they are 'Scottish', 'Irish', 'Italian', or that they are 'a mix'.

This evolution was linked to a particular structure of immigration that may have changed. Until recently, the move across the ocean, whether Atlantic or Pacific, could not be reversed. With the development of cheap air travel, it has become easier for migrants to maintain contact with family members on the other side. Those who come from the Caribbean particularly, often preserve international networks that look like those which urban blacks construct with their kin in the south. Many migrants from Taiwan, the Philippines and Korea may thus find themselves participating in two different systems of institutions and customs with different responsibilities on each side of the ocean. It remains to be seen whether this will strengthen the older generations in their struggles to maintain a kind of authority over their children that is not really allowed by America.

In their first years in the United States, migrants' relationship with America can remain relatively external and limited to the world of politics, education and work. Otherwise, one can conduct one's life in a neighbourhood inhabited mostly by others from one's own old country. Still, external contacts eventually have consequences on everyday life, particularly as children grow up in public schools where they encounter the children of migrants from other parts of the world, fight with them and, not so rarely, intermarry. Only the most exceptional effort can establish the wall that is necessary to prevent this from happening. Mennonites have succeeded. Hasidic Jews may be on the way to doing so. What will happen to the Muslims and Hindus that are now quite numerous is still unclear. But one should not discount a liberal, humanistic, democratic ideology which, through its declared neutrality towards religious (cultural) differences and its massive zeal in attacking anything or anyone who tries to limit individual freedom, has shown itself to be radically corrosive of any pattern that differs much from its own.

The future

Talcott Parsons, in the classic statement that opened this chapter, was arguing against the idea that 'the family' was dying out as an institution. He agreed that it appeared to have lost most of its traditional functions, but he attempted to demonstrate that other, fundamental functions would always be fulfilled within the confines of the family. The onslaught against his understanding of one of these functions, the 'stabilization of adult personalities' through a division of familial labour that would parallel 'natural' differences between men and women, has made a large part of his argument seem rather quaint. The other function he mentioned, 'early socialization of children', may still have some explanatory value if it is broadened. With the closing of orphanages and other such institutions, the collapse of utopian attempts at communal child-rearing has become complete. It may indeed be the case that nuclear-like

arrangements may be the easiest for human beings to construct, and that
America, through its emphasis on love and independence, will always
make it more difficult for broader networks to institutionalize themselves. There is little doubt that, in the foreseeable future, most children
in the United States will remain under the responsibility of a few adults,
most of whom are tied by intimate relationships to each other, and one of
whom at least is related biologically to the child. There is no reason not
to call such an arrangement a 'family'. This picture does not say much
about the exact nature of the relationship between the adults, or between
them and the child. To the dismay of many, and not simply among the
old and conservative, and barring a revolution or other cataclysm, there
is no mechanism in sight for the reinstitutionalization of heterosexual
marriage as the only legitimate setting for adult sexuality.

This, however, should not be overinterpreted. The picture that is
emerging is not quite a romantic one, particularly if one looks at it from
the point of view of the ideal-typical life cycle: it will certainly remain
common for a young adult to go through a period of 'one-night stands',
more or less committed 'relationships' and two or three marriages with
the attendant divorces. This ensures a lifetime of loss and mourning, and,
for those who can afford it, counselling. Any one of the arrangements
may constitute a 'family' in the above sense, particularly when children
cohabit in the household. The exact nature of the activities within these
households is the interesting question since, as all adults work outside the
home, and most children attend day-care centres, nurseries, schools, etc.,
not much besides sleeping and toileting may be happening there. In large
urban centres, the development of cheap restaurants and commercial
laundries appears to take even food preparation and clothes cleaning out
of the home. This allows for continued talk about the family losing
further function to other specialized institutions in an ever more detailed
division of labour. There is only one area that strongly argues for
continuing to think of the family as a central institution: education in its
relationship with the reproduction of social stratification. All evidence
points to the fact that this is always mediated by the family through its
organizing of the educational experiences of children. Parents do not set
school curricula, and they may not have much input on the organization
of schools. They are however the determining influence on the kind of
school their children attend. Given the enormous diversity of schools in
the United States, this is something that is not likely to change soon.

This is profoundly shocking to the American liberal imagination, and
signals the need to see children as the ultimate challenge to the realization
of democracy. The conception of children is, on the one hand, a moment
for the radical expression of the parents', and particularly the mother's,

freedom. The state may not enter the bedroom; it may not regulate abortion. Once the child breathes on his own, however, his reality as a child 'of' his parents becomes a problem, psychically and socially. America is founded on the fully individualized adult, the 'self-made man'. It constructs a person who stands alone, psychologically and financially, and who then enters into informal arrangements with other independent adults while keeping the right to break them at any time. This makes children problematic: they cannot display institutional independence. As human beings they are ideologically 'individuals', separate and different from their parents. As children, they are malleable persons who actively construct those who take care of them as somehow 'theirs'. Their immaturity however does not allow them to be very effective in imposing their will on their parents, for whom they may be, above all, a practical problem to be resolved – through baby-sitters, day-care centres, schools, etc. There is a strong political awareness that this situation may hurt children, so that the further withdrawal of the state in matters sexual and reproductive seems to be balanced by further inroads into what used to be 'private' family matters. Welfare agencies already have extensive authority over the family life of the poor. Schools, starting with sex education, and now through many programmes intended to help children with family problems (alcoholism, abuse, divorce, etc.), are slowly being given authority over middle-class parents. This is and will remain explosive.

This is a multiply paradoxical situation. It will drive institutional change and, in the long run, ideological evolution. Marriages will be even freer, the independence of children will be even greater. The couples will be ever more alone in building their relationship, and they will be further confused. They will be ever more jealous of their rights over their children, and the state will be ever more involved in what will be less and less of a private realm. These tensions, particularly if something major happened radically to challenge the astonishing success of the United States as a world power, could lead to radical transformation. Such moments are rare, however, and it would be surprising if, thirty years from now, the quotation with which I opened this chapter did not still apply. People will marry, and they will divorce. They will have children and worry about them. They will reproduce America, even as they resist it and question an ideology they cannot escape.

ELEVEN

Socialist Families

Basile Kerblay

Did you say 'socialist'?

In this chapter I do not refer to a type of civilization, since those countries that were 'socialist' belong to different cultural types and are at different stages in their development. Depending on which families we are considering, the characteristics they presented are common either to so-called traditional societies or to all industrial societies (nuclear family, birth control, lower birth rate, increased divorce rate). The scope of this chapter does not allow us to draw up an inventory of socialist families, and we have chosen instead to illustrate the diversity of family situations by taking examples, principally from the Soviet Union, because its history extended over three generations and influenced very different traditions: Russian, Caucasian and Muslim. In addition, I felt it would be interesting to explore how an extended peasant family such as the Yugoslav *zadruga* managed to adapt to the collectivist system, and to study the situation of families in a country like Poland, where the Communist Party had to share its monopoly of the prevailing ideology with the Catholic Church.

This diversity also reveals characteristics common to socialist countries as a whole, although no attempt to define the term has been made. Dictionaries use the term 'socialism' indifferently to designate national socialism as much as utopian socialism (Robert): the dictionary of the Académie Française (1877) even confused it with communism. The qualification 'socialist' is ambiguous because it could give rise to the notion that socialist families can be considered on the same level as Christian, Jewish or Muslim families on account of an interior experience specific to themselves, whereas the term here acquired meaning only in relation to an exterior environment which imposed a number of constraints on family activities.

These constraints were derived from the abolition of private ownership of the means of production (which was tolerated only within very narrow limits in agriculture, handicrafts and the service sector), which conferred on the socialist state as embodied by the Communist Party the monopoly of employment, so that incomes, leisure and the social promotion of families depended on it alone. The constitution recognized only such individual and family liberties as conformed to the social purposes defined by the authorities.

This was not a new phenomenon, since every kind of totalitarian ideology tries to dominate the family by modifying the laws which govern it. In the fifth and sixth centuries, the Catholic Church was able to secure its material and landed power bases by modifying the rules governing the transmission of property and marriage, in order to allow individuals who were concerned about the fate of their souls to bequeath their property to ecclesiastical institutions. The communist authorities went much further by attacking the productive inheritance of families: by expropriating capitalist entrepreneurs they meant to implement a return to the primitive equality of a classless society.

The term socialist 'revolution' implies a radical break with the past. As it happened, the family, irrespective of its social origins, was the depository of tradition and embodied the very society which had to be transformed. Thus from the start, in the the Soviet Union as much as in the 'people's democracies', the introduction of permissive civil legislation had the effect of dissolving family bonds established on the basis of law and religion, which were felt to have an oppressive effect on the freedom of married persons. At the same time an educational system was set up under which the education of the younger generations in the spirit of Marxist-Leninist ideology became the monopoly of the state.

Marx, Engels and Lenin: not the same struggle

It is useful at this point to recall the main postulates of Marxism-Leninism with regard to the family, in so far as they inspired the family policies adopted by states based on this ideology.

Engels's *Origin of the Family, Private Property and the State* (1884) formulated the link between family types and modes of production, and thus the necessary modification to the status of woman which would result from the transformation of the rule of private ownership. The exploitation of women would disappear with the advent of communism because their domestic functions and the education of their children would be incumbent on the state:

> Because the husband in the bourgeois family is the sole wage-earner, he dominates his family totally; he is the bourgeois, and his wife and children are the proletariat. True liberation can be won only when women participate fully and equally in production processes. The monogamous family will have to cease functioning as an economic unit. Full participation in productive work will become less arduous and household duties will be less demanding, much of household work will be carried out by public enterprise ... Healthy sexual relations are perverted as long as economic ties rather than love and affection bind the family together. In fact, in its very origins, the monogamous family is not based on love but is a business deal ... Once the monogamous family is abolished relations between the sexes will become a purely private matter, of no concern to Church, state or neighbours. Men and women will form binary unions for extended periods. These unions will be based solely on mutual affection and will be dissolved if that affection cools. All children in this future world will be extramarital. (*Origin of the Family* passim)

These words have been interpreted by commentators as legitimizing free

A lower middle-class Russian family, including representatives of the revolutionary intelligentsia. Roger Viollet.

love. In Russia, Alexandra Kollontai became the spokeswoman for this theory, which was inspired more by the philosopher Fourier's utopias than by Marxism. Lenin, in a letter to Clara Zetkin which she quoted in her *Reminiscences of Lenin* (1934) repudiated the

> tendency to reduce the modification of relations between the sexes, irrespective of their relationship to any ideology, directly to the economic basis of society. This would not be Marxism but rationalism. Certainly thirst must be slaked. But would a normal man drink from a glass when its rims have been sullied by dozens of other lips? Drinking water concerns but one person; with love, however, two beings are involved and it gives rise to a third. It is here that its social interest lies concealed and that its duty towards the collectivity is born.

Lenin differs from Marx in his conception of the political system even more than he does on the status of the family. Whereas Marx imagined a model of associative society, Lenin countered with a civil society, organized on the military model, centralized and controlled by the Communist Party. According to his unitary concept, power was no longer the result of a balance of forces but the expression of the dictatorship of the proletariat, with the mission of carrying the transformation of society through to its conclusion with the abolition of class. All family liberties and activities were recognized only within the perspective of this overriding purpose, the advent of the new man. Viewed in this light, the feminist movement and its struggle for votes for women appeared derisory and women were not to be granted any form of autonomy, since men and women were to unite in one and the same action to bring about socialism.

The plan on the testing-ground of history

The Tsar's abdication in 1917 opened the way to the revolutionaries to modify the social structures of the former regime. At the time they were confronted by two currents of opinion. The first was libertarian, bourgeois in origin and inspired by feminist ideals, and, in addition to the radical parties, it was largely shared by all those who were campaigning for the abolition of the Holy Synod's exorbitant rights over civil society, and notably divorce. At the same time, however, the Bolsheviks also had to contend with the popular and conservative current represented by peasant traditions. Having given the libertarians a free hand in the 1920s, the government attempted a compromise with the peasant tradition in the 1930s. This gradually resulted in the restoration of laws protecting the family.

The Russian feminist movement held its first congress in 1908 with 900 delegates, which revealed its breadth; in 1917 it had extracted from the provisional government the right for women to vote. In October 1917 a militant member, Alexandra Kollontai, was nominated by Lenin to be People's Commissioner at the social security department, where she was given the task of drafting the new family legislation to be incorporated into the Civil Code in 1923. These laws aimed at secularizing marriage, facilitating divorce by mutual consent or even when instigated by one spouse only, suppressing marital authority by granting women identical rights over their children, inheritance, choice of name, residence and work, and instituting equality between legitimate and natural children. In 1922 the amount of legally transmissible inheritance was reduced.

The *Zhenotdel*, the female section of the Central Committee which was created in 1919, was subsequently given the task of supervising the way this legislation was applied. Inessa Armand was at its head; she wanted to go even further by inviting women workers on the occasion of their first congress in 1918 to 'extirpate the old forms of family life and of educating children'.

Advances

The outbreak of the Civil War contributed to emancipation, because appeals were made to women to replace factory workers who had enlisted in the Red Army. Crèches and canteens were opened, but not in sufficient numbers for the state to take on the upkeep of all children. Lunacharski reckoned that there were 9 million homeless children, some of whom formed bands of young delinquents (*bezprizornye*). The children's homes could not take in more than 800,000, as Lenin's wife, Krupskaya, ascertained; she was hostile to utopian projects.

By speeding up the rural exodus, industrialization contributed in its turn to disrupting living conditions for town families (town populations tripled between 1920 and 1940). It was now no longer only bourgeois families like Dr Zhivago's which had to share their apartments with worker families; these in their turn had to share with new arrivals. Kléber Lejay reported observing up to nine people sharing three beds in a single room (*Le Populaire*, 22 February 1937). Food and lodgings were so hard to secure that abortion was frequently resorted to. Abortions were permitted from 1920 – in the first three months of pregnancy – and in 1926 private clinics were reopened because the hospitals could not meet the demand.

As is often the case in times of abrupt change, some minorities attempted new experiments by making a virtue of the necessity of living in common and transforming it into a communal ideal. Young *komsomols* co-resided in urban communes and adopted an iconoclastic style: they assumed revolutionary names such as Barricade or Guillotine, and men and women wore similar clothes. The ensuing generation conflict was exploited by the Bolsheviks to rouse children against their parents, even to the point of encouraging denunciations, as in the case of Pavlik Morozov, who was made a hero of the Soviet pantheon.

Although this phase of exaltation did not last in the towns, in the country, there were some 1,900 agrarian communes created after 1917 on a voluntary basis which were transformed into *artels* and did not disappear until 1930, when Stalin decided to condemn this form of grass-roots autonomous communism. In fact, the commune, unlike the latter-day *kolkhoz*, excluded all private ownership by families. Even meals were taken in common, and children were entrusted to nursery attendants, while all agricultural produce was shared on an egalitarian basis, although later on according to each member's work contribution.

The inspiration for this form of communism was not drawn from a single model. In it can be found traces of traditions derived from religious sects like the 'old-believers', who had founded flourishing communities in distant provinces in order to live according to their faith and safe from

Russian peasants. Anonymous photograph from the late nineteenth century. Bibliothèque des Arts Décoratifs, Paris. Photo: J. L. Charmet.

persecution. At the beginning of the twentieth century, the Tolstoyans and anarchists had imitated their example by creating communities of the Fourier type. However, the majority of communes were peasant in origin and inspired by ideals close to those promulgated by the revolutionary socialists and Marx. Had not the latter envisaged the traditional Russian peasant community, the *mir*, becoming, under certain conditions, the cell of the future socialist society (letter to Vera Zasulich)?

These 'phalansteries' should not be confused with traditional peasant communities, which periodically redistributed land among their members according to the number of mouths to be fed, but within which each family retained ownership of its farm and autonomy over its labour and revenues. Although families engaged in many forms of mutual assistance there was no obligation to do collective work, such as was imposed in a dramatic fashion in the *kolkhoz* during the phase of collectivization in 1929–30.

This collectivization was to introduce many modifications to family life: married children were induced to leave their paternal homes by the offer of additional plots of land; heads of family who had been respected as farm bosses were now no more than agricultural workers. The village community had to obey new notables – its elders having been eliminated as *kulaks* – who were brought in from outside on party orders. Thousands of families were deported, half the livestock perished between 1929 and 1933, and millions of people died during the famine in the Ukraine. The 1937 census revealed a shortfall of 17 million on the population estimates for the whole country.

Reverses

In 1935 the authorities were forced to accept a compromise with the peasantry, and in the following year to adopt measures protecting the family in accordance with popular aspirations. The 1935 *Kolkhoz* law guaranteed private ownership of a family farm with a few head of livestock and a small plot of land. As under the former regime, this property was indivisible: it belonged to the family group and not the head of the family, so that when he died the farm continued to be owned by the other family members living at home. Personal property could be transmitted according to the common rules of civil law.

By revising divorce procedures more restrictively, the Civil Code of 1937 gave satisfaction to ordinary women, who had resented the liberties granted in marriage and divorce matters as giving their husbands freedom to leave them at will. From then on, divorce would only be registered when both spouses had made an appearance, the procedure was no longer free and a deserting husband was obliged to pay alimony. On the other hand, measures taken to restrict the number of abortions conducted in hospitals by limiting the permitted categories produced an angry reaction in the towns, where housing conditions were steadily deteriorating (4 square metres per inhabitant in 1940). The Second World War with its 20 million dead had the effect of strengthening measures in the family's favour (decrees of 8 July 1944). From then on, only registered marriages were recognized, and divorce was subjected to arbitration by a tribunal and given greater publicity. Unmarried mothers were to be given financial assistance, and family benefit was to be paid on the birth of a fourth child (the number of beneficiaries was low, 5.5 per 100 families in 1979 as opposed to 13.8 per 100 in 1960).

When the Soviet Union extended its sphere of power to include the neighbouring states of eastern Europe, the Soviet model was not automatically copied by them. Although their civil legislation was identical, the measures they took to socialize private agriculture attempted to avoid the excesses of Soviet collectivization and were limited to restricting the size of peasant farms while retaining the rural elites. After their unfruitful attempts at collectivization, Yugoslavia and Poland reverted to a predominantly family form of agriculture (in Poland this sector represented 77 per cent of the cultivated area). In the Soviet Union too, private plots of land were allowed to a maximum size of 0.5 ha from 1981, if the family signed a contract for fattening cattle for sale by the state.

These accommodations with the peasantry reveal the ambiguity of official conceptions about the nature of the peasant family. For Lenin and his disciples, family farms embodied capitalism *par excellence*. They did not listen to those people who, like Chayanov in the 1920s, had tried to show that the peasants' motivations were not dictated by desire for profit and that the intensification of labour and the area under cultivation were determined primarily by families' needs in relation to the number of mouths to be fed.

Nowadays too, even though town and country children are provided with the same education, peasant families retain more specific features linked to the diversity of national cultures and to the survival of kinship groups or clans which have adapted successfully to the new institutions. The dichotomy between rural and urban families, which tends to disappear in industrialized countries under the impact of rapid urbanization of the countryside, is still very evident in most of the countries of eastern Europe, where many small towns retain their rural character. Thus we will begin with the rural family in attempting a closer look at the modifications which socialist rule effected among different traditions.

Rural families: socialism and national traditions

We can find a certain number of characteristics which are common to all the following examples borrowed from Russian, Yugoslav, Georgian, Armenian and Uzbek families.

First of all, the family group, even when limited to the nuclear family or extended over three generations, is never isolated in its activities of a kinship or clan nature. The individual always has the sense of belonging to a group larger than his family: he knows that he can count on his relatives or in-laws well beyond the boundaries of his village. In those countries where Christian traditions have endured, kinship also includes godparents who are chosen when children are baptized, and who then act

The oldest woman of an Uzbek village, Oypar Saidova of the Obraztsovy *kolkhoz*. Trip.

as marriage sponsors among families capable of enhancing their prestige or strengthening the bonds of mutual help between two family groups. This spiritual kinship also creates prohibitions in the matrimonial order, as was the case in former days with fraternization (*pobratistvo*), when two persons exchanged their baptismal crosses as a token of their spiritual bonding.

Secondly, although the agrarian laws set limits to the size of plots, and although collective agriculture took up most of the working time available to the adult members of a family, the family economy continued to supply basic food requirements. In the Soviet Union private plots and livestock supplied 70 per cent of family consumption and 25 per cent of cash income. Consequently the family group's productive functions, which had practically disappeared from the urban model, retained their full vitality in the countryside. This was the case with one family in two in the Soviet Union, and one in three in Poland.

This family economy was mainly based on female labour. A survey conducted in the Soviet Union in 1967 showed that, of the total time dedicated to the private sector, the men's share amounted to only 13 per cent and the women's to 87 per cent, in other words, an average rate of over eleven hours a day, taking into account the obligation to participate in collective labour on the *kolkhoz* or *sovkhoz*. Here too the division of labour continued to favour men: men operated the machinery, women performed manual tasks. This explains why, in every country of eastern Europe, girls were the first to leave the countryside.

Finally, while there was a tendency to devalue older people's experience, on account both of the younger generation's educational advance and of the modernization of agriculture, the old continued to be granted a degree of respect because they embodied wisdom and national tradition. In Serbia, daughters-in-law still have to serve their fathers-in-law before their own children, and while young adults no longer kiss their master's hand (*domaciu*), they salute him with an expression which recalls the former gesture, 'ljubim ruku!' (love to your hand).

The Yugoslav zadruga

The southern Slavs provide an illustration of the other extended groups to be found in the nineteenth century in Romania (*gospodaria*) and Russia (*semejnaja obshchina*). The Yugoslavs' *rodbinskaja zadruga* were founded on agnatic kinship, although the common ascendant was not necessarily alive or present. Such groups would gather between twenty and ninety members under the authority of a head (*stareshina*, or nowadays *domačin*) and would include married brothers and cousins, grandparents and their descendants, uncles and nephews.

These family groupings fell apart in the twentieth century under the influence of the market economy well before the establishment of socialist rule. The falling birth rate and agrarian reforms further served to speed up the disintegration of such polynuclear families.

Gossiaux (1982) noted the creation of *de facto* associations between brothers and neighbours (*srenja*) as 'tacit communities' within agricultural collectives (*opce zemljaradnicke zadruga*) in republics as different as Slovenia and Macedonia. These groups often made it possible to adapt to legal constraints limiting the area of agricultural exploitations and the income from them by involving tertiary occupations. The micro-*zadruga* was thus extended to sectors such as transport: several families would form an association to exploit a flotilla of boats.

As Gossiaux notes, nuclear families very often correspond to the first stage of the family life cycle because the whole polynuclear family is reconstituted when the children reach adulthood. These days, however, the villages are steadily emptying (two-thirds of Kossovo farmers have no successors) in a process which threatens the rapid demise of an original tradition.

In the Soviet Union informal associations between families in the same village could be observed, but these did not constitute tacit communities as they were restricted to co-operation in the sale of produce on the markets and the organization of collective labour. The tendency was to entrust the cultivation of particular farmlands to brigades or small teams (*zveno*) co-opted from from families known to each other and organized as autonomous units.

Armenian and Georgian families

In the Caucasus, family relationships have a special significance. The vitality of kinship groups in these regions is derived from the fact that in former times communal ownership was a means of excluding strangers from settling in the village. Family solidarity was the condition of survival in these valleys, which lie open to invaders. Dragadzé (1976) reported, after her stay in the village of Ratcha in northern Georgia, that fifty-one out of seventy-eight families shared the same patronym.

Marriages were made between the occupants of the *aouls* (fortified villages), but there was a rule prohibiting marriage between any couple sharing a common ancestor up to seven generations back. As in other Mediterranean countries, a family's respectability is linked to its descent. Belonging to the same paternal line creates obligations between brothers who consult each other on every decision which could affect the family's honour. The eldest represents the family. The husbands do the shopping in town.

Men in Georgia have to prove their manhood and knowledge of life to gain their peers' respect; they do so by ostentatious dress and a lavish manner when they meet other men in the café. In Armenia, it is still the tradition to pay due respect to the head of the family (*tanter*), who is either the father or the married son living with his widowed mother. Young people do not smoke in his presence and sit down only when invited to do so.

Women embody stability. They are respected for their modesty. In Georgia, if a quarrel breaks out between the men someone runs to fetch the women because the men make a point of behaving in their presence. In Armenia, the mistress of the house sits alone to receive a stranger; the spoon (*shereb*) at her side symbolizes the authority which she used to hold over her daughters-in-law. Nowadays, wives occupy a position equal to their husbands.

The Georgian rite of marriage includes the custom that the spouses have to tread on a plate as they cross the threshold of their new home, smashing it in the process; the spouse who breaks it will hold the reins in the home. Armenian marriages, like those among the neighbouring Muslims, take place in three stages: first, the future husband's family sends an envoy to discover the girl's inclinations and to secure her parents' agreement (*hnamhos*); then the betrothal (*hshandrek*) takes place, at which the marriage promise is formally expressed by the exchange of gifts; finally, in the following month, the wedding (*harsanik*), with a procession, religious ceremony and a meal in the home of the husbands' parents with over 100 guests. One week after her wedding, the bride pays her parents a visit.

Armenians particularly dote on their children, because they embody not only the perpetuation of their line but that of a people which, like the Jews, owes its survival only to the very strong unity of its families. However, once the age of reason has been reached, children have stricter discipline; adolescents show deferential reserve towards adult strangers, and young girls will seldom attempt to meet their eye.

The kin come forward to provide assistance in everyday life and for special purposes, particularly the settlement of disputes. During his ten years of office, the mayor of an Armenian village was only once asked to arbitrate in a quarrel between brothers. A group's solidarity is shown by the physical presence of all its members on great occasions. In Georgia, whole buses are hired for its funerals. A hospital operation or a university entrance examination will serve to bring the entire family from the village to surround the building and support the individual during his ordeal. An

Armenian woman has commented that in the event of failure, the humiliation is all the more acute because the news is instantly relayed to the entire family (Kaputikjan, 1983).

Kinship groups adapted remarkably well to Soviet institutions. They constituted networks which are suitable for all kinds of traffic, including traffic in influence. Their sense of honour gives security to transactions which need trust between individuals. Nepotism becomes a moral obligation to get someone into an institute, a responsible job or a position where there is money to be made, and this further enhances the group's power. A check in Daghestan revealed that all 120 employees in a medical institute belonged to the same family (*Pravda*, 18 April 1984). This makes for competition between clans, and indeed long-running family feuds, as described by the Abkhazi author F. Iskander in his *Sandro iz Chegema*, which provides a chronicle of Caucasian village life.

The affection which all feel for their own village and the problems encountered in finding work locally have resulted in an itinerant type of seasonal employment, which may involve market trading or construction work in other regions. These migrations do not, however, occur among the peoples of central Asia because their cultural habits are closely intertwined with family life and could not be recreated anywhere but their own village.

The Muslim families of central Asia

At the beginning of the twentieth century two family types could be distinguished in central Asia. First there were the exogamic nomads, the Kazakh, Kirghiz and Turkoman people for whom endogamy would not have been practicable within tribes of restricted size. Then there were the sedentary people of the oases, the Uzbeks and Tadjiks, who practised endogamy in order to preserve their collective inheritance and cultural identity from contact with other peoples. Nowadays this endogamy is no longer the rule and transhumance has replaced the nomadic way of life, while the women of the nomadic tradition, who were never forced into reclusion, achieved emancipation more easily than their more conservative sisters of the oases.

This emancipation was implemented in stages. Originally the *Sharia* (rules derived from the Quran) gave husbands almost exclusive powers over inheritance. However, the Soviet law of 1923 made equal shares between spouses the rule in cases of inheritance and divorce. Wives were given total freedom in matters of marriage and divorce, a right granted only to husbands by the *Sharia*, and this prevented parents from forcing girls into marriage in their absence. The custom had been to marry girls between the ages of twelve and fifteen, but from 1925 early marriage was prohibited, and in 1928 the Quranic tribunals were stripped of their powers.

Customs changed less rapidly than laws: 43 per cent of young girls were still married by the age of sixteen in 1937, but only 6 per cent ten years later. Strict moral standards are still rigidly applied, and any girl who loses her virginity will have trouble finding a husband. In order to get women out of the seclusion of their homes, the *Zhenotdel*, the women's section of the Communist Party Central Committee, organized a network of family circles (*oiljavi tugarak*) in the years 1925–7, which the male members of a family had to attend accompanied by either a mother or a sister. A 1931 law obliged firms to take on female workers.

These transformations to the status of women did little to modify marriage rituals which, as in the past, are celebrated in several phases. The marriage request (*djaouchy*) involves presenting gifts (*kalym*) to the betrothed girl. In earlier times the *kalym* would have been given to her father as compensation for the loss of a daughter and would have comprised payment in money or cattle. Parents still intervene in such arrangements on account of the considerable expenditure involved in the wedding preparations, but nowadays the actual decision depends only on the couple. The betrothal (*kuda tuser*) is then celebrated at the girl's home with a variety of entertainments. In former times, the betrothed couple would only meet after this. Their married life would begin on the night which they spent together prior to their wedding, thereby definitively committing both their families. In the event of either spouse dying, the bereaved spouse would be provided with a sister or brother of the deceased spouse according to the rules of sororate and levirate. Because of the expenditure involved in the wedding proper, which is celebrated according to the Islamic rite and provides an occasion for entertainment by professional performers, a family will often celebrate two weddings on the same day.

Polygamy used to be practised only by the urban bourgeoisie, because *kalym* meant that only rich men could allow themselves more than one wife, but it is no longer permitted. However, men have been known to register their first marriage with the civil state and a second with the mullah; in such cases only the legal spouse is the legally designated mother of the husband's children.

The birth of a child is the occasion for a party (*besnik toi*). Boys are circumcised five to seven days afterwards and often given their grandfather's name, in accordance with the belief that the child has inherited the grandfather's soul. If the grandfather is still alive, he is the first to be told of his grandson's birth.

Although the present-day Muslim family is conjugal, consisting on average of seven members (as compared with around thirty in the nineteenth century), traces of the extended family survived in different forms: in the *kolkhoz* brigades for carrying out collective work, consisting of former clans or clan sections composed of between twenty and forty families; in the custom of being buried in the same cemetery; and in living arrangements like those observed among the Uzbek *dourmen*, where several nuclear families live around a communal courtyard. The communal budget is managed by the mothers of the married men, who prepare hot meals for everyone; cattle are also held in common. On the other hand, the money which women earned by their work on the *kolkhoz* was their own, and not handed over to their mother-in-law. The Turkoman film-maker Khodjakuli Narliev's film *The Daughter-in-law* illustrates the modesty prevailing in family relationships. Silence means that each member is attuned to the others; in such contexts, the expression of their eyes often counts for more than their spoken exchanges.

Veils are no longer worn, except by a few elderly women. They served as proof of an inner life that can only be understood from a religious perspective, which itself is symbolized by the house. Here the only opening onto the street is the door, through which guests can reach the centre of the dwelling, an inner court open to the sky. The move to the towns cut women off from their previous female society and shut them off within the loneliness of the married couple. This was a profound break with a lifestyle rooted in Islamic tradition. Belonging to Islam – the community of the faithful – has replaced their tribal identification as the main means of identification for individuals. In appealing to social justice, a sense of honour and equality, Islam is not opposed to the ideals of communism, which makes it all the easier to confuse the two.

This desire for identification is also fostered by works of literature exalting the past (such as those written in Russian by the Kirghiz author Aitmatov). Bilingualism does not as such constitute a threat to national cultures because the language used for training recruits and in everyday conversation is often no more than 'kitchen' Russian. Islam has in fact created a barrier which people who claim to belong to different traditions find hard to cross. While the peoples of central Asia frequently engage in mixed marriages, these are far less common between these peoples and the Slavs. Indeed, the strong Russian minorities which have settled in the large towns of the region produce the occasional exception which only serves to confirm the general rule. Although 20 per cent of marriages in

Tashkent were registered as mixed, this percentage makes no distinction between the different nationalities. However, it cannot be disputed that the evolution among couples of the younger generation is, if not moving towards assimilation of the various nationalities, at least converging towards a family pattern inspired by the urban model.

Urban families: old and new roles

The label 'urban' is applied for lack of anything better to characterize a family model which has emerged from the advances in women's education and work outside the home and which is becoming general throughout the former Soviet populations. Furthermore, in many rural families the members either work in town or are employed in non-agricultural jobs. Thus the contrast between traditional and modern families is more a case of contrast between two generations than between two centres of residence.

How families are formed

The 1979 census showed that 87 per cent of the urban population and 91 per cent of the rural population in the Soviet Union lived in families, although in the early 1980s about a third of the urban population between twenty-five and thirty-five were unmarried. Some 2.7 million marriages are celebrated every year, which does not exclude the existence of non-registered households (estimated to be 1.5 million in 1970). It has also been observed that the proportion of men who remarry after a divorce is falling; it was 55 per cent in 1967 and 47 per cent in 1976. This applies even more to divorced women, 40 per cent of whom remarry.

People marry young: on average at twenty-one years seven months for girls and at twenty-three for boys. In 1972, 60.2 per cent of married women were aged under twenty-five, as opposed to 34 per cent of the generation born between 1919 and 1925. In the Ukraine and central Asia more than half of the women are under twenty at marriage. The age of conscription for men was lowered from twenty-two to twenty in order to promote the birth rate. This trend, however, was not observed in every socialist country.

Choice of spouse is to some extent dictated by social homogeneity. In 70 per cent of cases the spouses belong to the same milieu. In the countryside, the betrothed girl generally comes from another village. On the other hand, endogamy is customarily applied to the nationality of a spouse. Marriages between Russians and Ukrainians form the exception to this rule: 30 per cent of mixed marriages in the towns of the Ukraine, as opposed to 9 per cent in Tallin and only 5 per cent in the towns of Armenia. Sociologists note, however, that the spouses' degree of cultural homogeneity and level of education count for more than nationality. Academic qualifications are mentioned in marriage announcements, and are one reason why women between the ages of twenty and twenty-nine with degrees, who are twice as numerous in the countryside as men of the same educational level, have trouble finding husbands.

Study, employment and holidays present more frequent occasions for marriage than neighbourhood relations. Lonely individuals can find succour in clubs for single people and in marriage advertisements. Engagements (*sgovor*) or their substitute, 'going out', continue for one or two years in half of all cases, but nearly 40 per cent of marriages are celebrated after less than six months. An interval of one month is required between lodging a request and registering the marriage, which seems to be a useful precaution given the number of broken engagements, which numbered 10 per cent on average in Hungary, and 20 per cent in April 1983 in Moscow (*Literaturnaya Gazeta*, 33, 1983). In Russia proper 25 per cent of marriages are the result of pregnancy; in Georgia they prefer to get married after the birth of the first child.

Three-quarters of all couples are in paid employment; around 20 per cent have not finished their studies and are financially dependent on their parents because university grants do not cover all their expenses. In half of all cases, the young couple has to co-reside with one of the parents' families for the first few years; indeed, getting a separate flat depends on the number of their children, unless they have rich parents who can buy them a flat in a housing co-operative. A similar situation could be observed in the other socialist countries. In Poland in 1977, only 18 per cent of young couples had their own dwellings (*Trybuna Ludu*, 30–1 July 1977). Furnishings could be bought with the help of state loans.

Although marriages are celebrated in accordance with each nation's culture and traditions, only civil registration is recognized. This involves a ritual which is gaining in solemnity with the passage of time; it includes a procession to the registry office to the strains of a wedding march, as well as leaving flowers on the war memorial. While simple people make do with a dinner for their friends in the town restaurant, some weddings are more ostentatious. It has become the fashion to contribute towards the costs by presenting the newly-weds with gifts of cash or Giro cheques.

Family typologies in the former Soviet Union

In towns as in the countryside, the dominant type of family is nuclear (64 per cent of all families) with or without children. In 1970, only 16 per cent of all families consisted of three generations, and 14.8 were single-parent families with or without a grandparent.

Another differentiating factor relates to these families' place of residence. Urban families have widely varying housing conditions and services; such differences are often far more important than inequalities of income.

The inhabitants of a city like Moscow are privileged, although less than half of all working families take their meals in canteens or have their washing done in laundrettes, whereas in Poland in 1975, only 10 per cent of households took their meals outside the home. In Moscow, 80 per cent of families have a flat to themselves; in other cities, only two-thirds of couples are in the same position. At Nijni Novgorod, Novossibirsk, Tashkent, Tbilisi and Erevan, all of which were cities of more than a million inhabitants in 1982, the housing norm per inhabitant was only three-quarters the Moscow level, and expenditure on consumer goods only half the average in Moscow.

Incomes are often higher in worker than white-collar families, though the latter enjoy better-equipped homes and housing conditions. The average size per housing unit in the former Soviet Union did not exceed 16 square metres, compared with 48 square metres in the United States (*Argumenty i Fakty*, 4, 1990). There are no figures available for the exceptional privileges enjoyed by the communist rulers and *nomenklatura* (dachas, servants and official cars). From 1985 some of those dachas were assigned to public use and the number of official cars was cut by half (in a country where only 17 per cent of town and 14 per cent of country families owned a car in 1989, ibid., 7, 1990).

The range of incomes opened up considerably from 1985 to 1990. In 1989 monthly per capita income was estimated to be five times higher (three times in 1980) for 10 per cent of the most prosperous families than for the 10 per cent at the bottom of the scale (ibid., 45, 1990). In 1990, when the minimum living wage was around 100 roubles per month, 71 million Soviet citizens earned less than this and 28.8 million received more than 250 roubles per month, from a total worker population of 127 million (ibid.).

Family typologies must also take length of marriage into account because income and housing conditions evolve, generally improving, during the whole of the family life cycle.

The birth rate: impact of female education and employment

Neither income nor profession can be applied as criteria for differentiating between families according to the number of children. On the other hand, different national traditions and degrees of urbanization do enable comparisons to be drawn between the European regions, most of which are urban, and the predominantly rural Islamic republics, which have an average of five members per household and practise early marriage (see table 24).

It follows that regional variations are more significant than the Soviet national average (as compared with 3.6 members per household in Czechoslovakia; 3.4 in Poland; 3.0 in Hungary). In Moscow, in the 1970s, 22.3 per cent of couples had no children, 52.7 per cent had only one child (as opposed to 28.9 per cent in rural areas), and 2.8 per cent had three children or more (26.5 per cent in rural areas).

Here as elsewhere, it seems that the lower birth rate has its origins in female employment and women's education. The example of the Soviet Union shows that there was some delay before the recruitment of a female workforce had an effect on the birth rate.

The 1979 census in Bulgaria showed that there was no difference between the number of children for working and non-working women, but that there was a correlation with their level of education. Women educated at secondary or university level had half as many children as women with only primary education. In Poland in 1974, 42 per cent of working women with higher certificates did not have children. The optimum number of wanted children in white-collar families was 2.17 and among blue-collar workers 2.29, a figure lower than that given for the same period in the Soviet Union, which was 3.2 children. Since then this average has drawn closer to the Polish ideal at 2.2, far higher than the actual figure, which stands at 1.4 children in St Petersburg.

In the Soviet Union abortion was considered less dangerous than the pill and was the commonest form of birth control. The ratio of abortions to births was estimated at between 2 and 3 to 1. In Czechoslovakia it is estimated that at least a quarter of all pregnancies are terminated by abortion (see table 25). The chief reason given by Soviet women for limiting births was their inadequate income, which forced them to work (Hansson and Linden, 1983).

Female employment was burdened from the start with a heavy cultural handicap because illiteracy was most widespread among women. Nowadays educational equality has been achieved: in the former Soviet Union the percentage of women in higher education is even higher than that of

Table 24 Social indicators in the Soviet Union: regional variations (1978)

	Family size: number per household			Birthrate per nationality		Early nuptiality (17–19 yrs)	Urbanization percentage of toal
	1959	1979	Towns	Country			
Estonia	3.1	3.1	1.79	2.47		4.9	66
Russia (RSFSR)	3.6	3.3	1.76	2.47		9.1	64
Armenia	4.8	4.7	2.64	3.97		15.2	61
Azerbaijan	4.5	5.1	3.19	5.43		8.3	51
Uzbekistan	4.6	5.5	4.31	5.66		21.9	37
Turkestan	4.5	5.5	5.03	6.05		19.1	48
Tadjikistan	4.7	5.7	5.12	6.26		24.9	38
USSR (average)	3.8	3.5	1.88	3.24		–	57

Table 25　Number of abortions per 1,000 women aged between fourteen and fifty-five in 1986

USSR	118.6	Poland	16.5
Romania	90.2	United States	27.0
Czechoslovakia	34.5	United Kingdom	12.8

Source: *Sociologiceskie Issledovaja*, 3, 1989.

men (51 per cent of all students as opposed to 28 per cent in 1927–8). Indeed, women have made up more than 50 per cent of the whole employment sector since the Second World War.

　　Roughly speaking, agriculture, industry and the services sector each have a third share of the female workforce. It may be observed that women are employed predominantly in relatively low-paid jobs. Thus the health service employs women in 85 per cent of its workforce and pays them on average 30 per cent less than the average wage; 73 per cent of those employed in the national education sector are women, and 76 per cent of those in distribution, with wages equal to 87 and 75 per cent respectively of the national average. However, only a third of secondary school head teachers are women, and 10 per cent of firm directors or technical managers. Conversely, it is women who often carry out the manual tasks in the countryside, whereas men do the mechanized work, and it is women who perform the fiddly and unpleasant jobs in industry or construction work. Some occupations such as night work are not open to women, who can retire earlier than men, at the age of 55.

　　Professions such as teaching and health work are chosen by women because of their more flexible working hours, which allow them more time for the home. In the metalworking industry or the mines, where husbands earn high wages, more women stay at home than in other professions. In any case, material needs are not the only factors prompting women to seek work, since the wish to pursue a career increases in proportion to academic achievement.

Women: new awareness and old servitudes

What occurred in the Soviet Union, as in other industrialized countries, was a real transformation of female roles, although living conditions and the far slower evolution of male mentalities did not always allow these new aspirations to be manifested fully.

　　The evidence collated by Hansson and Linden (1983) reveals that women are demanding two things: on the one hand freedom in love, modelled on a certain image of femininity which combines the desire to please and to wear personalized clothes with that of contributing moral

Table 26 Female employment: repercussions on the birth rate in the Soviet Union

	Percentage of women in workforce in USSR	Generations	Percentage of worker families with three or more children
1922	25	1919/20	55
1940	39	1936/40	42
1945	56	1946/50	11
1960	47	1951/7	6

Source: N. Krupjanskaya, *Kultura i byt gornjakov Nizhnogo Tagila* (Mining culture and way of life in Nizhnij Tagil) *1917–1950.*

support and tenderness to the home in spite of being exhausted; on the other, the ability to establish themselves in a circle less narrow than the family. This is why girls feel that getting a degree is vital to their prestige and that without one they would be undervalued fiancées.

In practice, the dual role obliges women to take on conflicting attributes. Women attempt to equal men in the workplace, and they revert to being wives and mothers in the home. They dream of not having to choose. However, the advent of a child forces wives to sacrifice their careers unless they have a parent at home who can look after the baby, since state nurseries still leave much to be desired. 'I went to work as to a party, but once married I did not agree to putting my children in a boarding school because I suffered too much in my childhood, and I had to give up my work' (a reader, quoted in *Literaturnaya Gazeta*, 28 December 1983). 'I am a scientific researcher of mature age fascinated by my work, but if I had to choose between my career and my daughter's health, I would not hesitate a minute, I would choose family duties and suppress my own inclinations' (another reader, ibid.).

These family duties are not slight. They take up considerable time because the persistence of stereotypes burdens women with most of the work of caring for the home and bringing up the children.

Time/budget surveys in the Soviet Union established that married women in Moscow had to devote between three and three and a half hours per day to their homes, and in other cities even more time. Shopping absorbed between four and five hours a week and forced women to engage in real queuing marathons in rush hours and during shortages.

To sum up, the equality which women have acquired in the workplace has not yet been applied to their leisure time. Athough husbands can pursue their studies as well as working with a fair degree of ease, only 28 per cent of married women without children, 13 per cent after the birth of the first child and 9 per cent after the second manage to do so.

It is also the mother who takes on most educational functions, although the surveys reveal that she considers this task to be incumbent on her husband or a joint one (82 per cent). Grandparents also have a great deal of influence in everyday terms, notably during the first years of marriage, and their interference, which cannot be avoided when the couple co-resides with parents, is often resented. However, the presence of a *babushka* or granny in younger-generation families is becoming increasingly rare in the former Soviet Union. In Poland, a third of all child care is taken on by grandparents, a third by crèches and a third by mothers on maternity leave. The mother's level of culture will determine her child's educational future – until her influence is challenged by that of his schoolfellows.

In Russia today the gradual erosion of paternal authority is attributed to the feminization of school education and to the fact that it is no longer blindly accepted, as in the days when the differences between husbands' and wives' ages and levels of education allowed the men to assume the role of head of family. The crisis comes when spouses no longer communicate except about their everyday family concerns. The bread-and-butter aspect of their relationship is confined to an emotional zone where disappointment and criticism take precedence over shared pleasures. This means that they will live parallel lives, meeting only during their leisure periods, when their basic inequality becomes evident because married women have half as much free time as their husbands.

When all is said and done, what a woman learns from marriage is that the man, who seemed at their engagement so attentive and keen to do what she wanted, is no longer the virile hero of her favourite novels. She is to some extent frustrated by having to take on roles which she considers belong to her husband. However, the inverse is quite as common among worker families, when the husband makes all the decisions as well as choosing their friends. These friends are recruited from among colleagues at work (52 per cent), neighbours (23 per cent) and relatives (18 per cent).

Russian women nowadays no longer put up with this situation. They are influenced by the ethos which presides over their professional lives and relationships, and are competing for control of their family group. Letters written by husbands to the press suggest that this desire for independence sometimes conceals a wife's inability to run a household: it also reveals that men entertain an ideal which is closer to the traditional model of the stay-at-home wife than to that of the emancipated woman.

Sociologists and psychologists agree that married couples value harmony at home above the ironing of shirts. This is why, when the atmosphere of inner peace which is necessary for her children's development is no longer there, a wife will prefer divorce to a bad marriage.

Divorce

Married couples who have difficulty in communicating are clearly not limited to socialist countries. Divorce occurs just as frequently in the United States and Sweden as in the former Soviet Union. However, what may be more specific to the latter state is that when the social conventions were abolished, the intelligentsia developed more subtle barriers related to the woman's intellectual attainments. If her husband confuses Gogol with Hegel (pronounced Gegel in Russian), his conjugal love will suffer. To this must be added the circumstances peculiar to Russian life: the frequency of co-residence with parents at the start of married life and the greater mobility demanded of specialists, involving temporary separations. Literature is full of sentimental stories on the theme of seasonal love, the geologist away from home on fieldwork, for instance, while a fatal triangle grows up around the married man's colleague at work and his wife, neglected by her husband because of his professional obligations. As in those novels where the heroine makes advances to a distraught or indecisive man, in real life it is generally the wife who initiates divorce because the material independence which she has acquired makes the procedure less dramatic, and a broken marriage is no longer considered a disgrace.

Among the reasons given by women in divorce cases the most common are: broken emotional bonds (12 per cent) manifested by adultery (16 per cent); the husband's alcoholism (20 per cent); psychological tension resulting from the absence of harmonious sexual relations or poorly organized material conditions at home (10 per cent); interference by parents-in-law (3 per cent) and lengthy absences (4 per cent). Husbands cite incompatibility of character, adultery and incompetence by the woman in household matters. Deeper causes may often lie hidden behind these motives, relating to the spouses' lack of maturity. Indeed, 21 per cent of divorce petitions are filed less than a year after the marriage, and in three-fifths of cases less than five years; in 1981, 48 per cent of women and 30 per cent of men who had obtained a divorce were under twenty-five. In the traditionally Muslim countries, women still sometimes cite forced marriage or non-payment of *kalym* in their divorce petitions.

There have even been cases of girls imprisoned in their parents' house (*kaitarma*) to force a fiancé to fulfil his contract.

Tribunals generally grant mothers custody of children under ten, but recent judgements have tended to take children's interests into account by giving custody to the parent to whom they are most attached. Maintenance is set at a quarter of the husband's salary for the first child until the age of eighteen, a third for two children, and so on. However, non-payment cases are so frequent that on 6 February 1984 the Council of Ministers in the Soviet Union decided to give emergency payments of 20 to 50 roubles a month, depending on the number of children, while the defecting parent is being pursued. Divorce registration fees have been increased to cover these payments. Single mothers are also given priority crèche placements for their children and priority housing allocations. At the present time there are some 9 million homes with no father. The incidence of divorce varies according to the situation on the marriage market and the extent to which it is assisted by the legislation and national traditions in each of the former socialist countries.

These variations illustrate the impact of environment, depending on which region of the CIS or which country is involved. The province of Magadan, a pioneer frontier state in the far east, registers the highest incidence of divorce; the republics of the Caucasus and central Asia, where the model of the traditional family is still active, contrast with more emancipated countries such as Protestant Latvia or the Czech Republic. People divorce more frequently in Russia than in Catholic Lithuania, and in Orthodox Bulgaria than in Poland. This prompts an analysis of impact of the Catholic tradition on family life in that country.

Table 27 Divorce rates per 1,000 inhabitants

East European countries	1960	1976	1980	USSR	1969
Bulgaria	0.50	1.29	1.43	Armenia and Georgia	1.0
Czechoslovakia	1.12	2.67	2.67	Latvia	4.2
Hungary	1.66	2.56	2.58	Lithuania	1.1
Poland	0.50	1.11	1.15	Magadan (Far East)	9.4
USSR	1.30	3.35	3.50	Russia (RSFSR)	3.7
Yugoslavia	1.20	1.13	1.00	Tadjikistan	1.1

The Polish family

As in the other ex-socialist countries, the Polish family's evolution was subjected to the influence of common factors: industrialization, employment plans and the ideological and political monopoly of the Communist

Party. However, this monopoly was challenged by the long-established influence of the Church, which was identified with the Polish nation throughout its history. Because of this, it was the only institution of civil society that was able to escape communist control in a socialist country.

As with Poland's neighbours, female employment rates outside the home (30 per cent in 1950, 42 per cent in 1974) and women's level of education have risen markedly. In 1974, there were 139 female students aged under twenty-five per 100 male students of the same age in higher education. Nevertheless, the traditional ideals which exalt the notion of the mother in her home are still active and tend to make working mothers feel guilty.

According to a survey taken in 1975, 82 per cent of women under the age of thirty who were questioned declared that they worked out of economic necessity, and that two-thirds of them would be prepared to stop working if they could afford it. Those most attached to their work were the wives of private-sector agriculturalists who remained with their families.

Among men too, the female model is still that of the wife who devotes herself to her children, who works hard but can be confided in when problems crop up. Men like to think of themselves as cavaliers who delight in expressing their gratitude to women by kissing their hands, still a common practice, and by buying them flowers whenever they visit, in short by engaging in a form of courtesy which is also a way of signalling their distance from the stereotyped practices of official existence.

The Polish family's ideal number of children is close to the Russians' (2.3 children on average), which means that family planning is practised. Among workers of peasant origin, with whom the Church's influence is most strongly felt, the contraceptive methods used are those approved by priests. Among the intelligentsia, where respectability is no longer associated, as it used to be, with the practice of religion, a quarter of women use the rhythm method and very few the pill, which means that abortion is the most popular method of birth control, as it is in the former Soviet Union. More abortions than births were registered in Lodz and Warsaw in 1968.

The Catholic hierarchy's well-known disapproval did not prevent Parliament in 1976 confirming the 1956 law which legalized abortion. On this point, women's attitudes vary according to their milieu and level of education. A survey conducted in 1972 indicated that 43 per cent of women in the countryside were hostile to abortion, as opposed to 26 per cent in town; 33 per cent of women living in town who had received only primary education were opposed to it, compared with only 10 per cent among those with higher education.

A survey by Ewa Surfin into the way young people in Warsaw felt about the family showed that 73 per cent of them (as opposed to 34 per cent of a Parisian sample) stated that they experienced various degrees of conflict in their relations with their parents, that they had different ideas about roles and about the distribution of power, and that they enjoyed greater sexual freedom. This is explained as much by the cultural gap between the generations as by the specific material conditions in the eastern countries, such as having to live with their parents on account of housing problems and drawing inadequate incomes which prolong dependence on parents who hold the purse-strings (see *L'Évolution des modèles familiaux dans les pays de l'Est européen et en URSS*, Paris, 1988).

In fact, actual behaviour among Polish families in matters of sex, abortion and extramarital relations are no different from those in the 'Christian' societies of western Europe. On the other hand, west European families can face crises and difficulties better than families in the east, going by the divorce rates in big cities like Warsaw and Lodz which are themselves well below levels in Moscow and St Petersburg (5.4 to 5.9 per cent). This is because in the Polish scale of values the family is still the unit with which individuals prefer to identify (Novak, 1980). Szezpanski (1970) went still further in noting that opposition to socialism contributed to making the Polish family into the stronghold of the national spirit, and that the vitality of this micro-society was a factor for continuity which enabled it to counterbalance the changes introduced by the macro-structure.

Family politics and social ethics

The Polish case is exemplary because it illustrates the family microcosm's capacity for resistance to external pressures, whether from the Communist Party or the Church. This inertia allows traditions to be transmitted in spite of the authorities' monopoly in ideology and education. The Polish consitution (article 67), just like the Soviet consitution (article 67), obliged parents to prepare their children for a useful job and for becoming worthy members of socialist society. The state was thereby giving itself the right of looking into family life by means of of class counsellors in school and youth commissions on local councils. Tribunals could intervene where the parents' or grandparents' influence was considered harmful to the child's interests (for instance in cases of parental alchoholism, or encouragement to attend religious ceremonies).

However, what the schools were actually propounding was a conservative model of the family, one which perpetuated the authoritarian model inherited from peasant society. The stereotype of female and male roles recurs in the professional orientation given to schoolchildren at the same time as they were acquiring the political vocabulary which would serve as a reference in collective life and for official purposes.

Any action taken by the socialist state could only be indirect by creating conditions favourable to family life; it could neither induce people to marry nor force them to have children. Yet we should not underestimate the considerable transformations which the Soviet Union effected in the course of three generations, in urbanization, education and employment of women, social mobility, etc. An example is provided by an opinion poll taken in in Novossibirsk in 1967 from a sample of families belonging to the 1917 generation, 55 per cent of whom declared themselves to be members of the working class and 17.5 per cent of the intelligentsia. The results showed that in the next generation, 31 per cent of their sons and 41 per cent of their daughters had managed to establish themselves in the intellectual professions.

Pro-natalist incitements

Not all the results obtained conformed to official ideals. The lower birth rate, the increased number of divorces and the advance of juvenile delinquency all obliged the authorities to introduce family policies with a set of complex measures, from improving worker accommodation to granting financial assistance to families, less rigid timetables at work and the provision of consultation services for couples in crisis.

Czechoslovakia was the first country to adopt a policy of helping young households with loans for acquiring a home and furniture, and reducing repayments with each birth. Similar measures were taken in the Soviet Union on 22 January 1981 to help couples under thirty with one child; couples who were still childless were promised their own flat if they had a baby in the next three years of marriage. Also in 1981, 451 occupations were classed as too strenuous and closed to women (in 1957 the law had already been changed to ban women from underground mining work).

The example of East Germany, which succeeded in raising the birth rate from 10.6 per cent in 1973 to 14 per cent in 1981 (an increase of 34 per cent) by introducing 26 weeks' maternity leave paid at half the current wage, was contagious. The Soviet Union extended maternity leave to one year in 1982, with partial remuneration (35 to 50 roubles per month depending on the region) and the right to six months' further unpaid leave without pay while keeping one's job. In Hungary maternity leave was extended to three years on half-pay; the same applied to Poland but without remuneration. The organization of more flexible working hours for mothers meets a general wish, but the aspiration has only occasionally been realized.

The social infrastructure of crèches, services and shops was not sufficiently developed, and this always presented an obstacle to lightening domestic work for married women, or even abolishing it. In the Soviet Union around 30 per cent of children under the age of eight were taken into crèches, in Poland it was 8 per cent (1975), and in Hungary 11 per cent. Despite all this, equality with men ceased at 6 p.m. However, these ideals were surely based on the false assumptions that changing the environment would in itself suffice to change attitudes and behaviour; and that a socialist infrastructure would give birth to a socialist ethic.

While women's concept of themselves was undoubtedly modified, the male mentality evolved far less rapidly. The press is frequently bombarded with letters from mothers complaining about discrimination by their firm managers because of the privileges which they enjoy in the right to miss work in order to care for a sick child, and to choose their own holiday times.

Women who rebel against the dream

Many women became aware of the gulf between the official discourse exalting mothers of families and working women in Women's Day celebrations, and humdrum reality. This did not give rise to a structured feminist movement. The sporadic demonstrations at the 1980 Olympic Games in Moscow were paper tigers, quickly suppressed by the police, but they made public opinion in the West aware of the existence of a feminist movement with a variety of aims. The libertarian current is paralleled by more traditional currents based on spiritual demands.

Far more significant are the letters from female readers, regularly published in the press, making increasingly vehement statements about the difficulties inherent in the condition of women. This theme surfaced in contemporary Soviet literature, for instance in N. Baranskaia's novel, *Nedelia Kak Nedelia* (One week is like another) (*Novyi Mir*, November 1969, pp. 23–55), since imaginative writing was the only permitted means of conveying a political message in Russia.

However, none of these aspirations found expression in collective action, which would anyway have been impossible given the degree of police surveillance, because people still thought that change could come only from above. What was the point of dreaming about what could never happen, asked the women questioned by Hansson and Linden

(1983, pp. 11, 184). Their mothers had experienced far harsher times than they had; besides, the demands made by women for equality in the past only served to give more freedom to men. Their demands can be summed up as calls for better-organized town services, more comfortable dwellings, higher wages for their husbands, more space for emotional life, and freedom to travel abroad. In short, their attitudes were those of the middle classes in other industrialized countries.

More searching surveys, such as those conducted by Novak in Poland, showed that family ethics did not fully match the ideals of socialism. The primary point of identification for individuals was not the collective but the family group. The family's well-being and the children's health and education came before all other considerations. This is another reason why material worries and the race to acquire, which might wrongly be taken for a form of consumerism, assumed such importance. Because of their inability to transmit inheritance to their children, families became very keen to leave them another form of wealth, their culture, so that equality of opportunity was circumvented by the greater facilities available to the children of the intelligentsia where access to prestigious careers was concerned.

After the family, the restricted circle of friends – in a selective sense which does not correspond to the superficial use of the term in English – provides the second rank of attachments. Among friends, as with his own family, the individual can be fully himself and express himself without fear, abandoning the wooden language used in his professional life, and the double face which makes for frustration and aggression in relations with others. Thus the exaltation of the collective ended by engendering its antidote: a retreat into family life and appreciation of the home.

The collapse of the Soviet regime and its consequences for the family

The Soviet-style regimes which imposed specific constraints on family life collapsed when civil society, which had for so long been kept in the background, at last found a means of expression. There were many reasons for this collapse, the most important of which related to economics and personal outlook. The increasingly obvious dichotomy between real circumstances and collectivist ideals eventually weakened the social fabric and caused economic stagnation. The part played by families was less visible, but more profound. It was families that had preserved the free space whence came the surge of protest which prompted clear-thinking and courageous men to give a voice to the aspirations of their peoples, men like Vaclav Havel, Andrei Sakharov and Lech Walesa. Even before the breaching of the Berlin Wall on 9 November 1989, it was Poland – of all the countries in the eastern bloc the one in which the family had clung most strongly to its traditional values, backed by a Church reinvigorated by Karol Wojtyla's accession to the papacy – that gave birth to the movement which, in one form or another, spread over the whole of eastern Europe before finally, in August 1991, reaching Moscow, the very heart of the Soviet empire. Nothing would ever be the same again. All references to socialism disappeared from Russia's new constitution, and the Communist Party collapsed, with the USSR falling in pieces around it. Must we conclude from this that our preceding pages now have no more than a historical interest?

Feminist demands and freedom for the young

The regaining of independence by countries formerly under the Soviet yoke and the new freedom from fear in the former Soviet Union itself caused a radical change in the psychological climate which had for so long forced families back on themselves. Freedom of expression (*glasnost*) reopened the possibility of genuine debate. Debates over the family ranged over a wide area, from a renewed emphasis on its importance in education to a feminist revolt against a concept of gender roles which returned women to their status in earlier Eastern societies. The small number of women in public life (only 15% of deputies elected to the USSR People's Congress in 1989 were women) seems to indicate that most women give priority to motherhood (*Moscow News*, 8 January 1989). Moreover, Olga Voronina thinks that urban families are showing signs of developing matriarchy (*Sociologisheskie issledovaniya*, 2, 1988). The woman is often the more important, if not the only, parent, and because girls are generally better educated than boys, she has inherited the cultural duties which were formerly performed by the father. He, if we are to judge from recent films and novels, is a bird of passage in the family, and his psychological supremacy is much in doubt, since women prefer to rule undivided over their children.

It might have been expected that when Russian peasants were given leave to own property, this would help to perpetuate farming methods which vested authority in the head of the family. At the beginning of 1993 there were 184,000 independent working farms, a tiny number in comparison with the 8 million families engaged in collective agriculture – for return to the land offers few attractions to the younger generation.

The present climate is favourable to the penetration of Western customs and to freedom of behaviour: schoolchildren experimenting with sex, pornographic phone lines, sexual harassment in the office. The sensational press peddles an image of women which encourages them to think that their bodies are their chief asset. Escort services, modelling and striptease, if not prostitution, are the way to a lucrative career. The younger generation has seized the opportunity to raise the torch of libertarian ideals which was brandished by many participants in the Revolution of 1917. To this we can add the foreign-imported counter-culture – clothes, rock and roll, discos – which was been so sharply criticized by the conservative intelligentsia intent on preserving a national identity (Abramov, Belov, Vladimir Rasputin, Solzhenitsin and others).

The moral crisis and the awakening of nations

With the collapse of communist ideology, individuals lost all their vision of the future. Insecurity of outlook was joined by a feeling of physical insecurity caused by the upsurge in criminal behaviour of all kinds. The past has become the main point of reference in the search for a lost identity. It leads to the reawakening of nationalist, ethnic and religious instincts, along with their darker side: exclusion of 'outsiders' and the displacement of thousands of threatened families. In the former Soviet Union, the redefinition of relationships between the central authority, the republics and the autonomous regions, has transferred extensive powers of legislation over everything which affects the family and education. In the independent republics of central Asia the *kalym* is now practised openly. In Kazakhstan there is a proposal to restore polygamy so as to increase the proportion of Kazakhs among the population.

In Russia, religion is enjoying a certain increase in popularity con-sequent on the freedoms allowed to the various faiths. There has been an increase in Orthodox Christian baptisms (46 per cent of babies in 1990 as against 16 per cent in 1985), but church weddings are still the exception (9 per cent according to *Argumenty i fakty*, 29 (*sic*), 1990), although in the present chaotic situation marriage, we are told, is seen as a kind of refuge: whereas in 1985 45 per cent of boys and 30 per cent of girls in their final school year in Minsk refused to commit themselves to marriage, and up to 30 per cent of babies were abandoned in certain cities, today the illusion that marriage will bring longed-for stability, and the need for companionship, is strongly felt among young people (A. Spinavov, professor of psychology at Moscow University, *Argumenty i fakty*, 27 (*sic*), 1991). Nevertheless, the birth rate is going down, so much so that in 1992 the total population of Russia fell by 70,000 despite the influx of over a million refugees from neighbouring states. These

Basile Kerblay

demographic shifts, in spite of the advantages granted to families with
three children (who get priority for accommodation) or five children
(allowed retirement five years before the statutory age), witness to the
gravity of Russia's current economic crisis.

The economic crisis and the growth of inequality

In this period of transition to a market economy, families have been hard
hit by inflation and unemployment, which gnaw away at their income,
and by the loss of the social protection which formerly guaranteed secure
employment, free education and health care, low rents and stable prices.
The first wave of reform has dismantled the administration which used to
control production and distribution, but has yet to create the conditions
for a resumption of growth. Countries which embarked on similar
reforms some years earlier, such as Hungary and Poland, have had more
success in controlling inflation than Russia and Romania, which are
suffering cruelly from the inconstancies of a 'bazaar economy' (see tables
28 and 29).

The families most affected are those whose parents are in retirement,
and large families, because pensions and allowances lag behind the
upward spiral of prices. A third of Russian families have an income
which puts them below the poverty line (*Argumenty*, 24, June 1993). The
social hierarchy is gradually changing to the disadvantage of the intelligentsia, severely affected by restrictions, and the working class, hit by job
losses. Women are the first victims of unemployment (70 per cent of total

Table 28   Increase in the annual retail price index

	Bulgaria	Hungary	Poland	Romania	Russia	Czechoslovakia
1990	19.3	28.5	250.0	4.7	—	10.1
1991	474.0	36.5	60.0	350.0	160.0	58.0
1992	65.0	20.0	50.0	120.0	2,500.0	10–12 (*sic*)

Source: see table 29.

Table 29   Unemployment (percentage of the active population)

	Bulgaria	Hungary	Poland	Romania	Russia	Czechoslovakia
1900	1.6	1.7	6.1	1.6	—	1.3
1991	12.0	8.3	11.4	6.00	0.7	6.5
1992	16.0	10.0	18.0	12.0	1.4	12.0

Source: Marie Larigne, L'Europe de l'Est du plan au marché (Paris, 1992), p. 127; T. de
Montbrial (ed.), *Ramses 1993* (Paris, 1992), p. 190; *Argumenty i fakty*, 125 (June 1993).

registered unemployed in Russia on 1 January 1993). What will happen when major state enterprises are privatized, causing mass unemployment (an expected 15 million in the year 2000), is anyone's guess.

We can already see the emergence of a two-speed society, with hospitals charging for their services and private schools for the more fortunate children, while the 9 million families – a quarter of the urban population – who are unable to buy an apartment of their own join the endless waiting list (*Argumenty*, 39, October 1991).

Political reform and reluctance to change

However, the after-effects of communist education and family traditions are not without influence on the possible directions of change in the medium term. Tradition allows the father arbitrary authority over his children – with the result that every year 50,000 children run away from home (Igor Gamajunov, *Literaturnaya Gazeta*, 23 November 1992). The other problem is that of the overprotective mother. Both types of upbringing turn out passive individuals who seek security above all else. This makes it no easier to nurture democratic institutions which demand self-confidence and tolerance, together with an acceptance of the rules of competition and a willingness to take risks. Because privatization has been slow to catch hold, economic interests are still insufficiently diversified to encourage the emergence of a middle class and structured political parties. Political life, in a country with no tradition of democracy, is reduced to a personal combat between individuals, most of them members of the former *nomenklatura*. There is reason to fear that in the present situation a charismatic leader may be able to take advantage of the general longing for a restoration of authority by exploiting feelings of racial awareness. As for the national churches, which have never been independent of the current wielders of power: they have become inward-looking – which can only accentuate the drift into nationalism and xenophobia. It will take a long time for new attitudes to establish themselves in the family and in society.

Happily, there is a further lesson to be learned from the recent history of socialist Europe: 'Being and history are governed by their own sort of time. They do not blindly obey the whims of technocrats or political manipulators; they are not there to fulfil the predictions of such men. World and being have their secrets, which never cease to confound modern reason' (Vaclav Havel, inaugural speech to the Académie des sciences morales et politiques, *Le Monde*, 29 October 1992).

TWELVE

The Scandinavian Model

David Gaunt and Louise Nyström

Although people often confuse the Scandinavian or Nordic countries with each other, everyday life in each one is distinguished by a number of differences, relating above all to their geographical position, their natural resources and their methods of exploiting these resources. It is obvious that a culture based on deep-sea fishing, as is found in Iceland, will differ from another based on mining and industry, as in Sweden. These very distinct variations can be found even in those countries where private industry tends to settle in the southern zones, while the northern regions are affected by the chronic instability inherent in raw material production, by unemployment and consequently by emigration.

All the Nordic countries share the same spiritual inheritance, with Lutheran Protestantism as their official religion. The nineteenth and twentieth centuries saw the appearance of many free religious groupings, often of a puritan tendency, while the official Church's influence declined. Finland has a Russian Orthodox minority. The waves of immigration which followed the Second World War brought numerous Catholics and Muslims to the Nordic countries.

The farm has historically constituted the kernel of Scandinavian family life. The further south one went the more feudal the ownership of land became, whereas further north the farmers owned their farms. Wheat was grown to make bread, and in those regions where agriculture did not pay, cattle were reared for milk products. Good arable land was rare, the forests were dense, and in spite of the midnight sun the growing season was brief in the northern areas. In many regions people simply had to find another means of existence.

Many farmers turned themselves into jacks of all trades. Depending on

A family of agricultural workers, early twentieth century. Nordiska Museet, Stockholm.

their ecological environment, they would choose peddling, which could be profitable, or deep-sea herring fishing, which always paid; they would burn charcoal, cut stone, make tar or pitch, hunt and set snares or engage in forestry. Such were the various expedients resorted to by the family. Serfs alone were deprived of these opportunities.

Peasant families were generally restricted; they included six to twelve persons, two or three of whom were servants and two or three others children. Although it was possible for the grandparents to live on the farm as well, they normally lived in a separate house and took their meals at home. The slow rotation of farms and the scarcity of land for clearing pushed the average age at marriage back to over twenty-five for women and almost thirty for men. This high age reduced the number of children born to each family, and the very high rate of infant mortality limited the family group still further, holding population growth at a very low rate.

In Gotland, an island which was settled very early on, there was almost no land to colonize. Families thus tended to remain very small in order to avoid splitting up the farms. One of the techniques employed consisted of limiting the number of births, proof that a sort of family planning already existed in the eighteenth century. Another consisted of arranging marriages so that a brother–sister pair on one farm would simultaneously marry a brother–sister pair on a neighbouring farm. In other regions the way of life demanded a large workforce, and no birth control was practised. For the free peasants who mined iron in central Sweden, their year was made up of a succession of exhausting tasks: farming in summer, burning charcoal and woodcutting in winter, iron mining at the end of winter followed by smelting and freighting during the spring floods. These lucrative non-agricultural jobs enabled them to split their farms up into little plots, since mineral production rose with the number of workers engaged in it, and it was easy to purchase food from outside with the profits realized from the sale of foundry pig-iron (D. Gaunt, 1977).

The sole exception to this model was found in east and north Finland, where a scattered population was engaged in farming clearings in the forests. Land was not scarce here, but servants were. This explains the existence of huge households of thirty to forty persons, almost all related. Marriage was early, and births numerous. Not everyone lived beneath one roof, but their dwellings were grouped close together, and three or four brothers with their families would often share both work and meals. Some of these huge families were still in existence on the eve of the Second World War (Tornberg, 1972).

In the distant past Finland was historically linked to Sweden. Iceland and Norway were attached to Denmark, the similarity of their languages and administrative structures facilitating co-operation and a constant exchange of ideas between these countries. Of course Finland, with its distinctive language, is the exception, but the country is officially bilingual in Finnish and Swedish. Despite a fairly similar cultural environment, the Nordic countries also have their ethnic minorities, very old ones such as the Lapps and more recent settlements such as immigrant groups from Greece, Yugoslavia, Turkey and Latin America.

A tradition: control by the state

Where family and official regulations are concerned, the Nordic countries are to some extent modelled on each other. In general, governments exercise far greater power over private life than in other Western countries. This can be attributed only partly to the enduring electoral success of the social democratic parties. For even when parties to the right of the social democrats come to power, few changes to social policy are made. This is possibly because well before the emergence of the notion of the welfare state, Nordic governments continued to live according to their mercantilist inheritance of regulation and supervision. The famous church registers and the annual checks on each person's religious practice belonged to this tradition; fairly precise lists were held by parish ministers, local tax collectors and the military administration. These registers were opened in the seventeenth century and have served as starting points for the present-day very precise computerized supervision of the family.

Swedes were encouraged at an early date to learn to read, and their varying aptitudes were recorded by the priest on his annual visit of inspection. The same did not apply to learning writing skills. This was an ideal situation for the government; the population could read and assimilate royal proclamations, but very few people would have been able to write a letter of protest or draw up a petition (D. Gaunt, 1983a).

Although the general principles of the welfare state are universally acknowledged, differences exist. In Denmark and Sweden, state expenditure on social security programmes amounts to 30 per cent of the gross national product, but comes to only 17 per cent in Iceland, with Norway (21 per cent) and Finland (23 per cent) in between. As we have already stressed, this variation cannot be attributed solely to social democratic policy. Between 1945 and 1976 (and even earlier), Swedish social democrats enjoyed stable power, a predominance also exercised by the Norwegian Labour Party. However, Danish political life did not have this stability, and governments of the right and left have regularly succeeded one another. It is, however, very nearly the general opinion that all governments should use their taxes and social security programmes to remove existing inequalities. While there are occasional reports that the Scandinavians are growing somewhat tired of assistance 'from the cradle to the grave', they still think it their due.

Two ideologies predominate in Scandinavia: liberal and social democratic. While liberals (and conservatives) agree that the state should act as a safety net for those who, for one reason or another, are incapable of looking after themselves, social democratic ideology advocates the well-being of all with no distinction by class. Whereas in the liberals' view the state must ensure a minimum in matters of income, schooling, hospitals, housing, etc., social democrats think that social investment should aim at the highest quality and attract and be accessible to all. Let all hospitals, all schools and residential areas offer the highest possible quality, and all citizens will benefit. Thus it is in the interests of all to pay their taxes, because they contribute to improving the situation of the population as a whole. The richest will not be tempted to seek private solutions if the public institutions offer the best care to children and the elderly, the best instruction and the best housing conditions, etc. Thus the Scandinavian welfare state is modelled on the intersection of these two ideologies – the liberal safety net's guarantee of a minimum quality and the social democratic motto, 'The highest quality for each and all' (Hedborg and Meidner, 1984). Sweden has the clearest social democratic image of the welfare state, the 'Folk Home Model', which is why this country will be examined in greater detail in this chapter. In the process we will identify certain characteristics of the family situation in modern welfare-state society.

Working mothers: a new role for fathers

Over the last twenty years the same, or almost the same, proportion of women as men have entered the labour market in the Nordic countries. In 1992, around 90 per cent of all Swedish women aged between twenty-five and fifty-four were working, as opposed to 94 per cent of men in the same age group. Housewives are now to be found only among the oldest women; 40 per cent of women aged between fifty-five and sixty-four are not engaged in paid employment. Otherwise the main difference between men and women is that women prefer part-time employment. Women in the Nordic countries do paid work to a much greater extent than in other European countries. Like everywhere else, women have always worked and have often had heavier schedules than their husbands. This has, however, always been traditional both in the home and on the farm.

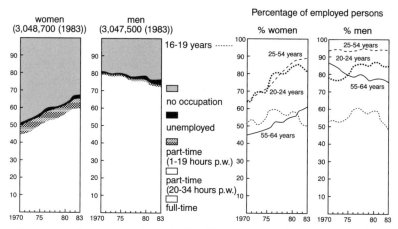

Figure 11   Percentage of people (16–74 years) in employment in Sweden

If we go back as far as the Viking period we can observe that women already had a well-defined sphere of their own within the whole body of work on the farm. They were responsible for everything that went on inside the house – cooking, housework and keeping the stores – and for looking after all the animals except horses and beef cattle, and they would also cultivate an orchard and vegetable garden. The keys which the wife wore at her belt were one of the symbols of her power. She also held her husband's keys, and nobody except the king could force her to hand over her bunch of keys or to broach a store. This economic distinction between female and male roles conferred on women power almost equal to that of men.

In regions where the men worked far away, such as the islands where they were mostly merchant sailors, or when hunting kept them far from home, women often assumed all the work of the farm. Examples of quasi-amazonian societies can be found in certain Danish islands, where the women cultivated the land, estates were transmitted from mother to daughter and women ran the local institutions. When the men came back, they took no part in this. They could even be seen quietly sitting alongside their wives as they drove to church with the wives holding the reins.

During industrialization a great number of outlets were opened to unmarried women – and not solely in the textile light manufacturing industries. Women were also employed at dangerous and exhausting jobs in the mines, foundries and sawmills and in the construction industry. There was nothing exceptional in their earning as much if not more than some of their husbands. Although the appearance of trade unions goes back to an earlier period, they only became truly efficient in the early twentieth century. The Scandinavian trade unions were and are more powerful than those in other Western countries. Some sociologists go so far as to claim that the success of the Swedish welfare state is derived from that of negotiations between unions and management (Hedborg and Meidner, 1984). The unions have almost always been adult male worker collectives fighting to secure the prohibition of female employment, for the good reason, they said, that the unions could secure wage rises only in a market where labour is scarce. Thus the unions were pursuing two aims: organizing all male workers, and eliminating cheap labour – women, children and the elderly. This was seldom openly said. Instead, the trade unions invoked humanitarian arguments. Every time there was an accident the local union would demand that women and children be excluded from the type of employment held to blame. Employers would often give in to the unions' demands in order to avoid a strike. With other forms of employment they used legislation against women; typography, a very remunerative form of night work, passed out of women's hands into those of men.

The unions wanted to see women at home with their children, and argued that a worker should earn a wage sufficient to meet his family's requirements. Although industrial jobs were male-dominated during the 1940s and 1950s, women found outlets in the service sector, which was then in full development, in teaching, the caring sector and office work. While it would be an exaggeration to claim that there are two labour markets, one for women and the other for men, it is certainly still true

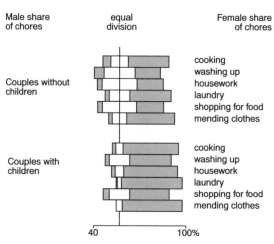

Figure 12 Division of tasks in homes where the wives are in full-time employment

that most women have jobs in the service sector and that men dominate the industrial sector. It is equally true that women are not as strongly placed on the labour market. Saving on public expenditure threatens typically female jobs. The domestic responsibilities (home, children) which women assume prevent them from working full-time and from aspiring to careers. An employer will always secretly weigh up the risks he incurs by employing a young woman, because he knows that she will demand her right to maternity leave and will also stay away when her children are ill. Though her leave is paid for by social security, her employer has to find and train a replacement.

Even though the role of fathers is growing all the time, it is generally women who adapt their work to the needs of their children. In Sweden, both parents are entitled to take parental leave together, extending to twelve months for each child (since 1980), but fathers generally take only a small part of it. Social security guarantees wages for one parent to care for a sick child, but in this case too it is the mother who stays at home. Since 1978, one parent is also able to reduce his working hours by 25 per cent, but fathers only rarely take advantage of this opportunity.

In the home, the same differences can be found as have been observed on the labour market. Apart from child care, women continue to take on the majority of household chores, whereas men are content to 'give a hand'. A mother devotes on average 5.7 hours a day to housework and raising her children, and a father 1.4 hours per day. However, he also takes charge of house, garden and car maintenance. Even in families where both parents work full-time, women carry out the majority of domestic tasks. Washing up and shopping are the main male household chores, whereas cooking, washing, ironing and mending clothes are almost exclusively female occupations.

Men's reluctance to divide household tasks equitably puts women in a situation where they are constantly rushing, and many complain of always being tired and short of sleep. They want to have well-kept homes, impeccable children and a balanced diet for their family – and they also want to succeed at work. They are obliged to apologize all the time: to their boss for getting to work late or having to take their children to the dentist; to their children for coming home late or having to do the vacuum-cleaning. Giving up outside work is not the solution – nowadays two incomes are necessary to balance the family budget – and the problem of household chores has to be solved in other ways. One obvious method is to persuade the men to carry out their responsibilities more fully, and another is to find a better way of everyday living. The communes, which we will mention further on, are one of the possible solutions.

Participation by men in family life requires fathers to assume a new role. This role is surrounded by considerable confusion which is not solely due to the fathers. Do the women and children really need them? The thousands of women who live on their own with their children have shown that they are not convinced this is the case, even though such families are economically unstable. With artificial insemination, it is now possible to give birth to children without any contact with a man. This particular climate disturbs some fathers. In addition, they read and hear it said everywhere that husbands ought to do the cooking, housework and washing, and that fathers ought to play a greater part in their children's upbringing and not content themselves with occasionally taking them fishing or to a football match.

In Sweden a certain number of men have taken advantage of their entitlement to parental leave to look after their new-born children, but these are more often young civil servants than middle-aged factory workers. There are also a good many families whose parents do not work the same hours, in order to avoid having to pay for child care. However, the greatest change perhaps lies in the fact that more and more fathers are growing deeply attached to their babies. Note for instance that almost all fathers are now present at the birth.

Recently, and in spite of the still limited nature of fathers' participation, a shadow has been cast over their new function. The fear is that excessively gentle fathers will engender disturbed children. Some developmental psychologists stress that we incur the risk of eliminating a parental duality which has always been necessary to develop the whole personality (Humble, 1984). Women have always symbolized tenderness and forgiveness, and men strictness and discipline. If this duality disappears, children will experience only forgiveness and will no longer be subjected to strictness or discipline. In the same way, when they reach puberty, children will no longer know which parent to choose to act as a touchstone for their identity crisis.

Other psychologists state that it is not good for the father to take too great a part in caring for a baby at six months, because this is the vital bonding stage with its mother and no one should replace her. While we have in all honesty no idea whether these fears are well founded or not (this is a field which requires more in-depth research), inflamed debates have taken place in which women have accused men of exercising a harmful influence on child development. One such debate ran throughout the summer of 1983, when the Swedish radio and newspapers were kept busy discussing the bad influence of 'velvet daddies' – meaning fathers who try to 'mother' their babies. Fathers who behave like mothers no doubt represent only a tiny minority, but the notion of velvet daddies was exploited to condemn the very concept of the new paternal role. This debate was preceded by another, concerning sexual abuse by fathers of their daughters. This was prompted by a proposal from the ministry of justice to legalize marriage between half-siblings. The power of the word 'incest' unleashed the public imaginations, and some were soon maintaining that the proposal envisaged legalizing incest, and in particular relations between fathers and daughters. Some of its opponents went so far as to present statistics proving that more than half of all girls had, at some time or another and in one way or another, been the object of sexual advances from their fathers. It was this that shook the 'men's movement' to its roots, for, taken to extremes, the debate about incest made all physical contact between father and daughter suspect. How were they to care for their children without touching them? How could they express their feelings without cuddling?

Needless to say, these debates about velvet daddies and incest have remained at a very superficial level. They are, however, clear evidence that the new role for fathers has not gained its true place in society. The fault cannot be blamed only on traditionalist fathers; mothers too, anxious about their children's well-being, cannot bring themselves entirely to trust their husbands. In any case, in order to enable the new role for fathers to make itself felt, it will have first of all to be accepted that men are men and women women, and that participation by fathers does not have to mean 'mothering'. Also, a great number of social experiments will have to be conducted before any consensus is reached about the new role for fathers.

The family module and its combinations

For a long time one of the most persistent myths of our age has been the end of the family institution. Some people hoped that the traditional bonds uniting husbands and wives, parents and children, would disappear to allow the whole person to flourish. Others blamed the collapse of the family on modern urban and industrial society, and judged this regrettable. This view has been shared by most governments since the 1930s. At the time, Alva Myrdal defined the problem with great clarity in *Folk och familj* 'Nation and Family,' 1944), in which she associated the crisis of society with the collapse of the family:

> The family is a social institution, meaning a system of human relations whose roots are deeply anchored in the past and which, as seems fairly normal, has not been able to adapt to the rapid and radical changes which have occurred during the last century in our economy and culture. The

family was not able either to turn these changes to its advantage or to avoid the damage which they could cause to the institution it represents. The family has been left to confront modernity with no defences.

Myrdal claimed that 'it is up to the state to guarantee that the life of the family retains its functions through the intervention of every sort of social programme.' It is astonishing that most of the programmes proposed by her were subsequently implemented. The notion of the collapse of the family and the decline which this would entail proved a political stroke of genius. The most radical social demands as a result came also to concern conservative politicians dreaming of a return to the good old times.

The irony remains, however, that during the whole period of the 'death throes of the family' in the 1940s and 1950s, the family continued to prosper in its conventional form. People were getting married more than ever before, and at younger and younger ages. Women were giving birth to children more than ever before and staying at home. Divorces were fairly few and the number of extramarital births was falling. Despite the crowd of intellectuals keen to write the family's epitaph, these tendencies remained stable from the 1920s until the late 1950s. Although we can nowadays establish that the intellectuals were wrong, they were no less anxious about the effects of obligatory schooling, the appearance of children's tribunals, the fall in the birth rate, relaxed divorce laws and premarital sexual relations, etc. What they forgot, however, is that the family is not a thing but a network of human relations, which survive even when their forms change.

Nowadays the greatest number of small families is to be found in Sweden. In 1990 an average-sized household numbered 2.1 persons. The size of the Danish household has slightly increased. Norway and Finland number on average three persons per household, more or less the same as in France, the United Kingdom, Belgium and Austria (Hemström, 1983). In Sweden and Denmark the fall in the birth rate, the rise in abortions and the high percentage of divorces exceed those in the other Nordic countries.

The existence of these restricted households in Sweden can be explained in both historical and cultural terms. Even before the creation of social security, Swedish households were somewhat restricted on account of the small number of children and the methods of land appropriation. However, although such small households proliferate, it is partly due to their high standard of living and to the absence of housing problems. Old people can live in their own place, and in our days they live longer, often after the death of one spouse. It is not exceptional for young people to leave the family home before the age of twenty, well before having children. Divorced couples serve to swell the number of one- or two-person households.

However, this official average of 2.1 persons per household may well prove to be an underestimate. It is often the case that young and middle-aged people are counted as unmarried when they are in fact living as couples. They will retain their own flat for convenience or in case their new relationship founders. The problem of taxes and benefits must also be taken into account. Single parents can obtain housing allocations as well as priority enrolment at crèches or schools. This form of 'double residence' came to worry the local authorities, and some years ago a survey was held in Stockholm to find out where single persons 'normally spent the night'. The aim was to uncover fraud in tax and housing allocation cases, but the public regarded the survey as an invasion of privacy, and the results were dubious.

In spite of this large proportion of one- and two-person households, the majority in Sweden live in families of three or more persons; furthermore, half the population is made up of families with children, and four-fifths of all children have at least one brother or sister (1980). Three-quarters of families with children are nuclear, a couple with its progeny. Non-nuclear families are constituted in equal proportions by one-parent families and mixed families, in which one or both parents have custody of a child born to a previous relationship. Around a quarter of Swedish children do not live with their father and mother, generally without the father. At least half of these children maintain close relations with the other parent, with whom they often stay for two days at a time.

Given the small size of these households, Sweden possesses the greatest number of housing units per capita in the Western world. These units are also smaller, with on average three rooms per dwelling, not counting the kitchen. The average space (persons per room) is almost equal to that in most other Western countries (Hemström, 1983).

When the 'Plan for a million homes' (1965–75) was implemented, the overpopulation and lack of space which had affected the habitat disappeared. Nowadays very few people live in overcrowded housing, and almost everyone has a modern home, apart from immigrants, especially those from Mediterranean countries, who live in great numbers beneath one roof. Socio-economic differences also entail differences in habitat.

The rapid modernization of the habitat led to the appearance of huge, uniform and characterless housing estates. During the 1960s people could not choose the geographical situation or type of their dwelling;

they had to accept what was built. It has since been possible to choose, and prosperous families opt for semi-detached homes, or detached houses in the suburbs. Thus a form of segregation has developed between poor families renting dwellings in large developments and wealthier families with their own suburban houses, a typical instance of more liberal ideas about housing.

In Sweden during the 1950s and 1960s it was almost possible to speak of an integrated urban population, at least in the new residential areas where there was a real social melting-pot in the neighbourhoods and schools. By the 1970s and 1980s, the population was divided geographically by class, income and nationality. Civil servants and members of the liberal professions could bring up their children in protected and pleasant districts where the houses are spacious and the friends they make in school share the same social environment.

Poor people and immigrants have remained in the large developments where life is difficult, services are lacking and the outside environment is often dilapidated. Nursery and primary-school teachers in these places encounter more problems, resulting in a rapid rate of staff turnover (Danermark, 1984). It would be going too far to depict all these areas as ghettos or unstable zones, but they are developing in an alarming manner and could in the future produce crime and disorder, especially if juvenile unemployment cannot be eliminated.

In most Nordic countries, the act of founding a family is not subjected to rigid principles. A good number of men and women live together for a while before getting married, and it is very common in Denmark and Sweden for people simply to go on cohabiting without ever celebrating their marriage. Thirty years ago this would have been thought antisocial and immoral. Nowadays, some people scarcely dare admit that they are really married. The laws and regulations have been adapted to leave almost no difference between married and cohabiting couples, and the Swedish census does not distinguish between them. Whether married or not, all couples are counted as living in a state of cohabitation. Thus it is hard to obtain precise figures for the number of marriages. On the other hand, the percentage of children born outside wedlock gives an idea: in Iceland 56, in Sweden 48, in Denmark 46 and in Norway 41 per cent of all births in 1991 were to parents who were unmarried. In Finland, the figure is somewhat lower: 25 per cent of all births in 1990.

The formation of a couple is a private matter. Gone are the complicated ceremonies attended by family and friends, whose presence used to mark the social significance of these rites of passage; no engagement party, no wedding, no presentation of gifts, in fact no specific moment to offer congratulations. This privatization can extend to relinquishing both baptism for the babies and wedding anniversaries, and to the absence of all formality when the family is dismantled. In contrast to couples united by the bonds of marriage, cohabiting couples can draw up their own contracts and make their wills as they please. Women, of course, retain their maiden name and the family can choose between two patronyms for the children. This can involve some practical difficulties, as in finding a telephone number or in knowing the surnames of one's friends' children. Giving the children their mother's name can accentuate the father's feeling of uselessness, although instances can be found where the man adopts his wife's name. This confusion of surnames also exists among married families. The only way of knowing whether people are married or not is still to ask them.

Swedish regional newspapers generally include a page dedicated to family news, featuring obituary columns, birth announcements and wedding photographs. In recent years, these wedding pictures have been showing not only the bride and groom but also their children grouped around them. Indeed, the ceremony often combines marriage with baptism. This is the case with couples who have already been cohabiting for seven or eight years; they attach little importance to the ceremony and are getting married simply to please their families.

Interviews have revealed that couples who cohabit do not do so as a reaction against the institution of marriage. The situation evolves progressively: first they are friends, then lovers, and finally the day comes when one of the two collects up his or her belongings and moves in with the other. If nobody in their circle of friends is married, they generally see no reason for getting married themselves – especially since all sanctions have disappeared. 'Marriage did not seem indispensable. We did the same as everyone' (Levin, 1979).

Some sociologists see cohabitation as the survival of a peasant tradition. The association is not obvious and is certainly debatable, but it is undeniable that premarital contacts did enjoy great freedom. The Nordic countries possessed ancient courtship traditions involving heavy petting; the further north one went, the more widespread these traditions were.

We can explain this very long and complicated history in a few words by stating that it was acceptable for a young bachelor to spend the night in the bed of a girlfriend who was also unmarried. In spite of appearances, this form of courtship was generally a chaste affair. Since the Scandinavians got married late, such couples would have been well into their twenties but were not considered adults on the social level. The young man would come on specific days, every Friday or Saturday. The girl would be waiting for him. The parents could not stop the boys from

Traditional courting. Nordiska Museet, Stockholm.

coming without finding themselves the butts of an aggressive *charivari* (Wikman, 1937).

Boys and girls thus began courting soon after Confirmation, but as long as they were adolescents it was mainly for fun and company. The boys would form small bands to go and visit all the girls in the village. They would gossip, play around and flirt a little, think up a few tricks to play or contrive to spy on an older couple who were overstepping the bounds of chastity. True physical intimacy began only when the marriage vow was almost a certainty, and more often than not it would not go beyond heavy petting. Of course, a great many prenuptial pregnancies occurred, but it must not be forgotten that it was the betrothal ceremony and not the church wedding which constituted the normal starting point for living together. In addition, it was not exceptional for thrifty farmers to house their male and female servants not only in the same room but even in the same bed, but that had nothing to do with the tradition of courtship.

Ever since the family became a private affair, all sorts of solutions and variants can be observed. Marriage and cohabitation represent the simplest of these. But there are also married couples who, while living in harmony, occupy separate flats. There are divorced couples who manage to dwell in the same part of town in order to take turns in having the children. Since it is hard for both spouses to find specialized jobs in the same area, the number of weekend families is steadily increasing. Some think that this mode of separate living gets rid of everyday problems and allows passion to be maintained at a maximum.

Divorce has grown more common, as it has everywhere else. Divorced people do not remain on their own for long. Around one fifth of children aged seven years live with only one biological parent. Nowadays, step-families are just as common as they were in the old agrarian society, but they no longer carry this name. Children sometimes call their step-father 'my pretend father' and in some districts of Stockholm the term 'plastic daddy' is current.

The norm now is for parents who get divorced to be automatically granted joint custody unless one of them refuses to take care of the children. This is merely a legal reform aimed at ridding the lawcourts of interminable and painful custody cases. Judges are not even concerned to find out which of the two spouses has caused the split, and when the two members of the couple consent to separate, the courts do not try to dissuade them and authorize the separation as a matter of routine. All this means that a considerable number of children are constantly circulating between parents, homes, brothers, half-brothers and friends. Nobody is absolutely convinced that this instability is not a cause of suffering for these children, but the few surveys which have been carried out reveal that some children appreciate this way of life and flourish in it, because they are not separated from their father or their mother. Nevertheless, a situation in which neither adult can take full responsibility, and where the parents are incapable of agreeing, can also be painful for their children. Is a couple which cannot conduct a successful relationship capable of solving the tricky problem of bringing up their children?

Who looks after the children?

Since both parents work, the question arises of who looks after the children. This is all the more acute in that young Swedes do not start school until they are seven years old (with a pre-school introductory year at the age of six). Furthermore, the school day is very short, three hours a day at nursery school and five in primary school. Then there are the holidays, twice as long for the children as their parents' five weeks. Thus, over a period of ten to fifteen years there is a chronic problem of child care when the parents are working. In the case of nursery school children, the problem covers the entire day, although even a nine-year-old child is not considered capable of coping on his own after school (albeit a certain number of young children at primary school come home to empty houses).

In Sweden, day nurseries take care of about 20 per cent of all children of pre-school age, starting at nine months. Other children are entrusted to minders, but half of all babies stay at home, some because their mother (or father) is on maternity leave, but most because their parents take turns at looking after them. As we have already explained, many mothers of small children work part-time and often have jobs with convenient working hours, such as night nurses, weekend shop assistants, office cleaners, etc. (Näsman et al., 1983). Thus when father comes home at five o'clock, it is time for mother to leave for work.

State nurseries are subsidized, but families are also required to contribute; keeping children at home thus represents a minor saving, but the parents see less of each other. The nurseries function only during the day, and are thus useless to parents who work evening or night shifts. However, it seems that the working classes are suspicious of nurseries, whose qualified teachers with their specialist opinions about educating children get on better with middle-class parents, and the proportion of middle-class children attending is far higher than that from working-class

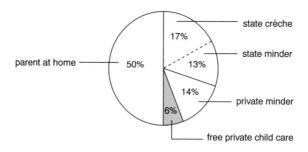

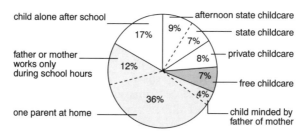

Figure 13   Child care in Sweden (1980). Above, the children are of pre-school age (0–6 years); below, of school age (7–10).

homes. Many working-class parents prefer to bring their children up without outside interference.

This brings us back to the question about the level of state intervention in the private life of the family. In the Nordic countries, the debate reflects the opposition between liberal and social democratic ideology. Everyone recognizes the advantages of family subsidies, medical aid, free schooling, maternity leave and nurseries for the children of working parents. Almost everyone will also recognize the advantages of housing aid for low-income families and training programmes for handicapped children. It is, however, more difficult to achieve consensus about proposals for the obligatory provision of nurseries for all infants or for projects to train parents in child education. A straightforward school reform allowing the school day to be extended with a few hours of optional activities (sport, chess, music and art) gave rise to massive protests among politicians as much as parents, who objected that the children would be too tired and that it would constitute an intrusion into the private life of the family. It is interesting to note that this Swedish proposal was not inspired by examples from other countries, such as French nurseries, or British schools where children start in their fifth year, usually after a year of nursery school. This is all the more striking, as the experience of longer school days in those countries could have helped Sweden to find a solution to the problem of child care provision better adapted to the mothers' work.

In general the state uses information campaigns to act on the way parents behave. A few years ago, the weightlifter Hoa-Hoa posed with his new-born baby for advertisements on buses and in the streets. Another information campaign by the government's social commission told people that they need six to eight slices of bread a day. In some cases adequate behaviour is prescribed by law. While alcohol for minors and the sale of drugs are of course prohibited, there is also the Swedish law of 1975 which forbids parents to punish their children by hitting or smacking them or subjecting them to humiliating treatment. It has not proved easy to apply this law, and everyone admits that it is very difficult to know what goes on behind closed doors. As for the children, it seems unthinkable that they should go and complain to the police. In reality, it is only a recommendation, which all psychologists would support, that parents do not chastise their children too often, treat them fairly and choose discussion rather than punishment. It is also a way of reminding parents that they have no 'right' to beat their children. The same was true in the past, for the ancient laws which allowed beating were abolished long ago, as in many other countries. The new law was formulated expressly for those cases where it might be disregarded. It must be hoped that the fate of ill-treated children has thus to some extent been improved, although punishment involving bodily harm has never been tolerated in Scandinavian families.

Instead dialogue is advocated as an educational principle in schools, nurseries and families. It is thought that by means of discussion, both child and adult will be able to agree on how to resolve their problems. By means of discussion, not only will the child change his attitude, but his parent or teacher will see things more clearly and be able to adapt his reaction accordingly.

In practice, the principle of dialogue implies that discipline and chatisement disappear, to be replaced by discussion. Teaching in schools and nurseries is given individually or in little groups, which requires numerous staff – one for every four children in the nurseries. The teachers have a large team of assistants, specialist helpers and trainee teachers. What is more, primary school classes are divided into two or three groups, with separate timetables, communal timetables and a few periods reserved for intensive work in small groups. Teachers are not allowed to apply any brutal method of correction but have to use persuasion to make their pupils work.

Primary schools, nurseries and leisure activity groups take all their decisions by means of general and democratic meetings. Any voting that takes place will always try to achieve consensus. During the first seven years of school no marks are allotted, but every term parents and pupils are invited to a private fifteen-minute meeting with the teacher to discuss the child's progress. Such meetings are also very common in nursery school. Parents are strongly advised to participate in schoolwork and are allowed to attend lessons when it suits them. Teacher–parent co-operation represents a sort of ideal, but needless to say some parents are reluctant to take part – they remember how strict schools were in their own childhood – and some teachers view intrusion by parents into their domain with a certain unease.

The educational principle of dialogue fits into a double context. The first is constituted by modern Scandinavian society, especially in the professional field. Over recent years, formal procedures at all levels have been given up in favour of informal discussion, of *ad hoc* groups, committees and workshops. Bureaucratic power structures are regarded with general suspicion, and mutual agreement is held in high regard. Since 1976, employers have had to discuss all changes with their employees before implementing them. This applies as much to the purchase of new equipment as to taking on new staff or even to closing the business.

Everyone except the king and queen is addressed in the familiar form with no distinction by age or social standing. Until the 1960s the polite form *Ni* and the third person singular were the only correct ways of addressing a superior: 'Would Miss Andersson kindly excuse my lateness?' Titles have since become rather embarrassing, and receiving a medal no less so. Complicated ceremonies – always associated with a form of inequality – are taboo.

The second precedent goes back to Ellen Key, reformer of conditions for children in Sweden, whose *Century of Childhood* (1900) reacted against the excessively austere education meted out to children. Instead of well-disciplined little gentlemen and ladies, she wanted to see children who really had the right to be children, according to principles very similar to those adopted by A. S. Neill in England.

In Scandinavia more than all other Western countries, these anti-authoritarian ideas must have had an influence on planning habitat layout. Every neighbourhood is obliged by law to provide adequate spaces for children to play in. There has to be a play area for small children for every residential block comprising thirty families. It must be protected from traffic and no more than 50 m from the house entrance. For bigger children, larger play areas are required as well as fields for ball games no more than 150 m from the entrance to the flats.

Since the 1960s, housing estates have been planned to be separate from road traffic. The blocks of flats are linked by bicycle and pedestrian paths to the play areas, schools, shops and other amenities. The road network stops at car parks set about 100 m from the dwellings.

Compared with other European countries, Scandinavia has extensive outdoor playground facilities for children. This is perhaps a consequence of the fairly late age at which schooling begins and the short school day, which allows the children more time for playing than in France or the United Kingdom. However, the Nordic climate restricts out-of-doors play to two hours a day for most of the year, which means that the children spend most of their time indoors. While their exterior environment is generally of a high quality, the same cannot be said of their indoor play-space.

Scandinavian families live in smaller dwellings than families in other Western countries. The greater part of the home is reserved for the adults, as for instance the living room and main bedroom. The children are allowed to play in their own room and in the kitchen. Bedrooms are small (about 10 square metres) and often shared by two children.

At home, most children of pre-school age engage in calm and silent activities (L. Gaunt, 1980). It is only very seldom that they play the creative and imaginative games which developmental psychologists consider essential for learning social skills.

The protected life which Scandinavian children lead means that the rate of child mortality due to accidents is lower there than in any other country. Nevertheless, every year one child in every six or seven ends up in hospital as the result of an accident. The number of accidents involving children exceeds the number of accidents at work. Most often children are injured at home or in their own neighbourhood. Thus, in spite of the attention paid to their safety, they live more dangerously than their parents do at work.

Traffic accidents are one of the major causes of serious injury. Half of all fatal accidents involving children occur on roads. The astonishing thing is that a large proportion of injured children are passengers in the car at the time of the accident. This must be the consequence of their many to-ings and fro-ings by car between their parents' homes, the nursery, sport centres, family and summer residences.

Safety at work is covered by law. Every workplace must have a safety department run by a workers' representative. Even accidents which are only near-misses have to be reported, and the employer is obliged to take adequate measures. Nothing of the kind exists to ensure the safety of children. Sweden has a government consultative council which addresses the problems of childhood environment, but there is no single municipal councillor in charge of this domain at local level. 'That's not in my brief' 'We haven't any money', 'No plans for improvement are pending', are the usual responses to complaints by parents about dangerous roads, damaged playground facilities, potholes, etc. This is perhaps one example demonstrating that dialogue, though much promoted, turns out in practice to be a one-way conversation. Dialogue is used to improve official policy in matters of child education and the diffusion of new laws, etc., but when parents want to submit their own proposals, they find the door shut.

The myth of the isolation of old people

In the old days peasants did not wait until they died of exhaustion in the middle of their fields to stop working. They would transmit their farms to their adult children and move into a little house nearby. It was quite common for the parents to draw up a contract with their children. In exchange for the farm, the old couple would be entitled to food, clothes, fuel, pocket money, etc. Thus there were neither legacies nor wills, and national laws on inheritance were circumvented. The different generations in one family would live close to each other, united by strong links of dependence. Nothing that we know about peasant families in the old days indicates that these links between generations were harmonious (D. Gaunt, 1983b).

On the contrary, old couples had every reason for anxiety. Their material existence was linked to the prosperity of their children. The new couple who took over the farm had the double burden of providing for their parents and their children. Often, when times were hard, these new farmers had no other solution but to get rid of their elders for good. Old people's homes were never very attractive, and it is not surprising that arsenic was nicknamed 'retirement powder'. Scandinavian folklore is full of hair-raising jokes and stories about the treatment of old relatives. While these seem to have been a way of letting off steam rather than authentic records they nevertheless provide good illustrations of the anguish underlying relations between the generations.

In the early days of the welfare state, its ideologists thought that old people's dependence on their families would become a thing of the past. Each family and household was to be self-sufficient, and links between the generations were to be broken. The idea of the nuclear family has survived and nowadays is viewed above all as an isolating factor.

Little girls nowadays have an average life expectancy of between seventy-eight and eighty years, and little boys will live between seventy-one and seventy-four years. This represents an advance since 1930 of about nine years for men and twelve for women. The greatest advance has been in Finland, where life expectancy for women has shifted from fifty-nine to seventy-nine years since the 1930s.

Never before have so many generations been alive at the same time. In the nineteenth century, becoming a grandmother was comparatively rare. Nowadays it is very usual to become a grandmother before the age of fifty, a great-grandmother at around seventy and, if one lives to ninety, there is a slight chance of becoming a great-great-grandmother. It is more than likely that a child born in our time will have many more relatives around him than a child born a century ago. Conversely he will have fewer brothers, sisters and cousins because of the fall in the birth rate. In the past, however, the ranks of brothers and sisters were decimated by infant mortality. Never before in the past did a child have so many chances of having two grandmothers, two grandfathers and even great-grandparents. Further, there is a far greater chance, too, that these grandparents will be active and in good health.

Old age pensions have been steadily rising since the 1940s and nowadays many retired Swedes enjoy a higher standard of living than families with children. They can afford travel, entertainment and luxuries which are not within the reach of their own children and grandchildren.

In many cases, financial aid now flows in the opposite direction, from old people to their children's families.

Most old people do not leave their homes, even once they have become handicapped. They are able to stay because of the high quality of their habitat and the system of home care, including medical care and help with the housework. As long as old people are still living as couples they rarely require to be taken in by specialized bodies such as retirement homes. As it is, even single persons over the age of eighty are seldom entrusted to institutional care. According to the Swedish census in 1991, 22 per cent of Swedes over eighty live in hospitals (long-term care) or in collective housing.

However, although it is apparently usual for old persons to live with one of their children or in an institution, a glance at the population as a whole gives a different picture. Three generations living together are to be found in only in 1 per cent of households. The most widespread model has the generations living in separate homes but close to each other. Retirement and improved living conditions have allowed greater intimacy to be enjoyed without giving rise to isolation. Almost half of all retired people have at least one child living within 15 km of their home: leaving out those with no children, two-thirds of all the elderly have children living within this distance.

Living nearby allows frequent visits. Around half of all old people maintain weekly contact with their close relatives, and only a small proportion (6 per cent in 1976) live alone without frequent family contacts.

The same model of intergenerational social life predominates in the other age groups. Around half of all families with children see their grandparents at least once a week, which means, of course, that there are many opportunities for contact between grandparents and grandchildren.

These figures apply to Sweden, but in this field there are very few differences to be observed between the Nordic countries. Thus, for many Swedish families, these close intergenerational links are part of their everyday life. Summer holidays and Christmas celebrations are family matters. Those who do not live close together will spend their holidays together; people newly settled in town will return to their native villages as soon as possible. The countryside is repopulated in summer; hamlets are transformed into summer houses, and new buildings spring up on the parents' land. Sweden can be said to be a country which has been urbanized by the mind but not by the heart. The real home is found in the country, and not in town. An amazing revival of amateur genealogists has been observed, haunting local archives in an attempt to trace their ancestors.

With the generations no longer weighed down by economic dependence and the heavy burden of responsibility, it seems that an affective and moral solidarity is developing. Although the entire care of old persons and children no longer falls on the intermediate generations, there are particular occasions when family responsibility is stimulated. Old people are cared for by relatives between visits from their home help, and grandparents are needed for baby-sitting. Temporary loans are provided and a hand is given with repairs to the home, fruit-picking, the garden or fishing (L. Gaunt, 1985).

Most Swedes and Finns agree in thinking that 'problems ought not go outside the family circle'. Problems about bringing up the children and marriage difficulties are preferably resolved without recourse to specialist counsellors (Liljeström and Dahlström, 1981; Haavio-Mannila, 1982).

With regard to the closeness of family ties, there are few differences between the social classes, with one exception. The liberal professions (lawyers, doctors, researchers, journalists, social workers, etc.) generally maintain far looser relations with their family than other social groups. University studies and a far more dispersed employment market often force them to live at a fair distance from their place of birth. A survey was conducted in 1980 which showed that only one in five middle-aged women practising a liberal profession lived within 15 km of her parents' home, as opposed to two in three blue-collar workers, office staff, farmers and managers of small private businesses (L. Gaunt, 1985).

It is very probable that this experience of moving away from parents, which is peculiar to the liberal professions, their need to find other social networks and their dependence on public institutions where children are concerned, are changing their vision of the family. The myth of the isolated nuclear family is thus perpetuated, because this is the experience of the most vocal group, and it is overlooked that the great majority live within a network of close family ties.

For the liberal professions, the remedy for isolation is found in a greater development of the neighbourhood spirit. A great deal of social work involves putting neighbours in touch with one another. Architects try to build neighbourhoods which encourage an atmosphere of solidarity between the residents. However, this work never seems to produce confirmed results. People prefer their family to their neighbours. One can ask one's family for help without the need for instant reciprocation; or, as a woman said, 'A difference of opinion with one's mother-in-law will be settled one day or another, whereas in the case of a neighbour, one avoids them.'

Private cars, telephones, long holidays and fast public transport make it easier to maintain uninterrupted contact with one's family. It also means that people are often en route to relatives. Improved living conditions make it easier to have these visitors to stay. The number of summer houses built on a close relative's land has also been seen to rise. Kinship has thus gradually become the heart of society, while at the same time the forms of the family are diversifying. Consequently neighbourhoods are now only places where people live, and not the sphere in which they develop their network of social relations.

The future: communes or kinship?

Over the whole of Scandinavia, as in other European countries, some groups are forming residential communes based on the notion of community spirit. Such groups are normally composed of intellectuals and are often created by architects. They contain families with children, and many of the parents have lived through the student revolts of the 1960s and early 1970s. They belong to men's and women's liberation movements and support anti-nuclear campaigns. They wish to live an alternative lifestyle, although many of them are well established in society, often as civil servants.

These communes are normally composed of separate private units, with large-scale communal amenities. The individual units are houses or flats of normal size composed of small private rooms with more spacious dining room and kitchen, utility room, games room and sauna. The collective amenities are held under a common contract, whereas the private units can be bought or rented individually. The number of families can vary from five to fifty (Kärnekull, 1980).

The people who live in these communes think that they can thus benefit from the combination of family and community life, which it is impossible to obtain in normal residential conditions. There are many advantages. Through being organized on a collective basis, household jobs are simplified and expenses are reduced. The evening meal is often prepared in common for the whole commune. By means of a rota, each person spends less time doing the shopping, cooking and washing up: 'Cooking spaghetti for twenty takes no longer than it does for four.' Buying food in bulk also saves time and money.

Women feel that it is easier to organize shared household tasks within a large group than with a single man. If everyone has agreed to take part in the housework, the cooking, the washing up and child care, men cannot get out of it as easily as in a normal family.

Children, it is thought, flourish in these communes. In them they find more than mere playfellows; they find a large group of brothers and sisters, and an adult is always nearby to provide help or comfort. The following advertisement was placed in a newspaper by a Danish woman: 'I am looking for a hundred parents for my child.' She got an impressive number of answers from parents who felt the same need. This was how one of the first Danish communes of this type was formed in the mid-1970s. Many others in Denmark were to imitate them, for the commune movement was particularly strong there.

The commune offers an excellent solution to the problem of organizing time for a number of intellectuals. Within it, they may also maintain a network of close friendships, even during the years when their children are small. As we have already indicated, this group often lives far away from its close family, and granny cannot come around in the evening to mind the children. As intellectuals, they see the advantages of sharing household tasks, and as members of the liberal professions they can count on discussion to resolve their problems. In fact, most of them spend their working day in meetings, seminars, consultations and therapy sessions.

The question however remains whether the commune is a solution for other social classes, in which strong kinship links increase family obligations but also reduce the need to live in a commune. Without the habit of discussion, would a manual worker not have difficulty getting his opinion across in a commune whose whole existence is based on agreement by everyone? It could also turn out to be difficult to adapt to the way of life in a community, especially those which are based on very strict principles.

The present situation – unstable families with their children within a stable kinship network – could well constitute the future for most Scandinavians. But there is a danger on the horizon. Are the narcissistic parents of today, who often put their own happiness before that of their children, capable of assuming the role of grandparents safeguarding their grandchildren's stability?

The family has survived other threats: poverty, industrialization, urbanization and female employment. There is thus every reason for believing that the family as an institution will also be able to overcome the problems of today.

THIRTEEN

Families in France

Martine Segalen and Françoise Zonabend

In a work like *A History of the Family* which looks at its subject from the perspective of time immemorial, any attempt to analyse contemporary family situations in France will present problems. If we make the attempt, we must assess the status of a vision which is necessarily bound to the present. In this field everything soon falls out of fashion, unlike the historical vision which enjoys the necessary distance to distinguish the major trends and relegate material, which may seem important to us today, to the rank of anecdote. While we may laugh at what hygienists and populationists were writing in the 1900s on account of their ideological load, our own demographers, who are equipped with proper statistical tools, often make mistakes when predicting the next twenty-five years. Do the clues floating on the surface of the very brief period which we will be discussing mark the beginning of a new era, or do they instead show that the trend will soon be reversed since, as has been fairly well established, demographic cycles alternate with the generations and their contrasting behaviour? Will we see today's babies, born to small families, producing larger sibling groups in twenty-five years time? How will family structures be affected by recession whose length and depth no one can yet predict?

Social changes and new mentalities

The family in France has never been subjected to so many studies as over the last twenty years. Although people were still referring to the 'crisis of the family' in the 1980s this certainly did not apply to research into the family. Moreover, themes have changed and the family is now being celebrated. Abundant statistical, sociological and psychological data are available for examining it, both at short range when following its demographic evolution, and from a distance, when the meaning and breadth of its transformations are to be appreciated. Historians, sociologists and ethnologists have co-operated successfully in producing a state-of-the-art picture of 'families in France', the term chosen in preference to 'French families' in order to stress their diversity and also to avoid the ideological content with which it is too often imbued. It is not our purpose to judge the family as a 'bastion', a 'rampart' or even a 'place in crisis'.

In an attempt to avoid the problems inherent in a contemporary analysis, we have tried to reveal, within the framework of the great trends presented in chapter 9, how families in France have retained some specific features, for instance the importance of the kinship group, and have acquired new ones, notably via the presence of immigrant groups. As we recall, France's economic evolution was characterized by its late economic revolution, by the preservation of its domestic base for industrial production, by the existence of a large agricultural population until the 1930s, and subsequently, from the 1950s, by massive and brutal population transfers to the conurbations, along with appeals to non-French workforces to participate in the post-war industrial development. More recently, France, like other European countries, has suffered rising unemployment and the increasing difficulties of the labour market. A new industrialization and urbanization process of this kind could not take place without consequences for the family.

Several models of household

Analysing the 1989 census provides a good snapshot of the diversity of households in France, and the picture which emerges shows a strong tendency to individualism, voluntary or enforced. Its most striking aspect, compared with data from twenty years earlier, is the way the family group has shrunk as a consequence of the fall in the birth rate: furthermore, the tendency is for co-residence between several households to disappear. We cannot be certain that the formidable rise in the number of those classified by the census as 'living alone' is the result of voluntary behaviour, although this certainly is the case with the lower birth rate and the separation of households. In 1989 one French household in four was composed of a single, widowed, divorced or unmarried person, generally elderly, with Paris as the capital of loneliness, where the proportion of persons living alone is one household in two.

The 1982 census stressed the fact that urban growth had halted and rural communities of less than 1,000 persons were developing, thus reversing a century-old trend. These facts have important consequences for family relations which can blossom through the existence of town–country relations; it is well known that many families are rooted in their landed property, even when there is not much of it. However, in the early 1990s, this trend seems to be in reverse. Thus, by looking back over the last twenty years, we can measure the intervening transformations in the structure of family groups living in France. Table 30 details (1) persons living alone; (2) single-parent families, meaning households with a single parent and one or more children, as in the case of widows, divorced persons and unmarried parents, in most cases women; (3) couples with or without children.

It is general knowledge that nowadays there are fewer legally consti-tuted couples and that divorces are on the increase. Marriages rose at a regular rate until 1972, when the number was over 400,000, but have since dropped to under 275,000 per annum in the early 1990s. It was in

Table 30   Household structures, France, 1968–1989

Households	1968	1975	1982	1989
Total	15 778 020	17 743 760	19 590 400	21 062 416
Single persons	3 198 240	3 935 100	4 816 680	5 617 107
	20.3%	22.2%	24.6%	26.7%
Men	1 021 720	1 312 300	1 665 660	1 970 510
	6.5%	7.4%	8.5%	9.4%
Women	2 176 520	2 622 800	3 151 020	3 646 597
	13.8%	14.8%	16.1%	13.7%
Other households	861 060	869 540	807 280	866 822
	5.5%	4.9%	16.1%	4.1%
One-parent families	658 280	726 320	846 820	1 097 461
	4.2%	4.1%	4.3%	5.2%
Man + children	132 060	140 980	122 900	146 933
	0.8%	0.8%	0.6%	0.7%
Woman + children	526 220	585 340	723 920	954 052
	3.3%	3.3%	3.7%	4.5%
Couples	11 060 440	12 212 800	13 119 620	13 453 482
	70.1%	68.8%	67.0%	63.9%
Married couples	10 739 687	11 870 842	12 382 220	12 185 415
	68.1%	66.9%	63.2%	57.9%
Unmarried couples	320 753	341 958	737 400	1 268 067
	2.0%	1.9%	3.8%	6.0%
Mean size of households	3.06	2.88	2.70	2.57

Sources: INSEE, census lists of 1968, 1975 and 1982; work survey, 1989.

the 1970s that the divorce curve for the whole of Europe was observed to climb rapidly: in France at the present time one marriage in three ends in divorce. The growing number of broken marriages, together with the reduced frequency of remarriage after divorce, should be interpreted as a challenge to the stability of the conjugal model. This seems all the more obvious when we consider the prevalence of juvenile cohabitation at the other end of the marriage sequence. Between 1957 and 1981, the number of extramarital couples in which the man is aged under thirty-five has risen from 155,000 to 400,000; in six years the proportion has more than doubled and is still growing. In 1990 there were 1,720,000 unmarried couples.

Finally, to these statistical signs of the frailty of the institutionalized couple we must add the rise in the number of extramarital births. It follows from the spread of contraceptive methods that such babies are wanted, and indeed they are increasingly seldom referred to as illegitimate; their birth rate has risen from 6 per cent between 1959 and 1966 to nearly 15 per cent in 1982 and 26 per cent in 1989.

These new models of conjugality can be placed with precision when we recall that, according to *Population et Sociétés* (April 1993), the total number of couples, married or otherwise, increased between 1982 and 1990. Projections by demographers like Hervé Le Bras and Louis Roussel in 1982 were based on the hypothesis that the final density of the marriage rate for the generations born between 1955 and 1959 will be set at between 80 and 85 per cent maximum. Even with these lower figures, the proportion of legally constituted couples will still be dominant, with a strong minority living in different family configurations, such as unmarried couples with or without children, single-parent families, recomposed families, divorced persons etc. What is new to France in the early 1990s is that these models are accepted in all their diversity. From being deviant forms, they have become new forms of normality accepted by society, contrary to the bourgeois ideology of the nineteenth century, which persisted into the 1960s and made the legally constituted family the sole and compulsory norm. A few years of juvenile cohabitation have allowed sociologists to observe that these free unions do not present a challenge to the homogamy which characterizes marriage. In so far as cohabitants choose each other, much as spouses do, from within matrimonial pools formed according to social class or educational level, their association no longer reeks of sulphur.

The variety of French households must be supplemented by that supplied by immigrant residents, less on account of their numerical importance than because of the collective fantasies in the form of racism which such households engender, and which are often experienced in terms of an alternative culture expressed in family attitudes. The proportion of immigrants living in France has not increased since 1957, and these 3,900,000 foreigners represent, as they did in 1931, around 6.5 per cent of the total population (Tribalat, 1991). Unlike pre-war immigrants, who were mostly of European origin sharing a Judaeo-Christian culture and have been assimilated into the French population via mixed marriages, the integration of more recent immigrants poses different problems according to the nationalities concerned. In fact, a strong proportion of immigrants to France are nowadays of African or Asian origin (48.5 and 8 per cent).

Just like the underqualified and unsettled workers at the beginning of industrialization, these immigrants supply strong contingents of isolated persons living in collective households, especially those whose origins lie in black Africa and North Africa (Brahimi-Tribalat, 1982). They form a sub-proletariat and experience an insecure and provisional way of life. Familialization undoubtedly provides a better means of social integration, according to a process observed in France in the case of provincials migrating to the cities. However, this familialization does not necessarily involve integration for every nationality. Eighty per cent of Spaniards, Italians (former immigrants) and Portuguese (recent immigrants) nowadays live in nuclear households comparable to French households. North African families are also becoming increasingly stabilized, in so far as the implementation of a restrictive immigration policy has ensured that recent arrivals in France are almost exclusively women and children coming to join a worker, thus helping to restore the balance of the sexes.

However, reconstituting their family units does not signify the end of their marginalization in relation to French families, as was the case with the Spaniards and Portuguese. The Muslim religion and notably the particular status which it confers on women have resulted in rejection from all sides, with second-generation immigrants often torn between conflicting aspirations. Although such immigrant families are under educated and the automatic first victims of unemployment, as well as being more fertile than families of French origin, they will gradually dissolve into the diversity of French family models when the cultural shocks which are being experienced on both sides have been assimilated.

The increase in transformations to the family

Until quite recently, all data relating to the family were the preserve of specialists who commented on it within the fastness of their scientific gatherings. Over the last few years, however, a new approach has been adopted, and this material has been put before the public. Since these figures are frequently published with dramatic commentaries, they have undoubtedly had some impact on individual attitudes. In the 1970s and 1980s not a week went by without a newspaper reporting a rise in juvenile cohabitation, studying the 'children of divorce', analysing the 'fertility crisis' or the 'rejection of children', or presenting marriage and divorce figures in order to announce that 'marriage is falling out of fashion', or describing the problems experienced by second-generation immigrants from North Africa, who feel ill at ease as individuals and in their families. One could well ask how much this kind of popularization has contributed to exacerbating the difficulties and accelerating the implementation of a family model not based on formal institutions, but only on a precariously formed couple, within which individuals are esteemed to the detriment of the collective feeling which the concept of the family always, to a greater or lesser degree, involves. Since the late 1980s the trend has been reversed, and the media are once again celebrating the family as a place of happiness and solidarity embodying modern values. One may well be amazed by these profuse new compliments, which seem to have developed in parallel with the crisis of the welfare state.

To what extent do the social and fiscal policies and laws which have gradually been introduced since the Second World War encourage the growth of the new type of couple, whose union lacks legitimacy only in that they have not gone through a registry office, but who are recognized and provided with a framework by the law and the social services just like married couples? Just like them, or better than them? A report on the 'Consequences of marital status as viewed by the legal, fiscal and social systems' presented to the Conseil Économique et Social (Economic and Social Council) by Evelyne Sullerot in 1983 concluded that French people were getting no encouragement whatsoever to marry. We can read in her report that

> Whereas the fixed aim of government is strict neutrality with regard to the choices made by couples and individuals, the effect of the laws and measures adopted over the years has been to handicap rather than favour marriage. This is derived from the fact that people can simultaneously benefit from the tax advantages given to unmarried and divorced people and the social advantages of marriage, which are equally granted to those cohabiting. The same person can even claim different civil status in different social services when it is advantageous.

Whether in relation to taxation or social assistance, 'those who do not accept legal responsibility for one another are assisted and often taxed less than those who do.' While all these measures were inspired by a just concern for freedom and neutrality with regard to individual situations, they have had the perverse effect of encouraging unions not sanctioned by law and contributing artificially to the rise in so-called illegitimate births. Sociologists find a remarkable illustration in all this of how complex the relationship between state and family is.

Our commentary on the figures relating to the structure of households cannot exhaust the whole subject of the family. Far from it: relations within the family group, between generations and relatives, and with those relatives and allied members who are dispersed in spatial terms but are designated by the term 'kin', cannot in fact be encapsulated by statistics. In order to study these themes, we must resort to monograph studies based on the psycho-sociological or ethnological approach.

A new economy of the couple

As we saw earlier, the constitution of couples has undergone successive identifiable phases over a number of distinct periods in the age of industrialization and urbanization: at the start, a variety of working-class families coexisted with bourgeois families and their constraining norms. The subsequent rise of the middle classes was accompanied by the return of women to the home, and thus by a strict redistribution of tasks. During this period, husbands had the task of earning the family's living, and wives that of maintaining an interior, which was particularly esteemed, and of bringing up their children, now fewer in number, through whom the family would achieve higher social status, while giving their husbands psychological support. Although this model was once believed to be both universal and traditional, it is now becoming truly dated as women enter the labour market and remain in it in spite of having children.

Sociology develops models which fall out of fashion like clothes and songs, and with the passage of time can be seen as the ideological products of their age. Thus Talcott Parsons (1943) considered the model of the couple with the father as sole provider to be a configuration particularly well adapted to the social and geographical mobility required by industrial and economic transformations. With the model of romantic marriage developed in the 1970s, and characterized by the spouses' 'companionate' relationship based on a bond of affection, people at the time liked to contrast it with the moneyed matches determined by mutual interest characteristic of bourgeois unions. But was the new model not derived from the glorification of individualism and freedom so dear to democratic countries in full spate of economic expansion?

At present, sociologists are analysing the effects of female employment on the couple, and their work will in its turn probably appear outmoded in a few years' time. Although the institution of the family is perennial, relationships between the individuals within it can evolve very quickly. Female employment is indeed another characteristic of the family in France. French women have always been employed on the labour market in greater numbers than the other women of Europe (with the exception of women in the former eastern bloc countries) and they have returned to it in massive numbers since the late 1960s. In 1986, women represented 44.6 per cent of the working population; in 56.4 per cent of couples with at least one employed member both partners were employed. No economic crisis seems to halt the trend to feminine employment, which affects all women, and especially young ones and the mothers of young children. In 1989, 77 per cent of women between twenty-five and forty-nine were employed, compared with 63 per cent in 1975.

We find that while an increasingly large proportion of the female population is combining marriage with work, this is certainly not a new situation. Over the last twenty-five years, however, sociologists have been specializing, studying the family and employment as separate subjects. Women had to enter the labour market in massive numbers before any connection was made between the two, and the fundamental interaction between family and working life was discovered. The repercussions of the two spheres of family and work are intertwined in many ways. To cite but a few examples, the woman's birth calendar – a fact of family life – is now adjusted to suit her work schedule; her choice of employment may be determined by proximity to home and flexibility of working hours; any deterioration in her working conditions or reduction in her salary will have consequences on her home life.

Although juvenile cohabitation and divorce, contraception and abortion are effectively accepted by French society to the point that these new forms of behaviour have given rise to laws expressing a more liberal attitude towards broken unions, voluntary limitation of births and interrupted pregnancies, society, as expressed through its legislation, does nothing to facilitate female employment.

The increase in women's work has been effected by young women in paid employment and by married women caring for one or two children. Consequently, the problem of providing care for pre-school children with working mothers arises, though this depends on the mother's job. For instance, 93 per cent of agriculturalists can keep their children at home while doing their work on the farm, but 81 per cent of office and commercial employees have to find child care outside the home. They generally resort to a baby-minder and only rarely to a crèche. An overall look at the ways of caring for young children shows that more than a quarter are cared for by a member of their family, 40.6 per cent by a paid minder outside the home, and only 8.6 per cent in crèches, most of which are in the cities, notably in the Paris conurbation. It is clear that there is an obvious lack of satisfactory child care places for young children in France in the 1990s; many crèches have waiting lists, showing that young parents now feel that this collective form of caring is the most suitable, although it was previously stigmatized because of its association with social assistance. The absence of adequate provision makes it difficult to evaluate precisely the importance of recourse to the kinship network, which basically means grandmothers, for help with looking after small children. Does this constitute a deliberate choice and would the kin be so frequently resorted to if the public services met these demands better?

According to Gokalp and David (1982) and Norvez (1982), the lack of child care also explains why pre-school attendance has boomed. By the age of three almost all French children are at school, a matter about which the public authorities and parents agree. The state considers it necessary to provide schooling for very young children in order to correct social and economic inequalities, and parents, for their part, find school a far less onerous form of child care than nurseries.

This explains in part why couples refuse to have a third child, since caring for it would present the working mother with considerable problems, and possibly force her to give up her job. Indeed, society's implicit reluctance to accept the fact that mothers work, or merely to pay lip service to the notion, is marked both by its refusal to develop programmes for the collective care of young children, and within the couple by its resistance to any redistribution of roles. It must be stressed here that the problems associated with women's desire to work place all couples in relatively similar situations, irrespective of their socio-professional standing.

Working women have to do 'double days' because they continue to assume the majority of domestic tasks, although men are more involved than they were. Sabine Chalvon-Demersay has observed, à propos the young cohabitants who seem to be promoting a new social model and vociferously proclaim the interchangeable nature of men and women, that at the end of the day it is the women who in practice take 'charge of supplies and the work of planning and budgeting' associated with domestic tasks (1983, p. 62).

The same traditional allocation of roles applies to child care. As time goes by, fathers gradually extricate themselves from the duties they assumed when their baby was born. Indeed, one need only ask who takes the child to nursery or school to see which duties fall on the mother and are not shared at all by the father, any more than other family duties are. Six children out of ten are always accompanied to nursery or school by their mother, and only one in ten always by their father. When both are working the same hours, three in four children are still accompanied by their mother. This does not mean that the father looks after the elder children; less than 5 per cent of schoolchildren are taken to or fetched from school by their fathers; 21 per cent go with their mothers and the rest either go on their own or with someone else.

In the case of domestic tasks, the traditional roles are still showing remarkable resistance. Not only do husbands take little part in them, but wives are satisfied with this unequal division of domestic chores. According to Catherine Gokalp and Henri Leridon, 58 per cent of working women questioned in 1981 felt that their husbands' participation was sufficient if he carried out only three out of the eight tasks listed in the survey. Feminists would say that this was evidence that women cherish their oppression, but others interpret this as showing that women do not want equality in the home since they appreciate having a preserve of their own.

Everything happens as though female employment were accepted on the condition that it does not disrupt home life or affect the standard of child care. This attitude is confirmed by the national survey conducted by Roussel and Bourguignon (1976, p. 126), in which wives still emerged as responsible for the upkeep of the household, and in particular for the care of young children, even when their employment was well accepted. There is no doubt that a situation pregnant with conflict was developing between women with their wish to work, and society and couples with their reluctance to help them. These conflicts can be resolved in various ways: women in top jobs are generally unmarried; those in intermediate jobs tend to limit their progeny; if there is too much conflict at home, they get divorced. The proportion of women seeking divorce has grown perceptibly, from 54.7 per cent in 1965 to 66 per cent in 1975, as Jacques Commaille has shown (1982, p. 55). This growth can be attributed in part to the new economic status of wives: being in paid work, they are autonomous on the economic level and can thus challenge the couple's very existence.

The constraints imposed by the presence of children, and the fact that society does little to assist working mothers, explain why marriage and childbirth act in different ways on husband and wife, as de Singly has stressed (1990). Although positive for the man, giving him a boost in the professional field, they are negative for his wife, interrupting her career and reducing her prospects of promotion. Married women with children may have started out with equal qualifications, but their careers will not be as good as those of men or unmarried women.

Society's ambiguous attitude to female employment is further characterized by the general acceptance that women, unlike men, have a choice. Women can choose whether or not to work (although, objectively speaking, this applies only to a few privileged categories), and whether or not to devote themselves to their children. The inference is that holding a job is obligatory for some and optional for others. Unlike men, whose behaviour is apparently motivated only by economic rationalism and professional ambition, women's entrance to the labour market is always related to the imperatives of family life, and they will still, more than ever, maintain close links with their family and children.

Couples in which both members are employed appear to be redefining themselves according to new aspirations which imperil the structure of family life, while simultaneously drawing strength from their dual employment. If the couple consists of no more than the association of two individuals pursuing autonomous aims and professional careers to which they are fully dedicated, then it incurs the risk of running into work-related conflicts. Take the case where one member is unemployed and finds a new job in another town: how will the other react in relation to his or her own professional commitment? Conversely, it can often be observed in the case of couples with dual professional careers, that their life outside work is centred on activities which allow them to share their free time, and in which all the members of the family group can join (Pitrou, 1983).

The interaction between a woman's professional life and her fertility also operates in two ways. The birth of children limits her professional future just as her career prospects restrict her opportunities for starting a family, since a woman's life is characterized by continuity between profession and family. These profound social changes in the model of the couple and its children cannot be summed up in terms of rejection of the couple and of motherhood. On the contrary, the birth of a child is part and parcel of the agenda adopted by new couples, which includes an extreme emotional investment in the child. However, what has definitively been rejected is large families, meaning three or more children. The arrival of a child presents material problems which the middle classes find hard to solve: these include the shortage of collective child care, lack of space at home and the expense involved. Having a third child would force the mother to stop working, and this, as we have seen, is contrary to women's aspirations. Not only is their pay needed, all the more so in an unstable financial situation, but women also find in their work a source of esteem and social contact even when employed in low-qualified jobs. Thus it is unlikely that the trend to female employment on the labour market will slow down, unless unemployment grows considerably worse, in which case women are, of course, the first victims; in 1992, 26 per cent of girls between fifteen and twenty-four were unemployed. In the same way, the number of children per couple does not seem due to rise. Opinion polls show that the model of the two-child couple is the more widespread the younger the generation questioned (Bastide, Girard and Roussel, 1982, p. 872).

Strong family networks

The fragility of these new households contrasts with the solidity of kinship groups, whose existence is now being rediscovered, having earlier been denied through unawareness of it (Segalen, 1991). It was assumed that all links with other conjugal units had been broken by industrialization, and research into the family was limited to the household, its formation and the relations between parents and children. Anthropology, by showing the social importance of kinship, has played a determining role in this area: sociologists and historians have resumed consideration of the ties which reach out extensively beyond the couple – married or not – and structure its relations within a larger whole consisting of parents, uncles and aunts, cousins, nephews and nieces.

While the importance of relations between a married couple and its parents was not unknown, there was a widespread idea that family relations ceased at this point and that people only met the other recognized members of their kinship group at purely symbolic celebrations marking various stages in life, including christenings, birthdays, weddings and funerals. On the whole, the general tendency was to reject everything of a family order in the private, affective and symbolic sphere, and to cut it off completely from the public world, from economic and institutional matters. Sociologists were in fact precisely contrasting the sort of society studied by anthropologists, in which all aspects of social life, especially those involving reproduction, are encompassed by kinship, with our society, in which family and socio-economic spheres are completely disconnected. This vision of a nuclear family cut off from the other members of its kinship group cannot be dissociated from the political contexts of its period, that of post-war economies in the throes of expansion, since all scientific discourse must to some extent reflect its period. Much in the same way that the formation of free unions seemed to announce the triumph of love, and the explosion of individual freedom proclaimed the defeat of the forces of fascism, so too the development of the welfare state restricted the family to a narrow sphere and deprived it of functions which it had previously assumed.

Sociologists are now placing a new emphasis on the strength of these family networks; it is, however, more a case of rediscovering them than of any sudden revival of the networks, which would be a curious parallel to a weakening of the couple.

Is the strength of family networks especially characteristic of French society? It may be so, when one recalls the size of the population in the agricultural sector until quite recently. French society ceased to be rural and peasant-based much later than English society. The strength of kinship groups may be attributed in part to their emergence from landed origins and from precise local terrains. Taking all social classes as a whole, many French people are the grandchildren of peasants, whereas in England the working and middle classes are the children and grand-children of workers who had long ago lost their rural origins. One feature common to kinship networks, irrespective of their social class, is that they integrate new normalities. Nowadays having a child without being married, or getting divorced no longer constitute reasons for breaking the links between generations or collateral lines. Young cohabi-tants receive considerable financial assistance from their parents, just as married children do.

Nowadays, kinship networks can be seen to function primarily through the transmission of goods and services between the generations (Gotman, 1988). Roussel and Bourguignon (1976) conducted surveys which reveal these new forms, detached from the traditional stages in the family life cycle: dowry has gone and less property is being bequeathed. In the more prosperous classes, economic transfers are made in the new form of building society savings schemes for children, by which an initial deposit will secure them a low-interest loan in the future. Intergenera-tional assistance can be observed at all levels as part of a larger framework of exchanges between kin, going well beyond the symbolic functions to which it was previously confined. Some authors speak of 'familial sociability', meaning frequent and regular meetings between family members as well as the exchange of goods and services. The latter may vary in form and intensity with the age of the people involved and their social category, but it is present throughout French society.

Retirement often provides parents with the opportunity to strengthen this sociability, which works both ways, because what the parents give in material time they get back in affection and psychological support, both of which are particularly necessary when they stop working. While the intensity of these relationships will obviously be moulded according to where the parties live and the means which parents and children have at their disposal, it is in general very deep. Among the working classes, as Guilbert (1983, p. 137) has shown, three out of four parents see their married children at least once a week. Retired parents can help in various ways, and themselves receive contributions in kind as well as financial and administrative assistance. When these retired relatives live in a house with a garden attached, a specific form of family sociability will emerge, based on the distribution of crates of fruit and vegetables, poultry and eggs by the parents to their children. Surplus produce from well-tended plots will serve to nourish family sociability in both the literal and the figurative sense, and what is called an underground economy will be grafted onto family networks. What is more, these will include not only parents and children but other more distant kin who will make a return for the goods under different forms.

The role of the information circulated among family networks is underestimated, although these can provide invaluable help in entering employment. A national survey showed that 22 per cent of young people had found their first job through the mediation of their family (Gokalp, 1981, p. 70). In this domain, the sons and daughters of agriculturalists, craftsmen and tradesmen receive the most assistance, since in their case the family network compensates for their lack of education; such recommendations are especially useful for those who cannot take examinations or acquire degrees.

Contemporary working-class familialism is expressed not only in the stability of the worker family unit, which is less affected than other social classes by divorce and the rise in cohabitation (Verret, 1983, Schwartz, 1990), but also in the multifunctionalism of family networks, which may be explained by the fact that the working classes are deprived of other forms of social contact.

At the other end of the social ladder, in a bourgeoisie which derives its legitimacy from the preceding generations, the group's social reproduction is ensured by maintaining very active kinship networks, in spite of the transformations which each couple introduces. Bourgeois identity is reproduced within these families which have, until recent generations, been characterized by a high birth rate. Married brothers and sisters maintain active links, and cousins often see one another, especially in the holidays, which are spent together in their great family houses in the provinces. Although the middle classes are not alone in spending their holidays in their parents' houses, this trait being very widespread among all social classes, the bourgeoisie is unique in possessing both the space and the means to accommodate all the grandchildren at the same time, so that cousins can establish bonds which remain firm all their lives, having been forged in their childhood.

It is from these reunions and memories that the image of *bon papa* and *bonne maman* emerges; these terms are used to designate the grand-parents, who are called 'pépé' and 'mémé' in other social classes. They refer to semi-mythical images of the ancestral figure. Bourgeois kinship networks are so integrated that the term *pièce rapportée* (always pronounced in inverted commas and with a smile) has been coined to designate spouses who marry into a sibling group. The term suggests the image of a close-knit group to which foreign elements attach themselves, finally fusing with it, though retaining the stigma of outsider status.

Between worker familialism and the vast kinship networks of the bourgeoisie lie the middle classes, whose family relationships can vary in intensity. Le Wita (1984) has demonstrated, in relation to Parisian families living in the thirteenth *arrondissement*, the importance of their kinship ties, which may function more on the symbolic than the material level. In their case, the intensity of their relationships varies with their level of academic achievement and depends on whether there is inherited property. A degree will ensure access to the labour market without the help of relatives; this is even more the case as a person rises higher up the qualifications and income ladder and his ability to present and 'sell' himself grows in value. The existence of family houses where the members can go for weekends and during holidays also contributes to the family's cohesion; such a place outside Paris provides a kind of mythical cradle for the detached line in the metropolis, and a symbolic means of identification which helps the dispersed members of the sibling group to overcome their relative separation. Perhaps it is these more prosperous classes – not, strictly speaking, the bourgeoisie – that find it easiest to manage the combination of family links and the relationships with friends developed in the social aspect of their leisure time.

The importance of family networks in France and the value set on identification with a line were marked in the 1980s by an obsession with reconstructing family trees. Not so long ago this pastime was one for aristocratic families in search of their quarterings. Nowadays thousands of French people take pride in their ancestors, even when these were people of no account, and enjoy discovering their roots and finding their place in a territory which geographical and social mobility caused their families to leave. Does this trend on the part of individuals and couples to enter their names in their genealogy portend a weakening of the family? On the contrary, ties are activated, solidarities formed and imaginations nourished by events like family parties bringing together 500 descendants of a single ancestor, which could never have happened as recently as thirty years ago. The kinship networks of French families bear witness to the family institution's powers of resistance and form part of the process of social reproduction of which they are the agents.

Social reproduction and social mobility

Genealogies provide a good insight into social and geographic mobility on the individual level, but they can also deceive, because a further feature peculiar to French society is that social mobility is less a result of internal promotion within a family line than of changes in the structure of society, as demonstrated in the work of Claude Thélot and Michel-Louis Lévy (1982, 1983). Considering the decline in the farming population since the 1950s, it is obvious that farmers' children have been leaving the countryside. In itself, this fact means that the gap between social categories shows no sign of dwindling and that social reproduction is still very strong. For instance, it is well known that civil service jobs are transmitted through families, with the top qualifications 'passing' from father to son. However, the same continuity can be observed in less prestigious professions, among post office and railway workers and in the police. More generally, it is the level of academic degree, and that vague qualification which Pierre Bourdieu has termed 'cultural heritage', which determine the way lines are maintained among occupational categories of comparable status. Marriage plays a considerable role in the process of duplication from one generation to the next. We now know, in the case of the upper bourgeoisie, that marriage ensures the reproduction of this social class by allowing in the groups which hold economic and political power. The endogamy of the great bourgeois families in the early period of capitalism, the archetype of which are the textile manufacturers in the north, has been replaced by a greater openness to a variety of professional groups at the top of the social ladder: senior civil servants, bank and company directors and politicians. The same social heredity can be noted at all levels of society.

Sociologists have a tendency to exaggerate the results of their analyses. They look at the curves for divorce, marriage and fertility rates and conclude that the traditional model of marriage and the family has collapsed. Let us say in the first instance that, going by the evidence in this book, there is no traditional model of the family. It has not stopped evolving, and several family types have coexisted in each period. Nor does the term 'crisis' seem any more appropriate. The dominant family model provides a firm point of reference for all forms of behaviour; acceptance of other models reflects a liberalization of attitudes, but is still a minority outlook. The fact that women continue to identify firmly with their role as mothers even when they are employed on the labour market shows that, though the couple is evolving and the family group assumes a variety of structures, the familial institution is still the dominant pattern, and its normative weight is still just as effective on the level of mental and symbolic images.

The fruitfulness of kinship networks and the reproductive power of the family put the hackneyed themes of the family in crisis and marriage outmoded in a new light. Viewed in all its variety, the family is an institution with considerable power in French society. Its strength comes from the support of other resistant forces, and the state can do little to change it.

Have family rituals endured or broken off?

The fact that the family institution has been maintained is partly due to its reliance on a set of unchanging features. The family occupies a designated space within which its identity is perpetuated; it lies at the centre of a network of relatives who succour it when required to do so; and it observes a number of rituals through which it is constantly taking stock of itself.

The family as a space for living

In France, as in the other agrarian societies of Europe, the early appropriation of land by individuals and the coalescence between unit of production and unit of residence caused the family to be defined very early on as a group of related persons living under one roof around the same hearth. Whatever its composition, a family is established in a space, a site where its social and familial life unfolds, and where a whole series of comportments of a semi-ritualized nature take place, which define each group's individuality. The quality of this space is no less important nowadays than it was in former times; it provides clues to the social standing, cultural milieu and regional origin of the group living there, and it constitutes an anchorage for the family's collective memory.

It is a commonplace that the aristocrat's dwelling has nothing in common with that of the bourgeois, which differs in turn from the peasant's. However, despite the diversity of all these types of dwellings and family spaces, which have nothing in common, they all possess the same specific value. These dwellings are now, as they were in former times, places for family memories and spaces with which families identify. Their furnishings and ornaments, all the knick-knacks they contain, are objects with a history of their own, which may be told in detail and constantly reiterated, as in this account by a Burgundian peasant woman recorded in 1970, which would not be out of place in other localities and other times:

> The table comes from the Grivots of Velbret; it was at my great-great-grandmother's and she gave it to my grandmother, which is how I got it. The dresser comes from my Vernet aunt's, mummy's godmother. The grandfather clock comes from my cousin's . . . the cupboard was a wedding present, it belonged to mummy, and my son took another, which came from an aunt. When my grandmother died, I got the little tureen, and my cousin got the big one; as for the two brass chandeliers, we each took one . . . Grandfather's rosary went to the eldest son. As for mummy's rosary, which came to me, I gave it to my youngest nephew when he made his First Communion. (Zonabend, 1984, p. 37)

Detailed records of goods received, shared and transmitted are kept; these objects and pieces of furniture, whose origins, history and future are known, constitute a tangible means of memorizing the family genealogy. In these dwellings the role and place of kinship relations is instantly established, and the family's endurance can instantly be read. In these ordered spaces, which are charged with representing family values, everything bears witness to the different stages of the family's constitution from generation to generation and in the course of a single generation.

It is also well known that while some families are capable of accumulating, sharing and redistributing, there are others which cannot. Modern life is forcing more and more families to give up their family houses. Generations no longer succeed each other in the same place, sibling groups disperse, and divorces and remarriages involve multiple changes of residence. However, in spite of all these hazards, it seems that every family has its share of souvenirs – objects, family papers and photographs – which serve to anchor its memories. Photographs, in particular, have come into increasingly general use, and tend to be given a place alongside traditional family emblems, sometimes even superseding them. They include portraits of ancestors and children, and of the ceremonies and feasts which punctuate family life; the function of such photographs, whether hung on walls or spread around on top of furniture, arranged on a sort of commemorative altar or carefully tucked away into the family album, is that of 'treasuring the family heritage' (Bourdieu, 1990). They are distributed and exchanged between the members of a kinship group and play a part in maintaining family relations. They are contemplated and commented on in these terms

A family record in photographs.

within the family and, along with family papers and inherited objects, they help to include newcomers and to strengthen group memories. Thus the social habits which photography has elicited constitute true rites for memorizing and integrating people into the family. The success and popularization of photography can be explained, among other features, by its ability to immortalize the family group and by its integration in the rites of passage which punctuate the life of the group.

Other forms of behaviour are also fostered in the context of this family intimacy and act as forces for the perpetuation and reproduction of the group. It is these rites of a convivial (meals taken in common) and a social nature (wakes and group prayers) and these codes of conduct (whether relatives kiss or shake hands), which vary between social classes, regions and sometimes families. The unity of the family group is strengthened by its participation in these semi-ritualized habits. By engaging in them, the group is in effect drawing a distinction between those who know them and those who do not, between the stranger who does not use them and its members who conform to them.

Such habits also make it possible to establish links with previous periods, times when ancestors were also performing the same gestures and conforming to the same practices. In this way the family's history is relived every day within the family space and will be continued in perpetuity. Holding on to a way of life specific to a particular family involves remaining in a time warp in which the members of the family are linked by this way of life to past and future generations. Both this intimate space within which the family lives and the codes of behaviour to which it is bound contribute to setting it within a collective family time.

Naming one's relatives

Every family in France, whatever its social origins or the period in which it is studied, is set within a kinship network formed of blood and allied relatives who are recognized by every member of the group. This collection of persons composes 'its' kin. The latter is easily identified, no less so in Western society than in others, via the terminology that we have elaborated to classify our kin.

This vocabulary is not well known in the case of past centuries. In fact, social anthropologists made no attempt to collate it in the periods when they were operating, when this terminology was still in use. As for historians, they have not yet started to research this subject through the archives and records they handle. This means that the few available bits of information have come from surveys conducted by ethnologists on contemporary social groups.

In France it appears from our way of 'talking family' that our kinship group is characterized by three main traits. Allied and blood relatives are clearly differentiated; the latter are classified according to a hierarchy and divided between paternal and maternal kin; finally, our dead relatives are included in the family just like the living.

It is probable that we used in former times to possess a far wider vocabulary for referring to alliance (Benveniste, 1969, pp. 245–6). English-speaking countries still distinguish between in-law relatives, meaning those allied by marriage or by marriage with a brother or sister, and step-relatives, meaning those allied by a parent's marriage (the mother's husband or the father's wife) or by a spouse's former marriage (children by a first spouse). In French-speaking countries, no difference is made between these kinds of allied relatives. Further, it is significant that in the towns, especially among the bourgeois classes, there is a tendency to assimilate the in-laws of blood relatives to the blood kin. The expression 'oncle par alliance' (uncle by marriage) is used less and less to designate the husband of the father's or mother's sister. Indeed, no distinction is made between him and a father's or mother's brother: both are 'uncles'.

Our relatives by alliance are thus essentially our spouse's blood relatives. And indeed, there are plenty of expressions indicating that these particular relatives are 'not part of the family', being *pièces rapportées* who do not come from the same stock. Even when they are referred to by means of terms borrowed from the vocabulary of kinship, the word used is preceded by *beau* or *belle* (in-law) as a sign of deference, or by 'wife of' or 'husband of', or followed by the formula 'by alliance' to indicate distance. Furthermore, specific terms are used to designate our close allies: *conjoint(e)* (spouse); *gendre* and *bru* (son-in-law and daughter-in-law). These last two terms are tending in urban circles to lose ground to *beau-fils* and *belle-fille*, providing an instance of how our vocabulary changes over time. Although we once employed *parâtre* and *marâtre* to designate our parents' spouses, the former term has fallen into disuse, and the latter has acquired such pejorative connotations that no one dares use it any more.

These ways of talking and modes of designating do indeed serve to indicate the particular status and place of these relatives. Proverbs also attest to it, since they all boil down in more or less the same way to the antagonism between parents-in-law and children-in-law: 'Every son-in-law and every daughter-in-law is a stranger' (Franche-Comté); 'A son-in-law's love is like the sun in winter' (Provence) (Segalen, 1983), not to mention the stereotyped stories on the prickly theme of relations between mother and daughter-in-law.

Hence it is not surprising that many features of family rituals are found to perform the essential function of linking and uniting the two groups of blood and allied relatives, especially when the marriage joining them was a 'family affair', intended to unite not only two people but also two partners, so as to favour the union of the two groups. Hence the propitiatory and well-meant noisy accompaniment to the wedding procession to ensure a good conjunction and favour the spouses' passage from one house to the other. Hence too the custom of mingling the two kinship groups in the procession, at the banquet and even at the celebration of mass on the following day for 'the dead of the two families'. In the wedding photograph, however, the solemn pictorial record of the alliance, the two kinship groups are still separated, each on its own side, behind its relative, and when the alliance is broken by death, each spouse may well be returned to his or her own family vault (Zonabend, 1973).

In fact, a true alliance will only be formed at the birth of a child. After all, it is with the new generation and through its mediation that allied relatives become blood relatives; children transform parents-in-law into grandparents, and spouses into fathers and mothers. Furthermore, it is by systematically choosing both the child's spiritual parents from its paternal and maternal lines respectively, in the societies of north-eastern Europe at any rate, and thus linking the two families' honours and services, that the bond between them is confirmed. Indeed, this role of the rituals of birth, that of bringing together allied relatives, explains in part why baptism was held in such affection. When it was banned during the Revolution, it was replaced by a republican form of godparenting.

Who, then, are these blood relatives? Every European society, now as in the past, employs a kinship terminology with five major categories of blood relatives. The kin by blood of a living individual is composed, in addition to his direct descendants, of his collaterals and their direct descendants, meaning his brothers and sisters, nephews and nieces, great-nephews and great-nieces; of his paternal grandfather's descendants, meaning his uncles and aunts whose descendants are his first cousins; then come the children of his paternal grandfather's father (i.e. his great-grandfather), whom he designates great-uncle, great-aunt, and whose descendants are his second cousins. Finally, beyond this kin classification, all strict designations in terms of category or genealogical ranking disappear, leaving only cousins in the vague sense, people to whom one knows one is related without being able to trace the exact ramifications of the kinship (see figure 14).

Formerly, there were local and provincial terminologies which existed alongside this national vocabulary. In Burgundy for instance, the group formed by the married couple and their unmarried children was designated by the generic locution *chez* together with its patronym, after which came *les propres*, the descendants of the maternal and paternal grandfather and grandmother and uncles. The group formed by great-uncle and second cousins was called *les parents à la mode de Bourgogne* (relatives in the manner of Burgundy). Beyond them, finally, came the cousins. In Lower Brittany today people distinguish between close relatives (*tud ker tost*, literally 'close kinsfolk'), and people who are distantly related, designated by the term *cousiné*; after these comes a third category of kin, the *pas parents du tout* (not related at all); it is among this group that marriages are preferentially formed (Segalen, 1991). In Quebec the members of the household were designated by the expression *chez nous*, with the term *les propres* or *les vrais* used to name the father's and mother's cousins and their descendants; after them came the grandparents' cousins and their descendants, who constituted relatives on the left or right buttock or thigh (*de la fesse, de la cuisse*)

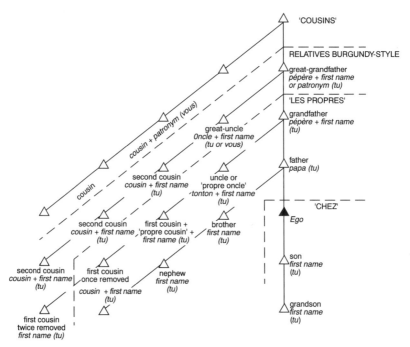

Figure 14 Terms of reference and ways of addressing kin in northern Burgundy; zones in which *tu* and *vous* are used

depending on whether the maternal or paternal side was meant, beyond which stretched the zone of *cousins* (Collard, 1979, p. 227). Quebecan nomenclature introduced a distinction between blood relatives on the paternal and maternal sides respectively, as relatives on the 'right' or 'left' side. This distinction can be seen in many other societies. In Albania, for instance, where 'kinship through blood' refers to paternal relatives and 'kinship by milk' to the maternal side; the same applies in Romania, where the distinction is between 'big' and 'little' kin.

Both in France and in other countries, the tendency is for these regional terms to disappear under the unifying and reductionist influence of national languages, but the attitudes remain. Thus there is not a single family in our contemporary society which does not distinguish between maternal and paternal kin. This is easily shown by tracing the course of any genealogy; greater recognition is always paid to one side, and its more numerous kin are entered with greater care. The same will happen on both sides of the genealogy, with some lines being retained and others lost. On the side or line which is retained and which is known about, the informant will mention every relative, detailing their origins and fates with care; the other side and the lines which he has decided to forget about will, however, present systematic lacunae and a dearth of information. In reality, people all use their genealogy in their own way and to manipulate their identity. The importance of genealogical memory is linked to the value accorded to one or other original line, and each genealogy prunes and cuts off its filiations in a sociologically significant manner. These differences of recall are not explained simply by demographic or geographic factors, but answer to the norms and social practices proper to each group studied.

Furthermore, this vocabulary of kinship has an obvious functional role; it enables us to know which family ceremonies we have to attend and, depending on one's ranking in the genealogy, whether one will be directly invited or 'notified' of it by other relatives. This vocabulary refers not only to a code of behaviour but also to a ceremonial protocol.

These family ways of doing things have obviously varied over time. In the old days the baptism of a new-born baby would take place very soon after birth and would never be the occasion of a great ceremony since only a few family members and its godparents would be involved. When the child made his First Communion, the circle of invited participants would broaden to include a few close relatives, and at his marriage the range of the invitations was extended to include cousins, but only those in the spouses' own age group. It was death which finally brought the entire kin together. In the same way the necessary participants for the proper performance of family rites were found within this kinship group:

when a marriage took place, the best man and maid of honour would be chosen from the spouses' brothers and sisters, with their uncles and first cousins serving as witnesses; their godparents, who had been chosen by preference from among grandparents or close collaterals, would lead the spouses to the altar. On the occasion of a death, the deceased person's close relatives were released from all direct obligations, and distant cousins would perform the requisite task of mourning. In the past, a 'well-constituted' family would be one which included all the members required for filling the roles imposed on the kin by the social system.

Finally, it was within this kindred, in which was embedded the family group, that were woven the principal solidarity networks the family could rely on. In Corsica, relatives to the fourth degree are bound to assist in vendettas. In peasant societies, the mutual-help groups formed for undertaking large-scale operations were basically composed of related members, among whom were also recruited the necessary electoral clients for establishing a local power base. Finally recent research by ethnologists has revealed the role played by the kindred in arranging marriages in these traditional societies, either between blood kin of varying degrees of closeness, or 'marriage linkages' between the blood relatives of of two families already related by marriage (Zonabend, 1981).

In our modern, urbanized, industrialized and populous societies, which are subjected to extensive migratory movements, the role of the kinship group is less immediately visible; in our opinion, however, kinship ties have too readily been judged to be in functional decline, as though the nuclear family group were at the present time sufficient in itself. In fact, these kinship networks still seem to be operative; through them status is perpetuated and social promotion is effected. They intervene above all to solve the sort of economic and social problems which families experience throughout their existence. Furthermore, historians and ethnologists have observed the preponderant place assumed by the kin in the ceremonies which punctuate the family life cycle. As links with the surrounding community are weakened, and with the loosening of age-group relationships, which previously acted as legitimizing or supervisory authorities, people draw closer to their kin. Thus marriage rites have been denuded of all those features whose purpose was to mark the couple's passage from one age group to another and to integrate it within village society: the procession with its noisy propitiatory accompaniment, and the visit to the married couple after their wedding night. In the same way, the young no longer start up *charivaris*, those night-time disturbances which once served to stigmatize an ill-matched marriage or deviant behaviour by a spouse.

This withdrawal into kinship groups, a sign of the privatization of behaviour, is accompanied by an altered weighting of the different family ceremonies. Nowadays there is no longer need for unobtrusiveness in celebrating birth, or for the precautions once taken to safeguard the vulnerable new-born baby. Baptism now takes place some time after birth, and a crowd of relatives is invited to attend the service and two lavish meals, which in their turn call for sumptuous gifts. First Communion is treated in the same way. Marriage on the other hand, if it takes place at all, involves only close relatives; finally death is marked by a gathering of the kin only if a religious ceremony is held, and the family wake is disappearing.

Thus the ceremonies linked to childhood and early life have gained the advantage over those associated with death and life's end. All of this can be seen as a consequence of the changes which have occurred in family demographies. Children, being few in number, have acquired a preponderant place in social and ceremonial life. The importance of children, and thus of life, is matched by the diminished consequence attending death in our societies. In all this, we must bear in mind the place assumed by kindred in our modern cultures; even today they seem to retain a 'social' power with functions as flexible as they are various.

This kindred group is characterized by a further feature: it is constituted not only of living but also of dead relatives. This becomes obvious enough when one persuades an individual to trace his genealogy; as he searches his memory for his kin he will enumerate both his living and deceased relatives as members of his kin. We know about societies in Ireland (Fox, 1978) in which people are capable of going back to the seventh ascendant generation in their genealogies without the help of the written word, whereas in ordinary circumstances our memory does not go back beyond the second or third ascendant generation. Indeed, we refer to written sources to supplement our failing recall, using public archives or family papers. These are the sources which the numerous amateur genealogists of today tap in order to draw up their family trees and compile their diagrams or 'family crosses'. Whether traced with the aid of memory or reconstructed by archival research, a genealogy will always involve a visit to the land of the dead members of the family, the deceased who make up lineages reaching far back in time. After all, what the individual is seeking via his genealogy is not himself as such, but himself as placed in a line of descent. He knows that he belongs to a line and is the depository of a destiny written generations ago, the bearer of names which are repeated from generation to generation, of a real symbolic patrimony of which one must become worthy – to the point that in some classes of society people speak of their need to defend it –

and one which in every case gives the family its unity and identity.

First names are generally culled from those borne by the members of paternal or maternal lines, living and dead. Until quite recently it was the custom, in France at least, for the eldest boy to be given his paternal grandfather's name, and the eldest girl that of her maternal grandmother, with a younger boy and girl receiving the maternal grandfather and paternal grandmother's names respectively. Other members of the sibling group would bear the names of collaterals chosen alternately from one or the other line. However, there are other norms for the giving of Christian names (see *'Formes de nomination en Europe'*, 1980) which all reveal cycles, repetitions of the same first names and continuous forms of transmission. In this way, first names are perpetuated in families and mark the incorporation of new members. However, the Christian name, received and constantly given again, is the embodiment of all the dead relatives who bore it. Thus these names have the function of uniting the living members of the family with the dead, who survive in their descendants. It is as though the real human losses occurring in the family group are continually made good with the help of these names. Hence the affection in which this use of family names is held in our societies, even if they survive only as subsidiary Christian names.

Although sibling and kinship groups tend to scatter and inheritance goods to dwindle, the names borne by ancestors remain to provide continuity. These symbolic signs are complemented by the rituals with which the family group punctuates its life cycle.

Rituals old and new

In the preceding paragraphs we mentioned a number of rituals, especially those accompanying birth and the development and disappearance of the domestic group. The marriage which founds it, the arrival of children which increases its members and finally death which marks its end, are moments which are everywhere and at all times accompanied by rituals whose function is to announce the passage from one stage to another. Hence the name 'rite of passage' given them by the social anthropologist Van Gennep (1909), showing that these rites were composed of a series of sequences (always the same ones: separation, margin, aggregation) with the task of marking and favouring the unproblematic accomplishment of these stages. As we observed above, the various relatives are actively present at all these rituals, both as participants and as authorities legitimizing the beginning of the family group, the additions to it and its disappearance. At the same time we pointed out how the weighting attributed to these different rituals has evolved in recent times.

This weighting may be explained in terms of evolving customs and of the demographic changes which have occurred in the population of western Europe, that is, increased longevity and lower child mortality. These aspects are undoubtedly behind the rise of those rituals commemorating the events which mark the life of the family; silver, gold and diamond weddings regenerating the alliance at the origin of the group; children's birthday parties recalling their birth and anniversary masses for deceased parents to ensure their remembrance year after year.

There are other family rituals, less spectacular because more intimate, such as those parties and ceremonies of a commonplace or solemn nature which punctuate the course of family life: family reunions at which dispersed kin gather for Christmas and Easter and the summer holidays, providing an opportunity for renewing family solidarities and reasserting kinship ties. People freely admit that such gatherings contribute to (re)vivifying and (re)creating the group. In fact, they provide everyone with material for learning – and learning more – about the bonds which unite them. While the absence of particular members, the sign of a quarrel or a death, is noticed, the unity of the group is expressed by those who are present. The purpose of these commemorative or festive ceremonies is also to provide continuity and permanence. The group is constantly re-formed by such occasions, and the principal family positions are always assumed at them, with the living members instantly taking over from the deceased, as this account bears witness:

> In my parents' time, around 1939, we had got into the habit of meeting up at their place on Easter Monday, we were eleven children, and my father too, there were eleven in his family . . . which meant that there were about forty to forty-five of us . . . When our parents died we said that we would go every year to my eldest sister's, who got my parents' house . . . all the children. We did enjoy meeting up again. When the meal was over, we would buy flowers and go and put them on my parents' grave . . . my brother said just before he died, he said, 'You know this reunion must go on until the end, until the last one.' Later on our children will do it . . .

It is these family positions within the narrow bounds of the nuclear family which the more recent rites seek to exalt. The social and cultural transformations which have occurred in Western society have, together with the dictates of fashion, effected a change in the choice of a child's first name. Eighteenth- and nineteenth-century calendars contained only a small number of first names, thus favouring identical names – and incidentally strengthening the bonds between the members of a community bearing the same name, since they could all wish each other a happy name-day. In our day individuality is emphasized by choosing names which are thought original and strange. Hence the new habit of celebrating birthdays rather than saints' days. Family time is no longer organized around the religious calendar, and likewise the village community now has hardly any part to play in its life. This new way of doing things defines yet again how preponderant is the place which the child now assumes in his family, which constantly marks the date of his arrival in the group. By the same token, over the passage of time, symbolized by the annual addition of a candle to his birthday cake, he is taught his role in the perpetuation of the family and the line whose patronym he bears.

In our societies, the place accorded to children is matched by the exaltation of women as mothers. Hence the invention at the start of the twentieth century of Mother's Day, by an American called Ann Jarvis. The Methodist Church in the United States, followed by Congress, made it an official celebration in 1914. It has since been adopted by most Western countries, first by Australia, then by Canada, Britain and Switzerland. In 1922 it passed to Germany, where it attained massive proportions under Nazi rule, and was then adopted by France under Pétain. By 1945 this 'day of celebration' appeared so obviously a fabrication of fascist regimes that people ceased to mark it for the next few years, but ten years after the war, Mother's Day blossomed again in both Germany and France.

The fact that our societies have taken up this ceremony with gusto, involving children through their schools, and creating the commercial mechanism to provide all the requisite publicity, clearly shows that its purpose is to emphasize the role of mothers in ensuring the continuity of the family. If our society is to keep continuity of identity, this bond between mother and children must be perpetuated. Western nations give so much attention to Mother's Day because the survival of our families, and thus of our societies, depends on the acceptance by women and men of their roles within their families.

Ritual is a reflection of the way man thinks about the world (Lévi-Strauss, 1981), and family rituals are not exempt: in their persistence and their novelty, they reflect the way people think about 'the family'.

FOURTEEN

The Family: What Next?

André Burguière, Christiane Klapisch-Zuber,
Martine Segalen and Françoise Zonabend

Nowadays it is no longer possible to look at the family and the way it has developed over time without integrating the aspects which are classically treated by historians of the family (demography, private life, family roles, relations between state and family) with other themes more specifically anthropological in nature, such as the place and role of the kin in the organization of the matrimonial field; structuration into clans, lineages, lines and kinship groups; social customs among kin; transmission of goods both material and symbolic; family life cycles and rites of passage. This is why we have constantly tried in *A History of the Family* to combine historical and ethnological problematics.

Having reached the end of this convoluted course from prehistoric groups to present-day societies, as pursued in these two volumes, the reader may well be asking what determined our choice of these particular periods and geographical entities rather than others.

We have to say straight away that we had no intention of aiming at an exhaustive study; clearly we could not take every geographical region into consideration. Thus we devoted ourselves to treating the great civilizations by emphasizing their enduring features as well as the moments when they broke up.

With each period, there was a risk that our choice would be to a great extent dictated by the nature of the sources which historians can lean on. In the case of ancient societies, the sources are primarily normative (religious or juridical texts) which encourage one to emphasize the family's ideological basis and possibly to overestimate its stability. Modern societies possess statistical sources (censuses, parish registers, etc.) and also an abundant literature of normative texts, novels and autobiographies, which cause historians to waver between two approaches: a description of family structures which eliminates the concept of evolution; and an analysis of practices which takes several factors and several evolutionary rhythms into account – economic and demographic situations as much as transformations of religious and affective attitudes.

Is it in fact legitimate to label family structures as rigid, and family practices as permanently innovatory? A *History of the Family* – and this is one of the advantages of an enterprise which has enabled us to compare periods and civilizations – can no longer give space to the evolutionary hypothesis, which has long persisted in the social sciences, of a progressive and universal passage from the traditional extended family to the modern nuclear family. Indeed, historians see the birth if not the triumph of the nuclear household as early as the Middle Ages, and possibly even in some ancient societies. The statistical sources for their part have revealed several forms of family organization existing on a European scale since the beginning of the modern age, with each one serving as the preferential model over an area which may or may not be well delimited.

The restricted family is predominant over the whole of north-western Europe, the Europe of great sedimentary basins, large-scale clearance programmes and great circuits of exchange. The stem family came to the fore in the mountains and pastures of Europe, from the Portuguese Minho to the Austrian Alps. Family communities, associated with share-cropping, non-division and great estates, triumphed in the east. It is only recently, since industrial societies evolved, swelling the towns, emptying the countryside and turning the household primarily into a unit of consumption, that the nuclear model seems to have been imposed everywhere.

The evolutionist hypothesis was based on the idea that the family corresponded, so to speak, to an archaic and pre-social stage of society and that it was thus quite naturally bound to shrink and dissolve as societies developed and diversified. This idea does not take adequate account of transformations to the family in the course of history, but it can cast light on the analysis of relations between the family group and its surrounding society. Let us for instance compare the nuclear model, which triumphed in the west in eighteenth-century Europe, with the great polynuclear households which predominated in the east, and with the Serbian *zadruga* or the peasant serf households on the great Russian estates.

In the west, the methods used in socializing children and managing the workforce, as illustrated by the custom of circulating children by placing them as servants with other families, and by the reluctance of married children to co-reside with their parents, involved the existence of institutions which were run either by the local society or by the state, and which assumed a large proportion of the duties incumbent on the family: education, justice and the care of isolated, aged or indigent persons. In eastern Europe, on the contrary, everything was run as though the great households could expect nothing of the world outside, and themselves assumed entire charge of the individual from cradle to grave.

Thus the western European type of family is a small, outward-looking unit, largely open to the circuits of exchange, to the market economy and to public life. In the eastern model, the family is a strongly integrating and autarkic unit, which appears to impede the development of the state and the unification of the market.

The process of modernizing societies takes place, not against the family, but with it. The family, whether a residential group or a network, provides support for individuals who have to uproot, move to town and make their way into new labour markets, as it did for the members of the bourgeoisie and the first capitalist enterprises. By looking at the history of the family we can see how wrong the previous hypotheses about its linear evolution were, and similarly, by studying the changes to the family associated with modernity, we are struck by the institution's many different ways of responding to new economic and social conditions.

The nineteenth century was characterized by a pyramidal social organization, with the bourgeois family at the apex. Its position was due to its economic capital, and it relied on its efficient kinship networks. This made it the advocate of a restricting norm, outside which every family comportment was stigmatized as deviant. Working-class families were targeted by social policies, which were aimed at combating attitudes felt to be at variance with the bourgeois model and eliminating the perils inherent in them.

In most industrialized countries, once the excesses of the first period of capitalism had been corrected, working-class and bourgeois aspirations fused in the nuclear family, based on a kinship network and centred on a small number of children. The social assistance policies which were implemented in the aftermath of the Second World War seemed to preside over this family cocoon, enveloped, thanks to economic prosperity, in a comfortable home environment. Women, however, wanted to get out and, since the 1970s, they have resumed the work they had so briefly abandoned. Whether part- or full-time, women want to stay in the labour market and to retain their economic independence. There is a growing trend not to consider such incomes as merely secondary in periods of recession, when two salaries are better than one. The freedom to work has been combined with the freedom to practise contraception;

for the first time in the history of mankind women have been offered the medical means of deciding for themselves how many children they wish to give birth to.

Are the shocks which the couple is undergoing today to be attributed to women's new independence? All the industrialized countries can show a correlation between the rise in the number of divorces and in female employment. What is more, a degree of uncertainty about the future can be observed, a refusal to commit oneself, a wish to resume one's independence more easily; all of these are ways of interpreting the development of cohabitation without the sanction of a legal tie.

Does the crisis of the married couple signify the death of the family? On the contrary, it seems to strengthen the kinship networks on which are based family lines, which will perhaps become female lines, since children continue to be raised by their mothers. These networks appear to have a great future in the industrialized societies, where granny and grandad 'booms' are taking place. The third age no longer consists simply of old people in care, but of healthy adults with time on their hands and regular incomes from retirement funds. Never before in the past have families been able to count so much on their affective and material aid; never have our ancestors been celebrated as much as they are today, when they have been given a new lease of life by intense geneaological research.

In the industrialized states, where the family is both nuclear and incorporated in a flexible kinship network, it appears as the dominant and universal model towards which societies tend in the course of their development. It might therefore be thought that the nuclear family is the sign of modernity, esteem for the individual and freedom from the constraints imposed by a weighty lineage or 'house'. However, this apparent standardization of family structures must not obscure the long-term permanent nature of old family models, on which economic and social changes are also based. In Japan, the industrial structure is influenced by its organization into 'houses', and semi-filial loyalties have persisted in the workplace. In Africa, not all family groups in the towns are nuclear, and they have not broken with their lineage solidarities, although the latter have been considerably shaken.

In the long run, there is no evidence that the advance towards a single model of the family can be continued in future decades. The condition of women and the evolution of fertility rates do not follow the same trends. Women's newly acquired independence in industrialized countries has been paralleled by the way they are kept indoors in Muslim countries, where religious fundamentalism is spreading. Industrial countries will see family structures and ideologies continuing to evolve in unpredictable directions, while in the Muslim world patriarchal family structures will grow stronger. Fertility levels are partly associated with changes to the condition of women and, while the average number of children per woman may fall, it will still be higher in the developing countries than in the old industrial nations.

The diminishing size of the nuclear family has two consequences: it restricts the number of first cousins, and in the long term it threatens the existence of the kinship network. If the single-child policy in China succeeds, within a few generations there will be no brothers, cousins, uncles or aunts. However, we know that kinship is above all a social phenomenon and could be replaced by fictive kindred, in the absence of real kindred.

Paradoxically enough, the contemporary world seems to be divided in half, between countries which encourage population growth and others trying to curb excessive increases. In both cases, the same risk is incurred, that of seeing their societies disappear sooner or later, either through shortage of people or through excessive numbers. Once this is understood, it is clear that every possible measure must be taken to palliate the perverse effects of demography.

China and India provide exemplary illustrations of the difficult balance which states must strike in order to impose a controlled population policy, but in countries where populations are smaller, the problems are no fewer. In such countries, action has been taken to increase the birth rate by social action and by developing medical research.

Of course these two sorts of measures are not on the same level: one sort is addressed to the whole of a society and tries to encourage couples to procreate by offering economic incentives; the others are of an individual order and try by scientific means to enable every human being to perpetuate himself. While the experiments conducted in most Western countries have made us aware of the forms and consequences of social population policy, little is yet known about the effects of medical research, and our imagination finds it difficult to grasp the scope and progress of developments in genetics. Nevertheless, the social repercussions of this research are immense, which is why we thought it important to ask questions from within the perspective of *A History of the Family*.

Every society expresses its concern to ensure its perpetuation, and to achieve a sort of immortality through its descendants. In every man and every woman can be found the same desire for self-perpetuation, which the procreation of children ensures by transmitting life from one person to another with the feeling that it will never cease. In every society this desire for descendants is fulfilled by setting up a system of marriage alliances to organize and give legitimacy to the procreation of children. It is consequently very understandable that every population should try to solve the problems of sterility.

In many cultures like those of ancient Greece and Rome, adoption, and sometimes the clandestine procreation of illegitimate children, have from earliest times provided the remedy. Nowadays, 'advanced' societies can resort to state-of-the-art medical technology, from artificial insemination to *in vitro* fertilization, borrowed wombs and surrogate mothers. While on the subject, we should remember that so-called primitive societies also dwelt long on the problem of sterility and thought up many solutions which we are now discovering. Multiple marriages; polyandry and polygyny; unions concluded in the name of a dead man or in the name of a different man or woman; adoption or gift of a child: these were all institutions which answered in different ways the need to remedy a particular individual's lack of descendants, whether through sterility (though this was not consciously perceived as such, especially where men were concerned) or early death. All these institutions were accepted and recognized by the prevailing moral code. In Western societies, however, the systematic official medical intervention tried in such cases encounters prejudice and has its repercussions on the status of the family.

The problem is undoubtedly primarily ethical in nature. May men give themselves the right to manipulate procreation – and soon their hereditary patrimony as well? The question is still open. We should equally ask what sort of repercussions genetic manipulation will have on the family.

What will become of descent when conception requires a supplementary parent introduced in the 'donor' or the possessor of the surrogate womb?

What will become of relations between the generations when the time of a child's birth can be manipulated by freezing the sperm or the embryo, or (even more so) by enabling a woman past the menopause to have a child by hormone treatment and thus extending what were thought to be the temporal limits to fertility?

What meaning will kinship links retain when it is enough to implant half of an embryo formed by *in vitro* fertilization to achieve the growth of a normal child, and when there is nothing to prevent the other half being implanted years or generations later on, thus giving birth to a real twin to the first-born child? The world could thus be peopled with brothers and sisters who would never know each another.

Finally, what will become of the family institution when children can be procreated without parents, now that it is possible for women to be artificially impregnated and then to separate permanently from the children they have borne?

We cannot provide definitive answers to all these questions. Indeed, who could, and is it really necessary? Wisdom consists perhaps in trying to imagine, prior to making a definitive statement, what could happen in such a world of fictitious kinship.

Let us point out first of all that we cannot envisage any society inventing a type of filiation which has not already been adopted by a group either today or in the past. We know that the possible combinations are finite in number – filiation passes either through men, or through women, or through both at once – and we cannot see any other system of filiation which a society could adopt without fundamentally attacking the very notion of kinship and consequently sapping the foundations of society.

Similarly we have seen that the family is a flexible institution, that it can assume multiple forms which combine social and biological elements in different ways, depending on place and period. Whether consanguineous or matrifocal, extended or nuclear, elementary or complex, irrespective of its form the family is still a family so long as humanity does not destroy the ideological edifice on which it is based, in other words, so long as people do not challenge the ban on incest or the marital exchange which ensues from it, or, over and above this, the explicit functions which the family is intended to fulfil in our world: raising children, sexual division of tasks and exercise of sexuality.

Nowadays advances in biology have shown that these ideological aspects of the family can be abolished and that its functions can be dissociated or distributed in other ways. Once the generations have been muddled up and kinship ties abolished, why not relax the prohibition on incest? Now that women can sell their reproductive capacities and procreate children in the general interest, why should we live in families?

At the same time as biologists are discovering the formidable possibilities in genetics, obstetricians and paediatricians are stressing the benefits of the osmosis between mother and baby during pregnancy and the traumatic effect of a difficult birth on the individual psyche.

Our societies, which have put such emphasis on individuality, are now also rediscovering the advantages of kinship networks; people are reacting to dispersion and migration by engaging in detailed and often fantasy-ridden research into their ancestral roots.

In these circumstances, need we believe that tomorrow will bring the end of the family?

Glossary

Acquest(s): assets acquired during marriage and belonging jointly to the spouses (hence the term 'joint ownership of acquests').

Affinity: relationship created through marriage. The terms 'affinal relative' or 'relationship' are also used.

Affrèrement (affrairement): French term for a contract binding relatives or unrelated individuals in order that they may live among themselves as brothers (see *tacit community*).

Agnate: related through the paternal line or by patrilinear descent.

Ancestry: the totality of generations and people from whom an individual is descended.

Anthroponym: all the names acquired by an individual in the course of his or her existence.

Avunculate: the relationship between an uncle (usually the mother's brother) and a nephew (usually the sister's son).

Avunculocal residence: the practice whereby boys live with an uncle (usually the mother's brother).

Bail d'enfant (or bail de tutelle): a French term (literally 'child lease') that denotes the awarding (sometimes by auction) of orphan children to those who undertake to assume responsibility for them at the lowest price.

Bilateral kinship: kin or kinship transmitted separately by the mother and by the father, with each filiation serving different ends (bilateral).

Bride price: the goods and/or services paid by the parents of the future husband to the parents of the future wife (see *matrimonial compensation, dowry*).

Broomstick marriage: a popular marriage ceremony, particularly widespread in

England, in which the bride and groom had only to jump over a broom for the marriage to be deemed valid.

Charivari (or rough music): a discordant, mocking, sometimes violent demonstration, organized by young people or other neighbours to ridicule and rebuke deviant social conduct, particularly an unconventional marriage (the remarriage of a widow, an exogamous marriage or a marriage in which there is a great disparity of age or social class between bride and groom).

Child exposure: abandonment of new-born babies or small children, mainly female, authorized or tolerated in certain societies, tantamount in fact to legal infanticide.

Clan: all the individuals who, by virtue of an assumed genealogical relationship, consider themselves descendants in a direct line, either paternal (patriclan) or maternal (matriclan), from a common mythical ancestor or ancestress. This common lineage may exist, by extension, through cognatic descent, in which case the term 'cognatic clan' is used.

Classificatory kinship: kinship system in which each term denotes several genealogical positions.

Cognatic: see *non-unilinear*

Cohabitants: persons, whether related or not, living under the same roof.

Collateral kinship: kin relationship, between siblings, i.e. between brothers and sisters, or between relatives descended from siblings.

Computation: method of calculating the degrees of kinship. There are two basic methods: Roman (or civil) computation, in which each degree of kinship corresponds to one step in the line of descent linking one individual to another through their common ancestor, and Germanic (or ecclesiastical) computation, in which the degrees of kinship are calculated by the number of generations separating two individuals from their common ancestor. For example, two first cousins are four degrees removed from each other in the Roman computation system and two degrees removed in the Germanic system.

Consanguinity: kinship between individuals claiming descent from a common ancestor.

Consorterie: a French term used to describe the legal integration of non-relatives into a family group.

Créantailles: old French word meaning engagement (used mainly in the areas where the *langue d'oïl* was spoken).

Descendants: all the generations and persons descended from one individual.

Descent: the set of social processes which define, from generation to generation, the kinship between individuals or membership of a social group.

Descriptive kinship: kinship system in which each term denotes a single genealogical position.

Double marriage: marriages between two brothers and two sisters or between two male and two female cousins.

Dowry: the goods and/or services offered by the family of the bride to her future husband. By extension, the term dowry has come to denote all matrimonial presentations, whether from the husband's or the wife's family.

Earnest: a sum of money or a symbolic gift given by the future husband or his family in order to seal a promise of marriage

Ego: individual from whom kinship is counted or extends.

Endogamous: denotes a marriage contracted within the family or local group.

Entail: see *fideicommissum*

Exogamous: denotes a marriage contracted outside the family or local group.

Family or life cycle: evolution of a domestic unit and the changes in size and structure that it undergoes from formation to dissolution.

Feu (hearth): fiscal definition of the household under the *ancien régime*.

Fictive, parallel, voluntary kinship: kinship created through various social procedures (for example, foster-brothers are said to be fictive kin).

Fideicommissum: a successional procedure inherited from Roman law and widely used in the seventeenth and eighteenth centuries in Italy and in southern France in order to exclude inherited land from partition by restricting it to a designated line of heirs (eldest sons, elder branch, etc.). Current term: entail.

Fief: a dwelling and, by extension, the right to an inheritance granted to a household in return for rent or certain services.

Frérèche: French term, denoting a group of married brothers, real or fictive, living communally in order to exploit an asset together (see *tacit community*).

Generation: all the individuals belonging to the same age group.

Homogamous: describes a marriage between a man and a woman of the same social background.

Hypergamic, hypogamic: used to describe a marriage between a man and a woman of different social standings. Looked at from the male point of view, a marriage is 'hypergamic' when the social status of the wife is superior to that of her husband; if the opposite is the case, the marriage is said to be 'hypogamic'.

Isogamy: choice of a marriage partner of the same social standing.

Isolate: geographical area or social space within which marriages are concluded (in-breeding area).

Joint ownership of acquests: a matrimonial settlement under which husband

and wife are the joint owners of assets acquired in the course of their marriage.

Kindred: all those individuals – consanguineal and, sometimes, affinal relations – to whom *Ego* considers himself related.

Kinship (nomenclature or vocabulary): the set of terms used by kin to denote their relationship to each other.

Legal portion: the minimum share of an inheritance to which each child is legally entitled, whatever the wishes of the testator.

Levirate: the remarriage of a woman to her deceased husband's brother.

Life-cycle servant: term coined by the English historian Peter Laslett to denote young people taken as servants into families other than their own, as much to complete their upbringing as to begin to earn their living.

Line: a kinship-group descended from a kinship-group within the space of a few generations; segment of a lineage.

Lineage: a kinship-group which considers itself to be descended either through the agnatic line (patrilineage), the uterine line (matrilineage) or bilaterally (cognatic lineage) from a common ancestor or ancestress who is known and has a name.

Lineal repurchase: repurchase by relatives of an asset belonging to the lineage that has been sold.

Majorat: a form of law of primogeniture, involving entailed property, particularly widespread in Spain (see *fideicommissum*).

Manse, *mas*: in medieval France, a peasant holding, including a dwelling house and agricultural land.

Maraîchinage: premarital contacts between young people, both permissive and ritualized, that used to be practised in some areas of northern Europe (a term coined in the Vendée region of France).

Marriage portion: see *dowry*, *widow's dower*.

Matriarchy: political system in which power is exercised by women. As far as is known, no society has ever existed with such a political system.

Matrilineal system: a descent system which counts only links through females (see also *uterine*).

Matrilocal residence: the practice whereby newly married couples live with or close to the bride's parents.

Matrimonial compensation: the goods and/or services offered by the future husband and his parents to the father and other relatives of his future wife (see *dowry*, *bride price*).

Morgengabe: German term (see *widow's dower*).

Mortmain: a feudal right that allowed the lord of the manor, in the event of there being no heirs, to tax or even to take possession of goods belonging to his vassals.

Natolocal residence: the practice whereby newly married couples live apart, each remaining with their own family.

Neolocal residence: the practice whereby newly married couples live in a place other than the one where their families live.

Non-unilinear: kinship transmitted by either the father or the mother. Also known as cognatic or bilateral descent.

Nubility: readiness or suitability for marriage.

Parallel or cross-cousins: children of siblings of either the opposite or the same sex. Thus the children of a brother and of a sister are known as 'cross-cousins', while those of two sisters or two brothers are known as 'parallel cousins'.

Parcenary: form of ownership or tenure in which heirs jointly agree not to divide up an inheritance.

Patriarchy: political system in which power is exercised by men, generally the oldest members of the community.

Patrilinear system: a kinship system which counts only links through males.

Patrilocal residence: the custom whereby newly married couples live with or near the husband's parents.

Penitential: a compilation of sins (the majority relating to sexuality) and the penalties they incur, drawn up for the use of clerics in the Middle Ages.

Phratry: all the individuals belonging to the same social group or who claim descent from a common ancestor, as in ancient Greece.

Polyandry: the practice or condition of being married to more than one husband at the same time.

Polygamy: legitimate marriage to more than one spouse simultaneously.

Polygyny: the practice or condition of being married to more than one wife at the same time.

Préciput: portion of an estate or inheritance devolving upon one of the co-heirs over and above his equal share with the others.

Primary, secondary marriage: in polygamy, the first marriage is called the primary marriage, while the others are termed secondary (also known as principal and subsidiary).

Primogeniture: systematic favouring of the eldest child, usually the eldest son, to the detriment of his younger siblings.

Provisional baptism: a baptism comprising only a sprinkling with consecrated water, administered to a new-born baby shortly after birth by the midwife or doctor when it was feared that the child might not survive.

Sibling: brother and sister born to the same father and mother; half-siblings are children who have either the same father or the same mother.

Société à maison: a legal entity owning a number of tangible and intangible assets which is perpetuated by the transmission of its name, fortune and titles, through a real or fictive line.

Son-in-law marriage: a form of marriage in which the son-in-law goes to live and work with his wife's parents.

Sororate: remarriage of a man to the sister of his dead wife.

Soulte: remuneration, in kind or cash, paid in compensation for the partition or tranmission of an inheritance.

Spiritual kinship: kinship established through relationships with godparents.

Tacit community: a group of conjugal units, related or not, living together communally on the basis of a tacit agreement rather than a written contract drawn up by a lawyer, in order jointly to exploit and enjoy an asset (see *frérèche*).

Teknonymy: the practice of designating or addressing a person by the name of his children.

Ultimogeniture: privilege granted to the last-born of a sibling group.

Unilineal descent: transmission of kinship either through the father (patrilineal system) or through the mother (matrilineal system).

Uterine: relative on the mother's side.

Uxorilocal residence: the practice whereby a newly married couple lives in the place where the wife lived before marriage.

Virilocal residence: the practice whereby a newly married couple lives in the place where the husband lived before marriage.

Widow's dower: the share of the marriage portion that the husband makes over to his wife in the event of his prior death. Whether determined in accordance with common law (customary dower) or voluntarily (mutually agreed dower), it is proportional to the wife's dowry or to the husband's property.

Youthful cohabitation: a term referring to a young unmarried couple setting up house together, as now widely accepted in Western countries.

Bibliography

Chapter 1   The One Hundred and One Families of Europe

Andorka, R. and Farago, J. 1983: 'Pre-industrial Household Structure in Hungary', in R. Wall (ed.), *Family Forms in Historic Europe*, Cambridge

Arbellot, G. 1970: *Cinq paroisses du Vallage, aux XVIIe et XVIIIe siècles*, Paris (microfiches)

Ariès, P. 1948: *Histoire des populations françaises et de leurs attitudes devant la vie depuis le XVIIIe siècle*, Paris

Ariès, P. 1960: 'Interprétation pour une histoire des mentalités', in H. Bergues (ed.), *La Prévention des naissances dans la famille*, Paris

Ariès, P. 1979: *Centuries of Childhood*, Harmondsworth

Baulant, M. 1972: 'La famille en miettes. Sur un aspect de la démographie du XVIIe siècle', *Annales ESC*, 4–5

Berkner, L. 1976: 'Inheritance Land Tenure and Peasant Family Structure: a German Regional Comparison', in J. Goody, J. Thirsk and E. P. Thomson (eds), *Family and Inheritance*, Cambridge

Biraben, J.-N. 1976: *Les Hommes et la peste en France et dans les pays européens des origines à 1850*, Paris

Burguière, A. 1972: 'De Malthus à Max Weber. Le mariage tardif et l'esprit d'entreprise', *Annales ESC*, 5

Burguière, A. 1979: 'Endogamie et communauté villageoise. Pratique matrimoniale à Romainville au XVIIIe siècle', *Annales de démographie historique*

Castan, N. 1971: 'La Criminalité familiale dans le ressort du parlement de Toulouse (1690–1730)', in 'Crimes et criminalités en France sous l'Ancien Régime', *Cahiers des Annales*

Castan, Y. 1974: *Honnêteté et relations sociales en Languedoc (1715–1780)*, Paris

Champeaux, E. 1933: 'Jus sanguinis', *Revue historique du droit français et étranger*, 4th series, XII

Chayanov, A. 1966: *Theory of Peasant Economy*, Homewood, Ill.

Claverie, E. and Lamaison, P. 1982: *L'Impossible Mariage*, Paris

Collomp, A. 1977: 'Alliance et filiation en haute Provence au XVIIIe siècle', *Annales ESC*, 3

Collomp, A. 1983: *La Maison du père. Famille et village en haute Provence aux XVIIe et XVIIIe siècles*, Paris

Cooper, J. 1976: 'Patterns of Inheritance and Settlement by Great Landowners from the XVth to the XVIIIth centuries', in J. Goody et al. (eds), *Family and Inheritance*, Cambridge

Czap, P. 1983: 'A Large Family: the Peasant's Greatest Wealth. Serf Household in Mishino Russia (1814–1858)', in R. Wall (ed.), *Family Forms in Historic Europe*, Cambridge

Delille, G. 1983: 'Dots des filles et circulation des biens dans les Pouilles aux XVIe–XVIIe siècles', *Mélanges de l'École française de Rome*, 95

Duby, G. 1973: *Hommes et structures du Moyen Âge*, Paris

Dupâquier, J. 1979a: *La Population rurale du Bassin parisien à l'époque de Louis XIV*, Paris

Dupâquier, J. 1979b: *La Population française aux XVIIe et XVIIIe siècles*, Paris

Durand, Y. 1971: *Les Fermiers généraux au XVIIIe siècle*, Paris

Durkheim, E. 1950: *Leçons de sociologie physique des mœurs et du droit*, Paris

Dyrvik, S. 1983: 'Domestiques et fonction productive. L'évolution des ménages norvégiens (1750–1850)', in *Actes du colloque de Trieste*, Paris

Elias, N. 1974: *La Société de cour*, Paris

Fauve-Chamoux, A. 1984: 'Les Structures familiales au royaume des familles souches. Esparros', *Annales ESC*, 3

Flandrin, J.-L. 1979: *Families in Former Times: Kinship, Household and Sexuality*, Cambridge

Fleury, M. and Henry, L. 1965: *Nouveau Manuel de dépouillement et d'exploitation de l'état civil ancien*, Paris

Flinn, M. 1981: *The European Demographic System, 1500–1870*, Brighton

Forster, R. 1971: *The House of Saulx-Tavanes: 1700–1830*, Baltimore

Garden, M. 1970: *Lyon et les Lyonnais au XVIIIe siècle*, Paris

Goody, J. 1976: 'Inheritance, Property and Women: some Comparative Considerations', in J. Goody et al. (eds), *Family and Inheritance*, Cambridge

Goody, J. 1983: *The Development of the Family and Marriage in Europe*, Cambridge

Goubert, P. 1959: *Familles marchandes sous l'Ancien Régime: les Danse et les Motte du Beauvaisis*, Paris

Hajnal, J. 1965: 'European Marriage Patterns in Perspective', in D. Eversley (ed.), *Population in History*, London

Hajnal, J. 1983: 'Two Kinds of Pre-industrial Household Formation System', in *Family Forms in Historic Europe*, Cambridge

Henry, L. and Levy, C. 1960: 'Ducs et pairs sous l'Ancien Régime. Caractéristiques démographiques d'une caste', *Population*, 5

Howell, C. 1976: 'Peasant Inheritance Customs in the Midlands, 1280–1700', in

J. Goody et al. (eds) *Family and Inheritance*, Cambridge

Joignon, L. 1984: *Stratégies patrimoniales et stratégies matrimoniales en Lorraine, aux XVIIe–XVIIIe siècles*, Paris (typescript)

Klapisch-Zuber, C. 1972: 'Household and Family in Tuscany in 1427', in Laslett

Klapisch-Zuber, C. and Herlihy, D. 1978: *Les Toscans et leurs familles*, Paris

Labatut, J.-P. 1972: *Les Ducs et pairs de France*, Paris

Labatut, J.-P. 1973: 'La Famille Gérard de Béarn sous l'Ancien Régime', in *Études européennes. Mélanges à V. L. Tapié*, Paris

Lamaison, P. 1979: 'Les Stratégies matrimoniales dans un système complexe de parenté. Ribennes en Gévaudan', *Annales ESC*

Laslett, P. 1972: *Household and Family in Past Time*, Cambridge

Laslett, P. 1977: *Family Life and Illicit Love in Earlier Generations*, Cambridge

Laslett, P. 1983a: 'Family and Household as Work Group and Kin Group: Areas of Traditional Europe Compared', in R. Wall (ed.), *Family Forms in Historic Europe*, Cambridge

Laslett, P. 1983b: *The World We Have Lost*, London

Lebrun, F. 1975: *La Vie conjugale sous l'Ancien Régime*, Paris

Le Play, P. 1875: *L'Organisation de la famille selon le vrai modèle signalé par l'histoire de toutes les races et de tous les temps*, Paris and Tours

Le Roy Ladurie, E. 1967: *Histoire du climat depuis l'An Mil*, Paris

Le Roy Ladurie, E. 1972: 'Structures familiales et coutumes d'héritages en France au XVIe siècle', *Annales ESC*, 4–5

Le Roy Ladurie, E. 1975: *Histoire de la France rurale*, vol. II, Paris

Le Roy Ladurie, E. 1982: *Love, Death and Money in the Pays d'Oc*, Harmondsworth

Macfarlane, A. 1970: *The Family of Ralph Josselin*, Cambridge

Marin-Muracciole, M. R. 1964: *L'Honneur des femmes en Corse*, Paris

Mause, L. de 1974: *The History of Childhood*, New York

Meyer, J. 1966: *La Noblesse bretonne au XVIIIe siècle*, Paris

Mezzario, R. 1980: *Il paese stretto. Strategie matrimoniali nella diocesi di Como, secoli XVI–XVII*, Turin

Mitterrauer, M. and Sieder, R. 1983: 'The Reconstruction of the Family Course', in R. Wall (ed.) *Family Forms in Historic Europe*, Cambridge

Möller, H. 1969: *Die kleinbürgerliche Familie im XVIII. Jahrhundert. Verhalten und Gruppenkultur*, Berlin

Nicolas, J. 1978: *La Savoie au XVIIIe siècle. Noblesse et bourgeoisie*, Paris

Palli, H. 1983: 'Estonian Households in the XVIIth–XVIIIth Century', in R. Wall (ed.), *Family Forms in Historic Europe*, Cambridge

Parsons, T. 1937: *The Structure of Social Action*, New York

Pedlow, G. W. 1982: 'Marriage, Family Size and Inheritance among Hessian Nobles (1650–1900)', *Journal of Family History*, vol. VII (4)

Poitrineau, A. 1980: 'Le Mariage auvergnat vu à travers les dispenses de consanguinité du diocèse de Clermont à la fin du XVIIIe siècle', in J. Ernard (ed.), *Aimer en France*, Clermont-Ferrand

Poni, C. 1983: 'Sharecropping Households and the Farm', in *Actes du Colloque de Trieste*, Paris

Poumarède, J. 1972: *Les Successions dans la France du Sud-Ouest au Moyen Âge*, Paris

Sabean, D. 1972: 'Famille et tenure paysanne: aux origines de la guerre des Paysans en Allemagne', *Annales ESC*, 4–5

Schmidtbauer, P. 1983: 'The Changing Household: Austrian Household Structure from the XVIIth to the XXth Century', in R. Wall (ed.), *Family Forms in Historic Europe*, Cambridge

Schofield, R. S. and Wrigley, E. A. 1981: *The Population History of England (1541–1871)*, London

Segalen, M. 1972: *Nuptialité et alliance*, Paris

Segalen, M. 1985: *Quinze générations de Bas-Bretons*, Paris

Shorter, E. 1977: *The Making of the Modern Family*, London

Stone, L. 1977: *The Family, Sex and Marriage in England (1500–1800)*, London

Stufford, M. 1976: 'Peasant Inheritance Customs in Cambridgeshire from the XVIth to the XVIIIth Century', in J. Goody et al. (eds), *Family and Inheritance*, Cambridge

Tönnies, F. 1979: *Gemeinschaft und Gesellschaft. Grundbegriffe der reinen Soziologie*, Darmstadt

Wheaton, R. 1979: 'Affinity and Descent in the XVIIth Century Bordeaux', in R. Wheaten and T. K. Haraven (eds), *Family and Sexuality in French History*, Philadelphia

Yver, J. 1966: *Essai de géographie coutumière. Égalité entre héritiers et exclusion des enfants dotés*, Paris

Chapter 2 Priest, Prince and Family

Ariès, P. 1960: 'Interprétation pour une histoire des mentalités', in H. Bergnes (ed.), *La Prévention des naissances dans la famille*, Paris

Ariès, P. 1979: *Centuries of Childhood*, Harmondsworth

Bardet, J.-P. 1983: *Rouen aux XVIIᵉ et XVIIIᵉ siècles*, Paris

Burguière, A. 1972: 'De Malthus à Max Weber. Le mariage tardif et l'esprit d'entreprise', *Annales ESC*, 4–5

Burguière, A. 1978: 'Le Rituel de mariage en France. Pratiques ecclésiastiques et pratiques populaires (XVIᵉ–XVIII siècles), *Annales ESC*, 3

Burguière, A. 1981: 'Pratique du charivari et répression religieuse dans la France de l'Ancien Régime', in J. Le Goff and J.-C. Schmidtt (eds), *Le Charivari*, Paris

Casey, J. 1983: 'Household Disputes and the Law in Early Modern Andalusia', in J. Bossy (ed.), *Disputes and Settlements*, Cambridge

Chartier, R., Compère, M. M. and Julia, D. 1976: *L'Éducation en France du XVIᵉ siècle au XVIIIᵉ siècle*, Paris

Depauw, J. 1972: 'Amour illégitime et société à Nantes au XVIIIe siècle', *Annales ESC*, 4–5

Dupâquier, J. 1979: *La Population française aux XVIIe et XVIIIe siècles*, Paris

Elias, N. 1978: *The History of Manners*, Oxford

Elias, N. 1994: *The Civilizing Process*, Oxford

Farge, A. (ed.) 1982: *Le Miroir des femmes*, Paris

Farge, A. and Foucault, M. 1982: *Le Désordre des familles*, Paris

Flandrin, J.-L. 1975: *Les Amours paysannes, XVIe–XIXe siècle*, Paris

Flandrin, J.-L. 1979: *Families in Former Times: Kinship, Household and Sexuality*, Cambridge

Flinn, M. W. 1981: *The European Demographic System, 1500–1820*, Brighton

Gelis, J. 1991: *History of Childbirth*, Cambridge

Gillis, R. 1983: 'Conjugal Settlements: Resort to Clandestine and Common Law Marriage in England and Wales (1650–1850)', in J. Bossy (ed.), *Disputes and Settlements*, Cambridge

Houlbrooke, R. A. 1984: *The English Family (1450–1700)*, London and New York

Kaplow, J. 1972: *The Names of Kings*, Basic Books, New York

Lafon, J. 1972: *Les Époux bordelais (1450–1850)*, Paris

Laget, M. 1982: *Naissances. L'Accouchement avant l'âge de la clinique*, Paris

Laslett, P. 1977: 'Long Term Trends in Bastardy in England', in *Family Life and Illicit Love in Earlier Generations*, Cambridge

Laslett, P. 1983: *The World We Have Lost*, London

Lebrun, F. 1975: *La Vie conjugale sous l'Ancien Régime*, Paris

Le Roy Ladurie, E. 1982: *Love, Death and Money in the Pays d'Oc*, Harmondsworth

Loux, F. 1978: *Le Jeune Enfant et son corps dans la médecine traditionnelle*, Paris

Menetra, J.-L. 1982: *Journal de ma vie*, ed. D. Roche, Paris

Mitterauer, M. 1983: *Ledige Mutter. Zur Geschichte unehelicher Geburten in Europa*, Munich

Molin, J.-B. and Mutembé, P. 1974: *Le Rituel de mariage en France du XIIe au XVIe siècle*, Paris

Möller, H. 1969: *Die kleinbürgerliche Familie im XVIII. Jht.*, Berlin

Noonan, J. T. 1986: *Contraception*, Cambridge, Mass.

Perrenoud, A. 1974: 'Malthusianisme et Protestantisme'. *Annales ESC*, 4

Pillorget, R. 1979: *La Tige et le rameau. Familles anglaises et françaises, XVIe–XVIIIe siècle*, Paris

Piveteau, C. 1957: *La Pratique matrimoniale en France d'après les statuts synodaux*, Paris (typescript)

Restif de La Bretonne, N. 1959: *Monsieur Nicolas*, ed. J.-J. Pauvert, Paris

Rossiaud, J. 1976: 'Prostitution, jeunesse et société dans les villes du Sud-Est au XVe siècle', *Annales ESC*, 2

Safley, Th. S. 1982: 'To Preserve the Marital State: the Basler Ehegericht (1550–1592)', *Journal of Family History*, 7

Shorter, E. 1977: *The Making of the Modern Family*, London

Stone, L. 1977: *The Family, Sex and Marriage in England (1500–1800)*, London

Wrigley, E. A. and Schofield, R. S. 1981: *The Population History of England (1541–1871)*, London

Chapter 3   Children of the Apocalypse: the Family in Meso-America and the Andes

Select sources

Anunciación, J. de la 1575: *Doctrina christiana muy cumplida . . .*, Mexico City

Cuevas, M. 1583: *Doctrina cristiana y catecismo para instrucción de los Indios compuesto por autoridad del Concilio Provincial . . . de 1583*, Ciudad de Los Reyes (Lima)

Cuevas, M. 1975: *Documentos inéditos del siglo XVI para la historia de Mexico*, Mexico City

Durán, D. 1967: *Historia de las Indias e islas de la Tierra Firme*, Mexico City

García Icazbalceta, J. 1947: *Don Fray Juan de Zumárraga, primer obispo y arzobispo de México*, Mexico City

Molina, A. (de) 1569: *Confesionario mayor en lengua mexicana y castellana*, Mexico City

Motolinia, Toribio de Benavente 1971: *Memoriales*, Mexico City

Pérez, M. 1713: *Farol indiano y guia de curas de Indios*, Mexico City

Polo de Ondegardo, J. 1916–17: *Informaciones acerca de la religión y gobierno de los Incas*, Lima

Poma de Ayala, F. G. 1980: *El primer nueva corónica y buen gobierno*, Mexico City

Ruiz de Alarcón, H. 1953: *Tratado de las supersticiones y costumbres gentílicas . . .*, Mexico City

Sahagún, B. de 1965: *Historia general de las cosas de Nueva España*, Mexico City

This list does not claim to be exhaustive but mentions simply those sources which have directly inspired certain passages in this chapter. To these should be added, on account of the information it contains the *Itinerario para parrocos de Indios*, published in Madrid in 1771 by the bishop of Quito, Alonso de la Peña Montenegro.

Pre-Hispanic and colonial periods

Aguirre Beltran, G. 1963: *Medicina y magia. El proceso de aculturación en el México colonial*, Mexico City

Aguirre Beltran, G. 1972: *La población negra de México*, Mexico City

Alberro, S. 1978: 'Noirs et mulâtres dans la société coloniale mexicaine d'après les archives de l'Inquisition, XVIᵉ–XVIIᵉ siècles', *Cahiers des Amériques latines* (Paris), XVII, 59–87

Alberro, S. 1981: *La actividad del Santo Oficio de la Inquisición en la Nueva España*, Mexico City

Alberro, S. et al. 1982: *Familia y sexualidad en Nueva España*, Mexico City

Arrom, S. M. 1976: *La mujer mexicana ante el divorcio eclesiástico, 1800–1857*, Mexico City

Arrom, S. M. 1980: *Women in Mexico City (1800–1857)*, University of Stanford, unpubl. thesis

Atondo, A. M. 1982: *La prostitución femenina en la ciudad de México, 1521–1621*, Mexico City, unpubl. thesis

Borah, W. and Cook, S. 1971–9: *Essays in Population History*, Berkeley

Bowser, F. P. 1974: *El esclavo africano en el Perú colonial*, Mexico City

Calnek, E. E. 1974: 'Conjunto urbano y modelo residencial en Tenochtitlan', in *Ensayos sobre el desarrollo urbano de México*, Mexico City, pp. 11–65

Carrasco, P. 1964: 'Family Structure of XVIth Century Tepoztlan', in *Process and Pattern in Culture*, Chicago, pp. 185–210

Carrasco, P. et al. 1976: *Estratificación social en la Mesoamérica prehispánica*, Mexico City

Dahlgren, B. 1954: *La Mixteca, su cultura e historia prehispánica*, Mexico City

Enciso, D. 1983: *El delito de bigamia en el México colonial. Siglo XVIII*, Mexico City, unpubl. thesis

Farriss, N. 1984: *Maya Society under Colonial Rule: the Collective Enterprise for Survival*, Princeton

Gibson, C. 1964: *The Aztecs under Spanish Rule: a History of the Indians of the Valley of Mexico, 1519–1580*, Stanford

Gruzinski, S. 1981: 'La Mère dévorante. Alcoolisme, sexualité et déculturation chez les Mexicas, 1500–1550', *Cahiers des Amériques Latines*, Paris, 20

Kellogg, S., 'Kinship and Social Organization in Early Colonial Tenochtitlan', in R. Spores (ed.), *Handbook of Middle American Indians*

Lockhart, J. 1968: *Spanish Peru, 1532–1560: a Colonial Society*, Madison

Lopez Austin, A. 1980: *Cuerpo humano e ideología. Las concepciones de los antiguos Nahuas*, Mexico City

Lounsbury, F. G. 1978: 'Aspects du système de patenté inca', *Annales ESC*, 33 (5–6)

Morner, M. 1974: *Raza y cambio en la Hispanoamérica colonial*, Mexico City

Muriel, J. 1974: *Los recognimientos de mujeros*, Mexico City

Murra, J. V. 1978: *La organización económica del estado inca*, Mexico City

Ortega, S. (ed.) 1986: *De la santidad a la perversion*, Mexico City
Phelan, J. L. 1967: *The Kingdom of Quito in the XVIIth Century*, Madison, Milwaukee and London
Quezada, N. 1975: *Amor y magia amorosa entre los Aztecas. Supervivencias en el México colonial*, Mexico City
Ripodas Ardanaz, D. 1977: *El matrimonio de Indias. Realidad social y regulación jurídica*, Buenos Aires
Spores, R. 1967: *The Mixtec Kings and their People*, Norman, Okla.
Wachtel, N. 1971: *La Vision des vaincus. Les Indiens du Pérou devant la conquête espagnole*, Paris
Zuidema, R. T. 1977: 'The Inca Kinship System: a New Theoretical View' in R. Bolton and E. Mayer (eds) *Andean Kinship and Marriage*. Washington

Ethnology and sociology

Mexico
Arizpe, S. L. 1973: *Parentesco y economía en una sociedad nahua*, Mexico City
Arizpe, S. L. 1975: *Indígenas en la ciudad de México. El caso de las Marías*, Mexico City
Arizpe, S. L. 1978: *Migración, etnicismo y cambio económico*, Mexico City
Foster, G. M. 1967: *Tzintzuntzan: Mexican Peasants in a Changing World*, Boston
Higgins, M. J. 1974: *Somos gente humilde. Etnogtafía de una colonia urbana de Oaxaca*, Mexico City
Kemper, R. V. 1976: *Campesinos en la ciudad. Gente de Tzintzuntzan*, Sepsetentas
Lewis, O. 1959: *Five Families: Mexican Case Studies in the Culture of Poverty*, New York
Lewis, O. 1961: *Children of Sánchez*, New York
Mintz, S. W. and Wolf, E. 1950: 'An Analysis of Ritual Co-parenthood (compadrazgo)', *Southwestern Journal of Anthropology*, VI, 341–68
Nutini, H. G. 1968: *San Bernardino Contla: Marriage and Family Structure in a Tlaxcalan Municipio*, Pittsburgh
Nutini, H. G. 1980: *Ritual Kinship: The Structure and Historical Development of the Compadrazgo System in Rural Tlaxcala*, Princeton
Nutini, H. G. et al. 1976: *Essays in Mexican Kinship*, Pittsburgh
Swartzbaugh, R. G. 1970: *Machismo: a Value System of a Mexican Peasant Class*, Ohio State University, unpubl. thesis

The Andes

Bernand, C. 1981: *Les Renaissants de Pindilig. Étude anthropologique de la déculturation d'une société paysanne du sud de l'Équateur, Province de Canar*, unpubl. thesis, Paris VII

Bolton, R. and Bolton, C. 1976: 'Concepción, embarazo y alumbramiento en una aldea qolla', *Antropología andina*, I, 58–74

Bolton, R. and Mayer, E. 1977: *Andean Kinship and Marriage*, Washington

Chungara, D. 1978: *Si on me donne la parole . . .* , Paris

Escobar, G. 1973: *Sicaya. Cambios culturales en una comunidad mestiza andina*, Lima

Isbell, B. J. 1971: 'No servimos mas. Un estudio de las consecuencias de la desaparición de un sistema de autoridad tradicional en un pueblo ayacuchano', *Revista del Museo nacional* (Lima), 37, 285–98

Nunez del Prado, O. 1969: 'El hombre y la familia. Su matrimonio y organización politicosocial en Q'ero', *Allpanchis* (Cuzco), I, 5–27

Orlove, B. S. 1974: 'Reciprocidad, desigualdad y dominación', in G. Alberti and E. Mayer (eds), *Reciprocidad e intercambio en los Andes peruanos*, Lima

Platt, T. 1982: *Estado boliviano y ayllu andino. Tierra y tributo en el Norte de Potosi*, Lima

Urbano, H. O. 1981: 'Del sexo, el incesto y los ancestros de Inkarrí. Mito, utopía e historia en las sociedades andinas', *Allpanchis*, XV (17–18), 77–104

Chapter 4   The Long March of the Chinese Family

Baker, H. 1968: *A Chinese Lineage Village: Sheung Shui*, London and Stanford

Baker, H. 1979: *Chinese Family and Kinship*, London

Buck, J. L. 1937: *Land Utilization in China*, Shanghai

Chiu, V. Y. 1966: *Marriage Laws and Customs of China*, Hong Kong

Cohen, M. L. 1976: *House United, House Divided: the Chinese Family in Taiwan*, New York and London

Fei, H. T. 1939: *Peasant Life in China*, London

Fei, H. T. 1983: *Chinese Village Close-up*, Beijing

Freedman, M. 1966: *Chinese Lineage and Society: Fukien and Kwangtung*, London

Gipoulon, C. 1976: *Pierre de l'oiseau Jingwei, Qiu Jin, femme et révolutionnaire en Chine au XIXe siècle*, Paris

Hsu, F. L. K. 1971: *Under the Ancestor's Shadow: Kinship, Personality and Social Mobility in China*, Stanford

Hua, C. M. 1981: *La Condition féminine et les communistes chinois en action. Yan'an 1935–1946*, Paris

Lang, O. 1946: *Chinese Family and Society*, New Haven

Levy, H. S. 1966: *Chinese Footbinding: the History of a Curious Erotic Custom*, Tokyo

Meijer, M. J. 1971: *Marriage Law and Policy in the Chinese People's Republic*, Hong Kong
Wolf, A. P. and Huang, C. S. 1980: *Marriage and Adoption in China*, Stanford
Wolf, M. 1972: *Women and the Family in Rural Taiwan*, Stanford

Chapter 5   The Family: Instrument and Model of the Japanese Nation

Bachnik, J. M. and Quinn, C. J., Jr, 1994: *Situated Meanings: Inside and Outside in Japanese Self, Society and Language*, Princeton
Befu, H. 1971: *Japan, an Anthropological Introduction*, New York
Bennett, J. W. and Ishino, I. 1963: *Paternalism in the Japanese Economy*, Minneapolis
Bernier, B. 1994: 'La Famille comme modèle/métaphore de l'entreprise au Japon', *L'Ethnographie* (Paris) 90 (1), no. 115 (Spring), 25–50
Coleman, S. 1983: *Family Planning in Japanese Society*, Princeton
De Vos, G. A. 1973: *Socialization for Achievement*, Berkeley
De Vos, G. A. 1984: *The Incredibility of Western Prophets: the Japanese Religion of the Family*, Amsterdam
Doi, T. 1982: *Le Jeu de l'indulgence*, Paris
Dore, R. P. 1958: *City Life in Japan*, Berkeley
Fukushima, M. (ed.) 1977: *Kazoku: seisaku to hô* (The family: politics and law), vol. 3: *Sengo nihon kazoku no dôkô* (Japanese family trends since the war), Tokyo
Fukutake, T. 1981: *Japanese Society Today*, Tokyo
Fukutake, T. 1982: *The Japanese Social Structure*, Tokyo
Fuse, A. and Tamamizu, T. (eds) 1982: *Gendai no kazoku* (The contemporary family), Tokyo
Gamo, M. 1977: 'Gendai no kazoku' (The contemporary family), *Jyurisuto* (special series), 6
Gamo, M. 1981: 'The Traditional Social Structure of Japan and Changes in it', in P. G. O'Neill (ed.), *Tradition and Modern Japan*, Tenterden
Hendry, J. 1981: *Marriage in Changing Japan*, London
Hirschmeier, J. and Yui, T. 1981: *The Development of Japanese Business (1600–1980)*. London
Hozumi, N. 1973: *Ancestor Worship and Japanese Law*, Plainview
Itô, M. 1982: *Kazoku kokka kan no jinruigaku* (Anthropology of the concept of family-state), Tokyo
Iwao, S. 1993: *The Japanese Woman: Traditional Image and Changing Reality*, Cambridge, Mass.
Jolivet, M. 1993: *Un pays en mal d'enfants*, Paris
Kôsaka, M. 1958: *Japanese Thought in the Meiji Era*, Tokyo
Koyama, T., Morioka, K. and Kumagai, F. (eds) 1981: 'Family and Household in Changing Japan', *Journal of Comparative Family Studies* 12 (3) (special number)

Koyano, S. 1980: 'Development of Sociological Studies on Family in Japan', *Sociologica Internationalis*, 18 (1–2)

Linhart, S. 'Changing Family Structure and Problems of the Older People in Japan: Present Trends and Prospects', in G. Fodella (ed.), *Social Structures and Economic Dynamics in Japan up to 1980*, Milan

Marshall, B.K. 1967: *Capitalism and Nationalism in Prewar Japan*, Stanford

Maruyama, M. 1979: *Thought and Behaviour in Modern Japanese Politics*, Tokyo and Oxford

Matsubara, H. 1983: *Kazoku no kiki* (The crisis of the family)

Minear, R. H. 1970: *Japanese Tradition and Western Law*, Cambridge, Mass.

Mito, T. 1994: *'Ie' to shite no Nihon shakai* (Japanese family as 'Ie'), Tokyo

Miyajima, T. and Beillevaire, P. 1983: 'Évolution du mode de vie et des attitudes à l'égard du travail au Japon', *Sciences Sociales du Japon Contemporain*, 4

Murakami, Y., Kumon, S. and Satô, S. 1979: *Bunmei to shite no ie shakai* (*Ie* society as civilization), Tokyo

Nakane, C. 1973: *Japanese Society*, Harmondsworth

Noguchi, P. H. 1990: *Delayed Departures, Overdue Arrivals, Industrial Familialism and the Japanese National Railways*, Honolulu

Nonoyama, H. 1977: *Gendai kazoku no ronri* (Logic of the contemporary family), Tokyo

Sano, C. 1973: *Changing Values of the Japanese Family*, Westport

Smith, R. J. 1974: *Ancestor Worship in Contemporary Japan*, Stanford

Takeda, A. 1989: *Kyôdai bun no minzoku* (Ethnology of fictive brotherhood), Tokyo

Vogel, E. F. 1967: 'Kinship Structure, Migration to the City, and Modernization', in R. P. Dore (ed.), *Aspects of Social Change in Modern Japan*, Princeton

Chapter 6   India: the Family, the State and Women

Agarwala, S. N. 1977: India's Population Problems, New York

Allen, M. A. and Mukerjee, S. N. 1982: 'Women in India and Nepal', *Australian National University Monographs on South Asia*, no. 8, Canberra

Altekar, A. S. 1959: *The Position of Women in Hindu Civilization*, Delhi

Ames, M. A. 1973: 'Structural Dimensions of Family Life in the Steel City of Jamshedpur, India', in M. Singer (ed.), *Entrepreneurship and Modernization of Occupational Cultures in South Asia*, Duke University Monograph and Occasional Papers Series, pp. 107–31

Bailey, F. G. 1958: *Caste and the Economic Frontier: a Village in Highland Orissa*, Bombay

Cain, M. 1982: 'Perspectives on Family and Fertility in Developing Countries', *Population Studies*, 36 (2), 159–75

Caldwell, J. C., Reddy, P. H. and Caldwell, P. 1983: 'The Causes of Marriage Change in South India', *Population Studies*, 37 (3), 343–61

Caldwell, J. C., Reddy, P. H. and Caldwell, P. 1984: 'The Determinants of Fertility Decline in Rural South India', in T. Dyson and N. Crook (eds), *India's*

Demography: Essays on the Contemporary Population, New Delhi

Carroll, L. 1983: 'Law, Custom and Statutory Social Reform: the Hindu Widow's Remarriage Act of 1958', *Indian Economic and Social History Review*, 20 (4), 363–88

Chambard, J.-L. 1974: 'La Société indienne est-elle une société bloquée? Essai sur la mobililité sociale en Inde', *France-Asie*, 4

Chambard, J.-L. 1980: *Atlas d'un village indien, Pirpasod, Madhya Pradesh*, Paris

Chandrasekhar, S. 1972: *Infant Mortality, Population Growth and Family Planning in India*, London

Conklin, G. H. 1973: 'Emerging Conjugal Role Patterns in a Joint Family System: Correlates of Social Change in Dharwar, India', *Journal of Marriage and the Family*, 35 (4), 742–8

Dandekar, K. and Unde, D. B. 1961: *Size and Composition of Households: Census of India 1961*, vol. 1, New Delhi

Derrett, J. D. M. 1978: *The Death of a Marriage Law: Epitaph for the Rishis*, Delhi

Desai, I. P. 1964: *Some Aspects of Family in Mahuva: a Sociological Study of Jointness in a Small Town*, Bombay

Dumont, L. 1969: 'Les Britanniques en Inde', in *Histoire du développement culturel et scientifique de l'humanité*, vol. V, Paris

Dumont, L. 1975: *Dravidien et Kariera. L'alliance de mariage dans l'Inde du Sud et en Australie*, Paris

Dumont, L. 1979: *Homo hierarchicus. Le système des castes et ses implications*, Paris

Epstein, T. S. 1960: 'Economic Development and Peasant Marriage in South India', *Man in India*, 40 (3), 192–233

Fox, R. 1969: *From Zamindar to Ballot Box: Community Change in a North Indian Market Town*, Ithaca

Fruzzetti, L. M. 1982: *The Gift of a Virgin: Women, Marriage and Ritual in a Bengali Society*, New Brunswick

Fuller, C. J. 1976: *The Nayars Today*, Cambridge

Gadgil, D. R. 1971: *The Industrial Evolution of India in Recent Times, 1860–1939*, Delhi

Goode, W. J. 1970: *World Revolution and Family Patterns*, London

Goody, J. and Tambiah, S. J. 1973: *Bridewealth and Dowry*, Cambridge

Gore, M. S. 1968: *Urbanization and Family Change*, Bombay

Heuzé, G. 1982: 'Unité et pluralité du monde ouvrier indien', *Purusartha 6* (Paris), 189–221

Jain, A. K. and Adlakha, A. L. 1982: 'Preliminary Estimates of Fertility Decline in India during the 1970's', *Population and Development Review*, 8 (3), 589–606

Jain, D. (ed.) 1975: *Indian Women*, Delhi

Kannan, C. T. 1963: *Intercastes and Intercommunity Marriages in India*, Bombay

Kessinger, T. 1975: 'The Peasant Farm in North India, 1848–1968, *Explorations in Economic History*, 12, 303–23

Kolenda, P. 1968: 'Region, Caste and Family Structure: a Comparative Study of the Indian "Joint" Family', in M. Singer and B. S. Cohn (eds), *Structure and Change in Indian Society*, Chicago

Kumar, R. 1983: 'Family and Factory: Women Workers in the Bombay Cotton Textile Industry, 1919–1939', *Indian Economic and Social History Review*, 20 (1), 81–110

Lardinois, R. 1977: 'Structures familiales et cycles familiaux dans un village d'Inde du Sud', *Cahiers ORSTOM*, Série sciences humaines, XIV (4), 409–20

Mahadevan, K. 1979: *Sociology of Fertility: Determinants of Fertility Differentials in South India*, New Delhi

Mamdani, M. 1972: *The Myth of Population Control: Family, Caste and Class in an Indian Village*, New York

Manushi, A Journal about Women in Society (monthly), New Delhi

Mehta, R. 1975: *Divorced Hindu Woman*, Delhi

Miller, B. D. 1981: *The Endangered Sex: Neglect of Female Children in Rural North India*, Ithaca

Minault, G. (ed.) 1981: *The Extended Family: Women and Political Participation in India and Pakistan*, Delhi

Mines, M. 1973: 'Tamil Muslim Merchants in India's Industrial Development', in M. Singer (ed.), *Entrepreneurship and Modernization of Occupational Cultures in South Asia*, Duke University Monograph and Occasional Papers Series, pp. 37–60

Mukerjee, R. 1976: *West Bengal Family Structures, 1946–1966: an Example of Viability of Joint Family*, Delhi

Mukerjee, S. 1976: *The Age Distribution of the Indian Population: A Reconstruction for the States and Territories, 1881–1961*, Honolulu

Mukherjee, M. 1983: 'Impact of Modernization on Women's Occupation: a Case Study of the Rice-Husking Industry of Bengal', *Indian Economic and Social History Review*, 20 (1), 27–45

Mukherjee, S. N. 1970: 'Class, Caste and Politics in Calcutta, 1815–1838', in E. Leach and S. N. Mukherjee (eds), *Elites in South Asia*, Cambridge

Nandy, A. 1980: *At the Edge of Psychology: Essays in Politics and Culture*, Delhi

Oddie, G. A. 1979: *Social Protest in India: British Protestant Missionaries and Social Reforms 1850–1900*, Delhi

Omvedt, G. 1980: *We Will Smash This Prison!* London

Owens, R. 1971: 'Industrialization and the Indian Joint Family', *Ethnology*, X (2), 223–50

Panigrahi, L. 1972: *British Social Policy and Female Infanticide in India*, New Delhi

Rajaram, I. 1983: 'Economics of Bride-Price and Dowry', *Economic and Political Weekly*, XVIII (8), 8 February

Ross, A. D. 1973: *The Hindu Family in its Urban Setting*, Delhi

Sarkar, T. 1984: 'Politics and Women in Bengal: the Conditions and Meaning of Participation', *Indian Economic and Social History Review*, 21 (1), 91–101

Singer, M. 1968: 'The Indian Joint Family in Modern Industry', in M. Singer and B. S. Cohn (eds), *Structure and Change in Indian Society*, Chicago

Srinavas, M. N. 1966: *Social Change in Modern India*, University of California Press

Srinivas, M. N. 1972: *Social Change in Modern India*, New Delhi

Srinavas, M. N. 1978: *Religion and Society among the Coorgs of South India*, Bombay

Srinivas, M. N. and Ramaswamy, E. A. 1977: *Culture and Human Fertility in India*, Delhi

Stern, H. 1982: 'L'Édification d'un secteur économique moderne: l'exemple d'une caste marchande du Rajasthan', *Purusartha* 6 (Paris), 135–57

Thomas, C. 1979: *L'Ashram de l'amour, le gandhisme et l'imaginaire*, Paris

Towards Equality 1974: Report of the Committee on the Status of Women in India, Government of India, Department of Social Welfare, Ministry of Education and Social Welfare, New Delhi

Vatuk, S. 1972: *Kinship and Urbanization: White-Collar Migrants in North India*, Berkeley

Verghese, J. 1980: *Her Gold and Her Body*, New Delhi

Vicziany, M. 1982: 'Coercion in a Soft State: the Family-Planning Programme of India', part I: 'The Myth of Voluntarism'; part II: 'The Sources of Coercion', *Pacific Affairs*, 55 (3), 373–402; (4), 557–92

Visaria, P. 1983: 'Level and Nature of Work Participation by Sex, Age and Marital Status in India, 1961', *Economic and Political Weekly*, XVIII, 19, 20 and 21 (May)

Chapter 7   Africa: the Family at the Crossroads

Antoine, P. and Guillaume, A. 1984: 'Une expression de la solidarité familiale à Abidjan. Enfants du couple et enfants confiés', Colloque international de Genève, *Les Familles d'aujourd'hui*

Augé, M. 1971: 'Traite précoloniale, politique, matrimoniale et stratégie sociale dans les sociétés lagunaires de basse Côte-d'Ivoire', *Cahiers sciences humaines de l'ORSTOM*, III (2)

Augé, M. (ed.) 1975: *Les Domaines de la parenté*, Paris

Balandier, G. 1955: *Sociologie actuelle de l'Afrique noire*, Paris

Balandier, G. 1974: *Anthropo-logiques*, Paris

Bazin, J. 1985: 'À chacun son Bambara', in J.-L. Amselle and E. Mbokolo (eds), *Ethnie, tribalisme et état en Afrique*, Paris

Bisilliat, J. and Fiéloux, M. 1983: *Femmes du Tiers Monde*, Paris

Bohannan, P. and L. 1953: *The Tiv of Central Nigeria*, London

Dozon, J.-P. 1985: *La Société bété (Côte-d'Ivoire)*, Paris

Dupire, M. 1960: *Planteurs autochtones et étrangers en basse Côte-d'Ivoire orientale*, Études Éburnéennes, 8

Étienne, P. and M. 1971: 'À qui mieux mieux, ou le mariage chez les Baoulé', in *Cahiers sciences humaines de l'ORSTOM*, VIII

Evans-Pritchard, E. E. 1968: *Les Nuer*, Paris

Fortes, M. 1953: 'The Structure of Unilinear Descent Groups', *American Anthropologist*, LV (1)

Gibbal, J.-M. 1974: 'La Magie à l'école', *Cahiers d'études africaines*, XIV (56)

Gibbal, J.-M. 1974: *Citadins et villageois dans la ville africaine: l'exemple d'Abidjan*, Paris

Godelier, M. 1973: 'Modes de production, rapports de parenté et structures démographiques', *La Pensée*, 172

Goody, J. 1986: *The Logic of Writing*, Cambridge

Hozelitz, B. F. 1960: *Sociological Aspects of Economic Growth*

Marie, A. 1984: *Espace, structures et pratiques sociales à Lomé. Étude de cas*, Paris

Monteil, V. 1971: *Islam noir*, Paris

Nicolas, G. 1981: *La Dynamique de l'Islam au sud du Sahara*, Paris

Radcliffe-Brown, A. R. and Forde, D. 1950: *African Systems of Kinship and Marriage*, London

Rey, P. P. 1971: *Colonialisme, néocolonialisme et transition au capitalisme*, Paris

Vidal, C. 1978: 'Guerre des sexes à Abidjan. Masculin, féminin', *Cahiers d'études africaines*, XVII

Chapter 8   The Arab World: the Family as Fortress

AARDES (Association algérienne pour la recherche démographique, économique et sociale), 1970: *Enquête sociodémographique*, IV: 'Rôles assignés aux hommes et aux femmes', Algiers

Annuaire de l'Afrique du Nord 1981. 1982: 'Maghrébins en France, émigrés ou immigrés?', Paris

Bchir, M. 1983: 'L'Inégalité devant la mort dans les pays arabes', Colloque sur *La Question démographique dans le monde arabe*, Tunis

Berque, J. 1969: *Les Arabes d'hier à demain*, Paris

Berque, J. 1985: *De l'Euphrate à l'Atlas*, Paris

Bouhdiba, A. 1967: 'Point de vue sur la famille tunisienne actuelle', *Revue tunisienne des sciences sociales*, 11

Bouhdiba, A. 1975: *La Sexualité en Islam*, Paris

Chamie, J. 1981: *Religion and Fertility: Arab Christian–Muslim Differentials*, Cambridge

CIEM (Centre interuniversitaire d'études méditerranéennes) 1984: *Villes et migrations internationales de travail dans le Tiers monde*, Poitiers

Cresswell, R. 1976: 'Lineage Endogamy among Maronite Mountaineers', in J.-C. Peristiany (ed.), *Mediterranean Family Structures*, Cambridge

EMF (World Survey on Fertility)
    Egypt (1983): *The Egyptian Fertility Survey, 1981*, Cairo

Jordan (1979): *Jordan Fertility Survey, 1976,* Amman
Morocco (1984): *Enquête nationale sur la fécondité et la planification de la famille au Maroc, 1979–80,* Rabat
Mauritania (1984): *Enquête nationale mauritanienne sur la fécondité, 1981,* Nouakchott
Sudan (1982): *The Sudan Fertility Survey, 1979,* Khartoum
Syria (1982): *Syria Fertility Survey, 1978,* Damascus
Tunisia (1982): *Enquête tunisienne sur la fécondité, 1978,* Tunis
Yemen (1983): *Yemen Arab Republic Fertility Survey, 1979,* Sanaa
Fargues, P. 1980: *Réserves de main-d'œuvre et rente pétrolière,* CERMOC, Beirut and Lyon
Fargues, P. 1986: 'Un siècle de transition démographique en Afrique méditerranéenne, 1885–1985', *Population,* 41–2
Khuri, F. 1970: 'Parallel Cousin Marriage Reconsidered', *Man,* 5
Le Bras, H. 1985: 'Les Jeux du hasard et du mariage', *Démographie et Sociologie,* Paris (Publications de la Sorbonne)
Mahfouz, N. 1983: *Passage des miracles,* Paris
Nasr, S. 1982: 'Formations sociales traditionnelles et sociétés urbaines au Proche-Orient', in *La Ville arabe dans l'Islam,* Tunis and Paris
OLPF (Lebanese family planning office) 1974: *Al Usra fî Lubnân* (The family in Lebanon), Beirut
Tabutin, D. 1976: *Mortalité infantile et juvénile en Algérie,* Paris
Taylor, E. 1984: 'Egyptian Migration and Peasant Wives', *Merip Reports* 124, Washington
Tillion, G. 1983: *The Republic of Cousins,* London
United Nations 1984: *Annuaire Démographique 1982,* New York
Vandevelde, H. 1985: 'Le Code algérien de la famille', *Maghreb-Machrek* 107, Paris
Zghal, A. 1967: 'Système de parenté et système coopératif dans les campagnes tunisiennes', *Revue tunisienne de sciences sociales,* 11
Zurayk, H. 1985: 'Women's Economic Participation', in F. Shorter and H. Zurayk, *Population Factors in Development Planning in the Middle-East,* Washington and Cairo

Chapter 9   The Industrial Revolution: from Proletariat to Bourgeoisie

Anderson, M. 1972: 'Household Structure and the Industrial Revolution: Mid-nineteenth Century Preston in Comparative Perspective', in P. Laslett (ed.), *Household and Family in Past Times,* Cambridge
Anderson, M. 1982: *Sociology of the Family,* Harmondsworth
Benveniste, É. 1969: *Le Vocabulaire des institutions indo-européennes,* vol. I, Paris
Boudon, R. 1984: *La Place du désordre,* Paris
Commaille, J. 1983: *Familles sans justice,* Paris

Duveau, G. 1946: *La Vie ouvrière en France sous le second Empire*, Paris
Faure, A. 1979: 'L'Épicerie parisienne au XIXe siècle ou la corporation éclatée', *Le Mouvement social*, 108, 113–30
Fohlen, C. 1955: *Une affaire de famille au XIXe siècle: Méquillet-Noblot*, Paris
Foucault, M. 1977: *Discipline and Punish*, London
Foucault, M. 1980: *The Will to Truth*, London
Hareven, T. K. 1977: 'Family Time and Industrial Time: Family and Work in a Planned Corporation Town, 1900–1924', in T. K. Hareven (ed.), *Family and Kin in Urban Communities*, New York
Hobsbawm, E. 1962: 'En Angleterre, révolution industrielle et vie matérielle des classes populaires', *Annales ESC*, 6 (November–December), 1047–61
Joseph, I. and Fritsch, P. 1977: 'Disciplines à domicile, l'édification de la famille', *Recherches*, 28 (November)
Leboutte, R. 1983: 'L'Apport des registres de population à la connaissance de la dynamique des ménages en Belgique au XIXe siècle', in *Strutture e rapporti familiari in epoca moderna: esperienze italiane e riferimenti europei*, International Congress, Trieste, 5–7 September (xerox)
Lequin, Y. 1977: *Les Ouvriers de la région lyonnaise*, Lyon
Levine, D. 1983: 'Unstable Population Theorizing', paper presented at the Conference *Transformations de l'Europe*, Bellagio, May (roneo)
Löfgren, O. 1984: 'Family and Household: Images and Realities. Cultural Change in Swedish Society', in R. R. Wilk and E. J. Arnould (eds), *Households, Comparative and Historical Studies of the Domestic Group*, Berkeley
Miterrauer, M. and Sieder, R. 1982: *The European Family: Patriarchy to Partnership from the Middle Ages to the Present*, Oxford
Navaillès, J.-P. 1982–3: 'Le Profit philanthropique: une réponse victorienne à la crise du logement ouvrier', *Milieux*, 11–12 (October 1982–January 1983), 50–61
Navaillès, J.-P. 1983: *La Famille ouvrière dans l'Angleterre victorienne*, Le Creusot, Écomusée
Pierrard, P. 1976: *La Vie quotidienne dans le Nord au XIXe siècle*, Paris
Polanyi, K. 1983: *La Grande Transformation. Aux origines politiques et économiques de notre temps*, Paris
Portet, F. 1978: *L'Ouvrier, la terre, la petite propriété. Jardin ouvrier et logement social*, Le Creusot, Écomusée
Rioux, J.-P. 1971: *La Révolution industrielle*, Paris
Robert, J.-L. 1981: 'La C.G.T. et la famille ouvrière, 1914–1918. Première approche', *Le Mouvement social*, 116, 47–66
Sandrin, J. 1982: *Enfants trouvés, enfants ouvriers*, Paris
Sewell, W. 1971: 'La Classe ouvrière de Marseille sous la IIe République. Structure sociale et comportement politique', *Le Mouvement social*, 76, 27–66
Sewell, W. 1983: *Gens de métier et révolutions*, Paris
Zunz, O. 1983: *Naissance de l'Amérique industrielle. Detroit 1880–1920*, Paris

Chapter 10   Love and Liberty: the Contemporary American Family

Generalities: symbolic framework and practical paradoxes

Bellah, Robert, et al. 1985: *Habits of the Heart: Individualism and Commitment in American Life*, Berkeley

Bumpass, Larry 1990: 'What's Happening to the Family? Interactions between Demographic and Institutional Change', *Demography*, 27, 483–98

Cherlin, Andrew 1981: *Marriage, Divorce, Remarriage*, Cambridge, Mass.

Furstenberg, Frank 1991: *Divided Families: What Happens to Children when Parents Part*. Cambridge, Mass.

Leichter, Hope and Mitchell, William 1978: *Kinship and Casework: Family Networks and Social Intervention*, New York

Newman, Cathy 1988: *Falling from Grace: the Experience of Downward Mobility in the American Middle Class*. New York

Ochs, Elinor and Schieffelin, Bambi 1984: 'Language Acquisition and Socialization: Three Developmental Stories and Their Implications', in R. Shweder and R. LeVine (eds), *Culture Theory*, Cambridge

Parsons, Talcott 1955: 'The American Family: Its Relations to Personality and to the Social Structure', in T. Parsons and R. F. Bales, *Family, Socialization and Interaction Process*, Glencoe

Perin, Constance 1977: *Everything in Its Place*, Princeton

Schneider, David 1980: *American Kinship: a Cultural Account*, Chicago

Varenne, Hervé 1977: *Americans Together: Structured Diversity in a Midwestern Town*, New York

Weston, Kath 1991: *Families We Choose: Lesbians, Gays, Kinship*, New York

History: puritans, industrials, workers

Demos, John 1970: *A Little Commonwealth: Family Life in Plymouth Colony*, New York

Greven, Philip 1970: *Four Generations: Population, Land and Family in Colonial Andover, Massachusetts*, Ithaca

Hareven, Tamara (ed.) 1977: *Family and Kin in Urban Communities*, New York

Hareven, Tamara and Langenbach, Randolph 1978: *Amoskeag: Life and Work in an American Factory-City*, New York

Lockridge, Kenneth 1970: *A New England Town: the First Hundred Years*, New York

Wallace, A. F. C. 1978: *Rockdale: the Growth of an American Village in the Early Industrial Revolution*, New York

Problems and controversies of everyday life: adolescence, education, old age

Coleman, James 1961: *The Adolescent Society: the Social Life of the Teenager and Its Impact on Education*, New York
Henry, Jules 1963: *Culture against Man*, New York
Hollingshead, A. B. 1949: *Elmtown's Youth: the Impact of Social Class on Adolescents*, New York
Jacobs, Jerry 1974: *Fun City: an Ethnographic Study of a Retirement Community*, New York
Kett, Joseph 1977: *Rites of Passage: Adolescence in America, 1790 to the Present*, New York
Myerhoff, Barbara 1978: *Number Our Days*, New York

Ethnic traditions: sublimation of difference

Glazer, Nathan, and Moynihan, Daniel 1963: *Beyond the Melting Pot: the Negroes, Puerto Ricans, Jews, Italians, and Irish of New York City*, Cambridge, Mass.
Schneider, David and Smith, Raymond 1973: *Class Differences and Sex Roles in American Kinship and Family Structure*, Englewood Cliffs
Sollors, Werner 1986: *Beyond Ethnicity: Consent and Descent in American Culture*, New York
Steinberg, Stephen 1981: *The Ethnic Myth: Race, Ethnicity, and Class in America*, New York
Yanagisako, Sylvia 1975: 'Two Processes of Change in Japanese-American Kinship', *Journal of Anthropological Research*, 31, 196–224

The poor: the American dilemma and its consequences

Dumont, Louis 1970: 'Caste, Racism and "Stratification": Reflexions of a Social Anthropologist', in his *Homo Hierarchicus*, tr. M. Sainsbury, Chicago
Garfinkel, Irwin 1986: *Single Mothers and Their Children: a New American Dilemma*, Washington
Gutman, Herbert 1976: *The Black Family in Slavery and Freedom, 1750–1925*, New York
Moynihan, Daniel 1967: 'The Negro Family: the Case for National Action', in L. Rainwater and W. Yancey (eds), *The Moynihan Report and the Politics of Controversy*, Cambridge, Mass. (first published 1965)
Myrdal, Gunnar 1962: *An American Dilemma: the Negro Problem and Modern Democracy*, New York
Shimkin, Demitri, Shimkin, E. and Frate, D. (eds) 1978: *The Extended Family in Black Societies*, The Hague

Stack, Carol 1975: *All Our Kin*, New York
Susser, Ida 1982: *Norman Street: Poverty and Politics in an Urban Neighbour-hood*, Oxford
Yanagisako, Sylvia 1977: 'Women-Centred Kin Networks in Urban Bilateral Kinship', *American Ethnologist*, 4, 207–26

Chapter 11   Socialist Families

Attwood, Lynne 1990: *The New Soviet Man and Woman: Sex Role Socialization in the USSR*, Basingstoke
Bennigsen, A. and Lemercier-Quelquejay, C. 1968: *L'Islam en Union soviétique*, Paris
Berelowitch, W. 1993: 'De la famille patriarcale à la découverte de l'individu', *Quelle Russie?*, série monde (Paris)
Bridger, Sue 1987: *Women in the Soviet Countryside*, Cambridge
Bridger, Sue 1990: 'Women in Contemporary Soviet Society', *Economy and Society* (November)
Browning, Genia K. 1987: *Women and Politics in the USSR*, Brighton
Buckley, Mary 1987: *Women and Ideology in the Soviet Union*, Brighton
Corrin, C. A. 1988: *The Situation of Women in Hungarian Society*, Ph.D. dissertation, Oxford
Cuisenier, J. and Raguin, C. 1967: 'De quelques transformations dans le système familial russe', *Revue française de sociologie*, VIII
Dragadze, Tamara 1988: *Rural Families in Soviet Georgia: a Case Study in Ratcha Province*, London
Geiger, K. 1968: *The Family in Soviet Russia*, Cambridge, Mass.
Gossiaux, J.-F. 1982: *Le Groupe domestique dans la Yougoslavie rurale*, thesis, EHESS (duplicated)
Hansson, C. and Linden, K. 1983: *Moscow Women*, New York
Hartchev, A. 1979: *Brak i sem'ja* (The urban family), Moscow
Heinen, Jacqueline 1990: 'Pologne/R.D.A. Impact des politiques sur le comporte-ment des femmes actives', *Sociétés contemporaines* (March)
Heitlinger, A. 1979: *Women and State Socialism: Sex Inequality in the Soviet Union and Czechoslovakia*, Montreal
Hirsch, Helga 1990: 'Zur Frauenfrage in Polen', *Frankfurter Heft*, 37
Kerblay, Basile (ed.) 1987: *Évolution des modèles familiaux de l'Est européen et en U.R.S.S.* Paris (Institut d'études slaves, *Cultures et sociétés de l'Est*, no. 9)
Jankova, Z. A. 1979: *Gorodskaja sem'ja* (The urban family), Moscow
Lapidus, G. W. 1968: *Women in Soviet Society*, Berkeley
Novak, S. 1980: 'Value Systems of Polish Society', *Polish Sociological Bulletin*, 2
Pugh, C. and Lewin, S. 1990: 'Women, Work and Housing in the Soviet Union in pre-Perestroika Times: Marxist Theory and Socialist Practice', *Netherlands Journal of Housing and Environmental Research*, 5
Seljacke obiteljske zadruga 1960 (Zagreb, Publikacija Etnoloskoga Zavada)

Sem'ja i semejnye obrjady u naradov srednej azii i Kazakhstana (The family and family rites among the peoples of central Asia and Kazakhstan) 1978, Moscow

Shaffer, Harry G. 1990: 'Frauen in der Sowjetunion', Jahrg 1990, p. 133.

Sovremennaja sem'ja (The contemporary family) 1982 (Moscow, Vypusk 7, Financy)

Szezpanski, J. 1970: *Polish Society*, New York

Trepper, Hartmute, Madonna mit Brecheisen', *Osteuropa*, 40, Jahrg 1990, p. 133

Vogyes, N. 1977: *The Liberated Female: Life, Work and Sex in Socialist Hungary*, Boulder

Yedlin, T. (ed.) 1980: *Women in Eastern Europe and the Soviet Union*, New York

Yvert-Jalu, M. H. 1976: 'Le Divorce en URSS', in A. Michel (ed.), *Femmes, sexisme et sociétés*, Paris

Yvert-Jalu, M. H. 1990: 'L'Avortement en Union soviétique', *Annales de démographie historique*

Chapter 12   The Scandinavian Model

Danermark, B. 1984: *Boendesegregationens utveckling i Sverige under efterkrigstiden*, Swedish Ministry of Housing, Ds Bo (4)

Fritzell, J. and Lundberg, O. (eds) 1994: *Vardgens villkor: levnadsförhällanden i sverige under tre decennier*, Stockholm

Gaunt, D. 1977: 'Pre-industrial Economy and Population Structure', *Scandinavian Journal of History*, 183–210

Gaunt, D. 1983a: *Familjeliv i Norden*, Stockholm

Gaunt, D. 1983b: 'The Property and Kin Relationships of Retired Farmers in Northern and Central Europe', in R. Wall (ed.), *Family Forms in Historic Europe*, Cambridge

Gaunt, D. 1987: 'Rural Household Organization and Inheritance in Northern Europe', *Journal of Family History*, 12 (1–3), 121–41

Gaunt, L. 1980: 'Can Children Play at Home?', in P. F. Wilkinson (ed.), *Innovation in Play Environments*, London

Gaunt, L. 1985: 'Housing the Extended Family in Sweden', in W. Vliet et al. (eds), *Housing Needs and Policy Approaches: Trends in Thirteen Countries*, Durham

Haavio-Mannila, E. 1982: 'Caregiving in the Welfare State', *Acta Sociologica*, 26, 61–82

Hedborg, A. and Meidner, R. 1984: *Folkhemsmodellen*, Stockholm

Hemström, E. 1983: *Utrymmesstandard i internationell jämförelse*, Swedish Ministry of Housing, Ds Bo (7)

Humble, K. 1984: 'Barn behöver sina föräldrar', in B. E. Andersson (ed.), *Familjebilder: myter, verklighet, visioner*, Stockholm

Key, E. 1900: *Barnets århundrade*, Stockholm

Kärnekull, K. 1980: 'Med bör jan i boendet', in *Vi bor för att leva*, Swedish Council for Building Research, vol. II

Lievin, B. 1979: *Om ogift samboende i Sverige*, Uppsala

Liljeström, R. and Dahlström, E. 1981: *Arbetarkvinnor i hem- arbets- och samhällsliv*, Stockholm

Myrdal, A. 1944: *Folk och familj*, Stockholm

Näsman, E. et al. 1983: *Föräldrars arbete och barns villkor- en kunskapsöversikt*, Stockholm

Tornberg, M. 1972: 'Storfamiljsinstitutionen i Finland', *Nord-nytt*, 4–17

Trost, J. 1994: *Familjen i Sverige*, Stockholm

Wilkman, K. R. V. 1937: *Die Einleitung der Ehe. Eine vergleichend ethnosoziologische Untersuchung über die Vorstufe der Ehe in den Sitten des schwedischen Volkstums*, Turku

Chapter 13   Families in France

Bastide, H., Girard, A. and Roussel, L. 1982: 'Une enquête d'opinion sur la conjoncture démographique', *Population*, 4–5, 867–904

Benveniste, É. 1969: *Le Vocabulaire des institutions indo-européennes*, Paris, vol. I

Bourdieu, P. 1990: *Photography: a Middle-brow Art*, Cambridge

Brahimi-Tribalat, M. 1982-3: 'Chronique de l'immigration', *Population* (1982), 1, 131–58, and (1983), 1, 137–60

Chalvon-Demersay, S. 1983: *Concubin, concubine*, Paris

Collard, C. 1979: 'L'Anthropologie de la parenté', in *Perspectives anthropologiques*, Montreal

Commaille, J. 1983: *Familles sans justice*, Paris

'Formes de nomination en Europe', 1980: special number of *L'Homme*, XX, 4

Fox, R. 1978: *Tory Islanders: a People of the Celtic Fringe*, London

Gokalp, C. 1981: 'Quand vient l'âge des choix', *Travaux et documents*, 95, Paris

Gokalp, C. and David, M.-G. 1982: 'La Garde des jeunes enfants', *Population et sociétés*, 161 (September)

Gokalp, C. and Leridon, H. 1983: 'La Participation du père aux activités domestiques', *Population et sociétés*, 175 (December), 4

Gotman, A. 1988: *Heriter*, Paris

Guilbert, J. 1983: 'La Vieillesse ouvrière', in *Actes du colloque 'Les Âges de la vie'*, vol. II, *Travaux et documents*, 102, Paris

Le Bras, H. and Roussel, C. 1982: 'Retard ou refus du mariage. L'évolution récente de la première nuptialité en France et sa prévision', *Population*, 6, 1009–44

Jolas, T., Verdier, Y. and Zonabend, F. 1970: 'Parler famille', *L'Homme*, X (3), 5–23

Lévi-Strauss, C. 1981: *The Naked Man*, London

Le Wita, B. 1984: 'La Mémoire familiale des Parisiens appartenant aux classes moyennes', *Ethnologie française*, 14 (1), 57–66

Norvez, A. 1982: 'La Première Enfance. Les 0–5 ans', in *Actes du colloque 'Les Âges de la vie'*, vol. I, *Travaux et documents*, 96, Paris

Parsons, T. 1943: 'The Kinship System of the Contemporary United States', *American Anthropologist*, 45 (January–March), 22–38

Pitrou, A. et al. 1983: *Trajectoires professionnelles et stratégies familiales, mars 1983*, Rapport d'ATP, CNRS, Paris (xerox)

Roussel, L. and Bourguignon, O. 1976: 'La Famille après le mariage des enfants. Étude sur les relations entre générations', *Travaux et documents*, 78, Paris

Schwartz, O. 1990: *Le monde privé des ouvriers. Hommes et femmes du Nord*, Paris

Segalen, M. 1983: *Love and Power in the Peasant Family*, Oxford

Segalen, M. 1991: *Fifteen Generations of Bretons*, Cambridge

Segalen, M. (ed.) 1991: *Jeux de familles*, Paris

Segalen, M. 1993: *Historical Anthropology of the Family*, Cambridge

Singly, F. de 1990: *Fortune et infortune de la femme mariée*, Paris

Thélot, C. 1982: *Tel père, tel fils?*, Paris

Thélot, C. and Lévy, M.-L. 1983: 'Grands-Parents, parents et enfants', *Population et sociétés*, 174 (November)

Tribalat, M. (ed.) 1991: 'Cent ans d'immigration. Etrangers d'hier, français d'aujourd'hui', *Travaux et documents*, 131, Paris

Van Gennep, A. 1909: *Les Rites de passage*, Paris and The Hague

Verret, M. 1983: 'La Famille ouvrière', *Projet*, 177 (July–August), 695–706

Zonabend, F. 1973: 'Les Morts et les vivants. Le cimetière de Minot en Châtillonnais', *Études rurales*, 52, 7–23

Zonabend, F. 1981: 'Le très proche et le pas trop loin. Réflexion sur l'organisation du champ matrimonial des sociétés à structures de parenté complexe', *Ethnologie française*, (4) 311–18

Zonabend, F. 1984: *The Enduring Memory*, Manchester

Index

Page references in italics refer to illustrations or their captions.